PRENTICE HALL
LITERATURE

10

Part 1

COMMON CORE EDITION ©

$20.00 —
txt
8/15

Upper Saddle River, New Jersey

Boston, Massachusetts

Chandler, Arizona

Glenview, Illinois

PEARSON

Cover Art: (Bkgd) ©Ted Mead/Getty Images, (L) ©James Forte/Getty Images, (B) ©Tom Merton/OJO Images/ Getty Images, (TL, BC) ©Blaine Harrington III/CORBIS, (CR) ©Uli Wiesmeier/zefa/CORBIS

Taken from:
Prentice Hall Literature, Grade 10, Common Core Edition
Copyright © 2012 by Pearson Education, Inc.
Published by Prentice Hall
Upper Saddle River, New Jersey 07458

This special edition published in cooperation with Pearson Learning Solutions.

All trademarks, service marks, registered trademarks, and registered service marks are the property of their respective owners and are used herein for identification purposes only.

Pearson Learning Solutions, 501 Boylston Street, Suite 900, Boston, MA 02116
A Pearson Education Company
www.pearsoned.com

Printed in the United States of America

2 3 4 5 6 7 8 9 10 0BRV 16 15 14 13

000200010271275771

CW

Acknowledgments appear on page R76, which constitutes an extension of this copyright page.

SAT is a registered trademark of the College Entrance Examination Board. ACT is a trademark owned by ACT, Inc.

Wikipedia® is a registered trademark of the Wikimedia Foundation, Inc. <http://www.wikimediafoundation.org>

Use of the trademarks implies no relationship, sponsorship, endorsement, sale, or promotion on the part of Pearson Education, Inc., or its affiliates.

Common Core State Standards © Copyright 2010. National Governors Association Center for Best Practices and Council of Chief State School Officers. All rights reserved.

"Understanding by Design" is registered as a trademark with the United States Patent and Trademark Office by the Association for Supervision of Curriculum Development (ASCD). ASCD claims exclusive trademark rights in the terms "Understanding by Design" and the abbreviation "UbD".

Pearson Education has incorporated the concepts of the Understanding by Design methodology into this text in consultation with Grant Wiggins, one of the creators of the Understanding by Design methodology. The Association for Supervision of Curriculum Development (ASCD), publisher of the "Understanding by Design Handbook" co-authored by Grant Wiggins, has not authorized, approved or sponsored this work and is in no way affiliated with Pearson or its products.

PEARSON

ISBN 10: 1-256-33181-3
ISBN 13: 978-1-256-33181-0

Master Teacher Board

Contributing Authors

The contributing authors guided the direction and philosophy of Pearson Prentice Hall Literature. *Working with the development team, they helped to build the pedagogical integrity of the program and to ensure its relevance for today's teachers and students.*

Grant Wiggins, Ed.D., is the President of Authentic Education in Hopewell, New Jersey. He earned his Ed.D. from Harvard University and his B.A. from St. John's College in Annapolis. Grant consults with schools, districts, and state education departments on a variety of reform matters; organizes conferences and workshops; and develops print materials and Web resources on curricular change. He is the coauthor, with Jay McTighe, of Understanding by Design and The Understanding by Design Handbook, the award-winning and highly successful materials on curriculum published by ASCD. His work has been supported by the Pew Charitable Trusts, the Geraldine R. Dodge Foundation, and the National Science Foundation. *The Association for Supervision of Curriculum Development (ASCD), publisher of the "Understanding by Design Handbook" co-authored by Grant Wiggins and registered owner of the trademark "Understanding by Design", has not authorized, approved, or sponsored this work and is in no way affiliated with Pearson or its products.*

Jeff Anderson has worked with struggling writers and readers for almost 20 years. Anderson's specialty is the integration of grammar and editing instruction into the processes of reading and writing. He has published two books, *Mechanically Inclined: Building Grammar, Usage, and Style into Writer's Workshop* and *Everyday Editing: Inviting Students to Develop Skill and Craft in Writer's Workshop,* as well as a DVD, *The Craft of Grammar.* Anderson's work has appeared in *English Journal.* Anderson won the NCTE Paul and Kate Farmer Award for his *English Journal* article on teaching grammar in context.

Arnetha F. Ball, Ph.D., is a Professor at Stanford University. Her areas of expertise include language and literacy studies of diverse student populations, research on writing instruction, and teacher preparation for working with diverse populations. She is the author of *African American Literacies Unleashed* with Dr. Ted Lardner, and *Multicultural Strategies for Education and Social Change.*

Sheridan Blau is Professor of Education and English at the University of California, Santa Barbara, where he directs the South Coast Writing Project and the Literature Institute for Teachers. He has served in senior advisory roles for such groups as the National Board for Professional Teaching Standards, the College Board, and the American Board for Teacher Education. Blau served for twenty years on the National Writing Project Advisory Board and Task Force, and is a former president of NCTE. Blau is the author of *The Literature Workshop: Teaching Texts and Their Readers,* which was named by the Conference on English Education as the 2004 Richard Meade Award winner for outstanding research in English education.

William G. Brozo, Ph.D., is a Professor of Literacy at George Mason University in Fairfax, Virginia. He has taught reading and language arts in junior and senior high school and is the author of numerous texts on literacy development. Dr. Brozo's work focuses on building capacity among teacher leaders, enriching the literate culture of schools, enhancing the literate lives of boys, and making teaching more responsive to the needs of all students. His recent publications include *Bright Beginnings for Boys: Engaging Young Boys in Active Literacy* and the *Adolescent Literacy Inventory.*

Doug Buehl is a teacher, author, and national literacy consultant. He is the author of *Classroom Strategies for Interactive Learning* and coauthor of *Reading and the High School Student: Strategies to Enhance Literacy;* and *Strategies to Enhance Literacy and Learning in Middle School Content Area Classrooms.*

Jim Cummins, Ph.D., is a professor in the Modern Language Centre at the University of Toronto. He is the author of numerous publications, including *Negotiating Identities: Education for Empowerment in a Diverse Society.* Cummins coined the acronyms BICS and CAPT to help differentiate the type of language ability students need for success.

Harvey Daniels, Ph.D., has been a classroom teacher, writing project director, author, and university professor. "Smokey" serves as an international consultant to schools, districts, and educational agencies. He is known for his work on student-led book clubs, as recounted in *Literature Circles: Voice and Choice in Book Clubs & Reading Groups* and *Mini Lessons for Literature Circles.* Recent works include *Subjects Matter: Every Teacher's Guide to Content-Area Reading* and *Content Area Writing: Every Teacher's Guide.*

Jane Feber taught language arts in Jacksonville, Florida, for 36 years. Her innovative approach to instruction has earned her several awards, including the NMSA Distinguished Educator Award, the NCTE Edwin A. Hoey Award, the Gladys Prior Award for Teaching Excellence, and the Florida Council of Teachers of English Teacher of the Year Award. She is a National Board Certified Teacher, past president of the Florida Council of Teachers of English and is the author of *Creative Book Reports* and *Active Word Play.*

Danling Fu, Ph.D., is Professor of Language and Culture in the College of Education at the University of Florida. She researches and provides inservice to public schools nationally, focusing on literacy instruction for new immigrant students. Fu's books include *My Trouble is My English* and *An Island of English* addressing English language learners in the secondary schools. She has authored chapters in the *Handbook of Adolescent Literacy Research* and in *Adolescent Literacy: Turning Promise to Practice.*

Kelly Gallagher is a full-time English teacher at Magnolia High School in Anaheim, California. He is the former co-director of the South Basin Writing Project at California State University, Long Beach. Gallagher wrote *Reading Reasons: Motivational Mini-Lessons for the Middle and High School, Deeper Reading: Comprehending Challenging Texts 4-12,* and *Teaching Adolescent Writers.* Gallagher won the Secondary Award of Classroom Excellence from the California Association of Teachers of English—the state's top English teacher honor.

Sharroky Hollie, Ph.D., is an assistant professor at California State University, Dominguez Hills, and an urban literacy visiting professor at Webster University, St. Louis. Hollie's work focuses on professional development, African American education, and second language methodology. He is a contributing author in two texts on culturally and linguistically responsive teaching. He is the Executive Director of the Center for Culturally Responsive Teaching and Learning and the co-founding director of the Culture and Language Academy of Success, an independent charter school in Los Angeles.

Dr. Donald J. Leu, Ph.D., teaches at the University of Connecticut and holds a joint appointment in Curriculum and Instruction and in Educational Psychology. He directs the New Literacies Research Lab and is a member of the Board of Directors of the International Reading Association. Leu studies the skills required to read, write, and learn with Internet technologies. His research has been funded by groups including the U.S. Department of Education, the National Science Foundation, and the Bill & Melinda Gates Foundation.

Jon Scieszka founded GUYS READ, a nonprofit literacy initiative for boys, to call attention to the problem of getting boys connected with reading. In 2008, he was named the first U.S. National Ambassador for Young People's Literature by the Library of Congress. Scieszka taught from first grade to eighth grade for ten years in New York City, drawing inspiration from his students to write *The True Story of the 3 Little Pigs!, The Stinky Cheese Man,* the *Time Warp Trio* series of chapter books, and the *Trucktown* series of books for beginning readers.

Sharon Vaughn, Ph.D., teaches at the University of Texas at Austin. She is the previous Editor-in-Chief of the *Journal of Learning Disabilities* and the co-editor of *Learning Disabilities Research and Practice.* She is the recipient of the American Education Research Association SIG Award for Outstanding Researcher. Vaughn's work focuses on effective practices for enhancing reading outcomes for students with reading difficulties. She is the author of more than 100 articles, and numerous books designed to improve research-based practices in the classroom.

Karen K. Wixson is Dean of the School of Education at the University of North Carolina, Greensboro. She has published widely in the areas of literacy curriculum, instruction, and assessment. Wixson has been an advisor to the National Research Council and helped develop the National Assessment of Educational Progress (NAEP) reading tests. She is a past member of the IRA Board of Directors and co-chair of the IRA Commission on RTI. Recently, Wixson served on the English Language Arts Work Team that was part of the Common Core State Standards Initiative.

Each unit addresses a BIG Question to enrich exploration of literary concepts and reading strategies.

Resources

Is there a difference between *reality* and *truth?*

★ INFORMATIONAL TEXT HIGHLIGHTED

PHLit Online!
www.PHLitOnline.com
Interactive resources provide personalized instruction and activities online.

Skills at a Glance

This page provides a quick look at the skills you will learn and practice in Unit 1.

Reading Skills

Make Predictions
  Use Your Prior Knowledge
  Ask Questions
Cause and Effect
  Reflect on Key Details
  Reread

Reading for Information

Analyze Structure and Format
Evaluate Sources

Literary Analysis

Theme
Central Idea
Plot and Foreshadowing
Author's Perspective
Comparing Styles
Conflict and Resolution
Author's Purpose
Comparing Irony and Paradox

Vocabulary

Big Question Vocabulary
Prefixes: *pro-, super-, inter-, ab-*
Roots: *-cred-, -strict-, -ver-, -ven-*
Using a Dictionary and Thesaurus
Independent Reading

Conventions

Common and Proper Nouns
Abstract and Concrete Nouns
Using Possessive Nouns Correctly
Personal Pronouns
Relative Pronouns
Revising Pronoun-Antecedent Agreement

Writing

Writing About the Big Question
Sequel
Description
Anecdote
Proposal
Timed Writing
Writing Workshop: Narrative Text: Autobiographical
  Narrative
Writing Workshop: Explanatory Text:
  Cause-and-Effect Essay

Speaking and Listening

Interview
Problem-Solving Group
Analyzing Media Messages

Research and Technology

Daily Observation Journal
Spreadsheet

 **Common Core State Standards
Addressed in This Unit**

Reading Literature RL.9-10.2, RL.9-10.4, RL.9-10.5,
RL.9-10.10

Reading Informational Text RI.9-10.2, RI.9-10.3,
RI.9-10.4, RI.9-10.6, RI.9-10.8, RI.9-10.10

Writing W.9-10.2, W.9-10.2.a, W.9-10.2.b, W.9-10.2.c,
W.9-10.2.d, W.9-10.2.e, W.9-10.2.f, W.9-10.3, W.9-10.3.a,
W.9-10.3.c, W.9-10.3.d, W.9-10.3.e, W.9-10.5, W.9-10.9,
W.9-10.9.a, W.9-10.9.b, W.9-10.10

Speaking and Listening SL.9-10.1, SL.9-10.1.a,
SL.9-10.1.b, SL.9-10.1.c, SL.9-10.1.d, SL.9-10.3, SL.9-10.5

Language L.9-10.1, L.9-10.1.b, L.9-10.2, L.9-10.2.c,
L.9-10.4, L.9-10.4.a, L.9-10.4.b, L.9-10.4.c, L.9-10.4.d,
L.9-10.5, L.9-10.6

[For the full wording of the standards, see the standards
chart in the front of your textbook.]

Can progress be made without *conflict?*

    ★ INFORMATIONAL TEXT HIGHLIGHTED

Interactive resources provide
personalized instruction and
activities online.

www.PHLitOnline.com

Skills at a Glance

This page provides a quick look at the skills you will learn and practice in Unit 2.

Reading Skills

Make Inferences
  Use Your Own Prior Knowledge and Experience
  Read On
Draw Conclusions
  Recognize Key Details
  Identify Patterns

Reading for Information

Analyze Text to Extend Ideas
Paraphrase to Connect Ideas

Literary Analysis

Character
Story Structure
Character and Characterization
Setting
Comparing Points of View
Theme
Symbolism and Allegory
Comparing Tones

Vocabulary

Big Question Vocabulary
Prefixes: *dis-, com-*
Suffixes: *-ence, -able, -ity, -ic, -tion, -id*
Word Origins

Conventions

The Principal Parts of Regular Verbs
Irregular Verbs
Revising to Apply Consistent Verb Tense
Action and Linking Verbs
Active and Passive Voice
Subject-Verb Agreement

Writing

Writing About the Big Question
Retelling
Letter / Book Review
Character Analysis
Narrative
Timed Writing
Writing Workshop: Narration: Short Story
Writing Workshop: Argument: Problem-
  and-Solution Essay

Speaking and Listening

Oral Reading
Group Discussion
Viewing and Evaluating a Speech

Research and Technology

Report on Sources
Research Summary

 Common Core State Standards Addressed in This Unit

Reading Literature RL.9-10.1, RL.9-10.2, RL.9-10.3, RL.9-10.4, RL.9-10.5, RL.9-10.6, RL.9-10.10
Reading Informational Text RI.9-10.4, RI.9-10.6, RI.9-10.10
Writing W.9-10.1, W.9-10.2, W.9-10.2.a, W.9-10.2.b, W.9-10.2.c, W.9-10.2.d, W.9-10.3, W.9-10.3.a, W.9-10.3.b, W.9-10.3.c, W.9-10.3.d, W.9-10.3.e, W.9-10.5, W.9-10.8, W.9-10.9.a, W.9-10.10
Speaking and Listening SL.9-10.1, SL.9-10.1.c, SL.9-10.1.d, SL.9-10.2, SL.9-10.3, SL.9-10.6
Language L.9-10.3, L.9-10.4, L.9-10.4.b, L.9-10.4.c, L.9-10.5, L.9-10.5.b, L.9-10.6
[For the full wording of the standards, see the standards chart in the front of your textbook.]

What kind of *knowledge* changes our lives?

★ INFORMATIONAL TEXT HIGHLIGHTED

Skills at a Glance

This page provides a quick look at the skills you will learn and practice in Unit 3.

Reading Skills

Main Idea
  Summarize
Ask Questions
Evaluate Persuasion
  Persuasive Techniques
  Distinguish Between Fact and Opinion

Reading for Information

Follow and Critique Technical Directions
Analyze Text Structures

Literary Analysis

Author's Point of View and Purpose
Rhetorical Mode
Word Choice and Tone
Expository Essay
Reflective Essay
Comparing Humorous Writing
Persuasive Writing and Rhetorical Devices
Analytic and Interpretive Essays
Comparing Authors' Purposes

Vocabulary

Big Question Vocabulary
Prefixes: *suc-, para-, em-, im-*
Roots: *-tact-, -tang-, -fig-, -scend-, -jur-*
Words With Multiple Meanings

Conventions

Direct and Indirect Objects
Subject Complements
Revising to Combine Short Sentences
Degrees of Adverbs
Degrees of Adjectives
Revising to Create Parallelism

Writing

Writing About the Big Question
Business Letter
Memoir
Letter
Critique
Timed Writing
Writing Workshop: Argument: Letter to the Editor
Writing Workshop: Argument: Persuasive Essay

Speaking and Listening

Humorous Persuasive Speech
Oral Recollection
Debate
Delivering a Persuasive Speech

Research and Technology

Cover Letter and Résumé

 Common Core State Standards Addressed in This Unit

Reading Literature RL.9-10.10
Reading Informational Text RI.9-10.2, RI.9-10.3, RI.9-10.4, RI.9-10.5, RI.9-10.6, RI.9-10.7, RI.9-10.8, RI.9-10.9, RI.9-10.10
Writing W.9-10.1, W.9-10.1.a, W.9-10.1.b, W.9-10.1.c, W.9-10.1.d, W.9-10.1.e, W.9-10.2, W.9-10.2.a, W.9-10.2.d, W.9-10.2.e, W.9-10.3.a, W.9-10.3.d, W.9-10.3.e, W.9-10.4, W.9-10.5, W.9-10.7, W.9-10.9.b, W.9-10.10
Speaking and Listening SL.9-10.1, SL.9-10.1.a, SL.9-10.3, SL.9-10.4, SL.9-10.6
Language L.9-10.1, L.9-10.1.a, L.9-10.2.c, L.9-10.3, L.9-10.4, L.9-10.4.a, L.9-10.4.b, L.9-10.4.c, L.9-10.4.d, L.9-10.5, L.9-10.6
[For the full wording of the standards, see the standards chart in the front of your textbook.]

Literature

▶ Poetry

Informational Text

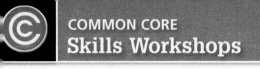

▶ Writing Workshops

▶ Vocabulary Workshops

▶ Communications Workshops

The Common Core State Standards will prepare you to succeed in college and your future career. They are separated into four sections—Reading (Literature and Informational Text), Writing, Speaking and Listening, and Language. Beginning each section, the College and Career Readiness Anchor Standards define what you need to achieve by the end of high school. The grade-specific standards that follow define what you need to know by the end of your current grade level.

© Common Core Reading Standards

College and Career Readiness Anchor Standards for Reading

Key Ideas and Details

1. Read closely to determine what the text says explicitly and to make logical inferences from it; cite specific textual evidence when writing or speaking to support conclusions drawn from the text.

2. Determine central ideas or themes of a text and analyze their development; summarize the key supporting details and ideas.

3. Analyze how and why individuals, events, and ideas develop and interact over the course of a text.

Craft and Structure

4. Interpret words and phrases as they are used in a text, including determining technical, connotative, and figurative meanings, and analyze how specific word choices shape meaning or tone.

5. Analyze the structure of texts, including how specific sentences, paragraphs, and larger portions of the text (e.g., a section, chapter, scene, or stanza) relate to each other and the whole.

6. Assess how point of view or purpose shapes the content and style of a text.

Integration of Knowledge and Ideas

7. Integrate and evaluate content presented in diverse formats and media, including visually and quantitatively, as well as in words.

8. Delineate and evaluate the argument and specific claims in a text, including the validity of the reasoning as well as the relevance and sufficiency of the evidence.

9. Analyze how two or more texts address similar themes or topics in order to build knowledge or to compare the approaches the authors take.

Range of Reading and Level of Text Complexity

10. Read and comprehend complex literary and informational texts independently and proficiently.

Grade 10 Reading Standards for Literature

Key Ideas and Details

1. Cite strong and thorough textual evidence to support analysis of what the text says explicitly as well as inferences drawn from the text.

2. Determine a theme or central idea of a text and analyze in detail its development over the course of the text, including how it emerges and is shaped and refined by specific details; provide an objective summary of the text.

3. Analyze how complex characters (e.g., those with multiple or conflicting motivations) develop over the course of a text, interact with other characters, and advance the plot or develop the theme.

Craft and Structure

4. Determine the meaning of words and phrases as they are used in the text, including figurative and connotative meanings; analyze the cumulative impact of specific word choices on meaning and tone (e.g., how the language evokes a sense of time and place; how it sets a formal or informal tone).

5. Analyze how an author's choices concerning how to structure a text, order events within it (e.g., parallel plots), and manipulate time (e.g., pacing, flashbacks) create such effects as mystery, tension, or surprise.

6. Analyze a particular point of view or cultural experience reflected in a work of literature from outside the United States, drawing on a wide reading of world literature.

Integration of Knowledge and Ideas

7. Analyze the representation of a subject or a key scene in two different artistic mediums, including what is emphasized or absent in each treatment (e.g., Auden's "Musée des Beaux Arts" and Breughel's *Landscape with the Fall of Icarus*).

8. (Not applicable to literature)

9. Analyze how an author draws on and transforms source material in a specific work (e.g., how Shakespeare treats a theme or topic from Ovid or the Bible or how a later author draws on a play by Shakespeare).

Range of Reading and Level of Text Complexity

10. By the end of grade 9, read and comprehend literature, including stories, dramas, and poems, in the grades 9–10 text complexity band proficiently, with scaffolding as needed at the high end of the range.

Grade 10 Reading Standards for Informational Text

Key Ideas and Details

1. Cite strong and thorough textual evidence to support analysis of what the text says explicitly as well as inferences drawn from the text.

2. Determine a central idea of a text and analyze its development over the course of the text, including how it emerges and is shaped and refined by specific details; provide an objective summary of the text.

3. Analyze how the author unfolds an analysis or series of ideas or events, including the order in which the points are made, how they are introduced and developed, and the connections that are drawn between them.

Craft and Structure

4. Determine the meaning of words and phrases as they are used in a text, including figurative, connotative, and technical meanings; analyze the cumulative impact of specific word choices on meaning and tone (e.g., how the language of a court opinion differs from that of a newspaper).

5. Analyze in detail how an author's ideas or claims are developed and refined by particular sentences, paragraphs, or larger portions of a text (e.g., a section or chapter).

6. Determine an author's point of view or purpose in a text and analyze how an author uses rhetoric to advance that point of view or purpose.

Integration of Knowledge and Ideas

7. Analyze various accounts of a subject told in different mediums (e.g., a person's life story in both print and multimedia), determining which details are emphasized in each account.

8. Delineate and evaluate the argument and specific claims in a text, assessing whether the reasoning is valid and the evidence is relevant and sufficient; identify false statements and fallacious reasoning.

9. Analyze seminal U.S. documents of historical and literary significance (e.g., Washington's Farewell Address, the Gettysburg Address, Roosevelt's Four Freedoms speech, King's "Letter from Birmingham Jail"), including how they address related themes and concepts.

Range of Reading and Level of Text Complexity

10. By the end of grade 9, read and comprehend literary nonfiction in the grades 9–10 text complexity band proficiently, with scaffolding as needed at the high end of the range.

© Common Core Writing Standards

College and Career Readiness Anchor Standards for Writing

Text Types and Purposes

1. Write arguments to support claims in an analysis of substantive topics or texts, using valid reasoning and relevant and sufficient evidence.

2. Write informative/explanatory texts to examine and convey complex ideas and information clearly and accurately through the effective selection, organization, and analysis of content.

3. Write narratives to develop real or imagined experiences or events using effective technique, well-chosen details, and well-structured event sequences.

Production and Distribution of Writing

4. Produce clear and coherent writing in which the development, organization, and style are appropriate to task, purpose, and audience.

5. Develop and strengthen writing as needed by planning, revising, editing, rewriting, or trying a new approach.

6. Use technology, including the Internet, to produce and publish writing and to interact and collaborate with others.

Research to Build and Present Knowledge

7. Conduct short as well as more sustained research projects based on focused questions, demonstrating understanding of the subject under investigation.

8. Gather relevant information from multiple print and digital sources, assess the credibility and accuracy of each source, and integrate the information while avoiding plagiarism.

9. Draw evidence from literary or informational texts to support analysis, reflection, and research.

Range of Writing

10. Write routinely over extended time frames (time for research, reflection, and revision) and shorter time frames (a single sitting or a day or two) for a range of tasks, purposes, and audiences.

Grade 10 Writing Standards

Text Types and Purposes

1. Write arguments to support claims in an analysis of substantive topics or texts, using valid reasoning and relevant and sufficient evidence.

   a. Introduce precise claim(s), distinguish the claim(s) from alternate or opposing claims, and create an organization that establishes clear relationships among claim(s), counterclaims, reasons, and evidence.

   b. Develop claim(s) and counterclaims fairly, supplying evidence for each while pointing out the strengths and limitations of both in a manner that anticipates the audience's knowledge level and concerns.

   c. Use words, phrases, and clauses to link the major sections of the text, create cohesion, and clarify the relationships between claim(s) and reasons, between reasons and evidence, and between claim(s) and counterclaims.

   d. Establish and maintain a formal style and objective tone while attending to the norms and conventions of the discipline in which they are writing.

   e. Provide a concluding statement or section that follows from and supports the argument presented.

2. Write informative/explanatory texts to examine and convey complex ideas, concepts, and information clearly and accurately through the effective selection, organization, and analysis of content.

   a. Introduce a topic; organize complex ideas, concepts, and information to make important connections and distinctions; include formatting (e.g., headings), graphics (e.g., figures, tables), and multimedia when useful to aiding comprehension.

   b. Develop the topic with well-chosen, relevant, and sufficient facts, extended definitions, concrete details, quotations, or other information and examples appropriate to the audience's knowledge of the topic.

   c. Use appropriate and varied transitions to link the major sections of the text, create cohesion, and clarify the relationships among complex ideas and concepts.

   d. Use precise language and domain-specific vocabulary to manage the complexity of the topic.

   e. Establish and maintain a formal style and objective tone while attending to the norms and conventions of the discipline in which they are writing.

   f. Provide a concluding statement or section that follows from and supports the information or explanation presented (e.g., articulating implications or the significance of the topic).

3. Write narratives to develop real or imagined experiences or events using effective technique, well-chosen details, and well-structured event sequences.

   a. Engage and orient the reader by setting out a problem, situation, or observation, establishing one or multiple point(s) of view, and introducing a narrator and/or characters; create a smooth progression of experiences or events.

    b. Use narrative techniques, such as dialogue, pacing, description, reflection, and multiple plot lines, to develop experiences, events, and/or characters.

    c. Use a variety of techniques to sequence events so that they build on one another to create a coherent whole.

    d. Use precise words and phrases, telling details, and sensory language to convey a vivid picture of the experiences, events, setting, and/or characters.

    e. Provide a conclusion that follows from and reflects on what is experienced, observed, or resolved over the course of the narrative.

Production and Distribution of Writing

4. Produce clear and coherent writing in which the development, organization, and style are appropriate to task, purpose, and audience.

5. Develop and strengthen writing as needed by planning, revising, editing, rewriting, or trying a new approach, focusing on addressing what is most significant for a specific purpose and audience.

6. Use technology, including the Internet, to produce, publish, and update individual or shared writing products, taking advantage of technology's capacity to link to other information and to display information flexibly and dynamically.

Research to Build and Present Knowledge

7. Conduct short as well as more sustained research projects to answer a question (including a self-generated question) or solve a problem; narrow or broaden the inquiry when appropriate; synthesize multiple sources on the subject, demonstrating understanding of the subject under investigation.

8. Gather relevant information from multiple authoritative print and digital sources, using advanced searches effectively; assess the usefulness of each source in answering the research question; integrate information into the text selectively to maintain the flow of ideas, avoiding plagiarism and following a standard format for citation.

9. Draw evidence from literary or informational texts to support analysis, reflection, and research.

    a. Apply *grades 9–10 Reading standards* to literature (e.g., "Analyze how an author draws on and transforms source material in a specific work [e.g., how Shakespeare treats a theme or topic from Ovid or the Bible or how a later author draws on a play by Shakespeare]").

    b. Apply *grades 9–10 Reading standards* to literary nonfiction (e.g., "Delineate and evaluate the argument and specific claims in a text, assessing whether the reasoning is valid and the evidence is relevant and sufficient; identify false statements and fallacious reasoning").

Range of Writing

10. Write routinely over extended time frames (time for research, reflection, and revision) and shorter time frames (a single sitting or a day or two) for a range of tasks, purposes, and audiences.

© Common Core
Speaking and Listening Standards

College and Career Readiness Anchor Standards for Speaking and Listening

Comprehension and Collaboration

1. Prepare for and participate effectively in a range of conversations and collaborations with diverse partners, building on others' ideas and expressing their own clearly and persuasively.

2. Integrate and evaluate information presented in diverse media and formats, including visually, quantitatively, and orally.

3. Evaluate a speaker's point of view, reasoning, and use of evidence and rhetoric.

Presentation of Knowledge and Ideas

4. Present information, findings, and supporting evidence such that listeners can follow the line of reasoning and the organization, development, and style are appropriate to task, purpose, and audience.

5. Make strategic use of digital media and visual displays of data to express information and enhance understanding of presentations.

6. Adapt speech to a variety of contexts and communicative tasks, demonstrating command of formal English when indicated or appropriate.

Grade 10 Speaking and Listening Standards

Comprehension and Collaboration

1. Initiate and participate effectively in a range of collaborative discussions (one-on-one, in groups, and teacher-led) with diverse partners on *grades 9–10 topics, texts, and issues,* building on others' ideas and expressing their own clearly and persuasively.

   a. Come to discussions prepared, having read and researched material under study; explicitly draw on that preparation by referring to evidence from texts and other research on the topic or issue to stimulate a thoughtful, well-reasoned exchange of ideas.

   b. Work with peers to set rules for collegial discussions and decision-making (e.g., informal consensus, taking votes on key issues, presentation of alternate views), clear goals and deadlines, and individual roles as needed.

   c. Propel conversations by posing and responding to questions that relate the current discussion to broader themes or larger ideas; actively incorporate others into the discussion; and clarify, verify, or challenge ideas and conclusions.

   d. Respond thoughtfully to diverse perspectives, summarize points of agreement and disagreement, and, when warranted, qualify or justify their own views and understanding and make new connections in light of the evidence and reasoning presented.

2. Integrate multiple sources of information presented in diverse media or formats (e.g., visually, quantitatively, orally) evaluating the credibility and accuracy of each source.

3. Evaluate a speaker's point of view, reasoning, and use of evidence and rhetoric, identifying any fallacious reasoning or exaggerated or distorted evidence.

Presentation of Knowledge and Ideas

4. Present information, findings, and supporting evidence clearly, concisely, and logically such that listeners can follow the line of reasoning and the organization, development, substance, and style are appropriate to purpose, audience, and task.

5. Make strategic use of digital media (e.g., textual, graphical, audio, visual, and interactive elements) in presentations to enhance understanding of findings, reasoning, and evidence and to add interest.

6. Adapt speech to a variety of contexts and tasks, demonstrating command of formal English when indicated or appropriate. (See grades 9–10 Language standards 1 and 3 for specific expectations.)

Common Core Language Standards

College and Career Readiness Anchor Standards for Language

Conventions of Standard English

1. Demonstrate command of the conventions of standard English grammar and usage when writing or speaking.

2. Demonstrate command of the conventions of standard English capitalization, punctuation, and spelling when writing.

Knowledge of Language

3. Apply knowledge of language to understand how language functions in different contexts, to make effective choices for meaning or style, and to comprehend more fully when reading or listening.

Vocabulary Acquisition and Use

4. Determine or clarify the meaning of unknown and multiple-meaning words and phrases by using context clues, analyzing meaningful word parts, and consulting general and specialized reference materials, as appropriate.

5. Demonstrate understanding of figurative language, word relationships, and nuances in word meanings.

6. Acquire and use accurately a range of general academic and domain-specific words and phrases sufficient for reading, writing, speaking, and listening at the college and career readiness level; demonstrate independence in gathering vocabulary knowledge when considering a word or phrase important to comprehension or expression.

Grade 10 Language Standards

Conventions of Standard English

1. Demonstrate command of the conventions of standard English grammar and usage when writing or speaking.
   a. Use parallel structure.
   b. Use various types of phrases (noun, verb, adjectival, adverbial, participial, prepositional, absolute) and clauses (independent, dependent; noun, relative, adverbial) to convey specific meanings and add variety and interest to writing or presentations.

2. Demonstrate command of the conventions of standard English capitalization, punctuation, and spelling when writing.

    a. Use a semicolon (and perhaps a conjunctive adverb) to link two or more closely related independent clauses.

    b. Use a colon to introduce a list or quotation.

    c. Spell correctly.

Knowledge of Language

3. Apply knowledge of language to understand how language functions in different contexts, to make effective choices for meaning or style, and to comprehend more fully when reading or listening.

    a. Write and edit work so that it conforms to the guidelines in a style manual (e.g., *MLA Handbook,* Turabian's *Manual for Writers*) appropriate for the discipline and writing type.

Vocabulary Acquisition and Use

4. Determine or clarify the meaning of unknown and multiple-meaning words and phrases based on *grades 9–10 reading and content,* choosing flexibly from a range of strategies.

    a. Use context (e.g., the overall meaning of a sentence, paragraph, or text; a word's position or function in a sentence) as a clue to the meaning of a word or phrase.

    b. Identify and correctly use patterns of word changes that indicate different meanings or parts of speech (e.g., *analyze, analysis, analytical; advocate, advocacy*).

    c. Consult general and specialized reference materials (e.g., dictionaries, glossaries, thesauruses), both print and digital, to find the pronunciation of a word or determine or clarify its precise meaning, its part of speech, or its etymology.

    d. Verify the preliminary determination of the meaning of a word or phrase (e.g., by checking the inferred meaning in context or in a dictionary).

5. Demonstrate understanding of figurative language, word relationships, and nuances in word meanings.

    a. Interpret figures of speech (e.g., euphemism, oxymoron) in context and analyze their role in the text.

    b. Analyze nuances in the meaning of words with similar denotations.

6. Acquire and use accurately general academic and domain-specific words and phrases, sufficient for reading, writing, speaking, and listening at the college and career readiness level; demonstrate independence in gathering vocabulary knowledge when considering a word or phrase important to comprehension or expression.

Introductory Unit

Building Academic Vocabulary

Academic vocabulary is the language you encounter in textbooks and on standardized tests and other assessments. Understanding these words and using them in your classroom discussions and writing will help you communicate your ideas clearly and effectively.

There are two basic types of academic vocabulary: general and domain-specific. **General academic vocabulary** includes words that are not specific to any single course of study. For example, the general academic vocabulary word *analyze* is used in language arts, math, social studies, art, and so on. **Domain-specific academic vocabulary** includes words that are usually encountered in the study of a specific discipline. For example, the words *factor* and *remainder* are most often used in mathematics classrooms and texts.

Common Core State Standards

Language
6. Acquire and use accurately general academic and domain-specific words and phrases sufficient for reading, writing, speaking, and listening at the college and career readiness level; demonstrate independence in gathering vocabulary knowledge when considering a word or phrase important to comprehension or expression.

General Academic Vocabulary

Word	Definition	Related Words	Word in Context
adapt (uh DAPT) *v.*	change or adjust	adaptable adaptation	Remember to adapt your reading rate to the text.
anticipate (an TIHS uh payt) *v.*	look forward to	anticipation anticipatory	Look for clues that anticipate future events.
awareness (uh WAIR nuhs) *n.*	having knowledge	aware	The author has a great awareness of his readers' interests.
background (BAK grownd) *n.*	conditions that surround or come before something		An author's background shapes his or her writing.
bias (BY uhs) *n.*	point of view before the facts are known	biased	The speaker allowed his bias to show.
character (KAR ihk tuhr) *n.*	moral strength; self-discipline	characteristic characteristically	Her character was revealed in Act II.
comprehend (kom prih HEHND) *v.*	grasp mentally; understand	comprehension	The side notes will help you comprehend new vocabulary.
conduct (KON duhkt) *n.*	the way a person acts; behavior		A speaker's conduct affects how the audience views her.
confirm (kuhn FURM) *v.*	establish the truth or correctness of something	confirmation confirmatory	Confirm whether the predictions are accurate.
context (KON tehkst) *n.*	circumstances that form the setting of an event	contextual	The context of a story may be historical.

Word	Definition	Related Words	Word in Context
convey (kuhn VAY) v.	communicate or make known		The poet uses imagery to convey feelings.
debate (dih BAYT) v.	argue or discuss	debatable debater	When you debate, support your arguments.
differentiate (dihf uh REHN shee ayt) v.	distinguish between	differ different	When reading an essay, differentiate between fact and opinion.
discern (duh ZURN) v.	tell the difference between two or more things; perceive	discernable discerning	Until I reached the end of the story, I couldn't discern the character's motives.
discourse (DIHS kawrs) n.	ongoing communication of ideas and information	discourser	Discourse in a group is an important way to hear different opinions.
distortion (dihs TAWR shuhn) n.	anything that shows something in an untrue way	distort	Avoid using unreliable sources that exhibit a distortion of facts.
evaluate (ih VAL yoo ayt) v.	determine the worth of something	evaluation	Rubrics help students evaluate their essays.
evolve (ih VOLV) v.	develop through gradual changes	evolution	Dealing with conflict allows Sam to evolve and grow.
explanation (ehks pluh NAY shuhn) n.	clarifying statement	explain explanatory	A technical document provides an explanation.
individual (ihn duh VIHJ oo uhl) adj.	relating to a single person or thing	individualism individuality	Work on an individual response, and then discuss the question.
inherent (ihn HIHR uhnt) adj.	existing naturally in something	inherence inherently	Revising is an inherent part of the process.
insight (ihn syt) n.	clear idea of the nature of things	insightful	A preface provides insight into an author's purpose.
integrity (ihn TEHG ruh tee) n.	willingness to stand by moral principles		Heroes typically display great integrity.
interact (ihn tuhr AKT) v.	relate to one another; affect another	interaction interactive	The characters interact with one another in the play.
interpretation (ihn tur pruh TAY shuhn) n.	explanation of the meaning of something	interpret interpretive	Sonnets may have more than one interpretation.
isolation (y suh LAY shuhn) n.	being alone or set apart	isolate isolated	Poems address complex feelings such as isolation.
manipulate (muh NIHP yuh layt) v.	control by use of influence, often in an unfair way	manipulation manipulative	Some speakers use bias to manipulate their audiences.

Word	Definition	Related Words	Word in Context
meaning (MEE nihng) *n.*	significance of something	meaningful	Break down long sentences to help determine their meaning.
misinterpret (mihs ihn TUR priht) *v.*	not understand correctly	interpret misinterpretation	If you misinterpret the instructions, you will build it wrong.
modified (MOD uh fyd) *v.*	changed; altered slightly	modification modifier	The cross-outs revealed that he had modified his essay.
motive (MOH tihv) *n.*	something that causes a person to act in a certain way	motivate motivation	The character's motive was revealed in the conclusion.
objective (uhb JEHK tihv) *adj.*	not dependent on another's point of view	objectively	Critics should take an objective and unbiased stance.
oppose (uh POHZ) *v.*	set against; disagree with	opposing opposition	If you oppose another student's opinion, reply respectfully.
perspective (puhr SPEHK tihv) *n.*	the way one sees things; viewpoint		I enjoy an essay more if I understand the author's perspective.
principles (PRIHN suh puhlz) *n.*	rules for right conduct; basics	principled	The principles of spelling are simple.
radical (RAD uh kuhl) *adj.*	changed to an extreme degree	radicalism radically	Beat poetry was a radical departure from classic poetry.
resolute (REHZ uh loot) *adj.*	showing a fixed purpose	resolutely	He is resolute about being honest in his article.
resolve (rih ZOLV) *v.*	reach a conclusion or decision	resolution resolved	How do the enemies resolve their conflicts?
respond (rih SPOND) *v.*	answer; react to	respondent response	How do you respond to the suspense?
responsibility (rih spon suh BIHL uh tee) *n.*	having to answer to someone; being accountable for success or failure	responsible	It is your responsibility to cite your sources when writing a research report.
revise (rih VYZ)	modify	revision	Revise your paper by fixing any errors.
subjective (suhb JEHK tihv) *adj.*	based on or influenced by a person's feelings or point of view	subjectively subjectivity	It is difficult not to be subjective when debating.
unify (YOO nuh fy) *v.*	combine into one	unification	To unify the ideas, we should add transitions.

Ordinary Language:
After reading further, I changed my original prediction.

Academic Language:
After reading further, I modified my original prediction.

Ordinary Language:
The author presents a unique view on the subject.

Academic Language:
The author presents a unique perspective on the subject.

Practice

Examples of various kinds of domain-specific academic vocabulary appear in the charts below. On a separate piece of paper, create your own domain-specific academic vocabulary charts in which you enter new academic vocabulary words as you learn them.

Social Studies: Domain-Specific Academic Vocabulary

Word	Definition	Related Words	Word in Context
absolutism (AB suh loo tiz uhm) *n.*	the principle or the exercise of complete and unrestricted power in government	absolute	The leader's absolutism restricted the freedom of citizens.
cartography (kahr TOG ruh fee) *n.*	the design and production of maps	cartographer	The geologist studied cartography and made maps.
ideology (ahy dee OL uh jee) *n.*	the beliefs that guide individuals and groups	idea	The communist ideology took hold of eastern Europe in the twentieth century.
mercantilism (MUR kuhn ti liz uhm) *n.*	commercialism; the practice of trade and commercial activity	merchant	Mercantilism was a large factor in the exploration of new lands.
radicalism (RAD I kuh liz uhm) *n.*	the favoring of drastic political, economic, or social reforms	radical	Radicalism in certain parts of the world has led to violence.

Create a chart for these social studies academic vocabulary words: *demobilization, democratization, nomination, resettlement,* and *reunification.*

Mathematics: Domain-Specific Academic Vocabulary

Word	Definition	Related Words	Word in Context
binary system (BY nuh ree SIS tuhm) *n.*	a system of counting or measurement based on powers of two	binary digit binaries	Computers use the binary system.
derivative (dih RIV uh tiv) *n.*	the rate of change of a function at any given instant	derive derived	We are going to learn about derivatives in advanced math.
dilation (dy LEY shuhn) *n.*	the transformation that changes the size of the image in geometry	dilate	We studied the dilation of images in our geometry class.
tangent (TAN juhnt) *n.*	a line in the plane of a circle that touches the circle at only one point	tangential	We were asked to find the tangent of a circle.
vector (VEK ter) *n.*	a quantity possessing both magnitude and direction	vectors	In geometry, we learned that a vector has both magnitude and direction.

Create a chart for these mathematics academic vocabulary words: *arc, continuity, correlation, density,* and *variance.*

Science: Domain-Specific Academic Vocabulary

Word	Definition	Related Words	Word in Context
fission (FISH uhn) *n.*	splitting of the nucleus of an atom or a cell	fissure	Some organisms reproduce by fission.
fusion (FYOO zhuhn) *n.*	in physics, the joining of two nuclei to form one new nucleus	fuse	Nuclear fission and fusion are opposite processes.
genetic mutation (juh NET ik myoo TEY shuhn) *n.*	any event that changes the genetic structure of an organism	genes mutate	Some genetic mutations lead to health problems.
isotope (AHY suh tohp) *n.*	multiple forms of an element that have the same number of protons but a different number of neutrons	isotopic	There are several isotopes of hydrogen.
organelle (awr guh NEL) *n.*	a part of a cell that has a specialized function	organ organism	Cell walls and nuclei are examples of organelles.

Create a chart for these science academic vocabulary words: *catalyst, chloroplast, organic, mitochondrion,* and *semiconductor.*

Art: Domain-Specific Academic Vocabulary

Word	Definition	Related Words	Word in Context
aesthetics (es THET iks) *n.*	the study of nature, beauty, and art	aesthetic aesthetician	We studied the aesthetics of ancient Greek sculpture.
analogous colors (uh NAL uh guhs KUHL ers) *n.*	colors that are next to each other on the color wheel	analogy	The difference between analogous colors is small.
formalist (FAWR muhl ihst) *n.*	anyone who places importance on how well artists design their works	formal formalize	The critic, a formalist, liked the artists' exhibit.
imitationist (im i TEY shuhn ihst) *n.*	one who favors realism in representing art subjects	imitate imitation	Because I like realism, I call myself an imitationist.
radial balance (REY dee uhl BAL uhns) *n.*	positioning objects around a central point	balanced radius	The sun is an example of an object with radial balance.

Create a chart for these art academic vocabulary words: *asymmetrical balance, emphasis, gradation, harmony,* and *symmetrical balance.*

Technology: Domain-Specific Academic Vocabulary

Word	Definition	Related Words	Word in Context
central processing unit (SEN truhl PROS es ihng YOO nit) *n.*	component of a computer that interprets and executes programs.	CPU	The central processing unit is the "brain" of a computer.
local network system (LOH kuhl NET wurk SIS tuhm) *n.*	a system for linking computers that are close to each other	LAN	Our local network system allows us to share files.
microprocessor (MY kroh pros es er) *n.*	the part of a computer that performs logical functions	micro processing	The information was fed into the microprocessor.
peripheral device (puh RIF er uhl dih VYS) *n.*	device that attaches to a computer to perform a specific function	peripheral peripherally	This scanner is the newest peripheral device I have.
shortcut key	key or combination of keys that executes a command	cut shortcut	I used a shortcut key to run the spell checker.

Create a chart for these technology academic vocabulary words: *copyright violation, desktop publishing, Internet service provider, invasion of privacy,* and *operating system.*

Increasing Your Word Knowledge

Increase your word knowledge and chances of success by taking an active role in developing your vocabulary. Here are some tips for you.

To own a word, follow these steps:

Steps to Follow	Model
1. Learn to identify the word and its basic meaning.	The word *examine* means "to look at closely."
2. Take note of the word's spelling.	*Examine* begins and ends with an *e*.
3. Practice pronouncing the word so that you can use it in conversation.	The *e* on the end of the word *examine* is silent. Its second syllable gets the most stress.
4. Visualize the word and illustrate its key meaning.	When I think of the word *examine*, I visualize a doctor checking a patient's health.
5. Learn the various forms of the word and its related words.	*Examination* and *exam* are forms of the word *examine*.
6. Compare the word with similar words.	*Examine, peruse,* and *study* are synonyms.
7. Contrast the word with similar words.	*Examine* suggests a more detailed study than *read* or *look at*.
8. Use the word in various contexts.	"I'd like to *examine* the footprints more closely." "I will *examine* the use of imagery in this poem."

Building Your Speaking Vocabulary

Language gives us the ability to express ourselves. The more words you know, the better able you will be to get your points across. There are two main aspects of language: reading and speaking. Using the steps above will help you acquire a rich vocabulary. Follow these steps below to help you learn to use this rich vocabulary in discussions, speeches, and conversations.

Steps to Follow	Tip
1. Practice pronouncing the word.	Become familiar with pronunciation guides to allow you to sound out unfamiliar words. Listening to audio books as you read the text will help you learn pronunciations of words.
2. Learn word forms.	Dictionaries often list forms of words following the main word entry. Practice saying word families aloud: "generate," "generated," "generation," "regenerate," "generator."
3. Translate your thoughts.	Restate your own thoughts and ideas in a variety of ways, to inject formality or to change your tone, for example.
4. Hold discussions.	With a classmate, practice using academic vocabulary words in discussions about the text. Choose one term to practice at a time, and see how many statements you can create using that term.
5. Tape-record yourself.	Analyze your word choices by listening to yourself objectively. Note places your word choice could be strengthened or changed.

Writing an Objective Summary

The ability to write objective summaries is key to success in college and in many careers. Writing an effective objective summary involves recording the key ideas of a text while demonstrating your understanding.

Common Core State Standards

Reading Literature
2. Determine a theme or central idea of a text and analyze in detail its development over the course of the text, including how it emerges and is shaped and refined by specific details; provide an objective summary of the text.
Reading Informational Text
2. Determine a central idea of a text and analyze its development over the course of the text, including how it emerges and is shaped and refined by specific details; provide an objective summary of the text.

What Is an Objective Summary?

An effective objective summary is a concise, complete, accurate, and objective overview of a text. Following are key elements of an objective summary:

- A good summary focuses on the main theme or central idea of a text and specific, relevant details that support that theme or central idea. Unnecessary supporting details are left out.

- Effective summaries are brief. However, the writer must be careful not to misrepresent the text by leaving out key elements.

- A summary should accurately capture the essence of the longer text it is describing.

- Finally, the writer must remain objective, that is, refrain from inserting his or her own opinions, reactions, or personal connections into the summary.

What to Avoid in an Objective Summary

- An objective summary is not a collection of sentences or paragraphs copied from the original source.

- It is not a long recounting of every event, detail, or point in the original text.

- Finally, a good summary does not include evaluative comments, such as the reader's overall opinion of or reaction to the piece.

- An objective summary is not the reader's interpretation or critical analysis of the work.

INFORMATIONAL TEXT

Model Objective Summary

Note the elements of an effective objective summary that are called out in the sidenotes. Then, write an objective summary of a text you have recently read. Review your summary, and delete any unnecessary details, opinions, or evaluations.

Summary of "The Gift of the Magi"

"The Gift of the Magi" by O. Henry is the ~~touching~~ story of a young couple named Jim and Della and what they give up in order to buy each other the perfect Christmas gift.

The story begins with Della counting the money she has scrimped to save. To her dismay, it only adds up to one dollar and eight-seven cents.

Della is looking around their humble flat when she comes up with an idea. Catching her reflection in the mirror, she decides that she will sell her most precious possession—her long, beautiful hair. She cries only a little before putting on her coat and going to a shop where she can sell her hair.

With the twenty dollars she receives for selling her hair and a dollar of her savings, Della buys Jim a chain to go with his most precious possession—a gold watch that had belonged to his father and to his grandfather before him.

At home, Della tries to fix her short hair by curling it and begins to prepare dinner. She prays that Jim still thinks she's pretty even without her long hair.

Jim arrives home on time, ~~right around 7 o'clock. Della notes that he is always on time~~. He does not react in any of the ways Della thought he might. She is terrified when she can't read the peculiar expression on his face. She begins to ramble about her hair growing back and tells him that she sold it for a good reason—to buy him a gift.

Finally, Jim assures Della that her cutting off her hair does not change how he feels about her, and he hands her a package. When she opens the gift, Della understands the odd expression on his face. Jim bought her the expensive hair combs she had wanted for a very long time, only now she doesn't have the hair to put them in.

Della assures him that her hair will grow back quickly, and then she presents Jim with the watch chain she bought him. ~~Jim tumbled down on the couch and put his hands under the back of his head and smiles.~~ He tells her that he sold the watch in order to buy her the combs.

The story ends with the narrator discussing the Magi—the wise men who began the tradition of giving Christmas gifts—and challenging the reader to consider whether Jim and Della were foolish or wise in their gift-giving. ~~I think most readers will agree that their gifts to each other were wise and heartfelt.~~

A one-sentence synopsis highlighting the theme or central idea of the story can be an effective start to a summary.

An adjective describing the story indicates an opinion and should not be included in an objective summary.

Relating the development of the text in chronological order makes a summary easy to follow.

Unnecessary details should be eliminated.

This sentence should be paraphrased rather than copied exactly from the story.

Key narration at the end of the story is included in the summary.

The writer's opinions should not appear in an objective summary.

Comprehending Complex Texts

Over the course of your academic years, you will be required to read increasingly complex texts as preparation for college and the workplace. A complex text is a work that contains challenging vocabulary, long, complex sentences, figurative language, multiple levels of meaning, or unfamiliar settings and situations.

The selections in this textbook provide you with a range of readings, including short stories, autobiography, poetry, drama, myths, and even science and history texts. Some of these texts will fall within your comfort zone; others will most likely be more challenging.

Strategy 1: Multi-draft Reading

Good readers develop the habit of revisiting texts in order to comprehend them completely. Get in the habit of reading a text or portions of a text two to three times in order to get the most out of your reading experience. To fully understand a text, try this multi-draft reading strategy:

1st Reading
On your first reading, read to gain the basic meaning of the text. If, for example, you are reading a story, look for the basics: who did what and to whom; what conflicts arise; how are conflicts resolved. If the text is nonfiction, look for main ideas and ways in which they are presented. If you are reading a lyric poem, identify the speaker, setting, and subject.

2nd Reading
During your second reading, focus on the artistry or effectiveness of the writing. Look for text structures and think about why the author chose those organizational patterns. Then, examine the author's creative use of language and its effects. For example, does the author employ metaphor, simile, or hyperbole? If so, what effect does that use of figurative language create?

3rd Reading
After your third reading, compare and contrast the text with others you have read that share an important feature. For example, once you have read Theodore Roosevelt's Inauguration Address (p. lix) and the excerpt from Dwight D. Eisenhower's speech (p. lxi), compare the way each speaker approaches the theme of national responsibility in a complex world. Evaluate the text's overall effectiveness and its central idea or theme.

 Common Core
State Standards

Reading Literature
10. By the end of grade 10, read and comprehend literature, including stories, dramas, and poems, at the high end of the grades 9–10 text complexity band independently and proficiently.

Reading Informational Text
9. Analyze seminal U. S. documents of historical and literary significance (e.g., Washington's Farewell Address, the Gettysburg Address, Roosevelt's Four Freedoms speech, King's "Letter from Birmingham Jail"), including how they address related themes and concepts.

10. By the end of grade 10, read and comprehend literary nonfiction at the high end of the grades 9–10 text complexity band independently and proficiently.

INFORMATIONAL TEXT

Independent Practice

As you read this text, practice the multi-draft reading strategy by completing a chart like the one below.

---

from Theodore Roosevelt's Inaugural Address, March 4 1905

... Our relations with the other powers of the world are important; but still more important are our relations among ourselves. Such growth in wealth, in population, and in power as this nation has seen during the century and a quarter of its national life is inevitably accompanied by a like growth in the problems which are ever before every nation that rises to greatness. Power invariably means both responsibility and danger. Our forefathers faced certain perils which we have outgrown. We now face other perils, the very existence of which it was impossible that they should foresee. Modern life is both complex and intense, and the tremendous changes wrought by the extraordinary industrial development of the last half century are felt in every fiber of our social and political being. Never before have men tried so vast and formidable an experiment as that of administering the affairs of a continent under the forms of a Democratic republic. The conditions which have told for our marvelous material well-being, which have developed to a very high degree our energy, self-reliance, and individual initiative, have also brought the care and anxiety inseparable from the accumulation of great wealth in industrial centers. Upon the success of our experiment much depends, not only as regards our own welfare, but as regards the welfare of mankind. ...

Multi-Draft Reading Chart

	My Understanding
1st Reading Look for key ideas and details that unlock basic meaning, concepts, and themes.	
2nd Reading Read for deeper meanings. Look for ways in which the author uses text structures and language to enhance meaning.	
3rd Reading Read to integrate your knowledge and ideas. Connect the text to others of its kind and to your own experience.	

Strategy 2: Close Read the Text

To comprehend a complex text, perform a close reading—a careful analysis of the words, phrases, and sentences within the text. As you close read, use the following tips to increase your understanding:

Tips for Close Reading
1. Break down long sentences into parts. Look for the subject of the sentence and its verb. Then, identify which parts of the sentence modify, or give more information about, its subject.
2. Reread passages. When reading complex texts, re-read difficult passages to make sure that you understand their meaning.
3. Look for context clues, such as the following: **a.** Restatement of an idea. For example, in this sentence, "wasted away" restates the verb *atrophy*.   He exercised so that his muscles would not **atrophy,** or <u>waste away,</u> because of disuse.   **b.** Definition of sophisticated words. In this sentence, the underlined information defines the word *monotonous*.   The **monotonous** song was <u>dull and unvarying</u>.   **c.** Examples of concepts and topics. In the following passage, the underlined text provides an example of the adjective *sparse*.   The **sparse** room <u>lacked proper furniture for guests and had no decorations on the walls</u>.   **d.** Contrasts of ideas and topics.   Abandoning his usual **veracity,** Eli <u>decided to fabricate a story</u> about why he missed practice.
4. Identify pronoun antecedents. If long sentences or passages contain pronouns, reread the text to make sure you know to what or whom the pronouns refer. In the following passage, the underlined pronouns all have the antecedent *love*.   Love has been accused of many things. *It* has caused wars, and *it* has brought peace. *It* drives people to insanity, and *it* cures disease. *It* allows the dead to live on, in the broken hearts of their survivors.
5. Look for conjunctions, such as *and, or,* and *yet,* to understand relationships between ideas.
6. Paraphrase, or restate in your own words, challenging passages in order to check your understanding. Remember that a paraphrase is a word-for-word rephrasing of an original text; it is not a summary.

INFORMATIONAL TEXT

Close-Read Model

As you read President Eisenhower's Address Before the General Assembly of the United Nations on December 8th, 1953, study the side notes that model ways to unlock meaning in the text.

 Common Core State Standards

Reading Informational Text 9. Analyze seminal U. S. documents of historical and literary significance (e.g., Washington's Farewell Address, the Gettysburg Address, Roosevelt's Four Freedoms speech, King's "Letter from Birmingham Jail"), including how they address related themes and concepts.

---

from "Atoms for Peace" by Dwight D. Eisenhower

Madame President, Members of the General Assembly:

. . .I know that the American people share my deep belief that if a danger exists in the world, it is a danger shared by all—and equally, that if hope exists in the mind of one nation, that hope should be shared by all...I feel impelled to speak today in a language that in a sense is new—one which I, who have spent so much of my life in the military profession, would have preferred never to use.

That new language is the language of atomic warfare. . .

Occasional pages of history do record the faces of the "Great Destroyers" but the whole book of history reveals mankind's never-ending quest for peace, and mankind's God-given capacity to build. It is with the book of history, and not with isolated pages, that the United States will ever wish to be identified. My country wants to be constructive, not destructive. It wants agreements, not wars, among nations. It wants itself to live in freedom, and in the confidence that the people of every other nation enjoy equally the right of choosing their own way of life.

So my country's purpose is to help us move out of the dark chamber of horrors into the light, to find a way by which the minds of men, the hopes of men, the souls of men everywhere, can move forward toward peace and happiness and well being. In this quest, I know that we must not lack patience. I know that in a world divided, such as ours today, salvation cannot be attained by one dramatic act. I know that many steps will have to be taken over many months before the world can look at itself one day and truly realize that a new climate of mutually peaceful confidence is abroad in the world. But I know, above all else, that we must start to take these steps—now.

Break down this long sentence. The speaker, *I*, is the subject, and *know* is the verb. The first phrase highlighted in green tells what the speaker knows. The last two phrases highlighted in green modify the word *belief*.

Search for context clues. The words highlighted in green can help you figure out the word highlighted in yellow.

The word "so" signals that a summarization of a key point is to come: America wants to help the world change direction.

Look for antecedents. The "we" refers to President Eisenhower and the members of the General Assembly of the United Nations.

Strategy 3: Ask Questions

Be an attentive reader by asking questions as you read. Throughout this textbook, we have provided questions for you following each selection. These questions are sorted into three basic categories that build in sophistication and lead you to a deeper understanding of the texts you read.

Here is an example from this text:

Some questions are about Key Ideas and Details in the text. To answer these questions, you will need to locate and cite explicit information in the text or draw inferences from what you have read.

Some questions are about Craft and Structure in the text. To answer these questions, you will need to analyze how the author developed and structured the text. You will also look for ways in which the author artfully used language and how those word choices impacted the meaning and tone of the work.

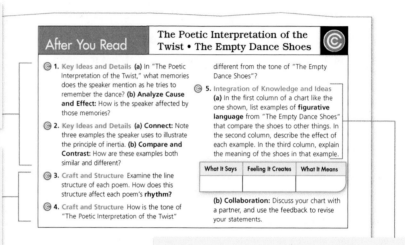

After You Read — The Poetic Interpretation of the Twist • The Empty Dance Shoes

1. Key Ideas and Details (a) In "The Poetic Interpretation of the Twist," what memories does the speaker mention as he tries to remember the dance? (b) Analyze Cause and Effect: How is the speaker affected by those memories?

2. Key Ideas and Details (a) Connect: Note three examples the speaker uses to illustrate the principle of inertia. (b) Compare and Contrast: How are these examples both similar and different?

3. Craft and Structure Examine the line structure of each poem. How does this structure affect each poem's rhythm?

4. Craft and Structure How is the tone of "The Poetic Interpretation of the Twist" different from the tone of "The Empty Dance Shoes"?

5. Integration of Knowledge and Ideas (a) In the first column of a chart like the one shown, list examples of figurative language from "The Empty Dance Shoes" that compare the shoes to other things. In the second column, describe the effect of each example. In the third column, explain the meaning of the shoes in that example.

What It Says	Feeling It Creates	What It Means

(b) Collaboration: Discuss your chart with a partner, and use the feedback to revise your statements.

Some questions are about the Integration of Knowledge and Ideas in the text. These questions ask you to evaluate a text in many different ways, such as comparing texts, analyzing arguments in the text, and using many other methods of thinking critically about a text's ideas.

Preparing to Read Complex Texts

Attentive Reading As you read literature on your own, bring your imagination and questions to the text. The questions shown below and others that you formulate as you read will help you learn and enjoy literature even more.

Common Core State Standards

Reading Literature/Informational Text
10. By the end of grade 9, read and comprehend literature, including stories, dramas, and poems, and literary nonfiction in the grades 9–10 text complexity band proficiently, with scaffolding as needed at the high end of the range.

When reading fiction, ask...

- Who is telling the story? Do I enjoy his or her voice?
- Does the story offer a message about life that I appreciate?
  — Key Ideas and Details

- Is the world of the story convincing? Do any details jolt me out of that world or seem wrong?
- Does the plot pull me along? Do I care what happens?
- Do the characters seem real? Do the reasons they feel and act as they do ring true? Do their words and thoughts sound authentic?
- Does the author use language well?
  — Craft and Structure

- Do I like the characters, or—at least—find them interesting?
- Do I believe the events of this story?
- Is the work fresh and original?
  — Integration of Ideas

As you read independently, ask similar types of questions to ensure that you fully enjoy and comprehend texts you read for both school and pleasure. We have provided sets of questions for you on the Independent Reading pages at the end of each unit.

EXEMPLAR TEXT

Model

Following is an example of a complex text. The sidenotes show sample questions that an attentive reader might ask while reading.

Sample questions:

---

from "Classifying the Stars" by Annie J. Cannon

To the People of the State of New York:

. . .The very beginning of our knowledge of the nature of a star dates back to 1672, when Isaac Newton gave to the world the results of his experiments on passing sunlight through a prism. To describe the beautiful band of rainbow tints, produced when sunlight was dispersed by his three-cornered piece of glass, he took from the Latin the word *spectrum*, meaning "an appearance."

. . .In 1814, more than a century after Newton, the spectrum of the Sun was obtained in such purity that an amazing detail was seen and studied by the German optician, Fraunhofer. He saw that the multiple spectral tings, ranging from delicate violet to deep red, were crossed by hundreds of fine dark lines. In other words, there were narrow gaps in the spectrum where certain shades were wholly blotted out.

We must remember that the word spectrum is applied not only to sunlight, but also to the light of any glowing substance when its rays are sorted out by a prism or a grating.

Key Ideas and Details What ideas are introduced in this paragraph? What assumptions does the author make?

Craft and Structure What organizational pattern does the writer use? How does the use of this pattern help to convey her ideas?

Integration of Knowledge and Ideas In what ways does the information in this text expand on or contradict what I already know?

 EXEMPLAR TEXT

Independent Practice

Write three to five questions you might ask yourself as you read this passage.

From "Circumference" by Nicholas Nicastro

The astrolabe . . . is a manual computing and observation device with myriad uses in astronomy, time keeping, surveying, navigation, and astrology. The principles behind the most common variety, the planispheric astrolabe, were first laid down in antiquity by the Greeks, who pioneered the notion of projecting three-dimensional images on flat surfaces. The device reached a high degree of refinement in the medieval Islamic world, where it was invaluable for determining prayer times and the direction of Mecca from anywhere in the Muslim world. The astrolabe was introduced to Europe by the eleventh century, where it saw wide use until the Renaissance....

Analyzing Arguments

The ability to evaluate an argument, as well as to make one, is an important skill for success in college and in the workplace.

What Is an Argument?

In literature and writing, an *argument* is the presentation of one side of a controversial or debatable issue. Through this type of argument, the writer logically supports a particular belief, conclusion, or point of view. A good argument is supported with strong reasoning and relevant, provable evidence.

**Common Core
State Standards**

Reading Informational Text
6. Determine an author's point of view or purpose in a text and analyze how an author uses rhetoric to advance that point of view or purpose.
8. Delineate and evaluate the argument and specific claims in a text, assessing whether the reasoning is valid and the evidence is relevant and sufficient; identify false statements and fallacious reasoning.
Language
6. Acquire and use accurately grade-appropriate general academic and domain-specific words and phrases; gather vocabulary knowledge when considering a word or phrase important to comprehension or expression.

Elements of Argument

Claim (assertion)—what the writer is trying to prove
Example: Grade point averages should be weighted.

Grounds (evidence)—the support used to convince the reader
Example: Because difficult classes require much more work, the extra effort should be acknowledged.

Justification—the link between the grounds and the claim; why the grounds are credible
Example: Because GPA is an indication of a student's ability to succeed in college, students who take challenging courses should be ranked above students who take easier classes even if they earn the same grade.

Evaluating Claims

When reading or listening to an argument, critically assess the claims that are made. Analyze the argument to identify claims that are valid or can be proved true. Also evaluate evidence that supports the claims. If there is little or no reasoning or evidence provided to support the claims, the argument may not be sound. Also, be on the lookout for logical fallacies, like those listed below.

Logical Fallacies

Although they can initially seem convincing, logical fallacies do not hold up in an examination of an argument.

- **False Causality:** The invalid idea that because B occurred after A, A caused B to happen
- *Ad Hominem:* An attack on a person's character, not on the person's position on an issue
- **Red Herring:** A provocative idea that is included in an argument to distract an audience's attention from the real issue under discussion
- **Begging the Question:** The premise or assumption that the argument is true because it is said to be true
- **Overgeneralization:** A conclusion that is based on little or no evidence

Model Argument

from "Thank Heaven for Little Girls" by Rich Stearns

The lyrics to Maurice Chevalier's most enduring song describe an idyllic view of little girls and the women they become. There is much in our art and literature that romanticizes girls and women and the role they play in our culture. But sadly, in our world today, being female often means being sentenced to a life of poverty, abuse, exploitation, and deprivation. Compared to her male counterpart, a girl growing up in the developing world is more likely to die before her fifth birthday and less likely to go to school. She is less likely to receive adequate food or health care, less likely to receive economic opportunities, more likely to be forced to marry before the age of 16 . . . Girls are forced to stay home from school to work. In fact, two thirds of the nearly 800 million illiterate people in the world are women. Only one in 10 women in Niger can read. Five hundred thousand women die every year from childbirth complications—that's one woman every minute . . . Women are denied property rights and inheritance in many countries. Worldwide, women own only 1 percent of the world's property. They work two-thirds of all the world's labor hours but earn just 10 percent of the world's wages. Being female, in much of our world, is not "heavenly."

And yet, in my opinion, the single-most significant thing that can be done to "cure" extreme poverty is this: protect, educate, and nurture girls and women and provide them with equal rights and opportunities—educationally, economically, and socially.

According to U.N. Secretary-General Kofi Annan: "No tool for development is more effective than the empowerment of women." This one thing can do more to address extreme poverty than food, shelter, health care, economic development, or increased foreign assistance. There is a saying in Ghana: "If you educate a man, you simply educate an individual, but if you educate a woman, you educate a nation." When a girl is educated, her income potential increases, maternal and infant mortality is reduced, her children are more likely to be immunized, the birth rate decreases, and HIV infection rates (especially in Africa) are lowered. She is more likely to acquire skills to improve her family's economic stability, and she is more likely to ensure that her daughters also receive an education. Educating girls pays dividend after dividend to the whole community. . .

The introduction explains the title and references a popular 1950s song to hook readers.

This paragraph describes the poverty and lack of freedoms that women face. Stearns will go on to argue that improving one (freedom) will improve the other (conditions of poverty).

Claim: Educating women relieves poverty.

Grounds: The claim is supported by a quotation from U.N. Secretary-General Kofi Annan and by a Ghanaian saying. Benefits from educating girls range from reducing infant mortality to improving economic stability. These benefits are assumed to address poverty and its effects.

Unstated Justification: The evidence comes from a wide range of sources: the U.N. Secretary-General, who is an authority on international issues; an African saying; and the summarized results of implied research.

A strong conclusion does more than simply restate the claim.

Analyzing Arguments **lxv**

The Art of Argument: Rhetorical Devices and Persuasive Techniques

Rhetorical Devices

Rhetoric is the art of using language in order to make a point or to persuade listeners. Rhetorical devices such as the ones listed below are accepted elements of argument. Their use does not invalidate or weaken an argument. Rather, the use of rhetorical devices is regarded as a key part of an effective argument.

Rhetorical Device	Examples
Repetition The repeated use of certain words, phrases, or sentences	Soldiers learn **true** greatness, **true** wisdom, and **true** strength.
Parallelism The repeated use of similar grammatical structures	Sports teach **the thrill of victory** and **the agony of defeat.**
Rhetorical Question Calling attention to an issue by implying an obvious answer	Isn't freedom worth fighting for?
Sound Devices The use of alliteration, assonance, rhyme, or rhythm	There are **d**ark **d**ays that lie ahead, but we will not be **d**efeated!
Simile and Metaphor Comparing two seemingly unlike things or asserting that one thing is another	**Patriotism** spread <u>like a fire</u> through the ranks of soldiers after the General's speech.

Persuasive Techniques

Persuasive techniques are often used in advertisements and in other forms of persuasion. Although techniques like the ones below may appear in formal arguments, they are less convincing than the use of logical reasoning and authoritative evidence.

Persuasive Technique	Examples
Bandwagon Approach/Anti-Bandwagon Approach Appeals to a person's desire to belong; encourages or celebrates individuality	Come see why more people choose to shop with us.
Emotional Appeal Evokes people's fear, anger, or desire	Join the army and protect our nation from those who would destroy our way of life.
Endorsement/Testimony Employs a well-known person to promote a product or idea	"I drink Happy Throat Tea before all of my concerts."
Loaded Language The use of words that are charged with emotion	They are suffering under a brutal dictator.
"Plain Folks" Appeal Shows a connection to everyday, ordinary people	"I grew up in a working-class neighborhood, just like this one."
Hyperbole Exaggerates to make a point	We face a thousand crises everyday.

INFORMATIONAL TEXT

Model Speech

The speech excerpted below includes rhetorical devices and persuasive techniques.

from "Duty, Honor, Country" by General Douglas MacArthur

Duty, Honor, Country: Those three hallowed words reverently dictate what you ought to be, what you can be, what you will be. They are your rallying points: to build courage when courage seems to fail; to regain faith when there seems to be little cause for faith; to create hope when hope becomes forlorn. Unhappily, I possess neither that eloquence of diction, that poetry of imagination, nor that brilliance of metaphor to tell you all that they mean...

> General MacArthur uses parallelism and repetition to emphasize the ideas of *duty, honor,* and *country.*

But these are some of the things they do. They build your basic character. They mold you for your future roles as the custodians of the nation's defense. They make you strong enough to know when you are weak, and brave enough to face yourself when you are afraid. They teach you to be proud and unbending in honest failure, but humble and gentle in success; not to substitute words for actions, not to seek the path of comfort, but to face the stress and spur of difficulty and challenge;... They give you a temper of the will, a quality of the imagination, a vigor of the emotions, a freshness of the deep springs of life, a temperamental predominance of courage over timidity, of an appetite for adventure over love of ease. They create in your heart the sense of wonder, the unfailing hope of what next, and the joy and inspiration of life. They teach you in this way to be an officer and a gentleman.

> Additional instances of parallelism clarify General MacArthur's ideas and make them more emotionally engaging.

And what sort of soldiers are those you are to lead? Are they reliable? Are they brave? Are they capable of victory? Their story is known to all of you. It is the story of the American man at arms...His name and fame are the birthright of every American citizen. In his youth and strength, his love and loyalty, he gave all that mortality can give....

> Rhetorical questions call attention to a change in the topic.

From one end of the world to the other, he has drained deep the chalice of courage. As I listened to those songs of the glee club, in memory's eye I could see those staggering columns of the First World War, bending under soggy packs on many a weary march, from dripping dusk to drizzling dawn, slogging ankle deep through mire of shell-pocked roads; to form grimly for the attack, blue-lipped, covered with sludge and mud, chilled by the wind and rain, driving home to their objective, and for many, to the judgment seat of God.

> MacArthur uses alliteration, which gives his descriptions more power.

I do not know the dignity of their birth, but I do know the glory of their death. They died unquestioning, uncomplaining, with faith in their hearts, and on their lips the hope that we would go on to victory. Always for them Duty, Honor, Country.

> Parallelism makes this phrase memorable and powerful.

> Repetition of key ideas from the beginning of the speech provides a satisfying conclusion.

Composing an Argument

**Common Core
State Standards**

Writing 1.a. Introduce precise claim(s), distinguish the claim(s) from alternate or opposing claims, and create an organization that establishes clear relationships among claim(s), counterclaims, reasons, and evidence.
1.b. Develop claim(s) and counterclaims fairly, supplying evidence for each while pointing out the strengths and limitations of both in a manner that anticipates the audience's knowledge level and concerns.
1.e. Provide a concluding statement or section that follows from and supports the argument presented.

Choosing a Topic

When writing an argument, choose a topic that matters—to people in general and to you personally. Brainstorm for topics you would like to address, and then choose the one that most interests you.

Once you have chosen a topic, check to be sure you can make an arguable claim. Ask yourself:

1. What am I trying to prove? What ideas do I need to communicate?
2. Are there people who would disagree with my claim? What opinions might they have?
3. Do I have evidence to support my claim? Is my evidence sufficient and relevant?

If you are able to put into words what you want to prove and can answer "Yes" to questions 2 and 3, you have an arguable claim.

Introducing the Claim and Establishing Its Significance

Before you begin writing, think about your audience and how much they already know about your topic. Then, provide only as much background information as necessary. Remember that you are not writing a summary of the issue—you are crafting an argument.

Once you have provided context for your argument, clearly state your claim, or thesis. A written argument's claim often, but not always, appears in the first paragraph.

Developing Your Claim with Reasoning and Evidence

Now that you have stated your claim, support it with evidence, or grounds. A good argument should be supported with at least three solid pieces of evidence. Evidence can range from personal experience to researched data or expert opinion. Understanding your audience's knowledge level, concerns, values, and possible biases can help you decide which types of evidence will have the strongest impact. Make sure your evidence is current and comes from a credible source. Do not forget to credit your sources.

Work to address opposing ideas, or counterclaims, within the body of your argument. Consider points you have made or evidence you have provided that a reader might challenge. Decide how best to respond to these counterclaims.

Writing a Concluding Statement or Section

Restate your claim in the conclusion of your argument, and synthesize, or pull together, the evidence you have provided. Make your conclusion powerful and memorable so that your readers continue to think about your points.

Practice

Complete an outline like the one below to help you plan your own argument.

Brainstorming for Topics:

_____

_____

The Topic That Most Interests Me Is _____ because

_____

Arguable Claim (Thesis): _____

What I Already Know About the Issue: _____

What I Need to Find Out About the Issue:

_____

Who Is My Audience and How Much Does My Audience Know About the Issue?

_____

Possible Sources of Evidence: _____

Grounds to Support My Claim (at least three strong pieces of evidence):

1. _____

2. _____

3. _____

Warrants for My Grounds (why my grounds are allowed to stand as evidence):

1. _____

2. _____

3. _____

Opposing Viewpoints to Consider: _____

Media Literacy Handbook

INTRODUCTION: Today, messages are transmitted across a variety of media modes, such as film, television, radio, and the Internet. As you interact with these messages each day—in images, advertisements, movies, and an array of different contexts—it is important to consider the potential influence of the medium.

- What is the intention of the message?
- How is it communicated?
- How do specific elements of the medium—such as color, image, or font—help convey the message?
- Why might the creator of the message have selected this medium?

These are the key issues of media literacy, the study of messages in the media and their impact.

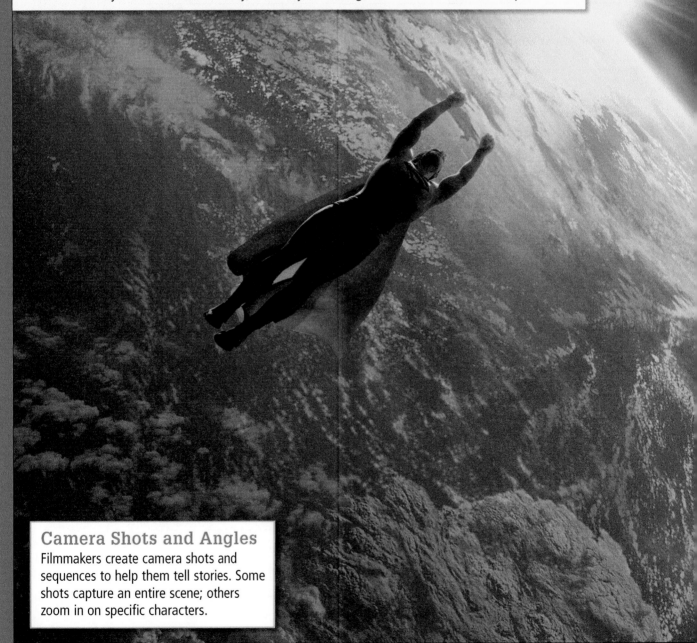

Camera Shots and Angles

Filmmakers create camera shots and sequences to help them tell stories. Some shots capture an entire scene; others zoom in on specific characters.

Special Effects

Filmmakers use special effects
to create on-screen illusions that
bring the imagination to life.

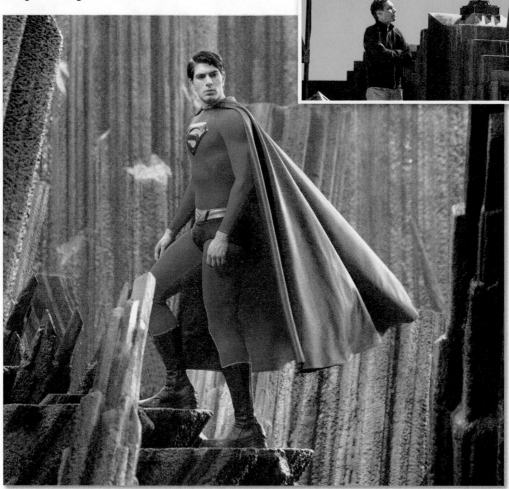

Questions About Film Techniques

- What effect is created by the choice of camera angle shown in the
  image at left? Choose another camera angle and explain how that
  shot might convey a different message than the one shown here.

- Study the images above. In what way does the use of special
  effects make the film better for viewers?

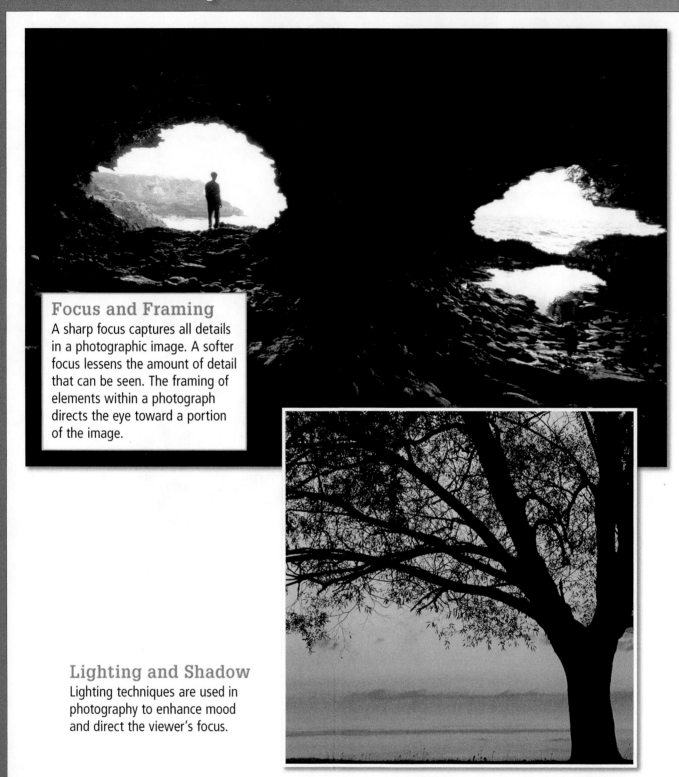

Focus and Framing

A sharp focus captures all details in a photographic image. A softer focus lessens the amount of detail that can be seen. The framing of elements within a photograph directs the eye toward a portion of the image.

Lighting and Shadow

Lighting techniques are used in photography to enhance mood and direct the viewer's focus.

Special Techniques

Most images you see today have been manipulated or changed in some way. Even a small change—such as an added graphic element or a difference in shading—can alter the mood of an image.

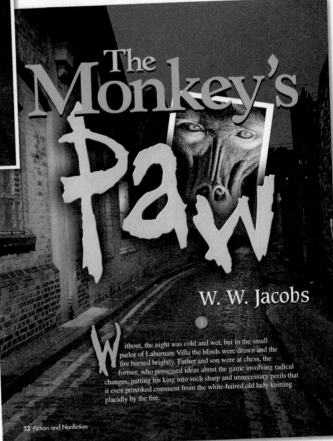

The Monkey's Paw

W. W. Jacobs

Without, the night was cold and wet, but in the small parlor of Laburnam Villa the blinds were drawn and the fire burned brightly. Father and son were at chess, the former, who possessed ideas about the game involving radical changes, putting his king into such sharp and unnecessary perils that it even provoked comment from the white-haired old lady knitting placidly by the fire.

32 Fiction and Nonfiction

Questions About Graphics and Photos

- What would be the effect if the images at left used different focuses?

- In what way does the use of color and light create mood in the photos at left?

- What special techniques were applied to the original photographs shown above? What effect does the use of special techniques create?

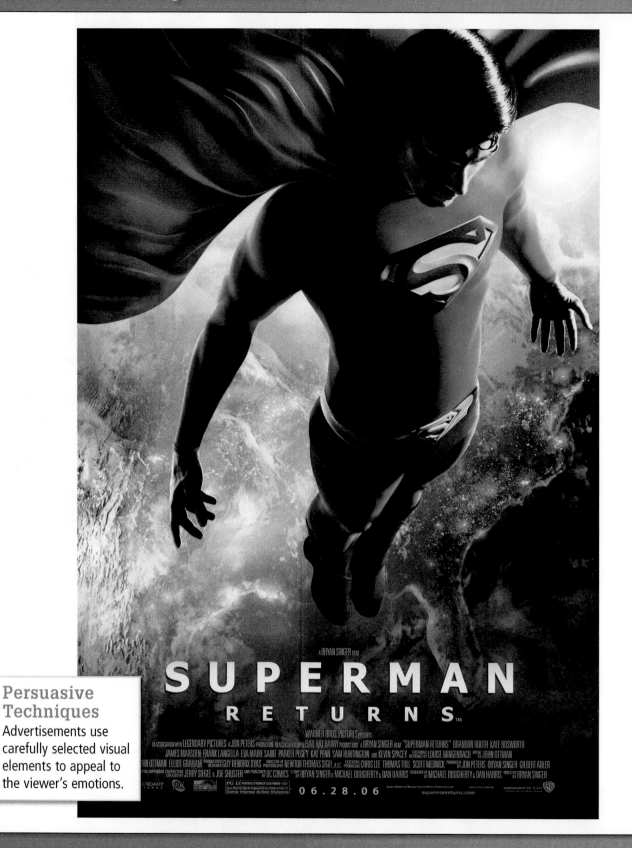

Persuasive Techniques

Advertisements use carefully selected visual elements to appeal to the viewer's emotions.

Text and Graphics

Newspaper and magazine layouts are constructed to capture the eye and quickly convey the important ideas of a story. The use of type fonts, images, and page space directs the eye to portions of the printed page.

Questions About Print Media

- What image or graphic dominates the advertisement at left? How does the image make the advertisement more effective?

- Which of the above grabs your attention: the image or the text on the magazine cover? Explain.

- What do you notice first on the newspaper's front page? What overall effect does the use of type size and fonts create?

How is this book organized?

- There are six units, each focusing on a specific genre.
- Each unit has a Big Question to get you thinking about important ideas and to guide your reading.
- A Literary Analysis Workshop begins each unit, providing instruction and practice for essential skills.

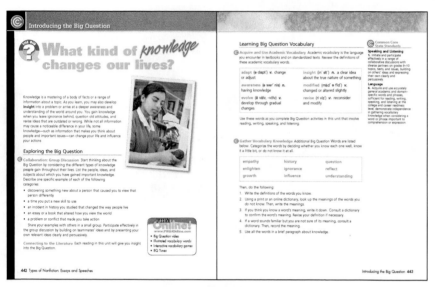

◀ At the beginning of the unit, **Introducing the Big Question** provides a reading focus for the entire unit. Use **academic vocabulary** to think, talk, and write about this question.

A **Literary Analysis Workshop** provides an overview of the unit genre, an in-depth exploration of Common Core State Standards, as well as models and practice opportunities. ▶

How are the literary selections organized?

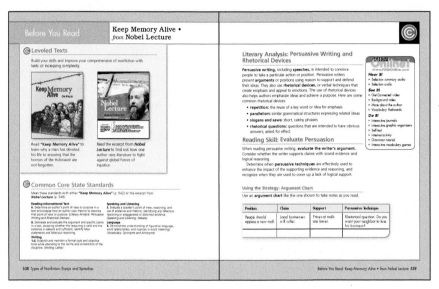

◀ **Before You Read** introduces two selection choices that both teach the same skills. Your teacher will help you choose the selection that is right for you.

Writing About the Big Question is a quick-writing activity that helps you connect the Big Question to the selection you are about to read.

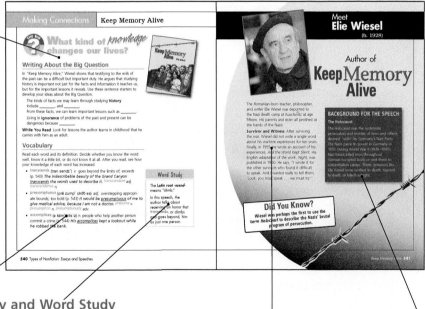

Vocabulary and Word Study introduce important selection vocabulary words and teach you about prefixes, suffixes, and roots.

Meet the Author and Background teach you about the author's life and provide information that will help you understand the selection.

How are the literary selections organized? *(continued)*

After You Read helps you practice the skills you have learned. ▼

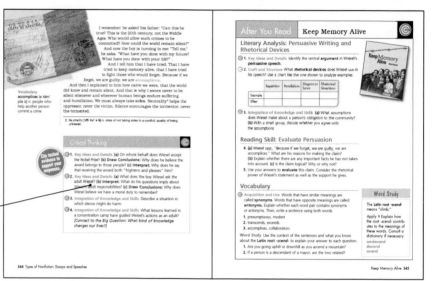

Critical Thinking questions help you reflect on what you have read and apply the Big Question to the selection.

Projects and activities help you deepen your understanding of the selection while strengthening your **writing, listening, speaking, and research skills.**

Integrated Language Skills provides instruction and practice for important grammar skills.

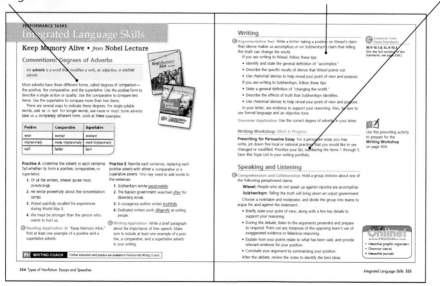

What special features will I find in this book?

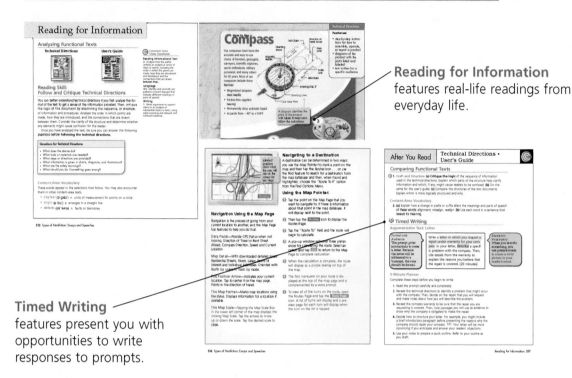

Reading for Information features real-life readings from everyday life.

Timed Writing features present you with opportunities to write responses to prompts.

◀ **Test Practice** features and **Assessment Workshops** enable you to test your knowledge of all major skills to help you succeed on standardized tests.

Is there a difference between *reality* and *truth?*

Fiction and Nonfiction

www.PHLitOnline.com

Hear It!
- Selection summary audio
- Selection audio
- BQ Tunes

See It!
- Author videos
- Big Question video
- Get Connected videos
- Background videos
- More about the authors
- Illustrated vocabulary words
- Vocabulary flashcards

Do It!
- Interactive journals
- Interactive graphic organizers
- Grammar tutorials
- Interactive vocabulary games
- Test practice

Is there a difference between *reality* and *truth?*

Reality and **truth** may seem like abstract ideas, but they can influence the way you see the world. The truth is something that has been proven or that we believe is so. However, the truth can be subjective, or influenced by each person's perceptions or life experiences. In contrast, reality refers to all the things that exist in the world. Our senses, such as sight and touch, help us discern what is real. However, things that are not concrete and observable can still exist.

Two people might watch the same event, for example, but observe different things. What is true about the event to one person is not true to the other. A video might seem more objective than a diary entry about an event, but even a recording is influenced by a whole variety of subjective factors, including decisions about editing and what to include on camera. Ultimately, although it is useful to think about how people perceive reality and truth, the answer is, to some extent, as individual as people themselves.

Exploring the Big Question

Collaboration: Group Discussion Start thinking about the Big Question. With a small group, list things that are true for some but may differ from reality or from other people's perception of the truth. Describe specific examples of each of the following, building on each other's ideas.

- Something that is easy for you and difficult for a friend
- Something that you and your parents see differently
- The solution to a political issue
- A scientific theory that has some uncertainty

For each example, discuss whether truth differs from reality. State your case clearly and persuasively.

Connecting to the Literature Each reading in this unit will give you additional insight into the Big Question.

PHLit Online!
www.PHLitOnline.com
- Big Question video
- Illustrated vocabulary words
- Interactive vocabulary games
- BQ Tunes

Learning Big Question Vocabulary

Common Core State Standards

Speaking and Listening
1. Initiate and participate effectively in a range of collaborative discussions with diverse partners on grade 9–10 topics, texts, and issues, building on others' ideas and expressing their own clearly and persuasively.

Language
6. Acquire and use accurately general academic and domain-specific words and phrases, sufficient for reading, writing, speaking, and listening at the college and career readiness level; demonstrate independence in gathering vocabulary knowledge when considering a word or phrase important to comprehension or expression.

Acquire and Use Academic Vocabulary Academic vocabulary is the language you encounter in textbooks and on standardized tests. Review the definitions of these academic vocabulary words.

comprehend (käm´ prē hend´) *v.* understand	**discern** (di surn´, di zurn´) *v.* tell the difference between two or more things
confirm (kən furm´) *v.* establish the truth or correctness of something	**evaluate** (ē val´ yoo āt´) *v.* determine the worth of something
context (kän´ tekst´) *n.* circumstances that surround an event or idea and give it meaning	**objective** (əb jek´ tiv) *adj.* not dependent on a person's viewpoint
differentiate (dif´ ər en shē āt´) *v.* distinguish between	**subjective** (səb jek´ tiv) *adj.* influenced by a person's viewpoint

Use these words as you complete Big Question activities in this unit that involve reading, writing, speaking, and listening.

Gather Vocabulary Knowledge Additional Big Question words are listed below. Categorize the words by deciding whether you know each one well, know it a little bit, or do not know it at all.

concrete	perception	uncertainty
evidence	reality	verify
improbable		

Then, do the following:

1. Write the definitions of the words you know.
2. Consult a print or online dictionary to confirm the meanings you wrote down. Revise your original definitions if necessary.
3. Using the dictionary, look up the meanings of the words you do not know. Then, rewrite the definitions in your own words.
4. Use all the words in a paragraph about a situation in which it is difficult to discover the truth because people's perceptions of reality are so different.

Elements of Fiction and Nonfiction

In **fiction,** an author tells of imaginary characters and events. In **nonfiction,** an author discusses facts or general ideas.

Fiction consists of **narratives,** or stories, that are products of an author's imagination. Not every detail in a work of fiction needs to be made up. For example, a short story may be set in a real place. Certain kinds of fiction routinely combine elements of the imaginary and the actual. In a historical novel, for example, an author may portray actual historical figures interacting with imaginary characters.

Nonfiction conveys factual information about real people, places, and events or discusses general ideas about the world. An author may describe a subject, explain how to perform a process, examine a theory, or try to convince readers to change their beliefs or take a particular course of action. Though nonfiction concerns fact, it may employ elements of fiction, such as striking language and artful pacing.

Comparison of Fiction and Nonfiction	
Fiction	**Nonfiction**
portrays imaginary people or animals, called **characters**	gives factual information about real people
describes a series of interrelated events, called the **plot**	gives factual information about real events and processes
depicts **conflicts,** or struggles between opposing forces, experienced by characters. These conflicts may be • **internal** psychological struggles, or • struggles with an **external** force.	tells of actual conflicts and real-world problems
is told from the **point of view,** or perspective, of an imaginary speaker called the **narrator.** The story may be told in the • **first-person point of view,** in which the narrator is a character in the story, or • **the third-person point of view,** in which the narrator is not a character in the story.	may be told from the point of view of the author, who is a real person, or may be written from a more **objective,** or neutral, point of view
takes place in a **setting**—a real or an imaginary time and place, including its beliefs and customs	provides factual information about real times, places, or cultures
often suggests a **theme,** or insight into life	often focuses on a **central idea,** or key concept

Major Forms of Fiction

There are three major forms of fiction.

Short stories are brief narratives. Their plots develop quickly and center around one or two main characters and a single, strong conflict and theme.

Novels are extended narratives that typically develop multiple characters, an extensive plot, and multiple conflicts. Novels often develop **subplots,** or distinct sequences of events that support or contrast with the main plot, and multiple themes.

Novellas are more concise than novels but lengthier than short stories. Novellas focus on a few main characters and a main plot, but they may develop characters and plots in more detail than a short story and may suggest more than one theme.

Major Forms of Nonfiction

Nonfiction may be divided into two large categories: functional texts and literary nonfiction.

Functional texts present facts and information intended to inform or educate the reader. Functional texts are generally objective: They do not express a particular author's point of view, and the writing style is usually clear and straightforward.

Literary nonfiction also presents facts about a subject, but it may employ literary elements such as descriptive language and dialogue to do so. As a result, it may entertain readers as well as inform them. Unlike functional texts, literary nonfiction may express the author's individual point of view.

The chart below lists and explains examples of functional texts and literary nonfiction.

In This Section

Elements of Fiction and Nonfiction

Determining Theme in Fiction

Determining Central Ideas in Nonfiction

Close Read: Theme in Fiction
• Model Text
• Practice Text

Close Read: Central Idea in Nonfiction
• Model Text
• Practice Text

After You Read

 Common Core State Standards

RL.9-10.2; RI.9-10.2
[For the full wording of the standards, see the standards chart in the front of your textbook.]

Examples of Functional Texts	Forms of Literary Nonfiction
Reports: detailed accounts of specific topics that • synthesize, or combine, information from a variety of sources • may organize and interpret the results of studies	**Personal narratives:** true stories by real people about their own lives • The author of an **autobiography** describes major events in his or her life. • The author of a **memoir** or **journal entry** describes a particular time or experience in detail.
Newsletters: collections of brief announcements, articles, and reports published at regular intervals that • can be either formal or informal in tone • appeal to a select audience targeted by the writer	**Biographies:** true accounts of a person's life that are written by someone else and that • describe the major events of the person's life • identify why the person is interesting or significant • may include the author's opinion of the person
Online reference sources: Web sites that are set up to provide information on a topic and that • may include audio or video content • identify their source on the home page or in a link	**Essays:** short literary works that focus on developing or explaining a central idea or concept and that • may be formal or informal • express the author's point of view

Determining Theme in Fiction

Common Core State Standards

Reading Literature

2. Determine a theme or central idea of a text and analyze in detail its development over the course of the text, including how it emerges and is shaped and refined by specific details; provide an objective summary of the text.

Themes—insights or messages about life—are often suggested through the words, actions, and fate of a story's characters.

Implied Theme A **theme** is an insight into human nature that emerges over the course of a work. Though a theme may be directly stated, more often it is *implied,* or suggested through elements of the work, as in the following example:

> **Character's Actions** Main character sacrifices friendship to make her business successful.
> **Character's Experience** Although she succeeds, she is unhappy.
> **Implied Theme** Friendship is more important than success.

Each detail in a work can contribute to the development and refinement of theme, as in this example:

> **Theme** Friendship is more important than success.
> **Introduction of Theme** To succeed, the main character breaks a promise to her friend.
> **Reinforcing Detail** Another character keeps a promise to a friend, though he loses money as a result.
> **Refining Detail** The main character loses her business, showing that friendship endures while success may be fleeting.

Different Interpretations of Theme Though themes emerge from the details of a work, which are the same for everyone, people may interpret the details differently. Review this summary of Charles Dickens's classic novel *A Christmas Carol.* Draw your own conclusion about its theme. Then, compare your ideas to the statements of theme that follow.

Example

Ebenezer Scrooge is a cold and greedy business owner who cares only about acquiring wealth. He refuses to help people in need, he has no friends, and he has lost contact with his relatives. He is also uncaring toward his employee, Bob Cratchit, who cannot afford medical care for one of his children. One Christmas Eve, three spirits visit Scrooge. They make him review his past, present, and future. As a result of these visits, Scrooge realizes he has been missing out on the most important things in life. He changes his ways, befriends his employee, helps the employee's child, and seeks out his relatives.

Possible Interpretations of Theme

- Human beings have the capacity to change their lives in wondrous ways.

- Love is more important than money.

- The love of a child can melt a cold heart.

Though these interpretations are all slightly different, each reflects the events in the novel and the lesson Scrooge learns. Whatever your interpretation of a story's theme, it should emerge from the key events and details in the work and the lessons that the main characters learn from them.

Determining Central Ideas in Nonfiction

 Common Core
State Standards

Reading Informational Text
2. Determine a central idea of a text and analyze its development over the course of the text, including how it emerges and is shaped and refined by specific details; provide an objective summary of the text.

The **central idea** of a nonfiction work is the work's main idea, supported by its details.

Central Ideas All nonfiction texts convey one or more **central ideas**—key concepts or main points that the author wants readers to understand and remember. In some works of nonfiction, the author directly states the central idea in the introduction. For example, the author of an essay may state the central idea in a **thesis statement** in the introductory paragraph. In some works of literary nonfiction, the central idea may be *implied,* or suggested, rather than stated directly. Readers determine the central idea by analyzing details to see what general idea they combine to support.

Author's Purpose and Central Ideas The three general **purposes,** or reasons, for writing are to **inform** or explain; to **persuade,** or try to convince readers to adopt a particular opinion or take a particular action; and to **entertain**. The author's purpose and the central idea in a work are directly related.

> **Example:**
> **Subject:** mobile phones
> **General purpose:** to inform
> **Specific purpose:** to inform readers about the origins of mobile phones
> **Central idea:** In 1973, Dr. Martin Cooper realized his vision of a portable personal phone when he placed the first mobile-phone call.

> **Example:**
> **Subject:** mobile phones
> **General purpose:** to entertain
> **Specific purpose:** to entertain readers by telling amusing stories about phones, leading them to reflect on modern life
> **Central idea:** After I got my first smartphone, I no longer had a life.

Development of Central Ideas In many works of nonfiction, the author devotes the entire work to a single central idea. That central idea is supported by each paragraph in the body of the work—each paragraph explains, illustrates, proves, or comments on some aspect of the central idea.

Each paragraph, in turn, has its own main idea, which supports the central idea of the work as a whole. The main idea of a paragraph is often stated directly in a **topic sentence** at or near its beginning. The details in the paragraph support its topic sentence. The example below illustrates the relationship between a central idea, topic sentences, and supporting details.

> **Example: Central Idea and Topic Sentences**
> **Central idea in introduction:** The state's graduated driver's license program has brought many benefits.
> **Topic sentence, paragraph 1 of body:** The number of fatal accidents involving teenagers has dropped significantly.
> **Topic sentence, paragraph 2 of body:** The total number of all accidents, including fender benders, has dropped.
> **Topic sentence, paragraph 3 of body:** Insurance rates for teen drivers have dropped.

The following detail helps support the topic sentence of the first paragraph in the body of the work:

Since our state instituted a graduated driver's license program, we have seen a 16-percent reduction in crashes for male teen drivers between the ages of sixteen and eighteen.

Close Read: Theme in Fiction

To discover the theme of a work, examine its use of literary elements and consider the message they suggest.

As you have learned, the theme of a literary work is the insight into human nature or life that the work conveys. Often, you must infer the author's theme or analyze main literary elements and related details to reach conclusions about what the author implies, or states indirectly. By making inferences, you will find deeper meaning in a work. Keep in mind that a work may suggest more than one theme, or main message. Use the tips in the chart to guide you.

Literary Elements as Clues to Theme

Title

The **title** is the name given to an individual literary work. As you read, ask these questions:

- Do the words in the title prompt ideas or stir emotions?
- Do the words suggest any universal themes —themes related to universal human concerns such as love, friendship, nature, or time?

Statements and Observations

Comments by the narrator or the main character may suggest or give insight into the theme. As you read, ask these questions:

- What do the characters say about each other? What do their words suggest about themselves?
- Which of the narrator's statements pertain to life or human beings in general?
- What sentences stand out in your mind? Why?

Setting

The **setting** refers to the time and place in which the events of a literary work occur. Setting includes the ideas, customs, beliefs, and values of a certain time and place. As you read, ask these questions:

- When and where do the events take place?
- What details help you picture the setting?
- What perspective does the setting offer on life or the world? (For example, is life in the setting a struggle? Is it calm? Simple? Full of pretense?)

Character

The **characters** are the people or animals that take part in the action of a literary work. As you read, ask:

- What are each character's traits, or qualities?
- Does the main character change, or develop, as a result of his or her experiences?
- What lesson in life does the character learn from his or her experiences?

Symbol

A **symbol** is a character, a place, an object, or an event that represents an idea, a quality, or a theme. For example, a wedding ring represents love and fidelity. As you read, ask these questions:

- What objects or events are emphasized?
- Are any of these objects or events strongly associated with a particular idea—are they symbols? What idea do they represent?
- What deeper meaning might they suggest?

Conflict and Plot

The **plot** of a narrative is the sequence of events that it tells. **Conflict,** or a struggle between opposing forces, drives the plot. As you read, ask:

- What are the main character's struggles?
- How does the character cope with these struggles?
- What does the character learn as a result of his or her experiences?

Model

About the Text Ray Bradbury's novel *Fahrenheit 451,* a work of science fiction, was published in 1953. The novel is set in a future totalitarian society that burns books to which the government and special-interest groups object. These include classic works of literature as well as religious texts. The Fahrenheit 451 of the title is the temperature at which books will burn.

Bradbury's concerns in the novel were shaped by contemporary events. World War II had pitted the United States against Nazi Germany and Fascist Italy, where censorship was routine. After the war, fear of Communism led some Americans to scrutinize each other for dissenting political beliefs. A person suspected of disloyalty might find his or her career ruined. At the same time, television gained popularity. By 1954, over half the households in the United States had a television set. In the background of Bradbury's novel, then, is a time when ideas were considered dangerous and television was beginning to take the place of reading.

---

from *Fahrenheit 451* by Ray Bradbury

It was a pleasure to burn.

It was a special pleasure to see things eaten, to see things blackened and *changed*. With the brass nozzle in his fists, with this great python spitting its venomous kerosene upon the world, the blood pounded in his head, and his hands were the hands of some amazing conductor playing all the symphonies of blazing and burning to bring down the tatters and charcoal ruins of history. With his symbolic helmet numbered 451 on his stolid head, and his eyes all orange flame with the thought of what came next, he flicked the igniter and the house jumped up in a gorging fire that burned the evening sky red and yellow and black. He strode in a swarm of fireflies. He wanted above all, like the old joke, to shove a marshmallow on a stick in the furnace, while the flapping pigeon-winged books died on the porch and lawn of the house. While the books went up in sparkling whirls and blew away on a wind turned dark with burning.

Montag grinned the fierce grin of all men singed and driven back by flame.

He knew that when he returned to the firehouse, he might wink at himself, a minstrel man, burnt-corked, in the mirror. Later, going to sleep, he would feel the fiery smile still gripped by his face muscles, in the dark. It never went away, that smile, it never ever went away, as long as he remembered.

Statements Bradbury ironically compares the hands of Montag, a destroyer, to the hands of a conductor, who creates something beautiful. The passage suggests that the theme concerns both creation and destruction.

Symbol The helmet symbolizes Montag's job, to destroy books and the knowledge and dissenting opinions they contain.

Setting The action takes place on a porch and lawn, which adds horror to this scene: Montag is attacking an ordinary house.

Theme The following themes are suggested by the details in the text:
- Humankind has the drive to destroy as well as to create.
- Censorship is driven by a passion for destruction.
- Violence and ignorance go hand in hand.

Independent Practice

About the Text This selection is an excerpt from Susan Vreeland's novel *Girl in Hyacinth Blue*, a work of historical fiction. The main character is Magdalena, the fictional daughter of artist Johannes Vermeer. Vermeer himself (1632–1675) was a real person, a famous painter who lived in Delft, a city in the Netherlands, during the seventeenth century.

Title Why might the daughter of an artist, in particular, like to look at things?

Setting What does this description of the setting suggest about Magdalena's world and her feelings about it? What theme do these details introduce?

"Magdalena Looking" by Susan Vreeland

Late one afternoon when Magdalena finished the clothes washing and her mother let her go out, she ran from their house by the Nieuwe Kerk across the market square, past van Buyten's bakery, over two cobbled bridges across the canals, past the blacksmith's all the way to Kethelstraat and the town wall where she climbed up and up the ochre stone steps, each one as high as her knee, to her favorite spot in all of Delft,[1] the round sentry post. From that great height, oh, what she could see. If only she could paint it. In one direction Schiedam Gate and beyond it the twin towers of Rotterdam Gate, and ships with odd-shaped sails the color of brown eggshells coming up the great Schie River from the sea, and in another direction strips of potato fields with wooden plows casting shadows over the soil like long fingers, and orchards, rows of rounded green as ordered as Mother wished their eleven young lives to be, and the smoke of the potteries and brickeries, and beyond that, she didn't know. She didn't know.

She stood there looking, looking, and behind her she heard the creak and thrum of the south windmill turning like her heart in the sea wind, and she breathed the brine[2] that had washed here from other shores. Below her the Schie lay like a pale yellow ribbon along the town wall. The longer she looked, the more it seemed to borrow its color from the sky. In the wind, the boats along the Schie docks with their fasteners clanking and their hollow bellies nudging one another made a kind of low rattling music she loved. It wasn't just today. She loved the sentry post in every kind of weather. To see rain pocking the gray sea and shimmering the stone bridge, to feel its cold strings of water on her face and hands, filled her to bursting.

---

1. **Nieuwe Kerk** (nü´ e kärk) . . . **van Buyten's** (fän bī´ tens) . . . **Kethelstraat** (kā´ tel strät) . . . **Delft** . . . *Nieuwe Kirk* means "New Church"; Kethelstraat is a street in the city; Delft is a manufacturing city on the Schie River in the Netherlands.
2. **brine** (brīn) saltwater.

She moved to a notch in the wall and just then a gust of wind lifted her skirts. The men on the bridge waiting with their bundles to go to sea shouted something in words she did not understand. She'd never tell Mother. Mother did not want her going there. The sentry post was full of guards smoking tobacco, Mother had said. There was some dark thing in her voice, as though she thought Magdalena should be afraid, but Magdalena did not know how to feel that then, or there.

Up there, high up above the town, she had longings no one in the family knew. No one would ever know them, she thought, unless perhaps a soul would read her face or she herself would have soul enough to speak of them. Wishes had the power to knock the breath out of her. Some were large and throbbing and persistent, some mere pinpricks of golden light, short-lived as fireflies but keenly felt. She wished for her chores to be done so she'd have time to race to the town wall every day before supper, or to the Oude Kerk[3] to lift the fallen leaves from her brother's grave. She wished her baby sisters wouldn't cry so, and the boys wouldn't quarrel and wrestle underfoot or run shouting through the house. Father wished that too, she knew. She wished there were not so many bowls to wash, thirteen each meal. She wished her hair shone flaxen in the sunlight of the market square like little Geertruida's.[4] She wished she could travel in a carriage across borders to all the lands drawn on her father's map.

She wished the grocer wouldn't treat her so gruffly when he saw her hand open out to offer four guilders,[5] all that her mother gave her to pay the grocery bill that was mounting into the hundreds, as far as she could tell. She wished he wouldn't shout; it sent his garlic breath straight into her nostrils. The baker, Hendrick van Buyten, was kinder. Two times so far he let Father pay with a painting so they could start over. Sometimes he gave her a still-warm bun to eat while walking home. And sometimes he put a curl of honey on it. She wished the grocer was like him.

She wished Father would take the iceboat to the Schie more often. He'd bought a fine one with a tall ivory sail. "Eighty guilders," Mother grumbled. "Better a winter's worth of bread and meat." On winter Sundays if the weather was clear, and if he was between paintings, it whisked them skimming across the

Characters What do you learn about Magdalena in this passage, and what possible themes do her thoughts suggest?

Statements and Observations What conflict over values does the mother's statement suggest, and what light do they shed on the theme?

---

3. **Oude Kerk** (ou´ de kārk)
4. **Geertruida's** (kher trī´ das)
5. **guilders** (gil´ dərz) *n.* The guilder is the basic unit of Dutch currency.

Practice continued

white glass of the canal. She'd never known such speed. The sharp cold air blew life and hope and excitement into her ears and open mouth.

She remembered wishing, one particular morning when Father mixed lead white with the smallest dot of lead-tin yellow[6] for the goose quill in a painting of Mother writing a letter, that she might someday have someone to write to, that she could write at the end of a letter full of love and news, "As ever, your loving Magdalena Elisabeth."

He painted Mother often, and Maria he painted once, draped her head in a golden mantle and her shoulders in a white satin shawl. She was older, fifteen, though only by eleven months. It might be fun to dress up like Maria did, and wear pearl earrings and have Father position her just so, but the only part she really wished for was that he would look and look and pay attention.

Characters What does Magdalena's greatest wish reveal about her? What does her wish add to your understanding of the theme?

More than all those wishes, she had one pulsing wish that outshone all the others. She wished to paint. Yes, me, she thought, leaning out over the stone wall. I want to paint. This and everything. The world from that vantage point stretched so grandly. Up there, beauty was more than color and shapes, but openness, light, the air itself, and because of that, it seemed untouchable. If only the act of wishing would make her able. Father only smiled queerly when she told him she wanted to paint, just as if she'd said she wanted to sail the seas, which, of course, she also wished, in order to paint what she would see. When she said so, that she wished to paint, Mother thrust into her hands the basket of mending to do.

Conflict and Plot What theme is suggested by the challenges Magdalena faces as a girl who lives in the seventeenth century?

Often from the edge of the room, she'd watch him work. Because he was always asking for quiet, with the little ones running through the room laughing or shouting, she didn't ask him many questions. He rarely answered anyway. Still, she studied how much linseed oil he used to thin the ultramarine,[7] and watched him apply it over a glassy layer of reddish brown. By magic, it made the dress he painted warmer than the blue on the palette. He would not let her go with him to the attic where he ground lead-tin yellow to powder, but he did send her to the apothecary[8] for the small bricks of it, and for linseed oil. Always there was money for that, but

---

6. **lead white . . . lead-tin yellow** references to pigments made from lead and tin and mixed with oil to produce paints of various colors.
7. **linseed oil . . . ultramarine** Linseed oil, made from the seed of the flax plant, can be used as the base for oil paint. Ultramarine is a rich blue.
8. **apothecary** (ə päth´ ə ker´ ē) n. historical term for a pharmacist; a dealer in medicines and various other preparations and chemicals.

she didn't know what to answer when the apothecary demanded the guilders for her brother's potions still owed after he died.

If only she could have colors of her own, and brushes. She wouldn't just paint pictures of women inside cramped little rooms. She'd paint them out in marketplaces, bending in the potato fields, talking in doorways in the sunlight, in boats on the Schie, or praying in the Oude Kerk. Or she'd paint people skating, fathers teaching their children on the frozen Schie.

Fathers teaching their children. The thought stopped her.

Looking from the sentry tower at a cloud darkening the river, she knew, just as she knew she'd always have washing and mending to do, that it would not be so. She'd worn herself out with wishing, and turned to go. She had to be home to help with supper.

On a spring day that began in no special way, except that she had climbed the town wall the afternoon before, and all over Delft lime trees lining the canals had burst into chartreuse[9] leaves, and light shone through them and made them yellower except where one leaf crossed over another and so was darker—on that spring-certain day, out of some unknown, unborn place came that scream. "I hate to mend," she shouted to the walls, to Mother, to anyone. "It's not making anything."

Father stepped into the room, looked at Mother and then scowled at Magdalena. It had been her job to keep her little brothers quiet for him, or shoo them out of doors, and here she was, the noisy one.

No one moved. Even the boys were still. At first she looked only at Father's hand smeared with ultramarine powder, not in his eyes, too surprised by the echo of her voice to fling out any additional defiance. She loved him, loved what he did with that hand, and even, she suspected, loved what he loved, though they had not spoken of it. When that thought lifted her face to his, she saw his cheeks grow softer, as if he noticed her in his house for the first time. He drew her over to the table by the window, brought the sewing basket, placed on her lap her

Characters What do Magdalena's thoughts suggest about women's lives during this time period? What theme about women is the writer suggesting?

Statements and Observations What does the author suggest is lacking in Magdalena's life? How does this suggestion reinforce your understanding of the theme?

Conflict and Plot What is the desire to "make" that leads to Magdalena's conflict with her family? How does this conflict develop the theme?

---

9. **chartreuse** (shär tro͞oz´) pale, yellowish green.

Practice continued

brother's shirt that needed buttons, adjusted the chair, opened the window, a little more, then less, and discovered that at a certain angle, it reflected her face. "If you sit here mending, I will paint you, Magdalena. But only if you stop that shouting." He positioned her shoulders, and his hands resting a moment were warm through the muslin[10] of her smock and seemed to settle her.

Mother rushed over to take away Geertruida's glass of milk.

"No, leave it, Catharina. Right there in the light."

Characters What message about the power of great art do these details suggest?

For days she sat there, still as she could for Father, and yet sewing a few stitches every so often to satisfy Mother. In that mood of stillness, all the things within her line of vision touched her deeply. The tapestry laid across the table, the sewing basket, the same glass repoured each day to the same level, the amber-toned map of the world on the wall—it plucked a lute string in her heart that these things she'd touched, grown as familiar to her as her own skin, would be looked at, marveled at, maybe even loved by viewers of his painting.

Setting What details suggest that Magdalena, like her father, has an artist's eye? How do these details reinforce the theme?

On sunny days the panes of window glass glistened before her. Like jewels melted into flat squares, she thought. Each one was slightly different in its pale transparent color—ivory, parchment, the lightest of wines and the palest of tulips. She wondered how glass was made, but she didn't ask. It would disturb him. Outside the window the market chattered with the selling of apples and lard and brooms and wooden buckets. She liked the cheese porters in their flat-brimmed red hats and stark white clothes. Their curved yellow carrying platforms stacked neatly with cheese rounds were suspended on ropes between pairs of them, casting brown shadows on the paving stones. Two platforms diagonally placed in the midground between their carriers would make a nice composition with the repeated shapes of those bulging cheese rounds. She'd put a delivery boy wheeling his cart of silver cod in the background against the guild hall, and maybe in the foreground a couple of lavender gray pigeons pecking crumbs.

The carillon[11] from Nieuwe Kerk ringing out the hour sounded something profound in her chest. All of it is ordinary to everyone but me, she thought.

---

10. **muslin** (muz´ lin) *n.* strong, plain cotton cloth.
11. **carillon** (kar´ ə län´) *n.* a set of tuned church bells.

All that month she did not speak, the occasion too momentous to dislodge it with words. He said he'd paint her as long as she didn't shout, and so she did not speak a word. Her chest ached like a dull wound when she realized that her silence did not cause him a moment's reflection or curiosity. When she looked out the corner of her eye at him, she could not tell what she meant to him. Slowly, she came to understand that he looked at her with the same interest he gave to the glass of milk.

Maybe it was because she wasn't pretty like Maria. She knew her jaws protruded and her watery, pale eyes were too widely set. She had a mole on her forehead that she always tried to hide by tugging at her cap. What if no one would want the painting? What then? It might be her fault, because she wasn't pretty. She wished he'd say something about her, but all he said, not to her directly, more to himself, was how the sunlight whitened her cap at the forehead, how the shadow at the nape of her neck reflected blue from her collar, or how the sienna of her skirt deepened to Venetian red[12] in the folds. It was never her, she cried to herself, only something surrounding her that she did not make or even contribute to knowingly. Another wish that never would come true, she saw then, even if she lived forever, was that he, that someone, would look at her not as an artistic study, but with love. If two people love the same thing, she reasoned, then they must love each other, at least a little, even if they never say it. Nevertheless, because he painted with such studied concentration, and because she held him in awe, she practiced looking calm for him as she looked out the window, but when she saw the canvas, what she intended as calm looked more like wistfulness.[13]

The painting was not bought by the brewer, Pieter Claesz van Ruijven,[14] who bought most of her father's work. He saw it, but passed over it for another. Disgrace seared her so that she could not speak that night. The painting hung without a frame in the outer kitchen where the younger children slept. Eventually the family had to give up their lodgings at Mechelen on the square, and take smaller rooms with Grandmother Maria on the Oude Langendijck.[15] Her father stopped taking the iceboat out to the Schie, sold it, in fact. He rarely

Characters What themes are reflected in Magdalena's relationship with her father?

---

12. **sienna** (sē en′ ə) . . . **Venetian** (və nē′ shən) **red** colors; sienna is a reddish or yellowish brown, and Venetian red is a brownish red.
13. **wistfulness** *n.* a mood of wishfulness or vague longing.
14. **Pieter Claesz van Ruijven** (pē ter kläs fän rī fen)
15. **Mechelen** (me′ khe len) . . . **Oude Langendijck** (ou′ de län en dīk) The Mechelen was an inn owned by the Vermeer family. The Oude Langendijck is a canal in Delft.

Practice continued

Conflict and Plot
What conflict does Magdalena have while helping to prepare her father's body for burial? What light does this conflict shed on the theme?

Characters How would you contrast Magdalena's youthful wishes and the reality of her adult life? Explain whether this contrast changes your understanding of the theme.

painted, the rooms were so cramped and dark, the younger children boisterous, and a few years later, he died.

When she washed him in his bed that last time, his fingers already cold, she had a thought, the shame of which prevented her from uttering: It would make a fine painting, a memorial, the daughter with towel and blue-figured washing bowl at bedside, her hand covering his, the wife exhausted on the Spanish chair clutching a crucifix, the father-husband, eyes glazed, looking to another landscape. While he painted everyone else, no one was there to paint him, to make him remembered. She yearned to do it, but the task was too fearsome. She lacked the skill, and the one to teach her had never offered.

Even though she asked for them, Mother sold his paints and brushes to the Guild of St. Luke. It helped to pay a debt. When Mother became sick with worry, Magdalena had the idea to take the painting to Hendrick van Buyten, the baker, because she knew he liked her. And he accepted it, along with one of a lady playing a guitar, for the debt of six hundred seventeen guilders, six stuivers,[16] more than two years' worth of bread. He smiled at her and gave her a bun.

Within a year, she married a saddlemaker named Nicolaes, the first man to notice her, a hard worker whose pores smelled of leather and grease, who taught her a pleasure not of the eyes, but, she soon realized, a man utterly without imagination. They moved to Amsterdam and she didn't see the painting again for twenty years.

In 1696, just after their only living child, Magritte, damp with fever, stopped breathing in her arms, Magdalena read in the Amsterdamsche Courant of a public auction of one hundred thirty-four paintings by various artists. "Several outstandingly artful paintings," the notice said, "including twenty-one works most powerfully and splendidly painted by the late J. Vermeer of Delft, will be auctioned May 16, 1:00, at the Oude Heeren Logement."[17] Only a week away. She thought of Hendrick. Of course he couldn't be expected to keep those paintings forever. Hers might be there. The possibility kept her awake nights.

Entering the auction gallery, she was struck again by that keenest of childhood wishes—to make a record not only of what she saw, but how. The distance

---

16. **stuivers** (stī´ fers) *n.* coins worth a fraction of a guilder; roughly, a dime.
17. **Oude Heeren Logement** (ou´ de her´ en lōzh mōn)

she'd come from that, and not even a child to show for it! She shocked herself by asking, involuntarily, what had been the point of having lived? Wishing had not been enough. Was it a mistake that she didn't beg him to teach her? Maybe not. If she'd seen that eventually, with help, she could paint, it might have made the years of birthing and dying harder. But then the birthing and dying would have been painted and the pain given. It would have served a purpose. Would that have been enough—to tell a truth in art?

She didn't know.

To see again so many of Father's paintings was like walking down an avenue of her childhood. The honey-colored window, the Spanish chair, the map she'd stared at, dreaming, hanging on the wall, Grandmother Maria's golden water pitcher, Mother's pearls and yellow satin jacket—they commanded such a reverence for her now that she felt they all had souls.

And suddenly there she was on canvas, framed. Her knees went weak.

Hendrick hadn't kept it. Even though he liked her, he hadn't kept it.

Almost a child she was, it seemed to her, gazing out the window instead of doing her mending, as if by the mere act of looking she could send her spirit out into the world. And those shoes! She had forgotten. How she loved the buckles, and thought they made her such a lady. Eventually she'd worn the soles right through, but now, brand-new, the buckles glinted on the canvas, each with a point of golden light. A bubble of joy surged upward right through her.

No, she wasn't beautiful, she owned, but there was a simplicity in her young face that she knew the years had eroded, a stilled longing in the forward lean of her body, a wishing in the intensity of her eyes. The painting showed she did not yet know that lives end abruptly, that much of living is repetition and separation, that buttons forever need resewing no matter how ferociously one works the thread, that nice things almost happen. Still a woman overcome with wishes, she wished Nicolaes would have come with her to see her in the days of her sentry post wonder when life and hope were new and full of possibility, but he had seen no reason to close up the shop on such a whim.

Character Do you think it would have been easier for Magdalena to bear her sorrows if she had been able to be an artist? Explain.

Symbol What might her father's painting of Magdalena represent?

Practice continued

Conflict and Plot
Why does Magdalena want the painting so much? In what way does her desire reinforce or add to the theme?

She stood on tiptoe and didn't breathe when her painting was announced. Her hand in her pocket closed tight around the twenty-four guilders, some of it borrowed from two neighbor women, some of it taken secretly from the box where Nicolaes kept money for leather supplies. It was all she could find, and she didn't dare ask for more. He would have thought it foolish.

"Twenty," said a man in front of her.

"Twenty-two," said another.

"Twenty-four," she said so loud and fast the auctioneer was startled. Did he see something similar in her face? He didn't call for another bid. The painting was hers!

"Twenty-five."

Her heart cracked.

The rest was a blur of sound. It finally went to a man who kept conferring with his wife, which she took as a good sign that it was going to a nice family. Forty-seven guilders. Most of the paintings sold for much more, but forty-seven was fine, she thought. In fact, it filled her momentarily with what she'd been taught was the sin of pride. Then she thought of Hendrick and a pain lashed through her. Forty-seven guilders minus the auctioneer's fee didn't come close to what her family had owed him.

She followed the couple out into the drizzle of Herengracht,[18] wanting to make herself known to them, just to have a few words, but then dropped back. She had such bad teeth now, and they were people of means. The woman wore stockings. What would she say to them? She didn't want them to think she wanted anything.

She walked away slowly along a wet stone wall that shone iridescent, and the wetness of the street reflected back the blue of her best dress. Water spots appeared fast, turning the cerulean[19] to deep ultramarine, Father's favorite blue.

---

18. **Herengracht** (her´ en khräkht) the "Gentleman's Canal"; one of the three main canals in the center of the city of Amsterdam.
19. **cerulean** (sə rōō´ lē ən) *adj.* sky-blue.

Light rain pricked the charcoal green canal water into delicate, dark lace, and she wondered if it had ever been painted just that way, or if the life of something as inconsequential as a water drop could be arrested and given to the world in a painting, or if the world would care.

She thought of all the people in all the paintings she had seen that day, not just Father's, in all the paintings of the world, in fact. Their eyes, the particular turn of a head, their loneliness or suffering or grief was borrowed by an artist to be seen by other people throughout the years who would never see them face to face. People who would be that close to her, she thought, a matter of a few arms' lengths, looking, looking, and they would never know her.

Conflict and Plot Do you think Magdalena's conflict is resolved? Explain why or why not.

Theme Consider Magdalena's wishes and conflicts as a child, as well as her experiences later in life, including her attempt to purchase her father's portrait of her. What message about unfulfilled dreams does this story convey? What other themes does the author suggest?

Close Read: Central Idea in Nonfiction

The central idea of a work of nonfiction emerges from and is supported by the details in the work.

In nonfiction works, an author often expresses the central, or main, idea in a **thesis statement.** For example, in an article about baseball, an author may state this thesis statement: Former catchers generally become good major league managers. To develop this central idea, the author might cite examples of former catchers who later excelled at managing. To further develop this idea, the author might then cite apparent exceptions to the rule and show how they actually prove it.

Sometimes, however, an author implies the central idea rather than stating it. If so, the reader must determine it by examining the supporting details in a work. For example, in an article about traffic safety, an author might describe several accidents that happened at a single intersection. These details imply the central idea that the particular intersection is dangerous.

As you read nonfiction selections, look for details that develop and support the central idea.

Clues to Central Idea	
The **title** is the name given to an individual work of nonfiction. Example: *"Perfect Pitch and Other Useful Skills for a Music Reviewer"*	A **thesis statement** is a direct statement of the central idea of a work, often found in the first paragraph. In each subsequent paragraph, a **topic sentence** generally states the central idea of the paragraph. The central idea in each paragraph helps support the central idea of the entire work. Example: *The point I want to stress is that exercise is essential to good health, as the following examples will illustrate.*
Support for Central Idea	
Statements of fact are statements that can be proven true. Example: *Water molecules consist of two atoms of hydrogen and one atom of oxygen.*	**Personal observations** are statements that an author makes based on his or her own firsthand knowledge and experiences. Example: *Having run the 20-mile marathon, I can tell you it's a tough endurance test.*
Expert opinion is information from an individual or a group that is an authority on a subject. Example: *According to the American Institute on Diet, raisins are an excellent source of potassium.*	An **anecdote** is a brief story that illustrates a point. Example: *The team was losing by 21 points, yet it managed to win the game. That shows what determination can do.*
Examples are specific illustrations of a general concept. Example: *The Community Service Club does volunteer work. For example, club members walk dogs at the town animal shelter on weekends.*	An **analogy** is a comparison of dissimilar things that focuses on an important similarity between them in order to aid understanding. Example: *Just as a single domino can topple several more, so can one revolution ignite many others.*

Model

About the Text While still in college, Anna Quindlen (b. 1953) began a career in journalism, writing for the *New York Post*. In 1986, she began writing a weekly column for *The New York Times*. In 1995, Quindlen left journalism for a time to devote herself to writing fiction and published four best-selling novels.

Quindlen's distinctive essayistic style is well suited to exploring the changes in national outlook after September 11, 2001. On that date, terrorists attacked the World Trade Center in New York City and the Pentagon in Washington, D.C. Quindlen responded in writing, mulling over the impact of the attacks on the nation's spirit. She published the following essay in *Newsweek* only weeks after the event.

from "A Quilt of a Country" by Anna Quindlen

With the end of the cold war, there was the creeping concern that without a focus for hatred and distrust, a sense of national identity would evaporate, that the left side of the hyphen—African-American, Mexican-American, Irish-American—would overwhelm the right. And slow-growing domestic traumas like economic unrest and increasing crime seemed more likely to emphasize division than community. Today the citizens of the United States have come together once more because of armed conflict and enemy attack. Terrorism has led to devastation—and unity.

Yet even in 1994, the overwhelming majority of those surveyed by the National Opinion Research Center agreed with this statement: "The U.S. is a unique country that stands for something special in the world." One of the things that it stands for is this vexing notion that a great nation can consist entirely of refugees from other nations, that people of different, even warring religions and cultures can live, if not side by side, then on either side of the country's Chester Avenues. Faced with this diversity there is little point in trying to isolate anything remotely resembling a national character, but there are two strains of behavior that, however tenuously, abet the concept of unity.

There is that Calvinist undercurrent in the American psyche that loves the difficult, the demanding, that sees mastering the impossible, whether it be prairie or subway, as a test of character, and so glories in the struggle of this fractured coalescing. And there is a grudging fairness among the citizens of the United States that eventually leads most to admit that, no matter what the

Title The title is an analogy that compares a quilt and a country. It provides a clue to the central idea of the text.

Personal Observations Based on the aftermath of the terrorist attacks, Quindlen makes the observation that the attacks unified Americans.

Facts Quindlen uses the results of a survey to support her claim that Americans are unified.

Topic Sentence This sentence states the central idea of the paragraph. The next sentence states the topic of the next paragraph, continuing to develop the central idea about American unity.

© EXEMPLAR TEXT

Model continued

Expert Opinion
Quindlen quotes the opinion of an expert to help support the idea that new immigrants are not very different from the immigrants who preceded them.

Example Quindlen uses a specific example to support the idea that the American people, regardless of their ancestry or country of birth, form a unified nation.

English-only advocates try to suggest, the new immigrants are not so different from our own parents or grandparents. Leonel Castillo, former director of the Immigration and Naturalization Service and himself the grandson of Mexican immigrants, once told the writer Studs Terkel proudly, "The old neighborhood Ma-Pa stores are still around. They are not Italian or Jewish or Eastern European any more. Ma and Pa are now Korean, Vietnamese, Iraqi, Jordanian, Latin American. They live in the store. They work seven days a week. Their kids are doing well in school. They're making it. Sound familiar?"

Tolerance is the word used most often when this kind of coexistence succeeds, but tolerance is a vanilla pudding word, standing for little more than the allowance of letting others live unremarked and unmolested. Pride seems excessive, given the American willingness to endlessly complain about them, them being whoever is new, different, unknown, or currently under suspicion. But patriotism is partly taking pride in this unlikely ability to throw all of us together in a country that across its length and breadth is as different as a dozen countries, and still be able to call it by one name. When photographs of the faces of all of those who died in the World Trade Center destruction are assembled in one place, it will be possible to trace in the skin color, the shape of the eyes and the noses, the texture of the hair, a map of the world. These are the representatives of a mongrel nation that somehow, at times like this, has one spirit. Like many improbable ideas, when it actually works, it's a wonder.

Central Idea The supporting details in the selection suggest the following central ideas:

- The unity of America as a nation is a complex and wonderful thing because the nation is founded on diversity.
- The unity of America is possible despite the diversity of American citizens because of two common attitudes: a love of struggle and a sense of fairness.

Independent Practice

About the Text In the course of writing *Girl in Hyacinth Blue,* Susan Vreeland did extensive research. In the article "Artful Research," she explains the necessity and benefits of research for writing fiction and shares some of her research methods.

"Artful Research" by Susan Vreeland

Is it possible for an ordinary person to climb over the area railings of #7 Eccles Street, either from the path or the steps, lower himself down from the lowest part of the railings till his feet are within two feet or three of the ground and drop unhurt? I saw it done myself but by a man of rather athletic build. I require this information in detail in order to determine the wording of a paragraph.

James Joyce[1] wrote this to his aunt once when he was out of Dublin. Can't you just imagine her muttering, "That boy! What will he think of next?" as she looks for her umbrella to go out in the rain and take the trolley to Eccles Street?

Excessive? Unnecessary? Stalling from the act of writing? Joyce's letter is instructive and revealing.

Similarly, I must admit that I sent my French translator on a mission to find out whether the carvings of heads on the façade of the Ministère de la Défense[2] on Boulevard Saint-Germain in Paris are repeats of the same face or different faces. Among other things, she told me I had the wrong street!

While some writers may be more cavalier, claiming that it's fiction, after all, I hold with the meticulous Joyce, not wholly out of allegiance to a recognized master, but for the sake of the richness of story that results. For me, research gives direction, depth, and authority to the writing; it doesn't just decorate a preconceived story with timely trivia.

Early research tends to be scattered, while one searches for the story, but later, usually during or after a first draft when one discovers in the work some needed information, it becomes pinpoint precise. At either time, an array of interesting material, some of it crucial, some merely useable, will emerge—and sometimes leap off the page. The results can be exciting. A single unexpected line can prompt a whole story. For example, the line in Jacob Presser's grim history, *Ashes in the Wind: The Destruction of Dutch Jewry,* indicating that in 1941, Jews were not allowed to keep pigeons, provided the genesis of my story "A Night Different from All Other Nights."

Anecdote What central idea is suggested by the anecdote about James Joyce?

Personal Observations What did Vreeland learn through her experiences with research? What central idea does she establish using her experiences?

Thesis Statement What central idea does Vreeland state here? Why might she have placed this thesis statement after her opening examples, rather than at the beginning?

Examples In what way does this example further develop Vreeland's central idea about the importance of research to fiction writing?

---

1. **James Joyce** (1882–1941) famed Irish writer noted for *Dubliners* (1914), a collection of short stories, and *Ulysses* (1922), a novel, among other works.
2. **Ministère de la Défense** (mēn i stär´ də là dā fäns´) the Ministry of Defense building in Paris, France.

Practice continued

That story is one of eight linked narratives comprising my composite novel, *Girl in Hyacinth Blue,* which traces an alleged Vermeer[3] painting in reverse chronology through the centuries, showing how defining moments in people's lives are lived under its influence. Besides the present, six time periods and numerous locales in the Netherlands are evoked: 1942 in Amsterdam; 1896 in Vreeland (yes, a real village located between Amsterdam and Utrecht); 1798 in The Hague during French rule: 1717 in Oling, Delfzijl, Westerbork, and Groningen (which I learned had been a university town since 1614, prompting my focal character to be a student); 1665 in Delft; and 1685 in Amsterdam. Naive in understanding what such a project entailed, I found that by the end, I had consulted seventy-six books.

Facts How did doing research help Vreeland shape one of her characters?

I'd been to the Netherlands only once, twenty-five years ago for three days, and I had never seen a Vermeer painting face to face. Blithely, I went ahead. I read books on Vermeer, Dutch art and social and cultural history, the Holocaust[4] as experienced in the Netherlands, the changing geography of the Netherlands as more land was reclaimed from the sea,[5] Erasmus' adages,[6] the history of costume, Passover and the practice of Jewish customs, Amsterdam's diamond trade, Dutch superstitions and treatment of witches, the French occupation, and the engineering of windmills and dikes.

Examples What central idea do these examples support?

Twenty printout pages from the Internet on the engineering of windmills (they vary regionally), on gears, wallowers, Archimedean screws, and drive shafts yielded one paragraph establishing the authority of my character the windmill engineer. More importantly, the research also suggested a metaphor appropriate for him:

I had fancied love a casual adjunct and not the central turning shaft making all parts move. I had not stood astonished at the power of its turning.

I would not have arrived at his critical self-assessment and the epiphany of the story without meandering through gears and drive shafts.

---

3. **Vermeer** (vər mir´) Jan (yän) Vermeer (1632–1675), renowned Dutch painter.
4. **the Holocaust** (häl´ ə kôst´) the persecution, imprisonment, and mass murder of Jews by Nazi Germany before and during the Second World War (1939–1945).
5. **reclaimed from the sea** Significant portions of the Netherlands were originally covered by water. To drain water from this land, the Dutch built a system of dikes (dams) and canals.
6. **Erasmus' adages** (i raz´ məs əz a´ di jəz) the sayings or brief observations of Desiderius (des´ ə dir´ ē əs) Erasmus (1469–1536), an influential Dutch scholar.

Here are ten research sources and approaches, beginning with the most obvious and ending with the ultimate—travel—that I used for either *Girl in Hyacinth Blue* or my subsequent novel, *The Passion of Artemisia,* which takes place in seventeenth-century Italy.

1. **Works on history, politics, and social conditions** A couple of titles might serve to show how I approached possible narratives from different angles: on the one hand, *Daily Life in Rembrandt's Holland;* on the other, *The Embarrassment of Riches: An Interpretation of Dutch Culture in the Golden Age.* Some I used as browser books; others, for specific information. Their bibliographies proved to be good sources for characters' names.

2. **Biography, autobiography, personal narrative, and oral history** The mere memory of *Anne Frank's Diary of a Young Girl* suggested that I create a young character the antithesis of Anne in terms of self-expression, yet suffering similar revelations.

3. **Geography books** These can give information about weather, topography, crops, industry, indigenous plants, birds, and other animals.

4. **Maps** Besides those available in travel bookstores, universities often have historical map collections. This was essential for *Girl* because I had to know if certain villages and canals existed at the time of each of the stories.

5. **Travel books** Those of the descriptive sort, the older the better, provide visual and cultural detail.

6. **Novels** Novels written at the time, written about the time, or set in the same place can be helpful in revealing attitudes, concerns, expressions, syntax, and diction.

7. **Paintings** Paintings done in the same time and place as one's fiction are excellent sources of information about costume, hairstyles, jewelry, household furnishings, landscape, available foods, flowers typical of the region, even the quality of light in a region, Vermeer's "trademark."

8. **Children's and juvenile fiction and nonfiction** Works for younger readers are sufficient in some cases and have the advantages of providing evocative illustrations and simplifying complicated political histories.

Personal Observations
What is Vreeland's purpose in listing resources she used to research her novels?

Practice continued

9. **Interviews and phone calls** Don't neglect the importance of interviews and phone calls. People are intrigued by novelists and are usually delighted to be consulted. For *Girl in Hyacinth Blue,* I consulted a pigeon breeder to learn why the owning of pigeons was prohibited to Jews under the German occupation and how homing pigeons "worked."

10. **Going there!** While travel is not always practical (I wrote *Girl in Hyacinth Blue* entirely while undergoing cancer treatment and could not travel), it will yield unexpected insights.

Personal Observations
What point does Vreeland make based on her personal experiences with research? How does it further develop her central idea?

So when does one stop researching and start writing? You write when the story comes to life, when it assumes some structure, when you can't help but start, not when you know everything you'll need to know. That's impossible to anticipate before you get into the heart of the writing. You might need to push yourself away from the safer act of research and leap into a first draft.

Don't get bogged down with fears of historical inaccuracy when writing a first draft. In one of the flood stories in *Girl in Hyacinth Blue,* the student needs to write a note. He's in a rowboat. He can't dip a pen in an inkwell. Did they have pencils in 1717? Look it up later. Keep writing. Keep the momentum going. If you don't know what they ate, leave it blank and get down the more important elements of the scene.

Personal Observations
How does this warning help focus Vreeland's central idea about research?

One caveat: Even if you put into your manuscript some fact delectable to you, recalling your delight in discovering it, if the story does not justify it, take it out. Type it up. Pin it on your wall. Use it elsewhere. But don't include it! The book is about characters, not about research.

1. **Key Ideas and Details** **(a)** Write an **objective summary** of "Magdalena Looking." Remember that an objective summary should contain only the most important details or events. It should not contain personal opinions. **(b)** Write an objective summary of "Artful Research."

2. **Key Ideas and Details** **(a)** In "Magdalena Looking," what is Magdalena's "one pulsing wish"? **(b) Interpret:** What obstacles prevent her from fulfilling her wish? Use details from the selection to explain your answer.

3. **Key Ideas and Details** **(a)** How do the time and cultural setting of "Magdalena Looking" influence the conflict she experiences? **(b) Draw Conclusions:** Do you think she would experience similar conflicts if she lived today? Explain.

4. **Key Ideas and Details** **(a) Cite:** Give three details from the story that show Magdalena's character. **(b) Draw Conclusions:** Describe Magdalena's character, based on the details you have chosen.

5. **Craft and Structure** **(a)** From whose point of view is "Magdalena Looking" told? **(b) Analyze:** How does the point of view help you understand the character of Magdalena?

6. **Key Ideas and Details** **(a) Support:** Identify details in the selection suggesting that Magdalena has artistic ability. Then, identify any opposing evidence—details that suggest she does not have talent. **(b) Synthesize:** Explain why the question of Magdalena's talent is crucial to the development of the story's theme.

7. **Key Ideas and Details** What do you think was Susan Vreeland's purpose in writing "Artful Research"? Use details from the essay to support your answer.

8. **Key Ideas and Details** **(a) Cite:** Give two examples that Vreeland uses in the essay to show the importance of research. **(b) Evaluate:** How convincing do you find each? Explain.

9. **Integration of Knowledge and Ideas** **(a) Apply:** In "Artful Research," Vreeland writes, "For me, research gives direction, depth, and authority to the writing. . . ." On a chart like the one below, note three passages from "Magdalena Looking" that may reflect what Vreeland means, and explain your choices. **(b) Collaboration:** Compare your chart with a classmate's, and discuss each passage chosen.

How Research Helps in Fiction

Passage	Why You Chose it

Ⓒ Leveled Texts

Build your skills and improve your comprehension of fiction with texts of increasing complexity.

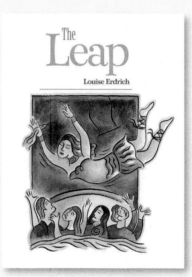

Read **"The Monkey's Paw"** to see how a mysterious object changes the lives of those who possess it.

Read **"The Leap"** to find out how a mother draws on her past as a circus performer to help her daughter.

Ⓒ Common Core State Standards

Meet these standards with either **"The Monkey's Paw"** (p. 32) or **"The Leap"** (p. 46).

Reading Literature
5. Analyze how an author's choices concerning how to structure a text, order events within it, and manipulate time create such effects as mystery, tension, or surprise. *(Literary Analysis: Plot and Foreshadowing)*

Spiral Review: RL.9-10.2

Writing
3. Write narratives to develop real or imagined experiences or events using effective technique, well-chosen details, and well-structured event sequences. **3.c.** Use a variety of techniques to sequence events so that they build on one another to create a coherent whole. *(Writing: Sequel)*

Speaking and Listening
1.a. Come to discussions prepared, having read and researched material under study; explicitly draw on that preparation by referring to evidence from texts and

other research on the topic to stimulate a thoughtful, well-reasoned exchange of ideas. *(Speaking and Listening: Interview)*

1.b. Work with peers to set rules for collegial discussions and decision-making, clear goals and deadlines, and individual roles as needed. *(Speaking and Listening: Interview)*

Language
2. Demonstrate command of the conventions of standard English capitalization, punctuation, and spelling when writing. *(Conventions: Common and Proper Nouns)*

5. Demonstrate understanding of figurative language, word relationships, and nuances in word meanings. *(Vocabulary: Analogies)*

Literary Analysis: Plot and Foreshadowing

A **plot** is the sequence of related events in a story. A typical plot revolves around a **conflict**—a struggle between opposing forces—and follows a structure, or pattern, like the one shown in the diagram below:

- **Exposition:** background on the characters and situation
- **Rising action:** events that intensify the conflict
- **Climax:** highest point of story tension at which outcome of conflict is revealed
- **Falling action:** events following climax
- **Resolution:** remaining issues resolved; conclusions or insights revealed by narrator

Writers use various techniques to add tension to a story. One technique is **foreshadowing**—giving details that hint at upcoming events.

To provide background on characters and their experiences, some authors choose to switch from present time to past time by using **flashback.** That is an interruption in the plot to describe an action of the past. After the flashback, the story returns to the present time of the action.

Using the Strategy: Plot Diagram

Use a diagram like the one here to help you track the plot of the story.

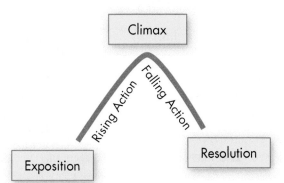

Reading Skill: Make Predictions

A **prediction** is a logical idea about what will happen. To make predictions, pay attention to story details and **use your prior knowledge.**

- Use knowledge of stories with similar plots to help you predict events.
- Use knowledge of human nature to help you predict how characters will act.

Is there a difference between *reality* and *truth?*

Writing About the Big Question

In "The Monkey's Paw," a family learns the truth behind a mysterious monkey's paw. Use this sentence starter to help you develop your ideas about the Big Question:

People may try to **verify** the truth by _____.

While You Read Look for explanations the characters offer to explain the truth behind the events in "The Monkey's Paw."

Vocabulary

Read each word and its definition. Decide whether you know the word well, know it a little bit, or do not know it at all. After you read, see how your knowledge of each word has increased.

- **grave** (grāv) *adj.* very serious and worrying (p. 35) *The doctor had a grave expression on her face when she gave John's family the bad news. gravely adv. gravity n.*

- **maligned** (mə līnd´) *adj.* spoken ill of (p. 36) *The CD, maligned by critics, was still a tremendous hit. malign v. malignant adj.*

- **credulity** (krə doo´ lə tē) *n.* tendency to believe too readily (p. 36) *Due to his credulity, Tim was unaware that the news report was fake. credulous adj. incredulous adj.*

- **furtively** (fur´ tiv lē) *adv.* secretively; sneakily; stealthily (p. 38) *When no one was looking, she reached furtively for the last slice of pie. furtive adj.*

- **apathy** (ap´ ə thē) *n.* lack of interest or emotion (p. 39) *The bored audience looked at the speaker with apathy. apathetic adj. apathetically adv.*

- **oppressive** (ə pres´ iv) *adj.* causing great discomfort; distressing (p. 41) *The heat was so oppressive that they finally opened a window. oppress v. oppression n.*

Word Study

The **Latin root -cred-** means "believe."

In this story, a character must monitor his **credulity**, or readiness to believe, as he hears a wild story about a supernatural object.

Meet
W. W. Jacobs
(1863–1943)

Author of
The Monkey's Paw

As a boy, William Wymark Jacobs traveled far and wide in his imagination. He lived in London, England, in a house near the docks, and he listened eagerly to the tales of adventure told by sailors whom he met there. These tales shaped the stories he wrote as an adult—stories in which everyday life is disrupted by strange and fantastic events. "The Monkey's Paw" is his most famous tale of the supernatural.

More Than Horror Although today W. W. Jacobs is best known for this tale of suspense, in his own lifetime he was famous as a humorist. In fact, he wrote works of various kinds, and he wrote them in quantity. When a collection of his works was published in 1931, it contained seventeen books!

BACKGROUND FOR THE STORY

The British View of India

"The Monkey's Paw" tells of an eerie object that arrives in England from India. From the late 1700s until 1947, India was a British colony. In letters and visits back home, British soldiers passed on information and misinformation about India's culture. Before long, India came to represent the mysterious and supernatural, as this story shows.

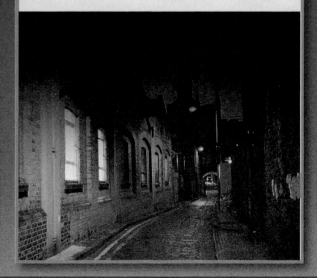

DID YOU KNOW?

Moviemakers have told the strange tale of "The Monkey's Paw" eight times! The first film version of the story was made in 1915. More recent remakes came out in 1996 and 2003.

The Monkey's Paw

W. W. Jacobs

I

Without, the night was cold and wet, but in the small parlor of Laburnam Villa the blinds were drawn and the fire burned brightly. Father and son were at chess, the former, who possessed ideas about the game involving radical changes, putting his king into such sharp and unnecessary perils that it even provoked comment from the white-haired old lady knitting placidly by the fire.

"Hark at the wind," said Mr. White, who, having seen a fatal mistake after it was too late, was amiably desirous of preventing his son from seeing it.

"I'm listening," said the latter, grimly surveying the board as he stretched out his hand. "Check."

"I should hardly think that he'd come tonight," said his father, with his hand poised over the board.

"Mate,"[1] replied the son.

"That's the worst of living so far out," bawled Mr. White, with sudden and unlooked-for violence; "of all the beastly, slushy, out-of-the-way places to live in, this is the worst. Pathway's a bog, and the road's a torrent. I don't know what people are thinking about. I suppose because only two houses on the road are let, they think it doesn't matter."

"Never mind, dear," said his wife, soothingly; "perhaps you'll win the next one."

Mr. White looked up sharply, just in time to intercept a knowing glance between mother and son. The words died away on his lips, and he hid a guilty grin in his thin gray beard.

"There he is," said Herbert White, as the gate banged to loudly and heavy footsteps came toward the door.

The old man rose with hospitable haste, and opening the door, was heard condoling with the new arrival. The new arrival also condoled with himself, so that Mrs. White said, "Tut, tut!" and coughed gently as her husband entered the room, followed by a tall, burly man, beady of eye and rubicund of visage.[2]

"Sergeant Major Morris," he said, introducing him.

The sergeant major shook hands, and taking the proffered seat by the fire, watched contentedly while his host got out tumblers and stood a small copper kettle on the fire.

At the third glass his eyes got brighter, and he began to talk, the little family circle regarding with eager interest this visitor from distant parts, as he squared his broad shoulders in the chair and spoke of wild scenes and doughty[3] deeds; of wars and plagues and strange peoples.

"Twenty-one years of it," said Mr. White, nodding at his wife and son. "When he went away he was a slip of a youth in the warehouse. Now look at him."

"He don't look to have taken much harm," said Mrs. White, politely.

---

1. **mate** *n.* checkmate, a chess move that prevents the opponent's king from escaping capture and so ends the game.
2. **rubicund** (rōō′ bə kund′) **of visage** (viz′ ij) having a red face.
3. **doughty** (dout′ ē) *adj.* brave.

Literary Analysis
Plot What important background information about the characters and their home is given in the exposition of this story?

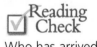
Reading Check
Who has arrived at the White's house?

"I'd like to go to India myself," said the old man, "just to look round a bit, you know."

"Better where you are," said the sergeant major, shaking his head. He put down the empty glass, and sighing softly, shook it again.

"I should like to see those old temples and fakirs and jugglers," said the old man. "What was that you started telling me the other day about a monkey's paw or something, Morris?"

"Nothing," said the soldier, hastily. "Leastways nothing worth hearing."

"Monkey's paw?" said Mrs. White, curiously.

"Well, it's just a bit of what you might call magic, perhaps," said the sergeant major, offhandedly.

His three listeners leaned forward eagerly. The visitor absent-mindedly put his empty glass to his lips and then set it down again. His host filled it for him.

"To look at," said the sergeant major, fumbling in his pocket, "it's just an ordinary little paw, dried to a mummy."

He took something out of his pocket and proffered it. Mrs. White drew back with a grimace, but her son, taking it, examined it curiously.

"And what is there special about it?" inquired Mr. White as he took it from his son, and having examined it, placed it upon the table.

"It had a spell put on it by an old fakir," said the sergeant major, "a very holy man. He wanted to show that fate ruled people's lives, and that those who interfered with it did so to their sorrow. He put a spell on it so that three separate men could each have three wishes from it."

His manner was so impressive that his hearers were conscious that their light laughter jarred somewhat.

"Well, why don't you have three, sir?" said Herbert White, cleverly.

The soldier regarded him in the way that middle age is wont to regard presumptuous youth. "I have," he said, quietly, and his blotchy face whitened.

"And did you really have the three wishes granted?" asked Mrs. White.

"I did," said the sergeant major, and his glass tapped against his strong teeth.

"And has anybody else wished?" persisted the old lady.

"The first man had his three wishes, yes," was the reply; "I don't know what the first

▼ Critical Viewing
What details of this man's appearance might make you think that he is "a very holy man"? [Support]

two were, but the third was for death. That's how I got the paw."

His tones were so grave that a hush fell upon the group.

"If you've had your three wishes, it's no good to you now, then, Morris," said the old man at last. "What do you keep it for?"

The soldier shook his head. "Fancy, I suppose," he said, slowly. "I did have some idea of selling it, but I don't think I will. It has caused enough mischief already. Besides, people won't buy. They think it's a fairy tale, some of them, and those who do think anything of it want to try it first and pay me afterward."

"If you could have another three wishes," said the old man, eyeing him keenly, "would you have them?"

"I don't know," said the other. "I don't know."

He took the paw, and dangling it between his forefinger and thumb, suddenly threw it upon the fire. White, with a slight cry, stooped down and snatched it off.

"Better let it burn," said the soldier, solemnly.

"If you don't want it, Morris," said the other, "give it to me."

"I won't," said his friend doggedly. "I threw it on the fire. If you keep it, don't blame me for what happens. Pitch it on the fire again, like a sensible man."

The other shook his head and examined his new possession closely. "How do you do it?" he inquired.

"Hold it up in your right hand and wish aloud," said the sergeant major, "but I warn you of the consequences."

"Sounds like the *Arabian Nights*,"[4] said Mrs. White, as she rose and began to set the supper. "Don't you think you might wish for four pairs of hands for me?"

Her husband drew the talisman from his pocket, and then all three burst into laughter as the sergeant major, with a look of alarm on his face, caught him by the arm. "If you must wish," he said, gruffly, "wish for something sensible."

Mr. White dropped it back in his pocket, and placing chairs, motioned his friend to the table. In the business of supper the talisman was partly forgotten, and afterward the three sat listening in an enthralled fashion to a second installment of the soldier's adventures in India.

"If the tale about the monkey's paw is not more truthful than those he has been telling us," said Herbert, as the door closed behind their guest, just in time for him to catch the last train, "we shan't make much out of it."

"Did you give him anything for it, Father?" inquired Mrs. White,

---

4. ***Arabian Nights*** collection of stories from the ancient Near East telling of fantastical adventures and supernatural beings.

Spiral Review
Theme What theme does Morris's story suggest to readers that the characters do not seem to perceive?

Vocabulary
grave (grāv) *adj.* very serious and worrying

Literary Analysis
Plot How does the information about the previous wishers foreshadow danger for the Whites?

Reading Check
According to the sergeant major, what is special about the monkey's paw?

Vocabulary

maligned (mə līnd´) *adj.* spoken ill of

credulity (krə dōō´ lə tē) *n.* tendency to believe too readily

regarding her husband closely.

"A trifle," said he, coloring slightly. "He didn't want it, but I made him take it. And he pressed me again to throw it away."

"Likely," said Herbert, with pretended horror. "Why, we're going to be rich, and famous and happy. Wish to be an emperor, Father, to begin with; then you can't be bossed around."

He darted round the table, pursued by the maligned Mrs. White armed with an antimacassar.[5]

Mr. White took the paw from his pocket and eyed it dubiously. "I don't know what to wish for, and that's a fact," he said, slowly. "It seems to me I've got all I want."

"If you only cleared the house, you'd be quite happy, wouldn't you?" said Herbert, with his hand on his shoulder. "Well, wish for two hundred pounds,[6] then; that'll just do it."

His father, smiling shamefacedly at his own credulity, held up the talisman, as his son, with a solemn face somewhat marred by a wink at his mother, sat down at the piano and struck a few impressive chords.

"I wish for two hundred pounds," said the old man distinctly.

A fine crash from the piano greeted the words, interrupted by a shuddering cry from the old man. His wife and son ran toward him.

"It moved," he cried, with a glance of disgust at the object as it lay on the floor. "As I wished it twisted in my hand like a snake."

"Well, I don't see the money," said his son as he picked it up and placed it on the table, "and I bet I never shall."

"It must have been your fancy, Father," said his wife, regarding him anxiously.

He shook his head. "Never mind, though; there's no harm done, but it gave me a shock all the same."

They sat down by the fire again while the two men finished their pipes. Outside, the wind was higher than ever, and the old man started nervously at the sound of a door banging upstairs. A silence unusual and depressing settled upon all three, which lasted until the old couple rose to retire for the night.

"I expect you'll find the cash tied up in a big bag in the middle of your bed," said Herbert, as he bade them good night, "and something horrible squatting up on top of the wardrobe watching you as you pocket your ill-gotten gains."

Herbert sat alone in the darkness, gazing at the dying fire, and seeing faces in it. The last face was so horrible and so simian[7] that he gazed at it in amazement. It got so vivid that, with a little uneasy

Reading Skill
Make Predictions
What do characters in stories about wishes usually learn? Predict the results of Mr. White's wish.

---

5. **antimacassar** (an´ ti mə kas´ ər) *n.* small cover for the arms or back of a chair or sofa.
6. **pounds** *n.* units of English currency, roughly comparable to dollars.
7. **simian** (sim´ ē ən) *adj.* monkeylike.

laugh, he felt on the table for a glass containing a little water to throw over it. His hand grasped the monkey's paw, and with a little shiver he wiped his hand on his coat and went up to bed. •

In the brightness of the wintry sun next morning as it streamed over the breakfast table Herbert laughed at his fears. There was an air of prosaic wholesomeness about the room which it had lacked on the previous night, and the dirty, shriveled little paw was pitched on the sideboard with a carelessness which betokened no great belief in its virtues.

"I suppose all old soldiers are the same," said Mrs. White. "The idea of our listening to such nonsense! How could wishes be granted in these days? And if they could, how could two hundred pounds hurt you, Father?"

"Might drop on his head from the sky," said the frivolous Herbert.

"Morris said the things happened so naturally," said his father, "that you might if you so wished attribute it to coincidence."

"Well, don't break into the money before I come back," said Herbert, as he rose from the table. "I'm afraid it'll turn you into a mean, avaricious[8] man, and we shall have to disown you."

His mother laughed, and following him to the door, watched him down the road, and, returning to the breakfast table, was very happy at the expense of her husband's credulity. All of which did not prevent her from scurrying to the door at the postman's knock, nor prevent her from referring somewhat shortly to retired sergeant majors of bibulous habits when she found that the post brought a tailor's bill.

"Herbert will have some more of his funny remarks, I expect, when he comes home," she said, as they sat at dinner.

"I dare say," said Mr. White, "but for all that, the thing moved in my hand; that I'll swear to."

"You thought it did," said the old lady soothingly.

"I say it did," replied the other. "There was no thought about it; I had just—What's the matter?"

His wife made no reply. She was watching the mysterious movements of a man outside, who, peering in an undecided fashion at the house, appeared to be trying to make up his mind to enter. In mental connection with the two hundred pounds, she noticed that the stranger was well dressed, and wore a silk hat of glossy newness. Three times he paused at the gate, and then walked on

Literary Analysis
Plot How does the conversation about the money foreshadow a problem?

Reading Check
For what does Mr. White wish?

---

8. avaricious (av´ ə rish´ əs) *adj.* greedy for wealth.

again. The fourth time he stood with his hand upon it, and then with sudden resolution flung it open and walked up the path. Mrs. White at the same moment placed her hands behind her, and hurriedly unfastening the strings of her apron, put that useful article of apparel beneath the cushion of her chair.

She brought the stranger, who seemed ill at ease, into the room. He gazed at her furtively, and listened in a preoccupied fashion as the old lady apologized for the appearance of the room, and her husband's coat, a garment which he usually reserved for the garden. She then waited patiently for him to broach his business, but he was at first strangely silent.

"I—was asked to call," he said at last, and stooped and picked a piece of cotton from his trousers. "I come from 'Maw and Meggins.'"

The old lady started. "Is anything the matter?" she asked, breathlessly. "Has anything happened to Herbert? What is it? What is it?"

Her husband interposed. "There, there, mother," he said, hastily. "Sit down, and don't jump to conclusions. You've not brought bad news, I'm sure, sir," and he eyed the other wistfully.

"I'm sorry—" began the visitor.

"Is he hurt?" demanded the mother, wildly.

The visitor bowed in assent. "Badly hurt," he said quietly, "but he is not in any pain."

"Oh, thank God!" said the old woman, clasping her hands. "Thank God for that! Thank—"

She broke off suddenly as the sinister meaning of the assurance dawned upon her and she saw the awful confirmation of her fears in the other's averted face. She caught her breath, and turning to her husband, laid her trembling old hand upon his. There was a long silence.

"He was caught in the machinery," said the visitor at length, in a low voice.

"Caught in the machinery," repeated Mr. White, in a dazed fashion, "yes."

He sat staring blankly out at the window, and taking his wife's hand between his own, pressed it as he had been wont to do in their old courting days nearly forty years before.

"He was the only one left to us," he said, turning gently to the visitor. "It is hard."

The other coughed, and, rising, walked slowly to the window. "The firm wished me to convey their sincere sympathy with you in your great loss," he said, without looking round. "I beg that you will understand I am only their servant and merely obeying orders."

There was no reply; the old woman's face was white, her eyes staring, and her breath inaudible; on the husband's face was a look such as his friend the sergeant might have carried into his first action.

"I was to say that Maw and Meggins disclaim all responsibility," continued the other. "They admit no liability at all, but in consideration of your son's services they wish to present you with a certain sum as compensation."

Mr. White dropped his wife's hand, and rising to his feet, gazed with a look of horror at his visitor. His dry lips shaped the words, "How much?"

"Two hundred pounds," was the answer.

Unconscious of his wife's shriek, the old man smiled faintly, put out his hands like a sightless man, and dropped, a senseless heap, to the floor. •

III

In the huge new cemetery, some two miles distant, the old people buried their dead, and came back to a house steeped in shadow and silence. It was all over so quickly that at first they could hardly realize it, and remained in a state of expectation as though of something else to happen—something else which was to lighten this load, too heavy for old hearts to bear.

But the days passed, and expectation gave place to resignation— the hopeless resignation of the old, sometimes miscalled apathy. Sometimes they hardly exchanged a word, for now they had nothing to talk about, and their days were long to weariness.

It was about a week after that the old man, waking suddenly in the night, stretched out his hand and found himself alone. The room was in darkness, and the sound of subdued weeping came from the window. He raised himself in bed and listened.

"Come back," he said, tenderly. "You will be cold."

"It is colder for my son," said the old woman, and wept afresh.

The sound of her sobs died away on his ears. The bed was warm, and his eyes heavy with sleep. He dozed fitfully, and then slept until a sudden wild cry from his wife awoke him with a start.

"*The paw!*" she cried wildly. "The monkey's paw!"

He started up in alarm. "Where? Where is it? What's the matter?"

She came stumbling across the room toward him. "I want it," she said quietly. "You've not destroyed it?"

"It's in the parlor, on the bracket," he replied, marveling. "Why?"

She cried and laughed together, and bending over, kissed his cheek.

Reading Skill
Make Predictions
Do you think the Whites will make another wish? Why or why not?

Vocabulary
apathy (ap´ə the) *n.* lack of interest or emotion

How do the Whites get their money?

"The other two wishes," she replied rapidly. "We've only had one."

Literary Analysis
Plot In what way does this new wish increase the tension of the story?

"I only just thought of it," she said hysterically. "Why didn't I think of it before? Why didn't *you* think of it?"

"Think of what?" he questioned.

"The other two wishes," she replied rapidly. "We've only had one."

"Was not that enough?" he demanded, fiercely.

"No," she cried triumphantly; "we'll have one more. Go down and get it quickly, and wish our boy alive again."

The man sat up in bed and flung the bedclothes from his quaking limbs. "You are mad!" he cried, aghast.

"Get it," she panted; "get it quickly, and wish—Oh, my boy, my boy!"

Her husband struck a match and lit the candle. "Get back to bed," he said unsteadily. "You don't know what you are saying."

"We had the first wish granted," said the old woman feverishly; "why not the second?"

"A coincidence," stammered the old man.

"Go and get it and wish," cried his wife, quivering with excitement.

The old man turned and regarded her, and his voice shook. "He has been dead ten days, and besides he—I would not tell you else, but—I could only recognize him by his clothing. If he was too terrible for you to see then, how now?"

"Bring him back," cried the old woman, and dragged him toward the door. "Do you think I fear the child I have nursed?"

He went down in the darkness, and felt his way to the parlor, and then to the mantelpiece. The talisman was in its place, and a horrible fear that the unspoken wish might bring his mutilated son before him ere he could escape from the room seized upon him, and he caught his breath as he found that he had lost the direction of the door. His brow cold with sweat, he felt his way round the table, and groped along the wall until he found himself in the small passage with the unwholesome thing in his hand.

Even his wife's face seemed changed as he entered the room. It was white and expectant, and to his fears seemed to have an unnatural look upon it. He was afraid of her.

"*Wish!*" she cried, in a strong voice.

"It is foolish and wicked," he faltered.

"*Wish!*" repeated his wife.

He raised his hand. "I wish my son alive again."

The talisman fell to the floor, and he regarded it fearfully. Then he sank trembling into a chair as the old woman, with burning eyes, walked to the window and raised the blind.

He sat until he was chilled with the cold, glancing occasionally at the figure of the old woman peering through the window. The candle-end, which had burned below the rim of the china candlestick, was throwing pulsating shadows on the ceiling and walls, until, with a flicker larger than the rest, it expired. The old man, with an unspeakable sense of relief at the failure of the talisman, crept back to his bed, and a minute or two afterward the old woman came silently and apathetically beside him.

Neither spoke, but lay silently listening to the ticking of the clock. A stair creaked, and a squeaky mouse scurried noisily through the wall. The darkness was oppressive, and after lying for some time screwing up his courage, he took the box of matches, and striking one, went downstairs for a candle.

At the foot of the stairs the match went out, and he paused to strike another; and at the same moment a knock, so quiet and stealthy as to be scarcely audible, sounded on the front door.

The matches fell from his hand and spilled in the passage. He stood motionless, his breath suspended until the knock was repeated. Then he turned and fled swiftly back to his room, and closed the door behind him. A third knock sounded through the house.

"*What's that?*" cried the old woman, starting up.

"A rat," said the old man in shaking tones—"a rat. It passed me on the stairs."

His wife sat up in bed listening. A loud knock resounded through the house.

"It's Herbert!" she screamed. "It's Herbert!"

She ran to the door, but her husband was before her, and catching her by the arm, held her tightly.

"What are you going to do?" he whispered hoarsely.

"It's my boy; it's Herbert!" she cried, struggling mechanically. "I forgot it was two miles away. What are you holding me for? Let go. I must open the door."

"Don't let it in," cried the old man, trembling.

"You're afraid of your own son," she cried, struggling. "Let me go. I'm coming, Herbert, I'm coming."

There was another knock, and another. The old woman with a sudden wrench broke free and ran from the room. Her husband followed to the landing, and called after her appealingly as she hurried downstairs. He heard the chain rattle back and the bottom bolt drawn slowly and stiffly from the socket. Then the old woman's voice, strained and panting.

"The bolt," she cried, loudly. "Come down. I can't reach it."

But her husband was on his hands and knees groping wildly on

Reading Check

Why is Mr. White afraid?

Literary Analysis

Plot How does the difference between what Mr. and Mrs. White are trying to do bring events to a climax?

the floor in search of the paw. If he could only find it before the thing outside got in. A perfect fusillade[9] of knocks reverberated through the house, and he heard the scraping of a chair as his wife put it down in the passage against the door. He heard the creaking of the bolt as it came slowly back, and at the same moment he found the monkey's paw, and frantically breathed his third and last wish.

The knocking ceased suddenly, although the echoes of it were still in the house. He heard the chair drawn back and the door opened. A cold wind rushed up the staircase, and a long loud wail of disappointment and misery from his wife gave him courage to run down to her side, and then to the gate beyond. The street lamp flickering opposite shone on a quiet and deserted road.

9. **fusillade** (fyoo′ sə lād′) *n.* rapid firing, as of gunshots.

Critical Thinking

> Cite textual evidence to support your responses.

1. **Key Ideas and Details** **(a)** How does each of the Whites react when first hearing the legend of the monkey's paw?
   (b) Contrast: How do the reactions of the mother and the father change?

2. **Key Ideas and Details** **(a)** What lesson does the fakir want to teach? **(b)** Does he succeed? Explain.

3. **Craft and Structure** **(a)** How does Mr. White word his first wish?
   (b) Discuss: In a group, discuss the strengths and weaknesses of other ways the wish could have been worded. Decide whether any version is foolproof. Share your decision with the class.

4. **Integration of Knowledge and Ideas** **(a)** Do the Whites begin to think that the legend of the monkey's paw is true? **(b)** How can you tell? *[Connect to the Big Question: Is there a difference between reality and truth?]*

The Monkey's Paw

Literary Analysis: Plot and Foreshadowing

© **1. Craft and Structure** What information about the paw is given in the **exposition?**

© **2. Craft and Structure (a)** Describe three events in the **rising action. (b)** Where does the story reach its **climax**?

© **3. Craft and Structure** Identify two details that **foreshadow** the tragic outcome of the first wish.

Reading Skill: Make Predictions

4. (a) Using a chart like the one shown, indicate how you used your prior knowledge to **make a prediction** about one of the wishes.

(b) Was your prediction close to the actual outcome? Explain.

Vocabulary

© **Acquisition and Use** An **analogy** shows the relationship between pairs of words. Use a word from the vocabulary list for "The Monkey's Paw" on page 30 to complete each analogy. Your choice should create a word pair that matches the relationship between the first two words given. Explain the relationship in each analogy.

1. ran : rapidly :: crept : _____

2. kindness : cruelty :: passion : _____

3. nourished : starved :: praised : _____

4. lighthearted : cheerful :: serious : _____

5. happiness : sadness :: doubt : _____

6. cautious : reckless :: unburdened : _____

Word Study Use the context of the sentences and what you know about the **Latin root -cred-** to explain your answer to each question.

1. Would you believe an *incredible* rumor?

2. Does someone who tells lies have *credibility?*

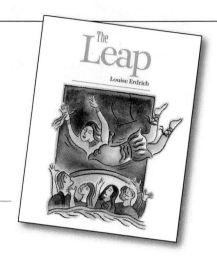

Writing About the Big Question

In "The Leap," a daughter thinks about the truth of her life by contemplating how much she owes her mother. Use these sentence starters to develop your ideas about the Big Question.

Decisions that people make can affect the **reality** of their lives by _____.

The choices people make can have **concrete** effects on _____.

While You Read Think about the choices that the characters make and how their choices affect their own lives and the lives of others.

Vocabulary

Read each word and its definition. Decide whether you know the word well, know it a little bit, or do not know it at all. After you read, see how your knowledge of each word has increased.

- **encroaching** (en krōch´ iŋ) *adj.* intruding on, especially in a gradual way (p. 47) *Toward afternoon, the <u>encroaching</u> clouds dimmed the sun.* encroach *v.* encroachment *n.*

- **commemorates** (kə mem´ ə rāts´) *v.* honors a memory (p. 47) *The memorial <u>commemorates</u> the soldiers who died defending their country.* commemoration *n.* memorial *n.* memory *n.*

- **extricating** (eks´ tri kāt´ iŋ) *n.* setting free; removing from a difficult situation (p. 50) *<u>Extricating</u> the kite from the tree proved to be very difficult.* extricate *v.* extrication *n.*

- **constricting** (kən strikt´ iŋ) *adj.* preventing freedom of movement; limiting (p. 51) *He found the sweater to be too <u>constricting</u>, so he bought a larger size.* constrict *v.* constriction *n.*

- **perpetually** (pər pech´ o͞o əl lē) *adv.* continuing forever; constantly (p. 52) *He was fired for being <u>perpetually</u> late to work.* perpetual *adj.* perpetuate *v.*

- **tentative** (ten´ tə tiv) *adj.* hesitant; not confident (p. 53) *I took a <u>tentative</u> bite of the odd dessert.* tentatively *adv.*

Word Study

The **Latin root -strict-** means "confine" or "squeeze."

In this story, a character thinks living in a small town can be **constricting**, because his experiences are confined within the boundaries of this small area.

©Thomas Victor

Author of

The Leap

Louise Erdrich's fiction and poetry celebrate life's richness. Born to a German American father and a French-Native American mother, Erdrich writes from the complex perspective of two distinct cultures.

A Family Tradition Erdrich grew up in North Dakota, where she often visited with her relatives in the Turtle Mountain Band of Chippewa, a Native American people. With little exposure to television or movies, Erdrich became fascinated by the storytelling tradition that surrounded her. "The people in our families made everything into a story," she explains. Her first published book, *Love Medicine*, a group of interrelated stories, brought Erdrich national acclaim.

BACKGROUND FOR THE STORY
Circus Families

Circus families often develop their own acts. They pass the specific skills involved, such as acrobatics or juggling, from one generation to the next. Many young circus performers, like the mother in "The Leap," bypass traditional schooling to develop the remarkable physical talents that they display to amazed audiences.

DID YOU KNOW?

Love Medicine was rejected by the first twenty-eight publishers to whom Erdrich sent it. When finally published, the book won rave reviews and the National Book Critics Circle Award.

The Leap

Louise Erdrich

My mother is the surviving half of a blindfold trapeze act, not a fact I think about much even now that she is sightless, the result of encroaching and stubborn cataracts.

She walks slowly through her house here in New Hampshire, lightly touching her way along walls and running her hands over knickknacks, books, the drift of a grown child's belongings and castoffs. She has never upset an object or as much as brushed a magazine onto the floor. She has never lost her balance or bumped into a closet door left carelessly open.

It has occurred to me that the catlike precision of her movements in old age might be the result of her early training, but she shows so little of the drama or flair one might expect from a performer that I tend to forget the Flying Avalons. She has kept no sequined costume, no photographs, no fliers or posters from that part of her youth. I would, in fact, tend to think that all memory of double somersaults and heart-stopping catches had left her arms and legs were it not for the fact that sometimes, as I sit sewing in the room of the rebuilt house in which I slept as a child, I hear the crackle, catch a whiff of smoke from the stove downstairs, and suddenly the room goes dark, the stitches burn beneath my fingers, and I am sewing with a needle of hot silver, a thread of fire.

I owe her my existence three times. The first was when she saved herself. In the town square a replica tent pole, cracked and splintered, now stands cast in concrete. It commemorates the disaster that put our town smack on the front page of the Boston and New York tabloids. It is from those old newspapers, now

Vocabulary
encroaching (en krōch´ iŋ) *adj.* intruding on, especially in a gradual way

commemorates (kə mem´ ə rāts´) *v.* honors a memory

Reading Check

What was the narrator's mother's profession?

historical records, that I get my information. Not from my mother, Anna of the Flying Avalons, nor from any of her in-laws, nor certainly from the other half of her particular act, Harold Avalon, her first husband. In one news account it says, "The day was mildly overcast, but nothing in the air or temperature gave any hint of the sudden force with which the deadly gale would strike."

I have lived in the West, where you can see the weather coming for miles, and it is true that out here we are at something of a disadvantage. When extremes of temperature collide, a hot and cold front, winds generate instantaneously behind a hill and crash upon you without warning. That, I think, was the likely situation on that day in June. People probably commented on the pleasant air, grateful that no hot sun beat upon the striped tent that stretched over the entire center green. They bought their tickets and surrendered them in anticipation. They sat. They ate caramelized popcorn and roasted peanuts. There was time, before the storm, for three acts. The White Arabians[1] of Ali-Khazar rose on their hind legs and waltzed. The Mysterious Bernie folded himself into a painted cracker tin, and the Lady of the Mists made herself appear and disappear in surprising places. As the clouds gathered outside, unnoticed, the ringmaster cracked his whip, shouted his introduction, and pointed to the ceiling of the tent, where the Flying Avalons were perched. •

They loved to drop gracefully from nowhere, like two sparkling birds, and blow kisses as they threw off their plumed helmets and high-collared capes. They laughed and flirted openly as they beat their way up again on the trapeze bars. In the final vignette of their act, they actually would kiss in midair, pausing, almost hovering as they swooped past one another. On the ground, between bows, Harry Avalon would skip quickly to the front rows and point out the smear of my mother's lipstick, just off the edge of his mouth. They made a romantic pair all right, especially in the blindfold sequence.

That afternoon, as the anticipation increased, as Mr. and Mrs. Avalon tied sparkling strips of cloth onto each other's face and as they puckered their lips in mock kisses, lips destined "never again to meet," as one long breathless article put it, the wind rose, miles off, wrapped itself into a cone, and howled. There came a rumble of electrical energy, drowned out by the sudden roll of drums.

Reading Skill
Make Predictions
What details help you predict that something will go wrong?

---

1. **Arabians** horses of the Arabian breed.

One detail not mentioned by the press, perhaps unknown—Anna was pregnant at the time, seven months and hardly showing, her stomach muscles were that strong. It seems incredible that she would work high above the ground when any fall could be so dangerous, but the explanation—I know from watching her go blind—is that my mother lives comfortably in extreme elements. She is one with the constant dark now, just as the air was her home, familiar to her, safe, before the storm that afternoon.

From opposite ends of the tent they waved, blind and smiling, to the crowd below. The ringmaster removed his hat and called for silence, so that the two above could concentrate. They rubbed their hands in chalky powder, then Harry launched himself and swung, once, twice, in huge calibrated beats across space. He hung from his knees and on the third swing stretched wide his arms, held his hands out to receive his pregnant wife as she dove from her shining bar.

It was while the two were in midair, their hands about to meet, that lightning struck the main pole and sizzled down the guy wires, filling the air with a blue radiance that Harry Avalon must certainly have seen through the cloth of his blindfold as the tent buckled and the edifice[2] toppled him forward, the swing continuing and not returning in its sweep, and Harry going down, down into the crowd with his last thought, perhaps, just a prickle of surprise at his empty hands.

My mother once said that I'd be amazed at how many things a person can do within the act of falling. Perhaps, at the time, she

---

2. **edifice** (ed´ i fis) *n.* large structure or building.

▲ **Critical Viewing**
What feelings might a scene like this inspire in an onlooker? **[Infer]**

Literary Analysis
Plot In what way do these descriptions of events increase the tension in the rising action?

Reading Check

What happens to Harry on the day of the gale?

was teaching me to dive off a board at the town pool, for I associate the idea with midair somersaults. But I also think she meant that even in that awful doomed second one could think, for she certainly did. When her hands did not meet her husband's, my mother tore her blindfold away. As he swept past her on the wrong side, she could have grasped his ankle, the toe-end of his tights, and gone down clutching him. Instead, she changed direction. Her body twisted toward a heavy wire and she managed to hang on to the braided metal, still hot from the lightning strike. Her palms were burned so terribly that once healed they bore no lines, only the blank scar tissue of a quieter future. She was lowered, gently, to the sawdust ring just underneath the dome of the canvas roof, which did not entirely settle but was held up on one end and jabbed through, torn, and still on fire in places from the giant spark, though rain and men's jackets soon put that out.

Three people died, but except for her hands my mother was not seriously harmed until an overeager rescuer broke her arm in extricating her and also, in the process, collapsed a portion of the tent bearing a huge buckle that knocked her unconscious. She was taken to the town hospital, and there she must have hemorrhaged,[3] for they kept her, confined to her bed, a month and a half before her baby was born without life.

Harry Avalon had wanted to be buried in the circus cemetery next to the original Avalon, his uncle, so she sent him back with his brothers. The child, however, is buried around the corner, beyond this house and just down the highway. Sometimes I used to walk there just to sit. She was a girl, but I rarely thought of her as a sister or even as a separate person really. I suppose you could call it the egocentrism[4] of a child, of all young children, but I considered her a less finished version of myself.

When the snow falls, throwing shadows among the stones, I can easily pick hers out from the road, for it is bigger than the others and in the shape of a lamb at rest, its legs curled beneath. The carved lamb looms larger as the years pass, though it is probably only my eyes, the vision shifting, as what is close to me blurs and distances sharpen. In odd moments, I think it is the edge drawing near, the edge of everything, the unseen horizon we do not really speak of in the eastern woods. And it also seems to me, although this is probably an idle fantasy, that the statue is growing more sharply etched, as if, instead of weathering itself into a porous mass, it is hardening on the hillside with each snowfall, perfecting itself. ●

---

3. **hemorrhaged** (hem´ ər ij'd´) *v.* bled heavily.
4. **egocentrism** (ē´ gō sen´ triz əm) *n.* self-centeredness; inability to distinguish one's own needs and interests from those of others.

It was during her confinement in the hospital that my mother met my father. He was called in to look at the set of her arm, which was complicated. He stayed, sitting at her bedside, for he was something of an armchair traveler and had spent his war quietly, at an air force training grounds, where he became a specialist in arms and legs broken during parachute training exercises. Anna Avalon had been to many of the places he longed to visit—Venice, Rome, Mexico, all through France and Spain. She had no family of her own and was taken in by the Avalons, trained to perform from a very young age. They toured Europe before the war, then based themselves in New York. She was illiterate.

It was in the hospital that she finally learned to read and write, as a way of overcoming the boredom and depression of those weeks, and it was my father who insisted on teaching her. In return for stories of her adventures, he graded her first exercises. He bought her her first book, and over her bold letters, which the pale guides of the penmanship pads could not contain, they fell in love.

I wonder if my father calculated the exchange he offered: one form of flight for another. For after that, and for as long as I can remember, my mother has never been without a book. Until now, that is, and it remains the greatest difficulty of her blindness. Since my father's recent death, there is no one to read to her, which is why I returned, in fact, from my failed life where the land is flat. I came home to read to my mother, to read out loud, to read long into the dark if I must, to read all night.

Once my father and mother married, they moved onto the old farm he had inherited but didn't care much for. Though he'd been thinking of moving to a larger city, he settled down and broadened his practice in this valley. It still seems odd to me, when they could have gone anywhere else, that they chose to stay in the town where the disaster had occurred, and which my father in the first place had found so constricting. It was my mother who insisted upon it, after her child did not survive. And then, too, she loved the sagging

Literary Analysis
Plot Which details in this paragraph provide additional exposition?

Vocabulary
constricting (kən strikt´ iŋ) adj. preventing freedom of movement; limiting

Reading Check

How do the narrator's mother and father first meet?

farmhouse with its scrap of what was left of a vast acreage of woods and hidden hay fields that stretched to the game park.

I owe my existence, the second time then, to the two of them and the hospital that brought them together. That is the debt we take for granted since none of us asks for life. It is only once we have it that we hang on so dearly. •

I was seven the year the house caught fire, probably from standing ash. It can rekindle, and my father, forgetful around the house and perpetually exhausted from night hours on call, often emptied what he thought were ashes from cold stoves into wooden or cardboard containers. The fire could have started from a flaming box, or perhaps a buildup of creosote inside the chimney was the culprit. It started right around the stove, and the heart of the house was gutted. The baby-sitter, fallen asleep in my father's den on the first floor, woke to find the stairway to my upstairs room cut off by flames. She used the phone, then ran outside to stand beneath my window.

When my parents arrived, the town volunteers had drawn water from the fire pond and were spraying the outside of the house, preparing to go inside after me, not knowing at the time that there was only one staircase and that it was lost. On the other side of the house, the superannuated[5] extension ladder broke in half. Perhaps the clatter of it falling against the walls woke me, for I'd been asleep up to that point.

As soon as I awakened, in the small room that I now use for sewing, I smelled the smoke. I followed things by the letter then, was good at memorizing instructions, and so I did exactly what was taught in the second-grade home fire drill. I got up, I touched the back of my door before opening it. Finding it hot, I left it closed and stuffed my rolled-up rug beneath the crack. I did not hide under my bed or crawl into my closet. I put on my flannel robe, and then I sat down to wait.

Outside, my mother stood below my dark window and saw clearly that there was no rescue. Flames had pierced one side wall, and the glare of the fire lighted the massive limbs and trunk of the vigorous old elm that had probably been planted the year the house was built, a hundred years ago at least. No leaf touched the wall, and just one thin branch scraped the roof. From below, it looked as though even a squirrel would have had trouble jumping from the tree onto the house, for the breadth of that small branch was no bigger than my mother's wrist.

Standing there, beside Father, who was preparing to rush back around to the front of the house, my mother asked him to unzip her dress. When he wouldn't be bothered, she made him understand.

Vocabulary
perpetually (pər pech′ o͞o əl lē) *adv.* continuing forever; constantly

Reading Skill
Make Preditions Based on facts in the story about Anna's past, what do you predict she will do next?

He couldn't make his hands work, so she finally tore it off and stood there in her pearls and stockings. She directed one of the men to lean the broken half of the extension ladder up against the trunk of the tree. In surprise, he complied. She ascended. She vanished. Then she could be seen among the leafless branches of late November as she made her way up and, along her stomach, inched the length of a bough that curved above the branch that brushed the roof.

Once there, swaying, she stood and balanced. There were plenty of people in the crowd and many who still remember, or think they do, my mother's leap through the ice-dark air toward that thinnest extension, and how she broke the branch falling so that it cracked in her hands, cracked louder than the flames as she vaulted with it toward the edge of the roof, and how it hurtled down end over end without her, and their eyes went up, again, to see where she had flown.

I didn't see her leap through air, only heard the sudden thump and looked out my window. She was hanging by the backs of her heels from the new gutter we had put in that year, and she was smiling. I was not surprised to see her, she was so matter-of-fact. She tapped on the window. I remember how she did it, too. It was the friendliest tap, a bit tentative, as if she was afraid she had arrived too early at a friend's house. Then she gestured at the latch, and when I opened the window she told me to

Vocabulary
tentative (ten´ tə tiv) adj.
hesitant; not confident

Reading Check

What steps does the narrator take when she realizes that there is a fire?

raise it wider and prop it up with the stick so it wouldn't crush her fingers. She swung down, caught the ledge, and crawled through the opening. Once she was in my room, I realized she had on only underclothing, a bra of the heavy stitched cotton women used to wear and step-in, lace-trimmed drawers. I remember feeling light-headed, of course, terribly relieved, and then embarrassed for her to be seen by the crowd undressed.

I was still embarrassed as we flew out the window, toward earth, me in her lap, her toes pointed as we skimmed toward the painted target of the fire fighter's net.

I know that she's right. I knew it even then. As you fall there is time to think. Curled as I was, against her stomach, I was not startled by the cries of the crowd or the looming faces. The wind roared and beat its hot breath at our back, the flames whistled. I slowly wondered what would happen if we missed the circle or bounced out of it. Then I wrapped my hands around my mother's hands. I felt the brush of her lips and heard the beat of her heart in my ears, loud as thunder, long as the roll of drums.

Spiral Review
Theme How does the mother turn a fall into a leap? What theme do her actions suggest?

Literary Analysis
Plot How is the conflict resolved?

Critical Thinking

Cite textual evidence to support your responses.

1. **Key Ideas and Details (a)** What does Anna decide to do when the circus tent pole is struck by lightning? **(b) Interpret:** In what sense does the narrator owe her life to her mother's decision?

2. **Key Ideas and Details (a)** Using details from the story, identify the two other ways in which the narrator owes her life to her mother. **(b) Compare and Contrast:** Compare the three ways in which the mother somehow saves the daughter's life. Note one difference and one similarity among them.

3. **Key Ideas and Details (a) Summarize:** Describe the scene at the end in which the mother leaps. **(b) Infer:** Why does the mother make the leap? **(c) Discuss:** In a group, discuss the qualities or ideas that the leap might represent. Choose one idea to share with the class.

4. **Integration of Knowledge and Ideas** In what ways is the narrator's view of reality shaped by the choices her mother has made? *[Connect to the Big Question: Is there a difference between reality and truth?]*

Literary Analysis: Plot and Foreshadowing

1. **Craft and Structure** What information about the mother is given in the **exposition**?

2. **Craft and Structure** **(a)** Describe three events in the **rising action.** **(b)** Where does the story reach its **climax**? Explain.

3. **Craft and Structure** What insight about the relationship between mother and daughter is presented in the **resolution** of the story?

4. **Craft and Structure** Give two examples of **foreshadowing** in the story. Give one example of a **flashback.**

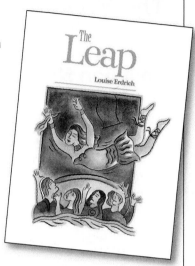

The Leap
Louise Erdrich

Reading Skill: Make Predictions

5. **(a)** Using a chart like the one shown, indicate how you used prior knowledge to **make a prediction** about the outcome of the story.

Story Detail

Similar Plots

How People Act

Prediction

(b) How closely did you predict the outcome of the story? Explain.

Vocabulary

Acquisition and Use An **analogy** shows the relationship between pairs of words. Use a word from the vocabulary list for "The Leap," on page 44, to complete each analogy. For each item, the new word pair should share the same relationship as the first two words. Explain the relationship in each analogy.

1. happiness : cheerful :: insecurity : _____
2. knowledge : teaching :: freedom : _____
3. receiving : giving :: retreating : _____
4. helps : aids :: honors : _____
5. towering : small :: expansive : _____
6. quickly : rapidly :: constantly : _____

Word Study Use the context of the sentences and what you know about the **Latin root -strict-** to explain your answer to each question.

1. Would a *strict* parent have many or few rules?
2. How would a *constrictor* snake kill its prey?

Word Study

The **Latin root -strict-** means "confine" or "squeeze."

Apply It Explain how the root -strict- contributes to the meanings of these words. Consult a dictionary if necessary.

district
restrict
stricture

Integrated Language Skills

The Monkey's Paw • The Leap

Conventions:
Common Nouns and Proper Nouns

A **noun** is a word that names a person, a place, or a thing. A **common noun** refers to any one of a certain kind of person, place, or thing. A **proper noun** names a specific person, place, or thing. Proper nouns always begin with capital letters. Look at these examples:

Common Nouns	Proper Nouns
writer	Louise Erdrich, W. W. Jacobs
city	St. Louis, Nairobi
athlete	Derek Jeter, Venus Williams

Practice A Identify the nouns in each sentence, and indicate whether they are common nouns or proper nouns.

1. Morris kept the withered paw of a monkey in his pocket.
2. Mr. White believes the legend and wishes for money.
3. When Herbert is killed at his job, his parents receive money from his employers.
4. Mrs. White tries to bring Herbert back to life using magic.

ⓔ **Reading Application** In "The Monkey's Paw," find three common nouns and three proper nouns.

Practice B Underline the common nouns in the following sentences. Then, substitute a proper noun, if possible, to make the sentence more precise.

1. The narrator's mother was part of the trapeze act.
2. The mother had traveled to many countries.
3. The storm that caused the circus tent to collapse occurred in the summer.
4. The narrator moved back to her hometown.

ⓔ **Writing Application** Use this model sentence to write two sentences with both common and proper nouns: *Anna's New Hampshire home contains few mementos of her life in the circus.*

PH **WRITING COACH** | Further instruction and practice are available in *Prentice Hall Writing Coach.*

Writing

Narrative Text Write a brief **sequel** to the story you read. For example, if you read "The Monkey's Paw," tell what happens when someone else finds the paw. If you read "The Leap," describe the mother's next daring rescue.

- Use a plot outline to plan your story so that events build on one another and create a satisfying whole.
- Try to capture the author's writing style. Use vivid details to describe events and create an appropriate tone.
- Use foreshadowing to build suspense.
- Add a flashback to help explain the characters' present actions.

Grammar Application Be sure to capitalize proper nouns correctly.

Writing Workshop: *Work in Progress*

Prewriting for Autobiographical Narrative For a narrative you may write, list places you have visited. Next to each, write words you associate with the place. Keep this Place List in your writing portfolio for later use.

Speaking and Listening

Comprehension and Collaboration In a small group, conduct an **interview** between a journalist and characters in the story you read.

- If you read "The Monkey's Paw," plan an exchange of ideas between a journalist and the Whites after the tragedy. Prepare questions that will focus the Whites' retelling of the story.
- If you read "The Leap," plan an exchange of ideas between a journalist who is writing about circus families and the narrator. Prepare questions that will help the narrator retell the main events of the story.

Follow these steps to plan and role-play the interview:

- Choose roles and set rules about how to ask and respond to questions appropriately.
- Demonstrate a knowledge of the subject through the questions asked and the responses given.

After the interview, evaluate the presentation. Discuss which questions and responses were most effective, using language that conveys maturity and respect. Summarize points of agreement and disagreement. Then, compile your responses in a brief report.

Common Core State Standards

L.9-10.2; W.9-10.3, W.9-10.3.c; SL.9-10.1.a, SL.9-10.1.b
[For the full wording of the standards, see page 28.]

Use this prewriting activity to prepare for the **Writing Workshop** on page 108.

PHLit Online!
www.PHLitOnline.com
- Interactive graphic organizers
- Grammar tutorial
- Interactive journals

Ⓒ Leveled Texts

Build your skills and improve your comprehension of nonfiction with texts
of increasing complexity.

Read the excerpt from **Swimming to Antarctica** to find out how one woman's fierce determination helps her complete a dangerous swim.

Read **"Occupation: Conductorette"** to see how a young girl's persistence helps her when she is faced with discrimination.

Ⓒ Common Core State Standards

Meet these standards with either the excerpt from **Swimming to Antarctica** (p. 62) or **"Occupation: Conductorette"** (p. 78).

Reading Informational Text
6. Determine an author's point of view or purpose in a text and analyze how an author uses rhetoric to advance that point of view or purpose. *(Literary Analysis: Author's Perspective)*

Writing
2.b. Develop the topic with well-chosen, relevant, and sufficient facts, extended definitions, concrete details, quotations, or other information and examples appropriate to the audience's knowledge of the topic. *(Writing: Description)*

Speaking and Listening
5. Make strategic use of digital media in presentations to enhance understanding of findings, reasoning, and evidence and to add interest. *(Speaking and Listening: Daily Observation Journal)*

Language
4.a. Use context as a clue to the meaning of a word or phrase. *(Vocabulary: Word Study)*
4.d. Verify the preliminary determination of the meaning of a word or phrase. *(Vocabulary: Word Study)*

Literary Analysis: Author's Perspective

The **author's perspective,** or point of view, in a literary work includes the judgments, attitudes, and experiences he or she brings to the subject. An author's perspective determines which details he or she includes, as in these examples:

- A writer with firsthand experience of an event might report his or her own reactions as well as generally known facts.
- A writer with a positive view of a subject might emphasize its benefits.

A work may combine several perspectives. For example, a writer might tell what it felt like to live through an event. In addition, the writer might express his or her present views of the experience. As you read, look for details, including specific words and phrases, that suggest the author's perspective.

Reading Skill: Make Predictions

As you read, **make predictions,** or develop ideas, about what will happen next. These predictions can be based on details in the text combined with your own background and experiences. You can check your predictions as you read.

- **Revise,** or adjust, your predictions as you gather more information.
- **Verify,** or confirm, predictions by comparing the outcome you predicted to the actual outcome.

To help you make, verify, and revise predictions, **ask questions** such as "Why did that happen?" and "What will be the result?"

Using the Strategy: Prediction Chart

Record your questions on a **prediction chart** like this one.

Prediction	Revise	Verify or Revise
What will happen?	What changes?	What actually happens?

Is there a difference between *reality* and *truth?*

Writing About the Big Question

In the excerpt from *Swimming to Antarctica,* a swimmer discovers how hard she can push her body to achieve a remarkable goal. Use this sentence starter to develop your ideas abut the Big Question.

Facing **uncertainty** about your ability to accomplish a difficult task is an opportunity to _____.

While You Read Look for details that reveal the realities Cox faces during her swim.

Vocabulary

Read each word and its definition. Decide whether you know the word well, know it a little bit, or do not know it at all. After you read, see how your knowledge of each word has increased.

- **venturing** (ven´ chər iŋ) *v.* attempting to do something that involves taking risks (p. 63) *The astronauts will be <u>venturing</u> into space next Tuesday. adventure n. venture n. venturesome adj.*

- **prolonged** (prō lôŋd´) *adj.* extended; lengthy (p. 65) *His <u>prolonged</u> absence is due to serious illness. prolong v.*

- **equilibrium** (ē´ kwi lib´ rē əm) *n.* a state of balance (p. 68) *See how well she keeps her <u>equilibrium</u> while walking on the balance beam! equilibrate v.*

- **abruptly** (ə brupt´ lē) *adv. happening suddenly; unexpectedly* (p. 68) *The diner <u>abruptly</u> stood up and ran from the restaurant. abrupt adj. abruptness n.*

- **gauge** (gāj) *v.* measure something's size, amount, extent or capacity (p. 70) *Use the map to <u>gauge</u> the distance between the two museums. gauge n.*

- **buffer** (buf´ ər) *v.* lessen a shock; cushion (p. 73) *A helmet helps <u>buffer</u> the impact of a fall. buffer n.*

Word Study

The **Latin prefix *pro-*** means "forth" or "forward."

In this story, the narra-tor endures **prolonged** exposure, or an extend-ed amount of time, to water that is freezing.

Meet
Lynne Cox
(b. 1957)

Author of

BACKGROUND FOR THE AUTOBIOGRAPHY
Cold-Water Swimming

Swimming in frigid water, as Lynne Cox does, puts great stress on the body. The body's core—the heart, lungs, and brain—must stay warm or normal muscle and brain function will be impaired, a condition called *hypothermia*. Water temperatures as "warm" as forty-four degrees Fahrenheit would kill most swimmers.

Raised in California, Lynne Cox got started breaking records when she was young. At age fourteen, she swam twenty-six miles from Catalina Island to the California coast. The next year, she broke the men's and the women's records swimming the English Channel.

Made to Swim Cox has a high percentage of body fat, evenly distributed around her body. This fat helps her float and provides insulation. Her unique body has allowed her to swim in waters ranging from the Bering Strait to Antarctica. Today, Lynne Cox stands as the most successful cold-water long-distance swimmer ever.

DID YOU KNOW?
During her swim around the Cape of Good Hope, Cox was chased by a shark.

In 2002, swimmer Lynne Cox attempted an ambitious feat—
swimming a mile in the frigid waters of Antarctica. Cox sailed on
the ship Orlova with a team of seven friends, including team leader
Barry Binder and her physicians, Susan Sklar, Gabriella Miotta,
and Laura King. Bob Griffith and Martha Kaplan, Cox's agent,
would scout for danger as Cox swam, while Dan Cohen stood by
as a rescue swimmer. Scott Pelley, a television producer, also came.
The ship's crew included Dr. Anthony Block and expedition leader
Susan Adie. Before attempting a mile, Cox tested her reactions on a
shorter swim.

from

Swimming to Antarctica

Lynne Cox

When I returned to my cabin, I thought for a long time about what I was about to attempt.

I had **mixed feelings** about the test swim. In some ways, it had given me **confidence**; I now **knew that I could** swim for twenty-two minutes in thirty-three-degree water. But it had also made me feel **uncertain**. It had been the most difficult and probably the most dangerous swim I had ever done. Part of me wanted to be **satisfied** with it. Part of me didn't want to attempt the mile. I was **afraid**.

The water temperature on the big swim would be a degree colder. Thirty-two degrees. That was a magic number, the temperature at which freshwater froze. I wondered if in thirty-two-degree water the water in my cells would freeze, if my body's tissues would become permanently damaged. I wondered if my mind would function better this time, if I would be able to be more aware of what was happening, or if it would be further dulled by the cold. Would my core temperature drop faster, more quickly than I could recognize? Would I be able to tell if I needed to get out? Did I really want to risk my life for this? Or did I want to risk failure?

The other part of me wanted to try, wanted to do what I had trained for, wanted to explore and reach beyond what I had done. That part of me was excited about venturing into the unknown. That part of me knew I would have felt a tremendous letdown if I didn't get a chance to try. I wanted to do it now.

The next morning, on December 15, 2002, Susan called me up to the bridge. She pointed out Water Boat Point. The tiny gray beach between steep glaciers was completely blocked by icebergs and brash ice.[1] There was no place to land.

We continued sailing south through the Gerlache Strait, past mountain-high glaciers and by ship-sized icebergs ranging in shades of blue from juniper berry to robin's-egg to light powder blue. In the protection of the Antarctic Peninsula, the wind dropped off and the sea grew calmer. When we reached Neko Harbor, about an hour later, Susan called me up to the bridge. She was excited. The beach was free of icebergs and brash ice. A landing was possible.

Now I would have a chance to swim the first Antarctic mile. I was thrilled and scared, but I tried to remain calm; I knew that the weather could suddenly change and the swim would be off. I met with Barry Binder, who said, "I'll get the crew into the Zodiacs[2] and come and get you when everything's set."

I walked to the ship's library, drank four eight-ounce cups of hot water, and ate two small croissants for breakfast—they were high in fat and carbohydrates, two sources of energy I would need for the swim. Then I started through the hallway to my cabin, where many of the *Orlova's* passengers were waiting, eager to find out if I was going to swim. They wished me luck and said they would wait for me at the finish. I stopped by Dan's cabin to ask him if he would jump into the water with me at the end of the swim. He was already in his dry suit, prepared to go. Everyone was doing what we had practiced. All I could do was to go back to my room and wait. Gabriella came in to take a core temperature; it was up to 100.4 degrees. Knowing I was venturing into unknown waters, I must have psyched myself

1. **brash ice** *n.* floating fragments of ice.
2. **Zodiacs** *n.* speedboats.

Literary Analysis
Author's Perspective
What do the opening sentences indicate about the author's attitude toward her swim?

Vocabulary
venturing (ven´ chər iŋ) *v.* attempting to do something that involves taking risks

Reading Skill
Make Predictions
Use details from the narrative to predict whether Cox will succeed or fail.

Reading Check
What will Cox attempt to do?

from Swimming to Antarctica **63**

up so much that I increased my body temperature. Gabriella left me alone while I put on my swimsuit and sweats. I rubbed sunscreen on my face, but not on my arms or legs; it could make my skin slippery, and if my crew needed me to get out of the water quickly, that would create a problem. The night before, three of the crew had spotted a pod of eight killer whales swimming into the Gerlache Strait. They hadn't been moving fast. I hoped they were still north of us.

I stared out the window at the brown crescent-shaped beach. There were snow-covered hills directly above the beach, and massive glaciers on either side. I picked out landmarks, places I could aim for, so I'd know if I was on or off course.

Literary Analysis
Author's Perspective
What details indicate that the writer feels fear and doubt before the swim?

Dr. Block caught me at the top of the stairs, just before we stepped out the door and onto the ramp, and asked if I would sit down on a step so he could trace two veins on my hands with a blue Magic Marker. It was just a precaution, he said, in case I needed emergency assistance; this way he would easily be able to find a vein to start an IV. I gave him my right hand and watched him draw the blue lines for the television camera. It gave me the creeps. Why did he have to do this now, right before I swam? Didn't he realize this kind of stuff psychs people out? *I know the swim is dangerous, but he could have done this hours ago, not just before I swam. Get over it*, I told myself. *Shake it off. Take a deep breath. Refocus. Take another breath. Good. Now think about the swim.* I smiled. *I'm so ready for this.*

Walking to the door, I peeked out and felt a blast of icy wind hit my face from the northwest. It was blowing in off the glaciers in gusts to twenty-five knots,[3] and the air temperature was thirty-two degrees. I felt the hair rising on my arms and my jaw tighten to suppress a shiver. I was much more nervous than I had been during my first swim. I had greater expectations of myself now. I wanted to swim the first Antarctic mile, and I knew I would be very disappointed if I didn't succeed.

> Why did he have to do this now, right before I swam?

I stared across the icy water at Neko Harbor's beach and felt excitement building within me. Quickly, before I could lose my chance, I pulled off my sweat suit and shoes and stuck them in a corner of the ship, climbed down the gangway, sat on the platform,

---

3. knots (näts) *n.* a rate of speed. One knot equals one nautical mile (6,076.12 feet) per hour.

and dangled my feet in the water. Surprisingly, it didn't feel any colder than it had two days before. I didn't realize then that the nerves on my skin's surface had been damaged from the first swim. I didn't know that the nerves that signaled danger weren't firing. I wasn't aware that my first line of defense was gone. I had no idea that prolonged exposure in thirty-two-degree water could cause permanent nerve and muscle damage. And I didn't know then that when an untrained person is immersed in water colder than forty degrees, their nerves are cooled down so they can't fire at the neuromuscular level. After only seven or eight minutes the person's body seizes up and [he or she] can't move. It was a good thing I didn't know any of this. All I knew was that I was ready. I took a deep breath, leaned back, and threw myself forward into the thirty-two-degree water.

When I hit the water, I went all the way under. I hadn't intended to do that; I hadn't wanted to immerse my head, which could over-stimulate my vagus nerve[4] and cause my heart to stop beating. Dog-paddling as quickly as I could, I popped up in the water, gasping for air. I couldn't catch my breath. I was swimming with my head up, hyperventilating.[5] I kept spinning my arms, trying to get warm, but I couldn't get enough air. I felt like I had a corset tightening around my chest. I told myself to relax, take a deep breath, but I couldn't slow my breath. And I couldn't get enough air in. I tried again. My body wanted air, and it wanted it now. I had to override that reaction of hyperventilating. I had to concentrate on my breath, to press my chest out against the cold water and draw the icy air into my lungs.

My body resisted it. The air was too cold. My body didn't want to draw the cold air deep into my lungs and cool myself from the inside. It wanted to take short breaths so the cold air would be warmed in my mouth before it reached my lungs. I was fighting against myself.

I noticed my arms. They were bright red, and I felt like I was swimming through slush. My arms were thirty-two degrees, as cold as the sea. They were going numb, and so were my legs. I pulled my hands right under my chest so that I was swimming on the upper inches of the sea, trying to minimize my contact with the water. I was swimming fast and it was hard to get enough air. I began to notice that the cold was pressurizing my body like a giant tourniquet. It was squeezing the blood from the exterior part of my body and pushing it into the core. Everything felt tight. *Focus on your breath*, I told myself. *Slow it down. Let it fill your lungs. You're*

---

4. **vagus** (vāg´ əs) **nerve** *n.* either of a pair of nerves running from the brain to the heart that regulate the heartbeat.
5. **hyperventilating** *v.* breathing so rapidly or deeply as to cause dizziness or fainting.

Vocabulary
prolonged (prō lôŋg´)
adj. extended; lengthy

Literary Analysis
Author's Perspective
How does this passage reflect both how it felt to live through the event and how it feels to look back on it?

Reading Skill
Make Predictions
Do these details verify your original prediction or lead you to revise it?

Reading Check

List two dangers Cox faces on her swim.

not going to be able to make it if you keep going at this rate.

It wasn't working. I was laboring for breath harder than on the test swim. I was in oxygen debt,[6] panting, gasping. My breath was inefficient, and the oxygen debt was compounding. In an attempt to create heat, I was spinning my arms wildly, faster than I'd ever turned them over before. Laura later told me that I was swimming at a rate of ninety strokes per minute, thirty strokes per minute quicker than my normal rate. My body was demanding more oxygen, but I couldn't slow down. Not for a nanosecond. Or I would freeze up and the swim would be over.

An icy wave slapped my face: I choked and felt a wave of panic rise within me. My throat tightened. I tried to clear my throat and breathe. My breath didn't come out. I couldn't get enough air in to clear my throat. I glanced at the crew. They couldn't tell I was in trouble. If I stopped, Dan would jump in and pull me out. I still couldn't get a good breath. I thought of rolling on my back to give myself time to breathe, but I couldn't. It was too cold. I closed my mouth, overrode everything my body was telling me to do, held my breath, and gasped, coughed, cleared my windpipe, and relaxed just a little, just enough to let my guard down and catch another wave in the face. I choked again. I put my face down into the water, hoping this time I could slow my heart rate down. I held my face in the water for two strokes and told myself, *Relax, just turn your head and breathe.* ●

▼ **Critical Viewing**
Explain whether or not any of the dangers faced by Cox are represented in this photograph.
[Connect]

6. **oxygen debt** *n.* an increased need for oxygen in the body brought on by intensive activity.

I choked and felt a wave of panic rise within me... I glanced at the crew. They couldn't tell I was in trouble.

could parallel shore again and head toward Neko Harbor. Barry knew I knew what I was doing. But the abrupt course change caught the Zodiac drivers by surprise. They scattered in different directions, trying to avoid ramming into each other and trying to catch up with me. The motor on the lead Zodiac on my left sputtered and stopped. The second Zodiac immediately pulled up beside me. I sprinted against the current.

"How long have I been swimming?"

"Twenty-one minutes," Barry said. He and all the crew were watching me intently, their faces filled with tension and concern.

I put my head down, and something suddenly clicked. Maybe it was because I knew shore was within reach, or maybe because I got a second wind; I don't know. But I was finally swimming strongly, stretching out and moving fluidly. My arms and legs were as cold as the sea, but I felt the heat within my head and contained in my torso and I thrilled to it, knowing my body had carried me to places no one else had been in only a bathing suit. I looked down into the water; it was a bright blue-gray and so clear that it appeared as if I were swimming through air. The viscosity of the water was different, too; it was thicker than any I had ever swum in. It felt like I was swimming through gelato. And I got more push out of each arm stroke than I ever had before. I looked at the crew. They were leaning so far over the pontoons, as if they were right there with me. I needed to let them know I was okay.

Literary Analysis
Author's Perspective
What information here reveals the writer's swimming expertise?

I lifted my head, took a big breath, and shouted, "Barry, I'm swimming to Antarctica!"

I saw the smiles, heard the cheers and laughs, and I felt their energy lift me. They were as thrilled as I was. I swam faster, extending my arms, pulling more strongly, reaching for the shores of Antarctica. Now I knew we were almost there.

Spiral Review
Central Idea How does the presence of her supporters help Cox win the conflict between her body and her mind?

The crew was shouting warnings about ice. I swerved around two icebergs. Some chunks looked sharp, but I was too tired to care. I swam into whatever was in my path. It hurt, but all I wanted now was to finish.

As we neared shore, I lifted my head and saw the other passengers from the *Orlova*, in their bright red and yellow hats and parkas, tromping down the snowbanks, spreading their feet and arms wide for balance, racing to the water's edge to meet us. I lifted my foot and waved and saw my crew break into bigger smiles.

I'm almost done, I thought. *I feel okay. I feel strong. I feel warm inside. My arms and legs are thirty-two degrees. But I feel good. I can stretch out my strokes and put my face in the water. Maybe I can go a little farther. Maybe I can see what more I can do. Maybe I can swim five or ten more minutes. Or maybe I should be happy with what I've*

Reading Check
What changes for Cox after she shifts her course?

---

10. crabbed *v.* moved sideways or diagonally.

done. *My skin is so cold I can't feel it, and when I stop swimming, I don't know how far my temperature's going to drop.* I looked at my watch. Twenty-three minutes. I'd been in a minute longer than two days before. *How much difference would a minute make? I asked myself. How much difference is there between thirty-two-degree and thirty-three-degree water? Remember what Dr. Keatinge[11] said: once your temperature starts to drop, it will drop very fast. If you continue swimming, you're going to cool down even more. Remember how hard you shivered last time? Remember how much work it was? Remember how uncomfortable you were? This is the place where people make mistakes, when they're tired and cold and they push too far into the unknown. You could really hurt yourself. Finish now. You've done a good job. Be satisfied with what you've done. Go celebrate with your friends.*

> My skin
> is so cold
> I can't
> feel it.

Turning in toward shore, I again lifted my foot and waved it, and my friends waved back and cheered. One hundred yards from shore, I saw chinstrap penguins sliding headfirst, like tiny black toboggans, down a steep snowbank. When they reached the base of the hill, they used their bristly tails like brakes, sticking them into the snow to stop their momentum. They waddled across the beach at full tilt, holding their wings out at their sides for balance. Reaching the water, they dove in headfirst, then porpoised across it, clearing it by one or two feet with each surface dive. They tucked their wings back by their sides so they would be more aerodynamic. When they neared the Zodiacs, they dove and flapped their wings under the water as if they were flying through air. It was amazing to think this was the only place they would fly. They zoomed under me in bursts of speed, and their bubbles exploded like white fireworks. More penguins joined in. One cannonballed off a ledge, another slipped on some ice and belly flopped, and three penguins swam within inches of my hands. I reached out to touch one, but he swerved and flapped his wings, so he moved just beyond my fingertips. I had no idea why they were swimming with me, but I knew it was a good sign; it meant there were no killer whales or leopard seals in the area.

---

11. Dr. Keatinge Cox's doctor on her swim across the Bering Strait.

When I reached knee-deep water, Dan jumped in, ran through the water, looped his arm through mine, and helped me stand. "Are you okay?" he asked.

"Yes. We made it!" I said.

Everyone around me was crying. Susan Adie helped Dan pull me up the incline. Martha wrapped a towel around my shoulders. Barry hugged me tightly. Laura and Susan began drying me off. I was so cold I was already starting to shiver hard. My legs were stiffer than after the other swim. The crew helped me into the Zodiac and I flopped onto the floor. Laura and Susan piled on top of me to protect me from the wind, and we pounded across the water, my head slamming into the Zodiac's floor. I managed to lift my head so that someone could place a hand under it to buffer the impact. I was so cold and stiff and shaking harder than before.

When we reached the Orlova, it took me a minute to stand, to gain my balance, and as I climbed the ramp's steps I clung to the railing and pulled myself up, shaking hard. By the time I reached the top of the ramp, my teeth were chattering and I was breathing harder and faster than when I had been swimming. I didn't like being so cold. I didn't like my body having to work so hard. My temperature had dropped to 95.5 degrees, and I couldn't control my shaking. I just let go, and my body bounced up and down with shakes and shivers.

Quickly Martha and Dan and the three doctors huddled around me like emperor penguins, and their combined comfort and body heat began to warm me. It seemed as if I would never stop shaking,

▲ **Critical Viewing**
Does this image of chinstrap penguins match what you imagined based on Cox's descriptions? Explain.
[Connect]

Vocabulary
buffer (buf´ ər) v. lessen a shock; cushion

☑ **Reading Check**

What is the outcome of Cox's attempt to swim a mile?

from Swimming to Antarctica **73**

and I was completely exhausted. Within half an hour my shivering had subsided to small body shudders. Once I was able to stand and maintain my balance, the doctors helped me pull on a special top and pants that had been designed by a friend. She had sewn pockets under the arms, in the groin area, and into a scarf and had placed chemical packs that emitted heat inside the pockets. Their placement in the clothing warmed the major blood-flow areas of my body so that I was heated from the inside out. It was effective, and within an hour my temperature was back to normal.

That night we celebrated with everyone aboard the Orlova. I had swum the first Antarctic mile—a distance of 1.06 miles, in fact—in thirty-two-degree water in twenty-five minutes. I had been able to do what had seemed impossible because I'd had a crew who believed in me and in what we as human beings were capable of. It was a great dream, swimming to Antarctica.

Literary Analysis
Author's Perspective
Which details show the difference between Cox's perspective before and after her swim?

Critical Thinking

Cite textual evidence to support your responses.

1. **Key Ideas and Details** **(a)** Using details from the selection, list three ways in which Cox prepares for her swim. **(b) Analyze Causes and Effects:** For each method of preparation, explain the effect it has or is intended to have.

2. **Key Ideas and Details** **(a)** What physical challenge causes Cox to struggle at the start of her swim? **(b) Analyze:** What does Cox's ability to overcome this challenge reveal about her?

3. **Key Ideas and Details** **(a)** Identify two instances in which Cox gives herself a pep talk. **(b) Summarize:** What is the main point Cox makes in each pep talk? **(c) Analyze:** Is each pep talk effective? Why?

4. **Key Ideas and Details** **(a) Speculate:** Identify two reasons Cox may have had for making the swim. **(b) Summarize:** List two of the dangers that Cox faced. **(c) Evaluate:** Explain whether the swim was worth the effort.

5. **Integration of Knowledge and Ideas** **(a)** What makes Cox able to push herself harder than she thought she could? **(b)** How does the reality of Cox's Antarctic swim differ from what she predicted it would be like? *[Connect to the Big Question: Is there a difference between reality and truth?]*

Literary Analysis: Author's Perspective

1. Key Ideas and Details **(a)** Using a chart like the one shown, analyze the **author's perspective** in the selection.

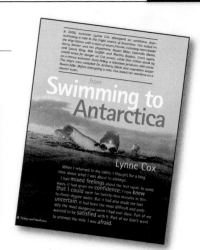

Author's Perspective	
Types of Details Included	**Examples of Each**
❏ researched facts ❏ personal experiences ❏ opinions ❏ attitudes	_____ _____ _____ _____

(b) Referring to your chart, briefly describe Cox's perspective.

2. Craft and Structure **(a)** List two ways in which Cox's story would be different if told by a news reporter. **(b)** Do you think Cox's firsthand point of view adds to the story's drama? Explain.

Reading Skill: Make Predictions

3. Identify details in the selection that you used to **verify a prediction.**

4. (a) Identify one prediction you **revised** as you read. **(b)** In a small group, discuss your predictions and explain why you revised them.

Vocabulary

Acquisition and Use Explain whether each sentence makes sense given the meaning of the underlined word. If a sentence does not make sense, revise it using the word correctly.

1. After <u>prolonged</u> workouts at the gym, he is finally back in shape.

2. The best tightrope walkers have no sense of <u>equilibrium</u>.

3. Open the windows; I need to <u>buffer</u> myself from the outside noise.

4. <u>Venturing</u> into the forest without a map is not a good idea.

5. After it is defrosted, <u>abruptly</u> cook the turkey for three hours.

6. An odometer helps you <u>gauge</u> how many miles you drive.

Word Study Use the context of the sentences and what you know about the **Latin prefix pro-** to explain your answer to each question.

1. If a runner *proceeds* to the finish line, has she finished the race?

2. Would a *progressive* idea look toward the future or the past?

Word Study

The **Latin prefix *pro-*** means "forth" or "forward."

Apply It Explain how the prefix *pro-* contributes to the meanings of these words. Consult a dictionary if necessary.

projectile
propeller
proficient

Is there a difference between *reality* and *truth?*

Writing About the Big Question

In "Occupation: Conductorette," a young girl experiences the harsh reality of prejudice. Use this sentence starter to develop your ideas about the Big Question.

People who are able to **comprehend** the truth behind problems in society must decide whether to _____ or

_____ .

While You Read Look for the ways the author challenges reality to fight for the job of streetcar conductor.

Vocabulary

Read each word and its definition. Decide whether you know the word well, know it a little bit, or do not know it at all. After you read, see how your knowledge of each word has increased.

- **self-sufficiency** (self´ sə fish´ ən sē) *n.* independence (p. 79) *His self-sufficiency helped him survive in the woods.* sufficient *adj.*

- **indignation** (in´ dig nā´ shən) *n.* anger that is a reaction to injustice or meanness (p. 80) *The indignation she felt towards the thief who stole her wallet was hard to put into words.* indignant *adj.*

- **dingy** (din´ jē) *adj.* dirty-looking; shabby (p. 81) *The dark walls made the room look dingy.* dingily *adv.* dinginess *n.*

- **supercilious** (sōō´pər sil´ ē əs) *adj.* expressing an attitude of superiority; contemptuous (p. 81) *The queen gave the peasant a supercilious smile.* superciliously *adv.* superciliousness *n.*

- **hypocrisy** (hi päk´ rə sē) *n.* the act of saying one thing but doing another (p. 81) *The environmentalist's hypocrisy was revealed when he littered.* hypocrite *n.* hypocritical *adj.*

- **dexterous** (deks´ tər əs) *adj.* having or showing mental skill (p. 83) *She showed how dexterous she was by quickly answering all the questions with ease.* dexterity *n.*

Word Study

The **Latin prefix** *super-* means "above."

In this excerpt, a young Maya Angelou tries to project confidence and show that she is above others by speaking in a **supercilious** manner, but she is really quite nervous.

Meet
Maya Angelou
(b. 1928)

Author of
Occupation:
Conductorette

Maya Angelou was born Marguerite Johnson in St. Louis, Missouri. *I Know Why the Caged Bird Sings,* the work from which this selection comes, is the first part of her autobiography.

Up From Hard Times Some of the communities in which Angelou grew up were segregated— African Americans were excluded from facilities, including schools, used by whites. Yet, Angelou rejects bitterness, saying, "The honorary duty of a human being is to love."

Angelou has had diverse experiences in life. She worked with Dr. Martin Luther King, Jr., in the civil rights movement. Afterward, she moved to Africa, where she lived from 1961 to 1966. Her literary success came in the 1970s.

BACKGROUND FOR THE AUTOBIOGRAPHY

Jobs and World War II

During the 1940s, the time Maya Angelou recalls, millions of American men went overseas to fight World War II. Their absence created new opportunities at home. Six million women went to work in industry to aid the war effort, taking jobs newly open to them. Although African Americans still faced prejudice, some found—or made—new opportunities for themselves.

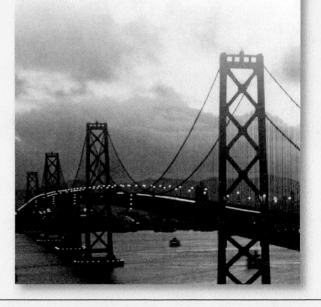

DID YOU KNOW?
Angelou read one of her poems at President William Jefferson Clinton's inauguration in 1993.

The young Angelou has
just returned to San
Francisco after an
adventure-filled trip.
Things are changing at
home, she discovers, and
her brother moves out
soon after her return.
Restless, and discontent,
Angelou ponders
her next step.

Occupation: Conductorette

from
I Know Why the Caged Bird Sings

Maya Angelou

I had it. The answer came to me with the suddenness of a collision. I would go to work. Mother wouldn't be difficult to convince; after all, in school I was a year ahead of my grade and Mother was a firm believer in self-sufficiency. In fact, she'd be pleased to think that I had that much gumption, that much of her in my character. (She liked to speak of herself as the original "do-it-yourself girl.")

Vocabulary
self-sufficiency
(self′ sə fish′ ən sē)
n. independence

Once I had settled on getting a job, all that remained was to decide which kind of job I was most fitted for. My intellectual pride had kept me from selecting typing, shorthand or filing as subjects in school, so office work was ruled out. War plants and shipyards demanded birth certificates, and mine would reveal me to be fifteen, and ineligible for work. So the well-paying defense jobs were also out. Women had replaced men on the streetcars as conductors and motormen, and the thought of sailing up and down the hills of San Francisco in a dark-blue uniform, with a money changer at my belt, caught my fancy.

Mother was as easy as I had anticipated. The world was moving so fast, so much money was being made, so many people were dying in Guam, and Germany,[1] that hordes of strangers became good friends overnight. Life was cheap and death entirely free. How could she have the time to think about my academic career?

To her question of what I planned to do, I replied that I would get a job on the streetcars. She rejected the proposal with: "They don't accept colored people on the streetcars."

I would like to claim an immediate fury which was followed by the noble determination to break the restricting tradition. But the truth is, my first reaction was one of disappointment. I'd pictured myself, dressed in a neat blue serge suit, my money changer swinging jauntily at my waist, and a cheery smile for the passengers which would make their own work day brighter.

From disappointment, I gradually ascended the emotional ladder to haughty indignation, and finally to that state of stubbornness where the mind is locked like the jaws of an enraged bulldog.

I would go to work on the streetcars and wear a blue serge suit. Mother gave me her support with one of her usual terse asides, "That's what you want to do? Then nothing beats a trial but a failure. Give it everything you've got. I've told you many times, 'Can't do is like Don't Care.' Neither of them have a home."

Translated, that meant there was nothing a person can't do, and there should be nothing a human being didn't care about. It was the most positive encouragement I could have hoped for.

---

1. **Guam** (gwäm), **and Germany** places where World War II (1939–1945) was fought. Guam is an island in the Pacific Ocean.

In the offices of the Market Street Railway Company, the receptionist seemed as surprised to see me there as I was surprised to find the interior dingy and the décor drab. Somehow I had expected waxed surfaces and carpeted floors. If I had met no resistance, I might have decided against working for such a poor-mouth-looking concern. As it was, I explained that I had come to see about a job. She asked, was I sent by an agency, and when I replied that I was not, she told me they were only accepting applicants from agencies.

The classified pages of the morning papers had listed advertisements for motorettes and conductorettes and I reminded her of that. She gave me a face full of astonishment that my suspicious nature would not accept.

"I am applying for the job listed in this morning's *Chronicle* and I'd like to be presented to your personnel manager." While I spoke in supercilious accents, and looked at the room as if I had an oil well in my own backyard, my armpits were being pricked by millions of hot pointed needles. She saw her escape and dived into it.

"He's out. He's out for the day. You might call tomorrow and if he's in, I'm sure you can see him." Then she swiveled her chair around on its rusty screws and with that I was supposed to be dismissed.

"May I ask his name?"

She half turned, acting surprised to find me still there.

"His name? Whose name?"

"Your personnel manager."

We were firmly joined in the hypocrisy to play out the scene.

"The personnel manager? Oh, he's Mr. Cooper, but I'm not sure you'll find him here tomorrow. He's . . . Oh, but you can try."

"Thank you."

"You're welcome."

And I was out of the musty room and into the even mustier lobby. In the street I saw the receptionist and myself going faithfully through paces that were stale with familiarity, although I had never encountered that kind of situation before and, probably, neither had she. We were like actors who, knowing the play by heart, were still able to cry afresh over the old tragedies and laugh spontaneously at the comic situations.

The miserable little encounter had nothing to do with me, the me

Vocabulary

dingy (din´ jē) *adj.* dirty-looking; shabby

supercilious (sōō´ pər sil´ ē əs) *adj.* expressing an attitude of superiority; contemptuous

hypocrisy (hi päk´ rə sē) *n.* the act of saying one thing but doing another

Reading Check

What major obstacle does Angelou face in her job quest?

of me, any more than it had to do with that silly clerk. The incident was a recurring dream, concocted years before by stupid whites and it eternally came back to haunt us all. The secretary and I were like Hamlet and Laertes[2] in the final scene, where, because of harm done by one ancestor to another, we were bound to duel to the death. Also because the play must end somewhere.

I went further than forgiving the clerk, I accepted her as a fellow victim of the same puppeteer.

On the streetcar, I put my fare into the box and the conductorette looked at me with the usual hard eyes of white contempt. "Move into the car, please move on in the car." She patted her money changer.

Her Southern nasal accent sliced my meditation and I looked deep into my thoughts. All lies, all comfortable lies. The receptionist was not innocent and neither was I. The whole charade we had played out in that crummy waiting room had directly to do with me, Black, and her, white.

I wouldn't move into the streetcar but stood on the ledge over the conductor, glaring. My mind shouted so energetically that the announcement made my veins stand out, and my mouth tighten into a prune.

I WOULD HAVE THE JOB. I WOULD BE A CONDUCTORETTE AND SLING A FULL MONEY CHANGER FROM MY BELT. I WOULD.

The next three weeks were a honeycomb[3] of determination with apertures for the days to go in and out. The Negro organizations to whom I appealed for support bounced me back and forth like a shuttlecock on a badminton court. Why did I insist on that particular job? Openings were going begging that paid nearly twice the money. The minor officials with whom I was able to win an audience thought me mad. Possibly I was.

Downtown San Francisco became alien and cold, and the streets I had loved in a personal familiarity were unknown lanes that twisted with malicious intent. Old buildings, whose gray rococo façades[4] housed my memories of the Forty-Niners, and Diamond Lil, Robert Service, Sutter and Jack London, were then imposing structures viciously joined to keep me out. My trips to the streetcar office were of the frequency of a person on salary. The struggle expanded. I was no longer in conflict only with the Market Street Railway

---

2. **Hamlet and Laertes** (lā ur´ tēz) characters in William Shakespeare's tragedy *Hamlet* who duel at the end of the play.
3. **honeycomb** (hun´ ē kōm´) *n.* wax structure, filled with holes, that bees build to store honey.
4. **rococo façades** (rə kō´ kō fə sädz´) elaborately designed building fonts.

but with the marble lobby of the building which housed its offices, and elevators and their operators.

During this period of strain Mother and I began our first steps on the long path toward mutual adult admiration. She never asked for reports and I didn't offer any details. But every morning she made breakfast, gave me carfare and lunch money, as if I were going to work. She comprehended the perversity of life, that in the struggle lies the joy. That I was no glory seeker was obvious to her, and that I had to exhaust every possibility before giving in was also clear.

On my way out of the house one morning she said, "Life is going to give you just what you put in it. Put your whole heart in everything you do, and pray, then you can wait." Another time she reminded me that "God helps those who help themselves." She had a store of aphorisms which she dished out as the occasion demanded. Strangely, as bored as I was with clichés, her inflection gave them something new, and set me thinking for a little while at least. Later when asked how I got my job, I was never able to say exactly. I only knew that one day, which was tiresomely like all the others before it, I sat in the Railway office, ostensibly waiting to be interviewed. The receptionist called me to her desk and shuffled a bundle of papers to me. They were job application forms. She said they had to be filled in triplicate. I had little time to wonder if I had won or not, for the standard questions reminded me of the necessity for dexterous lying. How old was I? List my previous jobs, starting from the last held and go backward to the first. How much money did I earn, and why did I leave the position? Give two references (not relatives).

Sitting at a side table my mind and I wove a cat's ladder of near truths and total lies. I kept my face blank (an old art) and wrote quickly the fable of Marguerite Johnson, aged nineteen, former companion and driver for Mrs. Annie Henderson (a White Lady) in Stamps, Arkansas.

I was given blood tests, aptitude tests, physical coordination tests, and Rorschachs,[5] then on a blissful day I was hired as the first Negro on the San Francisco streetcars.

Mother gave me the money to have my blue serge suit tailored, and I learned to fill out work cards, operate the money changer and punch transfers. The time crowded together and at an End of Days I was swinging on the back of the rackety trolley, smiling sweetly and persuading my charges to "step forward in the car, please."

---

5. **Rorschachs** (rôr´ shäks´) The Rorschach test is a method of analyzing an individual's personality using abstract images.

For one whole semester the street cars and I shimmied up and scooted down the sheer hills of San Francisco. I lost some of my need for the Black ghetto's shielding-sponge quality, as I clanged and cleared my way down Market Street, with its honky-tonk homes for homeless sailors, past the quiet retreat of Golden Gate Park and along closed undwelled-in-looking dwellings of the Sunset District.

My work shifts were split so haphazardly that it was easy to believe that my superiors had chosen them maliciously. Upon mentioning my suspicions to Mother, she said, "Don't worry about it. You ask for what you want, and you pay for what you get. And I'm going to show you that it ain't no trouble when you pack double."

She stayed awake to drive me out to the car barn at four thirty in the mornings, or to pick me up when I was relieved just before dawn. Her awareness of life's perils convinced her that while I would be safe on the public conveyances, she "wasn't about to trust a taxi driver with her baby."

When the spring classes began, I resumed my commitment with formal education. I was so much wiser and older, so much more independent, with a bank account and clothes that I had bought for myself, that I was sure that I had learned and earned the magic formula which would make me a part of the gay life my contemporaries led.

> **You ask for what you want, and you pay for what you get.**

Critical Thinking

Cite textual evidence to support your responses.

1. **Key Ideas and Details (a)** To what does Angelou compare her first encounter with the secretary at the railway company? **(b) Analyze Cause and Effect:** Explain how the streetcar conductorette's greeting changes Angelou's view of the meeting.

2. **Key Ideas and Details** Using details from the selection, explain why Angelou insists on becoming a conductorette.

3. **Key Ideas and Details (a) Interpret:** Find two passages in which Angelou's mother reacts to her quest, and explain what each shows about her mother's view of life. **(b) Draw Conclusions:** In what ways does her mother contribute to Angelou's success?

4. **Key Ideas and Details Summarize:** In a few sentences, objectively report what happens in the selection.

5. **Integration of Knowledge and Ideas** In what ways does Angelou challenge the accepted reality for African Americans in San Francisco? *[Connect to the Big Question: Is there a difference between reality and truth?]*

Literary Analysis: Author's Perspective

1. **Key Ideas and Details (a)** Using a chart like the one shown, analyze the **author's perspective** in the selection.

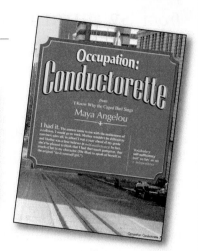

Author's Perspective	
Types of Details Included	**Examples of Each**
☐ researched facts ☐ personal experiences ☐ opinions ☐ attitudes	_____ _____ _____ _____

   (b) Use your chart to briefly describe Angelou's point of view.

2. **Key Ideas and Details** What is Angelou's present attitude toward her younger self? Consider her use of phrases such as "haughty indignation" to describe her reactions at the time.

Reading Skill: Make Predictions

3. Identify details in the selection that you used to **verify a prediction.**

4. **(a)** Identify one prediction you **revised** as you read. **(b)** In a small group, discuss your predictions and explain why you revised them.

Vocabulary

Acquisition and Use Explain whether each sentence makes sense given the meaning of the underlined word. If a sentence does not make sense, revise it using the word correctly.

1. She whines until her little brother makes her lunch for her—a clear sign of her <u>self-sufficiency</u>.
2. I painted the room a bright white to add to its <u>dingy</u> feeling.
3. When you ask him for help, give him a <u>supercilious</u> look.
4. Reading the thank-you letter gave him a great sense of <u>indignation</u>.
5. Known for his <u>hypocrisy</u>, he always said exactly what he felt.
6. Pat is such a <u>dexterous</u> thinker that she is never at a loss for words.

Word Study Use the context of the sentences and what you know about the **Latin prefix super-** to explain your answer to each question.

1. If a pet requires *supervision*, should it be left alone?
2. Does a *supervisor* generally give or receive orders?

Word Study

The **Latin prefix super-** means "above."

Apply It Explain how the prefix *super-* contributes to the meanings of these words. Consult a dictionary if necessary.

superimpose
superintendent
supersonic

Integrated Language Skills

from **Swimming to Antarctica** • Occupation: Conductorette

Conventions: Abstract and Concrete Nouns

A **noun** is a word that names a person, a place, or a thing.

Concrete nouns name specific things that can be directly experienced or perceived by the senses. The word *airplane* is a concrete noun because it names something you can see, feel, and hear.

Abstract nouns name ideas or concepts that cannot be seen, heard, felt, tasted, smelled, or directly experienced. *Justice* is an abstract noun because it is a concept that cannot be directly perceived by the senses.

Concrete Nouns	Abstract Nouns
The *pancakes* are still hot.	*Honesty* is an important *trait* for everyone.
My *sister* wanted a small *dog* with soft, fluffy *fur* and a wet *nose*.	Her greatest *wish* was for *peace* around the world.
The *car* was so loud I could not hear what my *mother* was saying.	*Democracy* is an important *tradition* in the United States.

Practice A Identify the noun or nouns in each sentence, and indicate whether they are concrete or abstract nouns. There are eleven in all.

1. To swim in cold water takes much endurance.

2. Lynne Cox needed a team to help her reach her goal.

3. A cold-water swimmer usually wears a wet-suit or a drysuit.

4. Cox relied on faith and determination.

Ⓒ **Reading Application** Find three concrete nouns and three abstract nouns in the excerpt from *Swimming to Antarctica*.

Practice B Label each noun as concrete or abstract. Then, use each word in a sentence.

1. gumption

2. streetcar

3. commitment

4. building

5. determination

Ⓒ **Writing Application** Using this sentence as a model, write two sentences with both concrete and abstract nouns: *Today is a basket of joy.*

PH **WRITING COACH** | Further instruction and practice are available in *Prentice Hall Writing Coach*.

Writing

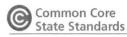 **Common Core State Standards**

W.9-10.2.b; SL.9-10.5
[For the full wording of the standards, see page 58.]

Explanatory Text Each selection provides information to help readers imagine an important scene. Write a brief **description** of either a scene in Antarctica or a 1940s streetcar ride.

- Use your prior knowledge and the information you learned from reading Cox's or Angelou's work to help you write your description.

- Consider your purpose and audience. Then, identify the mood, or atmosphere, you want to create, such as danger, beauty, or frustration.

- Carefully select details from the selection that fit the mood you want to create.

- Use precise words and sensory details to capture the scene and to develop your ideas. Organize details logically.

Grammar Application To make your description vivid, use specific concrete nouns more frequently than abstract nouns.

Writing Workshop: *Work in Progress*

Prewriting for Autobiographical Narrative Review the Place List in your writing portfolio. Use your notes to write a few lines about each item. Choose the one that is most meaningful to you and explain why. Save this Place Description in your writing portfolio for later use.

Use this prewriting activity to prepare for the **Writing Workshop** on page 108.

Research and Technology

Presentation of Knowledge and Ideas Keep a **daily observation journal** and use it to chart one of the following situations.

- If you read the excerpt from *Swimming to Antarctica*, keep a daily observation journal charting your speed or achievements in some activity, such as how many miles you run per day or how many words you type per minute.

- If you read "Occupation: Conductorette," observe someone who has a job you might want some day. Keep a journal to chart the person's work, recording important daily tasks and the time each one takes.

Follow these steps to complete the assignment:

- Using computer software, create a graph or chart that maps the information you discover in a clear and easily understood format. Then, write a summary of your findings.

- Present your findings, graphics, and summary orally in class. Consider your audience and purpose, and convey your ideas clearly and concisely.

Test Practice: Reading

Make Predictions

Fiction Selection

Directions: *Read the selection. Then, answer the questions.*

The day had been sunny, but as Jack was leaving his house, he noticed the sky was rapidly darkening. He heard his father calling.

"What's up, Dad?"

"Hurry," his father said. "To the cellar. A tornado is headed this way."

"Cool!" Jack responded.

"Not cool, Jack." Jack's father glanced outside. "Look—you can see it now!" Jack followed his father's gaze. A funnel-shaped cloud was swirling along the ground, twisting and pushing forward, absorbing debris as it moved. Jack and his father bolted to the cellar and huddled in a storage room. The wind howled overhead. When the roaring passed, Jack and his father peeked outside.

They were shocked to see that the house next door was missing its roof. Cars lay upside down in the street. When Jack and his father inspected their home, the only damage was a broken window. Jack looked at his father. "We're very lucky, aren't we?"

1. What information leads you to predict that a storm is coming?

   A. The sky was rapidly darkening.
   B. Jack heard his father calling.
   C. Debris was swirling in the funnel cloud.
   D. The roar of the tornado passed quickly.

2. What prior knowledge do you need to have to predict that Jack and his father will escape harm from the tornado?

   A. knowing how fast tornadoes can move
   B. knowing that the cellar is the safest place to be during a tornado
   C. knowing how tornadoes are formed
   D. knowing the damage tornadoes can cause

3. Which infomation does *not* help you predict that the tornado will cause damage?

   A. prior knowledge about tornadoes
   B. the description of the funnel cloud
   C. the description of the wind howling
   D. Jack's comment about being lucky

4. Based on the passage, you can predict that Jack—

   A. will never fear tornadoes.
   B. will not go outside if he sees a tornado.
   C. will rebuild his neighbor's roof.
   D. will study tornadoes to learn more.

Writing for Assessment

What do you predict Jack and his father will do immediately after the tornado? Write a short paragraph explaining your prediction.

Nonfiction Selection

Directions: *Read the selection. Then, answer the questions.*

A tornado, or twister, is a very violent type of storm. When it touches down on the ground, it can cause terrible devastation. A tornado's rotational, or twisting, speed is usually estimated at about 300 miles per hour but can reach nearly 500 miles per hour. A tornado can be recognized by its funnel cloud, which dips downward from the clouds of a strong thunderstorm. The funnel becomes darker as it touches the earth because of the debris it has sucked up.

A tornado moves forward at about 30 to 40 miles per hour, but can travel as fast as 70 miles per hour. Most tornadoes are only about 300 yards wide; however, one of the most destructive tornadoes ever to strike the United States was about one mile wide. Even though a tornado passes quickly, it can cause extreme destruction. The wind is so strong that blades of straw have been embedded in fence posts by tornadoes. In one case, a school with eighty-five students was destroyed and the students were carried about 450 feet by the twister. Surprisingly, not one of the students was injured.

1. Which of the following can you predict would suffer the most destruction from a tornado?

A. a concrete apartment building
B. an underground shelter
C. an outdoor carnival
D. a school's basement

2. If you knew exactly where a tornado was first sighted, which of the following details could help you predict how quickly to take cover?

A. Tornadoes are usually about 300 yards wide.
B. Winds can reach 300 miles per hour.
C. Tornadoes can move at 30 miles per hour.
D. Tornadoes cause terrible destruction.

3. Based on the passage, you can reasonably predict that—

A. small items such as pencils or pens can become deadly in a tornado.
B. most tornadoes will pass by without doing harm.
C. tornadoes do not usually injure people.
D. faster tornadoes pick up more debris.

4. What information is most helpful for predicting how much damage a tornado will cause?

A. the amount of debris that it picks up
B. the tornado's rotational speed
C. the shape of the funnel cloud
D. which storm generated the tornado

Writing for Assessment

Connecting Across Texts
What dangers might Jack have faced if he had not taken safety precautions? In a paragraph, use details from the two passages to support your answer.

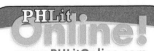

www.PHLitOnline.com
• Online practice
• Instant feedback

Analyzing Expository Texts

Feature Article

Newsletter

Common Core State Standards

Reading Informational Text
3. Analyze how the author unfolds an analysis or series of ideas or events, including the order in which the points are made, how they are introduced and developed, and the connections that are drawn between them.

4. Determine the meaning of words and phrases as they are used in a text, including figurative, connotative, and technical meanings; analyze the cumulative impact of specific word choices on meaning and tone.

Language
6. Acquire and use accurately general academic and domain-specific words and phrases, sufficient for reading, writing, speaking, and listening at the college and career readiness level; demonstrate independence in gathering vocabulary knowledge when considering a word or phrase important to comprehension or expression.

Reading Skill: Analyze Structure and Format

When you **analyze structure** and **format** in a text, you examine how the information is organized and presented. Authors make decisions about how words appear on a page in order to achieve specific **purposes.** Understanding how authors use structural features, or text features, can help you locate and analyze the information provided.

This chart shows some common structural features and their purposes.

Structural Feature	Purpose
Main heading	• Provides an overview of content
Subheading	• Introduces a specific topic within the main topic • Helps readers to quickly locate information
Bold or italic text	• Separates text on a page, making it easier to read • Calls attention to certain information
Illustration or other graphic	• Conveys visual information • Adds visual interest to a page

Content-Area Vocabulary

These words appear in the selections that follow. You may also encounter them in other content-area texts.

- **phrasings** (frāz´ ingz) *n.* groups of notes that form short, distinct passages of music

- **ensemble** (än säm´ bəl) *n.* group of musicians, actors, or dancers who perform together

- **repertoire** (rep´ ər twär) *n.* group of items, such as musical pieces, that are performed regularly

Feature Article

Features:

- a focused topic
- quotations from experts, participants, or observers
- photos, maps, or other informative graphics

Feel the City's Pulse?

It's Be-bop man!

By Ann Douglas

The main heading tells you that the article will be about be-bop music in the city.

In 1964, Thelonious Monk, one of the pioneers of be-bop and perhaps jazz's greatest composer, was asked by an interviewer to define jazz. Though Monk disliked questions and usually ignored them, this time he didn't miss a beat: "New York, man. You can feel it. It's around in the air. . . ."

Be-Bop was sometimes labeled "New York Jazz," and it is, in fact, the only major school of jazz to which the city can lay proprietary claim. Jazz of the '20s, dominated by Louis Armstrong, originated in New Orleans, migrating to New York only after a formative detour in Chicago. Armstrong inspired '30s swing, the music of the big bands led by Benny Goodman, Artie Shaw, Glenn Miller, Count Basie and Duke Ellington, the "mother bands," as Gillespie called them, whose music the be-boppers both emulated and revolutionized. . . . Bop's wide-ranging allusiveness, its quicksilver expressivity, angular dissonance and shockingly extended palette of pitches and rhythms echoed the international mix, the fluidity and speed of New York life.

Jamming After Hours

Bop began at roughly the same time as World War II, in 1940 when Monk, then 23, was hired to play with Kenny (Klook) Clarke, the man who transformed jazz drumming, at Minton's Playhouse in Harlem. Gillespie jammed with them after his regular engagement, and Parker[1] joined them a year later. When Minton's closed for the night, they adjourned to Clark Monroe's Uptown House, an after-hours club where an extraordinary teen-age drummer named Max Roach played in the band.

The nation's entrance into the war in late 1941 imposed gas rationing, entertainment taxes and curfews, sharply restricting travel. The swing bands were touring bands, and some of them continued to tour, but now everyone was looking for a long-term base in a big city, easily accessible by public transit. What hurt swing helped be-bop. The expense and risks of touring (especially down South) had been far greater for black musicians than for white.

The subheading breaks up the text for easier reading and explains what material will follow.

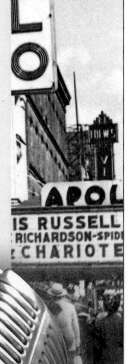

1. **Gillespie . . . Parker** Trumpeter Dizzy Gillespie and saxophonist Charlie Parker.

The cramped quarters of many city clubs suited the young bop musicians, eager to work with the small ensembles that maximized opportunities for experimentation. . . .

The word "be-bop," which both Monk and Gillespie claimed to have coined, described the music's unconventional stop-and-start form, especially Gillespie and Parker's witty eighth-note pair conclusions. The purpose of bop's irregular phrasings, side-sliding harmonies and whirlwind pace, was, in Kenny Clarke's words, to "raise the standards of musicianship," to tell people, "Whatever you go into, go into it intelligently." The be-boppers were the real New York intellectuals, the hippest, smartest men in town.

The map shows the locations of sites mentioned in the text.

SITES OF BOP'S TRIUMPHS AND TRAGEDIES

1. **Savoy Ballroom**, Lenox Avenue and 140th Street, Harlem. Charlie Parker played in this legendary jazz and dance hall with the Jay McShann Orchestra in his early days in New York.

2. **Minton's Playhouse**, 210 West 118th Street, Morningside Heights. Charlie Christian, Kenny Clarke, Thelonious Monk, Parker and Gillespie made musical history here in the early 1940s.

3. **St. Peter's Church**, 54th Street and Lexington Avenue, Manhattan (also its current site). Monk's funeral took place here on Feb. 22, 1982, with musicians playing for three hours.

4. **52nd Street**, between Fifth and Sixth Avenues, known as "The Street." A magical block of jazz clubs . . . including the Onyx, Spotlite, Three Deuces and Kelly's Stable.

Bold text helps to separate this list into clear sections.

5. **Birdland**, 1678 Broadway, at 53rd Street, Manhattan. It opened on Dec. 15, 1949, with dozens of (caged) birds on view and Charlie (Bird) Parker presiding.

6. **216 West 19th Street**
Eager to become "a New York musician," Gillespie lived here with his brother, . . . when he first came to town from Philadelphia in 1937, eating for 25 cents a day.

THE NEWSLETTER OF THE

HEALDSBURG JAZZ FESTIVAL

WINTER 2007
VOLUME 7
ISSUE 1

Dig Deeper into Jazz

The title indicates a specific area of interest—learning more about jazz.

JAZZ APPRECIATION COURSE STARTS IN HEALDSBURG

What is this "jazz" thing all about, anyway? Though we all know what we like—and we like jazz!—most of us don't know as much about it as we wish. Whether you're a novice or a fan, if you dig jazz, this is your chance to dig it deeper. Three fun, informative, and inexpensive mid-week Jazz Appreciation classes will begin February 28 at the Raven Film Center. The classes will mix live and recorded music with the expertise of the guest instructor to bring jazz history alive.

"Adult education has always been a missing component in the Healdsburg Jazz Festival," said artistic director Jessica Felix as she announced a new grant from the Healdsburg Area Affiliate of the Community Foundation, Sonoma County. The grant makes it possible to offer this three-part series on the history of jazz for area adults, extending the reach of the Festival's Jazz Education Program out of the schools and into the community at large."

"The goal of this series is to bring us all closer to understanding the depth and history of an art form that has grown out of the American experience," Jessica Felix explained.

Take three giant steps toward jazz enjoyment with our first-ever Jazz Appreciation Series, starting the last day of February. To learn more, see page 2 of this newsletter.

LEARN MORE ABOUT *Jazz Music With The*
HEALDSBURG JAZZ FESTIVAL'S JAZZ APPRECIATION COURSE

> A subheading introduces the topic covered in the second section of the newsletter.

THREE-PART SERIES AT THE RAVEN FILM CENTER, THEATER 2, 415 CENTER STREET

February 28th, March 28th, and May 9th. 6:30 to 9:30 pm

Open to all Ages, $10 per class, 3 for $25, half price for Senior Citizens (65 and over) and Students. Financial assistance available.

This class is made possible in part by a generous grant from the Healdsburg Area Affiliate of the Community Foundation, Sonoma County.

Class 1, February 28: Jazz History and Jazz Styles
Jazz educator, Ali Jackson explores the origins of jazz music with his celebrated *What is Jazz?*, a class, designed to make "America's Classical Music" accessible to a wide audience. What is jazz? Where did jazz come from? Who are the true pioneers and innovators of jazz? If you or a friend have asked these questions, *What is Jazz?* will provide the answers.
Class will use audio (CDs) and visual materials (DVDs).

> Boldface dates are followed by details for each event in the schedule.

Class 2, March 28: The Music Making Process
Dr. James Newton, internationally acclaimed musician, composer, educator and jazz historian, will introduce the class to the essential concepts of interaction within a jazz ensemble. The class will also demonstrate how a jazz combo approaches the interpretation of a composition, and Newton will be joined by a rhythm section to illustrate these concepts.
CDs, DVDs, and live music will be used as part of this class.

Class 3, May 9: Artists and Music of the Healdsburg Jazz Festival
Also taught by Dr. James Newton, this class will give participants a more informed perspective on the bands appearing at the 2007 Healdsburg Jazz Festival. The class will cover the stylistic practices of the artists and highlights of their careers, and explore the use of different size ensembles particularly as they relate to the jazz repertoire.
CDs and DVDs will be used as part of this class.

Comparing Expository Texts

 1. Key Ideas and Details (a) What is the author's **purpose** in each of the two documents? **(b)** How do the **structure and format** of each document support that purpose? **(c)** Which document do you think uses structural features more effectively to achieve the author's purpose? Explain your response.

Content-Area Vocabulary

2. (a) List a synonym, or word with a similar meaning, for *ensemble* and for *repertoire*. **(b)** Use *phrasings, ensemble,* and *repertoire* in a brief paragraph about music.

Timed Writing

Argument: Essay

> **Format**
> The prompt directs you to write a persuasive essay. Therefore, you should express an opinion and convince readers to agree with you.

Write a persuasive essay in which you take a position on the following quotation: "Music reflects culture. It is a central means by which a group asserts its relationship to past generations, distinguishes insiders from outsiders, and addresses the future." Support your response with details from the two texts. (25 minutes)

> **Academic Vocabulary**
> When you *take a position,* you state your opinion, or claim, on an issue. You *support* your position by defending it with evidence and examples.

5-Minute Planner

Complete these steps before you begin to write:

1. Read the prompt carefully to make sure you understand the assignment. Pay special attention to highlighted key words and phrases.
2. Review the article and newsletter, keeping in mind the quotation in the assignment. **TIP** Use structural features to find information.
3. Decide what position you will take on the quotation.
4. Note details from the two texts that support your position.
5. Prepare a quick outline for your essay. Then, refer to your notes and outline as you write.

Comparing Style

A writer's **style** is made up of the features that make his or her expression of ideas distinctive. Writers may use various styles, depending on their **purpose,** or reason for writing. Here are two important elements of style:

- **Diction,** or word choice, involves the types of words the writer uses. Writers may use words that are difficult or simple, abstract or concrete, old-fashioned or modern.

  Writers choose words that will help them achieve their purposes. In making their choices, writers consider the connotations, or emotional associations, of a word as well as its denotation, or definition.

- **Syntax,** or sentence structure, is related to the way words are organized to express ideas. When you analyze syntax, you consider the arrangement of words in phrases and sentences. You also consider what effect that arrangement has on the reader. One writer may write a series of short, punchy sentences, driving home each new idea. Another may play with readers, putting a key idea at the end of a long, twisty sentence.

Use a chart like the one shown to compare the writers' styles and purposes in "Marian Anderson, Famous Concert Singer" and "Tepeyac."

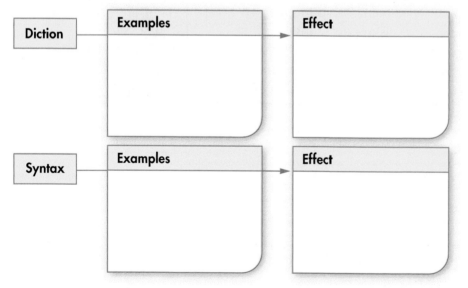

Diction	Examples	→	Effect
Syntax	Examples	→	Effect

**Common Core
State Standards**

**Reading Literature/
Informational Text**

4. Determine the meaning of words and phrases as they are used in the text, including figurative, connotative, and technical meanings; analyze the cumulative impact of specific word choices on meaning and tone.

Writing

2. Write informative/explanatory texts to examine and convey complex ideas, concepts, and information clearly and accurately through the effective selection, organization, and analysis of content. *(Timed Writing)*

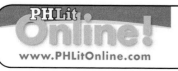
**PHLit
Online!**
www.PHLitOnline.com

- Vocabulary flashcards
- Interactive journals
- More about the authors
- Selection audio
- Interactive graphic organizers

THE BIG

Is there a difference
between *reality* and *truth?*

Writing About the Big Question

These selections show characters who grow as a result of the reality around them. Use this sentence starter to develop your ideas.

One person's **perception** of truth can be challenged when _____.

Meet the Authors

Langston Hughes (1902–1967)

Author of "Marian Anderson, Famous Concert Singer"

In the 1920s and 1930s, African American writers, artists, and musicians based in Harlem, a neighborhood in New York City, gave vivid, intense expression to the African American experience. The period is known as the Harlem Renaissance, and Langston Hughes is acknowledged as one of its dominant forces.

Jazz Rhythms on the Page Harlem Renaissance artists dedicated themselves to finding authentically African American styles. Hughes crafted a style, especially in his poetry, that reflected the rhythms and moods of jazz and blues music. (You can read one of Hughes's poems on page 736.)

Sandra Cisneros (b. 1954)

Author of "Tepeyac"

Born to a Mexican father and a Mexican American mother, Sandra Cisneros spent her childhood shuttling between Chicago and Mexico City. The only girl among seven children, Cisneros felt as if she had "seven fathers." Struggling to find her identity, she took refuge in reading and writing.

Winning Honors Although her family was not well-off, Cisneros managed to attend the prestigious Writers' Workshop at the University of Iowa. Her first novel, the autobiographical *The House on Mango Street* (1984), was a commercial and critical success, earning her the American Book Award from the Before Columbus Foundation in 1985.

Marian Anderson
FAMOUS CONCERT SINGER

Langston Hughes

Background Marian Anderson (1897?–1993) was one of the first African American singers to gain widespread recognition as a performer of classical music, including opera.

When Marian Anderson was born in a little red brick house in Philadelphia, a famous group of Negro singers, the Fisk Jubilee Singers, had already carried the spirituals all over Europe. And a colored woman billed as "Black Patti" had become famous on variety programs as a singer of both folk songs and the classics. Both

Negro and white minstrels had popularized American songs. The all-Negro musical comedies of Bert Williams and George Walker had been successful on Broadway. But no well-trained colored singers performing the great songs of Schubert, Handel, and the other masters, or the arias from famous operas, had become successful on the concert stage. And most people thought of Negro vocalists only in connection with spirituals. Roland Hayes[1] and Marian Anderson were the first to become famous enough to break this stereotype.

Marian Anderson's mother was a staunch church worker who loved to croon the hymns of her faith about the house, as did the aunt who came to live with them when Marian's father died. Both parents were from Virginia. Marian's mother had been a school-teacher there, and her father a farm boy. Shortly after they moved to Philadelphia where three daughters were born, the father died, and the mother went to work at Wanamaker's department store. But she saw to it that her children attended school and church regularly. The father had been an usher in the Union Baptist Church, so the congregation took an interest in his three little girls. Marian was the oldest and, before she was eight, singing in the Sunday school choir, she had already learned a great many hymns and spirituals by heart.

One day Marian saw an old violin in a pawnshop window marked $3.45. She set her mind on that violin, and began to save the nickels and dimes neighbors would give her for scrubbing their white front steps—the kind of stone steps so characteristic of Philadelphia and Baltimore houses—until she had $3.00. The pawnshop man let her take the violin at a reduced price. Marian never became very good on the violin. A few years later her mother bought a piano, so the child forgot all about it in favor of their newer instrument. By that time, too, her unusual singing voice had attracted the attention of her choir master, and at the age of fourteen she was promoted to a place in the main church choir. There she learned all four parts of all the hymns and anthems and could easily fill in anywhere from bass to soprano.

Sensing that she had exceptional musical talent, some of the church members began to raise money so that she might have singing lessons. But her first teacher, a colored woman, refused to accept any pay for instructing so talented a child. So the church folks put their money into a trust fund called "Marian Anderson's Future," banking it until the time came for her to have advanced training. Meanwhile, Marian attended South Philadelphia High School for Girls and took part in various group concerts, usually doing the solo parts. When she was fifteen she sang a group of

---

1. **Roland Hayes** (1887–1977) famous African American tenor.

Vocabulary
staunch (stônch) *adj.* steadfast; loyal

Literary Analysis
Style Identify an example of a direct, down-to-earth word or phrase in this passage.

Reading Check
What organization supported the development of Anderson's talent?

songs alone at a Sunday School Convention in Harrisburg and word of her talent began to spread about the state. When she was graduated from high school, the Philadelphia Choral Society, a Negro group, sponsored her further study and secured for her one of the best local teachers. Then in 1925 she journeyed to New York to take part, with three hundred other young singers, in the New York Philharmonic Competitions, where she won first place, and appeared with the orchestra at Lewisohn Stadium.

This appearance was given wide publicity, but very few lucrative engagements came in, so Marian continued to study. A Town Hall concert was arranged for her in New York, but it was unsuccessful. Meanwhile, she kept on singing with various choral groups, and herself gave concerts in churches and at some of the Negro colleges until, in 1930, a Rosenwald Fellowship made European study possible. During her first year abroad she made her debut in Berlin. A prominent Scandinavian concert manager read of this concert, but was attracted more by the name, *Anderson*, than by what the critics said about her voice. "Ah," he said, "a Negro singer with a Swedish name! She is bound to be a success in Scandinavia." He sent two of his friends to Germany to hear her, one of them being Kosti Vehanen who shortly became her accompanist and remained with her for many years.

Sure enough, Marian Anderson did become a great success in the Scandinavian countries, where she learned to sing in both Finnish and Swedish, and her first concert tour of Europe became a critical triumph. When she came back home to America, she gave several programs and appeared as soloist with the famous Hall Johnson Choir, but without financial success. However, the Scandinavian people, who had fallen in love with her, kept asking her to come back there. So, in 1933, she went again to Europe for 142 concerts in Norway, Sweden, Denmark, and Finland. She was decorated by the King of Denmark and the King of Sweden. Sibelius[2] dedicated a song to her. And the following spring she made her debut in Paris where she was so well received that she had to give three concerts that season at the Salle Gaveau.[3] Great successes followed in all the European capitals. In 1935 the famous conductor, Arturo Toscanini, listened to her sing at Salzburg.[4] He said, "What I heard today one is privileged to hear only once in a hundred years." It was in Europe that Marian Anderson began to be acclaimed by critics as "the greatest singer in the world."

When Marian Anderson again returned to America, she was a seasoned artist. News of her tremendous European successes

Vocabulary
lucrative (lōō′ krə tiv) *adj.* producing wealth; profitable
debut (dā byōō′) *n.* first public appearance

Literary Analysis
Style How do the words *sure enough* contribute to the informal, conversational diction?

2. **Sibelius** (si bā′ lē ơos) Jean Sibelius (1865–1957), a Finnish composer.
3. **Salle Gaveau** (sȧl ga vō′) concert hall in Paris, France.
4. **Salzburg** city in Austria noted for its music festivals.

had preceded her, so a big New York concert was planned. But a few days before she arrived at New York, in a storm on the liner crossing the Atlantic, Marian fell and broke her ankle. She refused to allow this to interfere with her concert, however, nor did she even want people to know about it. She wore a very long evening gown that night so that no one could see the plaster cast on her leg. She propped herself in a curve of the piano before the curtains parted, and gave her New York concert standing on one foot! The next day Howard Taubman wrote enthusiastically in *The New York Times*:

> Marian Anderson has returned to her native land one of the great singers of our time. . . . There is no doubt of it, she was mistress of all she surveyed. . . . It was music making that probed too deep for words.

A coast-to-coast American tour followed. And, from that season on, Marian Anderson has been one of our country's favorite singers, rated, according to *Variety*,[5] among the top ten of the concert stage who earn over $100,000 a year. Miss Anderson has sung with the great symphony orchestras, and appeared on all the major radio and television networks many times, being a particular favorite with the millions of listeners to the Ford Hour. During the years she has returned often to Europe for concerts, and

---

5. *Variety* a show-business newspaper.

▲ **Critical Viewing**
Does this photograph of Anderson's concert in Washington, D.C., support Hughes's description of her success? Explain.
[Support]

Spiral Review
Central Idea What central idea about Anderson does the reviewer's opinion help develop?

Reading Check
In which region of the world did Anderson first find success?

among the numerous honors accorded her abroad was a request for a command performance before the King and Queen of England, and a decoration from the government of Finland. Her concerts in South America and Asia have been as successful as those elsewhere. Since 1935 she has averaged over one hundred programs a year in cities as far apart as Vienna, Buenos Aires, Moscow, and Tokyo. Her recordings have sold millions of copies around the world. She has been invited more than once to sing at the White House. She has appeared in concert at the Paris Opera and at the Metropolitan Opera House in New York. Several colleges have granted her honorary degrees, and in 1944 Smith College made her a Doctor of Music.

In spite of all this, as a Negro, Marian Anderson has not been immune from those aspects of racial segregation which affect most traveling artists of color in the United States. In his book, *Marian Anderson*, her longtime accompanist, Vehanen, tells of hotel accommodations being denied her, and service in dining rooms often refused. Once after a concert in a Southern city, Vehanen writes that some white friends drove Marian to the railroad station and took her into the main waiting room. But a policeman ran them out, since Negroes were not allowed in that part of the station. Then they went into the smaller waiting room marked, COLORED. But again they were ejected, because *white* people were not permitted in the cubby hole allotted to Negroes. So they all had to stand on the platform until the train arrived.

The most dramatic incident of prejudice in all Marian Anderson's career occurred in 1939 when the Daughters of the American Revolution, who own Constitution Hall in Washington, refused to allow her to sing there. The newspapers headlined this and many Americans were outraged. In protest a committee of prominent people, including a number of great artists and distinguished figures in the government, was formed. Through the efforts of this committee, Marian Anderson sang in Washington, anyway—before the statue of Abraham Lincoln—to one of the largest crowds ever to hear a singer at one time in the history of the world. Seventy-five thousand people stood in the open air on a cold clear Easter Sunday afternoon to hear her. And millions more listened to Marian Anderson that day over the radio or heard her in the newsreels that recorded the event. Harold Ickes, then Secretary of the Interior, presented Miss Anderson to that enormous audience standing in the plaza to pay honor, as he said, not only to a great singer, but to the basic ideals of democracy and equality.

In 1943 Marian Anderson married Orpheus H. Fisher, an architect, and settled down—between tours—in a beautiful country house in Connecticut where she rehearses new songs to add to her already vast repertoire. Sometimes her neighbors across the fields can hear the rich warm voice that covers three octaves singing in English, French, Finnish, or German. And sometimes they hear in the New England air that old Negro spiritual, "Honor, honor unto the dying Lamb. . . ."

Friends say that Marian Anderson has invested her money in real estate and in government bonds. Certainly, throughout her career, she has lived very simply, traveled without a maid or secretary, and carried her own sewing machine along by train, ship, or plane to mend her gowns. When in 1941 in Philadelphia she was awarded the coveted Bok Award for outstanding public service, the $10,000 that came with the medallion she used to establish a trust fund for "talented American artists without regard to race or creed." Now, each year from this fund promising young musicians receive scholarships.

Vocabulary
repertoire (rep´ er twär´) *n.* a stock of works, such as songs, that a performer is prepared to present

Literary Analysis
Style Which words and phrases here give a direct illustration of Anderson's lifestyle?

Critical Thinking

1. **Key Ideas and Details** **(a)** According to Hughes, in what area had African American singers not received recognition before Anderson? **(b) Infer:** How can you explain this lack of recognition?

2. **Key Ideas and Details** **(a)** Identify one action Anderson's congregation took to help her career. **(b) Infer:** What does their decision to help suggest about Anderson's talent as a young girl? Explain.

3. **Key Ideas and Details** **(a) Summarize:** What type of difficulties did Anderson face when traveling in the United States? **(b) Infer:** What attitude led to these difficulties? **(c) Analyze:** In what sense was Anderson's outdoor concert in Washington, D. C., a response to this attitude?

4. **Integration of Knowledge and Ideas** In this biography, the narrator describes the reality of racial segregation practices during the 1930s and 1940s. How did Marian Anderson's career help expose the truth about racism during this time? Using details from the text, explain your answer. *[Connect to the Big Question: Is there a difference between reality and truth?]*

Cite textual evidence to support your responses.

TEPEYAC

Sandra Cisneros

Vocabulary
canopied (kan´ ə pēd)
adj. covered by a cloth
suspended from poles
or a framework

When the sky of Tepeyac[1] opens its first thin stars and the
dark comes down in an ink of Japanese blue above the
bell towers of La Basílica de Nuestra Señora,[2] above the
plaza photographers and their souvenir backdrops of La Virgen de
Guadalupe, above the balloon vendors and their balloons wearing
paper hats, above the red-canopied thrones of the shoeshine
stands, above the wooden booths of the women frying lunch in
vats of oil, above the *tlapalería*[3] on the corner of Misterios and
Cinco de Mayo, when the photographers have toted up their tripods
and big box cameras, have rolled away the wooden ponies I don't
know where, when the balloon men have sold all but the ugliest
balloons and herded these last few home, when the shoeshine men
have grown tired of squatting on their little wooden boxes, and the
women frying lunch have finished packing dishes, tablecloth, pots,
in the big straw basket in which they came, then Abuelito[4] tells the
boy with dusty hair, *Arturo, we are closed,* and in crooked shoes
and purple elbows Arturo pulls down with a pole the corrugated
metal curtains—first the one on Misterios, then the other on Cinco
de Mayo—like an eyelid over each door, before Abuelito tells him he
can go.

Literary Analysis
Style How many sen-
tences are included in
this first paragraph?

This is when I arrive, one shoe and then the next, over the
sagging door stone, worn smooth in the middle from the huaraches
of those who have come for tins of glue and to have their scissors
sharpened, who have asked for candles and cans of boot polish,

---

1. **Tepeyac** (tep ā yäk´) Tepeyac Hill lies in the northern part of Mexico City.
2. **La Basílica de Nuestra Señora** (lä bä sil´ ē kä dä nwäs´ trä sen yō´ rä) the Basilica
   [Church] of Our Lady, lying at the foot of Tepeyac Hill on the site where, according to
   legend, Juan Diego had a vision in 1531.
3. **tlapalería** (tlä pä lä rē´ ä) *n.* the Mexican equivalent of a hardware store.
4. **Abuelito** (ä bwä lē´ tō) *n.* affectionate Spanish term for "grandfather."

a half-kilo sack of nails, turpentine, blue-specked spoons, paintbrushes, photographic paper, a spool of picture wire, lamp oil, and string.

Abuelito under a bald light bulb, under a ceiling dusty with flies, puffs his cigar and counts money soft and wrinkled as old Kleenex, money earned by the plaza women serving lunch on flat tin plates, by the souvenir photographers and their canvas Recuerdo[5] de Tepeyac backdrops, by the shoeshine men sheltered beneath their fringed and canopied kingdoms, by the blessed vendors of the holy cards, rosaries, scapulars, little plastic altars, by the good sisters who live in the convent across the street, counts and recounts in a whisper and puts the money in a paper sack we carry home.

I take Abuelito's hand, fat and **dimpled** in the center like a valentine, and we walk past the basilica, where each Sunday the Abuela[6] lights the candles for the soul of Abuelito. Past the very same spot where long ago Juan Diego brought down from the *cerro*[7] the miracle that has drawn everyone, except my Abuelito, on their knees, down the avenue one block past the bright lights of the *sastrería*[8] of Señor Guzmán who is still at work at his sewing machine, past the candy store where I buy my milk-and-raisin gelatins, past La Providencia *tortillería* where every afternoon Luz María and I are sent for the basket of lunchtime tortillas, past the house of the widow Márquez whose husband died last winter of a tumor the size of her little white fist, past La Muñeca's mother watering her famous dahlias with a pink rubber hose and a skinny string of water, to the house on La Fortuna, number 12, that has always been our house. Green iron gates that arabesque[9] and scroll like the initials of my name, familiar whine and clang, familiar lacework of ivy growing over and between except for one small clean square for the hand of the postman whose face I have never seen, up the twenty-two steps we count out loud together—*uno, dos, tres*—to the supper of *sopa de fideo* and *carne guisada*—*cuatro, cinco, seis*—the glass of *café con leche*—*siete, ocho, nueve*—shut the door against the mad parrot voice of the Abuela—*diez, once, doce*—fall asleep as we always do, with the television mumbling—*trece, catorce, quince*—the Abuelito snoring—*dieciséis, diecisiete, dieciocho*—the grandchild, the one who will leave soon for that borrowed country—

---

5. **Recuerdo** (rā kwer´ tho) Spanish for "souvenir."
6. **Abuela** (ä bwā´ lä) *n.* Spanish for "grandmother."
7. **cerro** (se´ rō) *n.* Spanish for "hill."
8. **sastrería** (säs tre rē´ ä) *n.* tailor's shop.
9. **arabesque** (ar´ ə besk´) *v.* branch out in complex, intertwining lines (usually a noun referring to such lines).

Vocabulary
dimpled (dim´ pəld) *adj.* marked with small hollows or indentations

Reading Check

With whom does the narrator live in Tepeyac?

diecinueve, veinte, veintiuno—the one he will not remember, the one he is least familiar with—*veintidós, veintitrés, veinticuatro*—years later when the house on La Fortuna, number 12, is sold, when the *tlapalería*, corner of Misterios and Cinco de Mayo, changes owners, when the courtyard gate of arabesques and scrolls is taken off its hinges and replaced with a corrugated sheet metal door instead, when the widow Márquez and La Muñeca's mother move away, when Abuelito falls asleep one last time—*veinticinco, veintiséis, veintisiete*—years afterward when I return to the shop on the corner of Misterios and Cinco de Mayo, repainted and redone as a pharmacy, to the basilica that is crumbling and closed, to the plaza photographers, the balloon vendors and shoeshine thrones, the women whose faces I do not recognize serving lunch in the wooden booths, to the house on La Fortuna, number 12, smaller and darker than when we lived there, with the rooms boarded shut and rented to strangers, the street suddenly dizzy with automobiles and diesel fumes, the house fronts scuffed and the gardens frayed, the children who played kickball all grown and moved away.

Who would've guessed, after all this time, it is me who will remember when everything else is forgotten, you who took with you to your stone bed something irretrievable without a name.

Critical Thinking

1. Key Ideas and Details (a) List three details the narrator remembers about the market at Tepeyac. **(b) Synthesize:** What overall impression about the market do these details create? Explain your answer.

2. Key Ideas and Details Interpret: To what event is the narrator referring when she says, "the grandchild, the one who will leave soon for that borrowed country"?

3. Key Ideas and Details (a) Analyze: List two things that have changed in Tepeyac when the narrator returns. **(b) Draw Conclusions:** Why is the narrator surprised to discover at the end that "it is me who will remember"?

4. Integration of Knowledge and Ideas The narrator describes Tepeyac very realistically. What overall truth is she trying to convey with her detailed description? Explain. *[Connect to the Big Question: Is there a difference between reality and truth?]*

Comparing Styles

1. Craft and Structure (a) Explain how Hughes's **style** helps make Anderson seem accessible to readers, despite her fame. **(b)** How does Cisneros's style re-create the rushing flow of memories?

2. Craft and Structure (a) Using a chart like the one shown, compare each writer's style at the dramatic moment indicated.

	Hughes	Cisneros
Moment	**Washington, D.C., Concert**	**Concluding Realization**
type of words		
type of sentences		
similar to/different from rest of work?		

(b) Based on your chart, explain the ways in which each writer's style—or a shift in the writer's style—adds dramatic effect.

Timed Writing

Explanatory Text: Essay

Write an interpretive response to both texts that analyzes each author's specific purpose and the aesthetic effects of each author's use of stylistic devices. Then, decide which style is more effective in meeting the writer's purpose. **(30 minutes)**

5-Minute Planner

1. Read the prompt carefully and completely.

2. Consider these questions:

- What is each writer's purpose for writing?
- What stylistic devices, such as diction and syntax, does each author use?
- What role do stylistic devices play in helping each writer achieve his or her purpose?

3. Provide evidence and examples from the texts, including quotations.

4. Reread the prompt, and then draft your essay.

Writing Workshop

Write a Narrative

Narration: Autobiographical Narrative

Defining the Form **Autobiographical narratives** tell a story from the writer's own life. They can be as simple as a remembrance of a week-end vacation or as complex as the entire story of the writer's life. You might use elements of autobiographical narratives in journals, eyewitness accounts, and reflective essays.

Assignment Write an autobiographical narrative about an event in your life that changed you or helped you grow. Include these elements:

- ✓ a *clear sequence of events* involving you, the writer
- ✓ a *problem or conflict*
- ✓ *effective descriptions* of people, places, and events
- ✓ use of *dialogue* to show character
- ✓ an *insight* you gained as a result of this experience
- ✓ error-free grammar, including *correct use of possessive nouns*

To preview the criteria on which your autobiographical narrative may be judged, see the rubric on page 113.

 Writing Workshop: *Work in Progress*

Review the work you did on pages 57 and 87.

Prewriting/Planning Strategy

Create character and setting cards. To select a story from your life, consider events that were funny, exciting, unusual, or puzzling. Choose one and prepare to focus your narrative by identifying the main conflict or insight you want to explain. Write an index card for each important character or setting.

- For characters, include facts like name, age, and appearance. Also note personality, habits, and the person's role in your story.

- For settings, jot down precise physical details and sensory details, such as sights and sounds, to use in your descriptions.

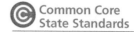 **Common Core State Standards**

Writing

3. Write narratives to develop real or imagined experiences or events using effective technique, well-chosen details, and well-structured event sequences.

3.a. Engage and orient the reader by setting out a problem, situation, or observation, establishing one or multiple point(s) of view, and introducing a narrator and/or characters; create a smooth progression of experiences or events.

3.c. Use a variety of techniques to sequence events so that they build on one another to create a coherent whole.

3.d. Use precise words and phrases, telling details, and sensory language to convey a vivid picture of the experiences, events, setting, and/or characters.

5. Develop and strengthen writing as needed by planning, revising, editing, rewriting, or trying a new approach, focusing on addressing what is most significant for a specific purpose and audience.

Reading-Writing Connection

To get a feel for narrative nonfiction, read the excerpt from *Swimming to Antarctica* by Lynne Cox on page 62.

Telling the Story

Organization is the order in which you present your ideas or the events and actions in your narrative. One common and effective technique is to sequence events in *chronological* order. To create a smooth sequence, a writer might begin by setting the scene and introducing the characters. Then, he or she might describe the action or event that occurs first in time and continue presenting the details of the narrative in the order that they took place.

Writers may use other techniques, such as *flashbacks,* or going back in time to describe an event that has an impact on their narrative. Writers also pace the presentation of the actions to show the changes in time and in the mood of the characters. For example, the first part of a narrative contains the rising action, or the actions and events that lead to the *climax*—the point of highest interest. After reaching the climax, writers reduce the suspense of their narrative until they reach a resolution, which is the point where the author ties up the loose ends.

Decide the point you want to make. Consider the impression you want to make on your readers. You may want to show how another person influenced your life. You might want to describe a suspenseful and frightening incident in which you narrowly escaped from injury. Perhaps you want to show how you reached an important decision.

Choose your details. Telling every single detail of an event usually bores the reader. Choose only those details that help you make your point, and try to convey vivid images.

Pace the action. Be sure to identify the climax before you begin writing. Then, pace the presentation of the events or actions to create tension or suspense as you build to the key moment of the climax.

Devise a plan for telling your story. Sequence events so that they build on one another in a logical way. Use this plot diagram to help structure your narrative.

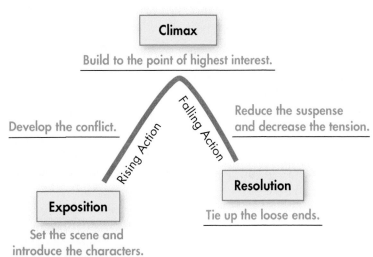

Climax

Build to the point of highest interest.

Develop the conflict.

Rising Action

Falling Action

Reduce the suspense and decrease the tension.

Resolution

Tie up the loose ends.

Exposition

Set the scene and introduce the characters.

Drafting Strategy

Use dialogue. *Dialogue*—the conversations between or among people in a narrative—can add interest to your writing. Use dialogue to advance the plot and show what characters are like. You might also create *interior monologues*, statements that reveal your exact thoughts at the time.

Narration	Dialogue
She told me not to go into the cave without a flashlight.	"Don't go into that cave without a flashlight," she warned me.

Dialogue also reflects the *point of view*, or perspective from which the narrative is told. In a *third-person* point of view, a voice outside the story relates the narrative. In a *first-person* point of view, the narrator or speaker is a character in the narrative. With a first-person point of view, the readers learn only what this character sees or hears.

Revising Strategies

Revise to clarify insight. Review your draft to make sure that you have clearly communicated the importance of the event you narrate. Underline sentences that show your reader what you learned. If necessary, add more of these sentences to explain your insight.

Check your conclusion. Provide a satisfying end to your narrative—one that follows from and reflects on the importance of the event you narrate.

Vary sentence length. Add interest by including both long and short sentences in your narrative. If you find a series of short, choppy sentences, combine some of them. Adding a short, energetic sentence to a passage of longer sentences can emphasize an exciting moment.

Varying Sentence Length	
I was lying in the hammock in the front yard. I was nearly asleep. The wind rustled in the trees. Cicadas were buzzing.	I was lying in the hammock in the front yard, nearly asleep. Wind rustled in the trees, and cicadas were buzzing.

Combining short sentences into a single longer one improves flow. Keeping a short sentence adds emphasis to the moment.

Common Core State Standards

Writing

3.a. Engage and orient the reader by setting out a problem, situation, or observation, establishing one or multiple point(s) of view, and introducing a narrator and/or characters; create a smooth progression of experiences or events.

3.b. Use narrative techniques, such as dialogue, pacing, description, reflection, and multiple plot lines, to develop experiences, events, and/or characters.

3.e. Provide a conclusion that follows from and reflects on what is experienced, observed, or resolved over the course of the narrative.

Language

2. Demonstrate command of the conventions of standard English capitalization, punctuation, and spelling when writing.

Using Possessive Nouns Correctly

A **possessive noun** indicates possession or ownership. An apostrophe must be used to form a possessive noun.

Identifying Incorrect Possessive Nouns You might find these three kinds of mistakes involving possessive nouns:

- nouns that are possessive but do not have an apostrophe
- possessive nouns that have an apostrophe in the wrong place
- nouns that are not possessive but include an apostrophe

Clarifying Your Meaning Thinking about what you mean will help you choose the correct possessive noun.

The student's essays were due on Friday. *(one student, many essays)*

The students' essays were due on Friday. *(more than one student)*

In the following example, the plural noun is not possessive. It should not have an apostrophe.

Wrong: The student's laughed.

Right: The students laughed.

Fixing Incorrect Possessive Nouns To fix the possessive nouns in your writing, look for any nouns that show ownership.

1. Ask yourself whether the noun is singular or plural.

2. Follow these rules to place the apostrophe correctly:

> A. Add an apostrophe and *s* to show the possessive case of most singular nouns.
>   the ocean's roar   Julia's bicycle   James's poem
>
> B. Add an apostrophe to show the possessive case of plural nouns ending in *s* or *es*.
>   the branches' leaves   the Canadians' houses
>
> C. Add an apostrophe and *s* to show the possessive case of plural nouns that do not end in *s* or *es*.
>   the people's stories   the children's department

PH **WRITING COACH**

Further instruction and practice are available in *Prentice Hall Writing Coach.*

Grammar in Your Writing

Scan your writing for apostrophes. You might find some in abbreviations, but others will be used in possessive nouns. Check that each possessive noun is punctuated correctly. Then, review your writing for possessives that are missing their apostrophes.

Student Model: Alexandria Symonds, Royersford, PA

 Common Core
State Standards

Language
2. Demonstrate command of the conventions of standard English capitalization, punctuation, and spelling when writing.

The Collision, or Hardly Extreme

Some people are simply not meant for extreme athletics, I thought to myself as I slowly regained consciousness. I am one of those people. I will never compete in the X Games; I should just stick to my orderly world where "sports" include Scrabble. I would have continued in this thought pattern, but a feeling like someone stabbing me in the eye with a dozen dull forks grabbed my attention instead.

I was bored that Saturday afternoon in May of 1998—so bored, in fact, that it seemed like a bright and creative idea to see if my old girly purple bike could be used for off-roading. The "off-road" in question was to be our front and back yards (the latter of which happened, incidentally, to back up to the North Carolina woods). I planned a fairly straightforward circuit around the house, complicated only slightly by the fact that our house sat on a hill.

It is prophesied that if the earth ever loses its gravitational pull, the moon will abandon its orbit and spin, instead, in a straight line into infinity. Something similar happened to me after a couple of laps around the house. I had reached a speed so high that I concentrated solely on pedaling to maintain it—forgetting, as it were, to turn at a pivotal point in the round. The difference, however, between the moon and me is that while the moon could spin into infinity unobstructed, there was a forest in my way.

I realized a split second too late that I hadn't made the turn and knew there was no use trying to do it now. In retrospect, I could have jumped off the bike, but logical thoughts rarely occur when one is hurtling toward a giant oak tree at 25 miles per hour. Instead, I stopped pedaling, closed my eyes, and braced myself for the impact.

I never actually felt it. When I opened my eyes, I was crumpled on the grass in a position I'm sure humans were never intended to take. My bike was tangled in my limbs, and a searing pain in my left eye was the only thing I could feel. After a bit of reflection about my "extreme" lack of foresight, I decided the best response was to scream as loudly as I could.

The events immediately following my ill-fated rendezvous with the tree are a blur; but I know that somehow I made it to the hospital, where I endured what seemed like endless tests and injections. I would be okay, but my recovery was a painful process. While the rest of me suffered only surface cuts and deep bruises, my left eye was swollen shut for a week. It was distended for months afterwards, and I still have some puffy scar tissue that causes my left eye to close more than the right when I smile.

Still, every time I get photos developed and notice this phenomenon, it serves as a reminder that I was simply not meant for any kind of physical activity more "extreme" than skipping.

Alexandria's thoughts provide an intriguing beginning for the narrative.

Specific details about Alexandria's state of mind and her bicycle add color and interest to the tale.

Alexandria's sense of humor gives a spark to the narrative.

Key details create a vivid picture and also keep the story moving.

Details here echo the beginning of the narrative and bring the story full circle.

Editing and Proofreading

Check your draft for errors in spelling, grammar, capitalization, and punctuation.

Focus on punctuating dialogue. Check that you have punctuated dialogue correctly. Quotation marks should surround a character's exact words or thoughts. As you edit, make sure that there is a closing quotation mark for every opening quotation mark. (For more on punctuating dialogue, see Quotation Marks on p. R53.)

Publishing and Presenting

Consider one of the following ways to share your writing:

Illustrate your narrative. Use photographs or drawings to illustrate people, places, or events in your narrative. Assemble a clean copy of your narrative, choosing an appropriate title and cover.

Deliver a narrative presentation. Rehearse reading your narrative aloud. Using a copy as a reading script, underline words that you will emphasize. Note places where you will vary your reading rate.

Reflecting on Your Writing

Jot down your answer to this question:

How did writing about the event help you to understand it?

Rubric for Self-Assessment

Find evidence in your writing to address each category. Then, use the rating scale to grade your work.

Spiral Review

Earlier in this unit, you learned about **common and proper nouns** (p. 56) and **abstract and concrete nouns** (p. 86). Check the capitalization of proper nouns in your narrative. Review your writing to make sure you used abstract and concrete nouns correctly.

Criteria	Rating Scale
	not very very
Focus: How clearly do you explain the insight gained from this experience?	1 2 3 4 5
Organization: How smooth is the progression of the sequence of events?	1 2 3 4 5
Support/Elaboration: How vivid and well structured are your descriptions of people, places, and events?	1 2 3 4 5
Style: How effective is your use of dialogue?	1 2 3 4 5
Conventions: How correct is your grammar, especially your use of possessive nouns?	1 2 3 4 5

Leveled Texts

Build your skills and improve your comprehension of fiction with texts of increasing complexity.

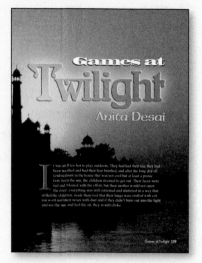

Read **"Contents of the Dead Man's Pocket"** to find out why a man risks his life on the ledge of a tall building.

Read **"Games at Twilight"** to experience the drama of a game of hide-and-seek from the point of view of a child.

Common Core State Standards

Meet these standards with either **"Contents of the Dead Man's Pocket"** (p. 118) or **"Games at Twilight"** (p. 139).

Reading Literature
5. Analyze how an author's choices concerning how to structure a text, order events within it, and manipulate time create such effects as mystery, tension, or surprise. *(Literary Analysis: Conflict and Resolution)*
Spiral Review: RL.9-10.2
Writing
3. Write narratives to develop real or imagined experiences or events using effective technique, well-chosen details, and well-structured event sequences. *(Writing: Anecdote)*
Speaking and Listening
1.a. Come to discussions prepared, having read and researched material under study; explicitly draw on that preparation by referring to evidence from texts and other research on the topic to stimulate a thoughtful,

well-reasoned exchange of ideas. **1.c.** Propel conversations by posing and responding to questions that relate the current discussion to broader themes or larger ideas; actively incorporate others into the discussion; and clarify, verify, or challenge ideas and conclusions. **1.d.** Respond thoughtfully to diverse perspectives, summarize points of agreement and disagreement, and qualify or justify their own views and understanding. *(Speaking and Listening: Problem-Solving Group)*
Language
1. Demonstrate command of the conventions of standard English grammar and usage when writing or speaking. *(Conventions: Personal Pronouns)*

Literary Analysis: Conflict and Resolution

The **conflict** in a short story is a struggle between two forces. Conflict drives a story's plot and influences the story's structure.

- In an **external conflict,** a character struggles against an outside force, such as an element of nature or another character.
- In an **internal conflict,** a character struggles with his or her own opposing desires, beliefs, or needs.

In many stories, the conflict intensifies until one force wins and a **resolution** of the conflict occurs. To build interest in a story's conflict, writers may hint at events to come or "stretch out" episodes that lead up to a crucial moment. In these ways, they create **suspense,** a rising curiosity or anxiety in readers.

Using the Strategy: Conflict Chart

As you read, use a chart like this one to record conflicts.

Force 1	Conflicts	Force 2
External storm	**External** Will boat arrive?	**External** sailors on ship headed to shore
Internal sailors' sense of duty	**Internal** Will sailors abandon ship?	**Internal** sailors' fear of storm

Reading Skill: Cause and Effect

A **cause** is an event, an action, or a situation that produces a result. An **effect** is the result produced. To better follow a story, **analyze causes and effects** as you read, determining which earlier events lead to which later events. Many stories are chains of cause and effect, in which one event leads to the next.

To analyze causes and effects, **reflect on key details** that the writer spends time explaining or describing. For example, a writer's description of a dangerous coastline prepares you to understand the cause-and-effect relationships leading to the sinking of a ship.

PHLit Online!
www.PHLitOnline.com

Hear It!
- Selection summary audio
- Selection audio

See It!
- Get Connected video
- Background video
- More about the author
- Vocabulary flashcards

Do It!
- Interactive journals
- Interactive graphic organizers
- Self-test
- Internet activity
- Grammar tutorial
- Interactive vocabulary games

Is there a difference between *reality* and *truth?*

THE BIG Q

Writing About the Big Question

In "Contents of the Dead Man's Pocket," a man's perception of reality shifts because of a terrifying experience. He discovers the truth about his life and his priorities. Use this sentence starter to develop your ideas about the Big Question.

Life-threatening situations may cause people to **evaluate** _____ because _____.

While You Read Look for moments when the main character experiences changes in his understanding of reality or truth.

Vocabulary

Read each word and its definition. Decide whether you know the word well, know it a little bit, or do not know it at all. After you read, see how your knowledge of each word has increased.

- **convoluted** (kän′ və loot′ əd) *adj.* twisted in a complicated way (p. 121) *The convoluted maze confused us.* convolution *n.*

- **verified** (ver′ ə fīd) *v.* proved to be true (p. 122) *He verified the results of the test by double-checking the scores.* verification *n.* verifiable *adj.*

- **deftness** (deft′ nis) *n.* skillfulness (p. 126) *She climbed with the deftness of a mountain goat.* deftly *adv.* deft *adj.*

- **imperceptibly** (im′ pər sep′ tə blē) *adv.* so slowly or slightly as to be barely noticeable (p. 127) *I did not notice when the fish nibbled imperceptibly at my bait.* imperceptible *adj.* perception *n.*

- **reveling** (rev′ əl iŋ) *v.* taking great pleasure or delight (p. 127) *When she got her first job, she could not stop reveling in her newfound independence.* revel *v.* reveler *n.* revelry *v.*

- **interminable** (in tur′ mi nə bəl) *adj.* endless or seeming endless (p. 130) *The wait seemed interminable to the impatient shopper.* interminably *adv.* terminate *v.*

Word Study

The **Latin root -ver-** means "true."

In this story, Tom **verified** a situation when he made sure that it was true.

opening. As he watched, the paper struck the bottom edge of the window and hung there for an instant, plastered against the glass and wood. Then as the moving air stilled completely, the curtains swinging back from the wall to hang free again, he saw the yellow sheet drop to the window ledge and slide over out of sight.

He ran across the room, grasped the bottom edge of the window and tugged, staring through the glass. He saw the yellow sheet, dimly now in the darkness outside, lying on the ornamental ledge a yard below the window. Even as he watched, it was moving, scraping slowly along the ledge, pushed by the breeze that pressed steadily against the building wall. He heaved on the window with all his strength and it shot open with a bang, the window weight rattling in the casing. But the paper was past his reach and, leaning out into the night, he watched it scud steadily along the ledge to the south, half plastered against the building wall. Above the muffled sound of the street traffic far below, he could hear the dry scrape of its movement, like a leaf on the pavement.

The living room of the next apartment to the south projected a yard or more farther out toward the street than this one; because of this the Beneckes paid seven and a half dollars less rent than their neighbors. And now the yellow sheet, sliding along the stone ledge, nearly invisible in the night, was stopped by the projecting blank wall of the next apartment. It lay motionless, then, in the corner formed by the two walls—a good five yards away, pressed firmly against the ornate corner ornament of the ledge, by the breeze that moved past Tom Benecke's face.

Literary Analysis
Conflict Explain how an external conflict here helps create suspense.

He knelt at the window and stared at the yellow paper for a full minute or more, waiting for it to move, to slide off the ledge and fall, hoping he could follow its course to the street, and then hurry down in the elevator and retrieve it. But it didn't move, and then he saw that the paper was caught firmly between a projection of the convoluted corner ornament and the ledge. He thought about the poker from the fireplace, then the broom, then the mop—discarding each thought as it occurred to him. There was nothing in the apartment long enough to reach that paper.

Vocabulary
convoluted (kän´ və lōōt´ id) *adj.* twisted in a complicated way

It was hard for him to understand that he actually had to abandon it—it was ridiculous—and he began to curse. Of all the papers on his desk, why did it have to be this one in particular! On four long Saturday afternoons he had stood in supermarkets counting the people who passed certain displays, and the results were scribbled on that yellow sheet. From stacks of trade publications, gone over page by page in snatched half hours at work and during evenings at home, he had copied facts, quotations, and figures onto that sheet. And he had carried it with him to the Public

Reading Check

What problem does Tom face?

Library on Fifth Avenue, where he'd spent a dozen lunch hours and early evenings adding more. All were needed to support and lend authority to his idea for a new grocery-store display method; without them his idea was a mere opinion. And there they all lay, in his own improvised shorthand—countless hours of work—out there on the ledge.

For many seconds he believed he was going to abandon the yellow sheet, that there was nothing else to do. The work could be duplicated. But it would take two months, and the time to present this idea . . . was *now*, for use in the spring displays. He struck his fist on the window ledge. Then he shrugged. Even if his plan were adopted, he told himself, it wouldn't bring him a raise in pay—not immediately, anyway, or as a direct result. It won't bring me a promotion either, he argued—not of itself. ●

Reading Skill
Cause and Effect
What might cause Tom to go after the paper?

But just the same, and he couldn't escape the thought, this and other independent projects, some already done and others planned for the future, would gradually mark him out from the score of other young men in his company. They were the way to change from a name on the payroll to a name in the minds of the company officials. They were the beginning of the long, long climb to where he was determined to be, at the very top. And he knew he was going out there in the darkness, after the yellow sheet fifteen feet beyond his reach.

By a kind of instinct, he instantly began making his intention acceptable to himself by laughing at it. The mental picture of himself sidling along the ledge outside was absurd—it was actually comical—and he smiled. He imagined himself describing it; it would make a good story at the office and, it occurred to him, would add a special interest and importance to his memorandum, which would do it no harm at all.

Reading Skill
Cause and Effect
What effect does Tom hope the story of his adventure will have on listeners?

To simply go out and get his paper was an easy task—he could be back here with it in less than two minutes—and he knew he wasn't deceiving himself. The ledge, he saw, measuring it with his eye, was about as wide as the length of his shoe, and perfectly flat. And every fifth row of brick in the face of the building, he remembered—leaning out, he verified this—was indented half an inch, enough for the tips of his fingers, enough to maintain balance easily. It occurred to him that if this ledge and wall were only a yard aboveground—as he knelt at the window staring out, this thought was the final confirmation of his intention—he could move along the ledge indefinitely.

On a sudden impulse, he got to his feet, walked to the front closet and took out an old tweed jacket; it would be cold outside. He put

Vocabulary
verified (ver´ ə fīd) *v.*
proved to be true

it on and buttoned it as he crossed the room rapidly toward the open window. In the back of his mind he knew he'd better hurry and get this over with before he thought too much, and at the window he didn't allow himself to hesitate.

He swung a leg over the sill, then felt for and found the ledge a yard below the window with his foot. Gripping the bottom of the window frame very tightly and carefully, he slowly ducked his head under it, feeling on his face the sudden change from the warm air of the room to the chill outside. With infinite care he brought out his other leg, his mind concentrating on what he was doing. Then he slowly stood erect. Most of the putty, dried out and brittle, had dropped off the bottom edging of the window frame, he found, and the flat wooden edging provided a good gripping surface, a half inch or more deep, for the tips of his fingers.

Now, balanced easily and firmly, he stood on the ledge outside in the slight, chill breeze, eleven stories above the street, staring into his own lighted apartment, odd and different-seeming now.

First his right hand, then his left, he carefully shifted his fingertip grip from the puttyless window edging to an indented row of bricks directly to his right. It was hard to take the first shuffling sideways step then—to make himself move—and the fear stirred in his stomach, but he did it, again by not allowing himself time to think. And now—with his chest, stomach, and the left side of his face pressed against the rough cold brick—his lighted apartment was suddenly gone, and it was much darker out here than he had thought.

Without pause he continued—right foot, left foot, right foot, left—his shoe soles shuffling and scraping along the rough stone, never lifting from it, fingers sliding along the exposed edging of brick. He moved on the balls of his feet, heels lifted slightly; the ledge was not quite as wide as he'd expected. But leaning slightly inward toward the face of the building and pressed against it, he could feel his balance firm and secure, and moving along the ledge was quite as easy as he had thought it would be. He could hear the buttons of his jacket scraping steadily along the rough bricks and feel them

Reading Check
Describe Tom's progress on the first part of his journey.

▲ **Critical Viewing**
Explain how this picture
helps you understand
Tom's feelings in the
story. **[Relate]**

catch momentarily, tugging a little, at each mortared crack. He
simply did not permit himself to look down, though the compulsion
to do so never left him; nor did he allow himself actually to think.
Mechanically—right foot, left foot, over and again—he shuffled
along crabwise, watching the projecting wall ahead loom steadily
closer . . .

Then he reached it, and, at the corner—he'd decided how he was
going to pick up the paper—he lifted his right foot and placed it
carefully on the ledge that ran along the projecting wall at a right
angle to the ledge on which his other foot rested. And now, facing
the building, he stood in the corner formed by the two walls, one
foot on the ledging of each, a hand on the shoulder-high indentation
of each wall. His forehead was pressed directly into the corner
against the cold bricks, and now he carefully lowered first one
hand, then the other, perhaps a foot farther down, to the next
indentation in the rows of bricks. ●

Very slowly, sliding his forehead down the trough of the brick
corner and bending his knees, he lowered his body toward the
paper lying between his outstretched feet. Again he lowered his
fingerholds another foot and bent his knees still more, thigh
muscles taut, his forehead sliding and bumping down the

brick V. Half squatting now, he dropped his left hand to the next indentation and then slowly reached with his right hand toward the paper between his feet.

He couldn't quite touch it, and his knees now were pressed against the wall; he could bend them no farther. But by ducking his head another inch lower, the top of his head now pressed against the bricks, he lowered his right shoulder and his fingers had the paper by a corner, pulling it loose. At the same instant he saw, between his legs and far below, Lexington Avenue stretched out for miles ahead.

He saw, in that instant, the Loew's theater sign, blocks ahead past Fiftieth Street; the miles of traffic signals, all green now; the lights of cars and street lamps; countless neon signs; and the moving black dots of people. And a violent instantaneous explosion of absolute terror roared through him. For a motionless instant he saw himself externally—bent practically double, balanced on this narrow ledge, nearly half his body projecting out above the street far below—and he began to tremble violently, panic flaring through his mind and muscles, and he felt the blood rush from the surface of his skin.

In the fractional moment before horror paralyzed him, as he stared between his legs at that terrible length of street far beneath him, a fragment of his mind raised his body in a spasmodic jerk to an upright position again, but so violently that his head scraped hard against the wall, bouncing off it, and his body swayed outward to the knife edge of balance, and he very nearly plunged backward and fell. Then he was leaning far into the corner again, squeezing and pushing into it, not only his face but his chest and stomach, his back arching; and his fingertips clung with all the pressure of his pulling arms to the shoulder-high half-inch indentation in the bricks.

He was more than trembling now; his whole body was racked with a violent shuddering beyond control, his eyes squeezed so tightly shut it was painful, though he was past awareness of that. His teeth were exposed in a frozen grimace, the strength draining like water from his knees and calves. It was extremely likely, he knew, that he would faint, to slump down along the wall, his face scraping, and then drop backward, a limp weight, out into nothing. And to save his life he concentrated on holding onto consciousness, drawing deliberate deep breaths of cold air into his lungs, fighting to keep his senses aware.

Then he knew that he would not faint, but he could neither stop shaking nor open his eyes. He stood where he was, breathing deeply, trying to hold back the terror of the glimpse he had had of

Reading Skill
Cause and Effect
What is the effect of Tom's glimpse of the avenue below?

Literary Analysis
Conflict What internal conflict does Tom's external conflict cause?

Reading Check
What event introduces a new obstacle in Tom's journey?

what lay below him; and he knew he had made a mistake in not making himself stare down at the street, getting used to it and accepting it, when he had first stepped out onto the ledge.

It was impossible to walk back. He simply could not do it. He couldn't bring himself to make the slightest movement. The strength was gone from his legs; his shivering hands—numb, cold and desperately rigid—had lost all deftness; his easy ability to move and balance was gone. Within a step or two, if he tried to move, he knew that he would stumble clumsily and fall.

Vocabulary
deftness (deft′ nis)
n. skillfulness

Seconds passed, with the chill faint wind pressing the side of his face, and he could hear the toned-down volume of the street traffic far beneath him. Again and again it slowed and then stopped, almost to silence; then presently, even this high, he would hear the click of the traffic signals and the subdued roar of the cars starting up again. During a lull in the street sounds, he called out. Then he was shouting "*Help!*" so loudly it rasped his throat. But he felt the steady pressure of the wind, moving between his face and the blank wall, snatch up his cries as he uttered them, and he knew they must sound directionless and distant. And he remembered how habitually, here in New York, he himself heard and ignored shouts in the night. If anyone heard him, there was no sign of it, and presently Tom Benecke knew he had to try moving; there was nothing else he could do.

Eyes squeezed shut, he watched scenes in his mind like scraps of motion-picture film—he could not stop them. He saw himself stumbling suddenly sideways as he crept along the ledge and saw his upper body arc outward, arms flailing. He saw a dangling shoestring caught between the ledge and the sole of his other shoe, saw a foot start to move, to be stopped with a jerk, and felt his balance leaving him. He saw himself falling with a terrible speed as his body revolved in the air, knees clutched tight to his chest, eyes squeezed shut, moaning softly.

Reading Skill
Cause and Effect
What causes Tom to begin moving?

Out of utter necessity, knowing that any of these thoughts might be reality in the very next seconds, he was slowly able to shut his mind against every thought but what he now began to do. With fear-soaked slowness, he slid his left foot an inch or two toward his own impossibly distant window. Then he slid the fingers of his shivering left hand a corresponding distance. For a moment he could not bring himself to lift his right foot from one ledge to the other; then he did it, and became aware of the harsh exhalation of air from his throat and realized that he was panting. As his right hand, then, began to slide along the brick edging, he was astonished to feel the yellow paper pressed to the bricks underneath his stiff fingers, and he uttered a terrible, abrupt bark that might have been a laugh or a moan. He opened his mouth and took the paper in his teeth, pulling it out from under his fingers.

By a kind of trick—by concentrating his entire mind on first his left foot, then his left hand, then the other foot, then the other hand—he was able to move, almost imperceptibly, trembling steadily, very nearly without thought. But he could feel the terrible strength of the pent-up horror on just the other side of the flimsy barrier he had erected in his mind; and he knew that if it broke through he would lose this thin artificial control of his body.

During one slow step he tried keeping his eyes closed; it made him feel safer, shutting him off a little from the fearful reality of where he was. Then a sudden rush of giddiness swept over him and he had to open his eyes wide, staring sideways at the cold rough brick and angled lines of mortar, his cheek tight against the building. He kept his eyes open then, knowing that if he once let them flick outward, to stare for an instant at the lighted windows across the street, he would be past help.

He didn't know how many dozens of tiny sidling steps he had taken, his chest, belly, and face pressed to the wall; but he knew the slender hold he was keeping on his mind and body was going to break. He had a sudden mental picture of his apartment on just the other side of this wall—warm, cheerful, incredibly spacious. And he saw himself striding through it, lying down on the floor on his back, arms spread wide, reveling in its unbelievable security. The impossible remoteness of this utter safety, the contrast between it and where he now stood, was more than he could bear. And the barrier broke then, and the fear of the awful height he stood on coursed through his nerves and muscles.

A fraction of his mind knew he was going to fall, and he began taking rapid blind steps with no feeling of what he was doing, sidling with a clumsy desperate swiftness, fingers scrabbling along the brick, almost hopelessly resigned to the sudden backward pull and swift motion outward and down. Then his moving left hand slid

Vocabulary

imperceptibly
(im´ pər sep´ tə blē) *adv.*
so slowly or slightly as
to be barely noticeable

reveling (rev´ əl iŋ)
v. taking great plea-
sure or delight

Reading Check

Why does Tom stop calling for help?

onto not brick but sheer emptiness, an impossible gap in the face of the wall, and he stumbled.

His right foot smashed into his left anklebone; he staggered sideways, began falling, and the claw of his hand cracked against glass and wood, slid down it, and his fingertips were pressed hard on the puttyless edging of his window. His right hand smacked gropingly beside it as he fell to his knees; and, under the full weight and direct downward pull of his sagging body, the open window dropped shudderingly in its frame till it closed and his wrists struck the sill and were jarred off.

For a single moment he knelt, knee bones against stone on the very edge of the ledge, body swaying and touching nowhere else, fighting for balance. Then he lost it, his shoulders plunging backward, and he flung his arms forward, his hands smashing against the window casing on either side; and—his body moving backward—his fingers clutched the narrow wood stripping of the upper pane.

For an instant he hung suspended between balance and falling, his fingertips pressed onto the quarter-inch wood strips. Then, with utmost delicacy, with a focused concentration of all his senses, he increased even further the strain on his fingertips hooked to these slim edgings of wood. Elbows slowly bending, he began to draw the full weight of his upper body forward, knowing that the instant his fingers slipped off these quarter-inch strips he'd plunge backward and be falling. Elbows imperceptibly bending, body shaking with the strain, the sweat starting from his forehead in great sudden drops, he pulled, his entire being and thought concentrated in his fingertips. Then suddenly, the strain slackened and ended, his chest touching the window sill, and he was kneeling on the ledge, his forehead pressed to the glass of the closed window.

Dropping his palms to the sill, he stared into his living room—at the red-brown davenport[2] across the room, and a magazine he had left there; at the pictures on the walls and the gray rug; the entrance to the hallway; and at his papers, typewriter and desk, not two feet from his nose. A movement from his desk caught his eye and he saw that it was a thin curl of blue smoke; his cigarette, the ash long, was still burning in the ash tray where he'd left it—this was past all belief—only a few minutes before.

His head moved, and in faint reflection from the glass before him he saw the yellow paper clenched in his front teeth. Lifting a hand from the sill he took it from his mouth; the moistened corner parted from the paper, and he spat it out.

---

2. **davenport** (dav´ ən pôrt´) *n.* large couch.

Literary Analysis
Conflict Why does this lengthy description at a moment of excitement add to the suspense?

Reading Skill
Cause and Effect
What key detail from the beginning of the story helps you understand the cause of Tom's situation?

For a moment, in the light from the living room, he stared wonderingly at the yellow sheet in his hand and then crushed it into the side pocket of his jacket.

He couldn't open the window. It had been pulled not completely closed, but its lower edge was below the level of the outside sill; there was no room to get his fingers underneath it. Between the upper sash and the lower was a gap not wide enough—reaching up, he tried—to get his fingers into; he couldn't push it open. The upper window panel, he knew from long experience, was impossible to move, frozen tight with dried paint.

Very carefully observing his balance, the fingertips of his left hand again hooked to the narrow stripping of the window casing, he drew back his right hand, palm facing the glass, and then struck the glass with the heel of his hand.

His arm rebounded from the pane, his body tottering, and he knew he didn't dare strike a harder blow.

But in the security and relief of his new position, he simply smiled; with only a sheet of glass between him and the room just before him, it was not possible that there wasn't a way past it. Eyes narrowing, he thought for a few moments about what to do. Then his eyes widened, for nothing occurred to him. But still he felt calm: the trembling, he realized, had stopped. At the back of his mind there still lay the thought that once he was again in his home, he could give release to his feelings. He actually would lie on the floor, rolling, clenching tufts of the rug in his hands. He would literally run across the room, free to move as he liked, jumping on the floor, testing and reveling in its absolute security, letting the relief flood through him, draining the fear from his mind and body. His yearning for this was astonishingly intense, and somehow he understood that he had better keep this feeling at bay.

He took a half dollar from his pocket and struck it against the pane, but without any hope that the glass would break and with very little disappointment when it did not. After a few moments of thought he drew his leg up onto the ledge and picked loose the knot of his shoelace. He slipped off the shoe and, holding it across the instep, drew back his arm as far as he dared and struck the leather heel against the glass. The pane rattled, but he knew he'd been a long way from breaking it. His foot was cold and he slipped the shoe back on. He shouted again experimentally, and then once more, but there was no answer.

LITERATURE IN CONTEXT

Science Connection

Physics

Tom is on the ledge with only a pane of glass between him and safety. Yet he is reluctant to hit the window to break the glass—with good reason. Tom understands Newton's third law of motion: for every action, there is an equal and opposite reaction. For example, the *action* of throwing a ball against a wall has the opposite *reaction* of the ball bouncing away from the wall.

Connect to the Literature

What opposite reaction does Tom fear will result if he hits the glass hard but does not break it?

Reading Check

In what way has Tom's situation improved? In what way does it remain the same?

Literary Analysis
Conflict What new
internal conflict does
Tom experience?

The realization suddenly struck him that he might have to wait
here till Clare came home, and for a moment the thought was
funny. He could see Clare opening the front door, withdrawing her
key from the lock, closing the door behind her, and then glancing
up to see him crouched on the other side of the window. He could
see her rush across the room, face astounded and frightened, and
hear himself shouting instructions: "Never mind how I got here!
Just open the wind—" She couldn't open it, he remembered, she'd
never been able to; she'd always had to call him. She'd have to get
the building superintendent or a neighbor, and he pictured himself
smiling and answering their questions as he climbed in. "I just
wanted to get a breath of fresh air, so—" •

He couldn't possibly wait here till Clare came home. It was the
second feature she'd wanted to see, and she'd left in time to see the
first. She'd be another three hours or—He glanced at his watch;
Clare had been gone eight minutes. It wasn't possible, but only eight
minutes ago he had kissed his wife goodbye. She wasn't even at the
theater yet!

It would be four hours before she could possibly be home, and he
tried to picture himself kneeling out here, fingertips hooked to these
narrow strippings, while first one movie, preceded by a slow listing
of credits, began, developed, reached its climax and then finally
ended. There'd be a newsreel next, maybe, and then an animated
cartoon, and then interminable scenes from coming pictures. And
then, once more, the beginning of a full-length picture—while all
the time he hung out here in the night.

He might possibly get to his feet, but he was afraid to try. Already
his legs were cramped, his thigh muscles tired; his knees hurt, his
feet felt numb and his hands were stiff. He couldn't possibly stay
out here for four hours, or anywhere near it. Long before that his
legs and arms would give out; he would be forced to try changing
his position often—stiffly, clumsily, his coordination and strength
gone—and he would fall. Quite realistically, he knew that he would
fall; no one could stay out here on this ledge for four hours.

A dozen windows in the apartment building across the street
were lighted. Looking over his shoulder, he could see the top of
a man's head behind the newspaper he was reading; in another
window he saw the blue-gray flicker of a television screen. No
more than twenty-odd yards from his back were scores of people,
and if just one of them would walk idly to his window and glance
out. . . . For some moments he stared over his shoulder at the
lighted rectangles, waiting. But no one appeared. The man reading

Vocabulary
interminable (in tʉr´
mi nə bəl) *adj.* endless
or seemingly endless

his paper turned a page and then continued his reading. A figure passed another of the windows and was immediately gone.

In the inside pocket of his jacket he found a little sheaf of papers, and he pulled one out and looked at it in the light from the living room. It was an old letter, an advertisement of some sort; his name and address, in purple ink, were on a label pasted to the envelope. Gripping one end of the envelope in his teeth, he twisted it into a tight curl. From his shirt pocket he brought out a book of matches. He didn't dare let go the casing with both hands, but, with the twist of paper in his teeth, he opened the matchbook with his free hand; then he bent one of the matches in two without tearing it from the folder, its red-tipped end now touching the striking surface. With his thumb, he rubbed the red tip across the striking area.

He did it again, then again, and still again, pressing harder each time, and the match suddenly flared, burning his thumb. But he kept it alight, cupping the matchbook in his hand and shielding it with his body. He held the flame to the paper in his mouth till it caught. Then he snuffed out the match flame with his thumb and forefinger, careless of the burn, and replaced the book in his pocket. Taking the paper twist in his hand, he held it flame down, watching the flame crawl up the paper, till it flared bright. Then he held it behind him over the street, moving it from side to side, watching it over his shoulder, the flame flickering and guttering in the wind.

There were three letters in his pocket and he lighted each of them, holding each till the flame touched his hand and then dropping it to the street below. At one point, watching over his shoulder while the last of the letters burned, he saw the man across the street put down his paper and stand—even seeming, to Tom, to glance toward his window. But when he moved, it was only to walk across the room and disappear from sight.

There were a dozen coins in Tom Benecke's pocket and he dropped them, three or four at a time. But if they struck anyone, or if anyone noticed their falling, no one connected them with their source, and no one glanced upward.

His arms had begun to tremble from the steady strain of clinging to this narrow perch, and he did not know what to do now and was terribly frightened. Clinging to the window stripping with one hand, he again searched his pockets. But now—he had left his wallet

Reading Skill
Cause and Effect
What effect does Tom hope the burning papers and the falling coins will have?

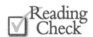

Reading Check
Why can't Tom wait for Clare to come home?

on his dresser when he'd changed clothes—there was nothing left but the yellow sheet. It occurred to him irrelevantly that his death on the sidewalk below would be an eternal mystery; the window closed—why, how, and from where could he have fallen? No one would be able to identify his body for a time, either—the thought was somehow unbearable and increased his fear. All they'd find in his pockets would be the yellow sheet. *Contents of the dead man's pockets,* he thought, *one sheet of paper bearing penciled notations— incomprehensible.*

He understood fully that he might actually be going to die; his arms, maintaining his balance on the ledge, were trembling steadily now. And it occurred to him then with all the force of a revelation that, if he fell, all he was ever going to have out of life he would then, abruptly, have had. Nothing, then, could ever be changed; and nothing more—no least experience or pleasure— could ever be added to his life. He wished, then, that he had not allowed his wife to go off by herself tonight—and on similar nights. He thought of all the evenings he had spent away from her, working; and he regretted them. He thought wonderingly of his fierce ambition and of the direction his life had taken; he thought of the hours he'd spent by himself, filling the yellow sheet that had brought him out here. *Contents of the dead man's pockets,* he thought with sudden fierce anger, *a wasted life.*

He was simply not going to cling here till he slipped and fell; he told himself that now. There was one last thing he could try; he had been aware of it for some moments, refusing to think about it, but now he faced it. Kneeling here on the ledge, the fingertips of one hand pressed to the narrow strip of wood, he could, he knew, draw his other hand back a yard perhaps, fist clenched tight, doing it very slowly till he sensed the outer limit of balance, then, as hard as he was able from the distance, he could drive his fist forward against the glass. If it broke, his fist smashing through, he was safe; he might cut himself badly, and probably would, but with his arm inside the room, he would be secure. But if the glass did not break, the rebound, flinging his arm back, would topple him off the ledge. He was certain of that.

He tested his plan. The fingers of his left hand clawlike on the little stripping, he drew back his other fist until his body began teetering backward. But he had no leverage now—he could feel that there would be no force to his swing—and he moved his fist slowly forward till he rocked forward on his knees again and could sense that his swing would carry its greatest force. Glancing down, however, measuring the distance from his fist to the glass, he saw that it was less than two feet.

Reading Skill
Cause and Effect
What key details explain why Tom grows angry?

Spiral Review
Theme What insight about himself does Tom experience? Is this insight also the story's theme? Explain.

It occurred to him that he could raise his arm over his head, to bring it down against the glass. But, experimenting in slow motion, he knew it would be an awkward . . . blow without the force of a driving punch, and not nearly enough to break the glass. •

Literary Analysis
Conflict
How do Tom's imaginings of what might happen build suspense?

Facing the window, he had to drive a blow from the shoulder, he knew now, at a distance of less than two feet; and he did not know whether it would break through the heavy glass. It might; he could picture it happening, he could feel it in the nerves of his arm. And it might not; he could feel that too—feel his fist striking this glass and being instantaneously flung back by the unbreaking pane, feel the fingers of his other hand breaking loose, nails scraping along the casing as he fell.

He waited, arm drawn back, fist balled, but in no hurry to strike; this pause, he knew, might be an extension of his life. And to live even a few seconds longer, he felt, even out here on this ledge in the night, was infinitely better than to die a moment earlier than he had to. His arm grew tired, and he brought it down and rested it.

Then he knew that it was time to make the attempt. He could not kneel here hesitating indefinitely till he lost all courage to act, waiting till he slipped off the ledge. Again he drew back his arm, knowing this time that he would not bring it down till he struck. His elbow protruding over Lexington Avenue far below, the fingers of his other hand pressed down bloodlessly tight against the narrow stripping, he waited, feeling the sick tenseness and terrible excitement building. It grew and swelled toward the moment of action, his nerves tautening. He thought of Clare—just a wordless, yearning thought—and then drew his arm back just a bit more, fist so tight his fingers pained him, and knowing he was going to do it. Then with full power, with every last scrap of strength he could bring to bear, he shot his arm forward toward the glass, and he said, "*Clare!*"

He heard the sound, felt the blow, felt himself falling forward, and his hand closed on the living-room curtains, the shards and fragments of glass showering onto the floor. And then, kneeling there on the ledge, an arm thrust into the room up to the shoulder, he began picking away the protruding slivers and great wedges of glass from the window frame, tossing them in onto the rug. And, as he grasped the edges of the empty window frame and climbed into his home, he was grinning in triumph.

He did not lie down on the floor or run through the apartment, as he had promised himself; even in the first few moments it seemed to him natural and normal that he should be where he was. He simply turned to his desk, pulled the crumpled yellow sheet from his pocket and laid it down where it had been, smoothing it out; then he absently laid a pencil across it to weight it down. He shook his head wonderingly, and turned to walk toward the closet.

There he got out his topcoat and hat and, without waiting to put them on, opened the front door and stepped out, to go find his wife. He turned to pull the door closed and the warm air from the hall rushed through the narrow opening again. As he saw the yellow paper, the pencil flying, scooped off the desk and, unimpeded by the glassless window, sail out into the night and out of his life, Tom Benecke burst into laughter and then closed the door behind him.

Critical Thinking

Cite textual evidence to support your responses.

1. **Key Ideas and Details** **(a) Analyze Cause and Effect:** At the start of the story, what long-term goals does Tom hope to achieve? **(b) Draw Conclusions:** What does his plan tell you about his character?

2. **Key Ideas and Details** **(a)** Why does Tom go out on the ledge? **(b) Connect:** Is his decision surprising? Explain using details from the story.

3. **Key Ideas and Details** **(a) Compare and Contrast:** Contrast Tom's attitude toward life at the beginning of the story with his attitude at the end. **(b) Infer:** What causes his attitude to change? **(c) Speculate:** What changes, if any, will Tom make as a result of this insight?

4. **Integration of Knowledge and Ideas** **(a) Evaluate:** Do you think a movie based on Finney's story would be as effective as the story itself? Why or why not? **(b) Discuss:** Share your response with a partner. Then, discuss the changes a filmmaker might make to the story and the reasons for such changes. Explain your ideas to the class.

5. **Integration of Knowledge and Ideas** How do Tom's perceptions of reality change during the course of the story? How can you tell? *[Connect to the Big Question: Is there a difference between reality and truth?]*

Contents of the Dead Man's Pocket

Literary Analysis: Conflict and Resolution

© **1. Key Ideas and Details (a)** What is the main **external conflict** in this story? Explain. **(b)** What is the main **internal conflict** in the story? Explain.

© **2. Craft and Structure (a)** Identify a moment in the story that has great **suspense. (b)** Which conflict helps to create this suspense? Explain.

© **3. Craft and Structure (a)** How are Tom's conflicts resolved? **(b)** Describe an alternative **resolution** the story might have had.

Reading Skill: Cause and Effect

4. (a) In your opinion, which single **cause** sets the story's cause-and-effect chain in motion? **(b)** Identify two **effects**—one short-term and one long-term—of this event. Use a diagram like this one.

Cause	Effect/Cause	Effect

5. (a) Identify a **key detail** early in the story that becomes important later on. **(b)** Analyze the causes and effects linked to this detail.

Vocabulary

© **Acquisition and Use** Answer each question. Explain your responses.

1. Should directions for dealing with an emergency be <u>convoluted</u>?

2. Can you trust information that has been <u>verified</u>?

3. Would you want a surgeon to display <u>deftness</u>?

4. If the temperature fell <u>imperceptibly</u>, would most people notice?

5. Is someone who is <u>reveling</u> expressing joy?

6. Would you be happy if your school day was <u>interminable</u>?

Word Study Use the context of the sentences and what you know about the **Latin root -ver-** to explain your answer to each question.

1. Does a judge expect *veracity* from those testifying in court?

2. Would you feel proud if your personal narrative was a *veritable* masterpiece?

Word Study

The **Latin root -ver-** means "true."

Apply It Explain how the root -ver- contributes to the meanings of these words. Consult a dictionary if necessary.

verification

aver

verdict

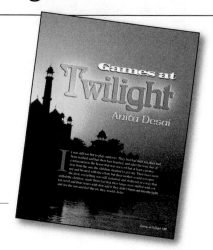

Is there a difference between *reality* **and** *truth?*

Writing About the Big Question

In "Games at Twilight," a boy tries to gain the respect of the older children by winning a game of hide-and-seek. Though it is just a game, it gives him a glimpse of a harsh reality. Use this sentence starter to develop your ideas about the Big Question.

Playing a game can change a person's **perception** of **reality** because _____.

While You Read Look for moments when the main character experiences changes in his understanding of reality or truth.

Vocabulary

Read each word and its definition. Decide whether you know the word well, know it a little bit, or do not know it at all. After you read, see how your knowledge of each word has increased.

- **livid** (liv´ id) *adj.* discolored, as by a bruise; red with anger (p. 140) *She became livid when she saw the bully bothering the first grade students.* *lividly adv. lividness n.*

- **intervened** (in´ tər vēnd´) *v.* came between (p. 140) *The moderator intervened because the two lawyers could not come to an agreement.* *intervention n. interval n.*

- **dejectedly** (dē jek´ tid lē) *adv.* in a depressed way (p. 142) *After losing the game, the players walked away dejectedly.* *dejection n. dejected adj.*

- **defunct** (dē fuŋkt´) *adj.* no longer in use or existence (p. 142) *The defunct computer now gathers cobwebs.* *function v.*

- **dogged** (dôg´ id) *adj.* stubborn (p. 146) *It took a day of dogged efforts to solve the puzzle.* *doggedness n. doggedly adv.*

- **elude** (ē lo̅o̅d´) *v.* escape or avoid (p. 146) *The toddler tried to elude us by hiding under a blanket.* *elusion n. elusive adj.*

Word Study

The **Latin root -ven-** means "come" or "go."

In this story, an older child **intervened**, or came between, arguing children.

roared and, clapping, they all chanted in melancholy unison: "Dip, dip, dip—my blue ship—" and every now and then one or the other saw he was safe by the way his hands fell at the crucial moment—palm on palm, or back of hand on palm—and dropped out of the circle with a yell and a jump of relief and jubilation.

Raghu was It. He started to protest, to cry "You cheated—Mira cheated—Anu cheated—" but it was too late, the others had all already streaked away. There was no one to hear when he called out, "Only in the veranda—the porch—Ma said—Ma said to stay in the porch!" No one had stopped to listen, all he saw were their brown legs flashing through the dusty shrubs, scrambling up brick walls, leaping over compost heaps and hedges, and then the porch stood empty in the purple shade of the bougainvillea and the garden was as empty as before; even the limp squirrels had whisked away, leaving everything gleaming, brassy and bare.

Only small Manu suddenly reappeared, as if he had dropped out of an invisible cloud or from a bird's claws, and stood for a moment in the center of the yellow lawn, chewing his finger and near to tears as he heard Raghu shouting, with his head pressed against the veranda wall, "Eighty-three, eighty-five, eighty-nine, ninety . . ." and then made off in a panic, half of him wanting to fly north, the other half counseling south. Raghu turned just in time to see the flash of his white shorts and the uncertain skittering of his red sandals, and charged after him with such a bloodcurdling yell that Manu

Reading Skill
Cause and Effect What key details suggest that the children use this rhyming game to choose who will be "it"?

Reading Check

What game do the children decide to play?

stumbled over the hosepipe, fell into its rubber coils and lay there weeping, "I won't be It—you have to find them all—all—All!"

"I know I have to, idiot," Raghu said, superciliously[2] kicking him with his toe. "You're dead," he said with satisfaction, licking the beads of perspiration off his upper lip, and then stalked off in search of worthier prey, whistling spiritedly so that the hiders should hear and tremble. •

Ravi heard the whistling and picked his nose in a panic, trying to find comfort by burrowing the finger deep—deep into that soft tunnel. He felt himself too exposed, sitting on an upturned flower pot behind the garage. Where could he burrow? He could run around the garage if he heard Raghu come—around and around and around—but he hadn't much faith in his short legs when matched against Raghu's long, hefty, hairy footballer legs. Ravi had a frightening glimpse of them as Raghu combed the hedge of crotons and hibiscus, trampling delicate ferns underfoot as he did so. Ravi looked about him desperately, swallowing a small ball of snot in his fear.

The garage was locked with a great heavy lock to which the driver had the key in his room, hanging from a nail on the wall under his work-shirt. Ravi had peeped in and seen him still sprawling on his string-cot in his vest and striped underpants, the hair on his chest and the hair in his nose shaking with the vibrations of his phlegm-obstructed snores. Ravi had wished he were tall enough, big enough to reach the key on the nail, but it was impossible, beyond his reach for years to come. He had sidled away and sat dejectedly on the flower pot. That at least was cut to his own size.

But next to the garage was another shed with a big green door. Also locked. No one even knew who had the key to the lock. That shed wasn't opened more than once a year when Ma turned out all the old broken bits of furniture and rolls of matting and leaking buckets, and the white ant hills were broken and swept away and Flit sprayed into the spider webs and rat holes so that the whole operation was like the looting of a poor, ruined and conquered city. The green leaves of the door sagged. They were nearly off their rusty hinges. The hinges were large and made a small gap between the door and the walls—only just large enough for rats, dogs, and, possibly, Ravi to slip through.

Ravi had never cared to enter such a dark and depressing mortuary of defunct household goods seething with such

---

2. **superciliously** (soo´ pər sil´ ē əs lē) *adv.* haughtily; in a manner expressing pride in oneself and scorn for the other person.

"It was dark, spooky in the shed. It had a muffled smell, as of graves."

unspeakable and alarming animal life but, as Raghu's whistling grew angrier and sharper and his crashing and storming in the hedge wilder, Ravi suddenly slipped off the flower pot and through the crack and was gone. He chuckled aloud with astonishment at his own temerity[3] so that Raghu came out of the hedge, stood silent with his hands on his hips, listening, and finally shouted "I heard you! I'm coming! Got you—" and came charging round the garage only to find the upturned flower pot, the yellow dust, the crawling of white ants in a mud-hill against the closed shed door—nothing. Snarling, he bent to pick up a stick and went off, whacking it against the garage and shed walls as if to beat out his prey.

Ravi shook, then shivered with delight, with self-congratulation. Also with fear. It was dark, spooky in the shed. It had a muffled smell, as of graves. Ravi had once got locked into the linen cupboard and sat there weeping for half an hour before he was rescued. But at least that had been a familiar place, and even

---

3. **temerity** (tə mer´ ə tē) *n.* recklessness; foolish boldness.

▲ **Critical Viewing**
What might Ravi find in a shed like the one shown in the photograph? **[Speculate]**

Spiral Review
Theme Which details in the description of the shed suggest a possible theme?

Reading Check

Where does Ravi decide to hide?

smelled pleasantly of starch, laundry and, reassuringly, of his mother. But the shed smelled of rats, ant hills, dust and spider webs. Also of less definable, less recognizable horrors. And it was dark. Except for the white-hot cracks along the door, there was no light. The roof was very low. Although Ravi was small, he felt as if he could reach up and touch it with his finger tips. But he didn't stretch. He hunched himself into a ball so as not to bump into anything, touch or feel anything. What might there not be to touch him and feel him as he stood there, trying to see in the dark? Something cold, or slimy—like a snake. Snakes! He leapt up as Raghu whacked the wall with his stick—then quickly realizing what it was, felt almost relieved to hear Raghu, hear his stick. It made him feel protected.

But Raghu soon moved away. There wasn't a sound once his footsteps had gone around the garage and disappeared. Ravi stood frozen inside the shed. Then he shivered all over. Something had tickled the back of his neck. It took him a while to pick up the courage to lift his hand and explore. It was an insect—perhaps a spider—exploring him. He squashed it and wondered how many more creatures were watching him, waiting to reach out and touch him, the stranger.

There was nothing now. After standing in that position—his hand still on his neck, feeling the wet splodge of the squashed spider gradually dry—for minutes, hours, his legs began to tremble with the effort, the inaction. By now he could see enough in the dark to make out the large solid shapes of old wardrobes, broken buckets and bedsteads piled on top of each other around him. He recognized an old bathtub—patches of enamel glimmered at him and at last he lowered himself onto its edge.

Literary Analysis
Conflict What internal conflict does Ravi now experience?

He contemplated slipping out of the shed and into the fray. He wondered if it would not be better to be captured by Raghu and be returned to the milling crowd as long as he could be in the sun, the light, the free spaces of the garden and the familiarity of his brothers, sisters and cousins. It would be evening soon. Their games would become legitimate. The parents would sit out on the lawn on cane basket chairs and watch them as they tore around the garden or gathered in knots to share a loot of mulberries or black, teeth-splitting jamun from the garden trees. The gardener would fix the hosepipe to the water tap and water would fall lavishly through the air to the ground, soaking the dry yellow grass and the red gravel and arousing the sweet, the intoxicating scent of water on dry earth—that loveliest scent in the world. Ravi sniffed for a whiff of it. He half-rose from the bathtub, then heard the despairing scream of one of the girls as Raghu bore down upon her. There was the sound of a crash, and of rolling about in the bushes, the shrubs, then screams and accusing sobs of, "I touched the den—" "You did not—" "I did—" "You liar, you did not" and then a fading away and silence again.

Ravi sat back on the harsh edge of the tub, deciding to hold out a bit longer. What fun if they were all found and caught—he alone left unconquered! He had never known that sensation. Nothing more wonderful had ever happened to him than being taken out by an uncle and bought a whole slab of chocolate all to himself, or being flung into the soda-man's pony cart and driven up to the gate by the friendly driver with the red beard and pointed ears. To defeat Raghu—that hirsute,[4] hoarse-voiced football champion—and to be the winner in a circle of older, bigger, luckier children—that would be thrilling beyond imagination. He hugged his knees together and smiled to himself almost shyly at the thought of so much victory, such laurels.[5] ●

---

4. **hirsute** (hʉr´ so͞ot´) *adj.* hairy.
5. **laurels** (lôr´ əlz) *n.* leaves of the laurel tree; worn in a crown as an ancient symbol of victory in a contest.

▲ **Critical Viewing**
Contrast the time of day in this image with the time of day at the beginning of the story. **[Contrast]**

Reading Check
What does Ravi hope happens?

There he sat smiling, knocking his heels against the bathtub, now and then getting up and going to the door to put his ear to the broad crack and listening for sounds of the game, the pursuer and the pursued, and then returning to his seat with the dogged determination of the true winner, a breaker of records, a champion.

It grew darker in the shed as the light at the door grew softer, fuzzier, turned to a kind of crumbling yellow pollen that turned to yellow fur, blue fur, gray fur. Evening. Twilight. The sound of water gushing, falling. The scent of earth receiving water, slaking its thirst in great gulps and releasing that green scent of freshness, coolness. Through the crack Ravi saw the long purple shadows of the shed and the garage lying still across the yard. Beyond that, the white walls of the house. The bougainvillea had lost its lividity, hung in dark bundles that quaked and twittered and seethed with masses of homing sparrows. The lawn was shut off from his view. Could he hear the children's voices? It seemed to him that he could. It seemed to him that he could hear them chanting, singing, laughing. But what about the game? What had happened? Could it be over? How could it when he was still not found?

It then occurred to him that he could have slipped out long ago, dashed across the yard to the veranda and touched the "den." It was necessary to do that to win. He had forgotten. He had only remembered the part of hiding and trying to elude the seeker. He had done that so successfully, his success had occupied him so wholly that he had quite forgotten that success had to be clinched by that final dash to victory and the ringing cry of "Den!"

With a whimper he burst through the crack, fell on his knees, got up and stumbled on stiff, benumbed legs across the shadowy yard, crying heartily by the time he reached the veranda so that when he flung himself at the white pillar and bawled, "Den! Den! Den!" his voice broke with rage and pity at the disgrace of it all and he felt himself flooded with tears and misery.

Out on the lawn, the children stopped chanting. They all turned to stare at him in amazement. Their faces were pale and triangular in the dusk. The trees and bushes around them stood inky and sepulchral,[6] spilling long shadows across them. They stared, wondering at his reappearance, his passion, his wild animal howling. Their mother rose from her basket chair and came toward him, worried, annoyed, saying, "Stop it, stop it, Ravi. Don't be a baby. Have you hurt yourself?" Seeing him attended to, the children went back to clasping their hands and chanting "The grass is green, the rose is red. . . . "

But Ravi would not let them. He tore himself out of his mother's grasp and pounded across the lawn into their midst, charging at them with his head lowered so that they scattered in surprise. "I won, I won, I won," he bawled, shaking his head so that the big tears flew. "Raghu didn't find me. I won, I won—"

It took them a minute to grasp what he was saying, even who he was. They had quite forgotten him. Raghu had found all the others long ago. There had been a fight about who was to be It next. It had been so fierce that their mother had emerged from her bath and made them change to another game. Then they had played another and another. Broken mulberries from the tree and eaten them. Helped the driver wash the car when their father returned from work. Helped the gardener water the beds till he roared at them and swore he would complain to their parents. The parents had come out, taken up their positions on the cane chairs. They had begun to play again, sing and chant. All this time no one had remembered Ravi. Having disappeared from the scene, he had disappeared from their minds. Clean.

"Don't be a fool," Raghu said roughly, pushing him aside, and even Mira said, "Stop howling, Ravi. If you want to play, you can

---

6. **sepulchral** (sə pul´ krəl) *adj.* of the tomb; gloomy.

Reading Skill
Cause and Effect
What effect had Ravi hoped for in hiding so well? What effect has it actually caused?

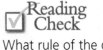

Reading Check
What rule of the game does Ravi forget?

stand at the end of the line," and she put him there very firmly.

The game proceeded. Two pairs of arms reached up and met in an arc. The children trooped under it again and again in a lugubrious[7] circle, ducking their heads and intoning

> "The grass is green,
> The rose is red;
> Remember me
> When I am dead, dead, dead, dead . . ."

And the arc of thin arms trembled in the twilight, and the heads were bowed so sadly, and their feet tramped to that melancholy refrain so mournfully, so helplessly, that Ravi could not bear it. He would not follow them, he would not be included in this funereal game. He had wanted victory and triumph—not a funeral. But he had been forgotten, left out and he would not join them now. The ignominy[8] of being forgotten—how could he face it? He felt his heart go heavy and ache inside him unbearably. He lay down full length on the damp grass, crushing his face into it, no longer crying, silenced by a terrible sense of his insignificance.

---

7. **lugubrious** (lə gō̄′ brē əs) *adj.* very sad, especially in an exaggerated or ridiculous way.
8. **ignominy** (ig′ nə min′ ē) *n.* shame and dishonor.

> # He would not follow them, he would not be included in this funereal game.

Critical Thinking

Cite textual evidence to support your responses.

1. **Key Ideas and Details (a)** How does Ravi think it would feel to be "the winner in a circle of older, bigger, luckier children"? **(b) Draw Conclusions:** What do his feelings show about his view of the other children?

2. **Key Ideas and Details (a) Infer:** Why do the other children stop searching for Ravi? **(b) Draw Conclusions:** What do the other children think of Ravi? Give details from the story to support your answer.

3. **Key Ideas and Details (a) Interpret:** What bitter lesson does Ravi learn at the end of the story? **(b) Apply:** Do you think that Ravi's sense of his "insignificance" will remain strong? Explain.

4. **Integration of Knowledge and Ideas** When does Ravi discover that his ideas about reality are not true? How does this discovery affect him? *[Connect to the Big Question: Is there a difference between reality and truth?]*

Literary Analysis: Conflict and Resolution

1. Key Ideas and Details (a) What is the main **external conflict** in this story? Explain. **(b)** What is the main **internal conflict** in the story? Explain.

2. Craft and Structure (a) Identify a moment in the story that has great **suspense. (b)** Which conflict helps to create this suspense? Explain your thinking.

3. Craft and Structure (a) Are Ravi's conflicts settled by the end of the story? Explain. **(b)** Describe an alternative **resolution** the story might have.

Reading Skill: Cause and Effect

4. (a) In your opinion, which **cause** sets the story's cause-and-effect chain in motion? **(b)** Identify two **effects** that depend on this event. Use a diagram like this one to record your answer.

Cause	Effect/Cause	Effect

5. (a) Find a key detail about the shed that links to later events.
(b) Explain the causes and effects to which this detail is linked.

Vocabulary

Acquisition and Use Answer each question. Explain your responses.

1. To inspire calm, would you paint a room in <u>livid</u> colors?

2. If a neutral person <u>intervened</u> in an argument, could it help the two sides resolve their differences?

3. Would an athlete sigh <u>dejectedly</u> after a game if she had won?

4. How many calls can you make on a <u>defunct</u> cell phone?

5. Is a lazy person likely to make a <u>dogged</u> effort?

6. Would you want to <u>elude</u> someone who has a gift for you?

Word Study Follow the directions for using a word that has the **Latin root -ven-.**

1. Use the verb *venture* to tell about a person who takes a risk.

2. Use the verb *convene* to tell about a group coming together.

Word Study

The **Latin root -ven-** means "come" or "go."

Apply It Explain how the root -ven- contributes to the meaning of these words. Consult a dictionary if necessary.

event
adventure
avenue

Integrated Language Skills

Contents of the Dead Man's Pocket • Games at Twilight

Conventions: Personal Pronouns

> **Pronouns** are words that are used in place of nouns or of words that work together as a noun. The words that pronouns replace are called antecedents.

The most common pronouns are **personal pronouns.** First-person pronouns refer to the person speaking. Second-person pronouns refer to the person being spoken to. Third-person pronouns refer to the person, place, or thing being spoken about. Look at the chart below to see first-, second-, and third-person pronouns in both singular and plural forms.

Personal Pronouns	Singular	Plural
First Person	I, me, my, mine	we, us, our, ours
Second Person	you, your, yours	you, your, yours
Third Person	he, him, his, she, her, hers, it, its	they, them, their, theirs

Practice A Identify the personal pronoun or pronouns in each sentence. Then, indicate whether they are first-, second-, or third-person pronouns.

1. Tom loses his paper when the wind blows it out the window.
2. He goes out on the ledge to retrieve it.
3. "You will not die today," he tells himself.
4. Tom wishes Clare were there to save him.

Ⓒ **Reading Application** In "Contents of the Dead Man's Pocket," find one example of each type of personal pronoun. Write the sentences in which they appear, circling and labeling the pronouns.

Practice B Rewrite each sentence, using a pronoun for each underlined word or words. Then, explain how the effect of the sentence changes.

1. The children hope to elude Raghu.
2. Ravi has never won the game before.
3. Though Ravi is frightened in the shed, Ravi hides in the shed for a long time.
4. "Victory will be Ravi's," thought Ravi.

Ⓒ **Writing Application** Find three sentences in "Games at Twilight" in which you could replace a noun or nouns with a personal pronoun. Rewrite these sentences with the substituting pronoun. What effect do these changes have?

PH WRITING COACH | Further instruction and practice are available in *Prentice Hall Writing Coach.*

Writing

**Common Core
State Standards**

L.9-10.1; W.9-10.3;
SL.9-10.1.a, SL.9-10.1.c,
SL.9-10.1.d
[For the full wording of the
standards, see page 114.]

Narrative Text Both "Contents of the Dead Man's Pocket" and "Games at Twilight" end with **irony**—a strong contrast between what a character or reader expects and what actually happens. Write an **anecdote,** or brief story, that has an ironic ending.

- Pick a character, a conflict, an expected end, and a twist.
- As you draft, carefully choose details that set up the expected outcome, but include hints that could explain an unexpected one.
- Pace the presentation of actions to accommodate time or mood changes.
- Finally, resolve the conflict with a well-structured ironic ending.

Grammar Application As you write your anecdote, be aware of your use of personal pronouns. Be sure the antecedents are clear.

Writing Workshop: *Work in Progress*

Prewriting for Cause-and-Effect Essay For an essay you may write, list three *why* questions on topics that interest you. Note sources that might have information on each topic. Keep this Why List in your writing portfolio.

Use this prewriting activity to prepare for the **Writing Workshop** on page 200.

Speaking and Listening

Comprehension and Collaboration Form a **problem-solving group** with classmates to find solutions to either Tom's or Ravi's problem.

- Identify the problem the character faces.
- Generate questions about the problem to determine an appropriate approach.
- Discuss strategies, supporting your ideas with reasons and examples. Make sure every group member participates.
- Summarize and evaluate comments as the discussion unfolds. Respond to one another respectfully and ask for clarification of any points you do not understand.
- At the end of the discussion, formulate one or two possible conclusions.
- Produce concise notes summarizing main discussion points. Use the notes to explain the potential solutions to classmates.

Share your ideas with the rest of the class.

PHLit
Online!
www.PHLitOnline.com
- Interactive graphic organizers
- Grammar tutorial
- Interactive journals

Leveled Texts

Build your skills and improve your comprehension of nonfiction with texts of increasing complexity.

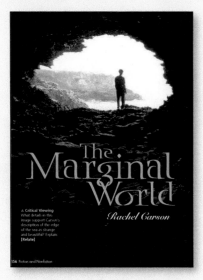

Read **"The Marginal World"** to learn about the enormous vitality of life at the edge of the sea.

Read **"Making History With Vitamin C"** to learn about the role vitamin C played in sea travel.

Common Core State Standards

Meet these standards with either **"The Marginal World"** (p. 156) or **"Making History with Vitamin C"** (p. 168).

Reading Informational Text
6. Determine an author's point of view or purpose in a text and analyze how an author uses rhetoric to advance that point of view or purpose. *(Literary Analysis: Author's Purpose)*

Writing
2.f. Provide a concluding statement or section that follows from the information or explanation presented. *(Research and Technology: Spreadsheet)*

9. Draw evidence from literary or informational texts to support analysis, reflection, and research. *(Writing: Proposal for a Documentary)*

Speaking and Listening
5. Make strategic use of digital media in presentations to enhance understanding of findings, reasoning, and evidence and to add interest. *(Research and Technology: Spreadsheet)*

Language
1.b. Use various types of phrases and clauses to convey specific meanings and add variety and interest to writing or presentations. *(Grammar: Relative Pronouns)*

5. Demonstrate understanding of figurative language, word relationships, and nuances in word meanings. *(Vocabulary: Antonyms)*

Literary Analysis: Author's Purpose

An **author's purpose** is his or her main reason for writing.

- An author may seek to inform, explain, persuade, describe, or entertain. He or she may also have more than one purpose.

- If an author's primary purpose is to inform or persuade, the author presents a **thesis**—the main point or claim about the subject. To explain and prove the thesis, the author supplies support: evidence, facts, and other details confirming the thesis.

- The author's purpose is also reflected in his or her rhetoric and style—the ways in which he or she uses language. Word choice, sentence length, and sentence complexity contribute to an author's style.

As you read, look for ways in which the authors achieve their purposes.

Reading Skill: Cause and Effect

A **cause** is an event, an action, or a situation that makes something happen. An **effect** is the event that results. To **analyze cause and effect,** determine which events cause which effects.

- **Reread** passages to determine whether some events in a sequence are the reason that other events happen.

- Look for cause-and-effect terms such as *because, as a result, for that reason,* and so on.

Using the Strategy: Sequence Chart

As you read, use a **sequence chart** like the one below to record connections between causes and effects.

Cause	Effect/Cause	Effect

Is there a difference between *reality* and *truth?*

Writing About the Big Question

Successful scientists, such as Rachel Carson, seek to discover truths through scientific inquiry. Use these sentence starters to develop your ideas about the Big Question.

Reality is sometimes best discovered by _____.

Scientists can find **evidence** of the wonders that exist in nature by _____.

While You Read Decide what "truth" the author is expressing by describing real things in the tidal pool in an imaginative way.

Vocabulary

Read each word and its definition. Decide whether you know the word well, know it a little bit, or do not know it at all. After you read, see how your knowledge of each word has increased.

- **elusive** (ē lōō′ siv) *adj.* hard to grasp mentally (p. 158) *The twisted plot made the movie too elusive for many viewers.* *elude v.*

- **mutable** (myōōt′ ə bəl) *adj.* changeable (p. 158) *His personality is mutable, and I never know how he will react.* *mutability n. mutation n.*

- **intertidal** (in′ tər tīd′′l) *adj.* pertaining to a shore zone bounded by the levels of low and high tide (p. 158) *When the tide is high, the intertidal zone is covered with water.* *tide n. tidal adj.*

- **ephemeral** (e fem′ ər əl) *adj.* short-lived (p. 160) *The fog was ephemeral; it lifted just after sunrise.*

- **marginal** (mär′ jə nəl) *adj.* at, on, or near the edge (p. 163) *The teacher wrote a few marginal comments on my final draft.* *margin n. marginally adv.*

- **manifestations** (man′ ə fes tā′ shənz) *n.* appearances; forms (p. 164) *Steam and ice are different manifestations of water.* *manifest v.*

Word Study

The **Latin prefix *inter-*** means "between" or "among."

In this selection, the author focuses on the part of the sea that is between the high tide and the low tide mark. Many plants and animals live in this **intertidal** zone.

Meet
Rachel Carson
(1907–1964)

Author of

The Marginal World

A lifelong lover of nature, Rachel Carson trained as a marine biologist at a time when few women pursued the study of the sea. She worked for the United States Fish and Wildlife Service and wrote poetically about nature in books like *The Sea Around Us,* which won the National Book Award.

A Crusade One day a friend wrote to complain that many birds had died on her property after it was sprayed for insects. Carson decided she had to show the world that people were damaging the environment with insecticides. In 1962, she published *Silent Spring,* a pioneering environmental work.

BACKGROUND FOR THE ESSAY
Tides

The pull of the moon's gravity is strongest on the part of Earth that is closest to the moon. As the Earth rotates, the area that is closest to the moon changes. The result is tides, the daily changes in the water level at the ocean shore. Each day, the edge of the shore is flooded and then exposed by the tides. Rachel Carson explores the creatures that live in this special zone.

DID YOU KNOW?
As a result of Carson's book *Silent Spring,* the insecticide DDT was eventually banned.

The Marginal World

Rachel Carson

▲ **Critical Viewing**
What details in this image support Carson's description of the edge of the sea as strange and beautiful? Explain.
[Relate]

The edge of the sea is a strange and beautiful place. All through the long history of Earth it has been an area of unrest where waves have broken heavily against the land, where the tides have pressed forward over the continents, receded, and then returned. For no two successive days is the shoreline precisely the same.

Literary Analysis
Author's Purpose
Which sentence in the opening paragraph states the author's thesis?

Vocabulary
elusive (ē lōō´ siv) *adj.* hard to grasp mentally
mutable (myōōt´ ə bəl) *adj.* changeable
intertidal (in tər tīd´ 'l) *adj.* pertaining to a shore zone bounded by the levels of low and high tide

Not only do the tides advance and retreat in their eternal rhythms, but the level of the sea itself is never at rest. It rises or falls as the glaciers melt or grow, as the floor of the deep ocean basins shifts under its increasing load of sediments, or as the earth's crust along the continental margins warps up or down in adjustment to strain and tension. Today a little more land may belong to the sea, tomorrow a little less. Always the edge of the sea remains an elusive and indefinable boundary.

The shore has a dual nature, changing with the swing of the tides, belonging now to the land, now to the sea. On the ebb tide it knows the harsh extremes of the land world, being exposed to heat and cold, to wind, to rain and drying sun. On the flood tide it is a water world, returning briefly to the relative stability of the open sea.

Only the most hardy and adaptable can survive in a region so mutable, yet the area between the tide lines is crowded with plants and animals. In this difficult world of the shore, life displays its enormous toughness and vitality by occupying almost every conceivable niche. Visibly, it carpets the intertidal rocks; or half hidden, it descends into fissures and crevices, or hides under boulders, or lurks in the wet gloom of sea caves. Invisibly, where the casual observer would say there is no life, it lies deep in the sand, in burrows and tubes and passageways. It tunnels into solid rock and bores into peat and clay. It encrusts weeds or drifting spars[1] or the hard, chitinous[2] shell of a lobster. It exists minutely, as the film of bacteria that spreads over a rock surface or a wharf piling; as spheres of protozoa, small as pinpricks, sparkling at the surface of the sea; and as Lilliputian[3] beings swimming through dark pools that lie between the grains of sand.

---

1. **spars** (spärz) *n.* pieces of wood or metal, such as masts or booms, for supporting sails on a ship.
2. **chitinous** (kī´ tin əs) *adj.* of the material that forms the tough outer covering of insects, crustaceans, and so on.
3. **Lilliputian** (lil´ ə pyōō´ shən) *adj.* tiny (from the name of the tiny people who inhabit Lilliput in *Gulliver's Travels* by Jonathan Swift).

▼ **Critical Viewing**
In what way are these creatures prepared for the life along the shore Carson describes? **[Draw Conclusions]**

The shore is an ancient world, for as long as there has been an earth and sea there has been this place of the meeting of land and water. Yet it is a world that keeps alive the sense of continuing creation and of the relentless drive of life. Each time that I enter it, I gain some new awareness of its beauty and its deeper meanings, sensing that intricate fabric of life by which one creature is linked with another, and each with its surroundings.

In my thoughts of the shore, one place stands apart for its revelation of exquisite beauty. It is a pool hidden within a cave that one can visit only rarely and briefly when the lowest of the year's low tides fall below it, and perhaps from that very fact it acquires some of its special beauty. Choosing such a tide, I hoped for a glimpse of the pool. The ebb was to fall early in the morning. I knew that if the wind held from the northwest and no interfering swell ran in from a distant storm the level of the sea should drop below the entrance to the pool. There had been sudden ominous showers in the night, with rain like handfuls of gravel flung on the roof. When I looked out into the early morning the sky was full of a gray dawn light but the sun had not yet risen. Water and air were pallid. Across the bay the moon was a luminous disc in the western sky, suspended above the dim line of distant shore—the full August moon, drawing the tide to the low, low levels of the threshold of the alien sea world. As I watched, a gull flew by, above the spruces. Its breast was rosy with the light of the unrisen sun. The day was, after all, to be fair. •

Later, as I stood above the tide near the entrance to the pool, the promise of that rosy light was sustained. From the base of the steep wall of rock on which I stood, a moss-covered ledge jutted seaward

Reading Skill
Cause and Effect What effect does the changing region have on the creatures that live there?

The shore is an ancient world, for as long as there has been an earth and sea there has been this place of the meeting of land and water.

☑ Reading Check
Name three places creatures may live along the shore.

into deep water. In the surge at the rim of the ledge the dark fronds of oarweeds swayed, smooth and gleaming as leather. The projecting ledge was the path to the small hidden cave and its pool. Occasionally a swell, stronger than the rest, rolled smoothly over the rim and broke in foam against the cliff. But the intervals between such swells were long enough to admit me to the ledge and long enough for a glimpse of that fairy pool, so seldom and so briefly exposed.

And so I knelt on the wet carpet of sea moss and looked back into the dark cavern that held the pool in a shallow basin. The floor of the cave was only a few inches below the roof, and a mirror had been created in which all that grew on the ceiling was reflected in the still water below.

Under water that was clear as glass the pool was carpeted with green sponge. Gray patches of sea squirts glistened on the ceiling and colonies of soft coral were a pale apricot color. In the moment when I looked into the cave a little elfin starfish hung down, suspended by the merest thread, perhaps by only a single tube foot. It reached down to touch its own reflection, so perfectly delineated that there might have been, not one starfish, but two. The beauty of the reflected images and of the limpid pool itself was the poignant beauty of things that are ephemeral, existing only until the sea should return to fill the little cave.

Whenever I go down into this magical zone of the low water of the spring tides, I look for the most delicately beautiful of all the shore's inhabitants—flowers that are not plant but animal, blooming on the threshold of the deeper sea. In that fairy cave I was not disappointed. Hanging from its roof were the pendent[4] flowers of the hydroid Tubularia, pale pink, fringed and delicate as the wind flower. Here were creatures so exquisitely fashioned that they seemed unreal, their beauty too fragile to exist in a world of crushing force. Yet every detail was functionally useful, every stalk and hydranth[5] and petallike tentacle fashioned for dealing with the realities of existence. I knew that they were merely waiting, in that moment of the tide's ebbing, for the return of the sea. Then in the rush of water, in the surge of surf and the pressure of the incoming tide, the delicate flower heads would stir with life. They would sway on their slender stalks, and their long tentacles would sweep the returning water, finding in it all that they needed for life.

And so in that enchanted place on the threshold

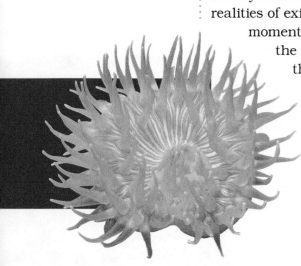

4. **pendent** (pen´ dənt) *adj.* dangling; hanging like a pendant on a necklace or charm.
5. **hydranth** (hī´ dranth´) *n.* one of the feeding individuals in a hydroid colony; the individuals are all attached at the base to a common tube.

of the sea the realities that possessed my mind were far from those of the land world I had left an hour before. In a different way the same sense of remoteness and of a world apart came to me in a twilight hour on a great beach on the coast of Georgia. I had come down after sunset and walked far out over sands that lay wet and gleaming, to the very edge of the retreating sea. Looking back across that immense flat, crossed by winding, waterfilled gullies and here and there holding shallow pools left by the tide, I was filled with awareness that this intertidal area, although abandoned briefly and rhythmically by the sea, is always reclaimed by the rising tide. There at the edge of low water the beach with its reminders of the land seemed far away. The only sounds were those of the wind and the sea and the birds. There was one sound of wind moving over water, and another of water sliding over the sand and tumbling down the faces of its own wave forms. The flats were astir with birds, and the voice of the willet[6] rang insistently. One of them stood at the edge of the water and gave its loud, urgent cry; an answer came from far up the beach and the two birds flew to join each other.

The flats took on a mysterious quality as dusk approached and the last evening light was reflected from the scattered pools and creeks. Then birds became only dark shadows, with no color discernible. Sanderlings[7] scurried across the beach like little ghosts, and here and there the darker forms of the willets stood out. Often I could come very close to them before they would start up in alarm—the sanderlings running, the willets flying up, crying. Black skimmers[8] flew along the ocean's edge silhouetted against the dull, metallic gleam, or they went flitting above the sand like large, dimly seen moths. Sometimes they "skimmed" the winding creeks of tidal water, where little spreading surface ripples marked the presence of small fish.

The shore at night is a different world, in which the very darkness that hides the distractions of daylight brings into sharper focus the elemental realities. Once, exploring the night beach, I surprised a small ghost crab in the searching beam of my torch. He was lying in a pit he had dug just above the surf, as though watching the sea and waiting. The blackness of the night possessed water, air, and beach. It was the darkness of an older world, before

▲ **Critical Viewing**
What features might make the skimmer particularly adept at catching fish? **[Interpret]**

Reading Check

What main qualities does Carson associate with life along the seashore?

---

6. **willet** (wil´ it) *n.* shorebird, about 16 inches long, with a long bill, found by shallow shores and other waters of North and South America.
7. **sanderlings** (san´ dər liŋz) *n.* small, gray-and-white shorebirds.
8. **skimmers** (skim´ ərz) *n.* shorebirds with bladelike bills, which they use to skim the surface of the water for small fish and crustaceans.

Spiral Review
Central Idea What meaning does Carson find in the ghost crab's existence at the edge of the sea?

Man. There was no sound but the all-enveloping, primeval sounds of wind blowing over water and sand, and of waves crashing on the beach. There was no other visible life—just one small crab near the sea. I have seen hundreds of ghost crabs in other settings, but suddenly I was filled with the odd sensation that for the first time I knew the creature in its own world—that I understood, as never before, the essence of its being. In that moment time was suspended; the world to which I belonged did not exist and I might have been an onlooker from outer space. The little crab alone with the sea became a symbol that stood for life itself—for the delicate, destructible, yet incredibly vital force that somehow holds its place amid the harsh realities of the inorganic world.

The sense of creation comes with memories of a southern coast, where the sea and the mangroves,[9] working together, are building a wilderness of thousands of small islands off the southwestern coast of Florida, separated from each other by a tortuous[10] pattern of bays, lagoons, and narrow waterways. I remember a winter day when the sky was blue and drenched with sunlight; though there was no wind one was conscious of flowing air like cold clear crystal. I had landed on the surf-washed tip of one of those islands, and then worked my way around to the sheltered bay side. There I found the tide far out, exposing the broad mud flat of a cove bordered by the mangroves with their twisted branches, their glossy leaves, and their long prop roots reaching down, grasping and holding the mud, building the land out a little more, then again a little more.

The mud flats were strewn with the shells of that small, exquisitely colored mollusk,[11] the rose tellin, looking like scattered

Reading Skill
Cause and Effect
Which details in this passage indicate cause-and-effect relationships?

---

9. **mangroves** (maŋ´ grōvz) *n.* tropical trees that grow in swampy ground with spreading branches. The branches send down additional roots, forming a cluster of trunks for each tree.
10. **tortuous** (tôr´ chōō əs) *adj.* full of twists and turns.
11. **mollusk** (mäl´ əsk) *n.* one of a large group of soft-bodied animals with shells, including clams and snails.

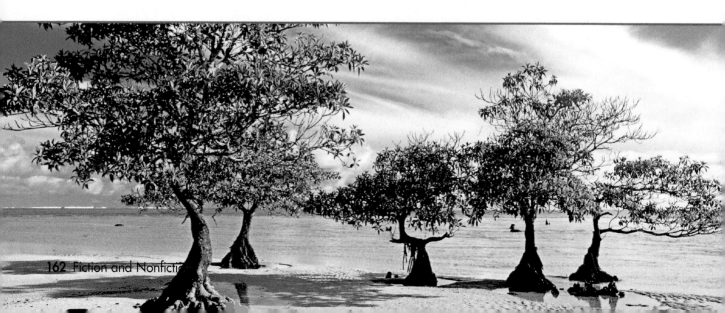

petals of pink roses. There must have been a colony nearby, living buried just under the surface of the mud. At first the only creature visible was a small heron in gray and rusty plumage—a reddish egret that waded across the flat with the stealthy, hesitant movements of its kind. But other land creatures had been there, for a line of fresh tracks wound in and out among the mangrove roots, marking the path of a raccoon feeding on the oysters that gripped the supporting roots with projections from their shells. Soon I found the tracks of a shore bird, probably a sanderling, and followed them a little; then they turned toward the water and were lost, for the tide had erased them and made them as though they had never been.

Looking out over the cove I felt a strong sense of the interchangeability of land and sea in this marginal world of the shore, and of the links between the life of the two. There was also an awareness of the past and of the continuing flow of time, obliterating much that had gone before, as the sea had that morning washed away the tracks of the bird.

The sequence and meaning of the drift of time were quietly summarized in the existence of hundreds of small snails—the mangrove periwinkles—browsing on the branches and roots of the trees. Once their ancestors had been sea dwellers, bound to the salt waters by every tie of their life processes. Little by little over the thousands and millions of years the ties had been broken, the snails had adjusted themselves to life out of water, and now today they were living many feet above the tide to which they only occasionally returned. And perhaps, who could say how many ages hence, there would be in their descendants not even this gesture of remembrance for the sea.

The spiral shells of other snails—these quite minute—left winding tracks on the mud as they moved about in search of food. They were horn shells, and when I saw them I had a nostalgic

Vocabulary
marginal (mär´ jə nəl)
adj. at, on, or near the edge

Reading Check

What realization does Carson come to during her encounter with the crab?

moment when I wished I might see what Audubon[12] saw, a century and more ago. For such little horn shells were the food of the flamingo, once so numerous on this coast, and when I half closed my eyes I could almost imagine a flock of these magnificent flame birds feeding in that cove, filling it with their color. It was a mere yesterday in the life of the earth that they were there; in nature, time and space are relative matters, perhaps most truly perceived subjectively in occasional flashes of insight, sparked by such a magical hour and place.

There is a common thread that links these scenes and memories—the spectacle of life in all its varied manifestations as it has appeared, evolved, and sometimes died out. Underlying the beauty of the spectacle there is meaning and significance. It is the elusiveness of that meaning that haunts us, that sends us again and again into the natural world where the key to the riddle is hidden. It sends us back to the edge of the sea, where the drama of life played its first scene on earth and perhaps even its prelude; where the forces of evolution are at work today, as they have been since the appearance of what we know as life; and where the spectacle of living creatures faced by the cosmic realities of their world is crystal clear.

---

12. **Audubon** (ôd´ ə bän´) John James Audubon (1785–1851), an ornithologist, a naturalist, and a painter famous for his paintings of North American birds.

Vocabulary
manifestations (man´ ə fes tā´ shənz) *n.* appearances; forms

Literary Analysis
Author's Purpose
In what way does this final paragraph relate to the thesis identified in the first paragraph?

Critical Thinking

Cite textual evidence to support your responses.

1. **Key Ideas and Details (a)** What does Carson mean when she says, "Only the most hardy and adaptable can survive in a place so mutable"? **(b)** How does she support this claim?

2. **Key Ideas and Details (a)** Name three creatures that Carson describes at length. **(b)** Explain how each demonstrates or symbolizes the power of life to endure in a harsh world.

3. **Key Ideas and Details Interpret:** What central idea, or lesson about life, does Carson draw from her observation of the "marginal world"? Support your answer with details from the work.

4. **Integration of Knowledge and Ideas** Carson wrote this essay about fifty years ago. Do you think she expresses a truth that is valid today? Explain your answer. *[Connect to the Big Question: Is there a difference between reality and truth?]*

Literary Analysis: Author's Purpose

© **1. Key Ideas and Details (a)** Explain Carson's main **purpose. (b)** Write a brief, objective summary stating Carson's **thesis** and main points.

© **2. Key Ideas and Details (a)** Use a diagram like this one to record details that **support** the author's thesis. Include at least five details. **(b)** Explain how each detail supports the thesis.

© **3. Key Ideas and Details** Identify two examples that persuasively support Carson's thesis about the "spectacle of life." Explain your choices.

Reading Skill: Cause and Effect

4. Identify the **cause** of water level changes in the "marginal world."

5. (a) Name two **effects** on creatures in the tidal zone caused by the changing water level. **(b)** For each effect, explain how the changing water level brings it about.

Vocabulary

© **Acquisition and Use Antonyms** are words that have opposite meanings, such as *day* and *night*. For each numbered word, choose the best antonym. Then, use each pair of antonyms in a sentence.

1. elusive: (a) unreal, (b) indefinable, (c) understandable

2. marginal: (a) buttery, (b) outside, (c) central

3. ephemeral: (a) enduring, (b) weak, (c) healthy

4. manifestations: (a) upheavals, (b) absences, (c) questions

5. mutable: (a) worried, (b) noisy, (c) permanent

6. intertidal: (a) watery, (b) deep-sea, (c) moving

Word Study Use the context of the sentences and what you know about the **Latin prefix *inter-*** to explain your answer to each question.

1. Would an *intermediate* course be very easy?

2. Does an *interstate* truck stay within the state?

Word Study

The **Latin prefix *inter-*** means "between" or "among."

Apply It Explain how the prefix *inter-* contributes to the meanings of these words. Consult a dictionary if necessary.

interfere
international
intermission

Is there a difference between *reality* and *truth?*

Writing About the Big Question

In "Making History With Vitamin C," you will learn that although there was proof that vitamin C prevented a terrible disease called scurvy, many people did not use this knowledge! Use this sentence starter to develop your ideas about the Big Question.

Even in the face of **evidence,** some people refuse to face the truth because _____.

While You Read Look for reasons that explain why many sailors ignored advice on avoiding scurvy.

Vocabulary

Read each word and its definition. Decide whether you know the word well, know it a little bit, or do not know it at all. After you read, see how your knowledge of each word has increased.

- **deficiency** (dē fish′ ən sē) *n.* lack of something essential (p. 168) *A calcium deficiency can cause weak bones.* deficient *adj.*

- **replenished** (ri plen′ isht) *v.* made complete or full again (p. 169) *She replenished the bowl with pretzels before it was empty.* replenishment *n.* replenish *v.*

- **incessant** (in ses′ ənt) *adj.* not stopping; constant (p. 169) *His incessant chatter gave me a headache.* incessantly *adv.* cease *v.*

- **alleviate** (ə lē′ vē āt′) *v.* lighten or relieve (p. 170) *The medicine should alleviate your headache and you will feel better.* alleviation *n.*

- **obscured** (əb skyoord′) *v.* made dark; blocked from view; hid (p. 171) *The tall person sitting in front of me obscured my view of the screen.* obscurely *adv.* obscurity *n.* obscure *v., adj.*

- **compulsory** (kəm pul′ sə rē) *adj.* required, mandatory (p. 172) *It is compulsory that the hikers stay on the safe trail, or they must leave the park.* compulsion *n.* compulsive *adj.* compel *v.*

Word Study

The **Latin prefix *ob-*** means "against," "over," or "in front of."

In this selection, the authors explain that the use of ineffective remedies for scurvy may have **obscured,** or covered over, our understanding of the power of vitamin C.

Making History With Vitamin C

Penny Le Couteur (b. 1943)
Jay Burreson (b. 1942)

Authors of "Making History With Vitamin C"

Born in New Zealand, Penny Le Couteur (lə k$\overline{oo}$′ tər) has taught chemistry for more than thirty years. Jay Burreson is also a chemist and runs a high-tech company. The two met in graduate school and have remained friends ever since.

Teaming Up The two friends decided to work together on a book "to tell the stories of the fascinating connections between chemical structures and historical episodes." Each chapter in this book, *Napoleon's Buttons*, examines a different molecule and its role in history.

Napoleon's Buttons takes its title from the chapter on tin. In extreme cold, tin will crumble. When the French leader Napoleon invaded Russia in 1812, his soldiers' tin buttons disintegrated in the freezing air. Many perished of cold in this defeat—some, perhaps, because of their tin buttons.

BACKGROUND FOR THE ESSAY

The Age of Discovery

In the 1300s, Europeans began sailing the known world in search of spices and other goods to trade. As navigation improved, they traveled farther. These adventurers risked shipwreck and losing their way. They also risked scurvy, the illness resulting from a lack of vitamin C, as "Making History With Vitamin C" explains.

DID YOU KNOW?

These two chemists propose that molecules helped shape history. For example, they claim that the pursuit of sugar led to the slave trade and the Industrial Revolution.

Making History With Vitamin C

Penny Le Couteur and Jay Burreson

Literary Analysis
Author's Purpose
What does the first paragraph suggest might be the thesis of this selection?

Vocabulary
deficiency (dē fish´ ən sē) *n.* lack of something essential

Reading Skill
Cause and Effect
Identify a cause and an effect of scurvy.

The Age of Discovery was fueled by molecules of the spice trade, but it was the lack of another, quite different molecule that almost ended it. Over 90 percent of his crew didn't survive Magellan's[1] 1519–1522 circumnavigation of the world—in large part due to scurvy, a devastating disease caused by a deficiency of the ascorbic acid molecule, dietary vitamin C.

Exhaustion and weakness, swelling of the arms and legs, softening of the gums, excessive bruising, hemorrhaging from the nose and mouth, foul breath, diarrhea, muscle pain, loss of teeth, lung and kidney problems—the list of symptoms of scurvy is long and horrible. Death generally results from an acute infection such as pneumonia or some other respiratory ailment or, even in young people, from heart failure. One symptom, depression, occurs at an early stage, but whether it is an effect of the actual disease or a response to the other symptoms is not clear. After all, if you were constantly exhausted and had sores that did not heal, painful and bleeding gums, stinking breath, and diarrhea, and you knew that there was worse to come, would you not be depressed, too?

Scurvy is an ancient disease. Changes in bone structure in Neolithic remains are thought to be compatible with scurvy, and hieroglyphs from ancient Egypt have been interpreted as referring to it. The word *scurvy* is said to be derived from Norse, the language of the seafaring Viking warriors who, starting in the ninth century, raided the Atlantic coast of Europe from their northern homelands in Scandinavia. A lack of vitamin-rich fresh fruit and vegetables would have been common on board ships and in northern communities during winter. The Vikings supposedly made use of

---

1. **Magellan's** (mə jel´ ənz) Ferdinand Magellan (ca. 1480–1521) was a Portuguese explorer in the service of Spain. He commanded the first expedition to sail around the world.

scurvy grass, a form of Arctic cress, on their way to America via Greenland. The first real descriptions of what was probably scurvy date from the Crusades in the thirteenth century. •

Scurvy at Sea

In the fourteenth and fifteenth centuries, as longer voyages were made possible by the development of more efficient sets of sails and fully rigged ships, scurvy became commonplace at sea. Oar-propelled galleys, such as those used by the Greeks and Romans, and the small sailing boats of Arab traders had stayed fairly close to the coast. These vessels were not seaworthy enough to withstand the rough waters and huge swells of the open ocean. Consequently, they would seldom venture far from the coast, and supplies could be replenished every few days or weeks. Access to fresh food on a regular basis meant that scurvy was seldom a major problem. But in the fifteenth century, long ocean voyages in large sailing ships heralded not only the Age of Discovery but also reliance on preserved food.

Bigger ships had to carry cargo and arms, a larger crew to handle the more complicated rigging and sails, and food and water for months at sea. An increase in the number of decks and men and the amount of supplies inevitably translated into cramped sleeping and living conditions for the crew, poor ventilation, and a subsequent increase in infectious diseases and respiratory conditions. Consumption (tuberculosis) and the "bloody flux" (a pernicious form of diarrhea) were common as, no doubt, were body and head lice, scabies, and other contagious skin conditions.

The standard sailor's food did nothing to improve his health. Two major factors dictated the seafaring diet. Firstly, aboard wooden ships it was extremely difficult to keep anything, including food, dry and mold free. Water was absorbed through wooden hulls, as the only water-proofing material available was pitch, a dark-colored, sticky resin obtained as a by-product of charcoal manufacture, applied to the outside of the hull. The inside of the hull, particularly where ventilation was poor, would have been extremely humid. Many accounts of sailing journeys describe incessant dampness, as mold and mildew grew on clothing, on leather boots and belts, on bedding, and on books. The standard sailor's fare was salted beef or pork and ship's biscuits known as hardtack, a mixture of flour and water without salt that was baked rock hard and used as a substitute for bread. Hardtack had the desirable characteristic of being relatively immune to mildew. It was baked to such a degree of hardness that it remained edible for

Vocabulary
replenished (ri plen´ isht) v. made complete or full again

incessant (in ses´ ənt) adj. not stopping; constant

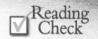

Reading Check
What problems did the lack of vitamin C in sailors' diets cause?

As for Resolution, Robin Brooks, Private Collection

decades, but it was extremely difficult to bite into, especially for those whose gums were inflamed by the onset of scurvy. Typically, ship's biscuits were weevil-infested, a circumstance that was actually welcomed by sailors as the weevil holes increased porosity and made the biscuits easier to break and chew.

The second factor governing diet on wooden ships was the fear of fire. Wooden construction and liberal use of highly combustible pitch meant that constant diligence was necessary to prevent fire at sea. For this reason the only fire permitted on board was in the galley and then only in relatively calm weather. At the first sign of foul weather, galley fires would be extinguished until the storm was over. Cooking was often not possible for days at a time. Salted meat could not be simmered in water for the hours necessary to reduce its saltiness; nor could ship's biscuits be made at least somewhat palatable by dunking them in hot stew or broth.

At the outset of a voyage provisions would be taken on board: butter, cheese, vinegar, bread, dried peas, beer, and rum. The butter was soon rancid, the bread moldy, the dried peas weevil infested, the cheeses hard, and the beer sour. None of these items provided vitamin C, so signs of scurvy were often evident after as little as six weeks out of port. Was it any wonder that the navies of European countries had to resort to the press-gang[2] as a means of manning their ships?

Scurvy's toll on the lives and health of sailors is recorded in the logs of early voyages. By the time the Portuguese explorer Vasco da Gama sailed around the southern tip of Africa in 1497, one hundred of his 160-member crew had died from scurvy. Reports exist of the discovery of ships adrift at sea with entire crews dead from the disease. It is estimated that for centuries scurvy was responsible for more death at sea than all other causes; more than the combined total of naval battles, piracy, shipwrecks, and other illnesses. ●

Astonishingly, preventives and remedies for scurvy during these years were known—but largely ignored. As early as the fifth century, the Chinese were growing fresh ginger in pots on board their ships. The idea that fresh fruit and vegetables could alleviate symptoms of scurvy was, no doubt, available to other countries in Southeast Asia in contact with Chinese trading vessels. It would have been passed on to the Dutch

Africa

Vocabulary
alleviate (ə lē′ vē āt′)
v. to lighten or relieve

---

2. **press-gang** men who round up other men to force them into naval or military service.

and been reported by them to other Europeans as, by 1601, the first fleet of the English East India Company is known to have collected oranges and lemons at Madagascar[3] on their way to the East. This small squadron of four ships was under the command of Captain James Lancaster, who carried bottled lemon juice with him on his flagship, the *Dragon*. Anyone who showed signs of scurvy was dosed with three teaspoons of lemon juice every morning. On arrival at the Cape of Good Hope, none of the men on board the *Dragon* was suffering from scurvy, but the toll on the other three ships was significant. Despite Lancaster's instructions and example, nearly a quarter of the total crew of this expedition died from scurvy—and not one of these deaths was on his flagship.

Some sixty-five years earlier the crew members on French explorer Jacques Cartier's second expedition to Newfoundland and Quebec were badly affected by a severe outbreak of scurvy, resulting in many deaths. An infusion of needles of the spruce tree, a remedy suggested by the local Indians, was tried with seemingly miraculous results. Almost overnight the symptoms were said to lessen and the disease rapidly disappeared. In 1593 Sir Richard Hawkins, an admiral of the British navy, claimed that within his own experience at least ten thousand men had died at sea from scurvy, but that lemon juice would have been an immediately effective cure.

There were even published accounts of successful treatments of scurvy. In 1617, John Woodall's *The Surgeon's Mate* described lemon juice as being prescribed for both cure and prevention. Eighty years later Dr. William Cockburn's *Sea Diseases, or the Treatise of their Nature, Cause and Cure* recommended fresh fruits and vegetables. Other suggestions such as vinegar, salt water, cinnamon, and whey were quite useless and may have obscured the correct action.

It was not until the middle of the following century that the effectiveness of citrus juice was proven in the first controlled clinical studies of scurvy. Although the numbers involved were very small, the conclusion was obvious. In 1747, James Lind, a Scottish naval surgeon at sea in the *Salisbury*, chose twelve of the crew suffering from scurvy for his experiment. He selected men whose symptoms seemed as similar as possible. He had them all eat the same diet: not the standard salted meat and hardtack, which these patients would have found very difficult to chew, but sweetened gruel, mutton broth, boiled biscuits, barley, sago, rice, raisins, currants, and wine. Lind added various supplements to this

---

3. **Madagascar** (mad´ ə gas´ kər) an island in the Indian Ocean off the southeast coast of Africa.

carbohydrate-based regime. Two of the sailors each received a quart of cider daily. Two others were dosed with vinegar, and another unfortunate pair received diluted elixir of vitriol (or sulfuric acid). Two more were required to drink half a pint of seawater daily, and another two were fed a concoction of nutmeg, garlic, mustard seed, gum myrrh, cream of tartar, and barley water. The lucky remaining pair was issued daily two oranges and one lemon each.

The results were sudden and visible and what we would expect with today's knowledge. Within six days the men who received the citrus fruit were fit for duty. Hopefully, the other ten sailors were then taken off their seawater, nutmeg, or sulfuric acid regimes and also supplied with lemons and oranges.

Lind's results were published in *A Treatise of Scurvy,* but it was another forty years before the British navy began the compulsory issue of lemon juice.

If an effective treatment for scurvy was known, why wasn't it acted upon and used routinely? Sadly, the remedy for scurvy, though proven, seems to have not been recognized or believed. A widely held theory blamed scurvy on a diet of either too much salted meat or not enough fresh meat rather than a lack of fresh fruit and vegetables. Also, there was a logistical problem: it was difficult to keep fresh citrus fruit or juice for weeks at a time. Attempts were made to concentrate and preserve lemon juice, but such procedures were time consuming, costly, and perhaps not very effective, as we now know that vitamin C is easily destroyed by heat and light and that long-term storage reduces the amount in fruits and vegetables.

Because of expense and inconvenience, naval officers, physicians, the British admiralty, and shipowners could see no way of growing sufficient greens or citrus fruit on heavily manned vessels. Precious cargo space would have to be used for this purpose. Fresh or preserved citrus fruit was expensive, especially if it was to be allocated daily as a preventive measure. Economy and the profit margin ruled—although, in hindsight, it does seem that this was a false economy. Ships had to be manned above capacity to allow for a 30, 40 or even 50 percent death rate from scurvy. Even without a high death rate, the effectiveness of a crew suffering from scurvy would have been remarkably low. And then there was the humane factor—rarely considered during these centuries.

Vocabulary
compulsory (kəm pul´ sə rē) *adj.* required, mandatory

Another element was the intransigence of the average crew. They were used to eating the standard ship's fare, and although they complained about the monotonous diet of salt meat and ship's biscuit when they were at sea, what they wanted in port was lots of fresh meat, fresh bread, cheese, butter, and good beer. Even if fresh fruit and vegetables were available, the majority of the crew would not have been interested in a quick stir-fry of tender crunchy greens. They wanted meat and more meat—boiled, stewed, or roasted. The officers, who generally came from a higher social class, where a wider and more varied diet was common, would have found eating fruit and vegetables in port to be normal and probably highly acceptable. It would not have been unusual for them to be interested in trying exotic new foodstuffs to be found in the locales where they made landfall. Tamarinds, limes, and other fruits high in vitamin C would have been used in the local cuisine that they, unlike the crew, might try. Scurvy was thus usually less of a problem among a ship's officers. •

Cook: Hundreds—Scurvy: Nil

James Cook of the British Royal Navy was the first ship's captain to ensure that his crews remained scurvy free. Cook is sometimes associated with the discovery of antiscorbutics, as scurvy-curing foods are called, but his true achievement lay in the fact that he insisted on maintaining high levels of diet and hygiene aboard all his vessels. The result of his meticulous standards was an extraordinarily good level of health and a low mortality rate among his crew. Cook entered the navy at the relatively late age of twenty-seven, but his previous nine years of experience sailing as a merchant seaman mate in the North Sea and the Baltic, his intelligence, and his innate seamanship combined to ensure his rapid promotion within the naval ranks. His first experience with scurvy came aboard the *Pembroke,* in 1758, on his initial voyage across the Atlantic Ocean to Canada to challenge the French hold on the St. Lawrence River. Cook was alarmed by the devastation this common affliction caused and appalled that the deaths of so many crew, the dangerous reduction of working efficiency, and even actual loss of ships were generally accepted as inevitable.

His experience exploring and mapping around Nova Scotia, the Gulf of St. Lawrence, and Newfoundland and his accurate observations of the eclipse of the sun greatly impressed the Royal Society, a body founded in 1645 with the aim of "improving natural knowledge." He was granted command of the ship *Endeavour* and instructed to explore and chart the southern oceans, to investigate

Reading Skill
Cause and Effect
In your own words, explain why the crew's food preferences were a cause of scurvy.

If an effective treatment for scurvy was known, why wasn't it acted upon and used routinely?

Reading
Check
What was James Cook's contribution to maintaining sailors' health?

new plants and animals, and to make astronomical observations of the transit of planets across the sun.

Less known but nonetheless compelling reasons for this voyage and for Cook's subsequent later voyages were political. Taking possession in the name of Britain of already discovered lands; claiming of new lands still to be discovered, including Terra Australis Incognita, the great southern continent; and the hopes of finding a Northwest Passage were all on the minds of the admiralty. That Cook was able to complete so many of these objectives depended to a large degree on ascorbic acid.

Consider the scenario on June 10, 1770, when the *Endeavour* ran aground on coral of the Great Barrier Reef just south of present-day Cooktown, in northern Queensland, Australia. It was a near catastrophe. The ship had struck at high water; a resulting hole in the hull necessitated drastic measures. In order to lighten the ship, the entire crew heaved overboard everything that could be spared. For twenty-three hours straight they manned the pumps as seawater leaked inexorably into the hold, hauling desperately on cables and anchor in an attempt to plug the hole by fothering, a temporary method of mending a hole by drawing a heavy sail under the hull. Incredible effort, superb seamanship, and good fortune prevailed. The ship eventually slid off the reef and was beached for repairs. It had been a very close call—one that an exhausted, scurvy-inflicted crew could not have summoned the energy to answer.

A healthy, well-functioning crew was essential for Cook to accomplish what he did on his voyages. This fact was recognized by the Royal Society when it awarded him its highest honor, the Copley gold medal, not for his navigational feats but for his demonstration that scurvy was not an inevitable companion on long ocean voyages. Cook's methods were simple. He insisted on maintaining cleanliness throughout the ship, especially in the tight confines of the seamen's quarters. All hands were required to wash their clothes regularly, to air and dry their bedding when the weather permitted, to fumigate between decks, and in general to live up to the meaning of the term *shipshape*. When it was not possible to obtain the fresh fruit and vegetables he thought necessary for a balanced diet, he required that his men eat the sauerkraut he had included in the ship's provisions. Cook touched land at every

▲ **Critical Viewing**
Do the actions of James Cook described in the essay seem to fit with his personality as suggested by this painting? Explain.
[Connect]

possible opportunity to replenish stores and gather local grasses (celery grass, scurvy grass) or plants from which he brewed teas.

This diet was not at all popular with the crew, accustomed as they were to the standard seamen's fare and reluctant to try anything new. But Cook was adamant. He and his officers also adhered to this diet, and it was by his example, authority, and determination that his regimen was followed. There is no record that Cook had anyone flogged for refusing to eat sauerkraut or celery grass, but the crew knew the captain would not hesitate to prescribe the lash for opposing his rules. Cook also made use of a more subtle approach. He records that a "Sour Kroutt" prepared from local plants was initially made available only to the officers; within a week the lower ranks were clamoring for their share.

Success no doubt helped convince Cook's crew that their captain's strange obsession with what they ate was worthwhile. Cook never lost a single man to scurvy. On his first voyage of almost three years, one-third of his crew died after contracting malaria or dysentery in Batavia (now Jakarta) in the Dutch East Indies (now Indonesia). On his second voyage from 1772 to 1775,

Reading Skill
Cause and Effect
What factors caused Cook to be successful in the Navy?

LITERATURE IN CONTEXT

History Connection

The Voyages of Captain James Cook (1728–1779)

First Voyage to the Pacific, 1768–1771: As first lieutenant of the ship *Endeavor*, Cook sails around the world from east to west; in New Zealand, he surveys the coast and proves it is not part of a vast southern continent.

Second Voyage to the Pacific, 1772–1775: As commander of the ship *Resolution*, he becomes the first navigator to cross the Antarctic Circle; he also charts Easter Island.

Third Voyage to the Pacific, 1776–1780: As commander of the *Resolution*, he explores Hawaii, which he names the Sandwich Islands.

Connect to the Literature What important point in the essay does the length of Cook's voyages, shown on the map, support?

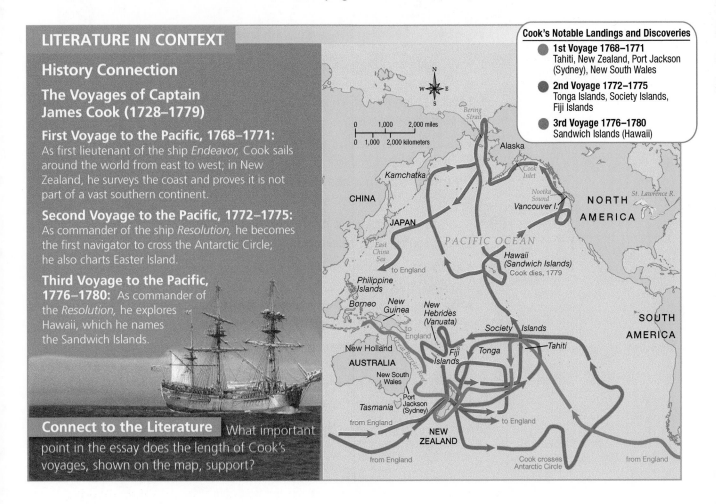

Cook's Notable Landings and Discoveries

- **1st Voyage 1768–1771**
  Tahiti, New Zealand, Port Jackson (Sydney), New South Wales
- **2nd Voyage 1772–1775**
  Tonga Islands, Society Islands, Fiji Islands
- **3rd Voyage 1776–1780**
  Sandwich Islands (Hawaii)

he lost one member of his crew to illness—but not to scurvy. Yet on that trip the crew of his companion vessel was badly affected by the problem. The commander, Tobias Furneaux, was severely reprimanded and instructed yet again by Cook on the need for preparation and administration of antiscorbutics. Thanks to vitamin C, the ascorbic acid molecule, Cook was able to compile an impressive list of accomplishments: the discovery of the Hawaiian Islands and the Great Barrier Reef, the first circumnavigation of New Zealand, the first charting of the coast of the Pacific Northwest, and first crossing of the Antarctic Circle.

Literary Analysis
Author's Purpose
What details about Captain Cook support the authors' thesis about the importance of vitamin C for the Age of Discovery?

Critical Thinking

Cite textual evidence to support your responses.

1. **Key Ideas and Details** **(a)** Before the eighteenth century, what was included in a typical sailor's diet? **(b) Analyze Cause and Effect:** Using details from the selection, explain why this diet led to widespread illness.

2. **Key Ideas and Details** **(a) Connect:** In what way did shipowners' concern about saving money add to the problem of scurvy? **(b) Interpret:** What does the delay in preventing and treating scurvy reveal about human nature?

3. **Key Ideas and Details** **Summarize:** What was Captain James Cook's contribution to eliminating scurvy?

4. **Key Ideas and Details** **(a) Speculate:** What modern food storage devices do you think would have been most helpful to navigators in the Age of Discovery? Why? **(b) Discuss:** Share your ideas with classmates in a group. Then, present your ideas to the class.

5. **Integration of Knowledge and Ideas** What are some reasons sailors and ships' captains failed to see the truth about the effectiveness of vitamin C? *[Connect to the Big Question: Is there a difference between reality and truth?]*

Literary Analysis: Author's Purpose

1. Key Ideas and Details (a) What is the authors' main **purpose** for writing? Explain. **(b)** Write a brief, objective summary stating the authors' **thesis** and main points.

2. Key Ideas and Details (a) Use a diagram like this one to record details that **support** the authors' thesis. Include at least five details. **(b)** Explain how each detail supports the thesis.

Detail		Thesis		Detail

3. Key Ideas and Details Identify two examples that show how the writers' choice of words helps them accomplish their purpose.

Reading Skill: Cause and Effect

4. Why was scurvy such a problem during the Age of Discovery? Name two **causes** from the text.

5. Explain the **effect** Captain Cook's shipboard dietary policies had on his voyages in the 1770s.

Vocabulary

Acquisition and Use Antonyms are words that have opposite meanings. For each numbered word below, choose the best antonym. Then, use each pair of antonyms in a sentence.

1. deficiency: (a) shortage, (b) obstacle, (c) surplus

2. replenished: (a) emptied, (b) forgave, (c) allowed

3. incessant: (a) failing, (b) brief, (c) filthy

4. alleviate: (a) oppose, (b) destroy, (c) increase

5. obscured: (a) revealed, (b) darkened, (c) pierced

6. compulsory: (a) necessary, (b) optional, (c) thoughtless

Word Study Use the context of the sentences and what you know about the **Latin prefix ob-** to explain your answer to each question.

1. Would a person who is *obstinate* be easily persuaded?

2. Would a lawyer *object* to a ruling in his favor?

Word Study

The **Latin prefix ob-** means "against," "over," or "in front of."

Apply It Explain how the prefix *ob-* contributes to the meanings of these words. Consult a dictionary if necessary.

obliterate

obstruction

obstacle

Integrated Language Skills

The Marginal World • Making History With Vitamin C

Conventions: Relative Pronouns

A **relative pronoun** is a pronoun that begins a subordinate clause. The relative pronoun relates the information in the clause to a noun or pronoun in the sentence.

Relative Pronouns				
that	**which**	**who**	**whom**	**whose**
This is the shell _that_ my brother gave me.	Cook insisted his crew drink lemon juice, _which_ saved many lives.	Carson is the author _who_ ignited environmental awareness in the public.	Cook was the captain with _whom_ men preferred to serve.	Captains _whose_ crews suffered from scurvy could have saved their men with lemon juice.

Practice A Copy the sentences. Circle the relative pronoun. Underline the noun and the clause that are connected by this relative pronoun.

1. Low tides expose the myriad of life that exists at the shore's edge.
2. A delicate starfish, whose reflection appears in the water, clings to the roof of the cave.
3. The little crab, which was scurrying near the water, was the only visible sign of life.
4. Creatures whose ancestors inhabited the sea for millions of years still exist in tidal waters.

Ⓒ **Reading Application** In "The Marginal World," find two sentences that contain a relative pronoun. Write the relative pronouns and the nouns to which the relative pronouns relate.

Practice B Complete the following sentences using a relative pronoun and a clause that relates to the noun.

1. Vitamin C is an important nutrient _____.
2. Early sailors, _____, often died from scurvy.
3. Victims of scurvy, _____, could have been saved by drinking lemon juice.
4. Captain Cook was a man _____.

Ⓒ **Writing Application** Using this sentence as a model, write two sentences with relative pronouns and a clause that relates to the noun: _Eating oranges, which contain vitamin C, prevents scurvy._

PH WRITING COACH Further instruction and practice are available in _Prentice Hall Writing Coach_.

Writing

Explanatory Text Both of these essays address topics that could be presented well in a film version. Write a **proposal for a documentary** on life at the edge of the sea or on Cook's efforts to prevent scurvy. First, reread the essay you chose for ideas. Then, write your own essay describing the documentary you propose to create. Include these elements:

- The main impression you want to convey
- Details about objects to be filmed and the places to be filmed
- Summaries of the actions and quotations to use from the essay
- Topics for comment by the narrator and actors

Grammar Application Check your proposal to make sure you have used relative pronouns correctly in any clauses that include them.

Writing Workshop: *Work in Progress*

Prewriting for Cause and Effect Look at the Why List in your writing portfolio and identify a question to research. While researching, note the progression of causes and effects that produced the final result. Keep these Cause-Effect Notes in your writing portfolio.

Research and Technology

Build and Present Knowledge Use computer software to create a **spreadsheet** based on one of the selections you read.

- If you read "The Marginal World," create a wildlife spreadsheet about living things you observe in your area. Include dates, times, and your observations. At the end of a week, write a conclusion about your environment. Compare your observations to Carson's.

- If you read "Making History With Vitamin C," create a personal diet spreadsheet. For one week, keep track of what you eat at each meal. Then, write a conclusion in which you compare your diet to that of typical sailors in Cook's day.

Use these suggestions when working on the assignment.

- Record many details for each observation. For example, for a wildlife spreadsheet, include detailed descriptions of all the plants, animals, and insects you observe. For a diet spreadsheet, record the ingredients of packaged foods.

- Review all your data carefully. Then, present your spreadsheet and conclusions to your class. Make sure that all of your conclusions flow directly from the data you gathered and that the connections are clear.

Common Core State Standards

L.9-10.1.b; W.9-10.2.f, W.9-10.9; SL.9-10.5
[For the full wording of the standards, see page 152.]

Use this prewriting activity to prepare for the **Writing Workshop** on page 200.

PHLit
Online!
www.PHLitOnline.com
- Interactive graphic organizers
- Grammar tutorial
- Interactive journals

Test Practice: Reading

Cause and Effect

Fiction Selection

Directions: *Read the selection. Then, answer the questions.*

"Ah-choo!" Lisa heard her brother George sneezing. He had been ill for two days, and Lisa could feel her throat getting itchy. "I knew I'd catch his cold," Lisa told her friend Keisha. "If he has a virus, I get it." Still, Lisa knew she could not miss school. "I need to review for the geometry exam tomorrow," she told her mother. "Keisha and I are studying after class."

"Okay, but be home early. If you don't get more rest, you will catch George's cold," her mother replied.

The next morning Lisa woke up with a throbbing headache. Her throat ached and she began sneezing and coughing.

"It looks like you're staying home today," her mother said. "You'll just have to miss the exam and make it up later."

That evening, Lisa phoned Keisha. "How was the exam?" asked Lisa. "I didn't go to school," Keisha replied, wheezing. "I have a cold, too."

"Great!" said Lisa. "We'll both spend the weekend in bed and then have to make up the exam on Monday. And all because of George!"

1. Which event occurs first?

    A. Lisa studies with Keisha for the exam.

    B. George has a cold.

    C. Lisa has a geometry exam.

    D. Lisa misses school.

2. What does Lisa suspect is causing her itchy throat?

    A. anxiety about her geometry exam

    B. lack of rest.

    C. an oncoming cold

    D. a sore throat

3. Which event is both a cause and an effect?

    A. Lisa catches a cold.

    B. George has a cold.

    C. Lisa makes up a math exam.

    D. Keisha spends the weekend in bed.

4. Which effect of the cold do both Lisa and Keisha experience?

    A. a sick brother

    B. a trip to the doctor

    C. a day home from school

    D. a failed geometry exam

Writing for Assessment

In a paragraph, describe the chain of events that occurs in this passage. What additional effects might George's cold have on his school, community, or family?

Nonfiction Selection

Directions: *Read the selection. Then, answer the questions.*

Most people occasionally suffer from the common cold. Although a cold is rarely serious, it can be uncomfortable and downright annoying. The first signs of a cold are a runny nose and sneezing, which are often followed by coughing, headache, fatigue, sore throat, and sometimes chills. Usually, no fever is involved.

Colds are caused by viruses. As many as 200 different viruses can cause colds. Colds are passed from one person to another. In fact, people can be carriers of cold viruses without having cold symptoms themselves. It takes only a short time to catch a cold from another person—as little as one to four days. Many colds are contracted in the fall, and cold epidemics can continue throughout the winter months. Scientists believe most colds occur during the cooler months because people spend more time indoors and have closer contact with people carrying cold viruses. No medicine is available that can cure the cold. Cold medicines simply help relieve cold symptoms. The most common treatment is resting and drinking fluids.

1. Which of the following is the direct cause of a cold?

   A. contact with a sick person
   B. staying indoors
   C. a virus
   D. cold weather

2. Which of the following is an effect of a cold?

   A. a high fever
   B. being confined to bed
   C. headache and tiredness
   D. drinking more fluids

3. According to the selection, which of the following causes people to catch colds?

   A. change of seasons
   B. contact with someone carrying the cold virus
   C. being outside in cold weather
   D. sneezing and coughing

4. Which of the following helps cure a cold?

   A. getting plenty of rest
   B. taking cold medicine
   C. staying indoors
   D. none of the above

Writing for Assessment

Connecting Across Texts

Lisa gets angry with her brother when she misses a geometry exam. In a paragraph, explain whether she is right to feel this way. Use details from each passage to support your response.

PHLit Online!
www.PHLitOnline.com
• Online practice
• Instant feedback

Reading for Information

Analyzing Functional and Expository Texts

Web Site

Primary Source

Common Core
State Standards

Reading Informational Text
6. Determine an author's point of view or purpose in a text.

Language
4.b. Identify and correctly use patterns of word changes that indicate different meanings or parts of speech.
6. Acquire and use accurately general academic and domain-specific words and phrases, sufficient for reading, writing, speaking, and listening at the college and career readiness level; demonstrate independence in gathering vocabulary knowledge when considering a word or phrase important to comprehension or expression.

Writing
2. Write informative/explanatory texts to examine and convey complex ideas, concepts, and information clearly and accurately through the effective selection, organization, and analysis of content. *(Timed Writing)*

Reading Skill: Evaluate Sources

When researching a topic, remember that not all the material you find will be completely accurate. Before you use material from a Web site or a primary source, **analyze the credibility** of the source. Do this by evaluating the text's validity and reliability. Use the following checklist.

Checklist for Evaluating Credibility of Sources

- ☐ Consider the author or sponsor. Might the source be biased?

- ☐ Check the information against a source you know is reliable.

- ☐ Check the date of the document or the "last updated" field on the Web page.

- ☐ For Web sites, check the ending of the URL.
  - Educational and governmental (".edu" and ".gov"): generally reliable
  - Nonprofit (".org"): may be unbiased, or may present only a specific point of view
  - Businesses and individuals (".com"): information of varying quality

Content-Area Vocabulary

These words appear in the selections that follow. You may also encounter them in other content-area texts.

- **excavate** (ek´ skə vāt´) *v.* create a hole by digging
- **millennia** (mə len´ ē ə) *n.* periods that each consist of one thousand years
- **vessels** (ves´ əlz) *n.* containers, often used to hold liquid, such as bowls or pots

The URL, or address, of the Web site, appears in the browser here. Check the ending of the URL to evaluate the site's credibility.

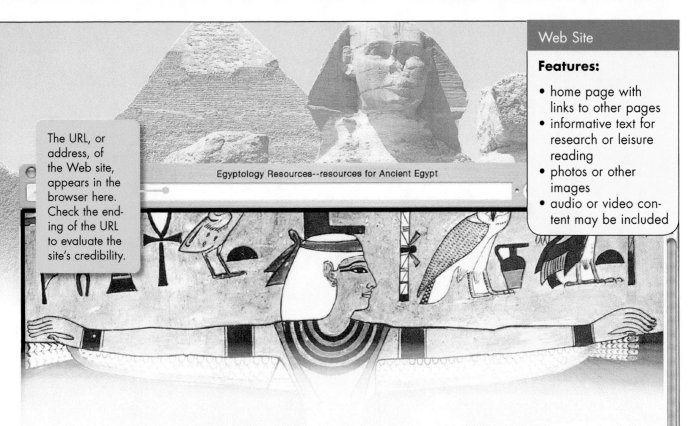

Egyptology Resources--resources for Ancient Egypt

EGYPTOLOGY RESOURCES

Popular local items

News & Gossip

Announcements

Bulletin Board

E-mail Addresses

Tomb of Sennefen

Beinlich Wordlist

Wilbour Library Acquisitions

Online Publications

Commercial Items

Server statistics

The first Egyptology site on the web

This page is set up with the kind assistance of the Newton Institute in the University of Cambridge to provide a World Wide Web resource for Egyptological information. The pages are not a publication of the Newton Institute, and all matters concerning them (e.g., comments, criticisms, and suggestions for items to include) should be sent to Nigel Strudwick.

Click here for guidelines on the format of material.

Click here for site history.

Main pages

Essential Resources

Institutions

Museums

Digs

Publishers, Booksellers

Journals, Magazines

Organizations, Societies

Interesting Egypt Pages

Personal Egypt Pages

Other Resources of Interest

Information on the individual who maintains this Web site is available by clicking his name. This information will help you evaluate the credibility of the site.

Q▾ Google

MUSEUMS ONLINE WITH EGYPTIAN COLLECTIONS

Many museums, of course, have WWW pages now. I have tried to select some of those which have more specific information on their Egyptian Collections, but I do also include the general Web presences of major museums with relevant material. Some of these links often go directly to the Egypt pages and bypass the home page. A more general set of links will be found in the ABZU indexes.

Each of these links brings users to the Web site of a museum that has Egyptian artifacts in its collection. Evaluate the credibility of any site you visit.

Egypt
- The Egyptian Museum, Cairo
- The Coptic Museum, Cairo

North America
- Museum of Fine Arts, Boston
- Metropolitan Museum, New York
- Michael C. Carlos Museum, Emory University, Atlanta
- Brooklyn Museum
- Oriental Institute, University of Chicago

Europe
- The British Museum, London COMPASS Project
- The Louvre, Paris
- Musées royaux d'art et d'art historie, Brussels
- Museo Egizio, Torino
- Agyptisches Museum und Papyrussammlung Berlin-Charlottenburg
- Allard Pierson Museum
- Carsten Niebuhr Institute, University of Copenhagen, Papyrus Collection

Back to Egyptology Resources home page

Interactive Dig

Primary Source

Features:

- informative text used for reference or research
- first-person perspective
- accounts of events given by an active participant or an eyewitness

Narmer's Temple: Week 1

by Renée Friedman

After a hiatus of 13 years, we've returned to the Predynastic Temple at Hierakonpolis. Dating to around 3500 B.C., it is Egypt's oldest. Excavations here in 1985, 1986–1987, and 1989 had revealed about half of a large (presumably) oval courtyard walled by a wooden fence, onto which fronted a main shrine with a façade composed of four large wooden pillars—now marked by four enormous postholes.

Our first order of business was to remove the sand that had accumulated over the **millennia** over the unexcavated portion of the courtyard floor in order to determine the full architectural layout of the vast complex. Of special interest was the area between the entrance to the compound and the entrance to the main shrine, as this might be where important things happened. With over 80cm of sand and debris covering this possible processional corridor, it is no wonder that the area was not cleared earlier. The volume of debris meant a lot of work, but it also, we hope, meant that the temple deposits below had a good chance of being undisturbed.

We got to work immediately. With Ramadan coming up, it was a race against time. We **excavate** with local workmen, who have worked with us for over 30 years. They come from the nearby village and ride their donkeys to work each day, since we can provide miles of free parking. Michael Hoffman, who directed the excavations, began training the villagers in 1969 and working for the expedition has become a family tradition. Now we are working with the sons and grandsons of the original crew, who have worked their way up from basket boy to valued excavator. They are not only skilled, but also interested and proud of their own local heritage. Trained to note the slightest change in the soil, they can point out areas of compaction, or texture differences, disturbance, etc. In a sandy site, where excavation balks are hard to maintain, and a prehistoric site, where detailed observation is critical, they make our work possible.

> The dig is described from a first-person perspective, which suggests the information is reliable.

Interactive Dig

Our workers are very good-natured. During the first week, the plan was to remove as much of the windblown sand and mixed debris as possible. This made for somewhat boring work as once we reached a level that looked good, I made them stop, and move over to the next square (we dig in 10×10m squares divided into 5×5m subunits) and begin again, saving the detailed work, brush work, sieving, and other less arduous tasks for the fasting days of Ramadan.

In the first six digging days, working from six in the morning until noon, we managed to clear seven 5×5m squares of about 50cm of sand to layers that look promising. The sand over the courtyard floor, however, was not entirely devoid of interesting things. We found a number of fragments of once beautifully polished stone **vessels** made of exotic stones imported from the Red Sea hills—diorite, basalt, alabaster, marble. We also recovered a crescent drill of flint used in the manufacture of these stone vessels. It probably originated from the workshops that surround the temple complex. Microdrills for boring out beads, and fragments of carefully knapped bifacial knives also turned up. The fine micro-retouch on the edge of what may have been a lance is amazing.

These objects, however, are no longer in their original place because of fertilizer digging. In the early part of the last century and before, farmers mined the rich soil of archaeological deposits as fertilizer for their fields, which is called *sebakh* in Arabic. The decayed organic debris of ancient sites provided a supply of nitrogen, necessary for the crops and before chemical fertilizer was easily available, mining the ancient levels was the only alternative. As a result, the low desert at Hierakonpolis looks like the valleys of the moon, with sand-filled pits surrounded by mountains of discarded predynastic artifacts that were of no interest to the farmers, who only wanted the midden in which they were found. Piles of potsherds, animal bone, grinding stones, lithics, and assorted other wonderful things cover the site—over two square miles. It was years before I ever looked up while walking to work here—the wealth of goodies on the ground was riveting and after a good rain (like the one we had on our very first day this season!) or a major sand storm, new wonders can always be found.

> The author demonstrates reliability by describing in detail how objects were found.

> The photo and caption indicate that the author was present for the work being described.

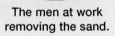

The men at work removing the sand.

Web Site • Primary Source

Comparing Functional and Expository Texts

1. Key Ideas and Details (a) Compare and contrast the possible disadvantages of using Web sites and primary sources for research. **(b)** Under what circumstances would you use either of these two sources?

Content-Area Vocabulary

2. (a) Explain how each of the following words is formed by adding a suffix to *excavate* and how the suffix changes the base word's meaning and part of speech: *excavation, excavator.* **(b)** Use each word in a sentence that shows its meaning.

Timed Writing

Explanatory Text: Essay

Format
The prompt calls for a brief essay. Therefore, you will need to present and support your ideas in three to five paragraphs.

Write a brief essay in which you evaluate the credibility of the Web site and the primary source document as sources of information on ancient Egypt. Note the features or techniques that make each source seem credible, as well as improvements that would make each source seem more credible. (20 minutes)

Academic Vocabulary
When you *evaluate* the credibility of a source, you analyze and make judgments about the source's quality and reliability.

5-Minute Planner

Complete these steps before you begin to write:

1. Read the prompt carefully.

2. Review the Web site and primary source document. Make notes about clues to each author's credibility and the features and techniques that make each source seem more credible. **TIP** Credibility of primary sources written in the first person often depends upon the author's purpose for writing or biases the author may have.

3. Note what elements of these two sources might be improved or what could be added to improve their credibility. Refer to your notes as you draft your essay.

Comparing Irony and Paradox

Irony is the effect created when a writer sets up contrasts between readers' or characters' expectations and reality. Irony may involve a discrepancy between appearance and reality, between expectation and outcome, or between stated meaning and intended meaning. A writer's use of irony often adds emotional intensity to a story or creates a sense of surprise when readers learn that a situation or a character has a different truth.

There are three main types of irony:

- In **situational irony,** an event directly contradicts strong expectations.

  Example: In a story in which two companions hide from an enemy, one of the two turns out to be an enemy operative.

- In **verbal irony,** a character says the opposite of what he or she really means.

  Example: After the enemy operative gives up his companion, the one betrayed says, "I'm glad I trusted you."

- In **dramatic irony,** the reader knows something a character does not.

  Example: During the whole story, readers know that the operative is actually a long-lost brother of the one he betrays—but neither of the characters are aware of this.

In addition to irony, writers may use **paradox**—a statement that seems contradictory but actually reveals a deeper truth. For example, consider the following statement: "One must sometimes be cruel to be kind." At first, the statement seems impossible—how can cruelty be kind? However, the statement makes sense when you consider that seemingly unkind words or actions can actually help someone face a painful truth or develop stronger skills.

In "Like the Sun" and "The Open Window," the writers use irony and paradox to explore contradictory ideas of honesty and deceit. As you read, use a diagram like the one shown to note examples of irony and paradox in these stories.

Common Core State Standards

Reading Literature

5. Analyze how an author's choices concerning how to structure a text, order events within it, and manipulate time create such effects as mystery, tension, or surprise.

Writing

2. Write informative/explanatory texts to examine and convey complex ideas, concepts, and information clearly and accurately through the effective selection, organization, and analysis of content. *(Timed Writing)*

2.b. Develop the topic with well-chosen, relevant, and sufficient facts; extended definitions, concrete details, quotations, or other information; and examples appropriate to the audience's knowledge of the topic. *(Timed Writing)*

Like the Sun		
Sekhar wants to be truthful.	*clashes with*	People dislike the truth.
Example of _____		

The Open Window		
Mr. Nuttel needs calm.	*clashes with*	Vera enjoys scaring him.
Example of _____		

Writing About the Big Question

In these stories, characters plan reasonable goals, but the outcomes are far from what they expect. Think about a time when things did not turn out as you had planned. Use these sentence starters to develop your ideas.

My **perception** of the situation was that _____.

In **reality,** though, _____.

Meet the Authors

R. K. Narayan (1906–2001)

Author of "Like the Sun"

R. K. Narayan spun his tales from the stuff of real life. His hometown of Mysore in southern India probably served as the basis for Malgudi, the setting for much of his fiction. Like the main character in "Like the Sun," Narayan's father was a schoolteacher, and Narayan studied music, a key element of the story, as a youth.

Crossing Languages A native Tamil speaker, Narayan wrote his novels and stories in English, a second language to many Indians. In addition to fiction, he wrote a memoir, *My Days,* and a noted English translation of the ancient Indian epic the *Mahabharata.*

Saki (1870–1916)

Author of "The Open Window"

Saki is the pen name of Hector Hugh Munro. Born to British parents in Burma (now Myanmar), Saki lived in England for most of his life. He began his career writing political satires for newspapers and later turned to fiction.

Humor and Wit Today, Saki is best known for his witty, sometimes cruel short stories, many of which feature humorous surprise endings. Many readers consider "The Open Window" to be one of the best examples of Saki's style.

Like _the_ Sun

R.K. Narayan

Truth,

Sekhar reflected, is like the sun. I suppose no human being can ever look it straight in the face without blinking or being dazed. He realized that, morning till night, the essence of human relationships consisted in tempering truth so that it might not shock. This day he set apart as a unique day—at least one day in the year we must give and take absolute Truth whatever may happen. Otherwise life is not worth living. The day ahead seemed to him full of possibilities. He told no one of his experiment. It was a quiet resolve, a secret pact between him and eternity.

The very first test came while his wife served him his morning meal. He showed hesitation over a tidbit, which she had thought was her culinary masterpiece. She asked, "Why, isn't it good?" At other times he would have said, considering her feelings in the matter, "I feel full up, that's all." But today he said, "It isn't good. I'm unable to swallow it." He saw her wince and said to himself, Can't be helped. Truth is like the sun.

Vocabulary
tempering (tem´ pər iŋ)
n. changing to make more suitable, usually by mixing with something

Spiral Review
Theme Based on the first two paragraphs, what thematic ideas do you think the author is developing? Explain.

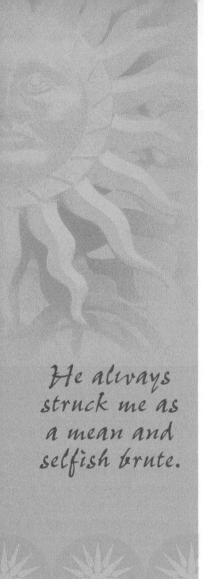

He always struck me as a mean and selfish brute.

Literary Analysis
Irony and Paradox
Why is it ironic that this is the day the headmaster will ask for Sekhar's opinion about his musical abilities?

Vocabulary
ingratiating (in grā´ shē āt´ iŋ) *adj.* acting in a way intended to win someone's favor

His next trial was in the common room when one of his colleagues came up and said, "Did you hear of the death of so-and-so? Don't you think it a pity?" "No," Sekhar answered. "He was such a fine man—" the other began. But Sekhar cut him short with: "Far from it. He always struck me as a mean and selfish brute."

During the last period when he was teaching geography for Third Form A,[1] Sekhar received a note from the headmaster: "Please see me before you go home." Sekhar said to himself: It must be about these horrible test papers. A hundred papers in the boys' scrawls; he had shirked this work for weeks, feeling all the time as if a sword were hanging over his head. The bell rang, and the boys burst out of the class.

Sekhar paused for a moment outside the headmaster's room to button up his coat; that was another subject the headmaster always sermonized about.

He stepped in with a very polite "Good evening, sir."

The headmaster looked up at him in a very friendly manner and asked, "Are you free this evening?"

Sekhar replied, "Just some outing which I have promised the children at home."

"Well, you can take them out another day. Come home with me now."

"Oh . . . yes, sir, certainly. . ." And then he added timidly, "anything special, sir?"

"Yes," replied the headmaster, smiling to himself. . . ."You didn't know my weakness for music?"

"Oh, yes, sir. . ."

"I've been learning and practicing secretly, and now I want you to hear me this evening. I've engaged a drummer and a violinist to accompany me—this is the first time I'm doing it full-dress, and I want your opinion. I know it will be valuable."

Sekhar's taste in music was well known. He was one of the most dreaded music critics in the town. But he never anticipated his musical inclinations would lead him to this trial. . . . "Rather a surprise for you, isn't it?" asked the headmaster. "I've spent a fortune on it behind closed doors. . . ."

They started for the headmaster's house.

"God hasn't given me a child, but at least let him not deny me the consolation of music," the headmaster said, pathetically, as they walked. He incessantly chattered about music: how he began one day out of sheer boredom; how his teacher at first laughed at him and then gave him hope; how his ambition in life was to forget himself in music.

At home the headmaster proved very ingratiating. He sat Sekhar on a red silk carpet, set before him several dishes of delicacies, and

---

1. Third Form A in British-style schools, an advanced class roughly equivalent to eighth grade in the United States school system.

fussed over him as if he were a son-in-law of the house. He even said, "Well, you must listen with a free mind. Don't worry about these test papers." He added half humorously, "I will give you a week's time."

"Make it ten days, sir," Sekhar pleaded.

"All right, granted," the headmaster said generously. Sekhar felt really relieved now—he would attack them at the rate of ten a day and get rid of the nuisance.

The headmaster lighted incense sticks. "Just to create the right atmosphere," he explained. A drummer and a violinist, already seated on a Rangoon mat, were waiting for him. The headmaster sat down between them like a professional at a concert, cleared his throat and began an alapana[2], and paused to ask, "Isn't it good Kalyani[3]?" Sekhar pretended not to have heard the question. The headmaster went on to sing a full song composed by Thyagaraja[4] and followed it with two more. All the time the headmaster was singing, Sekhar went on commenting within himself, He croaks like a dozen frogs. He is bellowing like a buffalo. Now he sounds like loose window shutters in a storm.

The incense sticks burnt low. Sekhar's head throbbed with the medley of sounds that had assailed his eardrums for a couple of hours now. He felt half stupefied. The headmaster had gone nearly hoarse, when he paused to ask, "Shall I go on?" Sekhar replied, "Please don't, sir; I think this will do. . . ." The headmaster looked stunned. His face was beaded with perspiration. Sekhar felt the greatest pity for him. But he felt he could not help it. No judge delivering a sentence felt more pained and helpless. Sekhar noticed that the headmaster's wife peeped in from the kitchen, with eager curiosity. The drummer and the violinist put away their burdens with an air of relief. The headmaster removed his spectacles, mopped his brow, and asked, "Now, come out with your opinion."

"Can't I give it tomorrow, sir?" Sekhar asked tentatively.

"No. I want it immediately—your frank opinion. Was it good?"

"No, sir. . . ." Sekhar replied.

"Oh! . . . Is there any use continuing my lessons?"

"Absolutely none, sir. . . ." Sekhar said with his voice trembling. He felt very unhappy that he could not speak more soothingly. Truth, he reflected, required as much strength to give as to receive. All the way home he felt worried. He felt that his official life was not going to be smooth sailing hereafter. There were questions of increment and

---

2. **alapana** (äl ä´ pä nä) in classical Indian music, an improvisational exploration of a melody, without a defined beat, and intended to showcase the talent of a singer.
3. **Kalyani** (käl yä´ nē) traditional Indian folk songs.
4. **Thyagaraja** (tē ä´ gä rä´ jä) (1767–1847) revered composer of Indian devotional songs.

▲ **Critical Viewing**
What can you conclude about the sitar (si tär´), a traditional Indian instrument, based on this image? Explain. **[Draw Conclusions]**

Reading Check

What does the headmaster request that Sekhar do that evening?

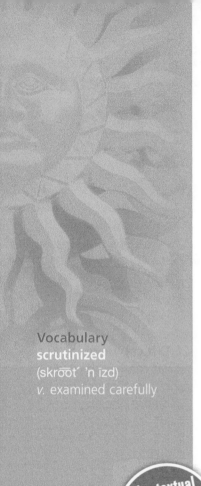

confirmation[5] and so on, all depending upon the headmaster's goodwill. All kinds of worries seemed to be in store for him. . . . Did not Harishchandra[6] lose his throne, wife, child, because he would speak nothing less than the absolute Truth whatever happened?

At home his wife served him with a sullen face. He knew she was still angry with him for his remark of the morning. Two casualties for today, Sekhar said to himself. If I practice it for a week, I don't think I shall have a single friend left.

He received a call from the headmaster in his classroom next day. He went up apprehensively.

"Your suggestion was useful. I have paid off the music master. No one would tell me the truth about my music all these days. Why such antics at my age! Thank you. By the way, what about those test papers?"

"You gave me ten days, sir, for correcting them."

"Oh, I've reconsidered it. I must positively have them here tomorrow. . . ." A hundred papers in a day! That meant all night's sitting up! "Give me a couple of days, sir. . . ."

"No. I must have them tomorrow morning. And remember, every paper must be thoroughly scrutinized."

"Yes, sir," Sekhar said, feeling that sitting up all night with a hundred test papers was a small price to pay for the luxury of practicing Truth.

Vocabulary
scrutinized
(skrōōt´ 'n izd)
v. examined carefully

---

5. **increment and confirmation** salary increase and job security.
6. **Harischchandra** (he rish chen´ dra) legendary Hindu king who was subject of many Indian stories. His name has come to symbolize truth and integrity.

Cite textual evidence to support your responses.

Critical Thinking

1. **Key Ideas and Details** **(a)** What experiment does Sekhar plan at the beginning of the story? **(b) Connect:** What conflict does this create for him?

2. **Key Ideas and Details** **Infer:** Is the headmaster pleased or angry that Sekhar has told him the truth about his music? Explain your inference.

3. **Key Ideas and Details** **(a) Draw Conclusions:** Are there any benefits to Sekhar's truth telling? **(b) Support:** Cite story details and logical reasons to support your conclusion.

4. **Integration of Knowledge and Ideas** Based on the results of Sekhar's experiment, do you think people prefer to hear reality through absolute truths, or do they prefer tempered truth? Explain. *[Connect to the Big Question: Is there a difference between reality and truth?]*

Literary Analysis
Irony and Paradox
How does Sekhar's experience contradict the idea that "honesty is the best policy"?

THE OPEN WINDOW

Saki (H.H. Munro)

"My aunt will be down presently, Mr. Nuttel," said a very self-possessed young lady of fifteen; "in the meantime you must try and put up with me."

Framton Nuttel endeavored to say the correct something that should duly flatter the niece of the moment without unduly discounting the aunt that was to come. Privately he doubted more than ever whether these formal visits on a succession of total strangers would do much towards helping the nerve cure which he was supposed to be undergoing.

"I know how it will be," his sister had said when he was preparing to migrate to this rural retreat; "you will bury yourself down there and not speak to a living soul, and your nerves will be worse than ever from moping. I shall just give you letters of introduction[1] to all the people I know there. Some of them, as far as I can remember, were quite nice."

---

1. **letters of introduction** letters introducing two strangers, written by someone who knows them both. The person to whom such a letter is written is obliged to provide hospitality to the person carrying the letter.

Framton wondered whether Mrs. Sappleton, the lady to whom he was presenting one of the letters of introduction, came into the nice division.

"Do you know many of the people round here?" asked the niece, when she judged that they had had sufficient silent communion.

"Hardly a soul," said Framton. "My sister was staying here, at the rectory, you know, some four years ago, and she gave me letters of introduction to some of the people here."

He made the last statement in a tone of distinct regret.

"Then you know practically nothing about my aunt?" pursued the self-possessed young lady.

"Only her name and address," admitted the caller. He was wondering whether Mrs. Sappleton was in the married or widowed state. An undefinable something about the room seemed to suggest masculine habitation.

"Her great tragedy happened just three years ago," said the child; "that would be since your sister's time."

"Her tragedy?" asked Framton; somehow in this restful country spot tragedies seemed out of place.

"You may wonder why we keep that window wide open on an October afternoon," said the niece, indicating a large French window that opened on to a lawn.

"It is quite warm for the time of the year," said Framton; "but has that window got anything to do with the tragedy?"

"Out through that window, three years ago to a day, her husband and her two young brothers went off for their day's shooting. They never came back. In crossing the moor to their favorite snipe-shooting ground[2] they were all three engulfed in a treacherous piece of bog.[3] It had been that dreadful wet summer, you know, and places that were safe in other years gave way suddenly without warning. Their bodies were never recovered. That was the dreadful part of it." Here the child's voice lost its self-possessed note and became falteringly human. "Poor aunt always thinks that they will come back some day,

Spiral Review
Theme Why is Vera's question, in which she seeks confirmation of Mr. Nuttel's ignorance, important?

Vocabulary
falteringly (fôl´ tər iŋ lē) *adv.* spoken hesitatingly or with a wavering voice

---

2. **snipe-shooting ground** area for hunting snipe—wading birds that live chiefly in marshy places and have long, flexible bills.
3. **bog** small swamp; wet, spongy ground.

they and the little brown spaniel that was lost with them, and walk in at that window just as they used to do. That is why the window is kept open every evening till it is quite dusk. Poor dear aunt, she has often told me how they went out, her husband with his white waterproof coat over his arm, and Ronnie, her youngest brother, singing, 'Bertie, why do you bound?' as he always did to tease her, because she said it got on her nerves. Do you know, sometimes on still, quiet evenings like this, I almost get a creepy feeling that they will walk in through that window—"

She broke off with a little shudder. It was a relief to Framton when the aunt bustled into the room with a whirl of apologies for being late in making her appearance.

"I hope Vera has been amusing you?" she said.

"She has been very interesting," said Framton.

"I hope you don't mind the open window," said Mrs. Sappleton briskly; "my husband and brothers will be home directly from shooting, and they always come in this way. They've been out for snipe in the marshes today, so they'll make a fine mess over my poor carpets. So like you menfolk, isn't it?"

She rattled on cheerfully about the shooting and the scarcity of birds, and the prospects for duck in the winter. To Framton, it was all purely horrible. He made a desperate but only partially successful effort to turn the talk on to a less ghastly topic; he was conscious that his hostess was giving him only a fragment of her attention, and her eyes were constantly straying past him to the open window and the lawn beyond. It was certainly an unfortunate coincidence that he should have paid his visit on this tragic anniversary.

"The doctors agree in ordering me complete rest, an absence of mental excitement, and avoidance of anything in the nature of violent physical exercise," announced Framton, who labored under the tolerably widespread delusion that total strangers and chance acquaintances are hungry for the least detail of one's ailments and infirmities, their cause and cure. "On the matter of diet they are not so much in agreement," he continued.

"No?" said Mrs. Sappleton, in a voice which only replaced a yawn at the last moment. Then she suddenly brightened into alert attention—but not to what Framton was saying.

"Here they are at last!" she cried. "Just in time for tea, and don't they look as if they were muddy up to the eyes!"

Framton shivered slightly and turned towards the niece with a look intended to convey sympathetic comprehension. The child was staring out through the open window with dazed horror in her eyes. In a chill shock of nameless fear Framton swung round in his seat and looked in the same direction.

Literary Analysis
Irony and Paradox
What kind of irony is involved when Mrs. Sappleton does not know about the tall tale Vera told Mr. Nuttel?

Vocabulary
delusion (di lōō′ zhan) *n.* an erroneous belief that is held despite evidence to the contrary

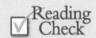
Reading Check
What does Vera say is her aunt's great tragedy?

In the deepening twilight three figures were walking across the lawn towards the window; they all carried guns under their arms, and one of them was additionally burdened with a white coat hung over his shoulders. A tired brown spaniel kept close at their heels. Noiselessly they neared the house, and then a hoarse young voice chanted out of the dusk: "I said, Bertie, why do you bound?"

Framton grabbed wildly at his stick and hat; the hall door, the gravel drive, and the front gate were dimly noted stages in his headlong retreat. A cyclist coming along the road had to run into the hedge to avoid imminent collision.

"Here we are, my dear," said the bearer of the white mackintosh,[4] coming in through the window; "fairly muddy, but most of it's dry. Who was that who bolted out as we came up?"

"A most extraordinary man, a Mr. Nuttel," said Mrs. Sappleton; "could only talk about his illnesses, and dashed off without a word of goodbye or apology when you arrived. One would think he had seen a ghost."

"I expect it was the spaniel," said the niece calmly; "he told me he had a horror of dogs. He was once hunted into a cemetery somewhere on the banks of the Ganges[5] by a pack of pariah dogs, and had to spend the night in a newly dug grave with the creatures snarling and grinning and foaming just above him. Enough to make anyone lose their nerve."

Romance at short notice was her specialty.

In the deepening twilight three figures were walking across the lawn towards the window...

4. **mackintosh** (mak´ in täsh´) *n.* waterproof raincoat.
5. **Ganges** (gan´ jēz) river in northern India and Bangladesh.

Critical Thinking

Cite textual evidence to support your responses.

@ 1. **Key Ideas and Details** **(a)** Why is Mr. Nuttel visiting the country? **(b) Interpret**: Why is this detail critical to the story?

@ 2. **Key Ideas and Details** **(a) Speculate:** Why does Vera tell Mr. Nuttel the story about the hunters' deaths? **(b) Connect:** Is it unusual for her to tell such stories? Explain.

@ 3. **Key Ideas and Details** **Compare and Contrast:** How are Mr. Nuttel and Vera similar and different? Use details from the story to support your answer.

@ 4. **Integration of Knowledge and Ideas** **(a)** How does Vera use aspects of reality to shape her story? **(b)** How is Mr. Nuttel's perception of the situation at the end of the story different from reality? *[Connect to the Big Question: Is there a difference between reality and truth?]*

Comparing Irony and Paradox

1. Craft and Structure (a) Analyze one example of **irony** in each story. For each example, identify and explain the elements that contrast with one another. **(b)** Did you identify situational, verbal, or dramatic irony? Explain.

2. Key Ideas and Details Explain how each story explores a **paradox:**

(a) "Like the Sun": Telling the truth is a virtue that leads to punishment.

(b) "The Open Window": The cure for Mr. Nuttel's illness makes him worse.

3. Craft and Structure Complete a diagram like this one to show how irony and paradox affect each story. Consider whether these devices simply add humor or whether they emphasize the impossible dilemmas facing a character.

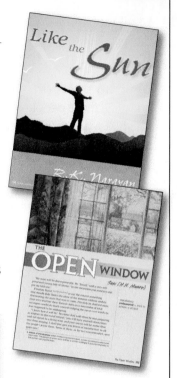

Like the Sun	The Open Window
Effect of Irony and Paradox:	Effect of Irony and Paradox:

Timed Writing

Explanatory Text: Essay

Both Narayan and Saki use irony or paradox to explore ideas. In an essay, compare and contrast how the authors present the concepts of truth and deception in these stories. Provide evidence from the texts to support your understanding. **(30 minutes)**

5-Minute Planner

1. Read the prompt carefully and completely.

2. Identify a few examples of irony or paradox in each story.

3. Draw a conclusion about the message each writer is expressing about truth, deception, and honesty.

4. Take notes on how the use of irony and paradox helps each writer express his message. Find quotations from the text that you can include to support your ideas.

5. Reread the prompt, and then draft your essay.

Writing Workshop

Write an Explanatory Text

Exposition: Cause-and-Effect Essay

Defining the Form Whenever something unusual happens, the first question most people ask is, "Why?" A **cause-and-effect essay** can satisfy a reader's curiosity. It might explain why a weird new fashion fad began or what happened as a result of a groundbreaking court decision. You might use elements of this form in research papers, informative articles, and reflective essays.

Assignment Write an essay in which you explain a cause-and-effect relationship. Include these elements:

✓ a thesis statement in which you clearly identify the cause-and-effect relationships you will explore

✓ an effective and *logical method of organization*

✓ well-chosen, relevant *supporting evidence* and examples that suit your audience and purpose

✓ *transitions* that smoothly and clearly connect your ideas

✓ error-free grammar, including *correct pronoun-antecedent agreement*

To preview the criteria on which your cause-and-effect essay may be judged, see the rubric on page 207.

 Writing Workshop: *Work in Progress*

Review the work you did on pages 151 and 179.

WRITE GUY
Jeff Anderson, M.Ed.

What Do You Notice?

Structure and Style

Read these sentences from Penny Le Couteur and Jay Burreson's "Making History with Vitamin C."

If an effective treatment for scurvy was known, why wasn't it acted upon and used routinely? Sadly, the remedy for scurvy, though proven, seems to have not been recognized or believed.

With a partner, discuss why these sentences are interesting. Consider the sentence structures and rhetorical strategies used.

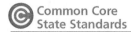 **Common Core State Standards**

Writing
2. Write informative/explanatory texts to examine and convey complex ideas, concepts, and information clearly and accurately through the effective selection, organization, and analysis of content.

5. Develop and strengthen writing as needed by planning, revising, editing, rewriting, or trying a new approach, focusing on addressing what is most significant for a specific purpose and audience.

7. Conduct short as well as more sustained research projects to answer a question or solve a problem; narrow or broaden the inquiry when appropriate.

Reading-Writing Connection

To get a feel for cause-and-effect essays, read "Making History With Vitamin C" by Penny Le Couteur and Jay Burreson on page 168.

Prewriting/Planning Strategies

Use one of the following ways to choose a topic and focus for your essay.

Make a list. Brainstorm for a list of scientific phenomena, historic events, or popular trends that you find interesting, important, or even confusing. Look over your list to choose a topic you would like to explore in an essay.

Scan a newspaper or magazine. Review print or online articles, looking for ideas that make you ask, "Why?" Identify possible topics and then conduct short research projects to learn more about the subjects that spark your interest. Review your research notes and choose a topic to address.

Narrow your topic. Once you have a topic, make sure that you can discuss it fully in your essay. If your topic is too broad, you may need to focus it. For example, you might not be able to answer "Why did the Great Depression happen?" in a short essay. Instead, you could focus your inquiry on why the stock market crashed in October of 1929.

Make a cause-and-effect chart. Organizing your ideas and details in a cause-and-effect chart can help you form a clear picture of the relationship you will discuss. One chart shown here presents three possible causes of one effect. The other chart classifies the possible effects of one cause.

PHLit
Online!
www.PHLitOnline.com
- Author video: Writing Process
- Author video: Rewards of Writing

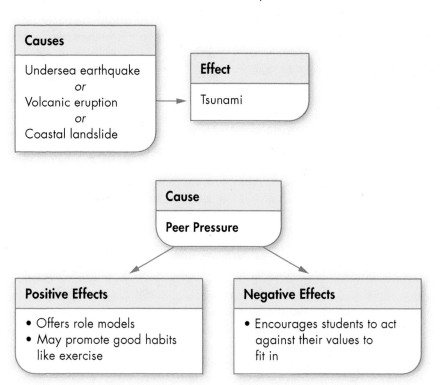

Causes
Undersea earthquake
or
Volcanic eruption
or
Coastal landslide

Effect
Tsunami

Cause
Peer Pressure

Positive Effects
• Offers role models
• May promote good habits like exercise

Negative Effects
• Encourages students to act against their values to fit in

Drafting Strategies

Clarify your analysis. Even if you are describing a complicated chain of effects, you will need a clear and direct introduction. Prepare a simplified cause-and-effect chart like the one shown on this page to organize your pre-writing ideas. It can show you which ideas are most essential to your topic.

Choose a logical organization. The structure you choose for your essay depends on the information you have.

- **Chronological order** makes sense for many cause-and-effect essays. You can start with the cause and then continue by describing its effects. Alternatively, you can start with the effect and then work through its causes one at a time.

- If you are describing multiple causes, consider using an **order-of-importance organization.** You might begin with your most important cause or save the most important cause for last.

When developing your organization, make sure your essay includes an introduction, a body, and a conclusion that supports your analysis.

Consider your audience. Think about how much your readers already know about your topic. Use precise words, and provide full explanations for any technical or unfamiliar words or events.

Use clear transitions. Specific words and phrases, called transitions, can help you introduce causes and effects. For example, use *therefore, consequently, as a result,* or *for that reason* to introduce effects. Refer to causes with transitions such as *because, since, as,* or *for the reason that.*

Also consider phrases that help you connect, contrast, and compare ideas. You might use *not only . . . but also* to join two related ideas. Other transitions, such as *however* and *on the other hand,* can clarify contrasting ideas.

Common Core State Standards

Writing

2.a. Introduce a topic, organize complex ideas, concepts, and information to make important connections and distinctions.

2.c. Use appropriate and varied transitions to link the major sections of the text, create cohesion, and clarify the relationships among complex ideas and concepts.

2.d. Use precise language and domain-specific vocabulary to manage the complexity of the topic.

2.f. Provide a concluding statement or section that follows from and supports the information or explanation presented.

Cause

Bicycles are built using new, stronger materials.

Effect

New bicycles are faster, more comfortable, and lighter.

Using Transitions

The buffalo nearly became extinct in the nineteenth century. George Grinnell worked to save the animal and protect it for future generations. Today, several herds are thriving in the wild.	*Because* the buffalo nearly became extinct in the nineteenth century, George Grinnell worked to save the animal and protect it for future generations. *As a result,* several herds are thriving in the wild today.

Writers on Writing

Susan Vreeland On Showing Causes and Effects

> Susan Vreeland is the author of "Magdalena Looking" (p. 10).

My story "Crayon, 1955" is drawn from a time in my childhood when my great-grandfather, an artist, came to our house to die. What occurred there in that intense time was magical: He introduced me to his world of art. The experience narrated here was the cause of my lifelong interest in art, and resulted, ultimately, in writing *Girl in Hyacinth Blue*.

"Re-visioning . . . is a coaxing process."
—Susan Vreeland

Professional Model:

from "Crayon, 1955"

"Jenny," he said the next day. His voice scraped [like a Popsicle stick across the sidewalk]. "Let me teach you to paint."

I wasn't sure I wanted him to. The room smelled bad, but not just because of his . . . paints. Once Mom said Gramp's blood ran with turpentine, which I thought was what made his skin waxy and yellow.

Practicing a secret style of shallow breathing, I sat on the edge of the bed and he held my hand inside his [spidery one] while I held the long brush. He squeezed so tightly, directing where my hand should go, that his long yellow nails jabbed into my palm. I curled up my toes and kept quiet. [Like a miracle,] in front of me appeared an unrolled white flower with an orange finger inside. "There's nothing so cheerful as a calla lily," he said as we worked. "They grow tall and graceful just like you, and one day, they open themselves to the world."

In my revision, I inserted images that a young girl might think — the simile of a Popsicle stick, and the visual adjective "spidery."

To convey sharply the resulting change in Jenny, in my revision I added, "like a miracle," an exaggerated simile revealing her astonishment.

In fiction, cause and effect are subtle, sometimes only a suggestion. Jenny's negative reactions to her grandfather change when the painting resulting from his teaching pleases her.

Revising Strategies

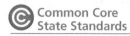
**Common Core
State Standards**

Writing

2.e. Establish and maintain a formal style and objective tone while attending to the norms and conventions of the discipline in which they are writing.

5. Develop and strengthen writing as needed by planning, revising, editing, rewriting, or trying a new approach, focusing on addressing what is most significant for a specific purpose and audience.

Language

1. Demonstrate command of the conventions of standard English grammar and usage when writing or speaking.

Look for careless repetition. Effective use of repetition helps to emphasize key ideas and create a memorable impact. Sloppy repetition, however, weakens your writing. Look for words that appear too often or too close together. Use a thesaurus to find words with related meanings or use a pronoun to replace a noun that you have used many times.

> **Too Much Repetition:** Bees *buzz* as a result of beating their wings *rapidly*. When an intruder approaches, bees beat their wings even more *rapidly*. As a result, *the bees' buzzing* grows louder.

> **More Effective:** Bees *buzz* as a result of beating their wings *rapidly*. When an intruder approaches, bees beat their wings *faster* and their *buzzing* grows louder.

Consider your style and tone. Use language that will further your purpose for writing. A formal style that is free of slang words and that creates a serious, objective tone is appropriate for cause-and-effect essays.

Color-code to identify related details. Each paragraph in your essay should have a strong, single focus. First, circle the topic sentence of each paragraph. If you cannot find a topic sentence, consider adding one. Then, underline sentences that contain details that support the topic of the paragraph.

Peer Review

After identifying topic sentences and supporting details, look at the sentences that are neither circled nor underlined. With a partner, discuss whether to rewrite or delete these sentences. You might also consider moving those sentences to a paragraph where they support the topic more effectively. After revising, explain your decisions to your partner.

Model: Revising to Strengthen Focus

Ice storms caused devastation throughout the Northeast. Power lines were downed by the heavy coating of ice, causing widespread electric outages. ~~People became bored without access to television.~~ Roads coated with ice became impassable.

> The writer deleted a sentence that offered useful information but did not relate to the topic of the paragraph.

Revising Pronoun-Antecedent Agreement

Antecedents are the nouns for which pronouns stand. A pronoun must agree with its antecedent in number, person, and gender.

Identifying Incorrect Pronoun-Antecedent Agreement In your writing, check each pronoun to make sure it agrees with its antecedent. Ask three things about the antecedent:

- *Number:* Is it singular or plural?
- *Person:* Is it first person (the one speaking), second person (the one being spoken to), or third person (the one spoken about)?
- *Gender:* Is it masculine, feminine, or neuter?

> Antecedent   Pronoun
> Marie Curie is known for her work with radium.
>
> Antecedent   Pronoun
> My father and I saw the experiment. We were amazed.

PH WRITING COACH
Further instruction and practice are available in *Prentice Hall Writing Coach*.

Special Problems With Agreement Use a plural personal pronoun with two or more antecedents joined by *and*.

Lewis and Clark described the expedition in their journal.

Use a singular personal pronoun with two or more antecedents joined by *or* or *nor*.

Neither Lewis nor Clark regretted his journey.

Fixing Agreement Errors To fix a pronoun and antecedent that do not agree, choose the pronoun that has the correct number, person, and gender.

1. Describe the number, person, and gender of the antecedent.
2. Choose a pronoun with the same number, person, and gender. Be sure you use the right pronoun case: nominative, objective, or possessive.

Grammar in Your Writing

Circle the pronouns in two paragraphs of your draft. Draw an arrow to the antecedent for each pronoun. Evaluate whether or not the pronoun and antecedent agree. Replace any incorrect pronouns.

Hurricane: Causes and Effects

Everyone dreads the hurricane season. When that time of year comes around, we all lock down and get ready for the harsh winds and power outages. The 2004 season started out with a bang. Large parts of the coast were torn apart as storms rolled in, one after another.

Causes of Hurricanes

Hurricanes form when weather patterns of different temperatures run into each other and start spinning. When a cold front out in the ocean, moving in one direction, comes in contact with a warm front moving in the opposite direction, winds start. These winds start moving in circular motions. As they spin, they pick up speed. These large areas of fast-moving winds generate tornadoes that pull water up into the storm. Hurricanes have high winds with tornadoes and carry large amounts of water.

When it starts, the storm is classified as a tropical depression. As it becomes stronger, it is called a tropical storm. If the wind speeds get high enough, the tropical storm is categorized as a hurricane.

Effects of Hurricanes: Damage to Property

When the storm hits land, it dumps all its water, and that is when it becomes the most destructive. Some of the water soaks into the ground, but often there is more water than the land can absorb. As a result, the water quickly runs off to lower areas. These run-offs are called flash floods. Flash floods can wash away land and possessions or destroy them by filling them with water. At the same time, hurricane winds can blow over trees and power lines. With the power out, repairs are hard to make quickly. This means power can be out for a week or longer. Hurricanes also bring lightning, which can cause fires in trees or houses.

Effects of Hurricanes: Damage to Business

During the late summer and fall of 2004, the state of Florida was hit by four major hurricanes: Charley, Frances, Ivan, and Jeanne. Each hurricane caused so much damage that it could not be repaired before the next storm hit. The damage was so bad that President Bush asked Congress for 7.1 billion dollars for repairs in Florida. Many people had to board up stores and wait in line for electric generators. In addition, relief workers were sent down to Florida to help deliver meals, water, and ice.

These storms not only caused trouble for the insurance companies, but also affected the citrus and tourism industries. The citrus growers in Florida lost about half of their grapefruit crop during Hurricane Frances. Tourism was also hurt because people do not want to travel into a disaster zone.

Conclusion

The hurricane season of 2004 was more intense than previous years. This is said to be from warm temperatures in the Atlantic Ocean and a decrease in wind shear. We hope that in the future we will better be able to predict and prepare for these hurricanes.

Andrew uses subheads to clearly organize the information. This paragraph explains what causes hurricanes.

Andrew breaks his discussion of the effects of hurricanes into two sections.

Andrew uses a specific detail to support his broader claims.

Editing and Proofreading

Review your draft to correct errors in grammar, spelling, capitalization, and punctuation.

Focus on usage errors. Check your writing for commonly confused words. Remember that *then* refers to time and *than* is used for comparisons. Use *since* to refer to a previous time, not to mean "because." If you are unsure about a word, consult a dictionary or usage guide.

Publishing and Presenting

Consider one of the following ways to share your writing:

Give a class presentation. Use your essay as the basis of a presentation. Use photographs, charts, maps, or diagrams to make your cause-and-effect relationships clear. Practice combining visuals with your writing, deciding when you will show each visual as you share the ideas from your essay.

Use e-mail. Share your writing electronically. Type your essay using word-processing software. Attach the file to an e-mail to a friend or relative. Save printouts of the essay and any responses in your writing portfolio.

Reflecting on Your Writing

Writer's Journal Jot down your answers to this question:
How did writing about your topic help you to understand it?

Rubric for Self-Assessment

Find evidence in your writing to address each category. Then, use the rating scale to grade your work.

Spiral Review
Earlier in the unit, you learned about **personal pronouns** (p. 150) and **relative pronouns** (p. 178). Review your draft carefully to be sure you have used these types of pronouns correctly.

Criteria	Rating Scale not very very				
Focus: How clearly do you identify the cause-and-effect relationship you explore?	1	2	3	4	5
Organization: How effectively do you organize your information?	1	2	3	4	5
Support/Elaboration: How strong are the details and examples you use as support?	1	2	3	4	5
Style: How effectively do you use transitions to connect your ideas?	1	2	3	4	5
Conventions: How correct is your grammar, especially your use of pronouns?	1	2	3	4	5

Vocabulary Workshop

Using a Dictionary and Thesaurus

Common Core
State Standards

Language
4. Determine or clarify the meaning of unknown and multiple-meaning words and phrases based on grades 9–10 reading and content, choosing flexibly from a range of strategies.
4.c. Consult general and specialized reference materials, both print and digital, to find the pronunciation of a word or determine or clarify its precise meaning, its part of speech, or its etymology.
4.d. Verify the preliminary determination of the meaning of a word or phrase.

A **dictionary** is an alphabetical listing of words. It gives definitions, parts of speech, etymologies, and more. Notice the information given in this dictionary entry.

Dictionary

Part of speech   Etymology

narrate (nar′āt; na āt′, nə-) *vt., vi.* **-rat′ed, -rat′ing** [< L *narratus*, pp. of *narrare*, to tell, akin to *gnarus*, acquainted with < IE **gnoro-* < base **gen-*, to KNOW] **1.** to tell (a story) in writing or speech **2.** to give an account of (happenings, etc.)

Definition

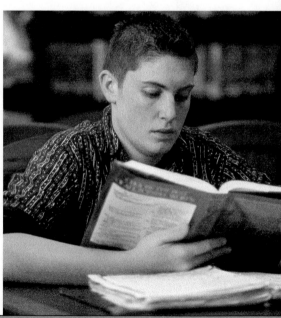

In addition to information about the work, a dictionary includes a guide to pronunciation. Most dictionaries provide a key to the symbols at the bottom of the page or in the front of the dictionary.

There are many kinds of dictionaries. One to know about is the *Oxford English Dictionary,* or OED. It tracks the usage of most English words over the past thousand years. The latest edition is available online and in a twenty-volume set. It is a very useful tool if you are studying the etymology, or origin, of a word in English.

A **thesaurus** is a reference book that lists synonyms, or words with similar meanings. You can use a thesaurus to increase your vocabulary or to find alternative words to express your meaning. Here's an example of a thesaurus entry:

Thesaurus

entertainer *n.* **1.** entertainer, performer, artist, dancer, hoofer **2.** actor, actress, player, thespian, mime, villain, character *v.* entertain, act, perform, dramatize, dance, play

Both dictionaries and thesauruses are available in print, in computer programs, and on the Internet.

Practice A Look up each word in a thesaurus. For each, write two words that have almost the same meaning.

1. disapproval
2. patience
3. talk

4. repeatedly
5. remember
6. joke

Practice B Use a dictionary to answer questions 1–7 and a thesaurus to respond to questions 8 and 9.

1. Some words have more than one dictionary definition. **(a)** What is the definition of *idle* in the following sentence? *Eliot sat idle all afternoon.* **(b)** What is another definition for this word?

2. **(a)** What is the adverb form of the word *sleepy*? **(b)** How would you use it in a sentence?

3. What is the meaning of the word *cuff* when used as a verb?

4. If the situation is *fraught* with danger, is it safe? Explain.

5. Which dictionary definition is correct for *sorry* as it is used the following sentence? *In Aunt Sarah's opinion, I was one sorry entertainer.*

6. Is it possible to use the word *revise* as a noun? Explain.

7. How many definitions does your dictionary give for the word *frost*?

8. Find three synonyms for *deadly.*

9. Rewrite this sentence twice using synonyms for *genuine*: *The painting turned out to be a genuine Van Gogh.*

PHLit Online!
www.PHLitOnline.com

- Illustrated vocabulary words
- Interactive vocabulary games
- Vocabulary flashcards

Activity Create a note card like the one shown for each of these words:

allay   unkempt   linear   quandary   naive

| Word: |
| Definition: |
| Pronunciation: |
| Sentence: |

Comprehension and Collaboration

Look up the following words in a dictionary or reliable online source. Find the earliest usage of each word and its definition. Then, locate a more modern definition of each word. Talk with a group about how the meaning of each word has changed over the years. Is the original meaning still used?

flaunt
cab
fragile
vandal

Read your sentences aloud. Then, in a group, trade cards and read each other's sentences. Check one another's pronunciation and usage. Refer to a dictionary if you disagree on the pronunciation or word meaning.

Communications Workshop

Analyzing Media Messages

Some television, radio, and Internet sources are truthful, thorough, and objective. Others offer information that is inaccurate, incomplete, or reported in a biased way. To evaluate media messages, stay alert and analyze claims critically.

Learn the Skills

Use the strategies to complete the activity on page 211.

Evaluate the content of the message. Carefully consider and evaluate what the message says.

- **Look for support for claims.** Note facts, statistics, quotations, and other evidence. If no support is provided, decide whether you have any reason to accept the claims in the message.

- **Consider bias.** People quoted in media may present biased, or one-sided, evidence. Consider the reasons a source might have to favor one version of events over another or to exaggerate or distort evidence. Note whether opposing viewpoints have been left out and why a speaker might omit them.

- **Look for faulty reasoning.** Ask yourself whether the claims made are contradictory or vague. Look for logical fallacies, such as insisting something is correct because most people think so.

- **Look for illegal statements.** There are laws to protect people from libel (false written statements) and slander (false spoken statements). Be alert to accusations that are not supported by facts.

Evaluate the style of the message. Once you understand a message's content, consider its delivery. Some media techniques sway viewers or misrepresent ideas.

- **Be aware of stereotypes.** Watch for stereotypes, or oversimplified ideas about a group of people. Many stereotypes are negative images based on race, gender, age, or role.

- **Detect cultural assumptions.** Media presentations can reflect basic assumptions about what is important or good. Think about whether you agree with such value judgments.

- **Be alert to charged or emotional language.** Listen for words and phrases that are meant to manipulate or affect your emotions.

- **Consider the impact of the medium.** Background music, images, and graphics may capture your attention. If they have been added only to stir emotions, they are not evidence.

Common Core State Standards

Speaking and Listening
3. Evaluate a speaker's point of view, reasoning, and use of evidence and rhetoric, identifying any fallacious reasoning or exaggerated or distorted evidence.

Practice the Skills

ⓒ **Presentation of Knowledge and Ideas** Use what you have learned in this workshop to perform the following task.

ACTIVITY: Analyze a Media Message

Using the Analysis Checklist as a guide, analyze a television newscast or advertisement. Then, share your analysis in a group discussion. Follow these steps.

- Watch the newscast or advertisement multiple times and observe carefully.
- As you watch, refer often to the Analysis Checklist.
- Take notes on your observations.
- Use your checklist and notes to present your ideas to a small group of classmates.

Analysis Checklist

Rating System

Poor   Excellent

1   2   3   4   5

Message Purpose

What is the main purpose of the message?

_____

_____

Use of Facts and Evidence

_____ Relevant Support   _____ Complete Support

_____ Unbiased Support   _____ Sound Reasoning

Message Style

_____ Relevance of Graphics or Images   _____ Avoidance of Charged Language

_____ Relevance of Music   _____ Avoidance of Stereotypes

Conclusions

Was the message trustworthy?

_____

_____

Did the message fulfill its purpose?

_____

_____

ⓒ **Comprehension and Collaboration** After you present your analysis of the media message to a small group, lead a brief discussion. Ask group members whether your observations are similar to or different from theirs. Make sure that everyone participates in the discussion.

Cumulative Review

I. Reading Literature/Informational Text

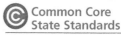

Common Core
State Standards

RL.9-10.1, RL.9-10.3, RL.9-10.4, RL.9-10.5; W.9-10.2
[For the full wording of the standards, see the standards chart in the front of your textbook.]

Directions: *Read the passage. Then, answer each question that follows.*

The Mummy's Curse

Death Shall Come on Swift Wings to Him Who Disturbs the Peace of the King.

These words, supposedly inscribed on the tomb of Egyptian King Tutankhamen, did not <u>deter</u> the intrepid English archaeologist Howard Carter. After years of searching, in 1922 Carter located King Tut's tomb. Archaeologists had long known that pharaohs were mummified at death and buried with riches to accompany them to the afterworld. To protect them from grave robbers, tombs were sealed with stone blocks or contained false passages. In some cases, the tombs were guarded by a curse.

After visiting England, Carter brought a canary back to Egypt. When Carter returned to his house after locating the tomb, his servant met him holding the dead bird. The servant claimed the bird had been killed by a cobra, a symbol of ancient Egyptian royalty, because Carter had violated the tomb. Carter ignored the warning. Upon the arrival in Egypt of his wealthy backer, Lord Carnarvon, Carter prepared to open the tomb.

Lord Carnarvon watched as Carter drilled a hole in the tomb door. Carter leaned through the hole, a candle in his hand.

"Can you see anything?" asked Lord Carnarvon.

"Yes, wonderful things," answered Carter.

The tomb contained a treasure trove, including a stone sarcophagus in which rested three gold coffins, nested inside each other. The innermost coffin held the mummy of King Tut. Everyone was excited about the find, and no one considered the curse. According to rumor, Carter had found a tablet inscribed with the curse, but hid it from his superstitious workers.

Shortly after the tomb was opened, the curse struck. Lord Carnarvon died from an infected bug bite. When King Tut's mummy was unwrapped, it had a wound in the same position as Lord Carnarvon's bug bite.

Within ten years, eleven people related to the discovery of King Tut's tomb had died of unnatural causes. Newspapers sensationalized the "mummy's curse" and claimed there were as many as twenty-one victims of the curse. Was this the hype of a sensationalist press, or did the curse exist?

Later investigation showed that of twenty-two people present when the tomb was opened, only six had died by 1934. Carter himself lived to the age of sixty-six, dying of natural causes.

1. Which event in the selection occurs first?

   A. The canary dies.
   B. King Tut's tomb is discovered.
   C. Lord Carnarvon dies.
   D. King Tut's mummy is unwrapped.

2. Which event is an example of **foreshadowing?**

   A. the death of Lord Carnarvon
   B. the arrival of Lord Carnarvon in Egypt
   C. the discovery of King Tut's tomb
   D. the death of the canary

3. Which of the following represents an **internal conflict** of a character?

   A. The servant fears the Mummy's curse.
   B. Carter dismisses the superstition.
   C. Lord Carnarvon pays for Carter's work.
   D. The reporters tell stories about the "curse."

4. **Vocabulary** Which word is closest in meaning to the underlined word *deter*?

   A. encourage
   B. destroy
   C. stop
   D. include

5. Which of the following best states the **author's purpose?**

   A. to persuade readers that the "mummy's curse" may have been exaggerated
   B. to persuade readers to study archaeology
   C. to entertain readers with a comic tale
   D. to inform readers about King Tut

6. Which of the following best describes the **author's perspective?**

   A. The author believes in the "mummy's curse."
   B. The author supports archaeological studies.
   C. The author views the story objectively.
   D. The author wants tombs to be undisturbed.

7. Which of the following is an example of **irony?**

   A. Carter eventually locates King Tut's tomb after years of searching.
   B. Lord Carnarvon attends the tomb's opening.
   C. The canary dies when the tomb is found.
   D. The mummy has a wound in the same location as Lord Carnarvon's bug bite.

8. Which of these sentences *best* increases the tension in the selection?

   A. Carter leaned through the hole, a candle in his hand.
   B. After years of searching, in 1922 Carter located King Tut's tomb.
   C. On one of his trips to England, Carter had brought a yellow canary back to Egypt.
   D. Carter himself lived to the age of sixty-six, dying of natural causes.

9. Which element common to fiction is *not* present in this nonfiction piece?

   A. ordered events
   B. dialogue
   C. suspense
   D. exposition

 Timed Writing

10. In a well-developed and logically organized essay, **explain** how the syntax and diction in the opening quotation reinforce the mysteriousness of the curse as described in the passage. **Support** your answer with details from the passage. [20 minutes]

 GO ON

II. Reading Informational Text

Directions: *Read the passage. Then, answer each question that follows.*

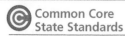 Common Core
State Standards

RI.9-10.3; L.9-10.1, L.9-10.3
[For the full wording of the standards, see the standards chart in the front of your textbook.]

The Ghost Crab

Have you ever taken an evening stroll on the beach and seen a small ghostly figure scurry across the sand and suddenly disappear? This was most probably a ghost crab, or *Ocypode quadrata,* also known as a sand crab. The name *ghost crab* comes from the creature's ability to blend in with the sand and to suddenly appear out of and disappear into the sand.

Habitat

Ghost crabs live on the sandy beaches along the eastern coastline of North America and South America. They live in burrows that can be as deep as three feet. Older crabs live farther from the water than younger crabs.

Appearance

Their body shell, or carapace, is usually square and can be up to two inches wide. They are gray or yellow-white on their top surface, but their underside is white. Ghost crabs have white or lavender pincers, are uneven in size, and have hairy legs. Their eyes, which sit atop long stalks, sense changes in light.

Diet

Ghost crabs are <u>omnivorous</u>. They will eat clams, insects, other crabs, and vegetation, as well as plant and animal detritus that washes up on the shore. They feed at night and burrow into the sand during daylight hours.

The following list shows some interesting facts about ghost crabs.
• At night, they face the moon when it is full.
• They can run up to ten miles per hour.
• At night, they wash water over their gills for oxygen.
• Their "periscope" eyes can see 360°.

1. If you wanted to draw a ghost crab, which feature in the text would help you locate the most useful information?

   A. the title
   B. the subhead *Habitat*
   C. the bulleted list
   D. the subhead *Appearance*

2. Which two ideas does the author connect?

   A. ghost crabs are pale / they seem to disappear
   B. crabs eat many things / they burrow
   C. crabs have pincers / they survive
   D. ghost crabs are fast / they feed at night

III. Writing and Language Conventions

Directions: *Read the passage. Then, answer each question that follows.*

(1) My dad and I had looked forward to our camping trip in the mountains for weeks. (2) Charlie, the family's black Labrador pup, was going along. (3) It was our first visit to the mountains.

(4) Our campsite was thickly lined with trees. (5) I inhaled the fresh mountain air, and, grabbing my fishing tackle, I strolled down the path to the lake with my dog. (6) The dog ran after me, ready for fun.

(7) "Watch out for bears, Joe," Dad called.

(8) "Okay!" I said, laughing. (9) As I rounded a bend, though, right in front of me was a small black bear ambling along the path. (10) Charlie's fur bristled. (11) The bear stopped cold, staring at me. (12) I froze, holding my breath until the bear finally turned and hurried off down the path.

(13) I've been camping a lot since then, but I'll never forget the dramatic events of that first trip.

1. Which of the following revisions to sentence 10 enhances the story's **conflict** and increases suspense?

  A. Charlie's black fur bristled.
  B. Charlie's fur bristled, his senses on full predator alert.
  C. Charlie stopped and his fur bristled.
  D. Charlie, his fur bristling, stopped suddenly.

2. How would you revise the **dialogue** in sentence 8 to better convey Joe's carefree attitude?

  A. "Yeah, sure!" I said, laughing.
  B. "Do you really think so?" I asked.
  C. "Thanks for the reminder!" I said.
  D. "Stop fooling around!" I cried.

3. What is the *best* way to add **sensory description** to sentence 4?

  A. Replace "trees" with "fragrant green pines."
  B. Replace "lined" with "wooded."
  C. Replace "campsite" with "camping area."
  D. Replace "Our campsite" with "Our chosen campsite."

4. Which **proper noun** should replace the **common noun** in sentence 6 for clarity?

  A. Joe
  B. Charlie
  C. Dad
  D. trail

5. Which **abstract noun** should be substituted for the phrase "the dramatic events" in sentence 13 in order to use precise language?

  A. joy
  B. boredom
  C. excitement
  D. melancholy

6. What is the correct way to write the **possessive noun** in sentence 2?

  A. the families black Labrador pup
  B. the familys' black Labrador pup
  C. the families' black Labrador pup
  D. Leave as is.

Performance Tasks

Directions: *Follow the instructions to complete the tasks below as required by your teacher.*

As you work on each task, incorporate both general academic vocabulary and literary terms you learned in this unit.

Ⓒ **Common Core State Standards**

RL.9-10.2, RL.9-10.4, RL.9-10.5; RI.9-10.2, RI.9-10.4, RI.9-10.6; W.9-10.2, W.9-10.9.a, W.9-10.9.b; SL.9-10.1.a–b, SL.9-10.4, SL.9-10.5; L.9-10.1, L.9-10.2

[For the full wording of the standards, see the standards chart in the front of your textbook.]

Writing

Ⓒ Task 1: Literature [RL.9-10.2; W.9-10.2, W.9-10.9.a]

Analyze Theme

Write an essay in which you analyze the development of the theme of a literary work from this unit.

- Choose a story from this unit that has a theme that you find interesting or compelling. Explain your choice.

- Provide a summary of the work, briefly describing the main characters and the story's key events.

- State the theme of the story in a sentence or two. Identify the theme as either stated or implied and provide justification for your decision.

- Explain how the theme is introduced in the story. For example, theme might first be suggested in dialogue or in descriptions of a character's inner struggles.

- Analyze the development of the theme by citing and explaining key details that shape the theme over the course of the story.

- Distinguish between significant details that contribute to the theme and minor or incidental details that do not shape the theme.

- Use all language conventions correctly, including capitalization of proper nouns.

Ⓒ Task 2: Informational Text [RI.9-10.2; W.9-10.2, W.9-10.9.b; L.9-10.1]

Analyze Central Idea

Write an essay in which you analyze the development of the central idea in a nonfiction work from this unit.

- Provide a brief summary of the work, explaining the central idea and the key points that support it.

- Explain how the author first presents the central idea. For example, it may be stated directly or implied though details.

- Analyze how the author supports and develops the central idea throughout the work. Cite key details from the work in your analysis and show how they help to deepen readers' understanding of the central idea.

- In your essay, be sure to follow the conventions of standard English grammar and usage.

Ⓒ Task 3: Informational Text [RI.9-10.6; W.9-10.9.b; L.9-10.1]

Analyze Author's Purpose

Write an essay in which you analyze an author's primary purpose in a nonfiction work from this unit.

- Select a nonfiction work from this unit, either functional text or literary nonfiction, in which the author's purpose is advanced by his or her style.

- State what you believe is the primary purpose of the text: to inform, to persuade, or to entertain. Then, discuss how the author's style—his or her special use of language—helps to achieve that purpose.

- Identify a specific purpose that the author is trying to achieve. Connect the author's style to the specific purpose by evaluating the effectiveness of the style he or she chose.

- Draw a conclusion about the relationship between the author's style and purpose.

- Establish and maintain a formal style in your essay.

- Be sure to follow the conventions of standard English grammar and usage. Check for correct pronoun-antecedent agreement.

Speaking and Listening

@ **Task 4: Informational Text** [RI.9-10.6; SL.9-10.4]

Analyze Author's Point of View

Prepare an oral presentation in which you analyze an author's point of view, or perspective, in a nonfiction work from this unit.

- Select a work of nonfiction from this unit, and determine the author's point of view in the work.

- Explain how the author's point of view is conveyed. Support your ideas with evidence from the text.

- Present your analysis logically, so that listeners are able to follow your reasoning.

- Organize and develop your presentation in ways that are appropriate to your purpose, audience, and task.

@ **Task 5: Literature/Informational Text** [RL.9-10.4; RI.9-10.4; SL.9-10.1.a–b]

Analyze an Author's Style

Lead a small group discussion analyzing the style of a work from this unit.

- Prepare for the discussion by analyzing the author's diction and syntax—his or her word choices and sentence structures. Consider the author's use of rhetorical devices or figurative language. Determine how these choices help to create the author's style.

- Create a list of discussion points, including specific questions you plan to ask. For example, to arrive at a description of the style of this work, you might ask whether the author's word choice is formal or informal, simple or sophisticated, or old-fashioned or contemporary. You might also discuss the function of style in the work (i.e., what style accomplishes), and how important style is to the overall meaning of the work.

- Make sure you guide the group to provide examples from the text to illustrate each point.

- As you lead the discussion, actively incorporate group members into the discussion. Clarify and challenge ideas while maintaining a collegial tone.

- At the conclusion of your discussion, review the key ideas that were expressed.

@ **Task 6: Literature** [RL.9-10.5; SL.9-10.5]

Analyze Cause and Effect

Prepare and deliver an oral presentation in which you analyze cause and effect in a literary work from this unit.

- Select a work from this unit in which cause and effect is important to the plot. Identify the specific cause (or causes) and effect (or effects).

- Describe how cause and effect fits within the structure of the text, how it affects the development of the plot, and how it contributes to the overall theme of the work.

- Present your analysis in a clear and logical way. Include supporting evidence from the text to validate your points.

- Incorporate digital media, such as a slide show, to help communicate your ideas. You may also create a poster or a handout to add interest to your presentation.

- When you are speaking, use adequate volume and clear pronunciation so that your audience can hear you easily.

THE BIG ?

Is there a difference between reality and truth?

At the beginning of Unit 1, you participated in a discussion of the Big Question. Now that you have completed the unit, write a response to the question. Discuss how your initial ideas have deepened or changed. Support your response with at least one example from literature and one example from an additional subject area or your own life. Use Big Question vocabulary words (see p. 3) in your response.

Featured Titles

In this unit, you have read a variety of fiction and literary nonfiction. Continue to read on your own. Select books that you enjoy, but challenge yourself to explore new topics, new authors, and works of increasing depth and complexity. The titles suggested below will help you get started.

Literature

Lord of the Flies
by William Golding
Berkley Publishing Group, 1954

In this **novel,** a plane crash leaves a group of boys stranded without adults on a deserted island, and life feels like an exotic vacation. A dark influence soon casts a shadow over the young survivors, and life turns dangerous and deadly. The reality that the boys face may challenge your ideas about human nature.

Revolutionary Petunias and Other Poems
by Alice Walker   EXEMPLAR TEXT

Walker's collection of **poetry** explores the similarities between love and revolution—both in terms of the devastation each can cause and the possibilities for dramatic breakthrough.

41 Stories
by O. Henry   EXEMPLAR TEXT

This collection of O. Henry's finest **short stories** whisks readers from a bustling city to a seedy saloon to a prison shoe shop. Wherever O. Henry takes you, you will find yourself discovering that reality and truth may not always be as they appear.

Animal Farm
by George Orwell

With idealism and stirring slogans, mistreated animals take over a farm and try to create a paradise of progress, justice, and equality. As the **novel** progresses, however, the reality of the situation points to far different truths. A hard-to-categorize mix of fable and political satire, this book is a bullet aimed squarely at totalitarianism in all its forms.

Rhinoceros
by Eugene Ionesco   EXEMPLAR TEXT

In this absurdist **drama,** Ionesco imagines a situation in which all the residents of a small French town slowly turn into rhinoceroses. This play is admired for its revealing look at the perils of conformity and the destructive nature of extremist ideologies.

Informational Texts

The Illustrated Book of Great Composers
by Wendy Thompson   EXEMPLAR TEXT

Herself a musician, Wendy Thompson has written a **reference book** that describes the lives and accomplishments of the most influential composers of classical music.

Euclid's Elements
by Euclid
Translated by Thomas L. Heath   EXEMPLAR TEXT

When the mathematician Euclid wrote this **treatise** in the third century B.C., he might as well have been planning a modern high school geometry course. Geometry students still learn the same axioms and proofs that Euclid proposed so many centuries ago. This translation includes all thirteen books written by this Greek "Father of Geometry."

Before Columbus: The Americas of 1491
by Charles C. Mann
Atheneum, 2009   EXEMPLAR TEXT

In this **nonfiction** book, the author vividly describes life in the Americas before Columbus. He tells how natives accomplished such feats as producing genetically engineered corn and building enormous pyramids.

Learning Big Question Vocabulary

Acquire and Use Academic Vocabulary Academic vocabulary is the language you encounter and use in classroom discussion, in textbooks, and on standardized tests. It is the language that helps to express and convey academic ideas. Review the definitions of these academic vocabulary words that relate to this unit's Big Question.

---

debate (dē bāt´) *v.* argue or discuss

motive (mōt´ iv) *n.* something that causes a person to act a certain way

oppose (ə pōz´) *v.* set against

radical (rad´ i kəl) *adj.* tending to make extreme changes in existing views, conditions, or institutions

resolve (ri zälv´, -zôlv) *v.* reach a conclusion or decision

unify (yo͞o´ nə fi´) *v.* combine into one

Use these words as you complete Big Question activities in this unit that involve reading, writing, speaking, and listening. Because they are related to the themes of progress and conflict, they will help you to express your thoughts effectively.

Gather Vocabulary Knowledge Additional Big Question words are listed below. Categorize the words by deciding whether you know each one well, know it a little bit, or do not know it at all.

---

adversity	concession	progress
change	confrontation	reconciliation
compromise	negotiate	struggle

Then, do the following:

1. Write the definitions of the words you know.

2. Using a print or an online dictionary, look up the meanings of the words you do not know. Then, write the meanings.

3. If you think you know a word's meaning, write it down. Consult a dictionary to confirm the word's meaning. Revise your definition if necessary.

4. If you are not sure of a word's meaning, consult a dictionary. Then, record the meaning.

5. Use all the words in a brief paragraph about progress.

Elements of a Short Story

A short story is a brief work of fiction. Like all fiction, short stories focus on characters in conflict.

A **short story** is a brief work of fiction that can usually be read in one sitting. Because short stories are compact, writers usually limit the number of characters, the range of settings, and the scope of the action.

Characters are the personalities that take part in the action of a story. An author portrays characters by using a set of techniques that are collectively called **characterization**, or **character development**. Descriptive details, dialogue, and other literary elements help readers understand characters' qualities, including their feelings, thoughts, motivations, and behavior.

The characters in a story interact within a **setting**, or a particular time and place. In some stories, the setting is simply a backdrop for the action. In other stories, the setting exerts a strong influence on characters, shaping their personalities and motivations.

In every story, characters face a **conflict** that sets the plot in motion. The **plot** is the sequence of interrelated events that make up the action. As events unfold, the plot develops to a **climax,** or high point of tension. The tension subsides as the plot reaches the **resolution,** when events come to a close.

All of the elements of a short story work together to suggest a theme, or central insight about life. A **theme** is not a summary of a story's events. Instead, it is a generalization about what the events mean. A theme may be stated explicitly, but more often it is implied. The reader must then examine the relationships among the story's elements to arrive at an interpretation of its theme.

All of the elements of a short story contribute to its deeper meaning, or theme.

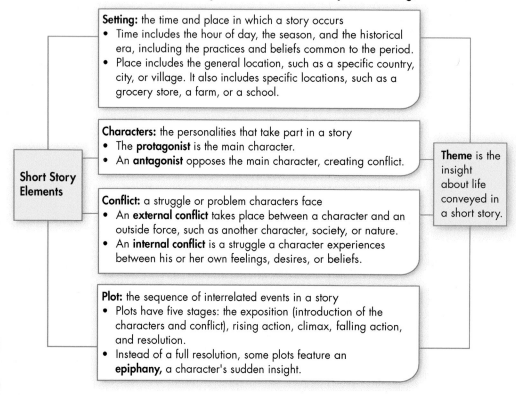

Genre and Structure A **genre** is a classification of works of fiction that share certain elements, such as character types, moods, and common plot patterns. Genres include mysteries, fantasy, and realistic fiction. Short stories appear in all fictional genres, from traditional tales with formulaic plots, to online experiments in which the reader decides who the characters are and what they do.

A story's **structure** is the way in which the events of the plot unfold and the reader learns about characters and situations. A story's structure is shaped, in part, by the story's genre. For example, a mystery story is usually structured around an intriguing problem and a protagonist who seeks to solve it. The plot usually involves many twists and turns that finally arrive at a logical, but surprising, resolution. A mystery writer is not obliged to follow that pattern and may break from the genre conventions. Some mystery writers, for instance, are as interested in relating complex characters as they are in relating complex plots. In general, however, a story's genre helps shape its structure.

In This Section

Elements of a Short Story

Analyzing Characters in a Short Story

Analyzing Structure in a Short Story

Close Read: Character Development and Story Structure
• Model Text
• Practice Text

After You Read

Common Core State Standards

RL.9-10.3, RL.9-10.5
[For the full wording of the standards, see the standards chart in the front of your textbook.]

Common Genres of Fiction	
Realistic	A story that portrays believable characters facing a true-to-life conflict in a realistic setting
	Example: A high-school athlete changes her priorities in life after an injury keeps her from playing sports.
Speculative (Science Fiction)	A story, often set in the future, in which actual or imagined science and technology play a central role
	Example: In the year 2090, humans declare war on androids after the machines attempt to overthrow the government.
Historical	A story set in the past that combines fictional characters with historical figures or events
	Example: A young man assists the Wright brothers at Kitty Hawk as they test various versions of their airplane.
Humorous	A story with comical characters and situations intended to amuse readers
	Example: Home alone, a bloodhound and a terrier join forces to track down and open a hidden bag of pet food.
Parody	An imitation of another story or writing style, intended to comment on or poke fun at the original
	Example: A retelling of a fairy tale in which characters are terrified, rather than delighted, by magical events.

Analyzing Characters in a Short Story

Complex characters are at the heart of most short stories.

Common Core
State Standards

Reading Literature 3. Analyze how complex characters develop over the course of a text, interact with other characters, and advance the plot or develop the theme.

Types of Characters Characters provide the moving force in most short stories. Their conflicts set off the plot and their actions and reactions keep it going. Characters can be classified according to the manner in which they are portrayed.

Types of Characters	
Flat, or Stock, Characters	Have just one or two traits
Round, or Complex, Characters	Have many traits, including both faults and virtues
Static Characters	Do not change during the story
Dynamic Characters	Change as a result of the experiences they undergo in the story

The main characters in most literary fiction are complex because they exhibit many different traits. Like real human beings, their personalities cannot be summed up in a word or simple phrase. However, complex characters may or may not be dynamic. For example, a complex character who undergoes a crisis may not change as a result.

All characters have **motivations,** or reasons for feeling and behaving as they do. Complex characters may have multiple or even **conflicting motivations.** For example, a character who desires to be true to his or her values may also want to fit in with a clique. Those two motivations conflict. They may cause the character to be confused, or to take actions that complicate his or her situation in unexpected ways.

Characterization is the method by which an author develops a character. In **direct characterization,** the **narrator**—the character or voice telling the story—directly states a character's traits.

> **Example: Direct Characterization**
> Lauren was always the first to volunteer to help, but then she never stopped reminding everyone about her good deeds. That was one of her greatest faults.

In **indirect characterization,** the narrator reveals a character's personality by describing a character's appearance, feelings, behavior, and thoughts, as well as his or her interactions with other characters. **Dialogue,** the words that characters speak, is one of the key tools an author uses to reveal character traits. The ways in which characters speak—their use of sarcasm, irony, body language, or hidden meanings—can be just as revealing as the statements they make. In the example shown below, dialogue reveals what the characters are like as well as what they think.

> **Example: Indirect Characterization**
> Matt stared at the huge pile of envelopes that he had to stuff for the fundraiser. "How will we finish in time?" he asked wearily.
>
> "Lauren said she'd be here to help," LaTise mumbled, rolling her eyes.
>
> Sarah added, "Then she'll spend the entire fundraiser announcing how she did it all by herself."
>
> Just then, Lauren walked in. "Never fear! I'm here to save the day!"

Analyzing Structure in a Short Story

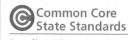 **Common Core State Standards**

Reading Literature 5.
Analyze how an author's choices concerning how to structure a text, order events within it, and manipulate time create such effects as mystery, tension, or surprise.

Story structure is the way in which events, characters, and situations are introduced and developed.

The foundation of a story's **structure** is its plot—the series of interrelated events that unfold as characters face a conflict. The order in which the author arranges events is an important part of that structure. **Chronological order,** in which events unfold in a sequence from beginning to end, is the most common structure. However, authors may vary that basic structure to create effects such as mystery, tension, or surprise. Consider the following narrative techniques.

Flashbacks interrupt the flow of a chronological sequence to describe earlier events. Flashbacks may take the form of a memory, a dream, or an actual relocation of the story into the past. Flashbacks may provide information about a character's past or insights into his or her motivations.

Flashback in a Chronological Sequence

Sequence	Event
First	Felicia waits for Nathan.
Second	Nathan arrives.
Third	They go to dinner.
Fourth	At dinner, Nathan asks Felicia to marry him.
Flashback	Felicia recalls the first time they met.
Fifth	Felicia says yes.

Parallel plots occur when an author develops two distinct storylines, with two sets of characters, in a single work. Parallel plots often explore similar conflicts among different groups of people. Often, these separate storylines ultimately join into a single, unified tale.

Pacing, the speed or rhythm of the writing, influences how readers experience a story. Slow pacing can create tension or suspense by delaying an anticipated event. Authors may slow the pace of events by adding detailed descriptions of the action or of a character's thoughts and feelings.

> **Example: Slow Pacing**
> Luis nervously stared at the clock. The hand trudged from one second to the next as though it were moving through mud. He counted along with each tick, dragging out the name of each number to match the sluggish twitches of the hand. "One . . . two . . . three . . ."
>
> His heart slowed, but his mind raced. If Jim arrived before the 3 o'clock train and found him, the whole scheme would fall apart.

By contrast, fast pacing creates a sense of energy and excitement. Short and even fragmented sentences and rapid cutting from detail to detail increase the story's pace.

> **Example: Fast Pacing**
> Luis stared at the clock. 2:55.
>
> He peered down the platform. A man in a suit was walking toward him. 2:56. He looked down the track. No train.
>
> The man drew closer. Was it Jim?
>
> Luis's heart pounded in his ears. 2:57. If Jim found him first the scheme would fail.
>
> The man was getting closer. Luis pulled down his hat. 2:58. Was that a train whistle? Time was running out.

Close Read: Character Development and Story Structure

Characters develop as a story progresses. Narrative structure organizes events and affects the reader's experience.

Complex, believable characters are the lifeblood of good stories. A character's history, perceptions, desires, and fears affect how he or she reacts to conflict. These reactions, in turn, move the plot forward and develop the theme. The story's structure helps the reader follow the unfolding of events and grasp the connections among details. As you read, look for clues to character and notice structural elements that organize the story.

Character Development	Structural Elements
Characterization Writers use many different techniques to reveal what characters are like. As you read, notice • direct statements that explain characters; • details that show characters' reactions to one another; • descriptions of how characters look, think, feel, and behave; • dialogue that indicates characters' attitudes, beliefs, or other qualities.	**Setting** The setting may be a backdrop or an active influence on the action. As you read, notice • details that describe the physical setting; • details that show values, beliefs, traditions, and cultural practices typical of the setting; • problems caused by the setting.
Characters' Motivations Characters' motivations, an aspect of characterization, play an essential role in a story. As you read, look for details that show • the reasons that characters feel, think, and behave as they do; • any opposing motivations that create internal conflict.	**Conflict and Plot** Conflict drives all plots. As you read, notice • the conflict that starts the story; • ways in which that conflict intensifies and is finally resolved; • the order of events; • causal relationships, or the way in which one event leads to another; • techniques that manipulate time, such as flashbacks or pacing.
Dynamic Characters Some characters are dynamic and change as a result of the events of a story, whereas others are static and do not. As you read, consider • how characters think, feel, and behave at the beginning of a story; • whether characters change by the end of the story; • what kinds of changes characters experience.	**Narrative Effects** Structural elements may create specific emotions in the reader. As you read, consider • emotional high points, such as suspense or excitement, and the story events that evoke these emotions; • changes in pacing and their effects.

Model

About the Text Langston Hughes (1902–1967) was a distinguished and prolific author who first came to prominence during the Harlem Renaissance of the 1920s. Although Hughes is probably best known as a poet, he was also a playwright, a song lyricist, a novelist, and an author of short stories.

In the following short story, Hughes depicts an unexpected meeting between former sweethearts in a New York City park. In little more than 400 words, Hughes vividly portrays a few moments in time—and a lifetime of regret.

"Early Autumn" by Langston Hughes

When Bill was very young, they had been in love. Many nights they had spent walking, talking together. Then something not very important had come between them, and they didn't speak. Impulsively, she had married a man she thought she loved. Bill went away, bitter about women.

Yesterday, walking across Washington Square, she saw him for the first time in years.

"Bill Walker," she said.

He stopped. At first he did not recognize her, to him she looked so old.

"Mary! Where did you come from?"

Unconsciously, she lifted her face as though wanting a kiss, but he held out his hand. She took it.

"I live in New York now," she said.

"Oh"—smiling politely. Then a little frown came quickly between his eyes.

"Always wondered what happened to you, Bill."

"I'm a lawyer. Nice firm, way downtown."

"Married yet?"

"Sure. Two kids."

"Oh," she said.

Setting The title suggests that the season of the year is important to the story's meaning. Autumn is a time of endings. The fact that the title says autumn comes early suggests that an ending comes too soon.

Conflict and Plot The first paragraph provides compact exposition that rapidly fills readers in on the characters' shared past and likely conflict.

Indirect Characterization Details emphasize the two characters' differences. Mary recognizes Bill, but she looks "so old" to him; she seems to seek a kiss, but he offers only his hand. Bill seems to have moved on, while Mary lingers over memories of this lost love.

Model continued

Dynamic Characters Mary has undergone many changes since she knew Bill. She is married, has children, and looks considerably older.

Conflict and Plot The chronological order is interrupted by a brief memory that provides important information about differences in the characters' ages.

Narrative Effects Autumn and dusk both represent endings. The fragmented description of the setting creates a broken and melancholy effect.

Motivation The detail about her son's name reinforces all the preceding details that suggest Mary still loves Bill. For Mary, their relationship did, indeed, end too early.

A great many people went past them through the park. People they didn't know. It was late afternoon. Nearly sunset. Cold.

"And your husband?" he asked her.

"We have three children. I work in the bursar's office at Columbia."

"You're looking very . . ." (he wanted to say *old*) ". . .well," he said.

She understood. Under the trees in Washington Square, she found herself desperately reaching back into the past. She had been older than he then in Ohio. Now she was not young at all. Bill was still young.

"We live on Central Park West," she said. "Come and see us sometime."

"Sure," he replied. "You and your husband must have dinner with my family some night. Any night. Lucille and I'd love to have you."

The leaves fell slowly from the trees in the Square. Fell without wind. Autumn dusk. She felt a little sick.

"We'd love it," she answered.

"You ought to see my kids." He grinned.

Suddenly the lights came on up the whole length of Fifth Avenue, chains of misty brilliance in the blue air.

"There's my bus," she said.

He held out his hand, "Good-bye."

"When . . ." she wanted to say, but the bus was ready to pull off. The lights on the avenue blurred, twinkled, blurred. And she was afraid to open her mouth as she entered the bus. Afraid it would be impossible to utter a word.

Suddenly she shrieked very loudly, "Good-bye!" But the bus door had closed.

The bus started. People came between them outside, people crossing the street, people they didn't know. Space and people. She lost sight of Bill. Then she remembered she had forgotten to give him her address—or to ask him for his—or tell him that her youngest boy was named Bill, too.

Independent Practice

About the Text C. J. Cherryh is known for her space opera series—books filled with romantic adventure, vivid details of alien cultures, and interstellar conflict. She enjoys excitement in her real life on Earth as well. Her adventures include outrunning a dog pack in Thebes, Greece, and falling down a chute in a cave on Crete. Referring to her home in the Pacific Northwest, Cherryh says, "I choose to live downwind of five active volcanoes."

In the following science-fiction story, Cherryh depicts the perils faced by the qhal, a human-like race, when they discover a way to travel through time. Cherryh says that "it's human to wish to relive yesterday or to leap ahead to a longed-for event. Science fiction allows you to fulfill that wish."

"The Threads of Time" by C. J. Cherryh

It was possible that the Gates were killing the qhal. They were everywhere, on every world, had been a fact of life for five thousand years, and linked the whole net of qhalur civilization into one present-tense coherency.

They had not, to be sure, invented the Gates. Chance gave them that gift . . . on a dead world of their own sun. One Gate stood—made by unknown hands.

And the qhal made others, imitating what they found. The Gates were instantaneous transfer, not alone from place to place, but, because of the motion of worlds and suns and the traveling galaxies—involving time.

There was an end of time. Ah, qhal *could* venture anything. If one supposed, if one believed, if one were very *sure,* one could step through a Gate to a Gate that would/might exist on some other distant world.

And if one were wrong?

If it did not exist?

If it never had?

Time warped in the Gate-passage. One could step across light-years, unaged; so it was possible to outrace light and time. Did one not want to die, bound to a single lifespan? Go forward. See the future. Visit the world/end worlds to come.

But never go back. Never tamper. Never alter the past.

There was an End of Time.

It was the place where qhal gathered, who had been farthest and lost their courage for traveling on. It was the point beyond which no one had courage, where descendants shared the world with living ancestors in greater and greater numbers, the jaded, the restless, who reached this age and felt their will erode away.

Setting Which clues in the opening paragraph suggest when and where this science fiction story takes place?

Narrative Effects How do the short, one-line paragraphs affect the pacing of the story?

Conflict and Plot What do these details tell you about the unusual way time and events will be ordered in this story?

Practice continued

Conflict and Plot What internal conflict for the qhal is described in these lines?

It was the place where hope ended. Oh, a few went farther, and the age saw them—no more. They were gone. They did not return.

They went beyond, whispered those who had lost their courage. They went out a Gate and found nothing there.

They died.

Or was it death—to travel without end? And what was death? And was the universe finite at all?

Some went, and vanished, and the age knew nothing more of them.

Those who were left were in agony—of desire to go; of fear to go farther.

Of changes.

This age—did change. It rippled with possibilities. Memories deceived. One remembered, or remembered that one had remembered, and the fact grew strange and dim, contradicting what obviously *was.* People remembered things that never had been true.

And one must never go back to see. Backtiming—had direst possibilities. It made paradox.

But some tried, seeking a time as close to their original exit point as possible. Some came too close, and involved themselves in time-loops, a particularly distressing kind of accident and unfortunate equally for those involved as bystanders.

Narrative Effects How do the varied lengths of paragraphs and sentences reinforce the sense of displacement in time the story describes?

Among qhal, between the finding of the first Gate and the End of Time, a new kind of specialist evolved: time-menders, who in most extreme cases of disturbance policed the Gates and carefully researched afflicted areas. They alone were licensed to violate the back-time barrier, passing back and forth under strict noninvolvement regulations, exchanging intelligence only with each other, to minutely adjust reality.

Evolved.

Agents recruited other agents at need—but at whose instance? There might be some who knew. It might have come from the far end of time—in that last (or was it last?) age beyond which nothing seemed certain, when the years since the First Gate were more than five thousand, and the Now in which all Gates existed was—very distant. Or it might have come from those who had found the Gate, overseeing their invention. Someone knew, somewhen, somewhere along the course of the stars toward the end of time.

But no one said.

It was hazardous business, this time-mending, in all senses. Precisely *what* was done was something virtually unknowable after it was done, for alterations in the past produced (one believed) changes in future reality. Whole time-fields, whose events could be wiped and redone, with effects which widened the farther down the timeline they proceeded. Detection of time-tampering was almost impossible.

> *A stranger wanted something to eat, a long time ago. He shot himself his dinner.*
>
> *A small creature was not where it had been, when it had been.*
>
> *A predator missed a meal and took another . . . likewise small.*
>
> *A child lost a pet.*
>
> *And found another.*
>
> *And a friend she would not have had. She was happier for it.*
>
> *She met many people she had never/would never meet.*
>
> *A man in a different age had breakfast in a house on a hill.*

Agent Harrh had acquired a sense about disruptions, a kind of extrasensory queasiness about a just-completed timewarp. He was not alone in this. But the time-menders (Harrh knew three others of his own age) never reported such experiences outside their own special group. Such reports would have been meaningless to his own time, involving a past which (as a result of the warp) was neither real nor valid nor perceptible to those in Time Present. Some time-menders would reach the verge of insanity because of this. This was future fact. Harrh knew this.

He had been there.

And he refused to go again to Now, that Now to which time had advanced since the discovery of the Gate—let alone to the End of Time, which was the farthest that anyone imagined. He was one of a few, a very few, licensed to do so, but he refused.

He lived scattered lives in ages to come, and remembered the future with increasing melancholy.

He had visited the End of Time, and left it in the most profound despair. He had seen what was there, and when he had contemplated going beyond, that most natural step out the Gate which stood and beckoned—

He fled. He had never run from anything but that. It remained, a recollection of shame at his fear.

Conflict and Plot What information about the past—or, in this story of time travel, the future—do these flashbacks provide?

Characterization The protagonist, Agent Harrh, appears for the first time in this paragraph. What do you learn about his personality in this introduction?

Dynamic Characters How has the experience of time travel changed Harrh?

Practice continued

A sense of a limit which he had never had before.

And this in itself was terrible, to a man who had thought time infinite and himself immortal.

In his own present of 1003 since the First Gate, Harrh had breakfast, a quiet meal. The children were off to the beach. His wife shared tea with him and thought it would be a fine morning.

"Yes," he said. "Shall we take the boat out? We can fish a little, take the sun."

Characterization
Describe what Harrh and his wife are like. Cite specific details from the text, both explicit and implied.

"Marvelous," she said. Her gray eyes shone. He loved her—for herself, for her patience. He caught her hand on the crystal table, held slender fingers, not speaking his thoughts, which were far too somber for the morning.

They spent their mornings and their days together. He came back to her, time after shifting time. He might be gone a month; and home a week; and gone two months next time. He never dared cut it too close. They lost a great deal of each other's lives, and so much— so much he could not share with her.

"The island," he said. "Mhreihrrinn, I'd like to see it again."

"I'll pack," she said.

And went away.

He came back to her never aged; and she bore their two sons; and reared them; and managed the accounts: and explained his absences to relatives and the world. *He travels,* she would say, with that right amount of secrecy that protected secrets.

And even to her he could never confide what he knew.

"I trust you," she would say—knowing what he was, but never what he did.

Dynamic Characters What dramatic change in his life is Harrh contemplating?

He let her go. She went off to the hall and out the door— He imagined happy faces, holiday, the boys making haste to run the boat out and put on the bright colored sail. She would keep them busy carrying this and that, fetching food and clothes—things happened in shortest order when Mhreihrrinn set her hand to them.

He wanted that, wanted the familiar, the orderly, the homely. He was, if he let his mind dwell on things—afraid. He had the notion never to leave again.

He had been to the Now most recently—5045, and his flesh crawled at the memory. There was recklessness there. There was disquiet. The Now had traveled two decades and more since he had first begun, and he felt it more and more. The whole decade of the 5040s had a queasiness about it, ripples of instability as if the whole fabric of the Now were shifting like a kaleidoscope.

And it headed for the End of Time. It had become more and more like that age, confirming it by its very collapse.

People had illusions in the Now. They perceived what had not been true.

And yet it *was* when he came home.

It had grown to be so—while he was gone.

A university stood in Morurir, which he did not remember.

A hedge of trees grew where a building had been in Morurir.

A man was in the Council who had died.

He would not go back to Now. He had resolved that this morning.

He had children, begotten before his first time-traveling. He had so very much to keep him—this place, this home, this stability—He was very well to do. He had invested well—his own small tampering. He had no lack, no need. He was mad to go on and on. He was done.

Motivation What are Harrh's reasons for wanting to stay?

But a light distracted him, an opal shimmering beyond his breakfast nook, arrival in that receptor which his fine home afforded, linked to the master gate at Pyvrrhn.

A young man materialized there, opal and light and then solidity, a distraught young man.

"Harrh," the youth said, disregarding the decencies of meeting, and strode forward unasked. "Harrh, is everything all right here?"

Harrh arose from the crystal table even before the shimmer died, beset by that old queasiness of things out of joint. This was Alhir from 390 Since the Gate, an experienced man in the force: he had used a Master Key to come here—had such access, being what he was.

Characterization What does the first rapid dialogue exchange between Harrh and Alhir tell you about these characters?

"Alhir," Harrh said, perplexed. "What's wrong?"

"You don't know." Alhir came as far as the door.

"A cup of tea?" Harrh said. Alhir had been here before. They were friends. There were oases along the course of suns, friendly years, places where houses served as rest-stops. In this too Mhreihrrinn was patient. "I've got to tell you— No, don't tell me. I don't want to know. I'm through. I've made up my mind. You can carry that where you're going. —But if you want the breakfast—"

"There's been an accident."
"I don't want to hear."
"He got past us."

Conflict and Plot What does this paragraph reveal about the conflict between Harrh and the time-menders?

Narrative Effects What effect is created by hinting at events without providing full information?

Practice continued

"I don't want to know." He walked over to the cupboard, took another cup. "Mhreihrrinn's with the boys down at the beach. You just caught us." He set the cup down and poured the tea, where Mhreihrrinn had sat. "Won't you? You're always welcome here. Mhreihrrinn has no idea what you are. My young friend, she calls you. She doesn't know. Or she suspects. She'd never say.—Sit *down.*"

Alhir had strayed aside, where a display case sat along the wall, a lighted case of mementoes of treasures, of crystal. "Harrh, there was a potsherd here."

"No," Harrh said, less and less comfortable. "Just the glasses. I'm quite sure."

"Harrh, it was very old."

"No," he said. "—I promised Mhreihrrinn and the boys—I mean it.

I'm through. I don't want to know."

"It came from Silen. From the digs at the First Gate, Harrh. It was a very valuable piece. You valued it very highly.—You don't remember."

"No," Harrh said, feeling fear thick about him, like a change in atmosphere. "I don't know of such a piece. I never had such a thing. Check your memory, Alhir."

"It was from the ruins by the *First Gate,* don't you understand?"

And then Alhir did not exist.

Harrh blinked, remembered pouring a cup of tea. But he was sitting in the chair, his breakfast before him.

He poured the tea and drank.

He was sitting on rock, amid the grasses blowing gently in the wind, on a clifftop by the sea.

He was standing there. "Mhreihrrinn," he said, in the first chill touch of fear.

But that memory faded. He had never had a wife, nor children. He forgot the house as well.

Trees grew and faded.

Rocks moved at random.

The time-menders were in most instances the only ones who survived even a little while.

Wrenched loose from time and with lives rooted in many parts of it, they felt it first and lived it longest, and not a few were trapped in backtime and did not die, but survived the horror of it and begot children who further confounded the time-line.

Narrative Effects
How does Alhir's sudden disappearance affect you as a reader?

Dynamic Characters
How has the loss of his memories affected Harrh? What insight about the relationship between memory and identity does this passage develop?

Time, stretched thin in possibilities, adjusted itself.

He was Harrh.

But he was many possibilities and many names.

In time none of them mattered.

He was many names; he lived. He had many bodies; and the souls stained his own.

In the end he remembered nothing at all, except the drive to live.

And the dreams.

And none of the dreams were true.

After You Read | The Threads of Time

1. **Key Ideas and Details (a)** How did the qhal acquire the ability to travel in time? **(b) Infer:** To what extent did they at first understand the consequences of what they were doing?

2. **Key Ideas and Details (a)** In his present of 1003, what changes does Harrh notice? **(b) Draw Conclusions:** Why are these changes significant?

3. **Key Ideas and Details (a) Describe:** How would you describe Mhreihrrinn? **(b) Classify:** Is she a dynamic or static character? Explain.

4. **Craft and Structure Analyze:** Is the character of Harrh developed mainly through direct or indirect characterization? Explain.

5. **Craft and Structure (a) Identify:** Note two techniques the author uses to manipulate the pace of the story. **(b) Analyze:** What effect is produced?

6. **Integration of Knowledge and Ideas (a)** Use a chart like the one shown to define key terms from the story.

Term	What It Means	Why It Is Important
the qhal		
Gate		
time-mender		
the Now		
End of Time		

(b) Collaboration: In a group, discuss your definitions.

Leveled Texts

Build your skills and improve your comprehension of short stories with texts of increasing complexity.

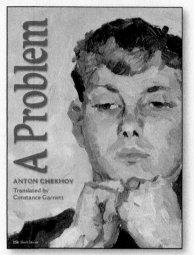

Read **"A Visit to Grandmother"** to see what happens when a son confronts his mother about his childhood.

Read **"A Problem"** to see how a group of uncles debates the fate of their irresponsible nephew.

Common Core State Standards

Meet these standards with either **"A Visit to Grandmother"** (p. 242) or **"A Problem"** (p. 256).

Reading Literature
3. Analyze how complex characters develop over the course of a text, interact with other characters, and advance the plot or develop the theme. *(Literary Analysis: Character and Characterization)*

Writing
3.a. Engage and orient the reader by setting out a problem, situation, or observation, establishing one or multiple point(s) of view, and introducing a narrator and/or characters; create a smooth progression of experiences or events.

3.b. Use narrative techniques, such as dialogue, pacing, description, reflection, and multiple plot lines, to develop experiences, events, and/or characters.

3.d. Use precise words and phrases, telling details, and sensory language to convey a vivid picture of the experiences, events, setting, and/or characters. *(Writing: Retellings)*

8. Gather relevant information from multiple authoritative print and digital sources; assess the usefulness of each source in answering the research question; integrate information into the text selectively to maintain the flow of ideas, avoiding plagiarism and following a standard format for citation. *(Research and Technology: Report on Sources)*

Language
4. Determine or clarify the meaning of unknown and multiple-meaning words and phrases based on grades 9–10 reading and content, choosing flexibly from a range of strategies. *(Vocabulary: Word Study)*

Literary Analysis: Character and Characterization

Story **characters** are the people, animals, or even objects who perform the actions and experience the events of a narrative. Writers use two main types of **characterization** to bring characters to life.

- **Direct characterization:** The writer tells readers exactly what a character is like—for example, "Hugo is generous to a fault."

- **Indirect characterization:** The writer reveals a character's traits through **dialogue** (the character's words), the character's actions and thoughts, and the interactions between the character and others.

To better understand characters and gain insight into the theme of a story, take note of the **character development**—changes a complex character undergoes or new aspects of the character the writer reveals.

Reading Skill: Make Inferences

An **inference** is a logical assumption based on details in a story. Making inferences helps you more fully understand story characters and the reasons that they act as they do. To make inferences about a character, **relate characters and events to your own experience,** and make assumptions based on that information. For example, if a story character mumbles and avoids eye contact, you may think of people you know who act this way, and you may infer that the character is shy.

Using the Strategy: Inference Chart

Use an **inference chart** like this one to help you relate your reading to your experiences.

Story Detail		Your Experience		Inference
The new captain's palms are sweating as she addresses the crew.	+	New camp counselors are nervous about whether campers will obey them.	→	The new captain is unsure of herself.

Writing About the Big Question

In "A Visit to Grandmother," a man must decide if he can believe his mother's version of a longstanding family conflict. Use these sentence starters to develop your ideas about the Big Question:

When people experience a misunderstanding, a **confrontation** may be helpful because _____.

Following a conflict, relationships might **change** because _____ _____.

While You Read Look for details that build up to a confrontation and decide whether progress can be made.

Vocabulary

Read each word and its definition. Decide whether you know the word well, know it a little bit, or do not know it at all. After you read, see how your knowledge of each word has increased.

- **indulgence** (in dul´ jəns) _n._ leniency; readiness to tolerate or forgive bad behavior (p. 244) _If you show the child too much indulgence, you may spoil her._ _indulge v. indulgent adj._

- **grimacing** (grim´ is iŋ) _v._ making a twisted face showing disgust or pain (p. 244) _She is grimacing because she has a splinter in her toe._ _grimace n._

- **meager** (mē´ gər) _adj._ of poor quality or small amount (p. 250) _Due to poor rainfall, there was only a meager crop._ _meagerly adv. meagerness n._

- **trace** (trās) _n._ tiny amount; hint (p. 250) _There was not even a trace of cake left._

- **fraud** (frôd) _n._ deceit; trickery (p. 251) _There are strict penalties for insurance fraud._ _fraudulent adj. fraudulently adv._

- **engaging** (en gāj´ iŋ) _adj._ attractive; pleasant (p. 252) _The doctor's engaging personality puts his patients at ease._ _engage v. engagingly adv. engagement n._

Word Study

The **Latin suffix -ence** means "quality of" or "state of."

In this story, a mother treats one of her sons with **indulgence,** or the state of yielding to his wishes, by not punishing him for improper behavior.

Author of

A Visit to Grandmother

William Melvin Kelley is a man of questions. He says, "I am not a sociologist or a politician or a spokesman. Such people try to give answers. A writer, I think, should ask questions."

Kelley's questions often explore the problems of belonging to a group. His first novel, *A Different Drummer,* reflects his belief in individualism.

A Community Artist At the same time, Kelley's work shows a strong connection to community. He belongs to the Black Arts Movement, the generation of writers, artists, dancers, and musicians that emerged in the 1960s and 1970s. Like others in the movement, he often addresses the moral, cultural, and political questions African Americans face.

BACKGROUND FOR THE STORY

Dialect

Dialect is the variety of a language spoken in a region or community. Some characters in "A Visit to Grandmother" speak in a southern dialect. In this dialect, *I reckon* means "I believe." *Fixin' to* replaces "about to."

DID YOU KNOW?

Introducing his class on writing fiction, Kelley notes that "Art may come from the heart, but craft comes from the brain."

L. WHEELER

◀ Critical Viewing
Predict what the grand-
mother in the story will
be like, judging from this
painting. [Predict]

A Visit to Grandmother

William Melvin Kelley

Chig knew something was wrong the instant his father kissed
her. He had always known his father to be the warmest of
men, a man so kind that when people ventured timidly into
his office, it took only a few words from him to make them relax,
and even laugh. Doctor Charles Dunford cared about people.

But when he had bent to kiss the old lady's black face, something
new and almost ugly had come into his eyes: fear, uncertainty,
sadness, and perhaps even hatred.

Ten days before in New York, Chig's father had decided suddenly
he wanted to go to Nashville to attend his college class reunion,
twenty years out. Both Chig's brother and sister, Peter and Connie,
were packing for camp and besides were too young for such an
affair. But Chig was seventeen, had nothing to do that summer, and
his father asked if he would like to go along. His father had given
him additional reasons: "All my running buddies got their diplomas
and were snapped up by them crafty young gals, and had kids
within a year—now all those kids, some of them gals, are your age."

The reunion had lasted a week. As they packed for home, his
father, in a far too offhand way, had suggested they visit Chig's
grandmother. "We this close. We might as well drop in on her and
my brothers."

Literary Analysis
Character and Characterization
What do you learn about GL through direct characterization?

Vocabulary
indulgence (in dul´ jəns)
n. leniency; readiness to tolerate or forgive bad behavior

So, instead of going north, they had gone farther south, had just entered her house. And Chig had a suspicion now that the reunion had been only an excuse to drive south, that his father had been heading to this house all the time.

His father had never talked much about his family, with the exception of his brother, GL, who seemed part con man, part practical joker and part Don Juan;[1] he had spoken of GL with the kind of indulgence he would have shown a cute, but ill-behaved and potentially dangerous, five-year-old.

Chig's father had left home when he was fifteen. When asked why, he would answer: "I wanted to go to school. They didn't have a Negro high school at home, so I went up to Knoxville and lived with a cousin and went to school."

They had been met at the door by Aunt Rose, GL's wife, and ushered into the living room. The old lady had looked up from her seat by the window. Aunt Rose stood between the visitors.

The old lady eyed his father. "Rose, who that? Rose?" She squinted. She looked like a doll, made of black straw, the wrinkles in her face running in one direction like the head of a broom. Her hair was white and coarse and grew out straight from her head. Her eyes were brown—the whites, too, seemed light brown—and were hidden behind thick glasses, which remained somehow on a tiny nose. "That Hiram?" That was another of his father's brothers. "No, it ain't Hiram; too big for Hiram." She turned then to Chig. "Now that man, he look like Eleanor, Charles's wife, but Charles wouldn't never send my grandson to see me. I never even hear from Charles." She stopped again.

"It Charles, Mama. That who it is." Aunt Rose, between them, led them closer. "It Charles come all the way from New York to see you, and brung little Charles with him."

Reading Skill
Make Inferences What feelings does the grandmother have upon seeing her son? Which details support your inference?

Vocabulary
grimacing (grim´ is iŋ)
v. making a twisted face showing disgust or pain

The old lady stared up at them. "Charles? Rose, that really Charles?" She turned away, and reached for a handkerchief in the pocket of her clean, ironed, flowered housecoat, and wiped her eyes. "God have mercy, Charles." She spread her arms up to him, and he bent down and kissed her cheek. That was when Chig saw his face, grimacing. She hugged him; Chig watched the muscles in her arms as they tightened around his father's neck. She half rose out of her chair. "How are you, son?"

Chig could not hear his father's answer.

She let him go, and fell back into her chair, grabbing the arms. Her hands were as dark as the wood, and seemed to become part of it. "Now, who that standing there? Who that man?"

---

1. Don Juan (dän´ wän´) a legendary nobleman, idle and immoral, who fascinates women.

"That's one of your grandsons, Mama." His father's voice cracked. "Charles Dunford, junior. You saw him once, when he was a baby, in Chicago. He's grown now."

"I can see that, boy!" She looked at Chig squarely. "Come here, son, and kiss me once." He did. "What they call you? Charles too?"

"No, ma'am, they call me Chig."

She smiled. She had all her teeth, but they were too perfect to be her own. "That's good. Can't have two boys answering to Charles in the same house. Won't nobody at all come. So you that little boy. You don't remember me, do you. I used to take you to church in Chicago, and you'd get up and hop in time to the music. You studying to be a preacher?"

"No, ma'am. I don't think so. I might be a lawyer."

"You'll be an honest one, won't you?"

"I'll try."

"Trying ain't enough! You be honest, you hear? Promise me. You be honest like your daddy."

"All right. I promise."

"Good. Rose, where's GL at? Where's that thief? He gone again?"

"I don't know, Mama." Aunt Rose looked embarrassed. "He say he was going by the store. He'll be back."

"Well, then where's Hiram? You call up those boys, and get them over here—now! You got enough to eat? Let me go see." She started to get up. Chig reached out his hand. She shook him off. "What they tell you about me, Chig? They tell you I'm all laid up? Don't believe it. They don't know nothing about old ladies. When I want help, I'll let you know. Only time I'll need help getting anywheres is when I dies and they lift me into the ground."

She was standing now, her back and shoulders straight. She came only to Chig's chest. She squinted up at him. "You eat much? Your daddy ate like two men."

"Yes, ma'am."

"That's good. That means you ain't nervous. Your mama, she ain't nervous. I remember that. In Chicago,

Literary Analysis
Character and Characterization
Name one trait of the grandmother that is suggested in the dialogue.

Reading Check

How does the grandmother react to the surprise visit?

she'd sit down by a window all afternoon and never say nothing, just knit." She smiled. "Let me see what we got to eat."

"I'll do that, Mama." Aunt Rose spoke softly. "You haven't seen Charles in a long time. You sit and talk."

The old lady squinted at her. "You can do the cooking if you promise it ain't because you think I can't."

Aunt Rose chuckled. "I know you can do it, Mama."

"All right. I'll just sit and talk a spell." She sat again and arranged her skirt around her short legs.

Chig did most of the talking, told all about himself before she asked. His father spoke only when he was spoken to, and then, only one word at a time, as if by coming back home, he had become a small boy again, sitting in the parlor while his mother spoke with her guests. •

When Uncle Hiram and Mae, his wife, came they sat down to eat. Chig did not have to ask about Uncle GL's absence; Aunt Rose volunteered an explanation: "Can't never tell where the man is at. One Thursday morning he left here and next thing we knew, he was calling from Chicago, saying he went up to see Joe Louis[2] fight. He'll be here though; he ain't as young and footloose as he used to be." Chig's father had mentioned driving down that GL was about five years older than he was, nearly fifty.

Uncle Hiram was somewhat smaller than Chig's father; his short-cropped kinky hair was half gray, half black. One spot, just off his forehead, was totally white. Later, Chig found out it had been that way since he was twenty. Mae (Chig could not bring himself to call her Aunt) was a good deal younger than Hiram, pretty enough so that Chig would have looked at her twice on the street. She was a honey-colored woman, with long eyelashes. She was wearing a white sheath.

At dinner, Chig and his father sat on one side, opposite Uncle Hiram and Mae; his grandmother and Aunt Rose sat at the ends. The food was good; there was a lot and Chig ate a lot. All through the meal, they talked about the family as it had been thirty years before, and particularly about the young GL. Mae and Chig asked questions; the old lady answered; Aunt Rose directed the discussion, steering the old lady onto the best stories; Chig's father laughed from time to time; Uncle Hiram ate.

"Why don't you tell them about the horse, Mama?" Aunt Rose, over Chig's weak protest, was spooning mashed potatoes onto his plate. "There now, Chig."

---

2. **Joe Louis** (1914–1981) U.S. boxer and the world heavyweight champion from 1937 to 1949.

◀ **Critical Viewing**
What does this image suggest about the life the grandmother and her family lead? **[Connect]**

Reading Check
How does Chig's father act during their visit?

"I'm trying to think." The old lady was holding her fork halfway to her mouth, looking at them over her glasses. "Oh, you talking about that crazy horse GL brung home that time."

"That's right, Mama." Aunt Rose nodded and slid another slice of white meat on Chig's plate.

Mae started to giggle. "Oh, I've heard this. This is funny, Chig."

Literary Analysis
Character and Characterization
How does the writer use indirect characterization to reveal GL's character?

The old lady put down her fork and began: Well, GL went out of the house one day with an old, no-good chair I wanted him to take over to the church for a bazaar, and he met up with this man who'd just brung in some horses from out West. Now, I reckon you can expect one swindler[3] to be in every town, but you don't rightly think there'll be two, and God forbid they should ever meet—but they did, GL and his chair, this man and his horses. Well, I wished I'd-a been there; there must-a been some mighty high-powered talking going on. That man with his horses, he told GL them horses was half-Arab, half-Indian, and GL told that man the chair was an antique he'd stole from some rich white folks. So they swapped. Well, I was a-looking out the window and seen GL dragging this animal to the house. It looked pretty gentle and its eyes was most closed and its feet was shuffling.

"GL, where'd you get that thing?" I says.

"I swapped him for that old chair, Mama," he says. "And made myself a bargain. This is even better than Papa's horse."

Well, I'm a-looking at this horse and noticing how he be looking more and more wide awake every minute, sort of warming up like a teakettle until, I swears to you, that horse is blowing steam out its nose.

"Come on, Mama," GL says, "come on and I'll take you for a ride." Now George, my husband, God rest his tired soul, he'd brung home this white folks' buggy which had a busted wheel and fixed it and was to take it back that day and GL says: "Come on, Mama, we'll use this fine buggy and take us a ride."

"GL," I says, "no, we ain't. Them white folks'll burn us alive if we use their buggy. You just take that horse right on back." You see, I was sure that boy'd come by that animal ungainly.

"Mama, I can't take him back," GL says.

"Why not?" I says.

"Because I don't rightly know where that man is at," GL says.

"Oh," I says. "Well, then I reckon we stuck with it." And I turned around to go back into the house because it was getting late, near dinner time, and I was cooking for ten.

"Mama," GL says to my back. "Mama, ain't you coming for a ride with me?"

---

3. **swindler** (swind´ lər) *n.* a cheater; a person who takes the money or property of others using deception.

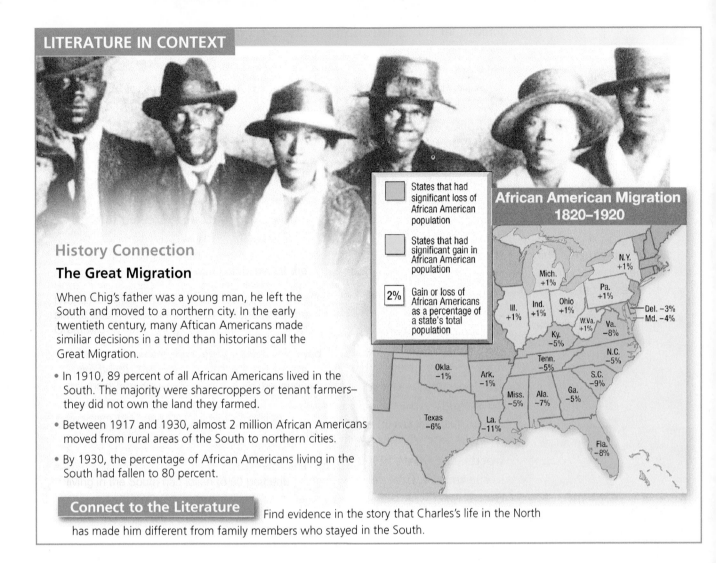

History Connection

The Great Migration

When Chig's father was a young man, he left the South and moved to a northern city. In the early twentieth century, many Aftican Americans made similiar decisions in a trend than historians call the Great Migration.

- In 1910, 89 percent of all African Americans lived in the South. The majority were sharecroppers or tenant farmers– they did not own the land they farmed.

- Between 1917 and 1930, almost 2 million African Americans moved from rural areas of the South to northern cities.

- By 1930, the percentage of African Americans living in the South had fallen to 80 percent.

Connect to the Literature Find evidence in the story that Charles's life in the North has made him different from family members who stayed in the South.

States that had significant loss of African American population

States that had significant gain in African American population

2% Gain or loss of African Americans as a percentage of a state's total population

African American Migration 1820–1920

N.Y. +1%
Mich. +1%
Pa. +1%
Ill. +1%
Ind. +1%
Ohio +1%
Del. –3%
Md. –4%
W.Va. +1%
Va. –8%
Ky. –5%
Okla. –1%
Ark. –1%
Tenn. –5%
N.C. –5%
S.C. –9%
Miss. –5%
Ala. –7%
Ga. –5%
Texas –6%
La. –11%
Fla. –8%

"Go on, boy. You ain't getting me inside kicking range of that animal." I was eying that beast and it was boiling hotter all the time. I reckon maybe that man had drugged it. "That horse is wild, GL," I says.

"No, he ain't. He ain't. That man say he is buggy and saddle broke[4] and as sweet as the inside of a apple."

My oldest girl, Essie, had-a come out on the porch and she says: "Go on, Mama. I'll cook. You ain't been out the house in weeks."

"Sure, come on, Mama," GL says. "There ain't nothing to be fidgety about. This horse is gentle as a rose petal." And just then that animal snorts so hard it sets up a little dust storm around its feet.

"Yes, Mama," Essie says, "you can see he gentle." Well, I looked at Essie and then at that horse because I didn't think we could be

---

4. **buggy and saddle broke** trained to carry a mounted rider or to pull a carriage.

Reading Check

What is the subject of the grandmother's story?

looking at the same animal. I should-a figured how Essie's eyes ain't never been so good.

"Come on, Mama," GL says.

"All right," I says. So I stood on the porch and watched GL hitching that horse up to the white folks' buggy. For a while there, the animal was pretty quiet, pawing a little, but not much. And I was feeling a little better about riding with GL behind that crazy-looking horse. I could see how GL was happy I was going with him. He was scurrying around that animal buckling buckles and strapping straps, all the time smiling, and that made me feel good. •

Then he was finished, and I must say, that horse looked mighty fine hitched to that buggy and I knew anybody what climbed up there would look pretty good too. GL came around and stood at the bottom of the steps, and took off his hat and bowed and said: "Madam," and reached out his hand to me and I was feeling real elegant like a fine lady. He helped me up to the seat and then got up beside me and we moved out down our alley. And I remember how colored folks come out on their porches and shook their heads, saying: "Lord now, will you look at Eva Dunford, the fine lady! Don't she look good sitting up there!" And I pretended not to hear and sat up straight and proud.

We rode on through the center of town, up Market Street, and all the way out where Hiram is living now, which in them days was all woods, there not being even a farm in sight and that's when that horse must-a first realized he weren't at all broke or tame or maybe thought he was back out West again, and started to gallop.

"GL," I says, "now you ain't joking with your mama, is you? Because if you is, I'll strap you purple if I live through this."

Well, GL was pulling on the reins with all his meager strength, and yelling, "Whoa, you. Say now, whoa!" He turned to me just long enough to say, "I ain't fooling with you, Mama. Honest!"

I reckon that animal weren't too satisfied with the road, because it made a sharp right turn just then, down into a gulley and struck out across a hilly meadow. "Mama," GL yells. "Mama, do something!"

I didn't know what to do, but I figured I had to do something so I stood up, hopped down onto the horse's back and pulled it to a stop. Don't ask me how I did that; I reckon it was that I was a mother and my baby asked me to do something, is all.

"Well, we walked that animal all the way home; sometimes I had to club it over the nose with my fist to make it come, but we made it, GL and me. You remember how tired we was, Charles?"

"I wasn't here at the time." Chig turned to his father and found his face completely blank, without even a trace of a smile or a laugh.

Reading Skill
Make Inferences Think of a person you know who likes to get attention. How does knowing this person help you understand GL's actions?

Vocabulary
meager (mē′ gər) *adj.* of poor quality or small amount

trace (trās) *n.* tiny amount; hint

"Well, of course you was, son. That happened in . . . in . . . it was a hot summer that year and—"

"I left here in June of that year. You wrote me about it."

The old lady stared past Chig at him. They all turned to him; Uncle Hiram looked up from his plate.

"Then you don't remember how we all laughed?"

"No, I don't, Mama. And I probably wouldn't have laughed. I don't think it was funny." They were staring into each other's eyes.

"Why not, Charles?"

"Because in the first place, the horse was gained by fraud. And in the second place, both of you might have been seriously injured or even killed." He broke off their stare and spoke to himself more than to any of them: "And if I'd done it, you would've beaten me good for it."

"Pardon?" The old lady had not heard him; only Chig had heard.

Chig's father sat up straight as if preparing to debate. "I said that if I had done it, if I had done just exactly what GL did, you would have beaten me good for it, Mama." He was looking at her again.

"Why you say that, son?" She was leaning toward him.

"Don't you know? Tell the truth. It can't hurt me now." His voice cracked, but only once. "If GL and I did something wrong, you'd beat me first and then be too tired to beat him. At dinner, he'd always get seconds and I wouldn't. You'd do things with him, like ride in that buggy, but if I wanted you to do something with me, you were always too busy." He paused and considered whether to say what he finally did say: "I cried when I left here. Nobody loved me, Mama. I cried all the way up to Knoxville. That was the last time I ever cried in my life."

"Oh, Charles." She started to get up, to come around the table to him.

He stopped her. "It's too late."

"But you don't understand."

"What don't I understand? I understood then; I understand now."

Tears now traveled down the lines in her face, but when she spoke, her voice was clear. "I thought you knew. I had ten children. I had to give all of them what they needed most." She nodded. "I paid more mind to GL. I had to. GL could-a ended up swinging if I hadn't. But you was smarter. You was more growed up than GL when you was five and he was ten, and I tried to show you that by letting you do what you wanted to do."

"That's not true, Mama. You know it. GL was light-skinned and had good hair and looked almost white and you loved him for that."

"Charles, no. No, son. I didn't love any one of you more than any other."

"That can't be true." His father was standing now, his fists

Spiral Review

Plot In what way does this family anecdote act as a flashback?

Vocabulary
fraud (frôd) *n.*
deceit; trickery

Literary Analysis
Character and Characterization
What new information helps to develop Charles's character?

What happens when GL takes his mother for a buggy ride?

clenched tight. "Admit it, Mama . . . please!" Chig looked at him, shocked; the man was actually crying.

"It may not-a been right what I done, but I ain't no liar." Chig knew she did not really understand what had happened, what he wanted of her. "I'm not lying to you, Charles."

Chig's father had gone pale. He spoke very softly. "You're about thirty years too late, Mama." He bolted from the table. Silverware and dishes rang and jumped. Chig heard him hurrying up to their room.

They sat in silence for a while and then heard a key in the front door. A man with a new, lacquered[5] straw hat came in. He was wearing brown and white two-tone shoes with very pointed toes and a white summer suit. "Say now! Man! I heard my brother was in town. Where he at? Where that rascal?"

He stood in the doorway, smiling broadly, an engaging, open, friendly smile, the innocent smile of a five-year-old.

Vocabulary
engaging (en gāj´ iŋ)
adj. attractive; pleasant

---

5. **lacquered** (lak´ erd) *adj.* coated with a hardened protective layer of resinous material, which gives a shine.

Critical Thinking

Cite textual evidence to support your responses.

1. **Key Ideas and Details (a)** What reason does Charles give for leaving home when he was fifteen? **(b) Hypothesize:** What other reasons might he have had? Support your answer with story details.

2. **Key Ideas and Details (a)** How does Charles react to Mama's story about GL and the horse? **(b) Compare and Contrast:** In what way does his reaction contrast with the way Mama feels about the story? **(c) Connect:** Explain why the story has this effect on Charles.

3. **Key Ideas and Details Speculate:** What might Charles's relationship with his mother be like in the future?

4. **Key Ideas and Details (a) Summarize:** Describe Mama's approach to raising her children. **(b) Evaluate:** Is her approach sound? Explain.

5. **Integration of Knowledge and Ideas** By finally confronting his mother about his feelings, has Chig's father made progress in repairing his relationship with his family? Explain. *[Connect to the Big Question: Can progress be made without conflict?]*

A Visit to Grandmother

Literary Analysis: Character and Characterization

1. **Key Ideas and Details** Use details from the story to compare and contrast the **characters** of Charles and GL.

2. **Key Ideas and Details** Give examples of **indirect characterization** used to portray Charles. Use a chart like this one.

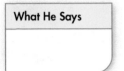

What He Says

What He Does

What Others Say About Him

3. **Key Ideas and Details** How does the character of Charles **develop** over the course of the story?

4. **Key Ideas and Details** **(a)** Give two examples of **dialogue** from Mama and two from Charles. **(b)** What do your examples show about how they differ?

Reading Skill: Make Inferences

5. **Make an inference** about Charles's feelings toward GL. On which story details is your inference based?

6. Make an inference about Chig's feelings toward his family. Support your inference with story details and your own experiences.

Vocabulary

Acquisition and Use Answer each question. Explain how the meaning of the underlined word influences your answer.

1. Would unlimited playtime be an <u>indulgence</u> for a child?
2. On what occasions might you see someone <u>grimacing</u>?
3. If there is a <u>trace</u> of mud on the rug, is a big cleanup necessary?
4. Would a child with a <u>meager</u> allowance have a large savings?
5. Would a bank allow a man known as a <u>fraud</u> to open an account?
6. Why would a politician want to have an <u>engaging</u> personality?

Word Study Use the context of the sentences and what you know about the **Latin suffix -ence** to explain your answer to each question.

1. Would a person's *negligence* help or hurt others?
2. Would you trust someone who demonstrates *competence*?

Word Study

The **Latin suffix -ence** means "quality of" or "state of."

Apply It Explain how the suffix *-ence* contributes to the meanings of these words. Consult a dictionary if necessary.

fraudulence
dependence
diligence

Can progress be made without *conflict?*

Writing About the Big Question

In "A Problem," an uncle argues with other family members to give his wayward nephew a second chance. Use this sentence starter to develop your ideas about the Big Question.

In order to help a loved one make an important **change** in his or her life, one should _____.

While You Read Look for clues that suggest Ivan Markovitch is successful in his efforts to help his nephew.

Vocabulary

Read each word and its definition. Decide whether you know the word well, know it a little bit, or do not know it at all. After you read, see how your knowledge of each word has increased.

- **pretense** (prē tens´) *n.* a pretending; a false show of something (p. 257) *She maintained a <u>pretense</u> of being friendly, but was really quite mean.* pretend *v.* pretentious *adj.*

- **candid** (kan´ did) *adj.* honest; direct (p. 257) *Stop telling tales, and give me a <u>candid</u> answer.* candidly *adv.* candor *n.*

- **lofty** (lôf´ tē) *adj.* elevated in character; noble (p. 258) *The dignitary's <u>lofty</u> ideals, such as equality and peace, are admirable.* loftily *adv.* loftiness *n.* aloft *adj.*

- **detestable** (dē tes´ tə bəl) *adj.* deserving hate or scorn; offensive (p. 259) *The factory's thick, foul-smelling smoke was <u>detestable</u> to her.* detest *v.* detestation *n.*

- **subdued** (səb dōōd´) *adj.* quiet; lacking energy (p. 262) *The boy was <u>subdued</u> after he was scolded.* subdue *v.*

- **edifying** (ed´ i fī in) *adj.* instructive in such a way as to improve morally or intellectually (p. 263) *The counselor's advice was generally quite helpful and <u>edifying</u>.* edify *v.* edification *n.*

Word Study

The **Latin suffix -able** means "worthy of; capable of being."

In this story, a character thinks his uncles are **detestable**, or worthy of being disliked, because they will not give in to his wishes.

Meet
Anton Chekhov
(1860–1904)

Author of
A Problem

Anton Chekhov grew up in the small coastal town of Taganrog in southern Russia. When the family moved to Moscow, he helped support them by writing comic sketches and light short stories. Although he attended medical school and became a doctor, Chekhov devoted himself to writing short stories and dramas.

A Diagnosis Chekhov said that "a writer is not a confectioner, a cosmetic dealer, or an entertainer. He is a man who has signed a contract with his conscience and his sense of duty." Some of Chekhov's works offer a diagnosis of nineteenth-century Russian society, showing how it trapped individuals into hopeless, unproductive lives. Other works humorously reveal universal human weaknesses. Today, he is regarded as one of the greatest modern writers and one of the most important dramatists of all time.

BACKGROUND FOR THE STORY
Money Lending

An IOU, or promissory note, is a promise to pay money or goods. In Russia at the time of this story, a person could "discount" an IOU, selling it to a moneylender for less than full value. Later, the person could "redeem" the note, buying it back by a certain date. In this story, a character commits a crime by forging an IOU and selling it to a moneylender.

DID YOU KNOW?
Chekhov's study of prisoner's lives, *The Island of Sakhalin*, helped reform the Russian prison system.

A Problem

ANTON CHEKHOV

translated by
Constance Garnett

The strictest measures were taken that the Uskovs' family secret might not leak out and become generally known. Half of the servants were sent off to the theater or the circus; the other half were sitting in the kitchen and not allowed to leave it. Orders were given that no one was to be admitted. The wife of the Colonel, her sister, and the governess, though they had been initiated into the secret, kept up a pretense of knowing nothing; they sat in the dining room and did not show themselves in the drawing room or the hall.

Sasha Uskov, the young man of twenty-five who was the cause of all the commotion, had arrived some time before, and by the advice of kind-hearted Ivan Markovitch, his uncle, who was taking his part, he sat meekly in the hall by the door leading to the study, and prepared himself to make an open, candid explanation.

The other side of the door, in the study, a family council was being held. The subject under discussion was an exceedingly disagreeable and delicate one. Sasha Uskov had cashed at one of the banks a false promissory note,[1] and it had become due for payment three days before, and now his two paternal uncles and Ivan Markovitch, the brother of his dead mother, were deciding the question whether they should pay the money and save the family honor, or wash their hands of it and leave the case to go to trial.

To outsiders who have no personal interest in the matter such questions seem simple; for those who are so unfortunate as to have to decide them in earnest they are extremely difficult. The uncles had been talking for a long time, but the problem seemed no nearer decision.

"My friends!" said the uncle who was a colonel, and there was a note of exhaustion and bitterness in his voice. "Who says that family honor is a mere convention? I don't say that at all. I am only warning you against a false view; I am pointing out the possibility of an unpardonable mistake. How can you fail to see it? I am not speaking Chinese; I am speaking Russian!"

"My dear fellow, we do understand," Ivan Markovitch protested mildly.

"How can you understand if you say that I don't believe in family honor? I repeat once more; fa-mil-y ho-nor false-ly un-der-stood is a prejudice! Falsely understood! That's what I say: whatever may be the motives for screening a scoundrel, whoever he may be, and helping him to escape punishment, it is contrary to law and unworthy of a gentleman. It's not saving the family honor; it's civic cowardice! Take the army, for instance. . . . The honor of the army is more precious to us than any other honor, yet we don't screen

---

1. **promissory note** written promise to pay a specified sum on demand; an IOU.

◀ **Critical Viewing**
Based on this painting, what do you expect the mood of the story will be? **[Predict]**

Vocabulary
pretense (prē tens´) n. a pretending; a false show of something

candid (kan´ did) adj. honest; direct

Reading Check

Why is Sasha in trouble?

our guilty members, but condemn them. And does the honor of the army suffer in consequence? Quite the opposite!"

The other paternal uncle, an official in the Treasury, a taciturn, dull-witted, and rheumatic man, sat silent, or spoke only of the fact that the Uskovs' name would get into the newspapers if the case went for trial. His opinion was that the case ought to be hushed up from the first and not become public property; but, apart from publicity in the newspapers, he advanced no other argument in support of this opinion.

The maternal uncle, kind-hearted Ivan Markovitch, spoke smoothly, softly, and with a tremor in his voice. He began with saying that youth has its rights and its peculiar temptations. Which of us has not been young, and who has not been led astray? To say nothing of ordinary mortals, even great men have not escaped errors and mistakes in their youth. Take, for instance, the biography of great writers. Did not every one of them gamble, drink, and draw down upon himself the anger of right-thinking people in his young days? If Sasha's error bordered upon crime, they must remember that Sasha had received practically no education; he had been expelled from the high school in the fifth class; he had lost his parents in early childhood, and so had been left at the tenderest age without guidance and good, benevolent influences. He was nervous, excitable, had no firm ground under his feet, and, above all, he had been unlucky. Even if he were guilty, anyway he deserved indulgence[2] and the sympathy of all compassionate souls. He ought, of course, to be punished, but he was punished as it was by his conscience and the agonies he was enduring now while awaiting the sentence of his relations. The comparison with the army made by the Colonel was delightful, and did credit to his lofty intelligence; his appeal to their feeling of public duty spoke for the chivalry of his soul, but they must not forget that in each individual the citizen is closely linked with the Christian. . . .

"Shall we be false to civic duty," Ivan Markovitch exclaimed passionately, "if instead of punishing an erring boy we hold out to him a helping hand?"

Ivan Markovitch talked further of family honor. He had not the honor to belong to the Uskov family himself, but he knew their distinguished family went back to the thirteenth century; he did not

---

2. **indulgence** (in dul´ jəns) *n.* forgiveness; tolerance.

forget for a minute, either, that his precious, beloved sister had been the wife of one of the representatives of that name. In short, the family was dear to him for many reasons, and he refused to admit the idea that, for the sake of a paltry fifteen hundred rubles,[3] a blot should be cast on the escutcheon[4] that was beyond all price. If all the motives he had brought forward were not sufficiently convincing, he, Ivan Markovitch, in conclusion, begged his listeners to ask themselves what was meant by crime? Crime is an immoral act founded upon ill-will. But is the will of man free? Philosophy has not yet given a positive answer to that question. Different views were held by the learned. The latest school of Lombroso,[5] for instance, denies the freedom of the will, and considers every crime as the product of the purely anatomical peculiarities of the individual.

"Ivan Markovitch," said the Colonel, in a voice of entreaty, "we are talking seriously about an important matter, and you bring in Lombroso, you clever fellow. Think a little, what are you saying all this for? Can you imagine that all your thunderings and rhetoric will furnish an answer to the question?" •

Sasha Uskov sat at the door and listened. He felt neither terror, shame, nor depression, but only weariness and inward emptiness. It seemed to him that it made absolutely no difference to him whether they forgave him or not; he had come here to hear his sentence and to explain himself simply because kind-hearted Ivan Markovitch had begged him to do so. He was not afraid of the future. It made no difference to him where he was: here in the hall, in prison, or in Siberia.

"If Siberia, then let it be Siberia, damn it all!"

He was sick of life and found it insufferably hard. He was inextricably involved in debt; he had not a farthing[6] in his pocket; his family had become detestable to him; he would have to part from his friends and his women sooner or later, as they had begun to be too contemptuous of his sponging on them. The future looked black.

Sasha was indifferent, and was only disturbed by one circumstance; the other side of the door they were calling him a scoundrel and a criminal. Every minute he was on the point of jumping up, bursting into the study and shouting in answer to the detestable metallic voice of the Colonel:

"You are lying!"

Reading Skill
Make Inferences Based on Sasha's thoughts, what can you infer about how mature he is?

Vocabulary
detestable (dē tes' tə bəl) *adj.* deserving hate or scorn; offensive

Reading Check

What is one reason Ivan Markovitch wants to help Sasha?

---

3. **rubles** (roō' belz) *n.* A ruble is the basic unit of Russian currency.
4. **escutcheon** (e skuch' ən) *n.* shield displaying a family's coat of arms, symbol of its nobility.
5. **Lombroso** Cesare Lombroso (1835–1909), an Italian criminologist who believed that criminals were of a distinct human type and were led to crime by hereditary, inborn characteristics.
6. **farthing** (fär' thiŋ) *n.* coin of little value.

"Criminal" is a dreadful word—that is what murderers, thieves, robbers are; in fact, wicked and morally hopeless people. And Sasha was very far from being all that. . . . It was true he owed a great deal and did not pay his debts. But debt is not a crime, and it is unusual for a man not to be in debt. The Colonel and Ivan Markovitch were both in debt. . . .

"What have I done wrong besides?" Sasha wondered.

He had discounted a forged note. But all the young men he knew did the same. Handrikov and Von Burst always forged IOU's from their parents or friends when their allowances were not paid at the regular time, and then when they got their money from home they redeemed them before they became due. Sasha had done the same, but had not redeemed the IOU because he had not got the money which Handrikov had promised to lend him. He was not to blame; it was the fault of circumstances. It was true that the use of another person's signature was considered reprehensible; but, still, it was not a crime but a generally accepted dodge, an ugly formality which injured no one and was quite harmless, for in forging the Colonel's signature Sasha had had no intention of causing anybody damage or loss.

"No, it doesn't mean that I am a criminal . . ." thought Sasha. "And it's not in my character to bring myself to commit a crime. I am soft, emotional. . . . When I have the money I help the poor. . . ."

Sasha was musing after this fashion while they went on talking the other side of the door.

"But, my friends, this is endless," the Colonel declared, getting excited. "Suppose we were to forgive him and pay the money. You know he would not give up leading a dissipated life, squandering money, making debts, going to our tailors and ordering suits in our names! Can you guarantee that this will be his last prank? As far as I am concerned, I have no faith whatever in his reforming!"

The official of the Treasury muttered something in reply; after him Ivan Markovitch began talking blandly and suavely again. The Colonel moved his chair impatiently and drowned the other's words with his detestable metallic voice. At last the door opened and Ivan Markovitch came out of the study; there were patches of red on his cleanshaven face.

"Come along," he said, taking Sasha by the hand. "Come and speak frankly from your heart. Without pride, my dear boy, humbly and from your heart."

Sasha went into the study. The official of the Treasury was sitting down; the Colonel was standing before the table with one hand in his pocket and one knee on a chair. It was smoky and stifling in the study. Sasha did not look at the official or the Colonel; he felt

suddenly ashamed and uncomfortable. He looked uneasily at Ivan Markovitch and muttered:

"I'll pay it . . . I'll give it back. . . ."

"What did you expect when you discounted the IOU?" he heard a metallic voice.

"I . . . Handrikov promised to lend me the money before now."

Sasha could say no more. He went out of the study and sat down again on the chair near the door. He would have been glad to go away altogether at once, but he was choking with hatred and he awfully wanted to remain, to tear the Colonel to pieces, to say something rude to him. He sat trying to think of something violent and effective to say to his hated uncle, and at that moment a woman's figure, shrouded in the twilight, appeared at the drawing room door. It was the Colonel's wife. She beckoned Sasha to her, and, wringing her hands, said, weeping:

"*Alexandre*, I know you don't like me, but . . . listen to me; listen, I beg you. . . . But, my dear, how can this have happened? Why, it's awful, awful! For goodness' sake, beg them, defend yourself, entreat them."

Sasha looked at her quivering shoulders, at the big tears that were rolling down her cheeks, heard behind his back the hollow, nervous voices of worried and exhausted people, and shrugged his shoulders. He had not in the least expected that his aristocratic relations would raise such a tempest over a paltry fifteen hundred rubles! He could not understand her tears nor the quiver of their voices. •

An hour later he heard that the Colonel was getting the best of it; the uncles were finally inclining to let the case go for trial.

"The matter's settled," said the Colonel, sighing. "Enough."

After this decision all the uncles, even the emphatic Colonel, became noticeably depressed. A silence followed.

"Merciful Heavens!" sighed Ivan Markovitch. "My poor sister!"

And he began saying in a subdued voice that most likely his sister, Sasha's mother, was present unseen in the study at that moment. He felt in his soul how the unhappy, saintly woman was weeping, grieving, and begging for her boy. For the sake of her peace beyond the grave, they ought to spare Sasha.

The sound of a muffled sob was heard. Ivan Markovitch was weeping and muttering something which it was impossible to catch through the door. The Colonel got up and paced from corner to corner. The long conversation began over again.

But then the clock in the drawing room struck two. The family council was over. To avoid seeing the person who had moved him to

Spiral Review
Plot What conflict are readers suddenly aware of in this scene?

Literary Analysis
Character and Characterization How does the writer reveal without directly stating it that Sasha is not sorry?

Vocabulary
subdued (səb dōōd´) *adj.* quiet; lacking energy

Reading Skill
Make Inferences Based on Ivan's response and your knowledge of families, make an inference about the uncles' feelings for Sasha's mother.

such wrath, the Colonel went from the study, not into the hall, but into the vestibule. . . . Ivan Markovitch came out into the hall. . . . He was agitated and rubbing his hands joyfully. His tear-stained eyes looked good-humored and his mouth was twisted into a smile.

"Capital," he said to Sasha. "Thank God! You can go home, my dear, and sleep tranquilly. We have decided to pay the sum, but on condition that you repent and come with me tomorrow into the country and set to work."

A minute later Ivan Markovitch and Sasha in their greatcoats and caps were going down the stairs. The uncle was muttering something edifying. Sasha did not listen, but felt as though some uneasy weight were gradually slipping off his shoulders. They had forgiven him; he was free! A gust of joy sprang up within him and sent a sweet chill to his heart. He longed to breathe, to move swiftly, to live! Glancing at the street lamps and the black sky, he remembered that Von Burst was celebrating his name day[7] that evening at the "Bear," and again a rush of joy flooded his soul. . . .

"I am going!" he decided.

But then he remembered he had not a farthing, that the companions he was going to would despise him at once for his empty pockets. He must get hold of some money, come what may!

"Uncle, lend me a hundred rubles," he said to Ivan Markovitch.

His uncle, surprised, looked into his face and backed against a lamppost.

"Give it to me," said Sasha, shifting impatiently from one foot to the other and beginning to pant. "Uncle, I entreat you, give me a hundred rubles."

---

7. **name day** feast day of the saint after whom a person is named.

Vocabulary
edifying (ed´ i fī´ iŋ)
adj. instructive in such a way as to improve morally or intellectually

They had forgiven him; he was free! A gust of joy sprang up within him and sent a sweet chill to his heart. He longed to breathe, to move swiftly, to live!

Reading Check

What decision do the uncles come to regarding Sasha?

His face worked; he trembled, and seemed on the point of attacking his uncle. . . .

"Won't you?" he kept asking, seeing that his uncle was still amazed and did not understand. "Listen. If you don't, I'll give myself up tomorrow! I won't let you pay the IOU! I'll present another false note tomorrow!"

Petrified, muttering something incoherent in his horror, Ivan Markovitch took a hundred-ruble note out of his pocketbook and gave it to Sasha. The young man took it and walked rapidly away from him. . . .

Taking a sledge, Sasha grew calmer, and felt a rush of joy within him again. The "rights of youth" of which kind-hearted Ivan Markovitch had spoken at the family council woke up and asserted themselves. Sasha pictured the drinking party before him, and, among the bottles, the women, and his friends, the thought flashed through his mind:

"Now I see that I am a criminal; yes, I am a criminal."

Literary Analysis
Character and Characterization In what way does Sasha's character develop at the end of the story?

Critical Thinking

Cite textual evidence to support your responses.

1. **Key Ideas and Details** **(a)** Why is Sasha in trouble? **(b) Compare and Contrast:** Use details from the story to compare the position each uncle takes toward Sasha's problem.

2. **Key Ideas and Details** **Infer:** How does Ivan Markovitch change the Colonel's mind?

3. **Key Ideas and Details** **(a)** Does Ivan Markovitch's attitude help or harm Sasha? Explain. **(b) Take a Position:** What should he have done when Sasha asked him for money after the family meeting?

4. **Key Ideas and Details (a) Evaluate:** Do you think what Sasha did should be punished as a crime? Why or why not? **(b) Relate:** What would you have done if you were one of Sasha's uncles? Explain.

5. **Integration of Knowledge and Ideas (a)** Did Ivan Markovitch make progress with the other uncles in his fight for Sasha? Why or why not? **(b)** Explain why you think Sasha did or did not learn his lesson after being given a second chance. *[Connect to the Big Question: Can progress be made without conflict?]*

Literary Analysis:
Character and Characterization

1. Key Ideas and Details Use details from the story to compare and contrast the **characters** of Ivan Markovitch and the Colonel.

2. Key Ideas and Details Give three examples of **indirect characterization** used to portray Sasha. Use a chart like this one.

What He Says

What He Does

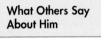
What Others Say About Him

3. Key Ideas and Details How does the character of Sasha **develop** over the course of the story?

4. Key Ideas and Details **(a)** Give two examples of **dialogue** from Sasha and two from Ivan. **(b)** What do your examples reveal about their differences?

Reading Skill: Make Inferences

5. Make an inference about how Sasha feels having been caught doing wrong. On which story details is your inference based?

6. Make an inference about Ivan's feelings at the end of the story. Support your inference with story details and your own experience.

Vocabulary

Acquisition and Use Answer each question. Explain how the meaning of the underlined word influences your answer.

1. Why might you expect a <u>candid</u> answer from a good friend?

2. When might it be a good idea to keep your conversation <u>subdued</u>?

3. Is someone who displays a <u>pretense</u> of wealth actually rich?

4. What <u>lofty</u> goals might an aspiring actor have?

5. Would you want to spend a lot of time with a <u>detestable</u> person?

6. When might a child expect an <u>edifying</u> speech from an adult?

Word Study Use the context of the sentences and what you know about the **Latin suffix -able** to explain your answer to each question.

1. If you have a *curable* disease, will you feel better soon?

2. When an athlete makes a *remarkable* play, do spectators cheer?

Word Study

The **Latin suffix -*able***
means "worthy of;
capable of being."

Apply It Explain how
the suffix -*able* contributes to the meanings of
these words. Consult a
dictionary if necessary.
admirable
calculable
negotiable

Integrated Language Skills

A Visit to Grandmother • A Problem

Conventions: Principal Parts of Regular Verbs

A **verb** is a word that expresses existence, action, or occurrence in a sentence. A verb has four **principal parts:** the present, the present participle, the past, and the past participle.

Most of the verbs in the English language form the present participle by adding *-ing* to the present. The past and the past participle of most verbs add *-ed* or *-d* to the present.

The Four Principal Parts of Verbs			
Present	**Present Participle**	**Past**	**Past Participle**
talk	(is) talking	talked	(have) talked
type	(is) typing	typed	(have) typed

Practice A Identify the verb in each sentence, and indicate whether it is the present, present participle, past, or past participle.

1. Chig has traveled with his father to the South.
2. Chig's grandmother tells stories about the past.
3. The aunts are passing the food to Chig.
4. Chig's father confronted his mother about his childhood.

ⓔ **Reading Application** In "A Visit to Grandmother," find one example of each principal verb part.

Practice B Identify the principal part of the italicized verb in each sentence. Then, rewrite each sentence using a different principal part.

1. Sasha *is waiting* for his uncles to finish their discussion.
2. "I always *borrow* money," Sasha explained.
3. Sasha *jumped* into a sledge and drove off.
4. Ivan Markovitch *has pleaded* Sasha's case to the uncles.

ⓔ **Writing Application** Rewrite this model sentence three times using the other principal parts of the verb: *Sasha prepared a candid explanation.*

PH WRITING COACH | Further instruction and practice are available in *Prentice Hall Writing Coach.*

Writing

Common Core State Standards

L.9-10.4; W.9-10.3.a, W.9-10.3.b, W.9-10.3.d, W.9-10.8
[For the full wording of the standards, see page 238.]

Narrative Text Write two brief **retellings** of the events that took place in the selection you read. For "A Visit to Grandmother," retell the story first as Mama would tell it and then retell the story from GL's viewpoint. For "A Problem," retell the story from the point of view, or perspective, of one of the uncles and then from Sasha's perspective.

- Use a story map or plot diagram to list the main events. Aim for a smooth progression of events.
- Identify details that will show the difference between the characters' perspectives and convey a vivid picture of each character.
- Use the pronoun *I* to write from the character's point of view.
- When you have completed a first draft, evaluate the draft for appropriate point of view.

Grammar Application For clarity, make sure to use the principal parts of verbs correctly in your retelling.

Writing Workshop: *Work in Progress*

Prewriting for a Short Story Select a character trait that would be suitable for a protagonist in a short story. Then, choose a trait for an antagonist. Provide brief descriptions of these two characters based on these traits. Save your Character Descriptions in your writing portfolio.

Use this prewriting activity to prepare for the **Writing Workshop** on page 328.

Research and Technology

Build and Present Knowledge Write a **report on sources** for a research project about either the Great Migration from the rural South or nineteenth-century Russian society.

Follow these steps to complete the assignment:

- Find three to four sources of varied types, including books, online material, CD-ROM references, or audiovisual materials.
- Evaluate the reliability of each source. Consider its date, the author's credentials, and its accuracy.
- Identify and evaluate each source's text features, such as the table of contents, glossary, index, charts, and graphs.
- As you read, identify complexities, look for discrepancies between sources, and note your thoughts and opinions.
- Use a style manual to cite publication information for each source correctly.
- In your report, assess the value of each source. Then, present your report to your class.

www.PHLitOnline.com
- Interactive graphic organizers
- Grammar tutorial
- Interactive journals

Leveled Texts

Build your skills and improve your comprehension of short stories with texts of increasing complexity.

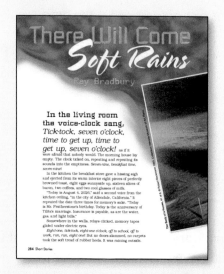

Read **"The Street of the Cañon"** to find out what happens when a mysterious stranger appears at a young woman's birthday party.

Read **"There Will Come Soft Rains"** to learn what happens when technology outlives its creators.

Common Core State Standards

Meet these standards with either **"The Street of the Cañon"** (p. 272) or **"There Will Come Soft Rains"** (p. 284).

Reading Literature
1. Cite strong and thorough textual evidence to support analysis of what the text says explicitly as well as inferences drawn from the text. *(Reading Skill: Make Inferences)*

4. Determine the meaning of words and phrases as they are used in the text, including figurative and connotative meanings; analyze the cumulative impact of specific word choices on meaning and tone. *(Literary Analysis: Setting)*

Spiral Review: RL.9-10.3

Writing
1. Write arguments to support claims in an analysis of substantive topics or texts, using valid reasoning and

relevant and sufficient evidence. *(Writing: Letter and Book Review)*

Speaking and Listening
6. Adapt speech to a variety of contexts and tasks, demonstrating command of formal English when indicated or appropriate. *(Speaking and Listening: Oral Reading)*

Language
4. Determine or clarify the meaning of unknown and multiple-meaning words and phrases based on *grades 9–10 reading and content,* choosing flexibly from a range of strategies. *(Vocabulary: Word Study)*

Literary Analysis: Setting

The time and the place of a story's events are called its **setting.** To establish a setting, writers use **description,** creating word-pictures that appeal to the senses. Settings shape stories in a few ways:

- Setting may affect a story's plot. In a story set in the Arctic wilderness, for example, characters will face challenges not found in a Caribbean resort hotel.

- A well-described setting helps readers understand the time and place of the action in a story. For example, a character from medieval times might be concerned with preserving his honor. A character from the Stone Age, however, might be concerned only with survival.

Before reading either selection, consult the author biographies and background notes. Then, consider the way the setting of the story reflects the time period in which it was written.

Using the Strategy: Setting Chart

To study setting, record details on a **setting chart** like this one.

Reading Skill: Make Inferences

An **inference** is a conclusion that you reach, based on evidence about information that is not stated in a text. Drawing inferences helps you make connections between facts or events. For instance, if a writer does not name a setting but describes extreme cold, hunters huddled in igloos, and a night that will last all winter, you can make the inference that the story is set in the Arctic.

After you make an inference, **read on** to find additional support for your inference. If new details contradict your inference, modify it.

PHLit
Online!
www.PHLitOnline.com

Hear It!
- Selection summary audio
- Selection audio

See It!
- Get Connected video
- Background video
- More about the author
- Vocabulary flashcards

Do It!
- Interactive journals
- Interactive graphic organizers
- Self-test
- Internet activity
- Grammar tutorial
- Interactive vocabulary games

Can progress be made without *conflict?*

Writing About the Big Question

In this selection, the towns of San Juan Iglesias and Hidalgo are in a quarrel. In the midst of the conflict, a mysterious man makes a bold move. Use these sentence starters to develop your ideas about the Big Question:

One possible **motive** for using humor during a quarrel is _____.

Forming personal connections with members of the opposing side is an important step towards **reconciliation** because _____.

While You Read Look for descriptions of the mysterious man's behavior and decide what may motivate his actions.

Vocabulary

Read each word and its definition. Decide whether you know the word well, know it a little bit, or do not know it at all. After you read, see how your knowledge of each word has increased.

- **nonchalantly** (nän´ shə länt´ lē) *adv.* casually; indifferently (p. 274) *Despite the insult, he shrugged <u>nonchalantly</u>.* nonchalance *n.*

- **audaciously** (ô dā´ shəs lē) *adv.* in a bold manner (p. 275) *He is usually so shy, so I was surprised to hear that he had behaved <u>audaciously</u>.* audacious *adj.* audacity *n.*

- **imperiously** (im pir´ ē əs lē) *adv.* arrogantly (p. 275) *She tends to be bossy and give orders <u>imperiously</u>.* imperious *adj.*

- **disdain** (dis dān´) *n.* a feeling or a show of a lack of respect (p. 276) *The men treated their captain with <u>disdain</u> by refusing to salute him when he walked by.* disdainful *adj.* disdainfully *adv.*

- **plausibility** (plô´ zə bil´ i tē) *n.* believability; seeming truth (p. 276) *Although his excuse has some <u>plausibility</u>, I just do not believe it.* plausible *adj.* plausibly *adv.*

- **apprehension** (ap´ rē hen´ shən) *n.* anxious feeling; fear (p. 280) *Filled with <u>apprehension</u>, the children slowly approached the abandoned house.* apprehensive *adj.* apprehensively *adv.*

Word Study

The **Latin suffix -*ity*** means "the quality of or state of being."

In this story, a man hopes the tone he uses has **plausibility**, or the quality of being believable, so his identity is not revealed.

Meet
Josephina Niggli
(1910–1983)

Author of

The Street of the Cañon

Josephina Niggli was born in Monterrey, Mexico, but she grew up on both sides of the border between Mexico and the United States. When Niggli was fifteen, her parents sent her to San Antonio, Texas, to attend school.

Writing for Stage and Screen Niggli published her first book shortly after her high school graduation. Later, she wrote plays. She found theater thrilling, writing, "Once you have experienced the emotion of having a play produced, you are forever lost to the ordinary world."

Later, Niggli worked on movie scripts in Hollywood. In 1945, she published *Mexican Village*, a collection of ten stories that capture the rich local color of Mexico.

Did You Know?
While still in college, Niggli won several prizes for her writing.

BACKGROUND FOR THE STORY

Courtship and Marriage in Old Mexico

Historically, in some parts of Mexico, a man had to ask a woman's family for permission to marry her. In others, the parents arranged the match. In the town in this story, a man and woman are considered engaged if they walk together in the plaza.

Dance in Tehuantepec, 1935. Diego Rivera. Los Angeles County Museum of Art.

The Street of the Cañon

JOSEPHINA NIGGLI

▲ **Critical Viewing**
What does this painting suggest about the setting of the story? **[Infer]**

It was May, the flowering thorn was sweet in the air, and the village of San Juan Iglesias in the Valley of the Three Marys was celebrating. The long dark streets were empty because all of the people, from the lowest-paid cowboy to the mayor, were helping Don Roméo Calderón celebrate his daughter's eighteenth birthday.

On the other side of the town, where the Cañon Road led across the mountains to the Sabinas Valley, a tall slender man, a package clutched tightly against his side, slipped from shadow to shadow.

Once a dog barked, and the man's black suit merged into the blackness of a wall. But no voice called out, and after a moment he slid into the narrow, dirt-packed street again.

The moonlight touched his shoulder and spilled across his narrow hips. He was young, no more than twenty-five, and his black curly head was bare. He walked swiftly along, heading always for the distant sound of guitar and flute. If he met anyone now, who could say from which direction he had come? He might be a trader from Monterrey, or a buyer of cow's milk from farther north in the Valley of the Three Marys. Who would guess that an Hidalgo man dared to walk alone in the moonlit streets of San Juan Iglesias?

Carefully adjusting his flat package so that it was not too prominent, he squared his shoulders and walked jauntily across the street to the laughter-filled house. Little boys packed in the doorway made way for him, smiling and nodding to him. The long, narrow room with the orchestra at one end was filled with whirling dancers. Rigid-backed chaperones[1] were gossiping together, seated in their straight chairs against the plaster walls. Over the scene was the yellow glow of kerosene lanterns, and the air was hot with the too-sweet perfume of gardenias, tuberoses,[2] and the pungent scent of close-packed humanity.

The man in the doorway, while trying to appear at ease, was carefully examining every smiling face. If just one person recognized him, the room would turn on him like a den of snarling mountain cats, but so far all the laughter-dancing eyes were friendly.

Suddenly a plump, officious little man, his round cheeks glistening with perspiration, pushed his way through the crowd. His voice, many times too large for his small body, boomed at the man in the doorway. "Welcome, stranger, welcome to our house." Thrusting his arm through the stranger's, and almost dislodging the package, he started to lead the way through the maze of dancers. "Come and drink a toast to my daughter—to my beautiful Sarita. She is eighteen this night."

In the square patio the gentle breeze ruffled the pink and white oleander bushes. A long table set up on sawhorses held loaves of flaky crusted French bread, stacks of thin, delicate tortillas, plates of barbecued beef, and long red rolls of spicy sausages. But most of all there were cheeses, for the Three Marys was a cheese-eating valley. There were yellow cheese and white cheese and curded

Reading Skill
Make Inferences
Make an inference about the towns of Hidalgo and San Juan Iglesias. What kinds of details might confirm your inference?

Literary Analysis
Setting To which senses does this description of the setting appeal?

Reading Check

What occasion is the village of San Juan Iglesias celebrating?

---

1. **chaperones** (shap´ ər ōnz´) older or married women who accompany and supervise the behavior of a young person in public.
2. **gardenias** (gär dēn´ yəz), **tuberoses** (tōōb´ rōz´ əs) two types of plant with especially sweet-smelling flowers.

Spanish Vocabulary

Set in Mexico, the story contains several Spanish words and terms, including

- **cañon** canyon; a narrow valley between high cliffs

- **tío** uncle

- **hola** Spanish exclamation meaning "hi"

- **don** title of respect meaning "sir"; often placed before a man's name

- **parada** literally, "parade"; a dance in which partners stride around together

Connect to the Literature

Why do you think Niggli included these terms in the story? **[Hypothesize]**

Vocabulary

nonchalantly (nän´ shə länt´ lē) *adv.* casually; indifferently

cheese from cow's milk. There was even a flat white cake of goat cheese from distant Linares, a delicacy too expensive for any but feast days.

To set off this feast were bottles of beer floating in ice-filled tin tubs, and another table was covered with bottles of mescal, of tequila, of maguey wine.

Don Roméo Calderón thrust a glass of tequila into the stranger's hand. "Drink, friend, to the prettiest girl in San Juan. As pretty as my fine fighting cocks, she is. On her wedding day she takes to her man, and may she find him soon, the best fighter in my flock. Drink deep, friend. Even the rivers flow with wine."

The Hidalgo man laughed and raised his glass high. "May the earth be always fertile beneath her feet."

Someone called to Don Roméo that more guests were arriving, and with a final delighted pat on the stranger's shoulder, the little man scurried away. As the young fellow smiled after his retreating host, his eyes caught and held another pair of eyes—laughing black eyes set in a young girl's face. The last time he had seen that face it had been white and tense with rage, and the lips clenched tight to prevent an outgushing stream of angry words. That had been in February, and she had worn a white lace shawl over her hair. Now it was May, and a gardenia was a splash of white in the glossy dark braids. The moonlight had mottled his face that February night, and he knew that she did not recognize him. He grinned impudently[3] back at her, and her eyes widened, then slid sideways to one of the chaperones. The fan in her small hand snapped shut. She tapped its parchment tip against her mouth and slipped away to join the dancing couples in the front room. The gestures of a fan translate into a coded language on the frontier. The stranger raised one eyebrow as he interpreted the signal.

But he did not move toward her at once. Instead, he inched slowly back against the table. No one was behind him, and his hands quickly unfastened the package he had been guarding so long. Then he nonchalantly walked into the front room.

The girl was sitting close to a chaperone. As he came up to her he swerved slightly toward the bushy-browed old lady.

"Your servant, señora. I kiss your hands and feet."

The chaperone stared at him in astonishment. Such fine manners were not common to the town of San Juan Iglesias.

"Eh, you're a stranger," she said. "I thought so."

---

3. **impudently** (im´ pyo͞o dənt lē) *adv.* in a shamelessly bold or provocative way.

"But a stranger no longer, señora, now that I have met you." He bent over her, so close she could smell the faint fragrance of talcum on his freshly shaven cheek.

"Will you dance the *parada* with me?"

This request startled her eyes into popping open beneath the heavy brows. "So, my young rooster, would you flirt with me, and I old enough to be your grandmother?"

"Can you show me a prettier woman to flirt with in the Valley of the Three Marys?" he asked audaciously.

She grinned at him and turned toward the girl at her side. "This young fool wants to meet you, my child."

The girl blushed to the roots of her hair and shyly lowered her white lids. The old woman laughed aloud.

"Go out and dance, the two of you. A man clever enough to pat the sheep has a right to play with the lamb."

The next moment they had joined the circle of dancers and Sarita was trying to control her laughter.

"She is the worst dragon in San Juan. And how easily you won her!"

"What is a dragon," he asked imperiously, "when I longed to dance with you?"

"Ay," she retorted, "you have a quick tongue. I think you are a dangerous man."

In answer he drew her closer to him, and turned her toward the orchestra. As he reached the chief violinist he called out, "Play the Virgencita, 'The Shy Young Maiden.'"

The violinist's mouth opened in soundless surprise. The girl in his arms said sharply, "You heard him, the *Borachita*, 'The Little Drunken Girl.'" •

Vocabulary

audaciously (ô dā´ shəs lē) *adv.* in a bold manner

imperiously (im pir´ ē əs lē) *adv.* arrogantly

Reading Check

Why does the stranger ask the girl's chaperone to dance?

With a relieved grin, the violinist tapped his music stand with his bow, and the music swung into the sad farewell of a man to his sweetheart:

> *Farewell, my little drunken one,*
> *I must go to the capital*
> *To serve the master*
> *Who makes me weep for my return.*

The stranger frowned down at her. "Is this a joke, señorita?" he asked coldly.

"No," she whispered, looking about her quickly to see if the incident had been observed. "But the Virgencita is the favorite song of Hidalgo, a village on the other side of the mountains in the next valley. The people of Hidalgo and San Juan Iglesias do not speak."

"That is a stupid thing," said the man from Hidalgo as he swung her around in a large turn. "Is not music free as air? Why should one town own the rights to a song?"

The girl shuddered slightly. "Those people from Hidalgo—they are wicked monsters. Can you guess what they did not six months since?"

The man started to point out that the space of time from February to May was three months, but he thought it better not to appear too wise. "Did these Hidalgo monsters frighten you, señorita? If they did, I personally will kill them all."

She moved closer against him and tilted her face until her mouth was close to his ear. "They attempted to steal the bones of Don Rómolo Balderas."

"Is it possible?" He made his eyes grow round and his lips purse up in disdain. "Surely not that! Why, all the world knows that Don Rómolo Balderas was the greatest historian in the entire Republic. Every school child reads his books. Wise men from Quintana Roo to the Río Bravo bow their heads in admiration to his name. What a wicked thing to do!" He hoped his virtuous tone was not too virtuous for plausibility, but she did not seem to notice.

"It is true! In the night they came. Three devils!"

"Young devils, I hope."

"Young or old, who cares? They were devils. The blacksmith surprised them even as they were opening the grave. He raised such a shout that all of San Juan rushed to his aid, for they were fighting, I can tell you. Especially one of them—their leader."

"And who was he?"

"You have heard of him doubtless. A proper wild one named Pepe Gonzalez."

Spiral Review
Plot What conflict does the stranger's cold reaction to the song help develop?

Vocabulary
disdain (dis dān´) *n.* a feeling or a show of a lack of respect

plausibility (plô´ zə bil´ i tē) *n.* believability; seeming truth

"And what happened to them?"

"They had horses and got away, but one, I think, was hurt."

The Hidalgo man twisted his mouth remembering how Rubén the candymaker had ridden across the whitewashed line high on the cañon trail that marked the division between the Three Marys' and the Sabinas' sides of the mountains, and then had fallen in a faint from his saddle because his left arm was broken. There was no candy in Hidalgo for six weeks, and the entire Sabinas Valley resented that broken arm as fiercely as did Rubén.

The stranger tightened his arm in reflexed anger about Sarita's waist as she said, "All the world knows that the men of Hidalgo are sons of the mountain witches."

"But even devils are shy of disturbing the honored dead," he said gravely.

"'Don Rómolo was born in our village,' Hidalgo says. 'His bones belong to us.' Well, anyone in the valley can tell you he died in San Juan Iglesias, and here his bones will stay! Is that not proper? Is that not right?"

To keep from answering, he guided her through an intricate dance pattern that led them past the patio door. Over her head he could see two men and a woman staring with amazement at the open package on the table.

▲ **Critical Viewing**
Compare the mood of this painting with the mood of the story. **[Compare and Contrast]**

Reading Skill
Make Inferences
Make an inference about the stranger's connection to the men who tried to raid the grave.

Reading Check

What did three men from Hidalgo try to do six months earlier?

His eyes on the patio, he asked blandly, "You say the leader was one Pepe Gonzalez? The name seems to have a familiar sound."

"But naturally. He has a talent." She tossed her head and stepped away from him as the music stopped. It was a dance of two *paradas.* He slipped his hand through her arm and guided her into place in the large oval of parading couples. Twice around the room and the orchestra would play again.

"A talent?" he prompted.

"For doing the impossible. When all the world says a thing cannot be done, he does it to prove the world wrong. Why, he climbed to the top of the Prow, and not even the long vanished Joaquín Castillo had ever climbed that mountain before. And this same Pepe caught a mountain lion with nothing to aid him but a rope and his two bare hands."

"He doesn't sound such a bad friend," protested the stranger, slipping his arm around her waist as the music began to play the merry song of the soap bubbles:

> *Pretty bubbles of a thousand colors*
> *That ride on the wind*
> *And break as swiftly*
> *As a lover's heart.*

The events in the patio were claiming his attention. Little by little he edged her closer to the door. The group at the table had considerably enlarged. There was a low murmur of excitement from the crowd.

"What has happened?" asked Sarita, attracted by the noise.

"There seems to be something wrong at the table," he answered, while trying to peer over the heads of the people in front of him. Realizing that this might be the last moment of peace he would have that evening, he bent toward her.

"If I come back on Sunday, will you walk around the plaza with me?"

She was startled into exclaiming, "Ay, no!"

"Please. Just once around."

"And you think I'd walk more than once with you, señor, even if you were no stranger? In San Juan Iglesias, to walk around the plaza with a girl means a wedding."

"Ha, and you think that is common to San Juan alone? Even the devils of Hidalgo respect that law," he added hastily at her puzzled upward glance. "And so they do in all the villages." To cover his lapse[4] he said softly, "I don't even know your name."

---

4. **lapse** (laps) *n.* slip; error.

Literary Analysis
Setting How does the time and place of the story affect the way Sarita responds to the stranger?

A mischievous grin crinkled the corners of her eyes. "Nor do I know yours, señor. Strangers do not often walk the streets of San Juan." •

Before he could answer, the chattering in the patio swelled to louder proportions. Don Roméo's voice lay on top, like thick cream on milk. "I tell you it is a jewel of a cheese. Such flavor, such texture, such whiteness. It is a jewel of a cheese."

"What has happened?" Sarita asked of a woman at her elbow.

"A fine goat's cheese appeared as if by magic on the table. No one knows where it came from."

"Probably an extra one from Linares," snorted a fat bald man on the right.

"Linares never made such a cheese as this," said the woman decisively.

"Silence!" roared Don Roméo. "Old Tío Daniel would speak a word to us."

A great hand of silence closed down over the mouths of the people. The girl was standing on tiptoe trying vainly to see what was happening. She was hardly aware of the stranger's whispering voice although she remembered the words that he said. "Sunday night—once around the plaza."

She did not realize that he had moved away, leaving a gap that was quickly filled by the blacksmith.

Old Tío Daniel's voice was a shrill squeak, and his thin, stringy neck jutted forth from his body like a turtle's from its shell. "This is no cheese from Linares," he said with authority, his mouth sucking in over his toothless gums between his sentences. "Years ago, when the great Don Rómolo Balderas was still alive, we had such cheese as this—ay, in those days we had it. But after he died and was buried in our own sainted ground, as was right and proper . . ."

"Yes, yes," muttered voices in the crowd. He glared at the interruption. As soon as there was silence again, he continued:

"After he died, we had it no more. Shall I tell you why?"

"Tell us, Tío Daniel," said the voices humbly.

"Because it is made in Hidalgo!"

The sound of a waterfall, the sound of a wind in a narrow cañon, and the sound of an angry crowd are much the same. There were no distinct words, but the sound was enough.

"Are you certain, Tío?" boomed Don Roméo.

"As certain as I am that a donkey has long ears. The people of Hidalgo have been famous for generations for making cheese like

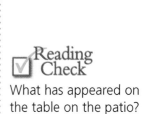

Reading Check
What has appeared on the table on the patio?

The Street of the Cañon **279**

Reading Skill
Make Inferences Do details here support your inference about the stranger's link with Hidalgo? Explain.

Vocabulary
apprehension
(ap´ rē hen´ shən) *n.* anxious feeling; fear

this—especially that wicked one, that owner of a cheese factory, Timotéo Gonzalez, father to Pepe, the wild one, whom we have good cause to remember."

"We do, we do," came the sigh of assurance.

"But on the whole northern frontier there are no vats like his to produce so fine a product. Ask the people of Chihuahua, of Sonora. Ask the man on the bridge at Laredo, or the man in his boat at Tampico, '*Hola,* friend, who makes the finest goat cheese?' And the answer will always be the same, 'Don Timotéo of Hidalgo.'"

It was the blacksmith who asked the great question. "Then where did that cheese come from, and we haters of Hidalgo these ten long years?"

No voice said, "The stranger," but with one fluid movement every head in the patio turned toward the girl in the doorway. She also turned, her eyes wide with something that she realized to her own amazement was more apprehension than anger.

But the stranger was not in the room. When the angry, muttering men pushed through to the street, the stranger was not on the plaza. He was not anywhere in sight. A few of the more religious crossed themselves for fear that the Devil had walked in their midst. "Who was he?" one voice asked another. But Sarita, who was meekly listening to a lecture from Don Roméo on the propriety of dancing with strangers, did not have to ask. She had a strong suspicion that she had danced that night within the circling arm of Pepe Gonzalez.

Critical Thinking

Cite textual evidence to support your responses.

1. **Key Ideas and Details (a)** What adjectives does the author use to describe the way the Hidalgo man walks into the village? **(b) Infer:** What does the man wish to prevent others from learning?

2. **Key Ideas and Details (a)** Whom does the Hidalgo man first ask to dance? **(b) Infer:** Why does he ask her?

3. **Key Ideas and Details (a) Summarize:** Why are the towns quarreling? **(b) Hypothesize:** What might the villagers have done to the stranger if they had known his identity? Explain your answer.

4. **Integration of Knowledge and Ideas** Why does the stranger risk danger to dance with Sarita and leave the gift? Explain your answer using details from the story. *[Connect to the Big Question: Can progress be made without conflict?]*

Literary Analysis: Setting

© **1. Craft and Structure** **(a)** Identify these aspects of the story's **setting:** the country, the town, and the historical period. **(b)** For each aspect, give an example of a **description** that helps make the setting vivid for readers.

© **2. Craft and Structure** Explain why the dangers the man from Hidalgo faces might not apply in a story set in a different town or time.

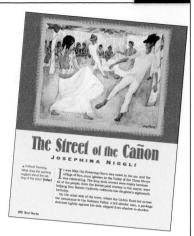

Reading Skill: Make Inferences

3. (a) Based on the information in the first three paragraphs of the story, what two **inferences** could you make about the stranger's plans? **(b)** For each inference, note at least one detail later in the story that either confirms it or disproves it. Record your answers in a chart like the one shown.

Inference	Confirming Details	Disproving Details

4. Make an inference concerning Sarita's feelings about the stranger at the end of the story. Give three details to support your inference.

Vocabulary

© **Acquisition and Use** Match each statement with a word from the vocabulary list on page 270. Explain each choice.

1. Some say that a good story should have this quality.

2. A conceited individual might act this way.

3. A nervous person may have difficulty behaving this way.

4. People with many fears often feel a sense of this.

5. A captain who treated his or her officers with this attitude would be disliked.

6. Extreme situations call for people to act this way.

Word Study Use the context of the sentences and what you know about the **Latin suffix -ity** to explain your answer to each question.

1. Could you read a letter that lacked *legibility*?

2. Is a movie that is known for its *complexity* easy to understand?

Word Study

The **Latin suffix -ity** means "the quality of or state of being."

Apply It Explain how the suffix -ity contributes to the meanings of these words. Consult a dictionary if necessary.

accessibility
activity
responsibility

Can progress be made without *conflict?*

Writing About the Big Question

In this story, the human race has achieved a high level of technology, but at a terrible cost. Use these sentence starters to develop your ideas about the Big Question:

A benefit of technological **progress** is _____.

A possible downside of new technology is _____.

While You Read Notice what technology allows the house to do during the course of one day. Then, determine if these advances are positive or negative.

Vocabulary

Read each word and its definition. Decide whether you know the word well, know it a little bit, or do not know it at all. After you read, see how your knowledge of each word has increased.

- **titanic** (tī tan´ ik) *adj.* powerful; of great size (p. 287) *A single titanic wave sank the ship.* titan *n.*

- **paranoia** (par´ ə noi´ ə) *n.* mental disorder characterized by delusions (p. 287) *His irrational fear of crowded places could be a sign of paranoia.* paranoid *adj.*

- **fluttered** (flut´ ərd) *v.* flapped or vibrated rapidly (p. 288) *The papers fluttered in the wind and then blew away.* flutter *n.*

- **manipulated** (mə nip´ yoō lāt´ id) *v.* managed or controlled through clever moves (p. 288) *The sculptor molded and manipulated the clay into different shapes.* manipulative *adj.* manipulation *n.*

- **tremulous** (trem´ yoō ləs) *adj.* trembling; quivering; timid; fearful (p. 289) *The cup shook in his tremulous hands.* tremulously *adv.*

- **oblivious** (ə bliv´ ē əs) *adj.* unaware (p. 291) *Oblivious to the shark that was quickly approaching, the turtle swam peacefully.* oblivion *n.* obliviously *adv.*

Word Study

The **Greek suffix -ic** means "having the characteristic of" or "pertaining to."

In this story, an event of **titanic** proportions, pertaining to giant consequences, has occurred.

©Thomas Victor

Author of
There Will Come
Soft Rains

Ray Bradbury, one of the world's most celebrated science-fiction and fantasy writers, was born in Waukegan, Illinois, and grew up near Lake Michigan. As a child, he was influenced by the stories of Edgar Allan Poe and developed a fascination with horror movies and futuristic fantasy.

Dreaming the Impossible Bradbury considers most of his work fantasy rather than science fiction, explaining, "Science fiction is the art of the possible. Fantasy is the art of the impossible." One of his dreams remains an impossible fantasy, at least for now—he wants to go to Mars. "But since it's not going to happen," he explains, "I don't worry about it."

BACKGROUND FOR THE STORY

The Atomic Age

Ray Bradbury published this story in 1950. Five years earlier, the United States had dropped the first atomic bombs on Japan. One year before the story was published, the Soviet Union had tested its own atomic device. This story reflects the fear at that time that these rival nations might unleash their deadly technology and destroy humanity.

The Body of a House, #5 of 8. © Robert Beckmann 1993. Collection: Nevada Museum of Art, Reno.

Did You Know?
In 2002, Bradbury was commemorated with a star on the Hollywood Walk of Fame.

There Will Come *Soft Rains*

Ray Bradbury

In the living room the voice-clock sang, *Tick-tock, seven o'clock, time to get up, time to get up, seven o'clock!* as if it were afraid that nobody would. The morning house lay empty. The clock ticked on, repeating and repeating its sounds into the emptiness. *Seven-nine, breakfast time, seven-nine!*

In the kitchen the breakfast stove gave a hissing sigh and ejected from its warm interior eight pieces of perfectly browned toast, eight eggs sunnyside up, sixteen slices of bacon, two coffees, and two cool glasses of milk.

"Today is August 4, 2026," said a second voice from the kitchen ceiling, "in the city of Allendale, California." It repeated the date three times for memory's sake. "Today is Mr. Featherstone's birthday. Today is the anniversary of Tilita's marriage. Insurance is payable, as are the water, gas, and light bills."

Somewhere in the walls, relays clicked, memory tapes glided under electric eyes.

Eight-one, tick-tock, eight-one o'clock, off to school, off to work, run, run, eight one! But no doors slammed, no carpets took the soft tread of rubber heels. It was

The Body of a House, #1 of 8. © Robert Beckmann 1993. Collection: Nevada Museum of Art, Reno.

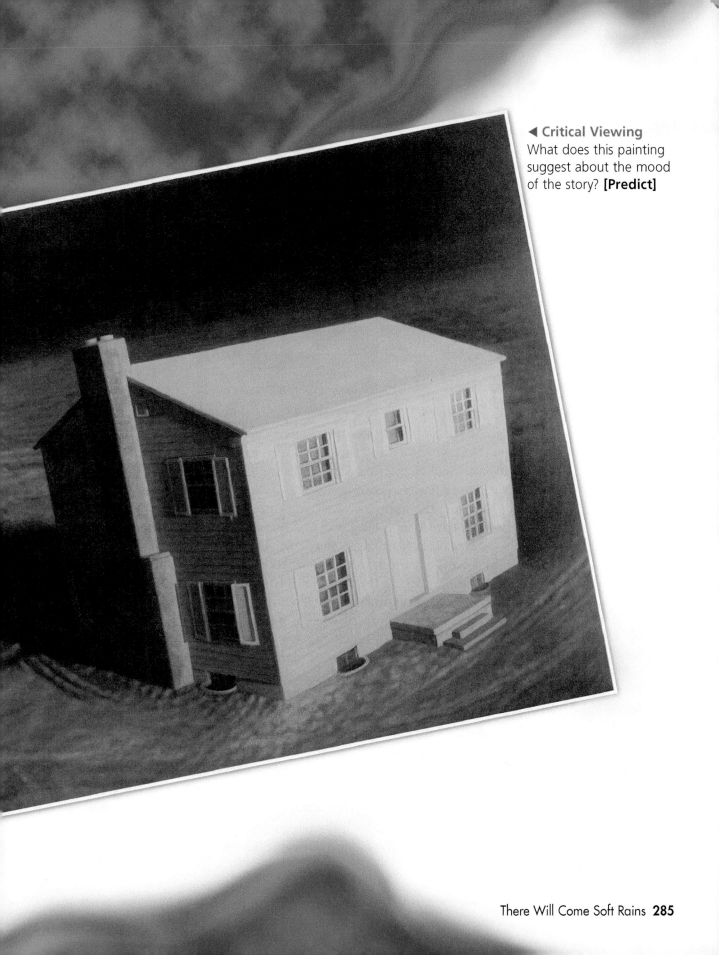

◀ **Critical Viewing**
What does this painting
suggest about the mood
of the story? **[Predict]**

The Body of a House, #2 of 8. © Robert Beckmann 1993. Collection: Nevada Museum of Art, Reno.

▶ **Critical Viewing**
Compare and contrast the house in this painting with the house at this point in the story. **[Compare and Contrast]**

Reading Skill
Make Inferences
Make an inference about the inhabitants of the house. What kinds of confirming details will you look for as you read on?

raining outside. The weather box on the front door sang quietly: "Rain, rain, go away; rubbers, raincoats for today . . ." And the rain tapped on the empty house, echoing.

Outside, the garage chimed and lifted its door to reveal the waiting car. After a long wait the door swung down again.

At eight-thirty the eggs were shriveled and the toast was like stone. An aluminum wedge scraped them into the sink, where hot water whirled them down a metal throat which digested and flushed them away to the distant sea. The dirty dishes were dropped into a hot washer and emerged twinkling dry.

Nine-fifteen, sang the clock, *time to clean.*

Out of warrens in the wall, tiny robot mice darted. The rooms were acrawl with the small cleaning animals, all rubber and metal. They thudded against chairs, whirling their mustached runners, kneading the rug nap, sucking gently at hidden dust. Then, like mysterious invaders, they popped into their burrows. Their pink electric eyes faded. The house was clean.

Ten o'clock. The sun came out from behind the rain. The house stood alone in a city of rubble and ashes. This was the one house left standing. At night the ruined city gave off a radioactive glow which could be seen for miles.

Ten-fifteen. The garden sprinklers whirled up in golden founts, filling the soft morning air with scatterings of brightness. The water pelted windowpanes, running down the charred west side where the house had been burned evenly free of its white paint. The entire west face of the house was black, save for five places. Here the silhouette[1] in paint of a man mowing a lawn. Here, as in a photograph, a woman bent to pick flowers. Still farther over, their images burned on wood in one titanic instant, a small boy, hands flung into the air; higher up, the image of a thrown ball, and opposite him a girl, hands raised to catch a ball which never came down.

The five spots of paint—the man, the woman, the children, the ball—remained. The rest was a thin charcoaled layer.

The gentle-sprinkler rain filled the garden with falling light.

Until this day, how well the house had kept its peace. How carefully it had inquired, "Who goes there? What's the password?" and, getting no answer from lonely foxes and whining cats, it had shut up its windows and drawn shades in an old-maidenly preoccupation with self-protection which bordered on a mechanical paranoia.

It quivered at each sound, the house did. If a sparrow brushed a window, the shade snapped up. The bird, startled, flew off! No, not even a bird must touch the house!

The house was an altar with ten thousand attendants, big, small, servicing, attending, in choirs. But the gods had gone away, and the ritual of the religion continued senselessly, uselessly. ●

Twelve noon.

A dog whined, shivering, on the front porch.

The front door recognized the dog voice and opened. The dog, once huge and fleshy, but now gone to bone and covered with sores, moved in and through the house, tracking mud. Behind it whirred angry mice, angry at having to pick up mud, angry at inconvenience.

For not a leaf fragment blew under the door but what the wall panels flipped open and the copper scrap rats flashed swiftly out. The offending dust, hair, or paper, seized in miniature steel jaws, was raced back to the burrows. There, down tubes which fed into the cellar, it was dropped into the sighing vent of an incinerator which sat like evil Baal[2] in a dark corner.

The dog ran upstairs, hysterically yelping to each door, at last realizing, as the house realized, that only silence was here.

It sniffed the air and scratched the kitchen door. Behind the door, the stove was making pancakes which filled the house with a rich baked odor and the scent of maple syrup.

---

1. **silhouette** (sil´ ə wet´) *n.* outline of a figure, filled in with a solid color.
2. **Baal** (bā´ əl) *n.* ancient Near Eastern deity, later associated with evil.

Vocabulary
titanic (tī tan´ ik) *adj.* powerful; of great size

Literary Analysis
Setting What new information have you learned about the setting of the story?

Vocabulary
paranoia (par´ ə noi´ ə) *n.* mental disorder characterized by delusions

What has happened to the rest of the city?

Vocabulary
fluttered (fluť ərd)
v. flapped or vibrated
rapidly

The dog frothed at the mouth, lying at the door, sniffing, its eyes turned to fire. It ran wildly in circles, biting at its tail, spun in a frenzy, and died. It lay in the parlor for an hour.

Two o'clock, sang a voice.

Delicately sensing decay at last, the regiments of mice hummed out as softly as blown gray leaves in an electrical wind.

Two-fifteen.

The dog was gone.

In the cellar, the incinerator glowed suddenly and a whirl of sparks leaped up the chimney.

Two thirty-five.

Bridge tables sprouted from patio walls. Playing cards fluttered onto pads in a shower of pips. Glasses manifested on an oaken bench with egg-salad sandwiches. Music played.

But the tables were silent and the cards untouched.

At four o'clock the tables folded like great butterflies back through the paneled walls.

Four-thirty.

The nursery walls glowed.

Animals took shape: yellow giraffes, blue lions, pink antelopes, lilac panthers cavorting in crystal substance. The walls were glass. They looked out upon color and fantasy. Hidden films clocked through well-oiled sprockets, and the walls lived. The nursery floor was woven to resemble a crisp, cereal meadow. Over this ran aluminum roaches and iron crickets, and in the hot still air butterflies of delicate red tissue wavered among the sharp aroma of animal spoors![3] There was the sound like a great matted yellow hive of bees within a dark bellows, the lazy bumble of a purring lion. And there was the patter of okapi[4] feet and the murmur of a fresh jungle rain, like other hoofs, falling upon the summer-starched grass. Now the walls dissolved into distances of parched weed, mile on mile, and warm endless sky. The animals drew away into thorn brakes and water holes.

It was the children's hour.

Five o'clock. The bath filled with clear hot water.

Six, seven, eight o'clock. The dinner dishes manipulated like magic tricks, and in the study a *click.* In the hearth a fire now blazed up warmly.

Nine o'clock. The beds warmed their hidden circuits, for nights were cool here.

Nine-five. A voice spoke from the study ceiling:

Literary Analysis
Setting How does this description show that the story is set in a time different from the present?

Vocabulary
manipulated (mə nip´ yo͞o lāt´ id) *v.* managed or controlled through clever moves

---

3. spoors (spo͝orz) *n.* droppings of wild animals.
4. okapi (ō kä´ pē) *n.* African animal related to the giraffe but with a much shorter neck.

The Body of a House, #4 of 8. © Robert Beckmann 1993.
Collection: Nevada Museum of Art, Reno.

"Mrs. McClellan, which poem would you like this evening?"
The house was silent.

The voice said at last, "Since you express no preference, I shall select a poem at random." Quiet music rose to back the voice. "Sara Teasdale. As I recall, your favorite. . . .

> *There will come soft rains and the smell of the ground,*
> *And swallows circling with their shimmering sound;*
>
> *And frogs in the pools singing at night,*
> *And wild plum trees in* tremulous *white;*
>
> *Robins will wear their feathery fire,*
> *Whistling their whims on a low fence-wire;*
>
> *And not one will know of the war, not one*
> *Will care at last when it is done.*
>
> *Not one would mind, neither bird nor tree,*
> *If mankind perished utterly;*

And Spring herself, when she woke at dawn
Would scarcely know that we were gone."

The fire burned on the stone hearth. The empty chairs faced each other between the silent walls, and the music played. •

At ten o'clock the house began to die.

The wind blew. A falling tree bough crashed through the kitchen window. Cleaning solvent, bottled, shattered over the stove. The room was ablaze in an instant!

"Fire!" screamed a voice. The house lights flashed, water pumps shot water from the ceilings. But the solvent spread on the linoleum, licking, eating, under the kitchen door, while the voices took it up in chorus: "Fire, fire, fire!"

The house tried to save itself. Doors sprang tightly shut, but the windows were broken by the heat and the wind blew and sucked upon the fire.

The house gave ground as the fire in ten billion angry sparks moved with flaming ease from room to room and then up the stairs. While scurrying water rats squeaked from the walls, pistoled their water, and ran for more. And the wall sprays let down showers of mechanical rain.

But too late. Somewhere, sighing, a pump shrugged to a stop. The quenching rain ceased. The reserve water supply which had filled baths and washed dishes for many quiet days was gone.

The fire crackled up the stairs. It fed upon Picassos and Matisses[5] in the upper halls, like delicacies, baking off the oily flesh, tenderly crisping the canvases into black shavings.

Now the fire lay in beds, stood in windows, changed the colors of drapes!

And then, reinforcements.

From attic trapdoors, blind robot faces peered down with faucet mouths gushing green chemical.

The fire backed off, as even an elephant must at the sight of a dead snake. Now there were twenty snakes whipping over the floor, killing the fire with a clear cold venom of green froth.

But the fire was clever. It had sent flame outside the house, up through the attic to the pumps there. An explosion! The attic brain which directed the pumps was shattered into bronze shrapnel on the beams.

---

5. Picassos (pi kä´ sōz) **and Matisses** (mä tēs´ ez) paintings by the celebrated modern painters Pablo Picasso (1881–1973) and Henri Matisse (1869–1954).

Spiral Review

Plot Which details make the house seem human? How does this characterization of the house intensify the rising action?

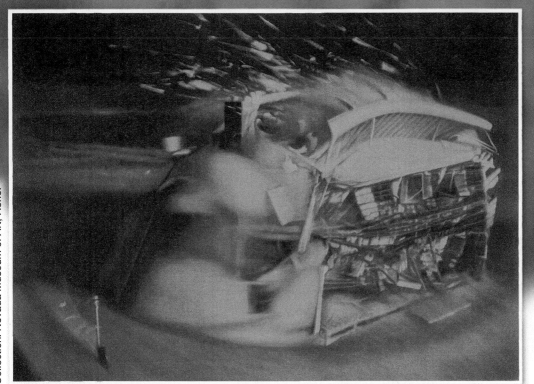

The Body of a House, #5 of 8. © Robert Beckmann 1993. Collection: Nevada Museum of Art, Reno.

The fire rushed back into every closet and felt of the clothes hung there.

The house shuddered, oak bone on bone, its bared skeleton cringing from the heat, its wire, its nerves revealed as if a surgeon had torn the skin off to let the red veins and capillaries quiver in the scalded air. Help, help! Fire! Run, run! Heat snapped mirrors like the first brittle winter ice. And the voices wailed Fire, fire, run, run, like a tragic nursery rhyme, a dozen voices, high, low, like children dying in a forest, alone, alone. And the voices fading as the wires popped their sheathings like hot chestnuts. One, two, three, four, five voices died.

In the nursery the jungle burned. Blue lions roared, purple giraffes bounded off. The panthers ran in circles, changing color, and ten million animals, running before the fire, vanished off toward a distant steaming river. . . .

Ten more voices died. In the last instant under the fire avalanche, other choruses, oblivious, could be heard announcing the time, playing music, cutting the lawn by remote-control mower, or setting an umbrella frantically out and in the slamming and opening front door, a thousand things happening, like a clock shop when each clock strikes the hour insanely before or after the other, a scene of maniac confusion, yet unity; singing, screaming, a few last cleaning mice darting bravely out to carry the horrid ashes away! And one voice, with sublime disregard for the situation, read poetry aloud in

Reading Skill
Make Inferences
Based on the details in this paragraph, what do you infer is happening?

Vocabulary
oblivious (ə bliv′ ē əs) *adj.* unaware

Reading Check
What starts the fire in the house?

the fiery study, until all the film spools burned, until all the wires withered and the circuits cracked.

The fire burst the house and let it slam flat down, puffing out skirts of spark and smoke.

In the kitchen, an instant before the rain of fire and timber, the stove could be seen making breakfasts at a psychopathic rate, ten dozen eggs, six loaves of toast, twenty dozen bacon strips, which, eaten by fire, started the stove working again, hysterically hissing!

The crash. The attic smashing into kitchen and parlor. The parlor into cellar, cellar into subcellar. Deep freeze, armchair, film tapes, circuits, beds, and all like skeletons thrown in a cluttered mound deep under.

Smoke and silence. A great quantity of smoke.

Dawn showed faintly in the east. Among the ruins, one wall stood alone. Within the wall, a last voice said, over and over again and again, even as the sun rose to shine upon the heaped rubble and steam:

"Today is August 5, 2026, today is August 5, 2026, today is . . ."

Critical Thinking

Cite textual evidence to support your responses.

1. **Key Ideas and Details (a)** List five automated tasks the house performs. **(b) Infer:** What is missing in the routine of activity that the house performs? **(c) Interpret:** What is a likely reason for this absence? Give details in support of your answer.

2. **Key Ideas and Details (a) Infer:** Why does the house continue its activity even when it no longer makes sense? **(b) Analyze:** What does this fact indicate about the human qualities the house lacks?

3. **Key Ideas and Details (a) Make a Judgment:** Do you think Bradbury gives a realistic view of the future of technology? Explain. **(b) Discuss:** Trade answers with a partner. After you have read your partner's response, discuss your answers. **(c) Reflect:** Afterward, write a sentence or two explaining whether your partner's views have influenced your own.

4. **Integration of Knowledge and Ideas** Are the technological advances described in the story more positive or negative? Explain. *[Connect to the Big Question: Can progress be made without conflict?]*

There Will Come Soft Rains

Literary Analysis: Setting

1. **Craft and Structure** **(a)** Identify these aspects of the story's **setting:** the place in which events occur; the historical period. **(b)** For each aspect, give an example of a **description** that helps make this setting vivid for readers.

2. **Craft and Structure** Explain why the setting of the story is also its main character.

Reading Skill: Make Inferences

3. **(a)** Based on information in the first two pages of the story, what two **inferences** could you make about events that occurred before the story opens? **(b)** For each inference, note at least one detail later in the story that either confirms it or disproves it. Record your answers in a chart like the one shown.

Inference	Confirming Details	Disproving Details

4. **(a)** What can you infer about the future of the house when the fire starts in the kitchen? **(b)** What information can you learn by reading on to confirm this inference?

Vocabulary

Acquisition and Use Match each statement with a word from the vocabulary list on page 282. Then, explain each choice.

1. This word might be used to describe a nervous person.
2. The flag did this in the breeze.
3. If you make an effort like this, you are working hard.
4. People who do not notice things can be described with this word.
5. People who see danger everywhere can be said to suffer from this.
6. If you adjusted a picture to make it brighter, you did this to it.

Word Study Use the context of the sentences and what you know about the **Greek suffix -ic** to explain your answer to each question.

1. Would a person be *emphatic* if he or she had a strong belief?
2. How might a person react to a *comedic* movie?

Word Study

The **Greek suffix -ic** means "having the characteristic of" or "pertaining to."

Apply It Explain how the suffix -ic contributes to the meanings of these words. Consult a dictionary if necessary.

dramatic
metallic
organic

Integrated Language Skills

The Street of the Cañon •
There Will Come Soft Rains

Conventions: Irregular Verbs

An **irregular verb** is a verb whose tenses are not formed according to the standard rules.

Unlike regular verbs, the past and the past participle of an irregular verb are not formed by adding *-ed* or *-d* to the present form. Some common irregular verbs are shown in the following chart.

The Four Principal Parts of Irregular Verbs			
Present	**Present Participle**	**Past**	**Past Participle**
lend	(is) lending	lent	(have) lent
fly	(is) flying	flew	(have) flown
spin	(is) spinning	spun	(have) spun
begin	(is) beginning	began	(have) begun

Practice A Identify which principal part each italicized verb represents.

1. The town church bells *rang* to announce the beginning of the party.
2. She *is eating* her birthday cake.
3. The guests *had begun* to dance.
4. People *ran* to see what the package contained.

Practice B Rewrite each sentence twice: once with the past form and once with the past participle form of the verb in parentheses.

1. The voice-clock _____ for the last time. (sing)
2. The garage door _____ up and down. (swing)
3. When the house _____ to die, it screamed, "Fire!" (begin)
4. The house _____ in its yard like a smoldering pile of trash. (sit)

Ⓒ **Reading Application** Find three sentences in "The Street of the Cañon" that contain irregular verbs. Write the irregular verbs and identify which of the principal parts the verbs represent.

Ⓒ **Writing Application** Write a paragraph about an automated machine such as a car alarm or an ATM. In your writing, use at least four different irregular verbs.

PH WRITING COACH | Further instruction and practice are available in *Prentice Hall Writing Coach*.

Writing

Argumentative Text Write a brief **letter to a friend** summarizing either "The Street of the Cañon" or "There Will Come Soft Rains." Then, rewrite the summary as part of a **book review** for newspaper readers.

- As you transfer your ideas into a new format, exclude information and arguments that are irrelevant to your book review.
- Change your language as needed for your new audience, replacing informal words with formal ones.
- Add information that a newspaper audience would expect to find in a review, such as information about the author.
- State your claim, or opinion of the story, and support it with examples.

Grammar Application Check your writing to make sure you have used the correct forms of irregular verbs.

Writing Workshop: *Work in Progress*

Prewriting for Narration: Short Story Using the Character Descriptions in your writing portfolio, make a chart of potential conflicts that the protagonist and antagonist could have. Choose one of these conflicts and add notes about how the two characters could resolve this conflict during the course of the story. Save your Potential Conflict chart in your writing portfolio.

Speaking and Listening

Comprehension and Collaboration Each of these stories can be compared to a well-known poem: Niggli's story bears similarity to Alfred Noyes's "The Highwayman"; Bradbury's story shares many similarities to the poem for which it was named, "There Will Come Soft Rains" by Sara Teasdale. Give an **oral reading** of the poem "The Highwayman" or the poem "There Will Come Soft Rains."

- Use a dictionary to look up the definitions and pronunciations of any words you do not know.
- Vary your tone of voice to reflect the poem's meaning. In addition, try different pacing to best capture its emotion and rhythm.
- Use gestures as appropriate.
- Spend time practicing the reading in front of a mirror, or ask friends or family members to listen to your reading and offer you suggestions.

After reading the poem to the class, lead a class discussion in a comparison of the poem and the story.

Common Core State Standards

L.9-10.4; SL.9-10.6; W.9-10.1
[For the full wording of the standards, see page 268.]

Use this prewriting activity to prepare for the **Writing Workshop** on page 328.

PHLit Online!
www.PHLitOnline.com
- Interactive graphic organizers
- Grammar tutorial
- Interactive journals

Test Practice: Reading

Make Inferences

Fiction Selection

Directions: *Read the selection. Then, answer the questions.*

David pulled Teacher from his backpack. "Review math lesson," he said into the device. David curled up on his bed as he listened to Teacher's smooth, mechanical voice. "Give the test," David said. As test questions appeared on the small screen, David used a stylus to record his answers. A light on his device blinked, and he touched the *pause* button.

"What's up, Jake?" he said, as the image of his best friend appeared.

"Meet me in the sky gym for some hoops."

"I've got a Spanish class," David answered.

"Bring Teacher. We can do the class together later," said Jake.

"Good idea," answered David. "See you at the gym." David pushed a button, and Jake's face was replaced on the screen with David's test.

David touched the *send* button without hesitation. Pushing Teacher into his pocket, he slipped on his anti-grav sneakers and left for the gym.

1. What inference can you make about the setting of this selection?

    A. It takes place in the future.
    B. It takes place in the twentieth century.
    C. It takes place long, long ago.
    D. It takes place in the present.

2. What detail helps you infer that sports activities are influenced by technology?

    A. having live video of a friend on the phone
    B. wearing "anti-grav sneakers"
    C. studying with an electronic "Teacher"
    D. postponing a class to play sports

3. Based on details in this passage, what inference can you make about David's education?

    A. He only reviews Spanish with Jake.
    B. Technology plays a role in his education.
    C. He wants to attend class in a school room.
    D. Teacher has taught him to speak Spanish fluently.

4. What can you infer about how technology enhances David's education?

    A. Technology helps him excel in athletics.
    B. He can contact his friends from school using technology.
    C. He can review material and take tests at his own pace.
    D. Teacher can answer all of David's questions about any subject.

Writing for Assessment

Using your own knowledge and details from this passage, what inferences can you make about how other areas of David's life besides his education might be affected by technology? Write a paragraph in which you explain your ideas.

Nonfiction Selection

Directions: *Read the selection. Then, answer the questions.*

Let's explore the implications of technological advancement on our students' lives now and on the lives of students in the future. The use of computers, the Internet, wireless systems, and hand-held mobile devices already impact our students' daily routines and some aspects of how we teach them. Information that once took hours or even days of library research to find can be retrieved in milliseconds. Research tools such as primary source documents and specialized reference books—previously found only in select libraries—can now be accessed easily. Along with the ease of accessibility, however, comes dangers. For example, some material found on the Internet contains misinformation. The act of using technology itself may cause unforeseen changes. I predict that both the dangers of technology and the advances in education due to technology will only increase.

1. Using the details in this text, you can infer that the writer is—

   A. a student.
   B. a teacher.
   C. a salesperson.
   D. an inventor.

2. You can infer that the remainder of this essay will elaborate on—

   A. positive and negative aspects of technology.
   B. positive aspects of technology.
   C. negative aspects of technology.
   D. the removal of technology from education.

3. Using your own knowledge, you can infer from the second sentence that the author—

   A. is aware of the ways in which students currently use technology.
   B. has limited knowledge about students.
   C. is confused about students' use of technology.
   D. is angry about students' use of technology.

4. After reading the last sentence, you can reasonably infer that the author—

   A. is in favor of increasing use of technology.
   B. is opposed to increasing use of technology.
   C. is ignorant about technology.
   D. has an open mind about technology.

Writing for Assessment

Connecting Across Texts
The author of this passage maintains that technology can have both positive and negative effects on students. Based on details from these two passages, what inferences can you make about the positive and negative effects of technology on David's education? Describe your conclusions in a paragraph.

PHLit Online!
www.PHLitOnline.com
- Online practice
- Instant feedback

Reading for Information

Analyzing Expository Texts

Technical Article

News Release

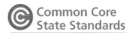
Common Core State Standards

Reading Informational Text
4. Determine the meaning of words and phrases as they are used in a text, including figurative, connotative, and technical meanings; analyze the cumulative impact of specific word choices on meaning and tone.

6. Determine an author's point of view or purpose in a text and analyze how an author uses rhetoric to advance that point of view or purpose.

Language
5.b. Analyze nuances in the meaning of words with similar denotations

Reading Skill: Analyze Texts to Extend Ideas

When you **extend ideas** presented in informational texts, you consider, judge, and build on those ideas. You do this through **analysis, evaluation,** and **elaboration.** To extend ideas, consider these questions:

Extending Ideas	Questions to Ask
Analysis	• What is the text about? • What kinds of details are presented? • What characteristics—text features and structures—are used to present information?
Evaluation	• How well are the main ideas presented and supported? • Is the text suited for its audience? Does it achieve its purpose?
Elaboration	• What connections can I make with the text? • What additional ideas and questions do I have about this topic?

Content-Area Vocabulary

These words appear in the selections that follow. You may also encounter them in other content-area texts.

* **phenomenon** (fə nom´ ə non) *n.* fact or event that can be observed

* **monitor** (mon´ ə tər) *v.* watch closely in order to control

* **mission** (mish´ ən) *n.* special work or service done on behalf of a government or military group

Tides

Joseph D. Exline, Ed.D., Jay M. Pasachoff, Ph.D., et al.

You're standing on a riverbank in the town of Saint John, Canada. In the distance there's a loud roaring sound, like a train approaching. Suddenly a wall of water twice your height thunders past. The surge of water rushes up the river channel so fast that it almost looks as if the river is flowing backward.

This thundering wall of water is an everyday event at Saint John. The town is located where the Saint John River enters the Bay of Fundy, an arm of the Atlantic Ocean. The Bay of Fundy is famous for its dramatic daily tides. When the tide comes in fishing boats float on the water near the piers, as shown in Figure 1A. But once the tide goes out, so much water flows back to sea that the boats are stranded on the muddy harbor bottom (Figure 1B).

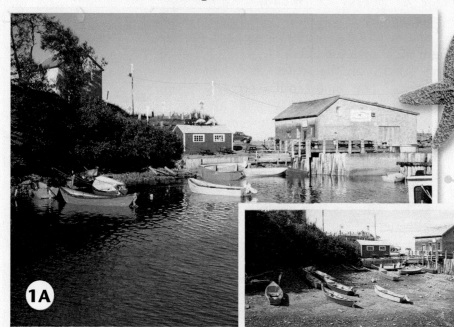

1A

1B

Figure 1 The Bay of Fundy in Canada is noted for its great differences in water level at high and low tide. **A.** Near the mouth of the bay, boats float in the Saint John River at high tide. **B.** At low tide, the boats are grounded.

Photographs, as well as diagrams and other graphics, are used to extend ideas presented in the text.

What Causes Tides?

The daily rise and fall of Earth's waters on its coastlines are called tides. As the tide comes in, the level of the water on the beach rises gradually. When the water reaches its highest point, it is high tide. Then the tide goes out, flowing back toward the sea. When the water reaches its lowest point, it is low tide. **Tides are caused by the interaction of Earth, the moon, and the sun.**

Figure 2 shows the effect of the moon's gravity on the water on Earth's surface. The moon pulls on the water on the side closest to it (point A) more strongly than it pulls on the center of the Earth. This pull creates a bulge of water, called a tidal bulge, on the side of Earth facing the moon. The water at point C is pulled toward the moon less strongly than is Earth as a whole. This water is "left behind," forming a second bulge.

In the places in Figure 2 where there are tidal bulges (points A and C), high tide is occurring along the coastlines. In the places between the bulges (points B and D), low tide is occurring. As Earth rotates, different places on the planet's surface pass through the areas of the tidal bulges and experience the change in water levels.

Moon

Earth

Tidal Bulges

Figure 2
The moon's pull on Earth's water causes tidal bulges to form on the side closest to the moon and the side farthest from the moon.

Day	Highest High Tide (m)	Lowest Low Tide (m)
1	1.9	0.2
2	2.1	0.1
3	2.3	0.0
4	2.4	-0.2
5	2.5	-0.2
6	2.6	-0.3
7	1.9	0.3

Figure 3
This table lists the highest high tides and lowest low tides at the mouth of the Savannah River at the Atlantic Ocean in Georgia for one week.

The Daily Tide Cycle

As Earth turns completely around once each day, people on or near the shore observe the rise and fall of the tides as they reach the area of each tidal bulge. The high tides occur about 12 hours and 25 minutes apart in each location. As Earth rotates, eastern-most points pass through the area of the tidal bulge before points farther to the west. Therefore, high tide occurs later the farther west you go along a coastline.

The Monthly Tide Cycle

Even though the sun is 150 million kilometers from Earth, it is so massive that its gravity also affects the tides. The sun pulls the water on Earth's surface toward it. In Figure 4 (next page), you can follow the positions of the Earth, moon, and sun at different times during a month.

Spring Tides Twice a month, at the new moon and the full moon, the sun and moon are lined up. Their combined gravitational pull produces the greatest range between high and low tide, called a spring tide. These tides get their name not because they occur during the spring season, but from an Old English word, *springen*, which means "to jump."

Tables present numerical data for you to analyze and evaluate.

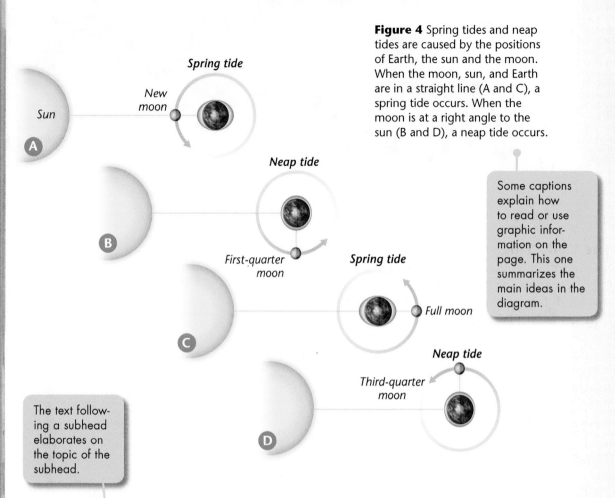

Figure 4 Spring tides and neap tides are caused by the positions of Earth, the sun and the moon. When the moon, sun, and Earth are in a straight line (A and C), a spring tide occurs. When the moon is at a right angle to the sun (B and D), a neap tide occurs.

Spring tide

New moon

Sun

A

Neap tide

B

First-quarter moon

Spring tide

Full moon

C

Neap tide

Third-quarter moon

D

Some captions explain how to read or use graphic information on the page. This one summarizes the main ideas in the diagram.

The text following a subhead elaborates on the topic of the subhead.

Neap Tides In between spring tides, at the first and third quarters of the moon, the sun and moon pull at right angles to each other. This line-up produces a neap tide, a tide with the least difference between low and high tide. During a neap tide, the sun's gravity pulls some of the water away from the tidal bulge facing the moon. This acts to "even out" the water level over Earth's surface, reducing the difference between high and low tides.

Information in the text elaborates on the information provided in the headline.

NASA News

Date: April 17, 2003 - RELEASE NO: 03-39
Contact: Rob Gutro

Black Water Turns the Tide on Florida Coral

In early 2002, a patch of "black water" spanning over 60 miles in diameter formed off southwestern Florida and contributed to severe coral reef stress and death in the Florida Keys, according to results published from research funded by the National Aeronautics and Space Administration (NASA), the U.S. Environmental Protection Agency and the National Oceanic and Atmospheric Administration (NOAA). The "black water" contained a high abundance of toxic and non-toxic microscopic plants.

Chuanmin Hu and other colleagues at the Institute for Marine Remote Sensing of the University of South Florida (USF), St. Petersburg, Fla., and colleagues from the Florida Fish and Wildlife Conservation Commission (FFWCC) and the University of Georgia, co-authored an article on this phenomenon that appeared as the cover story of a recent issue of the American Geophysical Union's Geophysical Research Letters.

You might evaluate the credibility of this information by noting the author's credentials.

"The water appeared black in satellite imagery because the concentration of the microscopic plants and other dissolved matters were high," Hu said. Because plants and dissolved matter absorb sunlight, they reduce the amount of light normally reflected from the ocean. When a red-tide bloom occurs the water takes on various hues of red or brown. While not all microscopic plants contribute to red tides, the darker hue created by both the plankton and the harmful algal blooms made the water appear black when seen from the satellite.

When Hu and his colleagues examined the data collected by divers from the dark water area in the Florida Keys, they discovered a 70 percent decrease in stony coral cover, a 40 percent reduction of coral species, and a near-elimination of sponge colonies at two reef sites after the dark water passed. By examining satellite images and field survey data, the authors concluded that the coral reef ecosystem was stressed by microscopic organisms and toxins contained in the dark water.

The "black water" event caused alarm among local fishermen, divers, and the public, as the color of the water was unusual and fish seemed to avoid this large area of dark water. Satellite instruments such as the Sea-viewing Wide Field-of-view Sensor (SeaWiFS) aboard Orbimage's SeaStar satellite and the Moderate Resolution Imaging Spectroradiometer (MODIS) aboard NASA's Terra and Aqua satellites provide information on ocean color that allows scientists to monitor the health of the water and the shallow benthic (ocean bottom) environment. The SeaWiFS and MODIS measurements of the dark water led to a number of investigations to help clarify the issues and to provide answers to the public's concerns.

> You can evaluate how well the data and statistics support the main idea of the article.

During January 2002, SeaWiFS detected the dark-colored water in the Florida Bight, just southwest of the Everglades. In fall 2001, the SeaWiFS images showed an extensive red tide off Florida's central west coast, near Charlotte Harbor.

Red tides occur every year off Florida and are known to cause fish kills, coral stress and mortality, and skin and respiratory problems in humans. They are caused by high concentration of microscopic plants called dinoflagellates. Other microorganisms called cyanobacteria can also cause harmful algal blooms. The waters containing this red tide migrated to the south along the coast. Winter storms caused large amounts of fresh water to drain from the Everglades into Florida Bight (the curve in the shoreline from the Keys north to Everglades National Park on the mainland), carrying high levels of nutrients such as silicate, phosphorus, and nitrogen to the sea. These caused a bloom of the microscopic marine plants known as diatoms in the same patch. The bloom turned the water dark and the "black water" patch re-circulated for several months in a slow clockwise motion off southwest Florida in the Florida Bight. Slowly, the dark water drifted farther south and toward the Florida Keys. By May 2002, the "black water" had moved through passages in the Florida Keys, dispersing into the Atlantic and the Gulf Stream. . . .

> To elaborate on these ideas, you might consult a resource on recent incidents of red tides.

NASA funded part of this research as part of its Earth Science mission to understand and protect our home planet. NASA's Earth Science Enterprise is dedicated to understanding the Earth as an integrated system and applying Earth System Science to improve prediction of climate, weather, and natural hazards using the unique vantage point of space.

Comparing Expository Texts

1. **Key Ideas and Details** **(a) Extend ideas** presented in the two texts by **analyzing** and comparing them. What different kinds of details do the two texts present? **(b) Evaluate** how well those details support the main ideas of each text. Which text offers better support? Explain. **(c) Elaborate** by describing how to improve the text that has less support.

Content-Area Vocabulary

2. (a) Explain the difference in meaning between the words in each pair: *mission/ work; phenomenon/event; monitor/watch.* **(b)** Choose a pair, and use each word in a sentence that shows its meaning.

Timed Writing

Analytical Text: Essay

Format
The prompt instructs you to write a *brief essay.* Therefore, your essay should be approximately three to five paragraphs long.

Both the technical article and the news release discuss tides, but from different perspectives. In a brief essay, identify each author's point of view and how it affects the tone and content of the text. Also, consider the combined information of the two sources and explain whether the authors' different perspectives cause discrepancies in the information presented. Support your response with details from the texts. (25 minutes)

Academic Vocabulary
When you *identify* something, you recognize and bring attention to it.

5-Minute Planner

Complete these steps before you begin to write:

1. Quickly review the two texts to compare the **perspectives,** tone, and content. **TIP** Consider the purpose of each text to better understand the author's perspective.

2. Note specific word and phrase choices to support your impressions.

3. **Synthesize,** or combine, the information in both texts by thinking about all the facts and details presented. Note any **discrepancies,** or conflicts, in the combined information.

4. Refer to your notes as you write your essay.

Comparing Literary Works

Comparing Points of View

Point of view is the perspective from which a story is told. Most stories are told from one of the following perspectives:

- **First-person point of view:** The narrator is one of the characters and refers to himself or herself with the pronouns *I* and *me*. One kind of first-person narrator is the **naïve first-person narrator.** This narrator understands less about events in the story than the readers do. For example, if the narrator of a story is a five-year-old, readers may have a clearer understanding of events in the story than does the child who describes them.

- **Third-person point of view:** The narrator does not participate in the action. Characters are referred to by the third-person pronouns *he, she, him, her, they,* and *them.* The narrator's point of view may be **omniscient** (all-knowing), or it may be **limited** (restricted to the perceptions of a single character).

By giving readers more information than the narrator or character has, writers can create **dramatic irony**—a contrast between what the readers know and what the narrator or character believes. Dramatic irony is a powerful device in fiction because it involves readers on an analytical, interpretive level as well as an emotional one. Effects such as tension and surprise can be created when readers' minds and hearts are engaged in a story.

Compare the use of point of view and its impact in "One Thousand Dollars" and "By the Waters of Babylon" by using a chart like the one shown.

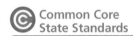 **Common Core State Standards**

Reading Literature
5. Analyze how an author's choices concerning how to structure a text, order events within it, and manipulate time create such effects as mystery, tension, or surprise.

Writing
2. Write informative/explanatory texts to examine and convey complex ideas, concepts, and information clearly and accurately through the effective selection, organization, and analysis of content. *(Timed Writing)*

Story	Point of View	What Reader Knows	What Character Knows	Effect of Contrast in Knowledge	Impact on Story

www.PHLitOnline.com

- Vocabulary flashcards
- Interactive journals
- More about the authors
- Selection audio
- Interactive graphic organizers

Can progress be made without *conflict?*

Writing About the Big Question

In each of these stories, the main character finds himself challenged by unusual circumstances. Both of these characters use conflict as a springboard toward **progress.** Use these sentence starters to develop your ideas about the Big Question.

Facing **adversity** could teach someone _____.

After a disagreement is **resolved**, a person may be able to _____.

Meet the Authors

O. Henry (1862–1910)
Author of "One Thousand Dollars"

A native of North Carolina, William Sydney Porter dropped out of school at age fifteen and by his twenties had made his way to Texas. After working for more than a decade as a bank teller, he was convicted— perhaps unjustly—of embezzling bank funds. In prison, he began to write short stories and took on the pen name O. Henry.

Hundreds of Stories Later Upon his release from jail, O. Henry settled in New York City, where he became a full-time and hugely successful short-story writer. He turned out nearly 300 tales, most of them featuring ironic twists of fate.

Stephen Vincent Benét (1898–1943)
Author of "By the Waters of Babylon"

Born in Bethlehem, Pennsylvania, Stephen Vincent Benét grew up listening to his father read poetry in the evenings. During World War I, Benét was barred from active army duty because of poor eyesight. Still, he took time off from his studies at Yale University to serve in the State Department during the war.

Touch of the Poet Benét considered himself a poet first and foremost. Much of his work centers on American history and the quest for American ideals. His interest in American history and folklore influenced his epic poem *John Brown's Body,* which won a Pulitzer Prize in 1929.

One Thousand Dollars

O. Henry

"One thousand dollars," repeated Lawyer Tolman, solemnly and severely, "and here is the money."

Young Gillian gave a decidedly amused laugh as he fingered the thin package of new fifty-dollar notes.

"It's such a confoundedly awkward amount," he explained, genially, to the lawyer. "If it had been ten thousand a fellow might wind up with a lot of fireworks and do himself credit. Even fifty dollars would have been less trouble."

"You heard the reading of your uncle's will," continued Lawyer Tolman, professionally dry in his tones. "I do not know if you paid much attention to its details. I must remind you of one. You are required to render to us an account of the manner of expenditure of this $1,000 as soon as you have disposed of it. The will stipulates that. I trust that you will so far comply with the late Mr. Gillian's wishes."

"You may depend upon it," said the young man, politely, "in spite of the extra expense it will entail. I may have to engage a secretary. I was never good at accounts."

Gillian went to his club. There he hunted out one whom he called Old Bryson.

Old Bryson was calm and forty and sequestered. He was in a corner reading a book, and when he saw Gillian approaching he sighed, laid down his book and took off his glasses.

"Old Bryson, wake up," said Gillian. "I've a funny story to tell you."

"I wish you would tell it to someone in the billiard room," said Old Bryson. "You know how I hate your stories."

"This is a better one than usual," said Gillian . . . ; "and I'm glad to tell it to you. It's too sad and funny to go with the rattling of billiard balls. I've just come from my late uncle's firm of legal corsairs. He leaves me an even thousand dollars. Now, what can a man possibly do with a thousand dollars?"

"I thought," said Old Bryson, showing as much interest as a bee shows in a vinegar cruet, "that the late Septimus Gillian was worth something like half a million."

"He was," assented Gillian, joyously, "and that's where the joke comes in. He's left his whole cargo of doubloons[1] to a microbe. That is, part of it goes to the man who invents a new bacillus and the rest to establish a hospital for doing away with it again. There are one or two trifling bequests on the side. The butler and the housekeeper get a seal ring and $10 each. His nephew gets $1,000."

"You've always had plenty of money to spend," observed Old Bryson.

"Tons," said Gillian. "Uncle was the fairy godmother as far as an allowance was concerned."

"Any other heirs?" asked Old Bryson.

"None." Gillian frowned . . . and kicked the upholstered leather of a divan uneasily. "There is a Miss Hayden, a ward of my uncle, who lived in his house. She's a quiet thing—musical—the daughter of somebody who was unlucky enough to be his friend. I forgot to say that she was in on the seal ring and $10 joke, too. I wish I had been. Then I could have had two bottles of brut, tipped the waiter with the ring, and had the whole business off my hands. Don't be superior and insulting, Old Bryson—tell me what a fellow can do with a thousand dollars."

Old Bryson rubbed his glasses and smiled. And when Old Bryson smiled, Gillian knew that he intended to be more offensive than ever.

"A thousand dollars," he said, "means much or little. One man may buy a happy home with it and laugh at Rockefeller.[2] Another could send his wife South with it and save her life. A thousand dollars would buy pure milk for one hundred babies during June, July, and August and save fifty of their lives. You could count upon a half hour's diversion with it at faro in one of the fortified art galleries. It would furnish an education to an ambitious boy.

---

1. **doubloons** (də blo͞onz´) *n.* old gold coins of Spanish or Spanish American origin, often associated with pirates.
2. **Rockefeller** John D. Rockefeller (1839–1937), a businessman who became the first American billionaire.

◄ **Critical Viewing**
Based on the details in this illustration, what might you speculate about this man? **[Infer]**

Vocabulary
stipulates (stip´ yə lāts´) *v.* includes specifically as part of an agreement

Literary Analysis
Point of View Whose thoughts are revealed in this short paragraph? Who reveals them?

Reading Check

What problem does young Gillian face?

I am told that a genuine Corot[3] was secured for that amount in an auction room yesterday. You could move to a New Hampshire town and live respectably two years on it. You could rent Madison Square Garden for one evening with it, and lecture your audience, if you should have one, on the precariousness of the profession of heir presumptive."

"People might like you, Old Bryson," said Gillian, almost unruffled, "if you wouldn't moralize. I asked you to tell me what I could do with a thousand dollars."

"You?" said Bryson, with a gentle laugh. "Why, Bobby Gillian, there's only one logical thing you could do. You can go buy Miss Lotta Lauriere a diamond pendant with the money, and then take yourself off to Idaho and inflict your presence upon a ranch. I advise a sheep ranch, as I have a particular dislike for sheep."

"Thanks," said Gillian, rising. "I thought I could depend upon you, Old Bryson. You've hit on the very scheme. I wanted to chuck the money in a lump, for I've got to turn in an account for it, and I hate itemizing."

Gillian phoned for a cab and said to the driver:

"The stage entrance of the Columbine Theatre."

Miss Lotta Lauriere was assisting nature with a powder puff, almost ready for her call at a crowded matinée, when her dresser mentioned the name of Mr. Gillian.

"Let it in," said Miss Lauriere. "Now, what is it, Bobby? I'm going on in two minutes."

"Rabbit-foot your right ear a little," suggested Gillian, critically. "That's better. It won't take two minutes for me. What do you say to a little thing in the pendant line? I can stand three ciphers[4] with a figure one in front of 'em."

"Oh, just as you say," carolled Miss Lauriere. "My right glove, Adams. Say, Bobby, did you see that necklace Della Stacey had on the other night? Twenty-two hundred dollars it cost at Tiffany's. But, of course—pull my sash a little to the left, Adams."

"Miss Lauriere for the opening chorus!" cried the call boy without.

Gillian strolled out to where his cab was waiting.

"What would you do with a thousand dollars if you had it?" he asked the driver.

"Open a s'loon," said the cabby promptly and huskily. "I know a place I could take money in with both hands. It's a four-story brick on a corner. I've got it figured out. Second story— . . . chop

---

3. **Corot** (kə rō') a painting by Jean (zhän) Baptiste (bȧ tēst') Camille (kȧ mē'y') Corot (1796–1875), a famous French painter.

4. **ciphers** (sī' fərz) n. zeroes.

Spiral Review

Character What does Bryson's advice to Gillian suggest about his opinion of Gillian?

Literary Analysis

Point of View Which details in the scene with Miss Lotta Lauriere would Gillian know first-hand? Which might he not know?

suey; third floor—manicures and foreign missions; fourth floor—poolroom. If you was thinking of putting up the cap—"

"Oh, no," said Gillian, "I merely asked from curiosity. I take you by the hour. Drive till I tell you to stop."

Eight blocks down Broadway Gillian poked up the trap[5] with his cane and got out. A blind man sat upon a stool on the sidewalk selling pencils. Gillian went out and stood before him.

"Excuse me," he said, "but would you mind telling me what you would do if you had a thousand dollars?"

"You got out of that cab that just drove up, didn't you?" asked the blind man.

"I did," said Gillian.

"I guess you are all right," said the pencil dealer, "to ride in a cab by daylight. Take a look at that, if you like."

He drew a small book from his coat pocket and held it out. Gillian opened it and saw that it was a bank deposit book. It showed a balance of $1,785 to the blind man's credit.

Gillian returned the book and got into the cab.

"I forgot something," he said. "You may drive to the law offices of Tolman & Sharp, at —— Broadway."

Lawyer Tolman looked at him hostilely and inquiringly through his gold-rimmed glasses.

"I beg your pardon," said Gillian, cheerfully, "but may I ask you a question? It is not an impertinent one, I hope. Was Miss Hayden left anything by my uncle's will besides the ring and the $10?"

"Nothing," said Mr. Tolman.

"I thank you very much, sir," said Gillian, and out he went to his cab. He gave the driver the address of his late uncle's home.

Miss Hayden was writing letters in the library. She was small and slender and clothed in black. But you would have noticed her eyes. Gillian drifted in with his air of regarding the world as inconsequent.

"I've just come from old Tolman's," he explained. "They've been going over the papers down there. They found a"—Gillian searched his memory for a legal term—"they found an amendment or a postscript or something to the will. It seemed that the old boy loosened up a little on second thoughts and willed you a thousand dollars. I was driving up this way and Tolman asked me to bring you the money. Here it is. You'd better count it to see if it's right." Gillian laid the money beside her hand on the desk.

Miss Hayden turned white. "Oh!" she said, and again "Oh!"

Reading Check

What are three ways other characters suggest Gillian spend the thousand dollars?

---

5. **poked up the trap** pushed open the roof door of the cab so that the driver would know that he wanted to get out.

Gillian half turned and looked out of the window.

"I suppose, of course," he said, in a low voice, "that you know I love you."

"I am sorry," said Miss Hayden, taking up her money.

"There is no use?" asked Gillian, almost light-heartedly.

"I am sorry," she said again.

"May I write a note?" asked Gillian, with a smile. He seated himself at the big library table. She supplied him with paper and pen, and then went back to her secrétaire.

Gillian made out his account of his expenditure of the thousand dollars in these words:

"Paid by the black sheep, Robert Gillian, $1,000 on account of the eternal happiness, owed by Heaven to the best and dearest woman on earth."

Gillian slipped his writing into an envelope, bowed and went his way.

His cab stopped again at the offices of Tolman & Sharp.

"I have expended the thousand dollars," he said, cheerily, to Tolman of the gold glasses, "and I have come to render account of it, as I agreed. There is quite a feeling of summer in the air—do you not think so, Mr. Tolman?" He tossed a white envelope on the lawyer's table. "You will find there a memorandum, sir, of the *modus operandi* of the vanishing of the dollars."

Without touching the envelope, Mr. Tolman went to a door and called his partner, Sharp. Together they explored the caverns of an immense safe. Forth they dragged as trophy of their search a big envelope sealed with wax. This they forcibly invaded, and wagged their venerable heads together over its contents. Then Tolman became spokesman.

"Mr. Gillian," he said, formally, "there was a codicil[6] to your uncle's will. It was intrusted to us privately, with instructions that it be not opened until you had furnished us with a full account of your handling of the $1,000 bequest in the will. As you have fulfilled the conditions, my partner and I have read the codicil. I do not wish to encumber your understanding with its legal phraseology, but I will acquaint you with the spirit of its contents.

"In the event that your disposition of the $1,000 demonstrates that you possess any of the qualifications that deserve reward, much benefit will accrue to you. Mr. Sharp and I are named as the judges, and I assure you that we will do our duty strictly according to justice—with liberality. We are not at all unfavorably disposed toward you, Mr. Gillian. But let us return to the letter of the codicil.

---

6. **codicil** (käd´ i səl) *n.* an addition to a will changing or explaining the instructions it gives.

"I have expended the thousand dollars," he said, cheerily, to Tolman of the gold glasses. . .

If your disposal of the money in question has been prudent, wise, or unselfish, it is in our power to hand you over bonds to the value of $50,000, which have been placed in our hands for that purpose. But if—as our client, the late Mr. Gillian, explicitly provides—you have used this money as you have used money in the past—I quote the late Mr. Gillian—in reprehensible dissipation among disreputable associates—the $50,000 is to be paid to Miriam Hayden, ward of the late Mr. Gillian, without delay. Now, Mr. Gillian, Mr. Sharp and I will examine your account in regard to the $1,000. You submit it in writing, I believe. I hope you will repose confidence in our decision."

Mr. Tolman reached for the envelope. Gillian was a little the quicker in taking it up. He tore the account and its cover leisurely into strips and dropped them into his pocket.

"It's all right," he said, smilingly. "There isn't a bit of need to bother you with this. I don't suppose you'd understand these itemized bets anyway. I lost the thousand dollars on the races. Good day to you, gentlemen."

Tolman & Sharp shook their heads mournfully at each other when Gillian left, for they heard him whistling gayly in the hallway as he started for the elevator.

Literary Analysis
Point of View How does the use of a limited third-person narrator help readers know more about what is in the envelope than Mr. Tolman knows?

Critical Thinking

1. **Key Ideas and Details (a)** According to his uncle's will, what must Bobby Gillian do after spending the thousand dollars? **(b) Infer:** What are Gillian's feelings about inheriting this amount?

2. **Key Ideas and Details (a) Infer:** Why does Gillian decide to give Miss Hayden the money but not tell the lawyers? **(b) Draw Conclusions:** What do these decisions tell you about his character? **(c) Compare and Contrast:** Compare what these decisions indicate about his character with your first impressions of him.

3. **Key Ideas and Details (a)** Why do you think Gillian lets Miss Hayden think that the money was willed to her by his uncle? **(b) Interpret:** What do you think Gillian hopes to gain by doing this?

4. **Integration of Knowledge and Ideas** Gillian deals with the conflict of being in love with Miss Hayden, who does not return his affection. **(a)** How does Gillian address this conflict? **(b)** Does dealing with this conflict help him to grow as a person? Explain. *[Connect to the Big Question: Can progress be made without conflict?]*

Cite textual evidence to support your responses.

BY THE WATERS OF BABYLON

STEPHEN VINCENT BENÉT

The north and the west and the south are good hunting ground, but it is forbidden to go east. It is forbidden to go to any of the Dead Places except to search for metal, and then he who touches the metal must be a priest or the son of a priest. Afterwards, both the man and the metal must be purified! These are the rules and the laws: they are well made. It is forbidden to cross the great river and look upon the place that was the Place of the Gods—this is most strictly forbidden. We do not even say its name though we know its name. It is there that spirits live, and demons—it is there that there are the ashes of the Great Burning. These things are forbidden—they have been forbidden since the beginning of time.

My father is a priest; I am the son of a priest. I have been in the Dead Places near us, with my father—at first, I was afraid. When my father went into the house to search for the metal, I stood by the door and my heart felt small and weak. It was a dead man's house, a spirit house. It did not have the smell of man, though there were old bones in a corner. But it is not fitting that a priest's son should show fear. I looked at the bones in the shadow and kept my voice still.

Then my father came out with the metal—a good, strong piece. He looked at me with both eyes but I had not run away. He gave me the metal to hold—I took it and did not die. So he knew that I was truly his son and would be a priest in my time. That was when I was very young—nevertheless, my brothers would not have done it, though they are good hunters. After that, they gave me the good piece of meat and the warm corner by the fire. My father watched over me—he was glad that I should be a priest. But when I boasted or wept without a reason, he punished me more strictly than my brothers. That was right.

After a time, I myself was allowed to go into the dead houses and search for metal. So I learned the ways of those houses—and if I saw bones, I was no longer afraid. The bones are light and old—sometimes they will fall into dust if you touch them. But that is a great sin.

I was taught the chants and the spells—I was taught how to stop the running of blood from a wound and many secrets. A priest must know many secrets—that was what my father said. If the hunters think we do all things by chants and spells, they may believe so—it does not hurt them. I was taught how to read in the old books and how to make the old writings—that was hard and took a long time. My knowledge made me happy—it was like a fire in my heart. Most of all, I liked to hear of the Old Days and the stories of the gods. I asked myself many questions that I could not answer, but it was good to ask them. At night, I would lie awake and listen to the

Vocabulary
purified (pyoor´ ə fīd´)
v. rid of impurities or pollution; made pure

Literary Analysis
Point of View Which words in the second paragraph on this page tell you that the story is written from the first-person point of view?

Vocabulary
nevertheless (nev´ ər *th*ə les´) *adv.* in spite of that; however

Reading Check

Why are the narrator and his father allowed to bring back metal from the "Dead Places"?

wind—it seemed to me that it was the voice of the gods as they flew through the air.

We are not ignorant like the Forest People—our women spin wool on the wheel, our priests wear a white robe. We do not eat grubs from the tree, we have not forgotten the old writings, although they are hard to understand. Nevertheless, my knowledge and my lack of knowledge burned in me—I wished to know more. When I was a man at last, I came to my father and said, "It is time for me to go on my journey. Give me your leave."

He looked at me for a long time, stroking his beard, then he said at last, "Yes. It is time." That night, in the house of the priesthood, I asked for and received purification. My body hurt but my spirit was a cool stone. It was my father himself who questioned me about my dreams.

He bade me look into the smoke of the fire and see—I saw and told what I saw. It was what I have always seen—a river, and, beyond it, a great Dead Place and in it the gods walking. I have always thought about that. His eyes were stern when I told him —he was no longer my father but a priest. He said, "This is a strong dream."

"It is mine," I said, while the smoke waved and my head felt light. They were singing the Star song in the outer chamber and it was like the buzzing of bees in my head.

He asked me how the gods were dressed and I told him how they were dressed. We know how they were dressed from the book, but I saw them as if they were before me. When I had finished, he threw the sticks three times and studied them as they fell.

"This is a very strong dream," he said. "It may eat you up."

"I am not afraid," I said and looked at him with both eyes. My voice sounded thin in my ears but that was because of the smoke.

He touched me on the breast and the forehead. He gave me the bow and the three arrows.

"Take them," he said. "It is forbidden to travel east. It is forbidden to cross the river. It is forbidden to go to the Place of the Gods. All these things are forbidden."

"All these things are forbidden," I said, but it was my voice that spoke and not my spirit. He looked at me again.

"My son," he said. "Once I had young dreams. If your dreams do not eat you up, you may be a great priest. If they eat you, you are still my son. Now go on your journey."

I went fasting, as is the law. My body hurt but not my heart. When the dawn came, I was out of sight of the village. I prayed and purified myself, waiting for a sign. The sign was an eagle. It flew east.

Literary Analysis
Point of View What details give the narrator credibility? Do you trust him? Why or why not?

▶ Critical Viewing
Why do you think the tribes in the story refer to a city like the one in this image as "the Place of the Gods"? **[Infer]**

Sometimes signs are sent by bad spirits. I waited again on the flat rock, fasting, taking no food. I was very still—I could feel the sky above me and the earth beneath. I waited till the sun was beginning to sink. Then three deer passed in the valley, going east—they did not wind me or see me. There was a white fawn with them—a very great sign.

I followed them, at a distance, waiting for what would happen. My heart was troubled about going east, yet I knew that I must go. My head hummed with my fasting—I did not even see the panther spring upon the white fawn. But, before I knew it, the bow was in my hand. I shouted and the panther lifted his head from the fawn. It is not easy to kill a panther with one arrow but the arrow went through his eye and into his brain. He died as he tried to spring— he rolled over, tearing at the ground. Then I knew I was meant to go east—I knew that was my journey. When the night came, I made my fire and roasted meat.

It is eight suns' journey to the east and a man passes by many Dead Places. The Forest People are afraid of them but I am not. Once I made my fire on the edge of a Dead Place at night and, next morning, in the dead house, I found a good knife, little rusted. That was small to what came afterward, but it made my heart feel big. Always when I looked for game, it was in front of my arrow, and twice I passed hunting parties of the Forest People without their knowing. So I knew my magic was strong and my journey clean, in spite of the law.

Toward the setting of the eighth sun, I came to the banks of the great river. It was half-a-day's journey after I had left the god-road— we do not use the god-roads now for they are falling apart into great blocks of stone, and the forest is safer going. A long way off, I had seen the water through trees but the trees were thick. At last, I came out upon an open place at the top of a cliff. There was the great river below, like a giant in the sun. It is very long, very wide. It could eat all the streams we know and still be thirsty. Its name is Ou-dis-sun, the Sacred, the Long. No man of my tribe had seen it, not even my father, the priest. It was magic and I prayed.

Literary Analysis
Point of View What might the reader understand about the Dead Places that John does not?

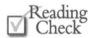
Reading Check

Where is the narrator journeying?

By the Waters of Babylon **317**

Then I raised my eyes and looked south. It was there, the Place of the Gods.

How can I tell what it was like—you do not know. It was there, in the red light, and they were too big to be houses. It was there with the red light upon it, mighty and ruined. I knew that in another moment the gods would see me. I covered my eyes with my hands and crept back into the forest.

Surely, that was enough to do, and live. Surely it was enough to spend the night upon the cliff. The Forest People themselves do not come near. Yet, all through the night, I knew that I should have to cross the river and walk in the places of the gods, although the gods ate me up. My magic did not help me at all and yet there was a fire in my bowels, a fire in my mind. When the sun rose, I thought, "My journey has been clean. Now I will go home from my journey." But, even as I thought so, I knew I could not. If I went to the place of the gods, I would surely die, but, if I did not go, I could never be at peace with my spirit again. It is better to lose one's life than one's spirit, if one is a priest and the son of a priest.

Nevertheless, as I made the raft, the tears ran out of my eyes. The Forest People could have killed me without fight, if they had come upon me then, but they did not come. When the raft was made, I said the sayings for the dead and painted myself for death. My heart was cold as a frog and my knees like water, but the burning in my mind would not let me have peace. As I pushed the raft from the shore, I began my death song—I had the right. It was a fine song.

"I am John, son of John," I sang. "My people are the Hill People.
    They are the men.
I go into the Dead Places but I am not slain.
I take the metal from the Dead Places but I am not blasted.
I travel upon the god-roads and am not afraid. E-yah! I have killed
    the panther, I have killed the fawn!
E-yah! I have come to the great river. No man has come there before.
It is forbidden to go east, but I have gone, forbidden to go on the
    great river, but I am there.
Open your hearts, you spirits, and hear my song.
Now I go to the Place of the Gods, I shall not return.
My body is painted for death and my limbs weak, but my heart is
    big as I go to the Place of the Gods!"

Literary Analysis
Point of View How does the use of a first-person narrator help readers appreciate John's thoughts and actions in this passage?

All the same, when I came to the Place of the Gods, I was afraid, afraid. The current of the great river is very strong—it gripped my raft with its hands. That was magic, for the river itself is wide and calm. I could feel evil spirits about me, in the bright morning; I could feel their breath on my neck as I was swept down the stream. Never have I been so much alone—I tried to think of my knowledge, but it was a squirrel's heap of winter nuts. There was no strength in my knowledge any more, and I felt small and naked as a new-hatched bird—alone upon the great river, the servant of the gods.

Yet, after a while, my eyes were opened and I saw. I saw both banks of the river—I saw that once there had been god-roads across it, though now they were broken and fallen like broken vines. Very great they were, and wonderful and broken—broken in the time of the Great Burning when the fire fell out of the sky. And always the current took me nearer to the Place of the Gods, and the huge ruins rose before my eyes.

I do not know the customs of rivers—we are the People of the Hills. I tried to guide my raft with the pole but it spun around. I thought the river meant to take me past the Place of the Gods and out into the Bitter Water of the legends. I grew angry then—my heart felt strong. I said aloud, "I am a priest and the son of a priest!" The gods heard me—they showed me how to paddle with the pole on one side of the raft. The current changed itself—I drew near to the Place of the Gods.

When I was very near, my raft struck and turned over. I can swim in our lakes—I swam to the shore. There was a great spike of rusted metal sticking out into the river—I hauled myself up upon it and sat there, panting. I had saved my bow and two arrows and the knife I found in the Dead Place but that was all. My raft went whirling downstream toward the Bitter Water. I looked after it, and thought if it had trod me under, at least I would be safely dead. Nevertheless, when I had dried my bow-string and restrung it, I walked forward to the Place of the Gods.

It felt like ground underfoot; it did not burn me. It is not true what some of the tales say, that the ground there burns forever, for I have been there. Here and there were the marks and stains of the Great Burning, on the ruins, that is true. But they were old marks and old stains. It is not true either, what some of our priests say, that it is an island covered with fogs and enchantments. It is not. It is a great Dead Place—greater than any Dead Place we know. Everywhere in it there are god-roads, though most are cracked and broken. Everywhere there are the ruins of the high towers of the gods.

◄ **Critical Viewing**
How does this image represent the natural dangers John has to overcome to get to the Place of the Gods? **[Infer]**

Spiral Review
Character What does John's anger about being taken past the Place of the Gods suggest about him?

Reading Check

How does John feel as he approaches the Place of the Gods?

▲ **Critical Viewing**
Which details in this image suggest that this cat might be "wild" and "unafraid of men"? **[Infer]**

Literary Analysis
Point of View Which details here suggest that John is a naive narrator—that the reader knows more about what John sees than John does?

How shall I tell what I saw? I went carefully, my strung bow in my hand, my skin ready for danger. There should have been the wailings of spirits and the shrieks of demons, but there were not. It was very silent and sunny where I had landed—the wind and the rain and the birds that drop seeds had done their work—the grass grew in the cracks of the broken stone. It is a fair island—no wonder the gods built there. If I had come there, a god, I also would have built.

How shall I tell what I saw? The towers are not all broken—here and there one still stands, like a great tree in a forest, and the birds nest high. But the towers themselves look blind, for the gods are gone. I saw a fish-hawk, catching fish in the river. I saw a little dance of white butterflies over a great heap of broken stones and columns. I went there and looked about me—there was a carved stone with cut-letters, broken in half. I can read letters but I could not understand these. They said UBTREAS. There was also the shattered image of a man or a god. It had been made of white stone and he wore his hair tied back like a woman's. His name was ASHING, as I read on the cracked half of a stone. I thought it wise to pray to ASHING, though I do not know that god.

How shall I tell what I saw? There was no smell of man left, on stone or metal. Nor were there many trees in that wilderness of stone. There are many pigeons, nesting and dropping in the could see that—and yet their wisdom could not but grow until all was peace.

Then I saw their fate come upon them and that was terrible past speech. It came upon them as they walked the streets of their city. I have been in the fights with the Forest People—I have seen men die. But this was not like that. When gods war with gods, they use weapons we do not know. It was fire falling out of the sky and a mist that poisoned. It was the time of the Great Burning and the Destruction. They ran about like ants in the streets of their city—poor gods, poor gods! Then the towers began to fall. A few escaped—yes, a few. The legends tell it. But, even after the city had become a Dead Place, for many years the poison was still in the ground. I saw it happen, I saw the last of them die. It was darkness over the broken city, and I wept.

All this, I saw. I saw it as I have told it, though not in the body. When I woke in the morning, I was hungry, but I did not think first of my hunger, for my heart was perplexed and confused. I knew the reason for the Dead Places but I did not see why it had happened. It seemed to me it should not have happened, with all the magic they had. I went through the house looking for an answer. There was so much in the house I could not understand—and yet I am a priest and the son of a priest. It was like being on one side of the great river, at night, with no light to show the way.

Then I saw the dead god. He was sitting in his chair, by the window, in a room I had not entered before and, for the first moment, I thought that he was alive. Then I saw the skin on the back of his hand—it was like dry leather. The room was shut, hot and dry—no doubt that had kept him as he was. At first I was afraid to approach him—then the fear left me. He was sitting looking out over the city—he was dressed in the clothes of the gods. His age was neither young nor old—I could not tell his age. But there was wisdom in his face and great sadness. You could see that he would have not run away. He had sat at his window, watching his city die—then he himself had died. But it is better to lose one's life than one's spirit—and you could see from the face that his spirit had not been lost. I knew that, if I touched him, he would fall into dust—and yet, there was something unconquered in the face.

That is all of my story, for then I knew he was a man—I knew then that they had been men, neither gods nor demons. It is a great knowledge, hard to tell and believe. They were men—they went a dark road, but they were men. I had no fear after that—I had no fear going home, though twice I fought off the dogs and once I was hunted for two days by the Forest People. When I saw my father again, I prayed and was purified. He touched my lips and my

Literary Analysis
Point of View In what way has John's view of the gods changed?

Reading Check
What event does John see in his vision?

breast, he said, "You went away a boy. You come back a man and a priest." I said, "Father, they were men! I have been in the Place of the Gods and seen it! Now slay me, if it is the law—but still I know they were men."

He looked at me out of both eyes. He said, "The law is not always the same shape—you have done what you have done. I could not have done it in my time but you come after me. Tell!"

I told and he listened. After that, I wished to tell all the people but he showed me otherwise. He said, "Truth is a hard deer to hunt. If you eat too much truth at once, you may die of the truth. It was not idly that our fathers forbade the Dead Places." He was right—it is better the truth should come little by little. I have learned that, being a priest. Perhaps, in the old days, they ate knowledge too fast.

Nevertheless, we make a beginning. It is not for the metal alone we go to the Dead Places now—there are the books and the writings. They are hard to learn. And the magic tools are broken—but we can look at them and wonder. At least, we make a beginning. And, when I am chief priest we shall go beyond the great river. We shall go to the Place of the Gods—the place newyork—not one man but a company. We shall look for the images of the gods and find the god ASHING and the others—the gods Lincoln and Biltmore[1] and Moses.[2] But they were men who built the city, not gods or demons. They were men. I remember the dead man's face. They were men who were here before us. We must build again.

1. **Biltmore** hotel in New York City.
2. **Moses** Robert Moses, former New York City municipal official who oversaw many large construction projects.

Literary Analysis
Point of View Does John's new understanding of the gods now match the reader's? Explain.

Critical Thinking

Cite textual evidence to support your responses.

1. **Key Ideas and Details** **(a) Infer:** What are the Dead Places and the Place of the Gods? **(b) Synthesize:** How does John's tribe view the Dead Places?

2. **Key Ideas and Details** **(a)** When is this story set? How can you tell? **(b) Infer:** What destroyed the city? Explain.

3. **Key Ideas and Details** **(a)** Why does John's father want to keep John's experience secret? **(b) Evaluate:** Do you agree with John's father? Explain.

4. **Integration of Knowledge and Ideas** **(a)** What progress does John make as a result of dealing with conflict? Explain. **(b)** Do you think he could have made this progress without facing conflict? Why or why not? *[Connect to the Big Question: Can progress be made without conflict?]*

Comparing Points of View

1. Craft and Structure Using a chart like the one shown, compare the way in which each author uses **point of view** to control the information his reader receives.

Story	Point of View	What Reader Knows	What Character Knows	Effect of Contrast in Knowledge	Impact of Story

2. Craft and Structure (a) Compare the ways in which the ending of each story surprises the reader. **(b)** For each story, explain how the author's choice of narrator helps prepare for this surprise.

3. Craft and Structure (a) Readers may find Gillian's final gesture moving because they see that none of the characters knows what he has done. How does point of view create this effect? **(b)** Compare this feeling with that created by the ending of "By the Waters of Babylon." Why might a modern reader feel humbled by the story's ending?

⏱ Timed Writing

Explanatory Text: Essay

Both stories use dramatic irony. In an essay, compare and contrast how the irony is achieved in these stories. Support your response with details from the texts. **(40 minutes)**

5-Minute Planner

1. Read the prompt carefully and completely.
2. Consider these questions for both stories:
   - How does the point of view develop dramatic irony?
   - What is the character or persona of the narrator?
   - How much do you trust the narrator to tell you the truth?
   - What is the nature of the truth that is revealed in the ending?
   - How does irony affect your response to the selection?
3. Reread the prompt, and then draft your essay.

Writing Workshop

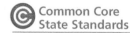 **Common Core State Standards**

Writing

3. Write narratives to develop real or imagined experiences or events using effective technique, well-chosen details, and well-structured event sequences.

3.a. Engage and orient the reader by setting out a problem, situation, or observation, establishing one or multiple point(s) of view, and introducing a narrator and/or characters; create a smooth progression of experiences or events.

5. Develop and strengthen writing as needed by planning, revising, editing, rewriting, or trying a new approach, focusing on addressing what is most significant for a specific purpose and audience.

Write a Narrative

Narration: Short Story

Defining the Form **Short stories** are a brief form of fiction that usually focuses on a limited number of characters. You might use elements of the short story in anecdotes, scripts, and reflective essays.

Assignment Write a short story about a main character who undergoes a change or learns something. Include these elements:

✓ a clear *setting*—the time and place of the story

✓ a *plot,* or series of events, that builds to a dramatic climax

✓ a *narrator* to tell the story

✓ effective descriptions using *sensory details*

✓ a *theme* that is revealed by the story's conclusion

✓ error-free grammar, including use of *consistent verb tense*

To preview the criteria on which your short story may be judged, see the rubric on page 333.

 Writing Workshop: *Work in Progress*

Review the work you did on pages 267 and 295.

Prewriting/Planning Strategy

Gather details about characters. Before you begin your draft, get to know the characters you will develop. Use a character chart like this one.

Character Chart	
Name	Kei
Appearance	Small frame, dark hair, intense brown eyes
Three Key Adjectives	smart, clumsy, ambitious
Goals	to be a great trumpet player
Habits or Quirks	taps his fingers
Likes	jazz, football, reading
Dislikes	TV, his boss at his after school job

Reading-Writing Connection

To get a feel for short stories, read "A Problem" by Anton Chekhov, on p. 256.

Using Your Imagination

Ideas are the building blocks of your story. They shape the plot, setting, and characters. As you generate ideas, begin with any one element—plot, setting, or characters—and develop the other two elements from there. Use these tips to engage your imagination and develop story ideas.

Imagining the Setting Create a setting you would choose if you could live anywhere or at any historical time. You can adapt most universal themes to any setting. For example, Shakespeare's play *Romeo and Juliet* is set in medieval Italy. The musical *West Side Story*, based loosely on the same plot, is set in 1950s New York City. Consider the setting before starting plot and character development. Often, the setting suggests the plot and characters. For example, a setting of a colony on a distant, inhospitable planet might suggest a struggle for survival.

Imagining the Plot Think about a dramatic moment in your life or the life of someone you know, or use newspapers or TV news to find an intriguing story. Turn the outlines of the personal event or news story into a short story. Remember that a short story is fiction, so you can add details or change the facts in order to make the story more interesting.

You might also use one of the universal themes of stories that can be adapted to any time or place. Examples include the following:

- A couple whose love is doomed, such as in *Romeo and Juliet*
- A hero who leads a desperate fight of good against evil
- A young person on a quest to save his or her family, tribe, or world

Imagining the Characters Think about the kind of character who would live in the setting or fit the plot you have chosen. As you develop your ideas, use a chart like the one shown to jot down notes.

	Plot	Setting	Character
Idea 1	a young boy struggles for survival in the wilderness	a remote area of the Rocky Mountains	a young Boy Scout who has wandered away during a camping trip
Idea 2			
Idea 3			

Drafting Strategies

Make a plot diagram. The plot of your story should include exposition to set up the characters, setting, and conflict. Rising action will build to a climax, or point of highest tension. Then, the falling action leads to the resolution. Create a plot diagram like the one shown here. Note major story events to create a logical, smooth progression.

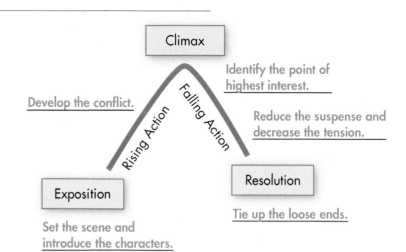

Keep pacing in mind. To keep your story moving, consider introducing the problem early in the story. Then, add details that intensify the problem. Using *flashbacks*—or material that occurred earlier than the present time of the narrative—is one way to add intensity. Flashbacks can be in the form of a character's memories, dreams, or accounts of past events, or they can simply be a shift in the narrative back to an earlier time. You might also delay the climax to create more suspense. After the climax, provide a conclusion in which a character or the narrator reflects on the events of the story.

Revising Strategies

Add dialogue to develop characters. Look for points where you can develop characters through dialogue and action. If your characters are from a specific region or background, including their dialect will help readers hear how they sound. Review your draft to identify direct statements that could be replaced with the characters' own words.

Revise to use active voice. Active voice is livelier and more engaging than the passive voice. In the passive voice, the action is done to the subject. In the active voice, the subject of the sentence performs the action.

> **Passive Voice:** The deadline was met by Krista and Rachel.

> **Active Voice:** Krista and Rachel met their deadline.

Add sensory details. Add sensory details to your writing to enable the reader to experience what you are describing. Sensory details are words that appeal to the senses: sight, smell, taste, touch, and hearing. Instead of writing *The pie smelled good,* you might say, *The freshly baked pie filled the house with the warm aroma of apples and cinnamon.* Using sensory language in this way allows readers to partake in your description.

Common Core State Standards

Writing

3.b. Use narrative techniques, such as dialogue, pacing, description, reflection, and multiple plot lines, to develop experiences, events, and/or characters.

3.c. Use a variety of techniques to sequence events so that they build on one another to create a coherent whole.

3.d. Use precise words and phrases, telling details, and sensory language to convey a vivid picture of the experiences, events, setting, and/or characters.

3.e. Provide a conclusion that follows from and reflects on what is experienced, observed, or resolved over the course of the narrative.

Revising to Apply Consistent Verb Tense

Correct use of verb tenses indicates when an event occurred. It is best to stay with a single tense. Mixing tenses unnecessarily can confuse the reader.

Six Basic Verb Tenses	
Present	He *arrives* today.
Past	He *arrived* yesterday.
Future	He *will arrive* tomorrow.
Present Perfect	He *has arrived* already.
Past Perfect	He *had arrived* earlier than expected.
Future Perfect	He *will have arrived* by next week.

Identifying Mixed Tenses To identify mixed tenses, first recognize the verb tenses you use. Compare these examples:

Mixed Tenses: Kei *has knocked* and *was waiting* patiently at the door. Nothing *happens*. Kei *had decided* to leave.

Consistent Tense: Kei *knocked* and *waited* patiently at the door. Nothing *happened*. Kei *decided* to leave.

Mixing tenses is necessary when your work refers to two different times.

> Past Perfect   Past
> Kei *had waited* for ten minutes before the door *opened*.

Fixing Errors To make sure that your verb tenses are consistent, find each verb in your writing.

1. Identify your overall verb tense as past, present, or future.

2. Review the verbs in your writing, circling each one.

3. If you find a verb that is not in your basic verb tense, make sure the tense shift is necessary.

4. Revise the verb if the shift is unnecessary.

Grammar in Your Writing

Review two paragraphs of your draft. Underline every verb and identify its tense. Use the steps you have just learned to fix confusing mixed tenses.

Student Model: Aubrey Weatherford, Broken Arrow, OK

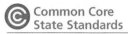

Common Core State Standards

Language
2.b. Spell correctly.

And Then the Rain Came

"Is it wrong for us to have a voice in our lives? We have to fight!" said the woman speaking to the crowd. Scarlett flashed instantly to the night of the fire. She could feel the young man holding her back; she could hear the child screaming in the burning building. She struggled to free herself, tears running down her face. Shaking herself back into reality, Scarlett walked slowly away from the park, the speaker's words fading as she went. There was a dull rumble in the distance, and a flicker of light illuminated the city around her. The cool breeze rustled her long skirt, and she began to quicken her pace for fear of being caught in the storm. Scarlett's mind was spinning, the speaker's words stirring her thoughts. The thought of speaking her opinion and of being able to choose whomever she wanted for public office, though she had never learned exactly what their jobs were—just the thought of having the choice was enough to excite her.

"Little Lady, you had better hurry on home now. There's a gonna be quite a storm a comin'." An old, wrinkled man had approached Scarlett from the shadows, seemingly trying to help. She was looking at him patiently.

"Hey you, crazy man, leave the lady alone. You go on home now, you worthless old fool!" A middle-aged businessman had approached the two.

"Don't talk to him that way! He wasn't bothering me!" Scarlett said. "You don't need to associate with street people like him. Go on home!"

"You have no right to speak to me in that fashion, good sir. I may associate with whomever I choose."

The businessman turned on his heel and left. "Thank yer for standing up for me, little lady. Mighty appreciative."

"It was nothing. You remind me so much of, oh, never mind," Scarlett replied.

"I am sure I will walk by here again sometime. I will look for you. Good day, sir." Though Scarlett did not see it, the old man began to come out of the shadows as she made her way down the crowded street, though his appearance had greatly changed. He was no longer a wrinkled, old man but a tall, young man with sandy hair and piercing eyes. Carefully, he watched as Scarlett hurried along the sidewalk. Tiny drops of rain began to fall from the ashen sky as Scarlett disappeared into the crowd. . . .

Aubrey introduces the main character in the first paragraph.

Sensory details describe the setting.

Aubrey develops the conflict through dialogue.

These details reveal an interesting twist in the plot.

Editing and Proofreading

Reread your story to correct errors in grammar, usage, and mechanics.

Focus on complete sentences and spelling. Check that all sentences in your draft contain a subject and a verb and express a complete thought. Also check your spelling. Words with double letters, such as *dilemma*, and words with two sets of double letters, such as *embarrass*, are often spelled incorrectly. Make up clues to help yourself remember any word that you often misspell.

Publishing and Presenting

Consider one of the following ways to share your writing:

Give a dramatic reading. Practice reading your story aloud, experimenting with pace, emphasis, and tone. Then, read your story to a group of classmates. After the presentation, discuss which of your story's elements were especially effective when presented dramatically.

Compile an anthology. Join with your classmates to create a class story anthology. Organize the stories by theme and illustrate them with suitable photographs or drawings. Place the collection in your class, school, or community library.

Reflecting on Your Writing

Writer's Journal Jot down your answers to this question:

How did writing a short story help you better understand the form?

Rubric for Self-Assessment

Find evidence in your writing to address each category. Then, use the rating scale to grade your work.

Spiral Review

Earlier in the unit, you learned about the **principal parts of regular verbs** (p. 266) and **irregular verbs** (p. 294). Review your draft to ensure you have formed verb tenses correctly and consistently.

Criteria	Rating Scale
	not very very
Focus: How clear is the story's theme or message?	1 2 3 4 5
Organization: How effectively does the plot build to a climax?	1 2 3 4 5
Support/Elaboration: How effective is your choice of details?	1 2 3 4 5
Style: How well do you describe the characters and setting?	1 2 3 4 5
Conventions: How correct is your grammar, especially your use of verb tense?	1 2 3 4 5
Ideas: How effective and interesting are your ideas for plot, setting, and characters?	1 2 3 4 5

Leveled Texts

Build your skills and improve your comprehension of short stories with texts of increasing complexity.

Read **"How Much Land Does a Man Need?"** to find out what happens when a man is never satisfied with what he has.

Read **"Civil Peace"** to find out what happens when a man chooses to make the most of what he has.

Common Core State Standards

Meet these standards with either **"How Much Land Does a Man Need?"** (p. 338) or **"Civil Peace"** (p. 358).

Reading Literature
2. Determine a theme or central idea of a text and analyze in detail its development over the course of the text, including how it emerges and is shaped and refined by specific details; provide an objective summary of the text. (*Literary Analysis: Theme*)
Spiral Review: RL.9-10.5
Writing
2.a. Introduce a topic; organize complex ideas, concepts, and information to make important connections and distinctions. **2.b.** Develop the topic with well-chosen, relevant, and sufficient facts, extended definitions, concrete details, quotations, or other information and examples appropriate to the audience's knowledge of the topic. **2.c.** Use appropriate and varied transitions to link the major sections of the text, create cohesion, and clarify the relationships among complex ideas and concepts.

(*Writing: Character Analysis*)
Speaking and Listening
1.c. Propel conversations by posing and responding to questions that relate the current discussion to broader themes or larger ideas; actively incorporate others into the discussion; and clarify, verify, or challenge ideas and conclusions. **1.d.** Respond thoughtfully to diverse perspectives, summarize points of agreement and disagreement, and, when warranted, qualify or justify their own views and understanding and make new connections in light of the evidence and reasoning presented. (*Speaking and Listening: Group Discussion*)

Language
5. Demonstrate understanding of figurative language, word relationships, and nuances in word meanings. (*Vocabulary: Antonyms*)

Literary Analysis: Theme

The **theme** of a literary work is the central idea it communicates about life. For example, a simple story might convey the theme "Honesty is the best policy." Another work might suggest, "Human suffering cannot be justified or explained." Frequently, writers' themes spring from the *historical context* of a selection, the social and cultural background of a story. The author's diction and use of figurative language contribute to the interpretation of the theme. To express a theme, a writer may take one of these approaches:

- Directly state the theme of the work, or have a character directly state it.

- Create patterns of story elements to suggest a larger meaning—for instance, by using language patterns or repeated phrases. In addition, a writer might contrast a generous man and his selfish brother to convey an idea about generosity.

In many cases, a theme reflects a **philosophical assumption**—the writer's basic beliefs about life. For instance, a writer may make the assumption that being generous leads to happiness and may explore that idea in his or her writing.

Reading Skill: Draw Conclusions

When you **draw a conclusion,** you reach a decision or form an opinion based on information in a text. To draw a conclusion identifying the theme of a work, **recognize key details.** Also, think about the characters' experiences and what they learn about life in the course of the story. Use that information to draw conclusions about theme.

Using the Strategy: Key Details Diagram

Use a **key details diagram** to help draw a conclusion about a selection.

Story Detail		Story Detail		Pattern
Greedy Joe invests in a crooked scheme. He loses his money.	+	Generous John tricks the crooks and saves Joe.	→	Being greedy causes harm. Being generous leads to solutions.

Can progress be made without *conflict?*

Writing About the Big Question

In "How Much Land Does a Man Need?", a man struggles to satisfy his desire for more land and prosperity. Use these sentence starters to help develop your ideas about the Big Question:

Making a **change** can improve the quality of your life as long as

_____ .

A person may **struggle** with finding happiness if _____ .

While You Read Note signs of the main character's discontent with his life. Then, decide whether he faces the biggest conflict with others or within himself.

Vocabulary

Read each word and its definition. Decide whether you know the word well, know it a little bit, or do not know it at all. After you read, see how your knowledge of each word has increased.

- **piqued** (pēkt) *adj.* annoyed or upset (p. 339) *I am* <u>*piqued*</u> *by the fact that you did not tell me that you would be late.* pique *n.* piqued *v.* piquant *adj.*

- **discord** (dis´ kôrd´) *n.* conflict; disagreement (p. 340) *The new referee's questionable call caused* <u>*discord*</u> *between the teams.* discordant *adj.* concord *n.* cordial *adj.*

- **forbore** (fôr bôr´) *v.* prevented oneself from doing something; refrained from (p. 342) *The quarterback* <u>*forbore*</u> *responding to the linebackers' taunts.* forbearance *n.* forbearingly *adv.*

- **aggrieved** (ə grēvd´) *adj.* wronged; suffering grief or injury (p. 343) *The tenants were* <u>*aggrieved*</u> *by the landlord's delay in fixing the hot-water tank.* aggrieve *v.* grievance *n.*

- **arable** (ar´ ə bəl) *adj.* suitable for growing crops (p. 344) *After two years of poor crops, the farmer was forced to seek out more* <u>*arable*</u> *land.* arability *adj.*

- **prostrate** (präs´ trāt´) *adj.* lying flat (p. 350) *After a tiring day, Randall lay* <u>*prostrate*</u> *on the couch.* prostration *n.*

Word Study

The **Latin prefix** *dis-* means "wrong," "bad," or "not."

In this story, **discord** arises when the peasants are not in accord, or agreement, with one another. They pursue individual interests instead of a common goal.

land to be had, the peasants would rush for it and it was taken up at once, so that unless you were sharp about it, you got none. It happened in the third year that he and a dealer together rented a piece of pasture land from some peasants, and they had already plowed it up, when there was some dispute and the peasants went to law about it, and things fell out so that the labor was all lost.

"If it were my own land," thought Pahom, "I should be independent, and there wouldn't be all this unpleasantness."

So Pahom began looking out for land which he could buy, and he came across a peasant who had bought thirteen hundred acres, but having got into difficulties was willing to sell again cheap. Pahom bargained and haggled with him, and at last they settled the price at fifteen hundred rubles, part in cash and part to be paid later. They had all but clinched the matter when a passing dealer happened to stop at Pahom's one day to get feed for his horses. He drank tea with Pahom, and they had a talk. The dealer said that he was just returning from the land of the Bashkirs,[5] far away, where he had bought thirteen thousand acres of land, all for a thousand rubles. Pahom questioned him further, and the dealer said:

▲ Critical Viewing
What assumptions could you make about the lifestyle of a peasant based on the details in this painting? **[Interpret]**

Reading Check

What information does the stranger who comes to visit give Pahom?

5. **Bashkirs** (bash kirz´) n. originally nomadic people who live in the plains of southwestern Russia.

"All one has to do is to make friends with the chiefs. I gave away about one hundred rubles' worth of silk robes and carpets, besides a case of tea, and I gave wine to those who would drink it; and I got the land for less than three kopecks[6] an acre." And he showed Pahom the title deed, saying:

"The land lies near a river, and the whole steppe[7] is virgin soil."

Pahom plied him with questions, and the dealer said:

"There's more land there than you could cover if you walked a year, and it all belongs to the Bashkirs. They're as simple as sheep, and land can be got almost for nothing."

"There, now," thought Pahom, "with my one thousand rubles, why should I get only thirteen hundred acres, and saddle myself with a debt besides? If I take it out there, I can get more than ten times as much for my money."

5

Pahom inquired how to get to the place, and as soon as the grain dealer had left him, he prepared to go there himself. He left his wife to look after the homestead, and started on his journey, taking his hired man with him. They stopped at a town on their way and bought a case of tea, some wine, and other presents, as the grain dealer had advised.

---

6. kopecks (kō′ peks′) *n.* units of Russian money, each equal to one hundredth of a ruble.
7. steppe (step) *n.* high grassland plains stretching from Hungary through Russia into central Asia.

On and on they went until they had gone more than three hundred miles, and on the seventh day they came to a place where the Bashkirs had pitched their round tents. It was all just as the dealer had said. The people lived on the steppe, by a river, in felt-covered tents. They neither tilled the ground nor ate bread. Their cattle and horses grazed in herds on the steppe. The colts were tethered behind the tents, and the mares were driven to them twice a day. The mares were milked, and from the milk kumiss[8] was made. It was the women who prepared the kumiss, and they also made cheese. As far as the men were concerned, drinking kumiss and tea, eating mutton, and playing on their pipes was all they cared about. They were all stout and merry, and all the summer long they never thought of doing any work. They were quite ignorant, and knew no Russian, but were good-natured enough.

As soon as they saw Pahom, they came out of their tents and gathered around the visitor. An interpreter was found, and Pahom told them he had come about some land. The Bashkirs seemed very glad; they took Pahom and led him into one of the best tents, where they made him sit on some down cushions placed on a carpet, while they sat around him. They gave him some tea and kumiss, and had a sheep killed, and gave him mutton to eat. Pahom took presents out of his cart and distributed them among the Bashkirs, and divided the tea amongst them. The Bashkirs were delighted. They talked a great deal among themselves and then told the interpreter what to say.

"They wish to tell you," said the interpreter, "that they like you and that it's our custom to do all we can to please a guest and to repay him for his gifts. You have given us presents, now tell us which of the things we possess please you best, that we may present them to you."

"What pleases me best here," answered Pahom, "is your land. Our land is crowded and the soil is worn out, but you have plenty of land, and it is good land. I never saw the likes of it."

The interpreter told the Bashkirs what Pahom had said. They talked among themselves for a while. Pahom could not understand what they were saying, but saw that they were much amused and heard them shout and laugh. Then they were silent and looked at Pahom while the interpreter said:

"They wish me to tell you that in return for your presents they will gladly give you as much land as you want. You have only to point it out with your hand and it is yours."

---

8. **kumiss** (ko͞o′ mis) *n.* fermented mare's or camel's milk that is used as a drink.

Reading Skill
Draw Conclusions
What details in this passage suggest that the Bashkirs have different priorities than Pahom?

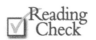

Reading Check
Where does Pahom decide to go next?

The Bashkirs talked again for a while and began to dispute. Pahom asked what they were disputing about, and the interpreter told him that some of them thought they ought to ask their chief about the land and not act in his absence, while others thought there was no need to wait for his return. ●

6

While the Bashkirs were disputing, a man in a large fox-fur cap appeared on the scene. They all became silent and rose to their feet. The interpreter said: "This is our chief himself."

Pahom immediately fetched the best dressing gown and five pounds of tea, and offered these to the chief. The chief accepted them and seated himself in the place of honor. The Bashkirs at once began telling him something. The chief listened for a while, then made a sign with his head for them to be silent, and addressing himself to Pahom, said in Russian:

"Well, so be it. Choose whatever piece of land you like; we have plenty of it."

"How can I take as much as I like?" thought Pahom. "I must get a deed to make it secure, or else they may say: 'It is yours,' and afterward may take it away again."

"Thank you for your kind words," he said aloud. "You have much land, and I only want a little. But I should like to be sure which portion is mine. Could it not be measured and made over to me? Life and death are in God's hands. You good people give it to me, but your children might wish to take it back again."

"You are quite right," said the chief. "We will make it over to you."

"I heard that a dealer had been here," continued Pahom, "and that you gave him a little land, too, and signed title deeds to that effect. I should like to have it done in the same way."

The chief understood.

"Yes," replied he, "that can be done quite easily. We have a scribe, and we will go to town with you and have the deed properly sealed."

"And what will be the price?" asked Pahom.

"Our price is always the same: one thousand rubles a day."

Pahom did not understand.

"A day? What measure is that? How many acres would that be?"

"We do not know how to reckon it out," said the chief. "We sell it by the day. As much as you can go around on your feet in a day is yours, and the price is one thousand rubles a day."

Pahom was surprised.

"But in a day you can get around a large tract of land," he said.

The chief laughed.

Reading Skill
Draw Conclusions
What details suggest that the Bashkirs view the land differently from Pahom?

"It will all be yours!" said he. "But there is one condition: If you don't return on the same day to the spot whence you started, your money is lost."

"But how am I to mark the way that I have gone?"

"Why, we shall go to any spot you like and stay there. You must start from that spot and make your round, taking a spade with you. Wherever you think necessary, make a mark. At every turning, dig a hole and pile up the turf; then afterward we will go around with a plow from hole to hole. You may make as large a circuit as you please, but before the sun sets you must return to the place you started from. All the land you cover will be yours."

Pahom was delighted. It was decided to start early next morning. They talked a while, and after drinking some more kumiss and eating some more mutton, they had tea again, and then the night came on. They gave Pahom a featherbed to sleep on, and the Bashkirs dispersed for the night, promising to assemble the next morning at daybreak and ride out before sunrise to the appointed spot.

"But there is one condition: If you don't return on the same day to the spot whence you started, your money is lost."

7

Pahom lay on the featherbed, but could not sleep. He kept thinking about the land.

"What a large tract I'll mark off!" thought he. "I can easily do thirty-five miles in a day. The days are long now, and within a circuit of thirty-five miles what a lot of land there will be! I'll sell the poorer land or let it to peasants, but I'll pick out the best and farm it myself. I'll buy two ox teams and hire two more laborers. About a hundred and fifty acres shall be plowland, and I'll pasture cattle on the rest."

Pahom lay awake all night and dozed off only just before dawn. Hardly were his eyes closed when he had a dream. He thought he was lying in that same tent and heard somebody chuckling outside. He wondered who it could be, and rose and went out, and he saw the Bashkir chief sitting in front of the tent holding his sides and rolling about with laughter. Going nearer to the chief, Pahom asked: "What are you laughing at?" But he saw that it was no longer the chief but the grain dealer who had recently stopped at his house and had told him about the land. Just as Pahom was going to ask: "Have you been here long?" he saw that it was not the dealer, but the peasant who had come up from the Volga long ago, to Pahom's old home. Then he saw that it was not the peasant either, but the Devil himself with hoofs and horns, sitting there and chuckling, and before him

Reading
Check

How large a tract of land does Pahom decide he will mark off?

History Connection

The Emancipation of the Serfs

Tolstoy published "How Much Land Does a Man Need?" in 1886, a year in which the question in the title was on many Russians' minds.

- In 1861, the ruler of Russia, Tsar Alexander II, freed the serfs
- The government bought land from the serfs' former masters and sold it to the serfs.
- In some parts of Russia, the price was unrealistically high. In other parts, the parcels were too small.
- To survive, some freed serfs rented land from landowners. Others worked for landowners or went to work in factories. Discontent grew, and many sought further reform.

Russia

1460	1649	1773–1774	1861
The freedom of peasants to leave the land they farmed is limited.	Russian peasants are enserfed.	Peasants rebel.	Alexander II ends serfdom in Russia.

Other Countries

England ends serfdom. **1600s**	France ends serfdom. **1789**	United States abolishes slavery. **1865**

Nineteenth Century Population of Russia

- **Nobles, Merchants, and Others** roughly one fifth
- **Privately Owned Serfs** roughly two fifths
- **State and Other Peasants** roughly two fifths

Connect to the Literature

Based on Pahom's story, what do you think Tolstoy thought of land reform in Russia? Explain.

Vocabulary
prostrate (präs´ trāt´) *adj.* lying flat

lay a man, prostrate on the ground, barefooted, with only trousers and a shirt on. And Pahom dreamed that he looked more attentively to see what sort of man it was lying there, and he saw that the man was dead, and that it was himself. Horror-struck, he awoke.

"What things one dreams about!" thought he.

Looking around he saw through the open door that the dawn was breaking.

"It's time to wake them up," thought he. "We ought to be starting."

He got up, roused his man (who was sleeping in his cart), bade him harness, and went to call the Bashkirs.

"It's time to go to the steppe to measure the land," he said.

The Bashkirs rose and assembled, and the chief came, too. Then they began drinking kumiss again, and offered Pahom some tea, but he would not wait.

"If we are to go, let's go. It's high time," said he.

8

The Bashkirs got ready and they all started; some mounted on horses and some in carts. Pahom drove in his own small cart with his servant and took a spade with him. When they reached the steppe, the red dawn was beginning to kindle. They ascended a hillock (called by the Bashkirs a *shikhan*) and, dismounting from their carts and their horses, gathered in one spot. The chief came up to Pahom and, stretching out his arm toward the plain:

"See," said he, "all this, as far as your eye can reach, is ours. You may have any part of it you like."

Pahom's eyes glistened: it was all virgin soil, as flat as the palm of your hand, as black as the seed of a poppy, and in the hollows different kinds of grasses grew breast-high.

The chief took off his fox-fur cap, placed it on the ground, and said:

"This will be the mark. Start from here, and return here again. All the land you go around shall be yours."

Pahom took out his money and put it on the cap. Then he took off his outer coat, remaining in his sleeveless undercoat. He unfastened his girdle[9] and tied it tight below his stomach, put a little bag of bread into the breast of his coat, and, tying a flask of water to his girdle, he drew up the tops of his boots, took the spade from his man, and stood ready to start. He considered for some moments which way he had better go—it was tempting everywhere.

"No matter," he concluded, "I'll go toward the rising sun."

He turned his face to the east, stretched himself, and waited for the sun to appear above the rim.

"I must lose no time," he thought, "and it's easier walking while it's still cool."

The sun's rays had hardly flashed above the horizon when Pahom, carrying the spade over his shoulder, went down into the steppe.

Pahom started walking neither slowly nor quickly. After having gone a thousand yards he stopped, dug a hole, and placed pieces of turf one on another to make it more visible. Then he went on; and now that he had walked off his stiffness he quickened his pace. After a while he dug another hole.

Pahom looked back. The hillock could be distinctly seen in the sunlight, with the people on it, and the glittering iron rims of the cartwheels. At a rough guess Pahom concluded that he had walked three miles. It was growing warmer; he took off his undercoat, slung it across his shoulder, and went on again. It had grown quite warm now; he looked at the sun—it was time to think of breakfast.

"The first shift is done, but there are four in a day, and it's too soon yet to turn. But I'll just take off my boots," said he to himself.

He sat down, took off his boots, stuck them into his girdle, and went on. It was easy walking now.

"I'll go on for another three miles," thought he, "and then turn

9. **girdle** (gᵤrd´l) *n.* old term for a belt or sash for the waist.

Literary Analysis
Theme How do Pahom's thoughts and actions now reflect his earlier attitude toward acquiring land?

Reading Check

At what sort of pace does Pahom set out?

to the left. This spot is so fine that it would be a pity to lose it. The further one goes, the better the land seems."

He went straight on for a while, and when he looked around, the hillock was scarcely visible and the people on it looked like black ants, and he could just see something glistening there in the sun.

"Ah," thought Pahom, "I have gone far enough in this direction; it's time to turn. Besides, I'm in a regular sweat, and very thirsty."

He stopped, dug a large hole, and heaped up pieces of turf. Next he untied his flask, had a drink, and then turned sharply to the left. He went on and on; the grass was high, and it was very hot.

Pahom began to grow tired: he looked at the sun and saw that it was noon.

"Well," he thought, "I must have a rest."

He sat down, and ate some bread and drank some water; but he did not lie down, thinking that if he did he might fall asleep. After sitting a little while, he went on again. At first he walked easily; the food had strengthened him; but it had become terribly hot and he felt sleepy. Still he went on, thinking: "An hour to suffer, a lifetime to live."

He went a long way in this direction also, and was about to turn to the left again, when he perceived a damp hollow: "It would be a pity to leave that out," he thought. "Flax would do well there." So he went on past the hollow and dug a hole on the other side of it before he made a sharp turn. Pahom looked toward the hillock. The heat made the air hazy: it seemed to be quivering, and through the haze the people on the hillock could scarcely be seen.

"Ah," thought Pahom, "I have made the sides too long; I must make this one shorter." And he went along the third side, stepping faster. He looked at the sun: it was nearly halfway to the horizon, and he had not yet done two miles of the third side of the square. He was still ten miles from the goal.

"No," he thought, "though it will make my land lopsided, I must hurry back in a straight line now. I might go too far, and as it is I have a great deal of land."

So Pahom hurriedly dug a hole and turned straight toward the hillock. •

9

Pahom went straight toward the hillock, but he now walked with difficulty. He was exhausted from the heat, his bare feet were cut and bruised, and his legs began to fail. He longed to rest, but it was impossible if he meant to get back before sunset. The sun waits for no man, and it was sinking lower and lower.

"Oh, Lord," he thought, "if only I have not blundered trying for

---

Spiral Review
Plot In what way do Pahom's pacing and the pacing of this part of the story work in parallel?

Reading Skill
Draw Conclusions
Based on details here and earlier, what conclusion can you draw about the chances for Pahom's success?

too much! What if I am too late?"

He looked toward the hillock and at the sun. He was still far from his goal, and the sun was already near the rim of the sky.

Pahom walked on and on; it was very hard walking, but he went quicker and quicker. He pressed on, but was still far from the place. He began running, threw away his coat, his boots, his flask, and his cap, and kept only the spade which he used as a support.

"What am I to do?" he thought again. "I've grasped too much and ruined the whole affair. I can't get there before the sun sets."

And this fear made him still more breathless. Pahom kept on running; his soaking shirt and trousers stuck to him, and his mouth was parched. His breast was working like a blacksmith's bellows, his heart was beating like a hammer, and his legs were giving way as if they did not belong to him. Pahom was seized with terror lest he should die of the strain.

Though afraid of death, he could not stop.

"After having run all that way they will call me a fool if I stop now," thought he.

And he ran on and on, and drew near and heard the Bashkirs yelling and shouting to him, and their cries inflamed his heart still more. He gathered his last strength and ran on.

The sun was close to the rim of the sky and, cloaked in mist, looked large, and red as blood. Now, yes, now, it was about to set! The sun was quite low, but he was also quite near his goal. Pahom could already see the people on the hillock waving their arms to make him hurry. He could see the fox-fur cap on the ground and the money in it, and the chief sitting on the ground holding his sides. And Pahom remembered his dream.

"There's plenty of land," thought he, "but will God let me live on it? I have lost my life, I have lost my life! Never will I reach that spot!"

Pahom looked at the sun, which had reached the earth: one side of it had already disappeared. With all his remaining strength he rushed on, bending his body forward so that his legs could hardly follow fast enough to keep him from falling. Just as he reached the hillock it suddenly grew dark. He looked up—the sun had already set!

"I can't get there before the sun sets."

He gave a cry: "All my labor has been in vain," thought he, and was about to stop, but he heard the Bashkirs still shouting and remembered that though to him, from below, the sun seemed to have set, they on the hillock could still see it. He took a long breath and ran up the hillock. It was still light there. He reached the top and saw the cap. Before it sat the chief, laughing and holding his sides. Again Pahom remembered his dream, and he uttered a cry: his legs gave way beneath him, he fell forward and reached the cap with his hands.

"Ah, that's a fine fellow!" exclaimed the chief. "He has gained much land!"

Pahom's servant came running up and tried to raise him, but he saw that blood was flowing from his mouth. Pahom was dead.

The Bashkirs clicked their tongues to show their pity.

His servant picked up the spade and dug a grave long enough for Pahom to lie in, and buried him in it.

Six feet from his head to his toes was all he needed.

Critical Thinking

Cite textual evidence to support your responses.

1. **Key Ideas and Details (a)** What event allows Pahom to buy his first parcel of land? **(b) Interpret:** What is his main reason for wanting this land? Support your answer with story details.

2. **Key Ideas and Details (a)** Explain the events that change Pahom's relations with his neighbors. **(b) Analyze Cause and Effect:** What effect does owning land have on his life?

3. **Craft and Structure (a)** If Pahom had no chances to acquire more land, do you think he could find happiness with what he already has? Explain. **(b) Discuss:** Share and discuss answers with a partner. **(c) Apply:** Based on your discussion, write a sentence explaining the author's attitude toward ambition.

4. **Key Ideas and Details (a) Summarize:** In a few sentences, sum up what happens on the last day of Pahom's life. Do not state your opinion of events; simply report them. **(b) Interpret:** Explain the meaning of the story's last sentence both as a description of Pahom's fate and as an answer to the title of the story.

5. **Integration of Knowledge and Ideas (a)** Is Pahom's main conflict with others or with himself? Explain. **(b)** Should Pahom's acquisition of increasingly large parcels of land be considered progress? Why or why not? *[Connect to the Big Question: Can progress be made without conflict?]*

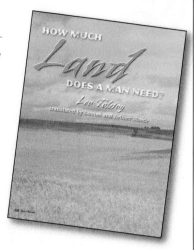

Literary Analysis: Theme

Ⓒ **1. Craft and Structure (a)** Using a chart like the one shown, analyze the episodes in which Pahom is given the chance to acquire property. **(b)** How are these episodes related?

Episode	Character's Response	Reasons for the Response	Result: Peace of Mind/Problems

(c) State the **theme** of the story, explaining how each event helps convey it.

Ⓒ **2. Key Ideas and Details** Tolstoy makes the **philosophical assumption** that people should not waste their lives on material things. How could Pahom have applied this belief to his life?

Reading Skill: Draw Conclusions

3. (a) Draw a conclusion about the Bashkirs' values based on their attitude toward land. **(b)** Which details in Tolstoy's depiction of the tribe contribute to the story's theme? Explain.

Vocabulary

Ⓒ **Acquisition and Use Antonyms** are words with opposite meanings. Rewrite the following sentences by replacing each word or phrase in italics with its antonym from the vocabulary list on page 336. Then, explain which version of each sentence makes more sense.

1. He *indulged* and ate half the cake.

2. After he took my bicycle, I was *forgiving* and lent him my radio.

3. I was *not hurt* by his insults, and I found his company enjoyable.

4. The *harmony* between the siblings made family dinners peaceful.

5. His land was *desert*, so he had no success with his crops.

6. Her body was *upright* and at attention as she received her medal.

Word Study Use the context of the sentences and what you know about the **Latin prefix dis-** to explain your answer to each question.

1. Are people living in *disharmony* good at working together?

2. What happens when a person is *disabled* in some way?

Word Study

The **Latin prefix dis-** means "wrong," "bad," or "not."

Apply It Explain how the prefix *dis-* contributes to the meanings of these words. Consult a dictionary if necessary.

disconnect
disembody
disregard

Can progress be made without *conflict?*

Writing About the Big Question

In "Civil Peace," a man and most of his family survive a civil war only to face new conflicts during peacetime. Use this sentence starter to develop your ideas about the Big Question.

Understanding what things are truly important in life can help a person overcome **adversity** because _____.

While You Read Look for things Jonathan, the story's main character, counts as blessings after the conflict of war ends.

Vocabulary

Read each word and its definition. Decide whether you know the word well, know it a little bit, or do not know it at all. After you read, see how your knowledge of each word has increased.

- **disreputable** (dis rep´ yo͞o tə bəl) *adj.* not respectable; having or deserving a bad reputation (p. 359) *The travel guide warned against* <u>disreputable</u> *street vendors.* *disreputably adv. disrepute n.*

- **amenable** (ə mē´ nə bəl) *adj.* responsive; open (p. 359) *The plans are not set, so I will be* <u>amenable</u> *to your suggestions.* *amenability n. amenably adv.*

- **destitute** (des´ tə to͞ot´) *adj.* lacking the basic necessities of life; poverty-stricken (p. 360) *The city provided housing for families left* <u>destitute</u> *by the flood.* *destitution n.*

- **inaudibly** (in ô´ də blē) *adv.* in a way that cannot be heard (p. 362) *No one can understand what Lydia says when she mumbles* <u>inaudibly</u>. *audible adj. inaudible adj. audio n.*

- **dissent** (di sent´) *n.* disagreement; refusal to accept a common opinion (p. 363) *The dictator would not tolerate* <u>dissent</u> *from his subjects.* *dissent v. dissenter n. assent v.*

- **commiserate** (kə miz´ ər āt´) *v.* sympathize with or show sorrow for (p. 364) *The coach will usually* <u>commiserate</u> *with his team after a tough loss.* *commiseration n. commiserative adj.*

Word Study

The **Latin prefix com-** means "together" or "with."

In this story, a character and his neighbors **commiserate,** or feel sorrow together, after he and his family are robbed.

Author of
Civil
Peace

Chinua (chin´ wä´) Achebe (ä chä´ bä) is renowned for novels and stories that explore the conflicts of modern Africans. Achebe was born into the Ibo tribe of Nigeria. He grew up to pursue a varied career as a university teacher and as a director for the Nigerian Broadcasting Corporation. According to one critic, "In the English language, he is the founding father of modern African literature."

Africans Face the West Achebe wrote his first and most celebrated novel, *Things Fall Apart* (1958), in an effort to accurately portray the disruption of Ibo tribal society by Western colonial rule.

BACKGROUND FOR THE STORY

The Nigerian Civil War

In 1960, the West African nation of Nigeria finally won independence from Britain. The Ibo (also spelled *Igbo*), one people of Nigeria, seceded from the new country, setting up the independent Republic of Biafra. A brutal civil war followed. In 1970, a defeated Biafra rejoined Nigeria. "Civil Peace" unfolds in the aftermath of this war.

DID YOU KNOW?

During the civil war in Nigeria, Achebe's house was bombed. He fled, leaving behind a book of his that he had nearly finished printing. When he returned, a single copy of the book remained.

Civil Peace

Chinua Achebe

Jonathan Iwegbu counted himself extraordinarily lucky. "Happy survival!" meant so much more to him than just a current fashion of greeting old friends in the first hazy days of peace. It went deep to his heart. He had come out of the war with five inestimable blessings—his head, his wife Maria's head and the heads of three out of their four children. As a bonus he also had his old bicycle—a miracle too but naturally not to be compared to the safety of five human heads.

The bicycle had a little history of its own. One day at the height of the war it was commandeered "for urgent military action." Hard as its loss would have been to him he would still have let it go without a thought had he not had some doubts about the genuineness of the officer. It wasn't his disreputable rags, nor the toes peeping out of one blue and one brown canvas shoe, nor yet the two stars of his rank done obviously in a hurry in biro,[1] that troubled Jonathan; many good and heroic soldiers looked the same or worse. It was rather a certain lack of grip and firmness in his manner. So Jonathan, suspecting he might be amenable to influence, rummaged in his raffia bag and produced the two pounds with which he had been going to buy firewood which his wife, Maria, retailed to camp officials for extra stock-fish and corn meal, and got his bicycle back. That night he buried it in the little clearing in the bush where the dead of the camp, including his own youngest son, were buried. When he dug it up again a year later after the surrender all it needed was a little palm-oil greasing. "Nothing puzzles God," he said in wonder.

He put it to immediate use as a taxi and accumulated a small pile of Biafran[2] money ferrying camp officials and their families across the four-mile stretch to the nearest tarred road. His standard charge per trip was six pounds and those who had the money were only glad to be rid of some of it in this way. At the end of a fortnight[3] he had made a small fortune of one hundred and fifteen pounds.

Then he made the journey to Enugu and found another miracle waiting for him. It was unbelievable. He rubbed his eyes and looked again and it was still standing there before him. But, needless to say, even that monumental blessing must be accounted also totally inferior to the five heads in the family. This newest miracle was his little house in Ogui Overside. Indeed nothing puzzles God! Only two houses away a huge concrete edifice some wealthy contractor had put up just before the war was a mountain of rubble. And here was Jonathan's little zinc house of no regrets built with mud blocks quite intact! Of course the doors and windows were missing and five sheets off the roof. But what was that? And anyhow he had returned to Enugu early enough to pick up bits of old zinc and wood and soggy sheets of cardboard lying around the neighborhood before thousands more came out of their forest holes looking for

Vocabulary
disreputable (dis rep´ yoo tə bəl) *adj.* not respectable; having or deserving a bad reputation

amenable (ə mē´ nə bəl) *adj.* responsive; open

Literary Analysis
Theme What do these stories of Jonathan's "blessings" have in common?

Reading Check

What are the five blessings for which Jonathan is grateful?

---

1. **biro** (bī´ rō) *n.* British expression for "ballpoint pen."
2. **Biafran** (bē äf´ rən) *adj.* of the rebellious southeastern region of Nigeria, which declared itself the independent Republic of Biafra in the civil war of 1967.
3. **fortnight** (fôrt´ nīt´) *n.* British English for "two weeks."

the same things. He got a destitute carpenter with one old hammer, a blunt plane and a few bent and rusty nails in his tool bag to turn this assortment of wood, paper and metal into door and window shutters for five Nigerian shillings or fifty Biafran pounds. He paid the pounds, and moved in with his overjoyed family carrying five heads on their shoulders.

His children picked mangoes near the military cemetery and sold them to soldiers' wives for a few pennies—real pennies this time—and his wife started making breakfast akara balls[4] for neighbors in a hurry to start life again. With his family earnings he took his bicycle to the villages around and bought fresh palm-wine which he mixed generously in his rooms with the water which had recently started running again in the public tap down the road, and opened up a bar for soldiers and other lucky people with good money.

At first he went daily, then every other day and finally once a week, to the offices of the Coal Corporation where he used to be a miner, to find out what was what. The only thing he did find out in the end was that that little house of his was even a greater blessing than he had thought. Some of his fellow ex-miners who had nowhere to return at the end of the day's waiting just slept outside the doors of the offices and cooked what meal they could scrounge together in Bournvita tins. As the weeks lengthened and still nobody could say what was what Jonathan discontinued his weekly visits altogether and faced his palm-wine bar.

But nothing puzzles God. Came the day of the windfall when

▲ Critical Viewing
Does the expression on this man's face suggest he has a personality similar to Jonathan's? Explain. **[Connect]**

Vocabulary
destitute (des´ tə to͞ot´) *adj.* lacking the basic necessities of life; poverty-stricken

---

4. akara (ə kär´ ə) **balls** *n.* deep-fried balls of ground beans.

after five days of endless scuffles in queues[5] and counterqueues in the sun outside the Treasury he had twenty pounds counted into his palms as ex-gratia[6] award for the rebel money he had turned in. It was like Christmas for him and for many others like him when the payments began. They called it (since few could manage its proper official name) *egg-rasher*.

As soon as the pound notes were placed in his palm Jonathan simply closed it tight over them and buried fist and money inside his trouser pocket. He had to be extra careful because he had seen a man a couple of days earlier collapse into near-madness in an instant before that oceanic crowd because no sooner had he got his twenty pounds than some heartless ruffian picked it off him. Though it was not right that a man in such an extremity of agony should be blamed yet many in the queues that day were able to remark quietly at the victim's carelessness, especially after he pulled out the innards of his pocket and revealed a hole in it big enough to pass a thief's head. But of course he had insisted that the money had been in the other pocket, pulling it out too to show

---

5. **queues** (kyo͞oz) *n.* British English for "lines."
6. **ex-gratia** (eks grā′ shē ə) as a favor (Latin).

Reading Skill
Draw Conclusions
What conclusion can you draw about Jonathan's attitude toward good and bad events? Explain.

Reading Check
What does Jonathan get in exchange for the rebel money he has saved?

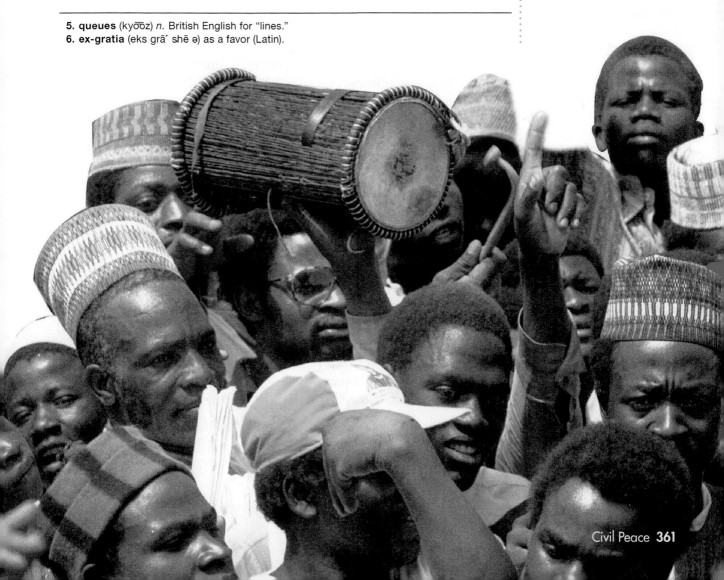

Geography Connection

Nigerian Civil War

Jonathan is delighted that his home in Enugu still stands—and for good reason. Enugu was at the center of the civil war that broke out in Nigeria in 1967. The war began when the eastern region of Nigeria declared itself the independent Republic of Biafra, with Enugu as its capital. The city was invaded by Nigerian federal troops just five months after independence. The war resulted in horrific famine as well as violence. It ended in 1970 with the defeat of Biafra and the reunification of Nigeria.

Connect to the Literature

Which of Jonathan's experiences can you connect to events of the Nigerian Civil War? Explain.

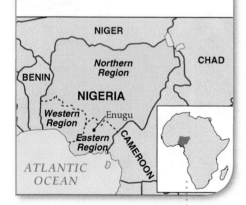

Vocabulary
inaudibly (in ôˊ də blē) *adv.* in a way that cannot be heard

its comparative wholeness. So one had to be careful.

Jonathan soon transferred the money to his left hand and pocket so as to leave his right free for shaking hands should the need arise, though by fixing his gaze at such an elevation as to miss all approaching human faces he made sure that the need did not arise, until he got home. •

He was normally a heavy sleeper but that night he heard all the neighborhood noises die down one after another. Even the night watchman who knocked the hour on some metal somewhere in the distance had fallen silent after knocking one o'clock. That must have been the last thought in Jonathan's mind before he was finally carried away himself. He couldn't have been gone for long, though, when he was violently awakened again.

"Who is knocking?" whispered his wife lying beside him on the floor.

"I don't know," he whispered back breathlessly.

The second time the knocking came it was so loud and imperious that the rickety old door could have fallen down.

"Who is knocking?" he asked them, his voice parched and trembling.

"Na tief-man and him people," came the cool reply. "Make you hopen de door."[7] This was followed by the heaviest knocking of all.

Maria was the first to raise the alarm, then he followed and all their children.

"Police-o! Thieves-o! Neighbors-o! Police-o! We are lost! We are dead! Neighbors, are you asleep? Wake up! Police-o!"

This went on for a long time and then stopped suddenly. Perhaps they had scared the thief away. There was total silence. But only for a short while.

"You done finish?" asked the voice outside. "Make we help you small. Oya, everybody!"

"Police-o! Tief-man-so! Neighbors-o! we done loss-o! Police-o! . . ."

There were at least five other voices besides the leader's.

Jonathan and his family were now completely paralyzed by terror. Maria and the children sobbed inaudibly like lost souls. Jonathan groaned continuously.

The silence that followed the thieves' alarm vibrated horribly. Jonathan all but begged their leader to speak again and be done with it.

---

7. **"Na tief-man . . . hopen de door"** (dialect) "I am a thief with my accomplices. Open the door."

"My frien," said he at long last, "we don try our best for call dem but I tink say dem all done sleep-o . . . So wetin we go do now? Sometaim you wan call soja? Or you wan make we call dem for you? Soja better pass police. No be so?"

"Na so!" replied his men. Jonathan thought he heard even more voices now than before and groaned heavily. His legs were sagging under him and his throat felt like sandpaper.

"My frien, why you no de talk again. I de ask you say you wan make we call soja?"

"No."

"Awrighto. Now make we talk business. We no be bad tief. We no like for make trouble. Trouble done finish. War done finish and all the katakata wey de for inside. No Civil War again. This time na Civil Peace. No be so?"

"Na so!" answered the horrible chorus.

"What do you want from me? I am a poor man. Everything I had went with this war. Why do you come to me? You know people who have money. We . . ."

"Awright! We know say you no get plenty money. But we sef no get even anini. So derefore make you open dis window and give us one hundred pound and we go commot. Orderwise we de come for inside now to show you guitar-boy like dis . . ."

A volley of automatic fire rang through the sky. Maria and the children began to weep aloud again.

"Ah, missisi de cry again. No need for dat. We done talk say we na good tief. We just take our small money and go nwayorly. No molest. Abi we de molest?"

"At all!" sang the chorus.

"My friends," began Jonathan hoarsely. "I hear what you say and I thank you. If I had one hundred pounds . . ."

"Lookia my frien, no be play we come play for your house. If we make mistake and step for inside you no go like am-o. So derefore . . ."

"To God who made me; if you come inside and find one hundred pounds, take it and shoot me and shoot my wife and children. I swear to God. The only money I have in this life is this twenty-pounds *egg-rasher* they gave me today . . ."

"Ok. Time de go. Make you open dis window and bring the twenty pound. We go manage am like dat."

There were now loud murmurs of dissent among the chorus: "Na lie de man de lie; e get plenty money . . . Make we go inside and search properly well . . . Wetin be twenty pound? . . ."

"Shurrup!" rang the leader's voice like a lone shot in the sky and silenced the murmuring at once. "Are you dere? Bring the money quick!"

Vocabulary
dissent (di sent´)
n. disagreement;
refusal to accept a
common opinion

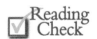

Reading
Check

Who are the people at Jonathan's door, and what do they want?

Vocabulary
commiserate
(kə miz´ ər āt´) *v.*
sympathize with or
show sorrow for

Spiral Review
Plot What pattern
from earlier in the
story is repeated here,
and what role does
the phrase "Nothing
puzzles God" play in
that pattern?

"I am coming," said Jonathan fumbling in the darkness with the key of the small wooden box he kept by his side on the mat.

At the first sign of light as neighbors and others assembled to commiserate with him he was already strapping his five-gallon demijohn[8] to his bicycle carrier and his wife, sweating in the open fire, was turning over akara balls in a wide clay bowl of boiling oil. In the corner his eldest son was rinsing out dregs of yesterday's palm-wine from old beer bottles.

"I count it as nothing," he told his sympathizers, his eyes on the rope he was tying. "What is *egg-rasher*? Did I depend on it last week? Or is it greater than other things that went with the war? I say, let *egg-rasher* perish in the flames! Let it go where everything else has gone. Nothing puzzles God."

---

8. demijohn (dem´ i jän´) *n.* large glass or earthenware bottle with a wicker cover.

Critical Thinking

Cite textual evidence to support your responses.

1. Key Ideas and Details (a) What are the "five inestimable blessings" for which Jonathan is grateful? **(b) Infer:** In what sense has the war enhanced Jonathan's appreciation for his life?

2. Key Ideas and Details (a) Explain how Jonathan reacts to the damage to his house. **(b) Connect:** Considering the other damage the war has caused, why might his reaction make sense?

3. Key Ideas and Details By giving the "egg-rasher" to the thieves, what does Jonathan hope to prevent? Explain.

4. Key Ideas and Details (a) In your own words, summarize Jonathan's reaction to the theft. **(b) Connect:** In what way is Jonathan's response consistent with his other responses to loss?

5. Integration of Knowledge and Ideas (a) How does Jonathan change as he experiences the conflicts in his life? **(b)** How might his life have changed without the conflict? *[Connect to the Big Question: Can progress be made without conflict?]*

Literary Analysis: Theme

1. Craft and Structure (a) Using a chart like the one shown, analyze the episodes that spark a response in Jonathan. **(b)** How are these episodes related?

Episode	Character's Response	Reasons for the Response	Result: Peace of Mind/Problems

(c) State the **theme** of the story, explaining how each event helps convey it.

2. Key Ideas and Details Achebe makes the **philosophical assumption** that in order to survive, we must be able to let go of what we have lost. How would Jonathan have behaved after the theft if he had refused to let go?

Reading Skill: Draw Conclusions

3. (a) Draw a conclusion about the thieves' response to the losses of war based on what they say and do. **(b)** Which details in Achebe's story contribute to its theme?

Vocabulary

Acquisition and Use Antonyms are words with opposite meanings. For each sentence, replace the word in italics with its antonym from the list on page 356. Explain which version makes more sense.

1. We should not give charity to the most *wealthy*.

2. People go to this bank because it is *respectable*.

3. In times of joy, people may get together to *celebrate*.

4. Ellen is *resistant* to trading bicycles with me because she likes hers.

5. His dog howled *audibly*, and the loud noise scared the cats away.

6. If there is *agreement* about going to the concert, I will buy a ticket.

Word Study Use the context of the sentences and what you know about the **Latin prefix com-** to explain your answer to each question.

1. What would happen to an egg under *compression?*

2. What effect would a *compromise* have on warring factions?

Word Study

The **Latin prefix com-** means "together" or "with."

Apply It Explain how the prefix com- contributes to the meanings of these words. Consult a dictionary if necessary.

compassion
compare
comfort

Integrated Language Skills

How Much Land Does a Man Need? •
Civil Peace

Conventions: Action and Linking Verbs

An **action verb** is a verb that shows physical or mental action.
A **linking verb** expresses state of being or tells what the subject
is by linking it to one or more words in the predicate.

Examples:

Action Verb: Li *worries* about her grades. (shows mental action)

Linking Verb: She *is* a good student. (links *She* to *good student*)

The most common linking verb is *be* in one of its forms—*is, are, was, were,* and so on. Other linking verbs include *feel* when used in a sentence such as "I feel ill" and *grew* when used in a sentence such as "He grew tall." To tell whether a verb is functioning as a linking verb, replace it with the appropriate form of *be*. If the sentence still makes sense, then the verb is a linking verb.

Testing Verbs to See if They Are Linking Verbs:

Action Verb: I *smelled* a rose. (cannot replace with a form of *be*)

Linking Verb: The rose *smelled* fragrant. (can replace with *was*)

Practice A Identify the verb in each sentence, and tell whether it is an action verb or a linking verb.

1. Pahom grows wheat on his land.
2. The land on the steppe is rich and fertile.
3. Pahom's tea tastes delicious.
4. Each year Pahom's parcel of land grows larger.

© **Reading Application** In "How Much Land Does a Man Need?," find two sentences with action verbs and two sentences with linking verbs.

Practice B For each word, write a sentence using the word as a linking verb and another sentence using the verb as an action verb.

1. look
2. grow
3. smell
4. feel

© **Writing Application** Use this sentence as a model to write two sentences that contain both action and linking verbs: *Jonathan realizes that his family is more valuable than any possession.*

PH WRITING COACH | Further instruction and practice are available in *Prentice Hall Writing Coach*.

Writing

Explanatory Text The fate of the characters in these selections is determined in large part by their personalities. Write a brief **character analysis** of Pahom or Jonathan. In your analysis, identify the character's main character traits including strengths and weaknesses.

- Review the text to analyze the character. Using a two-column chart, list strengths and weaknesses.

- As you draft, introduce the ideas you will convey. Elaborate on these strengths and weaknesses by providing examples of incidents and descriptions in the story that show these traits.

- Use phrases such as *for example* to link supporting details to your main idea. Include transitions such as *instead* to connect ideas.

Writing Workshop: *Work in Progress*

Prewriting for Problem-and-Solution Essay For an essay you may write, define a problem that you see in your school. Use this problem as the central circle of a web. Fill in spokes of the web with all the possible solutions. Put this Problem/Solution Web in your writing portfolio.

Speaking and Listening

Comprehension and Collaboration Hold a **group discussion** about the theme in Tolstoy's or Achebe's story. Begin by proposing and agreeing on a statement of the author's message. With your group, discuss ways in which the theme applies to your life or the lives of people today. Use persuasive techniques to support your ideas. To aid the discussion, follow these tips:

- Express your ideas in clear and inoffensive ways.

- Add to others' ideas and support your own viewpoints with details from the text. Include quotations that help to prove your ideas. When appropriate, adjust your ideas in light of the evidence presented by others.

- Allow your position to be challenged by the contributions of others.

- Clarify, illustrate, or verify a response when asked to do so. Ask other students follow-up questions to help members of the group clarify their own positions and to make new connections with previous statements.

- Make sure all members of the group have a chance to participate.

- As a group, decide on a single idea to share with the class.

Common Core State Standards

W.9-10.2.a, W.9-10.2.b, W.9-10.2.c; SL.9-10.1.c, SL.9-10.1.d
[For the full wording of the standards, see page 334.]

Use this prewriting activity to prepare for the **Writing Workshop** on page 420.

PHLit Online!
www.PHLitOnline.com
- Interactive graphic organizers
- Grammar tutorial
- Interactive journals

Leveled Texts

Build your skills and improve your comprehension of short stories with texts of increasing complexity.

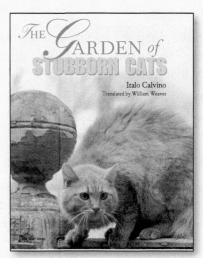

Read **"The Masque of the Red Death"** to see how a prince tries to use his power to evade death.

Read **"The Garden of Stubborn Cats"** to discover how the unexpected can spring up in the most ordinary places.

Common Core State Standards

Meet these standards with either **"The Masque of the Red Death"** (p. 372) or **"The Garden of the Stubborn Cats"** (p. 384).

Reading Literature
4. Determine the meaning of words and phrases as they are used in the text, including figurative and connotative meanings; analyze the cumulative impact of specific word choices on meaning and tone. *(Literary Analysis: Symbolism and Allegory)*

Spiral Review: RL.9-10.5
Writing
3. Write narratives to develop real or imagined experiences or events using effective technique, well-chosen details, and well-structured event sequences. **3.a.** Engage and orient the reader by setting out a problem, situation, or observation, establishing one or multiple point(s) of view, and introducing a narrator and/or characters; create a smooth progression of experiences or events. **3.b.** Use narrative techniques to develop experiences, events, and/or characters. *(Writing: Narrative)*

Speaking and Listening
2. Integrate multiple sources of information presented in diverse media or formats, evaluating the credibility and accuracy of each source. *(Research and Technology: Research Summary)*

Language
3. Apply knowledge of language to understand how language functions in different contexts, to make effective choices for meaning or style, and to comprehend more fully when reading or listening. *(Conventions: Active and Passive Voice)*

Literary Analysis: Symbolism and Allegory

Symbolism is a writer's use of symbols. A **symbol** is a type of figurative language in which a character, a place, a thing, or an event in a literary work stands for a larger idea. For example, a dog in a story may stand for loyalty. To create symbols, a writer may use these strategies:

- Call on traditional associations and connotations—a dog is a symbol of loyalty because dogs are often praised for that virtue.

- Create new associations—if a story character cherishes an object because it was his grandfather's, the object may come to symbolize family ties.

In most stories, the use of symbolism is subtle and open to interpretation. A story in which all characters, settings, events, and actions are clearly symbolic is called an **allegory.**

Using the Strategy: Symbol Diagram

Use a **symbol diagram** like this one to identify details that show that an object or a character symbolizes a larger meaning.

Reading Skill: Draw Conclusions

When you **draw a conclusion,** you make a decision or develop an opinion based on facts and details in a text. To draw a conclusion about the meaning of a symbol, **identify patterns** that suggest its larger meaning.

- Consider the repeated actions, qualities, and other details that the work associates with the symbol.

- Use any background knowledge you have to help you identify symbols.

- Develop an idea about the meaning of the symbol—the meaning that best explains its role in the work.

Can progress be made without *conflict?*

Writing About the Big Question

In "The Masque of the Red Death," a prince attempts to hide from a terrible death that is sweeping the kingdom. Use these sentence starters to develop your ideas about the Big Question.

People may **struggle** against the inevitable when _____.

Sometimes a **confrontation** is necessary in order to **resolve** a conflict because _____.

While You Read Look for descriptions of how the people behave at the masque, the grand ball that the prince hosts. Then, decide whether you think the writer believes people can avoid conflict.

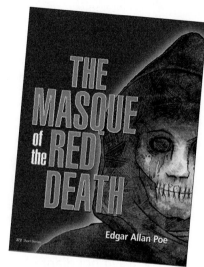

Vocabulary

Read each word and its definition. Decide whether you know the word well, know it a little bit, or do not know it at all. After you read, see how your knowledge of each word has increased.

- **profuse** (prō fyo͞os´) *adj.* giving or pouring forth freely, often to excess (p. 373) *Sheri offered her mother <u>profuse</u> apologies for forgetting her birthday.* *profusely adv. profusion n.*

- **august** (ô gust´) *adj.* impressive; majestic (p. 373) *The king was an <u>august</u> figure when he sat on his throne.* *augustly adv. augustness n.*

- **impeded** (im pēd´ əd) *v.* blocked; obstructed (p. 373) *The pillar I sat behind <u>impeded</u> my ability to see the stage.* *impediment n.*

- **cessation** (se sā´ shən) *n.* halt; stopping (p. 377) *After the sudden <u>cessation</u> of the car alarm, the silence seemed deep.* *cease v.*

- **decorum** (di kôr´ əm) *n.* behavior that is polite and correct for an occasion (p. 378) *The best man, lacking any <u>decorum</u>, showed up an hour late to the wedding.*

- **tangible** (tan´ jə bəl) *adj.* real and able to be touched (p. 380) *The dream was so vivid, that it almost seemed <u>tangible</u>.* *tangibly adv. tangibility n.*

Word Study

The **Latin suffix -tion** means "the act or quality of."

In this selection, there is a **cessation** of activity when the clock chimes the hour of midnight. All activity stops.

Meet
Edgar Allan Poe
(1809–1849)

Author of
The Masque of the Red Death

The son of traveling actors, Edgar Poe lost his mother at an early age. He was then raised by a wealthy Virginia family named Allan, from whom he took his middle name. After winning a writing contest with his story "MS. in a Bottle," Poe became a literary success, winning fame but not fortune. He died in poverty at the age of forty. Today, Poe is recognized as a master of the short story.

A Single Effect Poe believed that a work of fiction has the most impact if it can be read in one sitting and if all the elements work together to create a "single effect." He is best known for tales in which the single effect is horror. Poe also pioneered detective stories and science fiction.

BACKGROUND FOR THE STORY

The Black Death

In the 1300s, a plague called the Black Death swept across Europe, killing as many as 25 million people. Most of those who caught the disease died within three to five days after their symptoms appeared. Subsequent oubreaks of plague continued in Europe until recent times. Poe invented the "Red Death" for this story, but his tale plays on an age-old fear.

DID YOU KNOW?
The Mystery Writers of America call their annual awards "Edgars" in Poe's honor.

THE MASQUE of the RED DEATH

Edgar Allan Poe

The "Red Death" had long devastated the country. No pestilence had ever been so fatal, or so hideous. Blood was its Avatar[1] and its seal—the redness and the horror of blood. There were sharp pains, and sudden dizziness, and then profuse bleeding at the pores, with dissolution. The scarlet stains upon the body and especially upon the face of the victim, were the pest ban which shut him out from the aid and from the sympathy of his fellow men. And the whole seizure, progress and termination of the disease, were the incidents of half an hour.

But the Prince Prospero was happy and dauntless and sagacious. When his dominions were half depopulated, he summoned to his presence a thousand hale and lighthearted friends from among the knights and dames of his court, and with these retired to the deep seclusion of one of his castellated abbeys.[2] This was an extensive and magnificent structure, the creation of the prince's own eccentric yet august taste. A strong and lofty wall girdled it in. This wall had gates of iron. The courtiers, having entered, brought furnaces and massy hammers and welded the bolts. They resolved to leave means neither of ingress or egress[3] to the sudden impulses of despair or frenzy from within. The abbey was amply provisioned. With such precautions the courtiers might bid defiance to contagion. The external world could take care of itself. In the meantime it was folly to grieve, or to think. The prince had provided all the appliances of pleasure. There were buffoons, there were improvisatori, there were ballet dancers, there were musicians, there was Beauty, there was wine. All these and security were within. Without was the "Red Death."

It was toward the close of the fifth or sixth month of his seclusion, and while the pestilence raged most furiously abroad, that the Prince Prospero entertained his thousand friends at a masked ball of the most unusual magnificence.

It was a voluptuous scene, that masquerade. But first let me tell of the rooms in which it was held. There were seven—an imperial suite. In many palaces, however, such suites form a long and straight vista, while the folding doors slide back nearly to the walls on either hand, so that the view of the whole extent is scarcely impeded. Here the case was very different; as might have been expected from the duke's love of the bizarre. The apartments were so irregularly disposed that the vision embraced but little more than one at a time. There was a sharp turn at every twenty or thirty yards, and at each turn a novel effect. To the right and left, in the middle of each wall,

---

1. **Avatar** (av´ ə tär´) *n.* sign; outward manifestation of an unseen force.
2. **castellated abbeys** (kas´ tə lāt´ əd ab´ ēz) monasteries or convents (religious retreats) with towers like those of a castle.
3. **ingress** (in´ gres´) or egress (è» gres«) entry or exit.

Vocabulary
profuse (prō fyo͞os´) *adj.* giving or pouring forth freely, often to excess

august (ô gust´) *adj.* impressive; majestic

Reading Skill
Draw Conclusions
What details here support the conclusion that the prince thinks he can escape the plague?

Vocabulary
impeded (im pēd´ əd) *v.* blocked; obstructed

Reading Check
Why has Prince Prospero locked himself and his guests in his castle?

The Masque of the Red Death **373**

a tall and narrow Gothic window looked out upon a closed corridor which pursued the windings of the suite. These windows were of stained glass whose color varied in accordance with the prevailing hue of the decorations of the chamber into which it opened. That at the eastern extremity was hung, for example, in blue—and vividly blue were its windows. The second chamber was purple in its ornaments and tapestries, and here the panes were purple. The third was green throughout, and so were the casements. The fourth was furnished and lighted with orange—the fifth with white—the sixth with violet. The seventh apartment was closely shrouded in black velvet tapestries that hung all over the ceiling and down the walls, falling in heavy folds upon a carpet of the same material and hue. But in this chamber only, the color of the windows failed to correspond with the decorations. The panes here were scarlet—a deep blood color. Now in no one of the seven apartments was there any lamp or candelabrum amid the profusion of golden ornaments that lay scattered to and fro or depended from the roof. There was no light of any kind emanating from lamp or candle within the suite of chambers. But in the corridors that followed the suite, there stood, opposite to each window, a heavy tripod, bearing a brazier[4] of fire that projected its rays through the tinted glass and so glaringly illumined the room. And thus were produced a multitude of gaudy and fantastic appearances. But in the western or black chamber the effect of the firelight that streamed upon the dark hangings through the blood-tinted panes, was ghastly in the extreme, and produced so wild a look upon the countenances of those who entered, that there were few of the company bold enough to set foot within its precincts at all.

It was in this apartment, also, that there stood against the western wall a gigantic clock of ebony.[5] Its pendulum swung to and fro with a dull, heavy, monotonous clang; and when the minute-hand made the circuit of the face, and the hour was to be stricken, there came from the brazen lungs of the clock a sound which was clear and loud and deep and exceedingly musical, but of so peculiar a note and emphasis that, at each lapse of an hour, the musicians of the orchestra were constrained to pause, momentarily, in their performance, to hearken to the sound; and thus the waltzers perforce ceased their evolutions; and there was a brief disconcert[6] of the whole gay company; and, while the chimes of the clock yet rang, it was observed that the giddiest grew pale, and the more aged and sedate passed their hands over their brows as if in confused reverie or meditation. But when the echoes had fully ceased, a light laughter at once pervaded the assembly; the musicians looked at

Reading Skill
Draw Conclusions
Judging from the title of the story and the colors of the seventh room, what might the room represent?

---

4. **brazier** (brā´ zhər) *n.* metal pan or bowl used to hold burning coals.
5. **ebony** (eb´ ə nē) *n.* the black or dark wood of certain trees.
6. **disconcert** (dis kän´ sʉrt) *n.* embarrassment; confusion.

the walls, he made his way uninterruptedly, but with the same
solemn and measured step which had distinguished him from
the first, through the blue chamber to the purple—through the
purple to the green—through the green to the orange—through
this again to the white—and even thence to the violet, ere a decided
movement had been made to arrest him. It was then, however,
that the Prince Prospero, maddening with rage and the shame of
his own momentary cowardice, rushed hurriedly through the six
chambers, while none followed him on account of a deadly terror
that had seized upon all. He bore aloft a drawn dagger, and had
approached, in rapid impetuosity, to within three or four feet of the
retreating figure, when the latter, having attained the extremity of
the velvet apartment, turned suddenly and confronted his pursuer.
There was a sharp cry—and the dagger dropped gleaming upon
the sable carpet, upon which, instantly afterwards, fell prostrate
in death the Prince Prospero. Then, summoning the wild courage

Reading Check

How does Prince
Prospero react to the
stranger?

◀ **Critical Viewing**
In what way does this
image express the
fears of the revelers?
[Connect]

Vocabulary
tangible (tan´ jə bəl)
adj. real and able
to be touched

**Literary Analysis
Symbolism** How does
the use of a number
of symbols—the black
room, the clock, the un-
invited guest—show that
the story is an allegory?

of despair, a throng of the revelers
at once threw themselves into the
black apartment, and, seizing the
mummer, whose tall figure stood
erect and motionless within the
shadow of the ebony clock, gasped
in unutterable horror at finding the
grave cerements[13] and corpselike
mask which they handled with so
violent a rudeness, untenanted by
any tangible form.

And now was acknowledged
the presence of the Red Death.
He had come like a thief in the
night. And one by one dropped
the revelers in the blood-bedewed
halls of their revel, and died each
in the despairing posture of his
fall. And the life of the ebony clock
went out with that of the last of the
gay. And the flames of the tripods
expired. And Darkness and Decay
and the Red Death held illimitable
dominion over all.

---

13. cerements (ser´ ə mənts) *n.* burial wrapping for a corpse; shroud.

Critical Thinking

**Cite textual
evidence to
support your
responses.**

1. Key Ideas and Details (a) Why does Prince Prospero hide in his
palace? **(b) Contrast:** Contrast life outside the palace with life
inside it.

2. Key Ideas and Details (a) Use details from the story to describe
the rooms where the masquerade is held. **(b) Infer:** What do
these details suggest about the prince's tastes and values?

3. Key Ideas and Details (a) Why does the prince decide to hold
the masquerade? **(b) Evaluate:** What does the prince's response
to the Red Death suggest about the kind of person he is? Explain.

4. Integration of Knowledge and Ideas What message does
Poe convey about attempting to avoid conflict? Explain your
answer. *[Connect to the Big Question: Can progress be
made without conflict?]*

Literary Analysis: Symbolism and Allegory

1. Craft and Structure In the story, the stranger might be viewed as a **symbol** of death. **(a)** Describe two responses of the partygoers to the stranger. **(b)** How are these responses similar to ones associated with death? **(c)** Identify two other details supporting this interpretation of the stranger.

2. Craft and Structure This story can be read as an **allegory.** Explain what the ability of the uninvited guest to enter a fortified palace might symbolize.

THE MASQUE of the RED DEATH

Edgar Allan Poe

Reading Skill: Draw Conclusions

3. (a) In a chart like the one shown, identify the pattern of details that shows the importance of the clock. **(b)** Based on your chart, **draw a conclusion** about what the clock symbolizes.

Vocabulary

Acquisition and Use Words with similar meanings are called **synonyms.** For each set, choose the word that is *not* a synonym for the other two words. Explain.

1. plentiful; efficient; profuse

2. august; dignified; anguished

3. aided; hindered; impeded

4. end; cessation; hesitation

5. propriety; decisiveness; decorum

6. tangible; touchable; flavorful

Word Study Use the context of the sentences and what you know about the **Latin suffix -*tion*** to explain your answer to each question.

1. How would a positive job *evaluation* make you feel?

2. If you received a letter of *rejection,* would you be pleased?

Can progress be made without *conflict?*

Writing About the Big Question

In this story, stubborn cats fight to preserve their space. Use these sentence starters to develop your ideas about the Big Question.

A person may **oppose change** because _____.

Progress can sometimes create conflict when _____.

While You Read Note the differences between the world of cats and the world of humans. Then, decide whether nature and people must be in conflict.

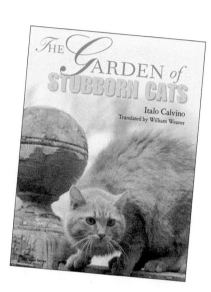

Vocabulary

Read each word and its definition. Decide whether you know the word well, know it a little bit, or do not know it at all. After you read, see how your knowledge of each word has increased.

- **itinerary** (ī tin´ ər er´ ē) *n.* route; travel plan (p. 385) *As part of our itinerary, we will be in Cleveland on Sunday.* *itinerant adj.*

- **intrigues** (in´ trēgz) *n.* plots; schemes (p. 386) *The twins whispered together and laughed, cooking up one of their intrigues.* *intrigue v. intriguing adj.*

- **squalid** (skwäl´ id) *adj.* foul or unclean (p. 387) *The restaurant was so squalid that the health board shut it down.* *squalor n. squalidly adv.*

- **futile** (fyo͞ot´ l) *adj.* not successful; useless (p. 390) *After a futile attempt to climb the steep and icy incline, the hikers had to seek another path.* *futilely adv. futility n.*

- **indigence** (in´ di jəns) *n.* poverty (p. 393) *Many lost their jobs, and the number of people living in indigence grew.* *indigent adj.*

- **consigned** (kən sīnd´) *v.* handed over; gave up or delivered (p. 395) *Thankfully, the stolen car was found and consigned to the owners.* *consignable adj. consignment n.*

Word Study

The **Latin suffix -id** means "the body of" or "connected with."

In this story, the cats lead Marcovaldo through **squalid** passageways, those that are filled with squalor, or dirt and grime.

Author of

THE GARDEN of STUBBORN CATS

The son of two Italian botanists, Italo Calvino was born in Cuba. He grew up in San Remo on the Italian Riviera and began his literary career in the Italian city of Turin.

A Writer of Fables According to Calvino, "A classic is a book that has never finished saying what it has to say." In this sense, Calvino's own works are classics. They say much more than appears on the page.

Though his ideas are complex, Calvino conveys them using events and characters as simple as those in a fable or fairy tale. Like a good fable, his stories blend reality and fantasy.

BACKGROUND FOR THE STORY

Marcovaldo

This story is one of the interrelated short stories in Italo Calvino's *Marcovaldo: or The Seasons in the City.* Set in a grim Italian industrial city in the 1950s and 1960s, the collection presents the adventures of Marcovaldo, an ordinary working man, as he uses his imagination to escape his surroundings.

DID YOU KNOW?

During World War II, Calvino joined the Italian Resistance to fight Italy's fascist dictatorship.

THE GARDEN of STUBBORN CATS

Italo Calvino

translated by William Weaver

The city of cats and the city of men exist one inside the other, but they are not the same city.

Few cats recall the time when there was no distinction: the streets and squares of men were also streets and squares of cats, and the lawns, courtyards, balconies, and fountains: you lived in a broad and various space. But for several generations now domestic felines have been prisoners of an uninhabitable city: the streets are uninterruptedly overrun by the mortal traffic of cat-crushing automobiles; in every square foot of terrain where once a garden extended or a vacant lot or the ruins of an old demolition, now condominiums loom up, welfare housing, brand-new skyscrapers; every entrance is crammed with parked cars; the courtyards, one by one, have been roofed by reinforced concrete and transformed into garages or movie houses or storerooms or workshops. And where a rolling plateau of low roofs once extended, copings, terraces, water tanks, balconies, skylights, corrugated-iron sheds, now one general superstructure rises wherever structures can rise; the intermediate differences in height, between the low ground of the street and the supernal[1] heaven of the penthouses, disappear; the cat of a recent litter seeks in vain the itinerary of its fathers, the point from which to make the soft leap from balustrade to cornice to drainpipe, or for the quick climb on the roof-tiles.

But in this vertical city, in this compressed city where all voids tend to fill up and every block of cement tends to mingle with other blocks of cement, a kind of counter-city opens, a negative city, that consists of empty slices between wall and wall, of the minimal distances ordained by the

---

1. **supernal** (soo pur´ nəl) *adj.* of the heavens; divine.

Literary Analysis
Symbolism What associations with cats is the author creating?

Vocabulary
itinerary (ī tin´ ər er´ ē) *n.* route; travel plan

Reading Check

Why is the city uninhabitable for cats?

building regulations between two constructions, between the rear of one construction and the rear of the next; it is a city of cavities, wells, air conduits, driveways, inner yards, accesses to basements, like a network of dry canals on a planet of stucco and tar, and it is through this network, grazing the walls, that the ancient cat population still scurries.

On occasion, to pass the time, Marcovaldo would follow a cat. It was during the work-break, between noon and three, when all the personnel except Marcovaldo went home to eat, and he—who brought his lunch in his bag—laid his place among the packing-cases in the warehouse, chewed his snack, smoked a half-cigar, and wandered around, alone and idle, waiting for work to resume. In those hours, a cat that peeped in at a window was always welcome company, and a guide for new explorations. He had made friends with a tabby, well fed, a blue ribbon around its neck, surely living with some well-to-do family. This tabby shared with Marcovaldo the habit of an afternoon stroll right after lunch; and naturally a friendship sprang up.

Following his tabby friend, Marcovaldo had started looking at places as if through the round eyes of a cat and even if these places were the usual environs of his firm he saw them in a different light, as settings for cattish stories, with connections practicable only by light, velvety paws. Though from the outside the neighborhood seemed poor in cats, every day on his rounds Marcovaldo made the acquaintance of some new face, and a miau, a hiss, a stiffening of fur on an arched back was enough for him to sense ties and intrigues and rivalries among them. At those moments he thought he had already penetrated the secrecy of the felines' society: and then he felt himself scrutinized by pupils that became slits, under the surveillance of the antennae of taut whiskers, and all the cats around him sat impassive as sphinxes, the pink triangles of their noses convergent on the black triangles of their lips, and the only things that moved were the tips of the ears, with a vibrant jerk like radar. They reached the end of a narrow passage, between squalid blank walls; and, looking around, Marcovaldo saw that the cats that had led him this far had vanished, all of them together, no telling in which direction, even his tabby friend, and they had left him alone. Their realm had territories, ceremonies, customs that it was not yet granted to him to discover.

On the other hand, from the cat city there opened unsuspected peepholes onto the city of men: and one day the same tabby led him to discover the great Biarritz Restaurant. ●

Vocabulary
squalid (skwäl′ id)
adj. foul or unclean

Anyone wishing to see the Biarritz Restaurant had only to assume the posture of a cat, that is, proceed on all fours. Cat and man, in this fashion, walked around a kind of dome, at whose foot some low, rectangular little windows opened. Following the tabby's example, Marcovaldo looked down. They were transoms through which the luxurious hall received air and light. To the sound of gypsy violins, partridges and quails swirled by on silver dishes balanced by the white-gloved fingers of waiters in tailcoats. Or, more precisely, above the partridges and quails the dishes whirled, and above the dishes the white gloves, and poised on the waiters' patent-leather shoes, the gleaming parquet floor, from which hung dwarf potted palms and tablecloths and crystal and buckets like bells with the champagne bottle for their clapper: everything was turned upside-down because Marcovaldo, for fear of being seen, wouldn't stick his head inside the window and confined himself to looking at the reversed reflection of the room in the tilted pane.

But it was not so much the windows of the dining-room as those of the kitchens that interested the cat: looking through the former you saw, distant and somehow transfigured, what in the

▲ **Critical Viewing**
In what way does this picture, like the story, express the idea of multiple perspectives on the world? **[Interpret]**

To what place does Marcovaldo follow the tabby?

The Garden of Stubborn Cats **387**

Architecture Connection

Architectural Features

The following building features are mentioned in the narrative:

- **balustrade** railing suported by posts
- **belvedere** long balcony with a roof
- **capitals** tops of columns
- **copings** top layer of a stone or brick wall, sloped to carry off water
- **cornice** overhanging part of a roof
- **transom** small window or shutter over a door or window

Connect to the Literature

Compare and contrast the purposes for which a cat and a person would use each of these features.

kitchens presented itself—quite concrete and within paw's reach—as a plucked bird or a fresh fish. And it was toward the kitchens, in fact, that the tabby wanted to lead Marcovaldo, either through a gesture of altruistic friendship or else because it counted on the man's help for one of its raids. Marcovaldo, however, was reluctant to leave his belvedere over the main room: first as he was fascinated by the luxury of the place, and then because something down there had riveted his attention. To such an extent that, overcoming his fear of being seen, he kept peeking in, with his head in the transom.

In the midst of the room, directly under that pane, there was a little glass fish tank, a kind of aquarium, where some fat trout were swimming. A special customer approached, a man with a shiny bald pate, black suit, black beard. An old waiter in tailcoat followed him, carrying a little net as if he were going to catch butterflies. The gentleman in black looked at the trout with a grave, intent air; then he raised one hand and with a slow, solemn gesture singled out a fish. The waiter dipped the net into the tank, pursued the appointed trout, captured it, headed for the kitchens, holding out in front of him, like a lance, the net in which the fish wriggled. The gentleman in black, solemn as a magistrate[2] who has handed down a capital sentence, went to take his seat and wait for the return of the trout, sautéed "à la meunière."[3]

If I found a way to drop a line from up here and make one of those trout bite, Marcovaldo thought, I couldn't be accused of theft; at worst, of fishing in an unauthorized place. And ignoring the miaus that called him toward the kitchens, he went to collect his fishing tackle.

Nobody in the crowded dining room of the Biarritz saw the long, fine line, armed with hook and bait, as it slowly dropped into the tank. The fish saw the bait, and flung themselves on it. In the fray one trout managed to bite the worm: and immediately it began to rise, rise, emerge from the water, a silvery flash, it darted up high, over the laid tables and the trolleys of hors d'oeuvres, over the blue flames of the crêpes Suzette, until it vanished into the heavens of the transom.

Marcovaldo had yanked the rod with the brisk snap of the expert fisherman, so the fish landed behind his back. The trout had barely touched the ground when the cat sprang. What little life the trout

---

2. **magistrate** (maj´ is trāt´) *n.* judge.
3. **sautéed "à la meunière"** (sô tād´ ä lä mə nyer´) rolled in flour, fried in butter, and sprinkled with lemon juice and chopped parsley.

still had was lost between the tabby's teeth. Marcovaldo, who had abandoned his line at that moment to run and grab the fish, saw it snatched from under his nose, hook and all. He was quick to put one foot on the rod, but the snatch had been so strong that the rod was all the man had left, while the tabby ran off with the fish, pulling the line after it. Treacherous kitty! It had vanished.

But this time it wouldn't escape him: there was that long line trailing after him and showing the way he had taken. Though he had lost sight of the cat, Marcovaldo followed the end of the line: there it was, running along a wall; it climbed a parapet, wound through a doorway, was swallowed up by a basement . . .

Literary Analysis
Symbolism Which details reinforce the contrast between a cat's view of the city and a human's view?

Marcovaldo, venturing into more and more cattish places, climbed roofs, straddled railings, always managed to catch a glimpse—perhaps only a second before it disappeared—of that moving trace that indicated the thief's path.

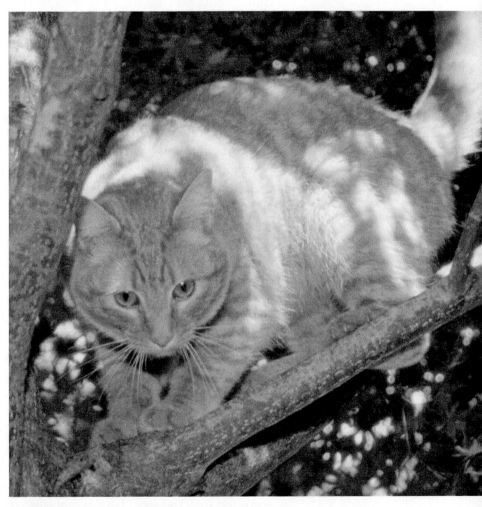

Now the line played out down a sidewalk, in the midst of the traffic, and Marcovaldo, running after it, almost managed to grab it. He flung himself down on his belly: there, he grabbed it! He managed to seize one end of the line before it slipped between the bars of a gate. •

Beyond a half-rusted gate and two bits of wall buried under climbing plants, there was a little rank[4] garden, with a small, abandoned-looking building at the far end of it. A carpet of dry leaves covered the path, and dry leaves lay everywhere under the boughs of the two plane-trees, forming actually some little mounds in the yard. A

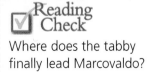

Reading Check
Where does the tabby finally lead Marcovaldo?

---

4. rank (raŋk) *adj.* growing vigorously and coarsely.

The Garden of Stubborn Cats **389**

layer of leaves was yellowing in the green water of a pool. Enormous buildings rose all around, skyscrapers with thousands of windows, like so many eyes trained disapprovingly on that little square patch with two trees, a few tiles, and all those yellow leaves, surviving right in the middle of an area of great traffic.

And in this garden, perched on the capitals and balustrades, lying on the dry leaves of the flowerbeds, climbing on the trunks of the trees or on the drainpipes, motionless on their four paws, their tails making a question-mark, seated to wash their faces, there were tiger cats, black cats, white cats, calico cats, tabbies, angoras, Persians, house cats and stray cats, perfumed cats and mangy cats. Marcovaldo realized he had finally reached the heart of the cats' realm, their secret island. And, in his emotion, he almost forgot his fish.

It had remained, that fish, hanging by the line from the branch of a tree, out of reach of the cats' leaps; it must have dropped from its kidnapper's mouth at some clumsy movement, perhaps as it was defended from the others, or perhaps displayed as an extraordinary prize. The line had got tangled, and Marcovaldo, tug as he would, couldn't manage to yank it loose. A furious battle had meanwhile been joined among the cats, to reach that unreachable fish, or rather, to win the right to try and reach it. Each wanted to prevent the others from leaping: they hurled themselves on one another, they tangled in midair, they rolled around clutching each other, and finally a general war broke out in a whirl of dry, crackling leaves.

After many futile yanks, Marcovaldo now felt the line was free, but he took care not to pull it: the trout would have fallen right in the midst of that infuriated scrimmage of felines.

It was at this moment that, from the top of the walls of the gardens, a strange rain began to fall: fish-bones, heads, tails, even bits of lung and lights.[5] Immediately the cats' attention was distracted from the suspended trout and they flung themselves on the new delicacies. To Marcovaldo, this seemed the right moment to pull the line and regain his fish. But, before he had time to act, from a blind of the little villa, two yellow, skinny hands darted out: one was brandishing scissors; the other, a frying pan. The hand with the scissors was raised above the trout, the hand with the frying pan was thrust under it. The scissors cut the line, the trout fell into the pan; hands, scissors and pan withdrew, the blind closed: all in the space of a second. Marcovaldo was totally bewildered.

---

5. **lights** term for animal organs used for catfood.

Spiral Review
Order of Events
What series of events brings Marcovaldo to the garden? What surprising discovery does he make there?

Vocabulary
futile (fyo͞ot´ l) *adj.* not successful; useless

Reading Skill
Draw Conclusions
Based on details of this event, what conclusion can you draw about whether the tabby has brought fish here before?

"Are you also a cat lover?" A voice at his back made him turn round. He was surrounded by little old women, some of them ancient, wearing old-fashioned hats on their heads; others, younger, but with the look of spinsters; and all were carrying in their hands or their bags packages of leftover meat or fish, and some even had little pans of milk. "Will you help me throw this package over the fence, for those poor creatures?"

All the ladies, cat lovers, gathered at this hour around the garden of dry leaves to take the food to their protégés.[6]

"Can you tell me why they are all here, these cats?" Marcovaldo inquired.

"Where else could they go? This garden is all they have left! Cats come here from other neighborhoods, too, from miles and miles around . . ."

"And birds, as well," another lady added. "They're forced to live by the hundreds and hundreds on these few trees . . ."

"And the frogs, they're all in that pool, and at night they never stop croaking . . . You can hear them even on the eighth floor of the buildings around here."

"Who does this villa belong to anyway?" Marcovaldo asked. Now, outside the gate, there weren't just the cat-loving ladies but also other people: the man from the gas pump opposite, the apprentices from a mechanic's shop, the postman, the grocer, some passers-by. And none of them, men and women, had to be asked twice: all wanted to have their say, as always when a mysterious and controversial subject comes up.

"It belongs to a Marchesa.[7] She lives there, but you never see her . . ."

"She's been offered millions and millions, by developers, for this little patch of land, but she won't sell . . ."

"What would she do with millions, an old woman all alone in the world? She wants to hold on to her house, even if it's falling to pieces, rather than be forced to move . . ."

"It's the only undeveloped bit of land in the downtown area . . . Its value goes up every year . . . They've made her offers—"

"Offers! That's not all. Threats, intimidation, persecution . . . You don't know the half of it! Those contractors!"

"But she holds out. She's held out for years . . ."

"She's a saint. Without her, where would those poor animals go?"

> *M*arcovaldo realized he had finally reached the heart of the cats' realm, their secret island.

Reading Check

What happens to Marcovaldo's trout?

---

6. **protégés** (prōt′ ə zhāz′) *n.* those guided and helped by another.
7. **Marchesa** (mär kā′ zä) *n.* title of an Italian noblewoman.

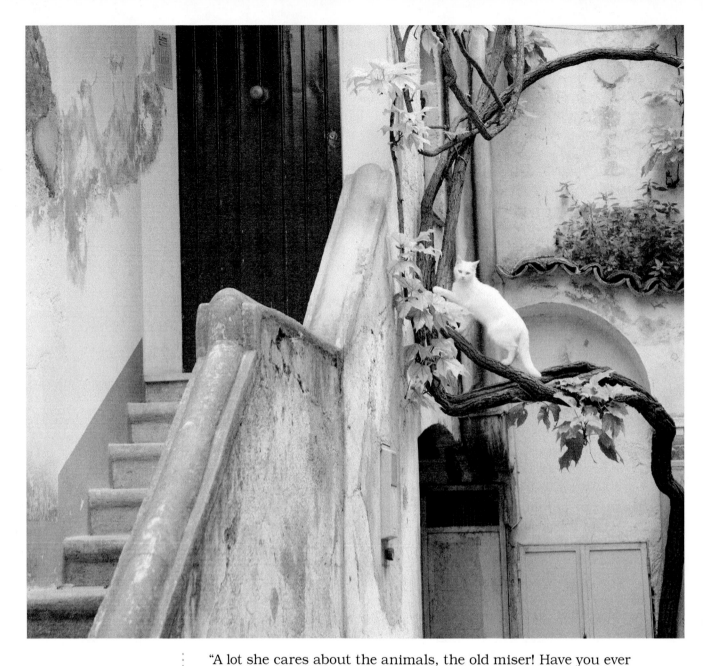

"A lot she cares about the animals, the old miser! Have you ever seen her give them anything to eat?"

"How can she feed the cats when she doesn't have food for herself? She's the last descendant of a ruined family!"

"She hates cats. I've seen her chasing them and hitting them with an umbrella!"

"Because they were tearing up her flowerbeds!"

"What flowerbeds? I've never seen anything in this garden but a great crop of weeds!"

Marcovaldo realized that with regard to the old Marchesa opinions were sharply divided: some saw her as an angelic being, others as an egoist and a miser.

Literary Analysis
Symbolism What relationship with the city do the Marchesa and her property represent?

"It's the same with the birds; she never gives them a crumb!"

"She gives them hospitality. Isn't that plenty?"

"Like she gives the mosquitoes, you mean. They all come from here, from that pool. In the summertime the mosquitoes eat us alive, and it's all the fault of that Marchesa!"

"And the mice? This villa is a mine of mice. Under the dead leaves they have their burrows, and at night they come out . . ."

"As far as the mice go, the cats take care of them . . ."

"Oh, you and your cats! If we had to rely on them . . ."

"Why? Have you got something to say against cats?"

Here the discussion degenerated into a general quarrel.

"The authorities should do something: confiscate the villa!" one man cried.

"What gives them the right?" another protested.

"In a modern neighborhood like ours, a mouse-nest like this . . . it should be forbidden . . ."

"Why, I picked my apartment precisely because it overlooked this little bit of green . . ."

"Green, hell! Think of the fine skyscraper they could build here!"

Marcovaldo would have liked to add something of his own, but he couldn't get a word in. Finally, all in one breath, he exclaimed: "The Marchesa stole a trout from me!"

The unexpected news supplied fresh ammunition to the old woman's enemies, but her defenders exploited it as proof of the indigence to which the unfortunate noblewoman was reduced. Both sides agreed that Marcovaldo should go and knock at her door to demand an explanation. ●

It wasn't clear whether the gate was locked or unlocked; in any case, it opened, after a push, with a mournful creak. Marcovaldo picked his way among the leaves and cats, climbed the steps to the porch, knocked hard at the entrance.

At a window (the very one where the frying pan had appeared), the blind was raised slightly and in one corner a round, pale blue eye was seen, and a clump of hair dyed an undefinable color, and a dry skinny hand. A voice was heard, asking: "Who is it? Who's at the door?", the words accompanied by a cloud smelling of fried oil.

"It's me, Marchesa. The trout man," Marcovaldo explained. "I don't mean to trouble you. I only wanted to tell you, in case you didn't know, that the trout was stolen from me, by that cat, and I'm the one who caught it. In fact the line . . ."

Vocabulary
indigence (in´ di jəns) *n.* poverty

"*She hates cats. I've seen her chasing them and hitting them with an umbrella!*"

Reading Check

Who owns the garden where the cats gather?

"Those cats! It's always those cats . . ." the Marchesa said, from behind the shutter, with a shrill, somewhat nasal voice. "All my troubles come from the cats! Nobody knows what I go through! Prisoner night and day of those horrid beasts! And with all the refuse people throw over the walls, to spite me!"

"But my trout . . ."

"Your trout! What am I supposed to know about your trout!" The Marchesa's voice became almost a scream, as if she wanted to drown out the sizzle of oil in the pan, which came through the window along with the aroma of fried fish. "How can I make sense of anything, with all the stuff that rains into my house?"

"I understand, but did you take the trout or didn't you?"

"When I think of all the damage I suffer because of the cats! Ah, fine state of affairs! I'm not responsible for anything! I can't tell you what I've lost! Thanks to those cats, who've occupied house and garden for years! My life at the mercy of those animals! Go and find the owners! Make them pay damages! Damages? A whole life destroyed! A prisoner here, unable to move a step!"

"Excuse me for asking: but who's forcing you to stay?"

From the crack in the blind there appeared sometimes a round, pale blue eye, sometimes a mouth with two protruding teeth; for a moment the whole face was visible, and to Marcovaldo it seemed, bewilderingly, the face of a cat.

"They keep me prisoner, they do, those cats! Oh, I'd be glad to leave! What wouldn't I give for a little apartment all my own, in a nice clean modern building! But I can't go out . . . They follow me, they block my path, they trip me up!" The voice became a whisper, as if to confide a secret. "They're afraid I'll sell the lot . . . They won't leave me . . . won't allow me . . . When the builders come to offer me a contract, you should see them, those cats! They get in the way, pull out their claws; they even chased a lawyer off! Once I had the contract right here, I was about to sign it, and they dived in through the window, knocked over the inkwell, tore up all the pages . . ."

All of a sudden Marcovaldo remembered the time, the shipping department, the boss. He tiptoed off over the dried leaves, as the voice continued to come through the slats of the blind, enfolded in that cloud apparently from the oil of a frying pan. "They even scratched me . . . I still have the scar . . . All alone here at the mercy of these demons . . ."

Winter came. A blossoming of white flakes

"All my troubles come from the cats! Nobody knows what I go through!"

decked the branches and capitals and the cats' tails. Under the snow, the dry leaves dissolved into mush. The cats were rarely seen, the cat lovers even less; the packages of fish-bones were consigned only to cats who came to the door. Nobody, for quite a while, had seen anything of the Marchesa. No smoke came now from the chimneypot of the villa.

One snowy day, the garden was again full of cats, who had returned as if it were spring, and they were miauing as if on a moonlight night. The neighbors realized that something had happened: they went and knocked at the Marchesa's door. She didn't answer: she was dead.

In the spring, instead of the garden, there was a huge building site that a contractor had set up. The steam shovels dug down to great depths to make room for the foundations, cement poured into the iron armatures, a very high crane passed beams to the workmen who were making the scaffoldings. But how could they get on with their work? Cats walked along all the planks, they made bricks fall and upset buckets of mortar, they fought in the midst of the piles of sand. When you started to raise an armature, you found a cat perched on top of it, hissing fiercely. More treacherous

▲ **Critical Viewing**
Compare this image with the garden in the story. **[Compare and Contrast]**

Vocabulary
consigned (kən sīnd')
v. handed over; gave up or delivered

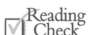
Reading
Check

How does the Marchesa feel about the cats?

pusses climbed onto the masons' backs as if to purr, and there was no getting rid of them. And the birds continued making their nests in all the trestles, the cab of the crane looked like an aviary[8] . . . And you couldn't dip up a bucket of water that wasn't full of frogs, croaking and hopping . . .

---

8. aviary (āʹ vē erʹ ē) *n.* building or large cage for housing many birds.

Critical Thinking

Cite textual evidence to support your responses.

1. **Key Ideas and Details (a)** What is the "negative city"? **(b) Infer:** How have changes in the city altered the way cats live?

2. **Key Ideas and Details (a)** How does Marcovaldo find the secret garden of the cats? **(b) Analyze:** List two details from the story that suggest such a garden is rare in the city.

3. **Integration of Knowledge and Ideas (a) Take a Position:** Should the garden of cats remain as it is, or should developers be free to build over it? Support your position. **(b) Discuss:** Share and discuss your opinions with a small group. **(c) Evaluate:** Choose the two best-supported opinions and share them with the class.

4. **Integration of Knowledge and Ideas (a)** How are nature and development at war with one another in this story? **(b)** Do you think the two can ever peacefully coexist? Explain. *[Connect to the Big Question: Can progress be made without conflict?]*

Literary Analysis: Symbolism and Allegory

© **1. Craft and Structure** The stubborn cats might be viewed as a force challenging order—they resist human attempts to control the city. **(a)** List two other forces—natural or human—that resist people's control of city space and life. **(b)** Using your answer, explain the meaning of the cats as a **symbol.**

© **2. Craft and Structure** This story can be read as an **allegory.** What does the final conflict between cats and humans symbolize?

Reading Skill: Draw Conclusions

3. (a) In a chart like the one shown, list two details showing the pattern in the Marchesa's relationship to other people in the city.

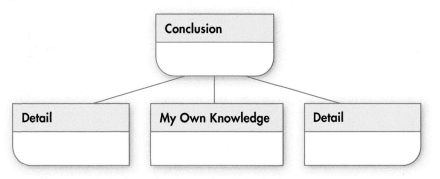

(b) Use your chart to **draw a conclusion** about what she may symbolize.

Vocabulary

© **Acquisition and Use** Words with similar meanings are called **synonyms**. For each set, choose the word that is *not* a synonym for the other two words. Explain.

1. schedule; itinerary; decision

2. intrigues; impulses; plots

3. dirty; nauseated; squalid

4. useless; futile; angry

5. indigence; poverty; laziness

6. delivered; agreed; consigned

Word Study Use the context of the sentences and what you know about the **Latin suffix -id** to explain your answer to each question.

1. If a deadline is *rigid*, can it be extended?

2. Should a mediator be *candid* in his or her judgments?

Integrated Language Skills

The Masque of the Red Death • The Garden of Stubborn Cats

Conventions: Active and Passive Voice

A verb is in the **active voice** when the subject performs the action. A verb is in the **passive voice** when the action is performed on the subject.

Verbs in the passive voice consist of a form of *be* followed by the past participle of the main verb. Usually, active voice is stronger. However, passive voice is used when the writer wants to emphasize the recipient of the action. Passive voice is also used when the subject performing the action is unknown.

Active Voice: The student *answered* the question.

Passive Voice: The question *was answered*.

Active Voice: Jeremy ate the last cookie.

Passive Voice: The last cookie was eaten by Jeremy.

Practice A Identify each verb or verb phrase as active or passive.

1. The costumes *produced* gaudy and fantastic appearances.
2. Thousands of friends *were invited* to the ball.
3. The clock's heavy clang *was heard* throughout the rooms.
4. The prince *stood* in the blue room.
5. The intruder *was* not *stopped* as he walked through the rooms.

Reading Application Choose four sentences from "The Masque of the Red Death," two in the active voice and two in the passive voice. Rewrite each sentence in the opposite voice.

Practice B Change the following sentences from passive voice to active voice. You may need to add words to indicate who performed the action.

1. Marcovaldo is led through alleys by the cat.
2. Marcovaldo's trout is taken by the Marchesa.
3. The fish bones are eaten by the cats.
4. The garden is destroyed and covered with a building.
5. The Marchesa was kept prisoner in her own apartment.

Writing Application Write a brief paragraph in the passive voice describing a cat you have seen. Then, rewrite the paragraph in the active voice. Discuss the effect of each paragraph on a reader.

PH WRITING COACH Further instruction and practice are available in *Prentice Hall Writing Coach*.

Writing

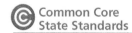 **Common Core State Standards**

L.9-10.3; W.9-10.3, W.9-10.3.a, W.9-10.3.b; SL.9-10.2
[For the full wording of the standards, see page 368.]

Narrative Text In both stories, symbols help convey important messages. Poe turns a clock into a symbol of doom. Calvino turns cats into a symbol of mischief and mystery. Write a brief **narrative** using another object or animal as a symbol. Follow these steps:

- In your narrative, develop an interesting, engaging plot.

- Describe your symbol using precise and vivid adjectives that suggest the qualities it represents. Provide information about its location or situation and its actions.

- Link your symbol to important events or give it a name that hints at what it symbolizes.

Grammar Application Make sure you have used the active voice to make your writing lively. Use the passive voice only when necessary.

Writing Workshop: *Work in Progress*

Prewriting for Problem-and-Solution Essay Take the Problem/Solution Web from your portfolio and highlight one solution. Clarify the solution with additional evidence, such as facts, reasons, or expressions of commonly accepted beliefs. Save this Solution Support List in your portfolio.

Use this prewriting activity to prepare for the **Writing Workshop** on page 420.

Research and Technology

Build and Present Knowledge Conduct library and Internet research to find out more about a topic related to one of the selections—either Poe's literary legacy or city planning. Consult three to four sources of varied types, including books, online sources, CD-ROM references, or audiovisual materials. Evaluate the accuracy and credibility of each source of information before you use it. Then, sum up your findings in a **research summary** and present it to your class. Use these suggestions:

- Use words suited to your audience's knowledge level. Explain technical terms such as *ratiocination* or *balustrade*.

- Anticipate and address listeners' potential misunderstandings and expectations. Make your ideas clear and easy to understand.

- At the end of your presentation, ask for questions and comments from the class.

Revise your summary based on feedback from the class.

PHLit
Online!
www.PHLitOnline.com
- Interactive graphic organizers
- Grammar tutorial
- Interactive journals

Test Practice: Reading

Draw Conclusions

Fiction Selection

Directions: *Read the selection. Then, answer the questions.*

Tiger had been Cassandra's cat since Cassandra was eight years old. Cassandra's father was in the army, and over the years her family moved from state to state, leaving behind friends, classmates, and favorite places. Then, Cassandra's father was sent overseas. Now, it was just Cassandra, her mom, and—until last weekend—Tiger. She and her mom had gone camping and had brought Tiger with them. He had enjoyed the trip, exploring the woods around the campground and snuggling up by Cassandra at night. As they packed to leave, they realized Tiger was gone. Cassandra and her mother spent hours searching for Tiger. Finally, they had to give up. Now at home, Cassandra lay on her bed, her mother sitting beside her. "You know, Sweetie," she said, "cats have amazing powers. We may yet see Tiger again." And somehow, Cassandra knew Tiger—and her dad—would come home someday.

1. Based on the passage, what can you conclude about Cassandra's life so far?

   A. It has been a life of upheaval and change.
   B. It has been exciting.
   C. It has been a life of stability and security.
   D. It has been happy.

2. What might Tiger symbolize to Cassandra?

   A. honesty and loyalty
   B. responsibility
   C. love and stability
   D. mystery

3. Based on details in this passage, what conclusion can you draw about how Cassandra probably feels about losing Tiger?

   A. She blames her mother for losing Tiger.
   B. She feels she has lost something important.
   C. She is glad to be relieved of the responsibility.
   D. She is excited about getting a new cat.

4. Which of the following is the *best* statement of this passage's theme?

   A. Pets are a great responsibility that most teenagers are not ready to handle.
   B. Pets can never replace a true friend.
   C. Cats are unpredictable and easily lost.
   D. Pets can be a source of comfort and stability in life.

Writing for Assessment

Consider the details in this passage. What conclusion can you draw about how Cassandra's mother feels about Tiger? Write a paragraph to explain your conclusion.

Nonfiction Selection

Directions: *Read the selection. Then, answer the questions.*

The ancestors of the domestic cat appeared in Egypt nearly 3,500 years ago. Ancient Egyptians considered the cat sacred and worshipped a cat-headed goddess called Bast. Egyptians often mummified cats, and even mummified mice, presumably as a source of food for the cats.

Cats first appeared in the art and literature of other cultures several thousand years ago: in Greece 2,600 years ago, in China 2,500 years ago, and in India 2,100 years ago. The cat appears in Arabia, Japan, and Britain by A.D. 900.

The cat is noted for its independence, frequent aloofness, and cleanliness, as well as its uncanny ability to find its way home over long distances. Over the centuries, it has been associated with superstitions. Black cats in particular have been associated with supernatural powers. Whatever the reason is, cats continue to fascinate many people. There are 37.7 million cat-owning households in the United States today.

1. Based on this passage, what can you conclude about humans' attitudes toward cats?

  A. All humans generally revere cats.
  B. Humans throughout the world have long been fascinated with cats.
  C. Humans generally dislike cats.
  D. Humans around the world find cats useful for removing pests from homes.

2. What can you conclude about the Egyptians' attitude toward cats?

  A. Egyptians believed cats live on in the afterworld just as they believed humans do.
  B. Egyptians believed that cats should be treated just like humans.
  C. Egyptians grieved over the death of a cat.
  D. Egyptians were afraid of cats.

3. Based on the details in this passage about cats, what could you reasonably conclude?

  A. Most cats are very clingy pets and cannot be left alone.
  B. The average cat has a good sense of direction.
  C. Few people keep cats as pets.
  D. Cats are not loyal to humans.

4. Based on details in the passage, the cat would make a good symbol for—

  A. affection.
  B. loyalty.
  C. the mysterious.
  D. justice.

Writing for Assessment

Connecting Across Texts
Based on details from these two passages, what can you conclude about the chances of Cassandra recovering Tiger? Explain your answer in a paragraph.

www.PHLitOnline.com
• Online practice
• Instant feedback

Reading for Information

Analyzing Argumentative and Expository Texts

Newspaper Editorial

Primary Source

 Common Core
State Standards

Reading Informational Text
3. Analyze how the author unfolds an analysis or series of ideas or events, including the order in which the points are made, how they are introduced and developed, and the connections that are drawn between them.

Language
4.b. Identify and correctly use patterns of word changes that indicate different meanings or parts of speech.
6. Acquire and use accurately general academic and domain-specific words and phrases, sufficient for reading, writing, speaking, and listening at the college and career readiness level; demonstrate independence in gathering vocabulary knowledge when considering a word or phrase important to comprehension or expression.

Reading Skills: Paraphrase to Connect Ideas

When you **paraphrase,** you use your own words to restate ideas presented in a text. Paraphrasing helps you to clarify meaning in a text so that you can determine the main idea and better understand how an author introduces, develops, and connects related ideas. Begin the process of paraphrasing by identifying key ideas and details in a text. Once you have identified the relevant ideas and details, restate them in your own words.

By paraphrasing ideas, you can better analyze how they are connected to each other. You can then more easily **connect** them to ideas in another text and **synthesize** content from the two sources. Use the following chart to guide your reading.

Guidelines for Paraphrasing and Connecting Ideas

- Paraphrase to identify the main ideas in source one.
- Look for similar or related ideas in source two.
- Synthesize the content from the sources by drawing a conclusion about the topic, based on your analysis of the main ideas.

Content-Area Vocabulary

These words appear in the selections that follow. You may also encounter them in other content-area texts.

- **regimes** (rə zhēmz´) *n.* systems or types of government; forms of rule
- **accelerate** (ak sel´ ər āt´) *v.* cause to happen sooner; speed up
- **proclaimed** (prō klāmd´) *v.* made known publicly and officially

Features:
- author's opinion about a current or a historical event
- background information and supporting arguments
- text written for a general or a specific audience

The New York Times

Editorial, November 10, 1999

The editorial begins with a statement of a main idea it will support: Gorbachev should be celebrated for his role in the fall of communism.

The Berlin Wall was bound to fall eventually. But that it came down as bloodlessly as it did 10 years ago this week is largely a tribute to one leader. Today Mikhail Gorbachev is a political pariah in Russia and increasingly forgotten in the West. But history will remember him generously for his crucial role in ending the cold war and pulling back the Iron Curtain that Stalin drew across Europe in 1945.[1]

Liquidating the Soviet empire was not what Mr. Gorbachev had in mind when he came to power in 1985. He was shrewd enough to recognize that radical changes were urgently needed to stave off economic and political bankruptcy in Russia and its European satellites.[2] . . .

Once Mr. Gorbachev lifted the lid with the openness of glasnost and the attempted economic restructuring of perestroika,[3] change took on a dynamic of its own. Similar energies were unleashed in the once-captive nations of Eastern Europe as it became clear that he would not send Soviet tanks to bail out the unpopular client regimes that had held sway there since World War II.

As political pressures began to build in the late 1980s, Mr. Gorbachev was left with two options. He could hurtle ahead toward full political and economic freedom. Or he could reverse course and crack down, as so many previous Soviet leaders had done. He chose to do neither. He was too much a creature of his Soviet Communist upbringing to subject his own power to the test of electoral democracy. But he was too enlightened to unleash the kind of thorough repression that might have preserved the Soviet empire for a few more years.

1. **Iron Curtain . . . 1945** At the end of the Second World War, in 1945, Europe was split between western countries, allied with the United States, and eastern countries, dominated by its rival, the Soviet Union, then led by Josef Stalin. West and East were said to be divided by an "iron curtain."
2. **European satellites** Eastern European countries dominated by the Soviet Union.
3. **glasnost** (glaz′ nōst) . . . **perestroika** (per′ ə strɑi′ kə) policies of Gorbachev's designed to reform the Soviet Union. Glasnost involved lifting restrictions on free speech; perestroika referred to attempts to reform the government and economy.

Although *glasnost* and *perestroika* are footnoted in the text, paraphrasing these definitions will help you understand them better.

Others stepped in to **accelerate** the transformations Mr. Gorbachev had begun, and in 1989 fixtures of the Soviet empire began to crumble. . . .

Through it all, Mr. Gorbachev and his like-minded foreign minister, Eduard Shevardnadze, stayed their hand, reflecting not only their idealism about reshaping East-West relations but also a pragmatic calculation that the Soviet Union could no longer afford an empire. For permitting its dissolution, Mr. Gorbachev paid a high price. Within two years he had been pushed from power in Moscow. . . .

History has passed Mr. Gorbachev by. But this week, especially, he deserves to be remembered for what he did and, perhaps more important, what he refused to do. With a wisdom and decency that is sadly rare in international power politics, he chose not to defend a dying system with a final, futile spasm of murderous force.

> The writer concludes the editorial with a statement that reinforces the main idea introduced in the first paragraph.

Voices from the Wall

Personal stories about the fall of the Berlin Wall

Where were you when the wall came down?

Not even two months after the Berlin Wall had been erected, I was born into the western part of this mysterious and fascinating city—I guess by accident. Who determined whether you were born to a family in the West or in the East? The small two-bedroom apartment where I grew up in the southern part of West Berlin (Neukoelln) was only 15 minutes walking distance from this world famous but horrific monument.

While graffiti was decorating the western exposure of this concrete monster, and interested tourists (and locals) could take a peek eastward from wooden watchtowers strategically positioned along the western demarcation line, a wide "death zone" or "no-man's land" extended from the Wall deep into East Berlin and was characterized by barbed wire, multiple rows of fences, wire-triggered explosive devices, watch dogs on mobile leashes and soldiers with rifles ready to shoot and kill those who dared to follow the soon-to-be-famous advertisement: "Let's Go West."

Seeing the Wall almost every day, being confined to "our" side and traveling on the rather bumpy East German autobahn "in transit" to West Germany, however, was part of our West Berlin normalcy.

In 1989, I was living in Schöneberg in the heart of West Berlin, right around the corner from Rathaus Schöneberg, the district's city hall. Rathaus Schöneberg had achieved some claim to fame when John F. Kennedy used it as the backdrop for his speech addressing a gigantic crowd of Berliners in 1963. The speech ended with the frequently quoted phrase: *"Ich bin ein Berliner"* (which does not mean: "I am a jelly-donut"). Kennedy's speech was directed to the population of West Berlin and was an assurance of America's commitment to—if necessary—defending the freedom of this encircled city. A few months after Kennedy's visit to West Berlin, he was assassinated in the streets of Dallas, Texas.

Paraphrasing the question the author poses will help clarify his main idea.

Paraphrasing this paragraph will ensure that you understand the situation described.

On November 9, 1989 late in the evening, I was watching the news on television in my cozy Schöneberg apartment. Gunter Schabowski, representative of the still-in-power East German government, was reading a declaration that surprisingly **proclaimed** East German citizens could—from now on—easily obtain travel permits to the West. It was apparently no longer required to provide unequivocal proof of a family emergency or similar hardship that would sometimes be accepted by East German authorities as justification for a "blitz-trip" to the golden West. Even in cases when a travel permit was granted, which was a rare event, the East German traveler's family had to stay behind to ensure his timely return to his beloved socialist fatherland. . . .

West Berliners lived in West Berlin and East Berliners were condemned to staying in East Berlin—that's the way it is. During the 28 years of my life that I had lived in this city, East Berliners traveling freely to West Berlin would be like running into polar bears in the Sahara desert. Thus, I did not pay too much attention to Schabowski's announcement and went to bed because I had to get up early the next day to go to work.

When I left my house the next morning I was stunned. Thousands of East German visitors had "arrived" and were hustling through the western part of the city. Visitors were waiting in long lines on sidewalks to receive their "Begrüssungsgeld" (welcome money), issued by the West German federal government through private banks. This was an unbelievable sight and the beginning of the probably most impressive political experience of my lifetime. The continuation of the story is well known.

I spent many days and nights in wintry Berlin witnessing pieces of the Wall being dismantled by East German soldiers and meeting people from the East. It was also the beginning of a period during which the West Berliners began to explore the other side of the iron curtain. Despite the physical proximity of East Berlin, this part of our city was largely unknown to us.

Four years after the fall of the Berlin Wall, in 1993, I moved to Seattle in the United States for job-related reasons. My wife is American. I am still captured by the events in November 1989 and will always remember them as a once-in-a-lifetime experience. . . .

Ich bin ein Berliner! And I will always be.

From Marco Mielcarek Seattle, Washington

To break down these long sentences into simpler parts, consider one detail at a time and restate the information in your own words.

Comparing Argumentative and Expository Texts

1. **Key Ideas and Details** **(a) Paraphrase** the first paragraph of the editorial. **(b)** Paraphrase each succeeding paragraph. **(c)** Based on your paraphrases, explain how the author introduces and develops his analysis.

2. **Key Ideas and Details** **(a)** Paraphrase the first paragraph of the primary source. **(b)** In what ways does the main idea in the editorial **connect** with the main idea of the primary source? Explain.

Content-Area Vocabulary

3. **(a)** Add the suffix *-ant* to the base word *accelerate*. Using a print or online dictionary, explain how changing the suffix alters the meaning and part of speech of the base word. **(b)** Do the same with the suffix *-ion*. **(c)** Use the words *accelerate, accelerant,* and *acceleration* in sentences that show their meanings.

Timed Writing

Argument: Response to Literature

Format
The prompt directs you to write a response to literature. Therefore, you must discuss your thoughts about a text you have read.

Each of these texts presents a different perspective on the same historical event, the fall of the Berlin Wall in 1989. Choose one of the texts and write a response to literature in which you describe what you found compelling about the text. Explain what effect the author's writing had on you, citing and paraphrasing sections of text to support your response. (40 minutes)

Academic Vocabulary
When you *cite* a section or passage from a text, you quote it as support for the argument or ideas you are presenting.

5-Minute Planner

Complete these steps before you begin to write:

1. Read the prompt carefully and completely. Look for key words.

2. Consider both your first and later responses to each text. Then, decide which one you find more compelling. If a text is unclear to you, paraphrase to understand it better.

3. Skim the text you have chosen and take notes about details and information you will include as support in your response.

4. Use your notes to draft an outline. Then, use your outline and notes to draft your response.

Comparing Literary Works

Comparing Tone in Fiction and Nonfiction

The **tone** of a work is the writer's attitude toward his or her subject and audience. A writer may treat a subject seriously or playfully, with anger or sadness, or in an objective tone that shows no emotion.

Tone is closely related to **voice** and **persona**—the personality that a writer shows to readers. The tone of a selection may also be affected by the author's **cultural experiences,** since these may help shape his or her attitude toward a subject. The two works you are about to read express very different cultural experiences. One is a work of fiction by a Latin American writer who lived under an oppressive regime. That experience is reflected in both the events and tone of her story. The other work is a personal essay by a Mexican American writer who explores the legacy of family heritage. The cultural experiences she discusses and the tone she uses reflect her admiration for diversity.

Tone may be conveyed by the details the writer chooses to include. It can also be developed in the **diction,** or word choice, that the writer uses. Finally, tone may be revealed in direct statements of the writer's feelings.

In these two selections, "The Censors" and "The Leader in the Mirror," Luisa Valenzuela and Pat Mora look at perceptions and values created by society. However, each writer's work expresses different cultural experiences and takes a different tone. Use a chart like the one shown to note elements in each essay that create its distinctive tone.

Common Core State Standards

Reading Literature
4. Determine the meaning of words and phrases as they are used in the text, including figurative and connotative meanings; analyze the cumulative impact of specific word choices on meaning and tone.
6. Analyze a particular point of view or cultural experience reflected in a work of literature from outside the United States, drawing on a wide reading of world literature.

Writing
1. Write arguments to support claims in an analysis of substantive topics or texts, using valid reasoning and relevant and sufficient evidence.

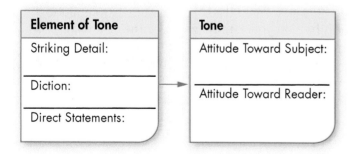

Element of Tone	Tone
Striking Detail: Diction: Direct Statements:	Attitude Toward Subject: Attitude Toward Reader:

www.PHLitOnline.com

- Vocabulary flashcards
- Interactive journals
- More about the authors
- Selection audio
- Interactive graphic organizers

Can progress be made without *conflict?*

Writing About the Big Question

In these selections, authors present the idea that facing **adversity** in everyday life can change a person. Consider how dealing with challenges could help someone grow. Use these sentence starters to develop your ideas about the Big Question.

Because I have **struggled** with_____, I know _____.

If someone asked me for advice on handling **conflict**, I would say ____.

Meet the Authors

Luisa Valenzuela (b. 1938)
Author of "The Censors"

Born in Buenos Aires, the capital of Argentina, Luisa Valenzuela has lived in places ranging from bustling New York City to Tepoztlán, Mexico, a little village where people still speak the ancient Aztec language. Valenzuela brings the same sense of adventure to her writing by changing spellings, creating new words, and using puns.

Politics and Writing Having lived under a repressive regime, Valenzuela is a strong defender of human rights. In "The Censors," she explores the dilemmas that life in a repressive society poses.

Pat Mora (b. 1942)
Author of "The Leader in the Mirror"

Pat Mora was born in El Paso, Texas, just across the United States border from Juarez, Mexico. A graduate of the University of Texas, she taught school and served as a museum director before becoming a full-time writer.

Celebrating Heritage As a young girl, Mora spoke Spanish at home but did not want her friends at school to know. Now, she celebrates her Mexican American background. "I write in part because Hispanic perspectives need to be part of our literary heritage," she explains.

The Censors

Luisa Valenzuela   *translated by* David Unger

Critical Viewing
What might this image suggest about the main character in the story? **[Preview]**

Background Like many other Latin American writers, Luisa Valenzuela often addresses political issues in her writing. Her native country, Argentina, now a democracy, has had an unfortunate history of censorship and other human rights violations. In the 1970s, a military regime took power, brutally hunting down suspected political foes and censoring news and mail. In "The Censors," Valenzuela explores the absurd aspects of such oppression.

Poor Juan! One day they caught him with his guard down before he could even realize that what he had taken as a stroke of luck was really one of fate's dirty tricks. These things happen the minute you're careless, as one often is. Juancito let happiness—a feeling you can't trust—get the better of him when he received from a confidential source Mariana's new address in Paris and knew that she hadn't forgotten him. Without thinking twice, he sat down at his table and wrote her a letter. The letter that now keeps his mind off his job during the day and won't let him sleep at night (what had he scrawled, what had he put on that sheet of paper he sent to Mariana?).

Juan knows there won't be a problem with the letter's contents, that it's irreproachable, harmless. But what about the rest? He knows that they examine, sniff, feel, and read between the lines of each and every letter, and check its tiniest comma and most accidental stain. He knows that all letters pass from hand to hand and go through all sorts of tests in the huge censorship offices and that, in the end, very few continue on their way. Usually it takes months, even years, if there aren't any snags; all this time the freedom, maybe even the life, of both sender and receiver is in jeopardy. And that's why Juan's so troubled: thinking that something might happen to Mariana because of his letters. Of all people, Mariana, who must finally feel safe there where she always dreamt she'd live. But he knows that the *Censor's Secret Command* operates all over the world and cashes in on the discount in air fares; there's nothing to stop them from going as far as that hidden Paris neighborhood, kidnapping Mariana, and returning to their cozy homes, certain of having fulfilled their noble mission.

Well, you've got to beat them to the punch, do what everyone tries to do: sabotage the machinery, throw sand in its gears, get to the bottom of the problem so as to stop it.

This was Juan's sound plan when he, like many others, applied for a censor's job—not because he had a calling or needed a job: no, he applied simply to intercept his own letter, a consoling albeit unoriginal idea. He was hired immediately, for each day more and more censors are needed and no one would bother to check on his references.

Ulterior motives couldn't be overlooked by the *Censorship Division*, but they needn't be too strict with those who applied. They knew how hard it would be for the poor guys to find the letter they wanted and even if they did, what's a letter or two when the new censor would snap up so many others? That's how Juan managed

Vocabulary
irreproachable (ir´ i prō´ chə bəl) *adj.* above criticism

ulterior (ul tir´ ē ər) *adj.* further; beyond what is openly stated or implied

Literary Analysis
Tone What does the author's use of phrases such as "beat them to the punch" and "throw sand in its gears" show you about her tone?

Reading Check
What does Juan fear may happen as a result of his letter?

to join the *Post Office's Censorship Division*, with a certain goal in mind.

The building had a festive air on the outside that contrasted with its inner staidness. Little by little, Juan was absorbed by his job, and he felt at peace since he was doing everything he could to get his letter for Mariana. He didn't even worry when, in his first month, he was sent to *Section K* where envelopes are very carefully screened for explosives.

It's true that on the third day, a fellow worker had his right hand blown off by a letter, but the division chief claimed it was sheer negligence on the victim's part. Juan and the other employees were allowed to go back to their work, though feeling less secure. After work, one of them tried to organize a strike to demand higher wages for unhealthy work, but Juan didn't join in; after thinking it over, he reported the man to his superiors and thus got promoted.

You don't form a habit by doing something once, he told himself as he left his boss's office. And when he was transferred to *Section F*, where letters are carefully checked for poison dust, he felt he had climbed a rung in the ladder.

By working hard, he quickly reached *Section E* where the job became more interesting, for he could now read and analyze the letters' contents. Here he could even hope to get hold of his letter, which, judging by the time that had elapsed, had gone through the other sections and was probably floating around in this one.

Soon his work became so absorbing that his noble mission blurred in his mind. Day after day he crossed out whole paragraphs in red ink, pitilessly chucking many letters into the censored basket. These were horrible days when he was shocked by the subtle and conniving ways employed by people to pass on subversive messages; his instincts were so sharp that he found behind a simple "the weather's unsettled" or "prices continue to soar" the wavering hand of someone secretly scheming to overthrow the Government.

▲ **Critical Viewing**
What similarities and differences exist between the building represented in this painting and the building in which Juan works? **[Connect]**

Vocabulary
staidness (stād´ nəs) *n.* state of being settled; calm

Literary Analysis
Tone Based on the details in this paragraph, what do you think is the author's attitude about Juan and his hard work as a censor?

His zeal brought him swift promotion. We don't know if this made him happy. Very few letters reached him in *Section B*—only a handful passed the other hurdles—so he read them over and over again, passed them under a magnifying glass, searched for microprint with an electronic microscope, and tuned his sense of smell so that he was beat by the time he made it home. He'd barely manage to warm up his soup, eat some fruit, and fall into bed, satisfied with having done his duty. Only his darling mother worried, but she couldn't get him back on the right track. She'd say, though it wasn't always true: Lola called, she's at the bar with the girls, they miss you, they're waiting for you. Or else she'd leave a bottle of red wine on the table. But Juan wouldn't overdo it: any distraction could make him lose his edge, and the perfect censor had to be alert, keen, attentive, and sharp to nab cheats. He had a truly patriotic task, both self-denying and uplifting.

His basket for censored letters became the best fed as well as the most cunning basket in the whole Censorship Division. He was about to congratulate himself for having finally discovered his true mission, when his letter to Mariana reached his hands. Naturally, he censored it without regret. And just as naturally, he couldn't stop them from executing him the following morning, another victim of his devotion to his work.

Spiral Review
Character Development How has Juan's job changed his attitude toward censorship?

Literary Analysis
Tone What does the last line of this selection contribute to the author's tone?

Critical Thinking

Cite textual evidence to support your responses.

1. **Key Ideas and Details** **(a)** What worries Juan at the start of the story? **(b) Infer:** From this concern, what can you tell about the situation in Juan's country?

2. **Key Ideas and Details** **(a)** Why does Juan apply for a job as a censor? **(b) Analyze:** What character traits make Juan a good censor?

3. **Key Ideas and Details** **(a)** How does Juan's career as a censor progress? **(b) Draw Conclusions:** Why does his attitude about censorship change?

4. **Integration of Knowledge and Ideas** **(a)** What advice would you give Juan on handling the conflicts he faces? **(b)** What details from the story would help you convince Juan to follow your advice? **(c)** Do you think this story suggests a positive outcome of the conflict? Why or why not? *[Connect to the Big Question: Can progress be made without conflict?]*

THE LEADER in the MIRROR

Pat Mora

Each year, the newspaper in my hometown of El Paso, Texas, honors the top five academic achievers from the local high schools at an annual banquet. Last year when I addressed the group, the room at the fancy hotel was full of proud students and their relatives.

The aspirations of the students were like a dose of powerful vitamins, filling parents, educators and guests with energy.

I began by congratulating the family members and teachers for being steady beacons[1] for those young people. In a society that undervalues families and educators, they had truly lived their commitments.

As I was planning the talk I would give to this group, I wondered how best to create an occasion for reflection. What could I say to the audience about the daily struggle to create a meaningful life?

I remembered planning parties for my children when they were young: the careful selection of party favors, the mementos for the guests to carry away. Since this banquet was to be a party of sorts, an academic celebration, I asked myself what favors I would choose for each place at the table.

I knew I would be very popular with the students if I could give them keys to a new red car or tickets to an island vacation. But I am a writer, not a millionaire. So I decided to give them imaginary gifts: Each student would receive confetti, a tape recorder, a photograph and a mirror—symbols and metaphors to take with them through life.

I hoped that most of the students were going to enroll in college. The confetti would be for their private celebrations, those solitary moments when they had passed a test that worried them, finished a difficult paper at 2 a.m., found a summer internship.[2] Sometimes, even when no one else is around, it's important to celebrate when we have struggled and succeeded—to sprinkle a little confetti on our own heads.

Why a tape recorder? I read them my poem "Immigrants."

Vocabulary
aspirations (as´ pə rā´ shənz) *n.* strong ambitions

Literary Analysis
Tone Which details here show you that the writer might be amused by students' values?

Reading Check

What does Mora say she used to do when planning parties for her children?

Immigrants
wrap their babies in the American flag,
feed them mashed hot dogs and apple pie,
name them Bill and Daisy,
buy them blonde dolls that blink blue
eyes or a football and tiny cleats
before the baby can even walk,
speak to them in thick English,
   hallo, babee, hallo,
whisper in Spanish or Polish
when the baby sleeps, whisper
in a dark parent bed, that dark
parent fear, "Will they like
our boy, our girl, our fine american
boy, our fine american girl?"

As a writer, I understand the value and necessity of knowing my past, of keeping that door open. My family stories are my catalyst for creativity. All of us have people in our lives whose voices merit saving if we'll only take the time.

Vocabulary
catalyst (kat´ ə list´) *n.* person or thing that triggers an event or action

▶ **Critical Viewing**
Drawing on the details in this photograph of El Paso, explain what sort of life Mora's audience might lead. **[Speculate]**

My own father was once a paper boy for the newspaper hosting the banquet. I might not have known that fact, nor his long history of hard work, had I not been listening to him with my tape recorder a few years ago. I did not want the students to wait as long as I had to begin preserving the rich inheritance of their family voices. The strength of their heritage would give them the courage to face the future.

My third gift was a photograph of the El Paso/Juarez border: the Chihuahua Desert. the Rio Grande,[3] a stern mountain, two sprawling border cities. Like our families, our geography is part of who we are.

When I was growing up on the U.S. side of that border, the society around me tried in subtle and not-so-subtle ways to convince me that my Mexican heritage was inferior to that of Anglo-Americans. I hope that today's educators on the border and throughout this nation are now committed to multiculturalism, to motivating the next generation to draw on their heritage as a resource for learning. The U.S. has been described as the first international country: Our varied cultures are our common wealth.

Borders—and if we're attentive, we realize we all live on borders, whether they are national or not—are sites of tension and sites for learning. Borders invite us to confront differences, inequities and stereotypes. They invite us to work for multicultural cooperation and to celebrate multilingual richness.

3. **El Paso** (el pas′ ō) / **Juárez** (hwä′ res) . . . **Chihuahua** (chi wä′ wä) . . . **Rio Grande** (rē′ ō grand′) El Paso is a city in Texas on the Rio Grande, the river forming the border between Texas and Mexico. Juárez, in the Mexican state of Chihuahua, is directly across the river.

Vocabulary
inheritance (in her′ i təns) *n.* gift handed down to a later generation

Literary Analysis
Tone What tone do the details and diction in this paragraph help to create?

Reading Check

What aspects of life does the writer intend the second and third gifts to reflect?

The final gift of the evening, a mirror, was for serious gazing. I asked the students if they saw a leader when they looked into their mirrors. My guess is that too many of our young people do not see themselves as leaders because they don't look, dress or sound like the images of leaders presented to us. But leaders come in all colors, shapes and sizes. Some are talkative while others are quiet, but they all share a determination to contribute to the society of the future.

I urged the students to look often in their mirrors and to ask themselves these questions: "Am I satisfied with this world? If not, what will I do to improve it?" For if we are shaped by our surroundings, we in turn shape them. We deceive ourselves if we believe that we can live neutral[4] lives.

One-third of this nation now traces its heritage to regions other than Western Europe. We will continue to squander[5] our talent if our leaders—in politics, science, business, education and the arts—do not reflect our grand variety. I urged the students (and all of us) to ponder the strength of the mountains around us, to rise to the challenges.

---

4. **neutral** ($n\overline{oo}'$ trəl) *adj.* not taking a position; lacking vivid color.
5. **squander** (skwän' dər) *v.* spend or use wastefully or extravagantly.

Critical Thinking

Cite textual evidence to support your responses.

1. **Key Ideas and Details (a)** On what occasion does Mora give her speech? **(b) Infer:** What does the invitation to give this speech show about Mora's achievements?

2. **Key Ideas and Details (a)** What "gifts" does Mora give the students? **(b) Interpret:** Explain the meaning or purpose of each. **(c) Connect:** In what way is each gift connected to the idea of respect for one's own cultural experiences and heritage?

3. **Key Ideas and Details** Which of Mora's gifts would you value the most? Explain your choice.

4. **Integration of Knowledge and Ideas** In this speech, Mora mentions that borders are "sites of tension and sites of learning." **(a)** Using examples from the speech, explain how tension and adversity have affected Mora's life. **(b)** How might tension lead to learning? *[Connect to the Big Question: Can progress be made without conflict?]*

Comparing Tones

ⓒ 1. Key Ideas and Details What is each author's attitude toward the following concepts? Cite textual evidence.

Valenzuela: (a) censorship **(b)** governments that censor

Mora: (c) heritage **(d)** consumer goods

ⓒ 2. Craft and Structure (a) Use a chart like the one shown to record words and phrases that express each writer's **tone**. Analyze each writer's attitude toward the perceptions created by a society.
(b) Based on your chart, write a sentence comparing the mixture of tones in each piece.

	Inspirational	Sarcastic	Analytical	Other
Diction				
Direct Statements				
Other Details				

ⓒ 3. Craft and Structure Based on the mix of tones in each piece, describe the **voice,** or "personality on the page," of each writer.

⏱ Timed Writing

Argumentative Text: Essay

In an argumentative essay, compare and evaluate the success of each author's writing style in conveying an idea to readers. Consider tone and diction and the way in which they shape readers' understanding. Support your response with details from each text. **(25 minutes)**

5-Minute Planner

1. Read the prompt carefully and completely.

2. Use these questions to gather details for your essay.

- How would you categorize each writer's tone and diction?
- How did each author's writing style affect your ability to understand her ideas?
- Which author did you find more successful? Why?

3. Review each text to locate textual evidence to support your ideas.

4. Reread the prompt, and then draft your essay.

Writing Workshop

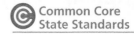
Common Core State Standards

Writing
1. Write arguments to support claims in an analysis of substantive topics or texts, using valid reasoning and relevant and sufficient evidence.

1.a. Introduce precise claim(s), distinguish the claim(s) from alternate or opposing claims, and create an organization that establishes clear relationships among claim(s), counterclaims, reasons, and evidence.

Write an Argumentative Text

Exposition: Problem-and-Solution Essay

Defining the Form Individuals, schools, communities, and even entire nations face problems. **Problem-and-solution writing** helps identify the problems and offers reasonable remedies. In this workshop, you will write a problem-and-solution essay on a subject of your choice.

Assignment Write a problem-and-solution essay to identify a problem in your school or community and present one or more solutions. Your essay should feature these elements:

- ✓ *a clear description* of a specific, real-life problem
- ✓ an *analysis* of the most important parts of the problem
- ✓ *proof, such as facts, anecdotes, or examples,* that shows the significance of the problem in a way your readers can understand
- ✓ *transitions* that link the parts of the essay to form a coherent whole
- ✓ *a complete explanation* of one or more possible solutions
- ✓ *your personal evaluation* of any solutions you discuss
- ✓ error-free grammar, *including correct subject-verb agreement*

To preview the criteria on which your problem-and-solution essay may be assessed, see the rubric on page 427.

 Writing Workshop: *Work in Progress*

Review the work you did on pages 367 and 399.

WRITE GUY
Jeff Anderson, M.Ed.

What Do You Notice?
Word Choice
The following passage is from Edgar Allan Poe's "The Masque of the Red Death." Read the passage several times.
The abbey was amply provisioned. With such precautions the courtiers might bid defiance to contagion.
With a partner, discuss the qualities that make this passage interesting.
Now, think about ways you might use word choice in your problem-and-solution essay.

Reading-Writing Connection

To get a feel for problem-and-solution essays, read "Nobel Lecture" by Alexander Solzhenitsyn on page 548.

Prewriting/Planning Strategies

Browse media sources. Look through newspapers, magazines, and Internet sites for recent stories that discuss a problem. Jot down problems for which you think you can offer solutions. Choose a topic from among these ideas.

Analyze your audience. Decide which people you want to reach—community members, students, or others. Consider that group's interests and needs. Conduct brief interviews to identify a problem that troubles your audience, and then choose a topic to pursue.

Categorize to narrow your topic. Some problems may be too large for your essay. Focus on manageable, local aspects of an issue.

- Write these categories: World, Nation, State, Town, and School. Identify one aspect of the problem for each category.

- Focus your essay on the aspect that you wrote under the local categories, such as "Town" or "School." For example, you cannot solve the problem of war in a few pages. However, you can write about the problem of bullies at school.

Evaluate possible solutions. After you have focused your essay on a specific and manageable problem, think about potential solutions. Brainstorm for practical and logical ways to solve the issue. Before you draft, use a chart to evaluate potential solutions. Be sure each solution can be supported with specific and concrete details. Then, consider the advantages and disadvantages of each solution. As you get ready to write, plan to offer the best solutions in your essay.

Problem	Solutions	Pros	Cons
Overcrowded computer lab Details: students have the same deadlines; all need the lab at the same times	1. Teachers split classes into three parts, each with separate deadlines.	Students won't need the lab at the same time.	Teachers will have to manage a lot of deadlines.
	2. Students sign up for lab time one week in advance.	Students will have to plan their work.	Some students may not sign up.

Drafting Strategies

Create an essay map. For additional support during drafting, write each important idea on an index card. Then, write each supporting detail, such as a fact or an example, on an index card. Using the index cards, arrange the ideas and details in different orders. Consider placing your most powerful idea near the end of the essay, before your personal evaluation. Once you have determined the best order, number the cards and use them as a map for your writing.

Write an outline. An outline gives you a quick overview of all your points. It also lets you figure out how best to structure, or order, the information and reasoning you want to present. The outlines here show two possible organizations for a problem-and-solution essay.

Common Core State Standards

Writing
1.c. Use words, phrases, and clauses to link the major sections of the text, create cohesion, and clarify the relationships between claim(s) and reasons, between reasons and evidence, and between claim(s) and counterclaims.
1.d. Establish and maintain a formal style and objective tone while attending to the norms and conventions of the discipline in which they are writing.

Outline A

I. Description of Problem
  A. One aspect
  B. Another aspect
II. Explanation of Solution
  A. How it solves the first aspect
  B. How it solves the second aspect
III. Personal Evaluation

Outline B

I. Description of Problem
  A. One aspect
  B. Another aspect
II. Explanation of First Solution
  A. Advantages
  B. Disadvantages
III. Explanation of Second Solution
  A. Advantages
  B. Disadvantages
IV. Personal Evaluation

Address your audience. Some audiences, such as your friends or young readers, might respond best to informal language. In general, though, audiences will respect your thinking more if you use formal language.

Informal: Face it—lots of us like to eat junk food for lunch.

Formal: When choosing their own meals, many students select foods with little nutritional value.

Stick to the facts. To convince your audience that the problem you describe is genuine, present factual information in an objective way rather than personal opinions. Reserve your opinions for your personal evaluation in the conclusion of your essay. Your personal evaluation should judge the quality of the solutions you included in your essay.

Use appropriate transitions. Show the relationships between your ideas by linking them with transitions. To show contrast, use transitions like *on the other hand.* To show cause-and-effect relationships, use transitions like *as a result.*

Writers on Writing

C. J. Cherryh On Revising to Tighten Sentences

C. J. Cherryh is the author of "The Threads of Time" (p. 231).

Knowing what to delete is as important as knowing what to write in the first place. The value of that advice is illustrated both by "The Threads of Time" and by the passage below, which I have written especially for this workshop. The last few sentences of "Threads" relate to the novel that the story originally introduced. Now that the story exists on its own, I'd like to strike that final passage. It's too late for that, but in the passage below, I show how the timely deletion of unnecessary words can tighten a narrative.

"Perfect sentences are created by good editing."
—C. J. Cherryh

Professional Model:

Original writing by C. J. Cherryh

"Well," I said, ~~taking a moment to look out at the sunset~~ gazing over the porch railing at the gathering dark, ~~of the porch which my grandfather had built,~~ ~~"I really think, well,~~ "it was about this time of evening, yes—back ~~sometime~~ in June. ~~when~~ I saw ~~a truly~~ something terrible ~~thing over there~~ in the garden, right over there by the rose bushes."

~~The little girl who was standing next to me on the porch looked.~~ Eight-year-old Susan glanced up at me, wide-eyed. ~~She had blue eyes. She was my sister's daughter. She was about eight. She looked very scared at first.~~

~~It wasn't fair to scare the girl. She was just like her mother. I used to tell her mother stories, too, when we were both kids in this house.~~ Then those eyes narrowed: "Mama said you~~'re~~ were a liar." ~~," she said.~~

Was I surprised? No. I knew my sister. ~~Her mother Louise never believed me, either.~~ Louise hated imagination: ~~and she missed a lot of~~ ever so many true things ~~sat~~ ~~that were~~ right under her nose, but she never believed ~~simply because she wouldn't believe~~ she saw them.

I really want the reader to hear the word "June." I set it off with a long dash. Then, I cut out the choppy, chattery little words, and set the rhythms of the sentence to land on "something terrible in the garden."

"Look" is a neutral word. "Glance" is sharp and fast. Choosing that word for "look" changes the impression in the reader's mind.

Do I need to spell out specifically who Louise is? Once the little girl talks about "mama" and I talk about "my sister," I trust my readers to figure it out.

Revising Strategies

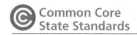 Common Core
State Standards

Writing
5. Develop and strengthen writing as needed by planning, revising, editing, rewriting, or trying a new approach, focusing on addressing what is most significant for a specific purpose and audience.

Language
3. Apply knowledge of language to make effective choices for meaning or style.

Ask questions to consider effectiveness. Review your draft to uncover illogical connections, weakly supported examples, or missing information. Ask yourself the following questions. If you have difficulty providing clear answers, adjust your writing.

- Is there a logical flow to my ideas?
- Did I provide enough details to support my ideas? Are there more facts, anecdotes, or examples that would be useful to include?
- Did I provide more details than I really need?
- Does every statement make sense? If not, what did I mean to say?
- Is this statement a fact or an opinion? If it is an opinion, am I sure I want to include it?
- Have I evaluated the solution I proposed?

Evaluate tone and style. The words you choose establish your **tone**—your attitude toward your subject and audience. When appropriate, you might want to present an optimistic or a pessimistic tone regarding a particular problem or solution.

Optimistic: Our challenge is to discover an effective solution.

Pessimistic: The difficulty will be in finding a workable solution.

Replace dull words. Word choice is also key to writing style. Replace any dull words and phrases with vivid, expressive writing, and define technical terms your readers may not know.

Flat: The board will make the final decision about the program.

Vivid: The fate of the program lies in the hands of the board.

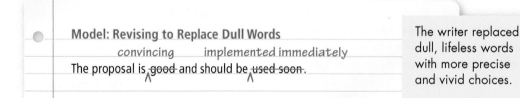

Model: Revising to Replace Dull Words

                convincing   implemented immediately
The proposal is ~~good~~ and should be ~~used soon~~.

The writer replaced dull, lifeless words with more precise and vivid choices.

Peer Review

Ask a partner to read your draft and then conduct a conference about your work. Your reader can ask about the overall structure as well as specific details. Use your discussion to guide your revisions.

Subject-Verb Agreement

For a subject and verb to agree, both must be singular or plural.

Identifying Errors Errors in agreement can occur when the subject and verb are separated by other words, phrases, or clauses. In the examples below, subjects are underlined, and verbs are set in italic type.

Singular Subject and Verb

> **Incorrect:** The <u>decision</u> of the board members *are* final.

> **Correct:** The <u>decision</u> of the board members *is* final.

Plural Subject and Verb

> **Incorrect:** <u>Students</u> who park here seldom *follows* the rules.

> **Correct:** <u>Students</u> who park here seldom *follow* the rules.

> Agreement errors also occur with compound subjects and with indefinite pronouns serving as subjects.

Identifying Indefinite Pronouns These are the most common indefinite pronouns categorized by number:

Singular:	anybody, anyone, each, either, every, everybody, neither, nobody, nothing, somebody, something
Plural:	both, few, many, others, several
Singular or Plural:	all, any, more, most, none, some

PH WRITING COACH

Further instruction and practice are available in *Prentice Hall Writing Coach*.

Fixing Errors To correct mismatched subjects and verbs, follow these steps:

1. Identify the subject and determine whether it is singular or plural.

2. Select the verb that matches the subject.

- For compound subjects joined by *and*, use the plural form.
- For singular subjects joined by *or* or *nor*, use the singular form.
- When the subject is an indefinite pronoun, use the appropriate form of the verb.

Grammar in Your Writing

Circle all the subjects in two paragraphs of your draft. For each subject, draw an arrow to the verb that tells what it does. Make sure that you have used the form of the verb that agrees with the subject.

Brand Names

A great majority of youth today have become walking advertisements. A person's worth is not based on the content of their character, but on the contents of their wallets. Labels have become the measure of merit, and the right clothing can lead to success and popularity. Society has forgotten the value of self-expression. Individuality has been dissolved in a world full of expensive brand names and styles. The problem has several main parts:

Expense: Students experience great pressure to purchase brand name clothes. However, these articles cost more than regular clothes, making it a challenge for many people to afford them. Despite these realities, those teens who do not own a popular brand are often shunned or ridiculed.

Sameness: Clothes should be a reflection of who you are, not an imitation of what you wish you were. For many teens, clothes no longer express their individuality. Instead, brand names express someone else's idea of who teens are supposed to be.

Poor Self-Esteem: We have a certain image of the ideal body, which has been fed to us by magazines, television, and movies. Girls are expected to be thin and tall, while boys should be muscular. However, everyone has a different body, and few fit these unrealistic images. The clothes that we are told to buy often suit only that one uncommon body type. The rest of the population is left to try to squeeze into stylish clothes or feel inferior. For many teens, self-esteem drops with every outfit they cannot wear.

The problem is complex, but there are some solutions:

Change the media: Magazines should feature models with more common body types wearing flattering clothing. Fewer television programs should be dedicated to fashion, and more should focus on human character. Department stores should offer a greater selection of sizes, styles, and prices. Clothing manufacturers might be able to make attractive but inexpensive clothes, so that costly brands do not have a fashion monopoly.

Change values: Adults should try to build children's identities so that teens are able to express themselves instead of copying whatever they are told is stylish. Schools could offer seminars on celebrating our personal distinctiveness.

Diversity is beautiful, yet it is far too often hidden beneath layers of conformity. Making more affordable and unique styles could lessen the problem of people being judged based on the brand of their clothes. Clothing can be a wonderful medium of self-expression, but only if we eliminate the pressure of dressing the same as everyone else.

In her introduction, Jacquelyn clearly explains the problem she will discuss.

The writer breaks the problem down into its elements.

Jacquelyn organizes her solutions into two main categories.

In her conclusion, the writer restates her key points.

Editing and Proofreading

Check your draft for errors in grammar, spelling, capitalization, and punctuation.

Focus on clear references. Make sure you have used *that* and *which* correctly. Use *that* to introduce adjective clauses that are essential to the meaning of the noun and *which* to introduce clauses that are not essential to the meaning of the noun.

Publishing and Presenting

Consider one of the following ways to share your essay with others:

Launch a discussion. Read your essay to your classmates. Then, allow your audience members to ask questions and propose their own solutions.

Submit your essay. If your essay focused on a matter of local interest, send it to your school or community newspaper. If your school or town has its own Web site, consider posting your essay. Create links to appropriate background information, and update your essay as new information becomes available.

Reflecting on Your Writing

Writer's Journal Jot down your answers to these questions:
How did writing about the work help you understand it?
Which strategy would you use again? Why?

Rubric for Self-Assessment

Find evidence in your writing to address each category. Then, use the rating scale to grade your work.

Criteria	Rating Scale
	not very / very
Focus: How well do you explain a problem?	1 2 3 4 5
Organization: How logically do you present one or more solutions?	1 2 3 4 5
Support/Elaboration: How effectively do you use facts, anecdotes, or examples to support your ideas?	1 2 3 4 5
Style: How confidently do you state your evaluations of the solutions?	1 2 3 4 5
Conventions: How correct is your grammar, especially your use of subject-verb agreement?	1 2 3 4 5

Spiral Review
Earlier in this unit, you learned about **action and linking verbs** (p. 366) and **active and passive voice** (tenses) (p. 398). Review your essay to be sure that you have often used action verbs and active voice.

PH WRITING COACH

Further instruction and practice are available in *Prentice Hall Writing Coach*.

Vocabulary Workshop

Word Origins

Words come into the English language from many sources. A word's **origin,** or source, is shown in its **etymology.** A word's etymology identifies the language in which the word first appeared and tells how its spelling and meaning have changed over time.

English as a language dates back to about the year 500, when Germanic tribes including Angles, Saxons, and Jutes settled in England. This first English language is known as Old English. In the years following 1066, English changed dramatically as a result of the Norman invasion, which brought Old French to England and produced what we now call Middle English. During a period known as the Renaissance, roughly between 1300 and 1500, there was a renewed interest in the classical languages of Greek and Latin that greatly influenced the English language. As a result, grammar, spelling, and pronunciation changed and Modern English emerged.

This chart shows how a few words first entered the English language.

Word	Definition	Origin
Thursday	the fifth day of the week	Old Norse word *Thorsdagr,* which means "Thor's day," a reference to the god of thunder in Norse mythology
martial	of or suitable for war	Latin word *martialis,* which means "of Mars," a reference to the god of war in Roman mythology
narcissistic	showing excessive self-love	reference to Narcissus, a young man in Greek mythology who falls in love with his own reflection

Common Core
State Standards

Language
4.c. Consult general and specialized reference materials, both print and digital, to find the pronunciation of a word or determine or clarify its precise meaning, its part of speech, or its etymology.

Practice A Look up each of the following words in a print or an online dictionary. Define each word and explain its origin.

1. psyche **2.** algebra **3.** Saturday

4. anger **5.** sleuth **6.** theater

PHLit
Online!
www.PHLitOnline.com
• Illustrated vocabulary words
• Interactive vocabulary games
• Vocabulary flashcards

Practice B Each numbered question contains a word that has come into the English language from the Greek, Latin, or Old Norse language or mythology. Use a dictionary to find each italicized word's origin and meaning. Then, use that information to answer the question.

1. How did the word *tantalizing* come to mean "tempting" or "enticing"?

2. What qualities does something *titanic* share with the Titans in Greek mythology?

3. What kind of days was the word *dismal* originally used to describe?

4. For which Norse god is *Wednesday* named?

5. What kind of journey is an *odyssey*, and which hero of Greek mythology took this kind of journey?

6. Why is the word *mercurial* used to describe someone who is lively and quick-witted?

Activity Use a print or an online dictionary to identify the source of each of the following English words. Then, use a graphic organizer like the one shown to explain how the English word and its source word are related. The first item has been completed as an example.

1. consequence **2.** agony **3.** detour **4.** thespian **5.** pendant

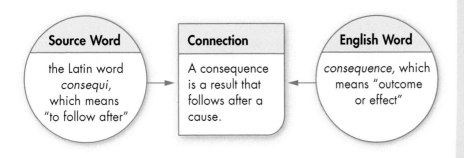

Source Word	Connection	English Word
the Latin word *consequi*, which means "to follow after"	A consequence is a result that follows after a cause.	*consequence*, which means "outcome or effect"

Comprehension and Collaboration

With a partner, research these words, which are all derived from ancient Greek theater. In writing, explain how each word's theatrical meaning relates to its everyday meaning.

catastrophe
antagonist
chorus

Viewing and Evaluating a Speech

Do not believe everything you hear in a speech, regardless of who presents it. Analyze the presenter's message and speaking skills as you listen.

Learn the Skills

Use the following strategies to help you complete the activity on page 431.

Identify the purpose. The purpose of a speech may be to pay tribute to someone, to inform, to entertain, or to persuade. Identifying the speaker's purpose will help you decide whether or not the presenter achieves his or her goal and therefore whether or not the speech is effective.

Assess the arguments. A speaker should present and support clear arguments, or ideas. Analyze the types of argument used by the speaker, such as *causation,* or making a connection between a cause and an effect; *analogy*, or comparing two situations to prove a point; and *authority,* or using an expert's credibility to support an argument.

Consider point of view. When listening to a speech, consider the speaker's point of view, which can be understood as the life experiences that have shaped the speaker and the perspective from which he or she presents information. A point of view can sometimes cause the speaker to be biased toward a certain way of thinking. An effective speaker presents both sides of an argument and anticipates opposing viewpoints.

Consider logic and accuracy. Use your knowledge to check the accuracy of statements. Look for fallacious, or faulty, reasoning, such as insisting that there is only one right solution to a problem.

Check language level. A good speaker chooses language suited to the audience. For example, if members of the audience are scientists, the speaker may use technical terms. When speaking to the general public, the speaker may use common terms instead.

Note word choice and style. A speaker may use formal or informal language, or he or she may use emotionally charged wording. Words with powerful connotations, or associations, can make a statement memorable or make opinions appear to be facts.

Look at nonverbal communication. A speaker communicates with more than words. The speaker's body language, eye contact, gestures, vocal tone, and pacing affect the audience's reaction.

Common Core State Standards

Speaking and Listening
3. Evaluate a speaker's point of view, reasoning, and use of evidence and rhetoric, identifying any fallacious reasoning or exaggerated or distorted evidence.

Practice the Skills

Presentation of Knowledge and Ideas Use what you've learned in this workshop to perform the following task.

ACTIVITY: Evaluate an Argument

Listen to a speech presented in your school or find one online or on television. Take notes to evaluate how the style and structure support or undermine the speaker's purpose and the speech's meaning. Answer the following questions in your notes.

- What is the speaker's main argument?
- How well do the details support this argument?
- Does the speaker appear biased in his or her point of view? Explain.
- Does the speaker make logical and accurate statements and avoid faulty reasoning? Explain.
- Is the speaker's word choice and use of connotations and emotionally charged language effective and suited to his or her audience? Explain.

As you listen to the speech, use the following Speech Checklist to analyze the purpose, point of view, and communication skills.

Speech Checklist

Rate how well the speaker did each of the following on a scale of 1 (very poor) to 5 (very good). Explain your ratings.

Purpose and Support
- [ ] conveyed a clear purpose   Rating: _____
- [ ] presented sufficient supporting arguments   Rating: _____
- [ ] avoided faulty reasoning   Rating: _____

Point of View
- [ ] conveyed a clear position without bias   Rating: _____
- [ ] presented opposing viewpoints fairly   Rating: _____

Communication Skills
- [ ] chose words with audience in mind   Rating: _____
- [ ] used effective body language,
      eye contact, and vocal tone   Rating: _____

Comprehension and Collaboration After you have evaluated the speech, work with a small group of classmates and compare your notes. Work together to build a consensus about whether the speaker's arguments, supporting details, and style effectively fulfilled his or her purpose.

Cumulative Review

I. Reading Literature

Directions: *Read the passage. Then, answer each question that follows.*

Common Core
State Standards

RL.9-10.1, RL.9-10.2, RL.9-10.3, RL.9-10.4; W.9-10.2
[For the full wording of the standards, see the standards chart in the front of your textbook.]

Futbol

Alex clutched the football under his arm and rubbed its rough surface. The plane was taking off. As he watched from his window seat, the cars on the freeway grew smaller and smaller, until they looked like toys. He gazed out over the city, trying to spot the football field at his old high school. He knew he would not see it again for a long time. Alex and his family were moving to Mexico City, Mexico. His dad had taken a job there.

"It will be an adventure, Alex," his dad had said when he announced the move. "You'll learn a new language and make new friends."

"But I'll have to leave my old friends—and football!" Alex had argued.

"They have football in Mexico—just not your kind."

"Very funny, dad! They call it *futbol*—we call it *soccer*. And I've never really played soccer." All during the conversation, Alex had tossed his football in the air, trying to imagine life without the game.

As soon as the family was settled in Mexico City, Alex enrolled in school. Although there were many English-speaking students, Alex still felt he didn't belong, like a <u>misfit.</u> He kept his football in his locker during the day and set it on the table by his bed at night.

One evening, a few months after the move, Alex's dad entered his room. "Alex, this is enough. You can't sit at home each night. I've enrolled you in a Saturday soccer league with kids from the neighborhood."

"You can't do that! I'm not going," Alex protested. "Those kids have played soccer all their lives!"

"Not all of them, Alex. Some are new to *futbol*."

"Futbol. Soccer. I've never played it. I'll look stupid."

"You were a wide receiver on the football team, and you know how to move. You'll do fine."

Saturday after Saturday, Alex went to the field, but he always watched on the sidelines as the boys played. Alex was an outsider. Afterwards, he would go home and toss his football in the air for hours. One Saturday, the ball came flying towards his spot on the sidelines, high over the heads of the players. Without thinking, Alex stepped forward and butted it back into play with his head. "Bueno! Bueno!" a dark-haired boy shouted at Alex with a grin. That afternoon, Alex picked up his football, gave it a pat, and put it on the top shelf in his closet.

1. Which of the following sentences is an example of direct characterization?

   A. Alex was an outsider.
   B. "It will be an adventure, Alex."
   C. Alex's dad entered his room.
   D. "Some are new to *futbol*."

2. Which statement best describes the **theme?**

   A. Change can be painful, but it opens doors to new experiences.
   B. People around the world are very similar.
   C. Moving to a different country is an exciting adventure.
   D. Not everyone is good at sports.

3. From which **point of view** is the story told?

   A. first person
   B. second person
   C. third person
   D. limited

4. **Vocabulary** What is the best definition of the underlined word *misfit?*

   A. someone who is not intelligent
   B. someone who feels out of place
   C. someone who feels superior
   D. someone who is disgusted

5. Which sentence best represents the **character development** that happens during the story?

   A. "Bueno! Bueno!" a dark haired boy shouted at Alex with a grin.
   B. That afternoon, Alex picked up his football, gave it a pat, and put it on the top shelf in his closet.
   C. He gazed out over the city, trying to spot the football field at his old high school.
   D. One Saturday, the ball came flying towards his spot on the sidelines, high over the heads of the players.

6. Which of the following statements includes the most **description?**

   A. He kept his football in his locker during the day and set it on the table by his bed at night.
   B. "And I've never really played soccer."
   C. He knew he would not see it again for a long time.
   D. As he watched from his window seat, the cars on the freeway grew smaller and smaller, until they looked like toys.

7. Which of the following best describes the **symbolic meaning** of Alex's football?

   A. his anger at his father for the move
   B. the family's move
   C. his source of comfort in new surroundings
   D. the football team's dedication

8. Which of the following does *not* describe the story's **setting?**

   A. an airplane
   B. a *futbol* field in Mexico City
   C. Alex's bedroom in Mexico
   D. a football field in the United States

9. The **dialogue** reveals that Alex's father—

   A. wants to leave Mexico City.
   B. believes Alex will adjust to *futbol*.
   C. has a high-paying job.
   D. knows how to play football.

⏱ Timed Writing

10. Write an informational essay in which you **describe** the character of Alex and **explain** how his character develops. Cite evidence from the text to support your analysis.

II. Reading Informational Text

Directions: *Read the passage. Then, answer each question that follows.*

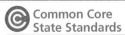

Common Core State Standards

RI.9-10.7; W.9-10.5; L.9-10.1, L.9-10.4.a
[For the full wording of the standards, see the standards chart in the front of your textbook.]

Association Football

In the United States, tens of thousands of kids play a game called *soccer.* Elsewhere the same ball game is called *association football,* or, in some countries, *futbol.* Around the world, about 40 million players are registered, plus there are thousands of others who play pickup games in streets, parks, school yards, and vacant lots, and even on beaches.

The game is played with two teams of eleven players each. The <u>ultimate</u> goal is to move the ball into the opposing team's goal net, without using the hands or arms. Players may bump the ball with their heads, hips, or knees, or they may kick the ball, but only the goalie, who stands in front of the goal, can touch the ball with his or her hands. The rules are simple, and the game can be played almost anywhere, which makes it the most popular game in the world, not only for players but for spectators as well.

Champions!

It was a brisk, overcast Sunday morning—the best kind for soccer. I walked on to the field and was greeted by high fives from my ten excited teammates. It was championship game day. Proud spectators with painted faces colored the stands, wildly waving striped flags and banners. "Today is the day," I thought to myself. "Nothing gets by these hands today." I put my gloves on and clapped my hands three times for good luck, a ritual I started years before on the streets in my neighborhood. The whistle sounded. I protected the goal, throwing my body in front of every shot. With 30 seconds of play left, the score was 1–0, our favor. Suddenly, I saw two fast and furious feet dribbling the ball toward my goal. I glanced at the clock—22 seconds left and counting down. I took a deep breath and put my hands up to block the shot I knew was coming. The fans roared. Teammates cheered. I did it! I shut the other team down. We had won the championship!

1. Both of these articles are about soccer. The article "Champions" would be more useful for—

A. learning how the game is played.
B. understanding the rules for playing soccer.
C. appreciating the excitement of watching a soccer game.
D. learning about the popularity of the game.

2. "Association Football" would be more useful for—

A. appreciating the fans.
B. understanding the stress on soccer players.
C. learning how soccer players feel.
D. learning the rules of soccer.

3. If these two articles were to continue, in which of them would you likely find statistics about soccer fans?

A. "Association Football"
B. "Champions"
C. Both articles
D. Neither article

4. Vocabulary What is the *best* definition of the underlined word *ultimate*?

A. most important
B. first
C. rule
D. lowest

III. Writing and Language Conventions

Directions: *Read the passage. Then, answer each question that follows.*

(1) The air lock doors were opened with a hiss. (2) As Mark stepped outside, he could feel the air, even through his protective suit. (3) Mark saw the sky as the sun set on Mars.

(4) "This is it, Joey," he is saying, looking down at the limp, furry, black body in his arms.

(5) He walked swiftly—bounced, really, in the thin gravity—away from the glowing glass dome of the city. (6) Carefully, Mark placed Joey's body in a shallow hole, kicking dirt back over it and mounding the grave with rocks. (7) Mark felt tears in his eyes, tears he couldn't wipe through his helmet. (8) Joey had been his first pet, brought to Mars when Mark's family moves there years earlier. (9) Losing him meant that his last tie to his old life on Earth was gone. (10) Mark was now completely Martian.

1. Which revision of sentence 3 most vividly describes the **setting** of the story?

   A. Mark could see the sun setting on Mars.
   B. Mark felt sadness as he watched the sun setting on Mars.
   C. The blackness of the sky was broken by the glow at the horizon—the sun setting on Mars.
   D. Mark watched the sun dip low in Mars's sky as he mourned the loss of his first pet, Joey.

2. What is the best way to incorporate **sensory details** in sentence 2?

   A. Replace "air" with "icy winds."
   B. Replace "he" with "Mark."
   C. Replace "suit" with "gear."
   D. Replace "protective" with "protecting."

3. How should the phrase "is saying" in sentence 4 be revised so that the **verb tense** is consistent in the story?

   A. says   C. said
   B. has said   D. keep as is

4. Which of the following is the *best* way to rewrite sentence 1 in the **active voice?**

   A. Hissing, the air lock doors were opened.
   B. Joey opened the air lock doors with a hiss.
   C. With a hiss, the air lock doors were opened.
   D. The air lock doors opened with a hiss.

5. How should sentence 8 be revised so that the **verb tense** in the sentence is consistent?

   A. Joey was his first pet, brought to Mars when Mark's family moved there.
   B. Joey was his first pet, brought to Mars when Mark's family moves there.
   C. Joey had been his first pet, brings to Mars when Mark's family had moved there.
   D. Joey is his first pet, brought to Mars when Mark's family will move there.

Performance Tasks

Directions: *Follow the instructions to complete the tasks below as required by your teacher.*

As you work on each task, incorporate both general academic vocabulary and literary terms you learned in this unit.

> © **Common Core State Standards**
>
> **RL.9-10.2, RL.9-10.3, RL.9-10.4, RL.9-10.5; RI.9-10.4; W.9-10.9.a, W.9-10.9.b; SL.9-10.1, SL.9-10.1.d, SL.9-10.4; L.9-10.1**
> [For the full wording of the standards, see the standards chart in the front of your textbook.]

Writing

© Task 1: Literature [RL.9-10.3; W.9-10.9.a]
Analyze the Development of a Complex Character

From this unit, choose a story that has characters with many or conflicting motivations. Write an essay analyzing the development of one of these complex characters.

- Identify the character you will analyze, and explain why you chose to analyze him or her.
- Explain what motivates the character to behave as he or she does. Include times during which the character's motivations conflict with each other.
- Analyze changes the character undergoes as a result of his or her experiences.
- Cite evidence from the text, including well-chosen, relevant details and direct quotations, to support your analysis.
- Use conventions of standard English in your writing. Ensure that all irregular verbs in your essay are in the correct form.

© Task 2: Literature [RL.9-10.4; W.9-10.9.a]
Analyze Setting

Write an essay analyzing how descriptions in a story from this unit evoke a sense of time and place.

- Identify the time and place in which the story is set.
- Quote vivid descriptions of setting from the story, including descriptions that appeal to one or more of the five senses.

- Evaluate the significance of setting in the story. For example, you might explain whether the setting helps shape the conflicts that characters experience or the events that take place in the story.
- Use conventions of standard English in your writing. Use the active voice throughout your essay unless you have a particular reason for using the passive voice.

© Task 3: Literature [RL.9-10.2; W.9-10.9.a]
Analyze the Theme of a Story

Write an essay in which you analyze the development of the theme of a story from this unit.

- Provide a short summary of the story in which you briefly identify the main characters and describe key events in the story's plot.
- State the theme of the story, and explain whether the theme is directly stated in the story or is implied.
- Describe how the theme is first presented in the story, citing specific details to support your ideas.
- Explain how the theme is shaped and refined over the course of the story.
- Use conventions of standard English as you write. Avoid mixing verb tenses unnecessarily.

Speaking and Listening

ⓒ Task 4: Literature [RL.9-10.4, SL.9-10.1.d]
Analyze Symbolism

Deliver a speech to your class in which you analyze the meaning of one or more symbols in a story from this unit.

- From the story, select a character, place, object, or event that stands for a larger idea.

- Identify the symbol you have chosen, and explain your interpretation of what it represents. Support your ideas with key details from the story.

- Explain whether the symbol is traditional—that is, it calls on ideas that people traditionally associate with the object or event—or whether the symbol is unique to the story.

- After you have finished your speech, encourage your classmates to ask questions and to offer their interpretations of the symbol.

- Respond thoughtfully to your classmates' interpretations, summarize points of agreement and disagreement, and make new connections in light of the reasoning they present.

ⓒ Task 5: Informational Text [RI.9-10.4; SL.9-10.4]
Analyze Word Choice

Prepare and deliver an oral presentation in which you analyze word choice in an informational text in this unit.

- Select an informational text in which word choice has a clear impact on meaning and tone. The text may be technical, historical, or reflective.

- Determine the tone, or author's attitude toward the subject, in the work. Provide examples of words and phrases that contribute to the tone.

- Analyze the specific word choices—for example, technical words, or words with specific connotations—that contribute to the meaning of the work.

- Draw a conclusion about the cumulative effect of word choice on the meaning and tone of the piece.

- Present your information clearly and in an organized way. Read portions of the text aloud to demonstrate your points.

ⓒ Task 6: Literature [RL.9-10.5; SL.9-10.1, SL.9-10.4]
Analyze the Point of View From Which a Story Is Told

Lead a small group discussion of the narrative point of view from which a story in this unit is told.

- Prepare for the discussion by identifying the story's point of view—first person, third person omniscient, or third person limited.

- Consider the effects of the narrative point of view on the story, including how it shapes readers' perceptions of the characters and whether a reader has more information or less information than the narrator or other characters have.

- Use details from the story to support your ideas about the narrative point of view.

- Prepare and pose relevant questions to the group. Involve all group members in the discussion. During the discussion, make new connections based on the points made by group members.

- To conclude your group discussion, review the main points made, as well as points of agreement and disagreement.

THE BIG ?

Can progress be made without conflict?

At the beginning of Unit 2, you participated in a discussion of the Big Question. Now that you have completed the unit, write a response to the question. Discuss how your understanding has deepened. Support your response with at least one example from literature and one example from an additional subject area or your own life. Use Big Question vocabulary words (see p. 223) in your response.

Featured Titles

In this unit, you have read a variety of short stories. Continue to read on your own. Select works that you enjoy, but challenge yourself to explore new authors and works of increasing depth and complexity. The titles suggested below will help you get started.

Literature

The Fall of the House of Usher and Other Tales
by Edgar Allan Poe

Poe's nightmarish **short stories** lead readers to the darkest experiences of the human condition—from a family confronting an ancient curse to a murderer losing his grasp on sanity.

Anton Chekhov: Selected Stories
by Anton Chekhov

Against the backdrop of Russia's bustling cities and rugged countryside, Chekhov brings vivid characters to life. This collection of renowned **short stories** shows everyday struggles portrayed with honesty and humor.

The Complete Poems of Percy Bysshe Shelley
by Percy Bysshe Shelley   EXEMPLAR TEXT ©

Shelley's collection of **poetry** explores many themes popularized by the nineteenth-century wave of writers known as The Romantics. His poems explore such topics as love, death, and nature with the type of passionate intensity for which the Romantic poets were famous.

The Prince and the Pauper
by Mark Twain
Signet, 1980

The sixteenth-century royal court and the boisterous London streets spring to life in this **novel** about a poor boy who exchanges identities with Edward Tudor, the prince of England.

The Collected Short Fiction of C. J. Cherryh
by C. J. Cherryh
Daw Books, 2008

From stories of an alien world threatened by a cooling sun to a tale of a woman cursed with unbelievable visions, this collection of **short stories** introduces readers to Cherryh's boundless imagination.

Informational Texts

Biography of an Atom
by Jacob Bronowski and
Millicent Selsam   EXEMPLAR TEXT

This **nonfiction** book by Millicent Selsam, a biologist and former science teacher, and Jacob Bronowski, an expert in both literature and science, explains atoms in a friendly, engaging way.

Up from Slavery
by Booker T. Washington
Signet, 2000

During his life, Booker T. Washington was a slave, an educator, an orator, and the founder of the Tuskegee University. In this **autobiography,** Washington tells the remarkable story of his struggles as he rose from houseboy to activist for social change.

Ancient Rome: Voyages Through Time
by Peter Ackroyd

Spanning centuries of war and conquest, this work of **historical nonfiction** brings the reader face to face with famous and infamous Roman rulers, along with the architectural marvels of their age—aqueducts, amphitheaters, spectacular temples, and the Circus Maximus.

Preparing to Read Complex Texts

Attentive Reading As you read literature on your own, bring your imagination and questions to the text. The questions shown below and others that you ask as you read will help you learn and enjoy literature even more.

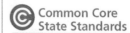
**Common Core
State Standards**

Reading Literature/Informational Text 10. By the end of Grade 10, read and comprehend literature, including stories, dramas, poems, and literary nonfiction at the high end of the grades 9–10 text complexity band independently and proficiently.

When reading short stories, ask yourself...

- Who is narrating the story? Is this voice part of the story or an outside observer?

- Do I find the narrator's voice interesting and engaging? Why or why not?

- Who is the story's main character? Is he or she interesting to me? Why or why not?

- Which characters do I like or admire? Which do I dislike? How do my reactions to the characters make me feel about the story as a whole?

- Is the setting of the story—the place, time, and society—believable and interesting? Why or why not?

- What does the story mean to me? Does it convey a theme or insight that I find important and true? Why or why not?

Key Ideas and Details

- What aspects of the story grab my attention right away? Which fail to grab my attention?

- Do I find anything about the story confusing? Do my questions get answered? Why or why not?

- Is there anything different or unusual in the way the story is structured? Do I find that structure interesting or distracting?

- Are there any passages or details that I find especially strong or beautiful?

- Do I understand why characters act and feel as they do? Do their thoughts and actions seem real? Why or why not?

- What questions do I have about characters and events?

Craft and Structure

- Does the story remind me of others I have read? If so, how?

- Have I gained new knowledge from reading this story? If so, what have I learned?

- Would I recommend this story to others? If so, to whom?

- Would I like to read other stories by this author? Why or why not?

Integration of Ideas

What kind of *knowledge* changes our lives?

Types of Nonfiction

PHLit
Online!
www.PHLitOnline.com

Hear It!
- Selection summary audio
- Selection audio
- BQ Tunes

See It!
- Author videos
- Big Question video
- Get Connected videos
- Background videos
- More about the authors
- Illustrated vocabulary words
- Vocabulary flashcards

Do It!
- Interactive journals
- Interactive graphic organizers
- Grammar tutorials
- Interactive vocabulary games
- Test practice

What kind of *knowledge* changes our lives?

Knowledge is a mastering of a body of facts or a range of information about a topic. As you learn, you may also develop **insight** into a problem or arrive at a deeper awareness and understanding of the world around you. You gain knowledge when you leave ignorance behind, question old attitudes, and revise ideas that are outdated or wrong. While not all information may cause a noticeable difference in your life, some knowledge—such as information that makes you think about people and important issues—can change your life and influence your actions

Exploring the Big Question

Collaboration: Group Discussion Start thinking about the Big Question by considering the different types of knowledge people gain throughout their lives. List the people, ideas, and subjects about which you have gained important knowledge. Describe one specific example of each of the following categories:

- discovering something new about a person that caused you to view that person differently
- a time you put a new skill to use
- an incident in history you studied that changed the way people live
- an essay or a book that altered how you view the world
- a problem or conflict that made you take action

   Share your examples with others in a small group. Participate effectively in the group discussion by building on teammates' ideas and by presenting your own relevant ideas clearly and persuasively.

Connecting to the Literature Each reading in this unit will give you insight into the Big Question.

PHLit Online!
www.PHLitOnline.com

- Big Question video
- Illustrated vocabulary words
- Interactive vocabulary games
- BQ Tunes

Learning Big Question Vocabulary

Common Core State Standards

Speaking and Listening
1. Initiate and participate effectively in a range of collaborative discussions with diverse partners on grades 9–10 topics, texts, and issues, building on others' ideas and expressing their own clearly and persuasively.

Language
6. Acquire and use accurately general academic and domain-specific words and phrases, sufficient for reading, writing, speaking, and listening at the college and career readiness level; demonstrate independence in gathering vocabulary knowledge when considering a word or phrase important to comprehension or expression.

Acquire and Use Academic Vocabulary Academic vocabulary is the language you encounter in textbooks and on standardized tests. Review the definitions of these academic vocabulary words.

adapt (ə dapt´) *v.* change or adjust	**insight** (in´ sīt´) *n.* a clear idea about the true nature of something
awareness (ə wer´ nis) *n.* having knowledge	**modified** (mäd´ ə fīd´) *v.* changed or altered slightly
evolve (ē välv´, -vôlv´) *v.* develop through gradual changes	**revise** (ri vīz´) *v.* reconsider and modify

Use these words as you complete Big Question activities in this unit that involve reading, writing, speaking, and listening.

Gather Vocabulary Knowledge Additional Big Question words are listed below. Categorize the words by deciding whether you know each one well, know it a little bit, or do not know it at all.

empathy	history	question
enlighten	ignorance	reflect
growth	influence	understanding

Then, do the following:

1. Write the definitions of the words you know.

2. Using a print or an online dictionary, look up the meanings of the words you do not know. Then, write the meanings.

3. If you think you know a word's meaning but are not certain, write your idea of the word's definition. Consult a dictionary to confirm the word's meaning. Revise your definition if necessary.

4. If a word sounds familiar but you do not know its meaning, consult a dictionary. Then, record the meaning.

5. Use all of the words in a brief paragraph about knowledge.

Elements of Essays and Speeches

Essays and speeches express an author's point of view about a single topic.

An **essay** is a short nonfiction work that conveys a central idea or key concept about a specific topic. It also expresses its author's **point of view,** or perspective, on the topic.

A **speech** is a nonfiction work that a speaker delivers to an audience. Like an essay, a speech usually presents a central idea and expresses the speaker's point of view on a topic.

Whether an author is writing an essay or a speech, he or she always has a **purpose,** or reason, for writing. A writer chooses details to include in an essay or speech based on his or her purpose. For example, a writer who wishes to warn of the dangers of pollution might include facts about its impact on health. Certain types of writing lend themselves to specific purposes:

- Expository writing **informs or explains.**
- Argumentative writing **persuades,** or convinces readers to believe or to do something.
- Narrative writing **entertains** by telling a story.

An author may have more than one purpose in a single work. For example, he or she might inform by telling an entertaining story about a topic. Usually, however, an author has one overriding purpose.

Effective essays and speeches employ the following elements in ways that suit the material, the circumstances of the writing, and the audience.

Elements of Essays and Speeches

Element	Definition
Author's Purpose	The author's main reason for writing
Central Idea	The author's main, or central, point
Point of View	The author's overall stance on the subject; an author's point of view reflects his or her beliefs, experiences, and values.
Structure	The organizational pattern the author uses to develop and present his or her ideas
Style	The author's distinct approach to writing. Stylistic elements include the author's **syntax** (sentence structure, length and variety) and **diction** (word choice).
Rhetorical Devices	Patterns of word choice, syntax, and meaning used to emphasize ideas, including *parallelism*, the use of similar grammatical structures to express related ideas
Tone	The author's emotional attitude toward his or her subject and audience.

Types of Essays

Essays are often categorized by their general purposes.

- An **expository essay** explains a topic by providing information about it or by exploring an idea related to it.

- A **persuasive essay, or argument,** attempts to convince readers to accept the writer's point of view on an issue or to take a particular course of action.

- A **reflective essay** presents experiences that inspired the writer's thoughts or feelings about a topic.

- A **narrative essay** tells the story of real events or experiences.

- A **descriptive essay** provides specific details to create an impression of a person, an object, or an experience.

An author may combine elements of different types of essays in order to fulfill a purpose. For example, in an argumentative essay persuading readers to exercise, an author might narrate a story about personal experiences with an exercise program.

Types of Speeches

When developing a speech, a writer must consider several factors: his or her purpose for writing, the occasion or event at which the speech will be delivered, and the audience. Imagine, for example, the differences between a speech for a school graduation ceremony and a speech for a surprise birthday party. The chart below shows possible occasions and audiences for several common types of speeches.

In This Section

Elements of Essays and Speeches

Analyzing the Development of Ideas

Close Read: Development of Ideas
- Model Text
- Practice Text

After You Read

 Common Core State Standards

RI.9-10.3, RI.9-10.4, RI.9-10.5, RI.9-10.6, RI.9-10.9

[For the full wording of the standards, see the standards chart in the front of your textbook.]

Type of Speech	Possible Occasion and Audience
Address: a formal, prepared speech that is usually delivered by someone of importance	A graduation speech, delivered by a principal to an audience of parents, faculty, staff, and students
Lecture: a prepared, often formal speech that informs or instructs an audience	A speech explaining a medical discovery, delivered by a scientist to doctors at a medical convention
Talk: an informal speech delivered in a conversational style	A report on a fundraiser, delivered by a student to other members of a volunteer club
Sermon: a prepared, often formal speech intended to teach or inspire	A speech about a religious figure, delivered by a pastor to the congregation of a church
Presentation: a prepared speech about a topic; may include visual aids	A multimedia presentation about a historical event, delivered by a student to a history class
Extemporaneous Speech: a speech delivered without preparation, usually in a conversational style	A toast at a wedding, delivered by a wedding guest to the bride and groom

Analyzing the Development of Ideas

Writers use a variety of techniques to **develop and support** the central ideas in their essays and speeches.

> **© Common Core State Standards**
>
> **Reading Informational Text**
> **3.** Analyze how the author unfolds an analysis or series of ideas or events, including the order in which the points are made, how they are introduced and developed, and the connections that are drawn between them.
> **5.** Analyze in detail how an author's ideas or claims are developed and refined by particular sentences, paragraphs, or larger portions of a text.

A writer will employ several different elements to fulfill his or her purpose and to develop the key ideas in an essay or speech. These elements include *support* for his or her claims; a specific *organizational structure; rhetorical devices; imagery and figurative language;* and effective *word choice.*

Types of Support Supporting a claim means giving readers valid reasons to believe it is true. Here are some types of support:

- **Facts,** or statements that can be proved true
- **Statistics,** or numerical data that presents important information on a subject
- **Descriptions,** or details that tell what something looks like, sounds like, and so on
- **Examples,** or specific cases that illustrate an idea
- **Reasons,** or statements that justify or explain a belief
- **Expert opinions,** or statements made by people who have special knowledge of a topic

The methods an author uses to support a claim depend upon his or her purpose and audience. Notice, for example, how the author relies on description in this persuasive speech to potential vacationers.

> **Example: Leave Winter Behind!**
> Take off those heavy boots and warm your feet on a soft, sandy beach. Listen to the call of the gulls as you gaze at aqua waves lapping a golden shore.

Organization of Ideas Authors organize ideas to emphasize the connections among them. In an effective essay or speech, key ideas are introduced, developed, and refined at all levels of the work. For example, a work may be divided into **sections** that introduce central ideas. **Paragraphs** develop and support those ideas, and **sentences** within the paragraphs present supporting details and connect one idea to another.

An author chooses the overall organizational structure that best fits his or her topic. In a long work, an author may employ several different methods of organization. The following are some common organizational patterns.

> **Example**
> **Organizational Structures**
>
> - **Chronological order** presents events in the order in which they happen.
> - **Spatial order** presents details from left to right, bottom to top, near to far, and so on.
> - **List organization** presents connected details consecutively or sorts them into categories.
> - **Comparison-and-contrast organization** groups ideas according to their similarities and differences.
> - **Cause-and-effect organization** shows how one event causes another.
> - **Problem-and-solution organization** identifies a problem, then presents ways to solve it.

Rhetorical Devices Rhetorical devices are language techniques that an author uses to support and emphasize central ideas, create rhythm, and make a work memorable. Although rhetorical devices by themselves are not sufficient to support a claim, they add force and appeal to a writer's work and aid readers in grasping, retaining, and accepting a writer's ideas. Some common rhetorical devices are listed below.

- **Repetition** is the reuse of a key word, phrase, or idea.

> **Example:** We will play with pride. We will play with sportsmanship. We will play to win.

- **Parallel structure** is the use of similar grammatical structures to express related ideas.

> **Example:** They will walk out of the darkness, into the light, beyond limitations.

- **Restatement** is the expression of the same idea in different words to strengthen a point.

> **Example:** We won't give up. Quitting is not an option.

- **Rhetorical questions** are inquiries that have obvious answers and that are asked for effect.

> **Example:** Do you really need to talk on your cell phone while you drive? Can't that call wait?

- **Analogies** are comparisons that show similarities between things that are otherwise not alike.

> **Example:** Our belief in this mission is a fire that keeps us warm.

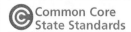

Common Core State Standards

Reading Informational Text
4. Determine the meaning of words and phrases as they are used in a text, including figurative, connotative, and technical meanings; analyze the cumulative impact of specific word choices on meaning and tone.

Imagery and Figurative Language In addition to rhetorical devices, authors use other creative methods to invigorate their writing. **Imagery** includes vivid details that appeal to the five senses of sight, sound, touch, taste, and smell. **Figurative language** is writing or speech that is not meant to be interpreted literally. It includes **figures of speech** that make unexpected comparisons or describe and explain in fresh, imaginative ways. Three common figures of speech are simile, metaphor, and personification.

- A **simile** is an indirect comparison that contains the word *like* or *as*: *My little brother is as annoying and tenacious as a swarm of mosquitoes.*

- A **metaphor** describes one thing as if it were another: *Each day is a gift.*

- **Personification** assigns human characteristics to a nonhuman subject: *The old car coughed, wheezed, and refused to move.*

Tone and Word Choice The tone of an essay or speech is the author's attitude toward his or her subject and audience. An author's tone may be formal or informal, ironic, amused, angry, sarcastic, or anything in between. Tone is revealed through an author's choice of words as well as the devices he or she uses. The **connotations,** or emotional associations, of words play a key part in creating tone.

> **Example: Humorous Essay**
> Finally, I finished writing my first draft. I admit it was a little rough. Well, maybe more than a little rough. To be honest, it was so rough you could sand wood with it.

Close Read: Development of Ideas

Analyzing literary nonfiction involves determining the author's point of view and evaluating the development of ideas within a work.

Writers of essays and speeches develop their ideas in ways that will fulfill their purpose and present their point of view. When you analyze a work, consider how the author introduces and supports a central idea. Identify the order in which ideas are presented, and note the logical connections among them. Finally, think about the elements the author uses to express ideas effectively, such as rhetorical devices and figures of speech, and consider how they work together to express meaning and create a tone. To guide you in your analysis, use the following questions:

Questions to Ask About Development of Ideas

Central Idea and Point of View
- What key point does the writer want me to understand?
- Where does the writer first introduce the point?
- What point of view, or position, does the author express in the central idea?
- What beliefs, values, or experiences are reflected in that point of view?

Methods of Development
- How does the author introduce and support the central idea or ideas?
- Does the author develop ideas in a way that strengthens his or her claims?
- Does the author provide enough support? If not, what ideas are unsupported?
- Is the support logical and convincing?

Organizational Structure
- What is the overall structure of the work?
- In what order are supporting details presented?
- What connections does the author make among the key ideas in the work?

Rhetorical Devices
- What rhetorical devices does the author use?
- Do these devices strengthen the author's arguments? Why or why not?
- Do these devices create emphasis or stir emotion? If so, how?

Imagery and Figurative Language
- Does the work contain vivid descriptions appealing to one or more of the five senses?
- Does the author make comparisons by using similes or metaphors?
- Does the author use personification to make a point?
- What are the effects of the figurative language in the work?

Tone and Word Choice
- Does the author use formal or informal language?
- What adjective or adjectives would you use to describe the author's tone?
- Does the tone fit the occasion? Does the tone support the author's purpose? How?

Model

About the Text When U.S. President Ronald Reagan addressed the students and faculty of Moscow State University in 1988, he stood before a "new" Soviet Union. The October Revolution of 1917 had helped establish the Soviet Union as a communist society, with a centrally planned economy and tight limits on freedom of speech and assembly. Now, led by Mikhail Gorbachev, the Soviets moved toward economic reform, including private ownership of some businesses, as well as expanded social freedoms.

Although reforms were taking root, President Reagan and other Western leaders pressed for faster, more comprehensive change.

Common Core
State Standards

Reading Informational Text
9. Analyze seminal U.S. documents of historical and literary significance, including how they address related themes and concepts.

from Address to Students at Moscow State University
by Ronald Reagan

But progress is not foreordained. The key is freedom—freedom of thought, freedom of information, freedom of communication. The renowned scientist, scholar, and founding father of this university, Mikhail Lomonosov, knew that. "It is common knowledge," he said, "that the achievements of science are considerable and rapid, particularly once the yoke of slavery is cast off and replaced by the freedom of philosophy." […]

The explorers of the modern era are the entrepreneurs, men with vision, with the courage to take risks and faith enough to brave the unknown. These entrepreneurs and their small enterprises are responsible for almost all the economic growth in the United States. They are the prime movers of the technological revolution. In fact, one of the largest personal computer firms in the United States was started by two college students, no older than you, in the garage behind their home. Some people, even in my own country, look at the riot of experiment that is the free market and see only waste. What of all the entrepreneurs that fail? Well, many do, particularly the successful ones; often several times. And if you ask them the secret of their success, they'll tell you it's all that they learned in their struggles along the way; yes, it's what they learned from failing. Like an athlete in competition or a scholar in pursuit of the truth, experience is the greatest teacher. […]

We are seeing the power of economic freedom spreading around the world. Places such as the Republic of Korea, Singapore, Taiwan have vaulted into the technological era, barely pausing in the industrial age along the way. Low-tax agricultural policies in the subcontinent mean that in some years India is now a net exporter of food. Perhaps most exciting are the winds of change that are

Point of View Here, Reagan expresses his central idea: that freedom is the key to progress. In doing so, he also reveals his point of view.

Methods of Development Reagan supports his central idea by connecting it to the related idea that freedom allows people to start businesses, which spurs economic growth.

Figurative Language Reagan uses similes to add emphasis and interest to his speech.

© EXEMPLAR TEXT

Model continued

blowing over the People's Republic of China, where one-quarter of the world's population is now getting its first taste of economic freedom. At the same time, the growth of democracy has become one of the most powerful political movements of our age. In Latin America in the 1970s, only a third of the population lived under democratic government; today over 90 percent does. In the Philippines, in the Republic of Korea, free, contested, democratic elections are the order of the day. Throughout the world, free markets are the model for growth. Democracy is the standard by which governments are measured.

We Americans make no secret of our belief in freedom. In fact, it's something of a national pastime. Every 4 years the American people choose a new president, and 1988 is one of those years. At one point there were 13 major candidates running in the two major parties, not to mention all the others, including the Socialist and Libertarian candidates—all trying to get my job. About 1,000 local television stations, 8,500 radio stations, and 1,700 daily newspapers—each one an independent, private enterprise, fiercely independent of the Government—report on the candidates, grill them in interviews, and bring them together for debates. In the end, the people vote; they decide who will be the next president. But freedom doesn't begin or end with elections.

Go to any American town, to take just an example, and you'll see dozens of churches, representing many different beliefs—in many places, synagogues and mosques—and you'll see families of every conceivable nationality worshiping together. Go into any schoolroom, and there you will see children being taught the Declaration of Independence, that they are endowed by their Creator with certain unalienable rights—among them life, liberty, and the pursuit of happiness—that no government can justly deny; the guarantees in their Constitution for freedom of speech, freedom of assembly, and freedom of religion. Go into any courtroom, and there will preside an independent judge, beholden to no government power. There every defendant has the right to a trial by a jury of his peers, usually 12 men and women—common citizens; they are the ones, the only ones, who weigh the evidence and decide on guilt or innocence. In that court, the accused is innocent until proven guilty, and the word of a policeman or any official has no greater legal standing than the word of the accused. Go to any university campus, and there you'll find an open, sometimes heated discussion of the problems in American society and what can be done to correct them. Turn on the television, and you'll see the legislature conducting the business of government right there before the camera, debating and voting on the legislation that will become the law of the land. March in any demonstration, and there are many of them; the people's right of assembly is guaranteed in the Constitution and protected by the police. Go into any union hall, where the members know their right to strike is protected by law. [...]

Methods of Development Reagan uses facts, statistics, and examples to support the key idea that Americans have the freedom to choose their presidents.

Tone and Word Choice Reagan uses simple, everyday language and sounds sincere, patriotic, and most importantly, believable.

Rhetorical Devices By using repetition and parallelism, Reagan emphasizes his key point that it is easy to find examples of the benefits of freedom.

But freedom is more even than this. Freedom is the right to question and change the established way of doing things. It is the continuing revolution of the marketplace. It is the understanding that allows us to recognize shortcomings and seek solutions. It is the right to put forth an idea, scoffed at by the experts, and watch it catch fire among the people. It is the right to dream—to follow your dream or stick to your conscience, even if you're the only one in a sea of doubters. Freedom is the recognition that no single person, no single authority or government has a monopoly on the truth, but that every individual life is infinitely precious, that every one of us put on this world has been put there for a reason and has something to offer. [. . .]

Your generation is living in one of the most exciting, hopeful times in Soviet history. It is a time when the first breath of freedom stirs the air and the heart beats to the accelerated rhythm of hope, when the accumulated spiritual energies of a long silence yearn to break free. I am reminded of the famous passage near the end of Gogol's[1] *Dead Souls.* Comparing his nation to a speeding troika,[2] Gogol asks what will be its destination. But he writes, "There was no answer save the bell pouring forth marvelous sound."

We do not know what the conclusion will be of this journey, but we're hopeful that the promise of reform will be fulfilled. In this Moscow spring, this May 1988, we may be allowed that hope: that freedom, like the fresh green sapling planted over Tolstoy's[3] grave, will blossom forth at last in the rich fertile soil of your people and culture. We may be allowed to hope that the marvelous sound of a new openness will keep rising through, ringing through, leading to a new world of reconciliation, friendship, and peace. [. . .]

Organizational Structure This section brings listeners full circle. Through rhetorical devices and memorable examples, Reagan sums up and explains the significance of his central idea.

Figurative Language Reagan ends his speech with a powerful appeal to his listeners, framed in figurative language: a comparison between freedom in Russia and a young tree.

1. **Gogol's** (gô′ gôlz) reference to Nikolai (nē′ kô lī′) Gogol (1809–1852), famous Russian novelist.
2. **troika** (troi′ kə) a Russian sled or carriage drawn by three horses.
3. **Tolstoy's** (täl′ stoiz′) reference to Leo Tolstoy (1828–1910), famous Russian novelist and thinker.

Independent Practice

About the Selection The dangers of high-altitude mountain climbing are severe. Many climbers fall sick or even die from illnesses caused by reduced oxygen. Others freeze or plummet to their deaths. Despite these risks, Erik Weihenmayer, a blind climber, had successfully reached the summits of five of the world's highest peaks by 1999. In that year, when Pasquale "PV" Scaturro, a geophysicist and expert climber, suggested an expedition to the top of Mount Everest, Weihenmayer readily agreed. He arranged sponsorship from the National Federation of the Blind and, with Scaturro, organized the expedition. The other members of the team included Sherm Bull and his son Brad; Ang Pasang, a Sherpa who had climbed Everest twice; and Weihenmayer's longtime mountaineering buddies Eric "Erie" Alexander, Jeff Evans, Chris Morris, and Mike O'Donnell. On May 25, 2001, Weihenmayer and many of his teammates reached the top of Mount Everest. This excerpt describes the final leg of that adventure.

"Everest" from *Touch the Top of the World* by Erik Weihenmayer

We left our tents a little before 9:00 p.m. on May 24. Because of our twenty-four-hour delay and the apprehension of other expeditions to share a summit day with me, we moved across the South Col with only one other team behind us. We had no worries of the typical horde clogging the fixed lines but could direct our full focus toward the mountain. The wind was blowing so loudly through the col that I couldn't hear the bells jingling from Chris's ice axe. Chris and I expected this, so for the first two hours he clanked his metal axe against rocks he passed. Finally, we worked our way around to the mountain's leeward[1] side, where Everest itself protected us from the wind. Chris had lost his voice, so his verbal directions were sparse. At each anchor, he'd hold the new line with his hand, so I could locate it and clip in. Chris was moving in front of me at his usual rock-solid pace, and I was right on his heels. We were making unbelievable time.

As we got higher up the mountain, four distinct changes had begun to work in my favor. Earlier, in the icefall, each step was very specific, but the terrain above the South Col consisted of steep forty-five-degree snow faces a hundred yards wide, intermingled with ten-to-fifty-foot crumbly rock steps. I could stay in the kicked boot holes of Chris or kick my own steps. Where I stepped had become less important than maintaining internal balance. I could breathe, scan my ice axe, and count on the next step. The slope was often so steep that I could lean forward and feel the rock or snow steps with my gloved hands, and I had trained myself long ago to save energy by landing my feet in the same holds my hands had just left. Finally, when I needed it most, the mountain had given me a pattern.

Imagery To which of the five senses does this descriptive language appeal?

Organizational Structure In what way does this sentence indicate a possible organizational pattern?

---

1. leeward (lē´ wərd´) *adj.* away from the wind.

The thin oxygen of extreme altitude reduced us to a crawl. It was like moving through a bizarre atmosphere of syrup mixed with a narcotic. My team, struggling just to put one foot in front of the other, moved so slowly, it gave me more time to scan my axe across the snow and feel my way forward. The third equalizer was the darkness. With just a trickle of light produced by headlamps, my sighted team could only see a few feet in front of them. Bulky goggles blocked their side vision, and oxygen masks covered much of their visual field. Also, the pure oxygen trickling through their masks would flow up and freeze the lenses of their goggles so that they constantly had to remove them to wipe the lenses clean. Those brief moments when eyes are exposed to the elements, corneas will freeze, and the intense rays of the sun reflecting off the snow cause instant snow blindness. Not once did I ever have to worry about these complications.

In addition, my teammates had chosen smaller masks that rode low and tight across their cheeks and hung mostly below their chins. This allowed climbers to see better and prevented pure oxygen from seeping into their lenses, but also allowed plenty of pure oxygen to escape into the wind. I, on the other hand, had the luxury of choosing the largest mask I could find and wore it high on my face, getting the most benefit from the oxygen flow and the ambient air around the mask. I'm sure I made a freakish sight with my gigantic mask covering my goggles, like a day long ago in wrestling practice when I had put my sweatshirt on backward, with the hood covering my face, and chased the terrified freshmen around the mat. The consistent terrain, the altitude, the mask, and the darkness were great equalizers. I wouldn't go so far as to claim these gave me an advantage, but it was a matter of perspective. The mountain had gotten desperately harder for everyone else, while it had gotten slightly easier for me.

For two and a half months, all the decisions, the logistics, the backup safety plans had been implemented and executed by PV, and now, somewhere below the Balcony, the exhausting burden of leadership finally took its toll. Suddenly feeling listless and unable to catch his breath even with his oxygen bottle at full flow, PV had arduously turned back. He managed to convince Brad and Sherm, next to him, that he was strong enough to descend alone, in retrospect, a ploy that might have turned deadly, but PV's weary brain had never stopped calculating the big picture. He had refused to divert any energy from the team's summit effort. Through periodic radio checks as PV dropped altitude, I could hear his characteristically hyper voice growing flat, and just below a steep ice bulge, only an hour from Camp Four, PV sat down in the snow.

Tone and Word Choice Describe the tone of these passages, in which the author notes that his blindness helps him avoid some of the problems faced by the other climbers.

Practice continued

"I'm very tired," he said. "I don't know if I can make it. I might need some assistance." PV's one warning before we left the tent was "If you sit down, you'll stay there." So, beginning to panic, I ripped my radio out of my pocket. "Is anyone near PV who can help him down?" I asked. "Is anyone reading me?" I repeated myself several times to empty static.

Methods of Development Why does Weihenmayer provide background details about Dr. Gipe?

A few weeks earlier, Dr. Gipe had received the sad news that a close family friend had been killed in a skiing accident; a three-thousand-foot day in the Death Zone just didn't seem fair to his family, so that night, he had never left his tent. His decision was a tough one to make, but extremely fortunate for PV's sake. "This is Gipe at the South Col," finally came over the radio. "I'm strapping on my crampons right now. I'm going out to get PV." Dr. Gipe met PV about a half an hour from camp, up again and staggering slowly toward the tents.

With the first crisis of the night averted, Chris and I plodded up a steep gully, which led us to the Balcony, a flat snow platform, ten feet wide. Michael Brown arrived first at about 2:00 a.m., with Chris and me right behind. All night, the weather had remained clear, with high clouds to the southeast and distant lightning flashes illuminating the sky, but at the Balcony, our luck suddenly ran out. We walked into a blasting storm. Wind and horizontal snow raked our down suits and covered us with a layer of ice. The lightning strikes were now on top of us, exploding like a pyrotechnic[2] show. Chris later said he couldn't see his feet through the blowing snow, which stopped us short, since the southeast ridge above narrowed to fifteen feet wide. Mike O.'s and Didrik's headlamps had simultaneously flickered out, and one of Didrik's crampons had popped off. "Someone come and help us," Mike yelled over the radio. Charley headed back and found them sitting in the snow only twenty feet away.

Tone and Word Choice How would you describe the tone at this point? Identify two words that help to create this tone, and explain the connotations, or emotional associations, of each.

Chris and I huddled together in the wind, waiting for the others to arrive. "What do you think, Big E?" he asked. "It's lookin' pretty grim." When the others trickled in, Sherm wanted to go on; Charley wanted to turn back, and Erie thought we should wait. For forty-five minutes, we waited, periodic arguments breaking out whether to go on or descend. I was beginning to shiver and forced myself to bounce up and down, and to windmill my arms. We were so close, and I was feeling strong. Turning back was a crushing proposition, but I also wasn't willing to go bullheadedly forward and throw my life away. My mind was starting to settle on the possibility of turning back, when Kevin's voice from Base Camp crackled over my radio. Throughout the expedition, Kevin had been learning to read the satellite weather reports we received every few days over the Internet. From the weather map, it appeared the storm was moving rapidly to the northeast toward Bhutan, and where we

---

2. **pyrotechnic** (pī′ rə tek′ nik) *adj.* of or pertaining to fireworks; here, brilliant; dazzling.

stood on the Balcony, we were directly northeast of Base Camp. "Hey you guys, don't quit yet," his voice sounded urgent. "The storm's cleared down here. It just might pass over you."

"Weather is also clearing here," Kami said from Camp Two below. Chris glanced over at me. Beyond my right hip, shining through the storm clouds, he could see a star. "Let's see if this thing breaks up," he said. Sherm must have felt good tidings, too, because he pushed on. Chris and I followed.

Following the narrow exposed southeast shoulder, I felt the first warmth of the sun about 4:00 a.m.; so high up, no other mountain blocked the sunrise. The weather had thankfully turned spectacular.

Still hours below the South Summit, we were stalled out again. The fixed lines, running up the steepest slope yet, had been frozen over by a hard windswept crust of snow. Jeff and Brad moved ahead, pulling the lines free, an exhausting job at twenty-eight thousand feet. The job was quickly wearing Jeff down, but he said later that with each gasping breath as he heaved the rope free, he envisioned the two of us standing on top together. Soon he was beginning to feel faint and dizzy. As he knelt in the snow, Brad, behind him, examined his oxygen equipment and assessed that his regulator, connecting the long tube of his mask to his bottle, had malfunctioned. The internal valves responsible for regulating flow were notoriously prone to freezing shut. "Who's got an extra regulator?" Brad called out over the radio, but tired bodies and brains could not recall who had thrown in the extras in the presummit shuffle. "My day's finished if I can't find the extra," Jeff yelled testily.

It may not have been PV's time to summit, but he wasn't through benefiting the team. "Calm down," he advised, lying weakly on his back in his tent. "Everyone take a deep breath. Ang Pasang and Sherm are carrying the extra regulators." Luckily, Ang Pasang was only a hundred feet behind. Together, Brad and Ang Pasang screwed on Jeff's new regulator.

By 8:00 a.m., we had struggled on to the South Summit, 28,700 feet. After a short rest, Chris took off for the summit, cranking it into "Morris gear," and Luis took over in front of me. From the South Summit, the true summit is still at least two hours away across the three-hundred-foot-long knife-edge ridge, up the fifty-foot vertical Hillary Step, and finally traversing up a long slightly broader ridge to the summit.

Jeff, exhausted from his two-hour struggle pulling lines, stopped short in front of me. "I'm wasted. I've gotta go down," he said reluctantly. "This'll have to be my summit."

Central Idea Why are these details significant?

Organizational Structure What organizational structure is Weihenmayer using in this passage?

Practice continued

Tone and Word Choice What are two adjectives that describe the author's tone in this passage? Citing specific examples, explain how he uses the connotative meaning of words to create this tone.

Methods of Development What key idea is developed and supported by this anecdote?

For a moment I wanted to goad him on the way we had done each other on winter training climbs of Colorado fourteeners. "If you wanna turn back, just say the word," we'd jab. "Of course, I'll have to tell everyone you were a whiney little crybaby." But 28,700 feet above sea level wasn't the place to motivate with bravado or ego, so assessing that he was strong enough to get down, I rested a hand on Jeff's shoulder and wished him a safe descent. Jeff had been with me from the beginning, practically introducing me to the mountains. He had shown extraordinary patience as I stumbled along experimenting with brand-new trekking poles. We had even stood together on the summit of Denali[3] and El Capitan,[4] so I knew that reaching the summit of Mt. Everest without him wouldn't feel complete. Suddenly, a wave of heavy exhaustion passed over me, and I felt weary and crumpled. "Maybe I'll go down too," I readied my lips to say, but then Luis was crunching through the snow in front of me, and I forced myself to revive.

Down-climbing the twenty-foot vertical snow face on the backside of the South Summit leading onto the knife-edge ridge went against my survival instinct. The ridge is the width of a picnic table and always heavily corniced[5] with snow. To the left is an eight-thousand-foot drop into Nepal, and on the right, a twelve-thousand-foot drop into Tibet. PV had told me that while crossing the ridge on his 1998 attempt, he had driven his ice axe into the snow and, after withdrawing it, had stared through the small hole into the early morning light of Tibet. In 1995, on Brad's second attempt, a climber in front of him had taken his first step onto the ridge just before the entire right half of it dropped away. The climber jumped back to safety, but a second later he would have ridden the cornice into Tibet. This year, the ridge was drier and more stable. Frozen boot steps traversed along the lefthand side. I'd scan my pole until it dropped into a boot mark, then cautiously lower my foot. I knew I couldn't make a mistake here: six hard steady breaths, another solid step, and a relaxed, focused mind like clear water.

Climbing the Hillary Step, I felt I was in my element, feeling the rock under my gloves. I stuck the crampon points of my right foot tenuously into a tiny crack and the left points into a cornice of snow, slid my ascender as high as it would go on the rope, and stood up and quickly reached for the next knob of rock. At the top, I awkwardly belly-flopped onto a flat ledge, slowly pulled myself to my feet, and began traversing the last slope to the summit. For forty minutes I trudged upward. My heavy sluggish muscles felt as if they were pushing through wet cement. With each step closer, the real possibility of standing on

---

3. **Denali** (di nä´ lē) name of the National Park in which Mt. McKinley is located.
4. **El Capitan** (el´ ka´ pē tan´) a peak in the Sierra Nevada mountain range in the Yosemite Valley of central California.
5. **corniced** (kôr´ nist) *adj.* in architecture, having a projecting decorative strip atop a wall or building; here, characterized by overhanging masses of snow or ice.

top began to trickle through my focused brain. I had speculated success in a conceptual way and as a way to motivate myself when I was down, but it was dangerous to believe it as a fact. A team could be turned back for so many reasons at any time. Just keep moving, I thought. You're not there yet.

Then a body moved down the slope toward me and I felt thin wiry arms beneath a puffy down suit wrapping around me. "Big E!" The voice rasped, so hollow and wispy, I had trouble recognizing it as Chris. His voice tried to say more, but his quaking words dissipated in the wind. Then he leaned in against my ear. "Big E"—his voice gave way to tears, then struggled out in an immense effort— "you're about to stand on top of the world." Then he quickly let go and hurriedly moved down the slope.

Luis and I linked our arms, and in a few steps, the earth flattened and the massive sky closed around me on all sides. "This is Erik, Luis, and Ang Pasang," I said over the radio. "We're on the top. I can't believe it; we're on the top."

"You're the best, Big E!" Kevin yelled from Base Camp. "I love you guys." I could hear the entire Base Camp crew cheering behind him.

"You're the strongest man in the world," PV said.

I turned around, surprised to hear more crampons moving up behind me. "I wasn't gonna let you stand on top and hear about it the rest of my life," Jeff said, with a little pep left in his voice. One of the greatest joys of my summit was that Jeff hadn't turned back at all. From the South Summit, he had watched us down-climb onto the knife-edge ridge and move toward the Hillary Step. Later he told me, "I simply had to follow." Behind Jeff came Erie, Michael B., Didrik, Charley, and Mike O. Sherm had been the first on the team to summit, becoming the oldest man in history to stand on the top of the world, but better than his record was the fact that his son, Brad, had stepped onto the summit right behind him. Nineteen team members made it to the summit: eleven Westerners and eight Sherpas, the most from one team to reach the top in a single day. So it was a crowded summit as we all stood together, hugging and crying on a snow platform the size of a single-car garage.

Another storm was rolling in from the north. "Weather's changing fast," PV called up on the radio. "You guys need to go down immediately." I turned to head down with Erie, when Jeff said, "Wait a second, Big E. You'll only be here once in your life. Look around. Think about where you are and what you've done." So I suspended my nerves for a moment, reached down and touched the

Rhetorical Devices
What emotion is conveyed through the repetition in these sentences?

Practice continued

snow through my gloved hand, listened to the Sherpa prayer flags flapping in the wind, and heard the infinite sound of space around me, as on my first rock climb. After I had gone blind almost twenty years ago, I would have been proud to find the bathroom, so I said a quick prayer and thanked God for giving me so much. Then it was time to go down.

We descended through heavy snowfall but, thankfully, little wind. Erie took over guiding me, down the Hillary Step, across the knife edge, and contrary to his fears that he wouldn't be strong enough to make the top, he was stronger and more lucid on the way down from Everest's summit than most were on the top of a peak in Colorado. Reaching our tents at about 3:00 p.m., I hugged Erie. "Today," I said, "you were my guardian angel. I'm glad you're here."

That night, Kevin radioed up to report that he had called Ellie on the sat phone with the news. "She screamed loud enough to break the neighbors' windows." He laughed. The next days were exhausting as we fought our way through the screaming wind of the South Col, down the Lhotse Face—where my rubbery legs refused to obey my brain—and finally one last trip through the icefall. At the bottom, in Superman's Palace, of course, the whole team was waiting, and the party lasted long after the sun had sunk below Pumori.

Point of View What is the author's point of view regarding his critics?

Despite our success, plenty of detractors voiced their opinions on Internet chat rooms and in letters to the editor. I've heard all the ridiculous assumptions.

"Now that a blind guy's climbed it, everyone's going to want to climb it. They're going to think it's easy. People will probably get hurt."

"Why are people thinking this is such a big deal? Anyone can be short-roped to the top by nineteen seeing-eye guides."

My teammates constantly come to my rescue with carefully crafted comebacks like "Before you start spouting a bunch of lies over a public forum, get your facts straight, dude!"

"Don't let 'em get to you," Chris Morris said after I shared with him their comments. "You climbed every inch of that mountain, and then some."

I knew he was right. There were some who would never be convinced, others who still had no idea what to think, but many others for whom the climb forced a higher expectation of their own possibilities. I don't climb mountains to prove to anyone that blind people can do this or that. I climb for the same reason an artist paints a picture: because it brings me great joy. But I'd be lying if I didn't admit my secret satisfaction in facing those cynics and blowing through their doubts, destroying their negative stereotypes, taking their very narrow parameters of what's possible and what's not, and shattering them into a million pieces.

When those parameters are rebuilt, thousands and thousands of people will live with fewer barriers placed before them, and if my climbs can play a small role in opening doors of opportunity and hope for those who will come after us, then I am very proud of what we were able to achieve . . .

Central Idea What is the central idea of this selection?

After You Read

"Everest" *from* Touch the Top of the World

1. **Integration of Knowledge and Ideas Speculate:** Why might it matter to people around the world that a blind man climbed Mount Everest?

2. **Integration of Knowledge and Ideas (a) Identify:** Identify two challenges that the altitude presents to the climbers. **(b) Connect:** In what ways is Weihenmayer's blindness a benefit as he meets these challenges? **(c) Generalize:** Based on his experience, what statements can you make about turning negatives into positives?

3. **Key Ideas and Details Analyze:** Use a chart like the one shown to analyze decisions made by individuals or the team on Mount Everest.

4. **Key Ideas and Details (a)** How do some critics respond to Weihenmayer's success in reaching the summit of Mount Everest? **(b) Analyze:** Based on the details of Weihenmayer's climb, how would you answer those critics?

5. **Craft and Structure Analyze:** In what ways does Weihenmayer balance his own perspective with the views of others? Explain.

6. **Integration of Knowledge and Ideas (a)** What new insights and skills did Weihenmayer develop because he lost his sight? **(b) Connect:** In what ways could learning about Weihenmayer's climbing experiences change someone else's life?

Decision	Results of Decision	Importance to the Team's Success

© Leveled Texts

Build your skills and improve your comprehension of nonfiction with texts of increasing complexity.

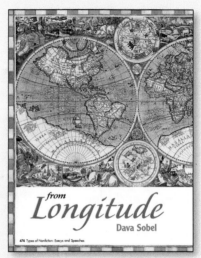

Read **"The Spider and the Wasp"** to find out how a wasp ensures the survival of its young by conquering a large and potentially deadly spider.

Read the excerpt from *Longitude* to learn how the demands of computing longitude have challenged people for hundreds of years.

© Common Core State Standards

Meet these standards with either **"The Spider and the Wasp"** (p. 464) or the excerpt from *Longitude* (p. 474).

Reading Informational Text
2. Determine a central idea of a text and analyze its development over the course of the text, including how it emerges and is shaped and refined by specific details; provide an objective summary of the text. *(Reading Skill: Main Idea)*

4. Determine the meaning of words and phrases as they are used in a text, including figurative, connotative, and technical meanings; analyze the cumulative impact of specific word choices on meaning and tone. *(Literary Analysis: Expository Essay)*

Spiral Review: RI.9-10.3
Writing
2.e. Establish and maintain a formal style and objective tone while attending to the norms and conventions of the

discipline in which they are writing. *(Writing: Business Letter)*

Speaking and Listening
4. Present information, findings, and supporting evidence clearly, concisely, and logically such that listeners can follow the line of reasoning and the organization, development, substance, and style are appropriate to purpose, audience, and task. *(Speaking and Listening: Humorous Persuasive Speech)*

Language
3. Apply knowledge of language to understand how language functions in different contexts, to make effective choices for meaning or style, and to comprehend more fully when reading or listening. *(Literary Analysis: Expository Essay; Speaking and Listening: Humorous Persuasive Speech)*

Literary Analysis: Expository Essay

An **expository essay** is a brief nonfiction work in which an author informs by explaining, defining, or interpreting an idea. Often, the writer reaches a conclusion through reasoning, or logic.

   Diction, or the author's word choice, sets one expository essay off from another. Diction may be formal, informal, sophisticated, or slangy. It may include *technical language,* such as scientific terms. The writer's word choice and sentence structure have an impact on a text's meaning and **tone**. The tone reflects the author's attitude toward his or her subject and affects the reader's perception.

Using the Strategy: Diction and Tone Chart

As you read, use a diction and tone chart like this one to find examples of the author's diction and to describe the tone it creates.

	Example of Diction	Description of Diction	Tone
"The Spider and the Wasp"	The hunter cannot exist without the hunted; if the latter should perish from the earth, the former would, too.	**Formal:** latter, former **Old-fashioned:** perish	scholarly philosophical
Longitude	Any sailor worth his salt can gauge his latitude well enough by the length of the day…	**Technical language:** gauge his latitude **Idiomatic expression:** worth his salt	not too formal friendly informative

Reading Skill: Main Idea

To fully understand an essay, **analyze main,** or **central, ideas** and **supporting details**—recognize each main point the writer makes and identify its relation to the ideas or facts that explain or illustrate it. To help you organize your thoughts, pause occasionally to summarize what you have read. When you **summarize,** you briefly restate the central ideas and key details from the text.

What kind of *knowledge* changes our lives?

Writing About the Big Question

In "The Spider and the Wasp," a spider's instinctive responses leave it vulnerable to attack by a wasp. Use this sentence starter to develop your ideas about the Big Question.

An example of a situation in which it would be important to **adapt** or **revise** a behavior based on instinct and gut reaction is _____.

While You Read Look for examples of how the spider uses information provided by its body to protect itself under normal circumstances.

Vocabulary

Read each word and its definition. Decide whether you know the word well, know it a little bit, or do not know it at all. After you read, see how your knowledge of each word has increased.

- **instinct** (in´ stiŋkt´) *n.* an inborn pattern of behavior, as opposed to a learned skill (p. 465) *As soon as they hatch, sea turtles use instinct to find their way to the sea.* *instinctive adj. instinctual adj.*

- **customarily** (kus´ tə mer´ ə lē) *adv.* usually; by habit or tradition (p. 465) *Senior citizens customarily receive discounts.* *custom n. customary adj.*

- **distinct** (di stiŋkt´) *adj.* clearly different; separate (p. 466) *There are two distinct sides to the issue.* *distinction n. distinctive adj.*

- **tactile** (tak´ təl) *adj.* related to the sense of touch (p. 467) *I enjoy the tactile sensations of stroking a rabbit's fluffy fur.* *tactility n. intact adj.*

- **formidable** (fôr´ mə də bəl) *adj.* causing fear or dread (p. 467) *He is such a formidable enemy, that few dare to cross him.* *formidably adv.*

- **evoking** (ē vōk´ iŋ) *v.* drawing forth emotions or responses (p. 468) *His experimental plays are known for evoking mixed responses from the audience.* *evocation n. evocative adj.*

Word Study

The **Latin roots -tact-** and **-tang-** mean "touch" or "feel."

This essay describes a particular kind of tarantula that has three **tactile** responses that cause it to react when touched.

Author of

The
Spider
and the
Wasp

The Russian thinker Alexander Petrunkevitch (pə trōon´ kə vich) was one of the first scientists to explore the secret world of spiders. He classified at least 274 species.

From Politics to Poetry Although Petrunkevitch spent countless hours observing spiders, he did not bury himself away from the world in science. Inspired by his father, who had been jailed for supporting democratic reforms in the Russian government, the younger Petrunkevitch was politically active. He also translated many English poems into Russian.

BACKGROUND FOR THE ESSAY

Instinct vs. Intelligence

Petrunkevitch's essay helps readers understand the distinction between instinct and intelligence. An animal's instincts cannot change, even when they lead to harm. Some animals, however, show intelligence: They learn and adjust their behavior to fit their experience.

Did You Know?
The scientific names for several spider species are based on Petrunkevitch's name.

The Spider and the Wasp

Alexander Petrunkevitch

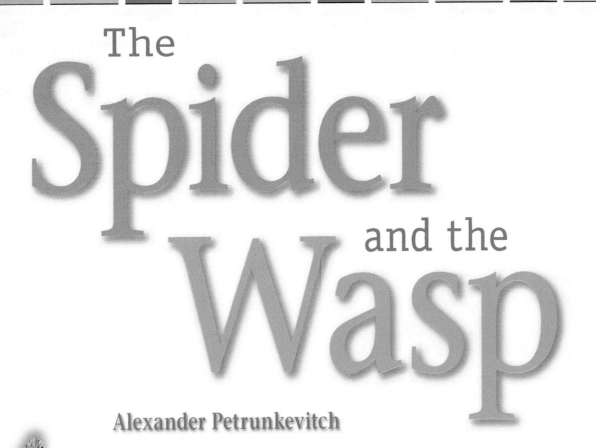

To hold its own in the struggle for existence, every species of animal must have a regular source of food, and if it happens to live on other animals, its survival may be very delicately balanced. The hunter cannot exist without the hunted; if the latter should perish from the earth, the former would, too. When the hunted also prey on some of the hunters, the matter may become complicated.

This is nowhere better illustrated than in the insect world. Think of the complexity of a situation such as the following: There is a certain wasp, *Pimpla inquisitor*, whose larvae feed on the larvae of the tussock moth. *Pimpla* larvae in turn serve as food for the larvae of a second wasp, and the latter in their turn nourish still a third wasp. What subtle balance between fertility and mortality must exist in the case of each of these four species to prevent the extinction of all of them! An excess of mortality over fertility in a single member of the group would ultimately wipe out all four.

This is not a unique case. The two great orders of insects, Hymenoptera and Diptera, are full of such examples of interrelationship. And the spiders (which are not insects but members of a separate order of arthropods) also are killers and victims of insects.

The picture is complicated by the fact that those species which are carnivorous in the larval stage have to be provided with animal food by a vegetarian mother. The survival of the young depends on the mother's correct choice of a food which she does not eat herself.

In the feeding and safeguarding of their progeny[1] the insects and spiders exhibit some interesting analogies to reasoning and some crass examples of blind instinct. The case I propose to describe here is that of the tarantula spiders and their arch-enemy, the digger wasps of the genus Pepsis. It is a classic example of what looks like intelligence pitted against instinct—a strange situation in which the victim, though fully able to defend itself, submits unwittingly to its destruction.

Most tarantulas live in the tropics, but several species occur in the temperate zone and a few are common in the southern U.S. Some varieties are large and have powerful fangs with which they can inflict a deep wound. These formidable-looking spiders do not, however, attack man; you can hold one in your hand, if you are gentle, without being bitten. Their bite is dangerous only to insects and small mammals such as mice; for a man it is no worse than a hornet's sting.

Tarantulas customarily live in deep cylindrical burrows, from which they emerge at dusk and into which they retire at dawn. Mature males wander about after dark in search of females and occasionally stray into houses. After mating, the male dies in a few weeks, but a female lives much longer and can mate several years in succession. In a Paris museum is a tropical specimen which is said to have been living in captivity for 25 years.

---

1. **progeny** (präj´ ə nē) *n.* offspring; young.

A fertilized female tarantula lays from 200 to 400 eggs at a time; thus it is possible for a single tarantula to produce several thousand young. She takes no care of them beyond weaving a cocoon of silk to enclose the eggs. After they hatch, the young walk away, find convenient places in which to dig their burrows and spend the rest of their lives in solitude. Tarantulas feed mostly on insects and millipedes. Once their appetite is appeased, they digest the food for several days before eating again. Their sight is poor, being limited to sensing a change in the intensity of light and to the perception of moving objects. They apparently have little or no sense of hearing, for a hungry tarantula will pay no attention to a loudly chirping cricket placed in its cage unless the insect happens to touch one of its legs.

But all spiders, and especially hairy ones, have an extremely delicate sense of touch. Laboratory experiments prove that tarantulas can distinguish three types of touch: pressure against the body wall, stroking of the body hair, and riffling of certain very fine hairs on the legs called trichobothria.[2] Pressure against the body, by a finger or the end of a pencil, causes the tarantula to move off slowly for a short distance. The touch excites no defensive response unless the approach is from above where the spider can see the motion, in which case it rises on its hind legs, lifts its front legs, opens its fangs and holds this threatening posture as long as the object continues to move. When the motion stops, the spider drops back to the ground, remains quiet for a few seconds and then moves slowly away.

The entire body of a tarantula, especially its legs, is thickly clothed with hair. Some of it is short and woolly, some long and stiff. Touching this body hair produces one of two distinct reactions. When the spider is hungry, it responds with an immediate and swift attack. At the touch of a cricket's antennae the tarantula seizes the insect so swiftly that a motion picture taken at the rate of 64 frames per second shows only the result and not the process of capture. But when the spider is not hungry, the stimulation of its hairs merely causes it to shake the touched limb. An insect can walk under its hairy belly unharmed.

The trichobothria, very fine hairs growing from disklike membranes on the legs, were once thought to be the spider's hearing organs, but we now know that they have nothing to do with sound.

---

2. **trichobothria** (trik´ ə bäth´ rē ə)

Spiral Review
Series of Ideas
Explain how the ideas stated in this paragraph connect to those expressed in the paragraphs that immediately precede and follow it.

> But all spiders, and especially hairy ones, have an extremely delicate sense of touch.

Vocabulary
distinct (di stiŋkt´) *adj.* clearly different; separate

Reading Skill
Main Idea Which sentence in this paragraph states the main idea?

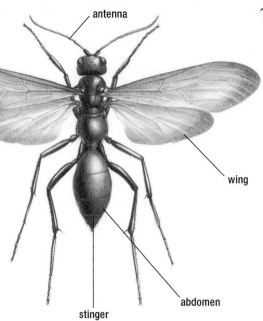

antenna

wing

abdomen

stinger

They are sensitive only to air movement. A light breeze makes them vibrate slowly, without disturbing the common hair. When one blows gently on the trichobothria, the tarantula reacts with a quick jerk of its four front legs. If the front and hind legs are stimulated at the same time, the spider makes a sudden jump. This reaction is quite independent of the state of its appetite.

These three tactile responses—to pressure on the body wall, to moving of the common hair, and to flexing of the trichobothria—are so different from one another that there is no possibility of confusing them. They serve the tarantula adequately for most of its needs and enable it to avoid most annoyances and dangers. But they fail the spider completely when it meets its deadly enemy, the digger wasp Pepsis.

These solitary wasps are beautiful and formidable creatures. Most species are either a deep shiny blue all over, or deep blue with rusty wings. The largest have a wing span of about four inches. They live on nectar. When excited, they give off a pungent odor—a warning that they are ready to attack. The sting is much worse than that of a bee or common wasp, and the pain and swelling last longer. In the adult stage the wasp lives only a few months. The female produces but a few eggs, one at a time at intervals of two or three days. For each egg the mother must provide one adult tarantula, alive but paralyzed. The tarantula must be of the correct species to nourish the larva. The mother wasp attaches the egg to the paralyzed spider's abdomen. Upon hatching from the egg, the larva is many hundreds of times smaller than its living but helpless victim. It eats no other food and drinks no water. By the time it has finished its single gargantuan meal and become ready for wasphood, nothing remains of the tarantula but its indigestible chitinous skeleton.[3]

The mother wasp goes tarantula-hunting when the egg in her ovary is almost ready to be laid. Flying low over the ground late on

Vocabulary
tactile (tak´ təl) *adj.* related to the sense of touch
formidable (fôr´ mə də bəl) *adj.* causing fear or dread

Reading Check

What three tactile responses do spiders have?

---

3. **chitinous** (kī´ tin əs) **skeleton** tough outer covering of an insect's body. The external skeleton gives an insect's body its structure, as an insect has no internal skeleton.

Studying Animal Behavior

Ethology—the scientific study of animal behavior in the wild—has helped scientists better understand the role of instinct in animal interactions. For instance, Konrad Lorenz (lōr´ ens´), shown below, discovered that instinct causes a baby bird to imprint on, or become attached to, the first moving creature it sees after hatching—even if that creature is a human scientist, not the bird's mother!

Connect to the Literature

Judging from Petrunkevitch's essay, what two concepts are a key concern for ethologists?

Vocabulary
evoking (ē vōk´ iŋ)
v. drawing forth emotions or responses

a sunny afternoon, the wasp looks for its victim or for the mouth of a tarantula burrow, a round hole edged by a bit of silk. The sex of the spider makes no difference, but the mother is highly discriminating as to species. Each species of Pepsis requires a certain species of tarantula, and the wasp will not attack the wrong species. In a cage with a tarantula which is not its normal prey, the wasp avoids the spider, and is usually killed by it in the night.

Yet when a wasp finds the correct species, it is the other way about. To identify the species the wasp apparently must explore the spider with her antennae. The tarantula shows an amazing tolerance to this exploration. The wasp crawls under it and walks over it without **evoking** any hostile response. The molestation is so great and so persistent that the tarantula often rises on all eight legs, as if it were on stilts. It may stand this way for several minutes. Meanwhile the wasp, having satisfied itself that the victim is of the right species, moves off a few inches to dig the spider's grave. Working vigorously with legs and jaws, it excavates a hole 8 to 10 inches deep with a diameter slightly larger than the spider's girth. Now and again the wasp pops out of the hole to make sure that the spider is still there.

When the grave is finished, the wasp returns to the tarantula to complete her ghastly enterprise. First she feels it all over once more with her antennae. Then her behavior becomes more aggressive. She bends her abdomen, protruding her sting, and searches for the soft membrane at the point where the spider's leg joins its body—the only spot where she can penetrate the horny skeleton. From time to time, as the exasperated spider slowly shifts ground, the wasp turns on her back and slides along with the aid of her wings, trying to get under the tarantula for a shot at the vital spot. During all this maneuvering, which can last for several minutes, the tarantula makes no move to save itself. Finally the wasp corners it against some obstruction and grasps one of its legs in her powerful jaws. Now at last the harassed spider tries a desperate but vain defense. The two contestants roll over and over on the ground. It is a terrifying sight and the outcome is always the same. The wasp finally manages to thrust her sting into the soft spot and holds it there for a few seconds while she pumps in the poison. Almost immediately the tarantula falls paralyzed on its back. Its legs stop twitching; its heart stops beating. Yet it is not dead, as is shown by the fact that if taken from the wasp it can be restored to some sensitivity by being kept in a moist chamber for several months.

After paralyzing the tarantula, the wasp cleans herself by dragging her body along the ground and rubbing her feet, sucks the drop of blood oozing from the wound in the spider's abdomen, then grabs a leg of the flabby, helpless animal in her jaws and drags it down to the bottom of the grave. She stays there for many minutes, sometimes for several hours, and what she does all that time in the dark we do not know. Eventually she lays her egg and attaches it to the side of the spider's abdomen with a sticky secretion. Then she emerges, fills the grave with soil carried bit by bit in her jaws, and finally tramples the ground all around to hide any trace of the grave from prowlers. Then she flies away, leaving her descendant safely started in life. •

▲ Critical Viewing
Does the spider appear to be responding to the wasp as Petrunkevitch describes? Explain. **[Connect]**

In all this the behavior of the wasp evidently is qualitatively different from that of the spider. The wasp acts like an intelligent animal. This is not to say that instinct plays no part or that she reasons as man does. But her actions are to the point; they are not automatic and can be modified to fit the situation. We do not know for certain how she identifies the tarantula—probably it is by some olfactory or chemotactile sense[4]—but she does it purposefully and does not blindly tackle a wrong species.

On the other hand, the tarantula's behavior shows only confusion. Evidently the wasp's pawing gives it no pleasure, for it tries to move away. That the wasp is not simulating sexual stimulation is certain, because male and female tarantulas react in the same way to its advances. That the spider is not anesthetized by some odorless secretion is easily shown by blowing lightly at the tarantula and making it jump suddenly. What, then, makes the tarantula behave as stupidly as it does?

No clear, simple answer is available. Possibly the stimulation by the wasp's antennae is masked by a heavier pressure on the spider's body, so that it reacts as when prodded by a pencil. But the explanation may be much more complex. Initiative in attack is not in the nature of tarantulas; most species fight only when

Literary Analysis
Expository Essay How does the writer link his descriptions of behavior to the concepts identified at the beginning of the essay?

Reading Check
What does the wasp do to the tarantula?

---

4. **olfactory** (äl fak´ tə rē) . . . **chemotactile** (kē´ mō tak´ təl) **sense** An olfactory sense is a sense of smell. A chemotactile sense involves sensitivity by touch to the presence of specific chemicals.

cornered so that escape is impossible. Their inherited patterns of behavior apparently prompt them to avoid problems rather than attack them. For example, spiders always weave their webs in three dimensions, and when a spider finds that there is insufficient space to attach certain threads in the third dimension, it leaves the place and seeks another, instead of finishing the web in a single plane. This urge to escape seems to arise under all circumstances, in all phases of life, and to take the place of reasoning. For a spider to change the pattern of its web is as impossible as for an inexperienced man to build a bridge across a chasm obstructing his way.

In a way the instinctive urge to escape is not only easier but often more efficient than reasoning. The tarantula does exactly what is most efficient in all cases except in an encounter with a ruthless and determined attacker dependent for the existence of her own species on killing as many tarantulas as she can lay eggs. Perhaps in this case the spider follows its usual pattern of trying to escape, instead of seizing and killing the wasp, because it is not aware of its danger. In any case, the survival of the tarantula species as a whole is protected by the fact that the spider is much more fertile than the wasp.

Critical Thinking

1. **Key Ideas and Details (a)** What do newly hatched digger wasps feed on? **(b) Compare and Contrast:** Using examples from the essay, compare the ways in which the wasp and the tarantula each provide for their young.

2. **Craft and Structure** The author says the tarantula rises "as if it were on stilts" to let the wasp explore it. How does this description help you picture the tarantula's actions?

3. **Key Ideas and Details (a) Classify:** In a two-column chart, collect examples of instinctive behavior and intelligent behavior from the essay. **(b) Analyze:** Identify the positive and the negative consequences of each behavior you list.

4. **Integration of Knowledge and Ideas** For an animal in conflict, do you think instinct or intelligence provides a greater advantage? Explain. *[Connect to the Big Question: What kind of knowledge changes our lives?]*

Literary Analysis: Expository Essay

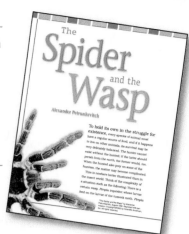

1. Key Ideas and Details (a) What phenomenon does Petrunkevitch explain in this **expository essay? (b)** How does the essay help readers see the difference between instinct and intelligence?

2. Craft and Structure Describe the **diction** in and the **tone** of the essay. Support your answer with analysis of specific word choices.

Reading Skill: Main Idea

3. Make a chart like the one shown to identify the **main**, or **central, ideas** and the **supporting details** in the essay. In each box, write the author's main idea about the topic in your own words. Then, find and record supporting details for each main idea.

Spider's Sense of Touch	Spider's Response to Wasp	Wasp's Handling of Spider
Detail Detail	Detail Detail	Detail Detail

4. In your own words, **summarize** the essay.

Vocabulary

Acquisition and Use Write a one-sentence answer to each question. Then, explain how the meaning of the underlined word helped you.

1. What is one <u>instinct</u> that all dogs have?

2. At what time do you <u>customarily</u> wake up?

3. How do scientists decide if two spiders belong to <u>distinct</u> species?

4. What fabric do you think has a lot of <u>tactile</u> appeal?

5. What traits make a grizzly bear a <u>formidable</u> creature?

6. Would a surprise party be effective in <u>evoking</u> a positive response?

Word Study Use the context of the sentences and what you know about the **Latin roots -tact-** and **-tang-** to explain your answers.

1. Why is it important for scientists to have *tangible* evidence?

2. Is someone who has *tact* in touch with the feelings of others?

Word Study

The **Latin roots -tact-** and **-tang-** mean "touch" or "feel."

Apply It Explain how the roots contribute to the meanings of these words. Consult a dictionary if necessary.

contact
intact
tangent

What kind of *knowledge* changes our lives?

from
Longitude
Dava Sobel

Writing About the Big Question

In the excerpt from *Longitude*, the author presents a history of the search for information about longitude. Use this sentence starter to develop your ideas about the Big Question.

New discoveries and inventions allow for **growth** in a person's **understanding** of the world because _____.

While You Read Look for steps taken throughout history to reach an understanding of longitude.

Vocabulary

Read each word and its definition. Decide whether you know the word well, know it a little bit, or do not know it at all. After you read, see how your knowledge of each word has increased.

- **haphazardly** (hap´ haz´ ərd lē) *adv.* in an unplanned or a disorganized way (p. 476) *Dirty clothes lay* <u>haphazardly</u> *thrown about the messy room.* *haphazard adj. haphazardness n.*

- **configuration** (kən fig´ yə rā´ shən) *n.* arrangement of parts; pattern (p. 476) *We stood in a circular* <u>configuration</u>. *configurative adj. configure v. figure n.*

- **converge** (kən vʉrj´) *v.* to come together (p. 476) *Relatives from across the country will* <u>converge</u> *at the reunion.* *convergence n.*

- **derived** (di rīvd´) *v.* reached by reasoning (p. 477) *We* <u>derived</u> *the answer by solving the equation.* *derivation n. derivative n.*

- **contested** (kən test´ əd) *v.* tried to disprove or invalidate something; disputed (p. 481) *She* <u>contested</u> *the false charges with the credit card company.* *contest n. contestant n.*

- **impervious** (im pʉr´ vē əs) *adj.* not affected by (used with *to*) (p. 481) *In my new parka, I am* <u>impervious</u> *to cold weather.* *imperviously adv. imperviousness n.*

Word Study

The **Latin root -fig-** means "form" or "shape."

In this essay, the author explains that although the world changes its **configuration**, its contours and how boundaries are formed, the lines of latitude and longitude stay fixed.

Meet
Dava Sobel
(b. 1947)

Author of
Longitude

As a child in the Bronx, New York, Dava Sobel enjoyed trips on her family's sailboat, navigated by one of her parents. Years later, she would transform a chapter of navigation history into her first bestseller, *Longitude*.

Curiosity and Inspiration Sobel attended the Bronx High School of Science and went on to become an award-winning science reporter for *The New York Times* and various magazines. In November 1993, she attended a conference about navigation. She became fascinated by the historic contributions of clockmaker John Harrison.

While researching the history of longitude, Sobel stumbled onto the topic of her next book: Italian Renaissance astronomer Galileo and his daughter. She wrote about their relationship in *Galileo's Daughter*.

BACKGROUND FOR THE ESSAY

Navigation

Navigation is the science of finding the position and direction of a craft such as a ship or plane. Since ancient times, mapmakers and sailors have used a system of imaginary lines—longitude and latitude—to identify positions on the Earth's surface.

Did You Know?

While researching *Longitude*, Sobel traveled to London for research and to stand directly on the prime meridian.

from Longitude

Dava Sobel

*W*hen I'm playful
I use the meridians
of longitude and parallels
of latitude for a seine, and
drag the Atlantic Ocean
for whales.

—Mark Twain
Life on the Mississippi

*O*nce on a Wednesday excursion when I was a little girl, my father bought me a beaded wire ball that I loved. At a touch, I could collapse the toy into a flat coil between my palms, or pop it open to make a hollow sphere. Rounded out, it resembled a tiny Earth, because its hinged wires traced the same pattern of intersecting circles that I had seen on the globe in my schoolroom—the thin black lines of latitude and longitude. The few colored beads slid along the wire paths haphazardly, like ships on the high seas.

My father strode up Fifth Avenue to Rockefeller Center with me on his shoulders, and we stopped to stare at the statue of Atlas,[1] carrying Heaven and Earth on his.

The bronze orb that Atlas held aloft, like the wire toy in my hands, was a see-through world, defined by imaginary lines. The Equator. The Ecliptic. The Tropic of Cancer. The Tropic of Capricorn. The Arctic Circle. The prime meridian. Even then I could recognize, in the graph-paper grid imposed on the globe, a powerful symbol of all the real lands and waters on the planet.

Today, the latitude and longitude lines govern with more authority than I could have imagined forty-odd years ago, for they stay fixed as the world changes its configuration underneath them—with continents adrift across a widening sea, and national boundaries repeatedly redrawn by war or peace.

As a child, I learned the trick for remembering the difference between latitude and longitude. The latitude lines, the *parallels*, really do stay parallel to each other as they girdle the globe from the Equator to the poles in a series of shrinking concentric[2] rings. The meridians of longitude go the other way: They loop from the North Pole to the South and back again in great circles of the same size, so they all converge at the ends of the Earth. ●

Lines of latitude and longitude began crisscrossing our worldview in ancient times, at least three centuries before the birth of Christ. By A.D. 150, the cartographer and astronomer Ptolemy had plotted them on the twenty-seven maps of his first world atlas. Also for this landmark volume, Ptolemy listed all the place names in an index, in alphabetical order, with the latitude and longitude of each—as well as he could gauge them from travelers' reports. Ptolemy himself had only an armchair appreciation of the wider world. A common misconception of

Vocabulary
haphazardly (hap´ haz´ ərd lē) *adv.* in an unplanned or a disorganized way

configuration (kən fig´ yə rā´ shən) *n.* arrangement of parts; pattern
converge (kən vʉrj´) *v.* to come together

▼ **Critical Viewing**
How does this image convey the endurance of the system of longitude and latitude? **[Interpret]**

1. **Fifth Avenue . . . Rockefeller Center . . . Atlas** landmarks in the borough of Manhattan of New York City. Rockefeller Center features a statue of Atlas, the Greek giant condemned to carry the heavens on his shoulders.
2. **concentric** (kən sen´ trik) *adj.* having a center in common.

his day held that anyone living below the Equator would melt into deformity from the horrible heat.

The Equator marked the zero-degree parallel of latitude for Ptolemy. He did not choose it arbitrarily but took it on higher authority from his predecessors, who had derived it from nature while observing the motions of the heavenly bodies. The sun, moon, and planets pass almost directly overhead at the Equator. Likewise the Tropic of Cancer and the Tropic of Capricorn, two other famous parallels, assume their positions at the sun's command. They mark the northern and southern boundaries of the sun's apparent motion over the course of the year.

Ptolemy was free, however, to lay his prime meridian, the zero-degree longitude line, wherever he liked. He chose to run it through the Fortunate Islands (now called the Canary and Madeira Islands) off the northwest coast of Africa. Later mapmakers moved the prime meridian to the Azores and to the Cape Verde Islands,[3] as well as to Rome, Copenhagen, Jerusalem, St. Petersburg, Pisa, Paris, and Philadelphia, among other places, before it settled down at last in London. As the world turns, any line drawn from pole to pole may serve as well as any other for a starting line of reference. The placement of the prime meridian is a purely political decision.

Here lies the real, hard-core difference between latitude and longitude—beyond the superficial difference in line direction that any child can see: The zero-degree parallel of latitude is fixed by the laws of nature, while the zero-degree meridian of longitude shifts like the sands of time. This difference makes finding latitude child's play, and turns the determination of longitude, especially at sea, into an adult dilemma—one that stumped the wisest minds of the world for the better part of human history.

Any sailor worth his salt can gauge his latitude well enough by the length of the day, or by the height of the sun or known guide stars above the horizon. Christopher Columbus followed a straight path across the Atlantic when he "sailed the parallel" on his 1492 journey, and the technique would doubtless have carried him to the Indies had not the Americas intervened.

The measurement of longitude meridians, in comparison, is tempered by time. To learn one's longitude at sea, one needs to know what time it is aboard ship and also the time at the home

3. **Azores** (ā´ zôrz´) . . . **Cape Verde** (vʉrd) **Islands** two island groups in the Atlantic Ocean; the Azores are off Portugal and the Cape Verde Islands are off the westernmost point of Africa.

Vocabulary
derived (di rīvd´) *v.* reached by reasoning

Reading Skill
Main Idea What main idea does the writer support using examples like Rome and Copenhagen?

A common misconception of his day held that anyone living below the Equator would melt into deformity from the horrible heat.

Reading Check

Name an important contribution made to science or navigation by Ptolemy.

Science Connection

Longitude and Latitude

The lines of longitude and latitude form an imaginary grid that can be used to name the exact location of any place on Earth.

- The **equator** is the line of latitude on which all points are the same distance from the North and South poles. The sun appears directly overhead at the equator on March 21 and September 21 of each year.

- The **Tropic of Cancer** is 23° 27′ north of the equator. It marks the northernmost latitude at which the sun can appear directly overhead— an event that occurs at noon on June 20 or 21.

- The **Tropic of Capricorn,** at 23° 27′ south, is the southernmost latitude at which the sun can appear directly overhead. The sun reaches its highest position at this tropic at noon on December 20 or 21.

- The **prime meridian** is the line of longitude chosen as the 0° line.

Connect to the Literature

What does this information indicate about how sailors determine latitude by the sun?

port or another place of known longitude—at that very same moment. The two clock times enable the navigator[4] to convert the hour difference into a geographical separation. Since the Earth takes twenty-four hours to complete one full revolution of three hundred sixty degrees, one hour marks one twenty-fourth of a spin, or fifteen degrees. And so each hour's time difference between the ship and the starting point marks a progress of fifteen degrees of longitude to the east or west. Every day at sea, when the navigator resets his ship's clock to local noon when the sun reaches its highest point in the sky, and then consults the home-port clock, every hour's discrepancy between them translates into another fifteen degrees of longitude.

Those same fifteen degrees of longitude also correspond to a distance traveled. At the Equator, where the girth of the Earth is greatest, fifteen degrees stretch fully one thousand miles. North or south of that line, however, the mileage value of each degree decreases. One degree of longitude equals four minutes of time the world over, but in terms of distance, one degree shrinks from sixty-eight miles at the Equator to virtually nothing at the poles.

Precise knowledge of the hour in two different places at once—a longitude prerequisite so easily accessible today from any pair of cheap wristwatches—was utterly unattainable up to and including the era of pendulum clocks.[5] On the deck of a rolling ship, such clocks would slow down, or speed up, or stop running altogether. Normal changes in temperature encountered en route from a cold country of origin to a tropical trade zone thinned or thickened a clock's lubricating oil and made its metal parts expand or contract with equally disastrous results. A rise or fall in barometric pressure, or the subtle variations in the Earth's gravity from one latitude to another, could also cause a clock to gain or lose time.

For lack of a practical method of determining longitude, every great captain in the Age of Exploration[6]

---

4. **navigator** (nav´ ə gāt´ ər) *n.* a person skilled in locating the position and plotting the course of a ship or an aircraft.
5. **pendulum** (pen´ dyo͞o ləm) **clocks** clocks whose timekeeping movement is regulated by a pendulum, a weight swinging freely from a fixed point.
6. **Age of Exploration** the period from about 1450 to about 1700, when European navigators sailed to new territories and founded colonies in Africa, the Americas, and Asia.

became lost at sea despite the best available charts and compasses. From Vasco da Gama to Vasco Núñez de Balboa, from Ferdinand Magellan to Sir Francis Drake[7]—they all got where they were going willy-nilly, by forces attributed to good luck or the grace of God.

As more and more sailing vessels set out to conquer or explore new territories, to wage war, or to ferry gold and commodities between foreign lands, the wealth of nations floated upon the oceans. And still no ship owned a reliable means for establishing her whereabouts. In consequence, untold numbers of sailors died when their destinations suddenly loomed out of the sea and took them by surprise. In a single such accident, on October 22, 1707, at the Scilly Isles near the southwestern tip of England, four home-bound British warships ran aground and nearly two thousand men lost their lives. ●

---

7. **Vasco da Gama** (väs´ kô də gä´ mə) . . . **Vasco Núñez de Balboa** (väs´ kô nōo´ nyeth *the* bal bō´ ə) . . . **Ferdinand Magellan** (mə jel´ ən) . . . **Sir Francis Drake** famous explorers of the fifteenth and sixteenth centuries.

Reading Skill
Main Idea Which detail in this paragraph supports Sobel's idea that not knowing one's longitude was dangerous?

Reading Check

What key technical problem prevented sailors from measuring longitude accurately?

Literary Analysis
Expository Essay
How do the details in this
paragraph contribute to
the author's tone?

The active quest for a solution to the problem of longitude persisted over four centuries and across the whole continent of Europe. Most crowned heads of state eventually played a part in the longitude story, notably King George III of England and King Louis XIV of France. Seafaring men such as Captain William Bligh of the Bounty and the great circumnavigator Captain James Cook, who made three long voyages of exploration and experimentation before his violent death in Hawaii, took the more promising methods to sea to test their accuracy and practicability.

Renowned astronomers approached the longitude challenge by appealing to the clockwork universe: Galileo Galilei, Jean Dominique Cassini, Christiaan Huygens, Sir Isaac Newton, and Edmond Halley,[8] of comet fame, all entreated the moon and stars for help. Palatial observatories were founded at Paris, London, and Berlin for the express purpose of determining longitude by the heavens. Meanwhile, lesser minds devised schemes that depended on the yelps of wounded dogs, or the cannon blasts of signal ships strategically anchored—somehow—on the open ocean.

In the course of their struggle to find longitude, scientists struck upon other discoveries that changed their view of the universe. These include the first accurate determinations of the weight of the Earth, the distance to the stars, and the speed of light.

▶ **Critical Viewing**
Does the appearance of Harrison's marine watch reflect its world-altering importance? Explain. **[Support]**

As time passed and no method proved successful, the search for a solution to the longitude problem assumed legendary proportions, on a par with discovering the Fountain of Youth, the secret of perpetual motion, or the formula for transforming lead into gold.[9] The governments of the great maritime nations—including Spain, the Netherlands, and certain city-states of Italy—periodically roiled the fervor by offering jackpot purses for a workable method. The British Parliament, in its famed Longitude Act of 1714, set the highest bounty of all, naming a prize equal to a king's ransom (several million dollars in today's currency) for a "Practicable and Useful" means of determining longitude.

▲ **King George III**

8. **Galileo Galilei** (gal´ ə lā´ ō gal´ ə lā ē) . . . **Jean-Dominique Cassini** (zhän dō mi nēk´ kä sē´ nē) . . . **Christiaan Huygens** (hī´ gənz) . . . **Sir Isaac Newton . . . Edmond Halley** (hal´ ē) pioneering astronomers and scientists of the sixteenth through the eighteenth centuries. Their work redefined people's picture of the universe, replacing traditional views with modern ones.

English clockmaker John Harrison, a mechanical genius who pioneered the science of portable precision timekeeping, devoted his life to this quest. He accomplished what Newton had feared was impossible: He invented a clock that would carry the true time from the home port, like an eternal flame, to any remote corner of the world.

Harrison, a man of simple birth and high intelligence, crossed swords with the leading lights of his day. He made a special enemy of the Reverend Nevil Maskelyne, the fifth astronomer royal, who contested his claim to the coveted prize money, and whose tactics at certain junctures can only be described as foul play.

With no formal education or apprenticeship to any watchmaker, Harrison nevertheless constructed a series of virtually friction-free clocks that required no lubrication and no cleaning, that were made from materials impervious to rust, and that kept their moving parts perfectly balanced in relation to one another, regardless of how the world pitched or tossed about them. He did away with the pendulum, and he combined different metals inside his works in such a way that when one component expanded or contracted with changes in temperature, the other counteracted the change and kept the clock's rate constant.

Vocabulary
contested (kən test´ əd) *v.* tried to disprove or invalidate something; disputed
impervious (im pʉr´ vē əs) *adj.* not affected by

Reading Check

What important device did Harrison invent?

---

9. **Fountain of Youth . . . lead into gold** three imaginary goals seriously pursued by inquirers. The Fountain of Youth was supposed to restore youth. Perpetual motion would allow people to generate power endlessly without consuming fuel. A formula to turn the cheap metal lead into the precious metal gold was sought for centuries by alchemists.

Spiral Review
Series of Ideas In what way does this paragraph develop the drama of Sobel's account? What point about science does it support?

His every success, however, was parried by members of the scientific elite, who distrusted Harrison's magic box. The commissioners charged with awarding the longitude prize—Nevil Maskelyne among them—changed the contest rules whenever they saw fit, so as to favor the chances of astronomers over the likes of Harrison and his fellow "mechanics."[10] But the utility and accuracy of Harrison's approach triumphed in the end. His followers shepherded Harrison's intricate, exquisite invention through the design modifications that enabled it to be mass produced and enjoy wide use.

An aged, exhausted Harrison, taken under the wing of King George III, ultimately claimed his rightful monetary reward in 1773—after forty struggling years of political intrigue, international warfare, academic backbiting, scientific revolution, and economic upheaval.

All these threads, and more, entwine in the lines of longitude. To unravel them now—to retrace their story in an age when a network of orbiting satellites can nail down a ship's position within a few feet in just a moment or two—is to see the globe anew.

---

10. **"mechanics"** skilled workers and tradesmen, of a lower class than merchants or aristocrats.

Critical Thinking

Cite textual evidence to support your responses.

1. **Key Ideas and Details (a)** According to Sobel, what two methods can sailors use to estimate their latitude? **(b) Apply:** Using one of these methods, how could you tell whether you were at the equator—the zero-degree latitude?

2. **Key Ideas and Details Analyze:** Briefly explain why the invention of an accurate clock was crucial to solving the problem of determining longitude.

3. **Key Ideas and Details Analyze Cause and Effect:** Why did Harrison have difficulties getting his solution to the problem of longitude recognized?

4. **Integration of Knowledge and Ideas (a)** Identify two ways in which the world would be different without Harrison's clocks. **(b)** Would you say longitude is a life-changing development? Explain. *[Connect to the Big Question: What kind of knowledge changes our lives?]*

Literary Analysis: Expository Essay

© **1. Key Ideas and Details (a)** What event does Sobel explain in this **expository essay? (b)** Briefly explain how she uses facts about astronomy and navigation to help readers understand the significance of this event.

© **2. Craft and Structure** Describe the **diction** in and the **tone** of the essay. Support your answer with analysis of specific word choices.

Reading Skill: Main Idea

3. Using a chart like the one shown, identify the **main,** or **central, ideas** and the **supporting details** in the essay.

4. In your own words, **summarize** the essay.

Vocabulary

© **Acquisition and Use** Write a one-sentence answer to each question. Then, explain how the meaning of the underlined word helped you.

1. What might a room look like if it is <u>haphazardly</u> decorated?

2. Has he <u>derived</u> a correct conclusion if he was missing information?

3. What is the <u>configuration</u> of the desks in your classroom?

4. Do you think anyone is truly <u>impervious</u> to criticism?

5. How could you determine if two streets <u>converge</u>?

6. What tone would you find at a debate over a <u>contested</u> election?

Word Study Use the context of the sentences and what you know about the **Latin root -*fig-*** to explain your answer to each question.

1. If a room becomes *transfigured,* will it look different?

2. What are you doing if you *reconfigure* a chart?

Word Study

The **Latin root -*fig-*** means "form" or "shape."

Apply It Explain how the root -*fig-* contributes to the meanings of these words. Consult a dictionary if necessary.

effigy
figment
figurine

Integrated Language Skills

The Spider and the Wasp •
from Longitude

Conventions: Direct and Indirect Objects

A **direct object** is a noun or pronoun that receives the action of an action verb. An **indirect object** is used with a direct object and names the person or thing that something is given to or done for.

To find the direct object of a verb, answer the question "[verb] *whom?*" or "[verb] *what?*"

Example: Sam threw Fred the ball.

Threw what? ANSWER: the ball (direct object)

To find the indirect object of a verb, answer the question "[verb] *to or for whom?*" or "[verb] *to or for what?*"

Example: Sam threw Fred the ball.

Threw to whom? ANSWER: Fred (indirect object)

Indirect objects may appear only between verbs and direct objects in sentences.

Practice A Identify the verb and direct and indirect objects in each sentence. Then, tell whether each object is a direct object or an indirect object.

1. Tarantulas attack insects.
2. Digger wasps give tarantulas a sting.
3. A spider's hair throws the brain impulses.
4. The wasp attaches her egg to the spider.
5. The writer told us the story of the spider and the wasp.

© Reading Application In "The Spider and the Wasp," find two sentences that have both direct and indirect objects. Identify and label the verb and the objects in each sentence.

Practice B Identify the action verb and direct object in each sentence below. Then, rewrite each sentence, adding an indirect object, if possible.

1. The author's father bought a ball.
2. The sailors showed the compass.
3. Harrison presented a clock.
4. The king granted the prize money.
5. Astronomers gave the results of their long research study.

© Writing Application Write two sentences about using maps using the following grammatical order: subject, action verb, indirect object, direct object.

PH WRITING COACH Further instruction and practice are available in *Prentice Hall Writing Coach*.

Writing

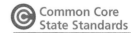

Common Core State Standards

W.9-10.2.e; SL.9-10.4; L.9-10.3
[For the full wording of the standards, see page 460.]

Explanatory Text Write a **business letter** in which you imagine that you are either a scientist requesting funds to do more research on tarantulas and wasps, or John Harrison explaining your invention to King George III. (For the format of a business letter, see page 532.) Maintain an objective style and formal tone appropriate for a business letter and for your audience and purpose.

If you read "The Spider and the Wasp," follow these suggestions.

- Explain why tarantulas and wasps are of scientific interest, and summarize what we currently know, as reported by Petrunkevitch.

- Tell what mysteries could be solved with additional research.

If you read the excerpt from *Longitude,* follow these suggestions.

- Briefly describe your clock and explain how it determines longitude.

- Mention the resistance you have met from the Royal Society.

Grammar Application In your letter, include at least one sentence with a direct object and indirect object.

Writing Workshop: *Work in Progress*

Prewriting for a Letter to the Editor For a letter to the editor you may write, list several issues in the news that spark your interest. Write two important facts or examples for each issue. Then, choose one issue about which to write. Put this Issues List in your writing portfolio.

Use this prewriting activity to prepare for the **Writing Workshop** on page 532.

Speaking and Listening

Comprehension and Collaboration Deliver a **humorous persuasive speech** in which you encourage your audience to view wasps and tarantulas as pets, or propose moving the prime meridian to your hometown.

- Plan humorous approaches to meet your audience's interests.

- Formulate a clear thesis—the main idea you want to get across.

- Support your ideas with facts, examples, and reasons.

- Address specific concerns your audience may have, anticipating and answering any objections.

- Choose effective language. Slang might seem contemporary, but formal language might command respect. Use figurative language such as similes, metaphors, or imagery to make your message vivid.

PHLit Online!
www.PHLitOnline.com

- Interactive graphic organizers
- Grammar tutorial
- Interactive journals

Ⓒ Leveled Texts

Build your skills and improve your comprehension of nonfiction with texts of increasing complexity.

Read **"The Sun Parlor"** to learn what happens when a woman puts her pride in a room ahead of her respect for a child.

Read the excerpt from **"In Commemoration: One Million Volumes"** to see how a boy cultivates his love of books throughout his life.

Ⓒ Common Core State Standards

Meet these standards with either **"The Sun Parlor"** (p. 490) or the excerpt from **"In Commemoration: One Million Volumes"** (p. 500).

Reading Informational Text
3. Analyze how the author unfolds an analysis or series of ideas or events, including the order in which the points are made, how they are introduced and developed, and the connections that are drawn between them. *(Literary Analysis: Reflective Essay)*

Spiral Review: RI.9-10.5
Writing
3.d. Use precise words and phrases, telling details, and sensory language to convey a vivid picture of the experiences, events, setting, and/or characters.

3.e. Provide a conclusion that follows from and reflects on what is experienced, observed, or resolved over the course of the narrative. *(Writing: Memoir)*

Speaking and Listening
4. Present information, findings, and supporting evidence clearly, concisely, and logically such that listeners can follow the line of reasoning and the organization, development, substance, and style are appropriate to purpose, audience, and task. *(Speaking and Listening: Oral Recollection)*

Language
6. Acquire and use accurately general academic and domain-specific words and phrases, sufficient for reading and writing at the college and career readiness level; demonstrate independence in gathering vocabulary knowledge when considering a word or phrase important to comprehension or expression. *(Vocabulary: Word Study)*

Literary Analysis: Reflective Essay

A **reflective essay** is a brief nonfiction work in which a writer presents the experiences that shaped or inspired his or her thoughts on a topic. In a reflective essay, a writer

- tells of an event, a time period, or an idea from his or her own life and experience.
- introduces and develops reflections on his or her topic, weaving connections between personal experience and a point of general interest, such as a lesson about life.
- may focus his or her reflections on a specific object, scene, occasion, place, or idea.

Look for these characteristics of a reflective essay as you read.

Reading Skill: Main Idea

To fully understand an essay, **analyze central,** or **main, ideas** and **supporting details**—recognize each main point that the writer makes and identify the ideas or facts that explain or illustrate it. To help you analyze, **ask questions** like these as you read:

- What is the topic of this passage?
- What is the main point being made?
- Which details support this point?

Using the Strategy: Main Ideas and Supporting Details Chart

As you read, record details on a **main ideas and supporting details chart** like this one. After you have read, consider what you know about the issue the writer develops and identify other questions you may have.

What kind of *knowledge* changes our lives?

The Sun Parlor
Dorothy West

Writing About the Big Question

In "The Sun Parlor," a woman learns an important lesson about values. Use these sentence starters to develop your ideas about the Big Question.

Understanding what is truly important in life is valuable because _____.

Learning from past mistakes can lead to personal **growth** when _____.

While You Read Notice the author's attitude toward the sun room, and compare it with the way she seems to feel about her niece.

Vocabulary

Read each word and its definition. Decide whether you know the word well, know it a little bit, or do not know it at all. After you read, see how your knowledge of each word has increased.

- **lavished** (lav′ isht) *v.* gave with extreme generosity (p. 491) *She lavished candy on us, and we had to borrow a bag to carry it home.* *lavish adj. lavishly adv. lavishness n.*

- **subordinate** (sə bôrd′ 'n it) *adj.* below another in importance or rank (p. 491) *A private is subordinate to a general.* *subordinate n. subordinately adv. subordination n.*

- **rejuvenation** (ri jo͞o′ və nā′ shən) *n.* the act of making new, youthful, or energetic again (p. 492) *A warm bath is a good method for rejuvenation.* *rejuvenate v. rejuvenator n. juvenile n.*

- **convalesce** (kän′ və les′) *v.* regain strength and health (p. 494) *A few days at home will give you time to convalesce after the accident.* *convalescence n. convalescent adj.*

- **cajoling** (kə jōl′ iŋ) *n.* coaxing with flattery (p. 494) *I resisted her cajoling and did not sign up for the play.* *cajole v. cajoler n. cajolingly adv.*

- **succinct** (sək siŋkt′) *adj.* clearly and briefly stated (p. 494) *If your essay is too wordy, revise to make it more succinct.* *succinctly adv. succinctness n.*

Word Study

The **Latin prefix suc-** is another spelling of the prefix **sub-,** meaning "under," "less or lower than," or "following after."

In this essay, the author imagines how something could be said in a more **succinct** way, using fewer words.

Author of

The Sun Parlor

Dorothy West enjoyed a comfortable childhood—one made possible by her family's fiery ambition and hard work. Her father, a former slave, came north and built a successful business in Boston.

A Lifetime of Writing By the age of fourteen, West was winning local writing competitions in Boston. A few years later, in 1926, she moved to New York City and contributed to the Harlem Renaissance, an outpouring of African American creativity in the 1920s.

West wrote short stories, novels, and essays. She spent the last half of her life in Oak Bluffs, the village in Martha's Vineyard that is the setting for "The Sun Parlor."

BACKGROUND FOR THE ESSAY
Parlors and Sun Parlors

In past eras, many houses, like the one described in "The Sun Parlor," included a room called the parlor. An early version of the modern living room, the parlor was a place for family members to visit with guests or with each other. A sun parlor, or solarium, enclosed mostly by glass, was intended for enjoying the sun and for reading and talking.

Did You Know?

Oprah Winfrey made West's second novel, *The Wedding,* into a television movie.

The *Sun Parlor*

Dorothy West

*T*his is a tale with a moral. I will try not to tax your attention too long. But I have to go way back to begin because it begins with my childhood. It is about houses and children, and which came first.

There were four of us children, well-schooled in good manners, well-behaved almost all of the time, and obedient to the commands of grown-ups, the power people who could make or break us.

We lived in a beautiful house. The reason I knew that is because all my mother's friends said so, and brought their other friends to see it. On the day appointed for the tour, which included inspection of every room on every floor, my mother would gather us around her and say in her gentlest voice, "I'm sorry, children, but Mrs. So-and-so is coming today and bringing a friend to see our house. You children keep clean and play quietly while they're here. It's not a real visit. They won't stay long. It'll be over before you can say Jack Robinson."

Most often a first-time caller, having lavished praise on everything she saw, including us, proceeded out without any further remarks. But there were others who, when they saw four children good as gold, did not see beyond their size, and asked my mother in outspoken horror, "How can you bear to let children loose in a lovely house like this?"

Every time it happened we were terrified. What would happen to us if my mother decided her house was too good for us and she hated the sight of us? What would we do, where would we go, would we starve?

My mother looked at our stricken faces, and her own face softened and her eyes filled with love. Then she would say to her inquisitor, though she did not say it rudely, "The children don't belong to the house. The house belongs to the children. No room says, *Do not enter.*"

I did not know I could ever forget those sentiments. But once, to my lasting regret, I did. With the passage of years I took my place with grown-ups, and there was another generation, among them the little girl, Sis, who was my mother's treasure. The summer she was eight was the one time I forgot that a child is not subordinate to a house.

We had a cottage in the Highlands of Oak Bluffs of unimpressive size and appearance. My mother loved it for its easy care. It couldn't even stand in the shade of our city house, and there certainly were no special rules for children. No one had ever looked aghast at a child on its premises.

Except me, the summer I painted the sun parlor. I am not a painter, but I am a perfectionist. I threw my whole soul into the project, and worked with such diligence and

◀ **Critical Viewing** Based on this painting, what feelings do you think will be described in the essay? **[Connect]**

Vocabulary
lavished (lav´ isht) *v.* gave with extreme generosity

subordinate (sə bôrd´ 'n it) *adj.* below another in importance or rank

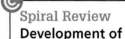

Spiral Review
Development of Ideas What central idea does the author introduce in her opening paragraphs? What is its connection to the rest of the essay?

Reading Check

What does the author say she regrets forgetting?

painstaking care that when the uncounted hours ended I felt that I had painted the Sistine Chapel.[1]

School vacation began, and Sis arrived for the long holiday, the car pulling up at the edge of the brick walk, and Sis streaking into the house for a round of hugs, then turning to tear upstairs to take off her travel clothes and put on her play clothes, and suddenly her flying feet braking to a stop in front of the sun parlor, its open door inviting inspection.

She who was always in motion, she who never took time for a second look at anything, or cared whether her bed was smooth or crumpled, or noticed what was on her plate as long as it was something to eat—she, in the awakening that came when she was eight, in her first awareness of something outside herself, stood in the doorway of the sun parlor, her face filled with the joy of her discovery, and said in a voice on the edge of tears, "It's the most beautiful room I ever saw in my whole life."

I did not hear her. I did not really hear her. I did not recognize the magnitude of that moment. I let it sink to some low level of my subconscious. All I saw was that her foot was poised to cross the threshold of my chapel.

I let out a little cry of pain. "Sis," I said, "please don't go in the sun parlor. There's nothing in there to interest a child. It's not a place for children to play in. It's a place for grown-ups to sit in. Go and change. Summer is outside waiting for you to come and play wherever you please."

In a little while the sounds of Sis's soaring laughter were mingling with the happy sounds of other vacationing children. They kept any doubt I might have had from surfacing. Sis was surely more herself running free than squirming on a chair in the sun parlor.

All the same I monitored that room, looking for smudges and streaks, scanning the floor for signs of scuffing. The room bore no scars, and Sis showed no trace of frustration.

The summer flowed. My friends admired the room, though they did it without superlatives. To them it was a room I had talked about redoing for a long time. Now I had done it. So much for that.

The summer waned, and Sis went home for school's reopening, as did the other summer children, taking so much life and laughter with them that the ensuing days recovered slowly. ●

Then my mother's sister, my favorite aunt, arrived from New York for her usual stay at summer's end. She looked ten years younger than her actual years. She seemed to bounce with energy, as if she had gone through some process of rejuvenation. We asked her for the secret.

---

1. **the Sistine Chapel** (sis´ tēn´ chap´ əl) place of worship in the Vatican, Rome, the Pope's residence. The chapel is famed for scenes painted on its walls and ceiling by Michelangelo.

Reading Skill
Main Idea Which details support the idea that Sis's reaction is exceptional?

Literary Analysis
Reflective Essay How is this experience connected to the lesson that the author learned from her mother?

Vocabulary
rejuvenation
(ri jōō´ və nā´ shən) n. the act of making new, youthful, or energetic again

I did not hear her. I did not really hear her.

There was no way for us to know in the brimful days that followed that there really was a secret she was keeping from us. She had had a heart attack some months before, and she had been ordered to follow a strict set of rules: plenty of rest during the day, early to bed at night, take her medicine faithfully, carefully watch her diet.

She was my mother's younger sister. My mother had been her babysitter. She didn't want my mother to know that she was back to being a baby again, needing to be watched over, having to be put down for a nap, having to be spoon-fed pap. She kept herself busy around the clock, walking, lifting, sitting up late, eating her favorite foods and forgetting her medicine.

▲ **Critical Viewing**
Do you think this painting reflects the author's description of the summer children? Why or why not? **[Connect]**

☑ Reading Check
What is the matter with West's aunt?

▶ Critical Viewing
In what way does this painting suggest a room apart from the rest of the house, like the sun parlor? [Connect]

Reading Skill
Main Idea What main idea do these details about the aunt's stay in the sun parlor suggest?

Vocabulary
convalesce (kän′ və les′) v. regain strength and health

cajoling (kə jōl′ iŋ) n. coaxing with flattery

succinct (sək siŋkt′) adj. clearly and briefly stated

And then one day standing over the stove involved in the making of a meal that a master chef might envy, she collapsed, and the doctor was called, and the doctor called the ambulance.

She was in the hospital ten days. When she was ready to come home to convalesce, we turned the sun parlor into a sickroom, for the stairs to the upper story were forbidden to her. At night we who, when she slept upstairs, would talk family talk back and forth from our beds far into the night, without her we were now quiet, not wanting our voices to wake her if she was asleep, knowing her recovery depended on rest and quiet.

But at night she slept fitfully. The sleeping house and separation from the flock were unbearable. She was afraid of the sun parlor, seeing it as an abnormal offshoot from the main part of the house, its seven long windows giving access to so many imagined terrors. She did not know if we would hear her if she called. She did not know if she would ever get well.

She did not get well. She went back to the hospital, and for our sakes was brave in her last days, comforting us more than we comforted her.

When it was over, we took the sickbed away and restored the sun parlor to its natural look. But it did not look natural. The sadness resisted the sun's cajoling. It had settled in every corner. The seven long windows streaming light did not help. I closed the door and locked it.

My mother saw the closed door and the key in my hand. She said as a simple statement of fact, "A little girl wanted to love that room, and you wouldn't let her. We learn so many lessons as we go through life."

> "We learn so many lessons as we go through life."

"I know that now," I said. "I wish I had known it then."

Another summer came, and with it Sis. The sun parlor door was open again, the room full of light with the sadness trying to hide itself whenever she passed. I did not know how to say to her, "You can go in the sun parlor if you want to." I did not know whether she knew it had been a sickroom, and might say, "Take your sun parlor and you-know-what," though in less succinct phrasing. I did not know if she yet knew that nothing can be the same once it has been different.

Other summers passed, older family members died, and mine became the oldest generation. I was living on the Island year-round in the winterized cottage. The sun parlor was just another everyday room, its seven long windows reduced to three of standard size, most of the furniture replaced for sturdier sitting.

Sis was married, a mother, coming to visit when she could—coming, I think, to look for bits and pieces of my mother in me, wanting to see her ways, hear her words through me.

It was a year ago that I asked her the question that had been on my mind, it seems, forever. A dozen times I had bitten it off my tongue because I did not know what she might answer.

"Sis," I said, "do you remember the summer I painted the sun parlor and acted as if I thought more of it than I thought of you? I'm not asking you to forgive me. All I want to know is if sometimes my mother said to you when I went out, 'She's gone.'" My mother always referred to me as "she" when she was annoyed with me. "'She said she'd be gone awhile. You go play in that sun parlor if you want to. There's nothing in there you can hurt. Nothing in that room is worth as much as a child.'"

I saw her lips beginning to part. And I felt my heart trembling.

"I don't want to know the answer. Please don't tell me the answer. I had to ask the question. It's enough for me that you listened."

She smiled.

Literary Analysis
Reflective Essay What lesson about life has the author learned?

Critical Thinking

Cite textual evidence to support your responses.

1. **Key Ideas and Details** **(a)** What project does West take on to improve the sun parlor? **(b) Infer:** Why does she tell Sis not to go into the room? **(c) Connect:** Does West's response to Sis reflect what her mother taught her about respect for children? Explain.

2. **Key Ideas and Details** **(a) Compare and Contrast:** Using details from the selection, contrast Sis's first reaction to the parlor with her reactions to other things. **(b) Interpret:** What does West mean by calling Sis's reaction part of an "awakening"?

3. **Craft and Structure** **(a)** At what point near the end of the essay does the author switch from the past to the present? **(b)** How does this order of ideas help her explain the lesson she learned?

4. **Integration of Knowledge and Ideas** **(a)** What does West mean when she says to Sis, "It's enough for me that you listened"? **(b)** Explain how the statement could also indicate the reason West wrote the essay. **(c)** In a group, discuss why it is important to West that people "listen." Work together to develop an explanation, and then present it to the class. *[Connect to the Big Question: What kind of knowledge changes our lives?]*

Literary Analysis: Reflective Essay

1. Key Ideas and Details Using a chart like the one shown, analyze West's use of the sun parlor as a focus for her **reflective essay.** For each detail you list, explain its connection to the sun parlor.

| Feelings | | The Sun Parlor | | Events or Facts |

2. Craft and Structure (a) Explain what point the author makes through the feelings and events she connects with the sun parlor. **(b)** Explain how she organizes details in her essay to build toward this point.

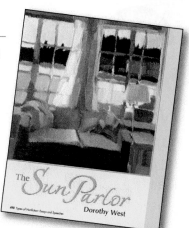

The **Sun Parlor**
Dorothy West

490 Types of Nonfiction: Essays and Speeches

Reading Skill: Main Idea

3. (a) Reread the first six paragraphs. What is the topic of this section? **(b)** What is the **main idea? (c)** What details support it?

4. (a) What is the next main idea you find in the essay? **(b)** Identify three **supporting details** that develop this idea.

5. (a) After reading the essay, identify one further question you have. **(b)** Where could you look to find the answer?

Vocabulary

Acquisition and Use For each sentence, write a new sentence with the same meaning using a word from the list on page 488.

1. I gave in to my brother's wheedling and lent him my new game.

2. The lesser-known actors must share a dressing room.

3. They showered praise on us for our successful fund drive.

4. The complete recovery of her knee after surgery was a wonder.

5. After she broke her leg, my sister had to stay home for a month to regain her strength and health.

6. He is a good debater because his responses are clear and brief.

Word Study Use the context of the sentences and what you know about the **Latin prefix suc-** to explain your answer to each question.

1. If books you requested from the library arrive in *succession*, will you receive them all at the same time?

2. Will a person with strong willpower easily *succumb* to others?

Word Study

The **Latin prefix suc-** is another spelling of the prefix **sub-,** meaning "under," "less or lower than," or "following after."

Apply It Explain how the prefix *-suc-* contributes to the meanings of these words. Consult a dictionary if necessary.

succeed
successor
succor

What kind of *knowledge* changes our lives?

from In Commemoration:
ONE MILLION VOLUMES

Rudolfo A. Anaya

Writing About the Big Question

In the excerpt from "In Commemoration: One Million Volumes," Anaya reflects on how a devotion to words and knowledge has shaped his life. Use these sentence starters to develop your ideas about the Big Question.

In addition to books and libraries, _____ may **influence** a person's desire to learn new things because _____.

One way to **enlighten** a person about new experiences and information is to _____.

While You Read Look for the different ways Anaya has gained knowledge throughout his life.

Vocabulary

Read each word and its definition. Decide whether you know the word well, know it a little bit, or do not know it at all. After you read, see how your knowledge of each word has increased.

- **infinite** (in´ fə nit) *adj.* beyond measure or comprehension; endless (p. 501) *The number of stars in the sky seems infinite.* *infinitely adv. infinity n. finite adj.*

- **inherent** (in hir´ ənt) *adj.* inborn; natural; characteristic (p. 502) *Her inherent sweetness makes it hard for her to get angry.* *inherently adv.*

- **paradox** (par´ ə däks´) *n.* a statement or situation that seems contradictory (p. 503) *What a paradox it is for him to confess that he never tells the truth! paradoxical adj. paradoxically adv.*

- **dilapidated** (də lap´ ə dāt´ id) *adj.* shabby; broken down (p. 503) *The dilapidated chair broke when I sat on it. dilapidate v. dilapidation n.*

- **enthralls** (en thrôlz´) *v.* captivates; fascinates (p. 505) *This book enthralls me, and I cannot wait to read more. enthrallment n.*

- **poignant** (poin´ yənt) *adj.* emotionally moving; piercing (p. 506) *The poignant scene with the abandoned puppies always makes me cry. poignancy n. poignantly adv.*

Word Study

The **Greek prefix *para-*** means "beside" or "beyond."

In this essay, the author explains that books are a **paradox** because they provide answers to questions but also make the reader want to go beyond that information in order to learn more.

Meet
Rudolfo A. Anaya
(b. 1937)

Author of
In Commemoration:
ONE MILLION
VOLUMES

Rudolfo A. Anaya was born and raised in the rural village of Pastura in New Mexico. As a child, Anaya's imagination was nourished by *cuentos*—stories that Mexican Americans passed down from one generation to the next.

Teaching and Learning While teaching high school English, Anaya wrote *Bless Me, Ultima,* a highly praised novel about a young boy growing up in New Mexico. The novel was published in 1972. A strong voice of the Mexican American experience, Anaya is considered a founder of Chicano literature. He went on to teach at the University of New Mexico until his retirement in 1993. In his writing, though, he plays the student as much as the teacher. He explains, "Writing novels seems to be the medium which allows me to bring together all the questions I ask about life."

BACKGROUND FOR THE ESSAY
Libraries
In this essay, Anaya is astounded by the size of the University of New Mexico's library. Libraries perform a variety of functions. For example, a neighborhood library may preserve local history. A university library supports the research of scholars in a variety of subject areas. The Library of Congress guards the historical and cultural records of the United States.

DID YOU KNOW?
In 2002, Anaya was awarded a National Medal of the Arts; he has also received the Mexican Medal of Friendship.

from In Commemoration:

ONE MILLION VOLUMES

Rudolfo A. Anaya

A MILLION VOLUMES.
A MAGIC NUMBER.
A MILLION BOOKS TO READ, TO LOOK AT, TO HOLD IN ONE'S HAND, TO LEARN, TO DREAM. . . .

I have always known there were at least a million stars. In the summer evenings when I was a child, we, all the children of the neighborhood, sat outside under the stars and listened to the stories of the old ones, los viejitos.[1] The stories of the old people taught us to wonder and imagine. Their adivinanzas[2] induced the stirring of our first questioning, our early learning.

I remember my grandfather raising his hand and pointing to the swirl of the Milky Way which swept over us. Then he would whisper his favorite riddle:

> Hay un hombre con tanto dinero
> Que no lo puede contar
> Una mujer con una sábana tan grande
> Que no la puede doblar.

> There is a man with so much money
> He cannot count it
> A woman with a bedspread so large
> She cannot fold it

We knew the million stars were the coins of the Lord, and the heavens were the bedspread of his mother, and in our minds the sky was a million miles wide. A hundred million. Infinite. Stuff for the imagination. And what was more important, the teachings of the old ones made us see that we were bound to the infinity of that cosmic dance of life which swept around us. Their teachings created in us a thirst for knowledge. Can this library with its million volumes bestow that same inspiration?

I was fortunate to have had those old and wise viejitos as guides into the world of nature and knowledge. They taught me with their stories; they taught me the magic of words. Now

---

1. los viejitos (lôs byā hē´ tôs) *n.* Spanish for "the old ones."
2. adivinanzas (a *th*ē vē nan´ sas) *n.* Spanish for "riddles."

◀ **Critical Viewing**
How does this painting convey a sense of wonder and imagination? **[Connect]**

Vocabulary
infinite (in´ fə nit) *adj.* beyond measure or comprehension; endless

Reading Check

What does Anaya learn to appreciate from the *viejitos*?

Vocabulary
inherent (in hir´ ənt)
adj. inborn; natural;
characteristic

Literary Analysis
Reflective Essay Which
period in his life is the
writer describing?

Reading Skill
Main Idea What main
idea is supported by
details about the writer's
grandfather's stories?

Spiral Review
**Development of
Ideas** Explain how this
passage helps the writer
develop connections
between the theme of
wonder and the theme
of learning.

the words lie captured in ink, but the magic is still there, the power inherent in each volume. Now with book in hand we can participate in the wisdom of mankind.

Each person moves from innocence through rites of passage into the knowledge of the world, and so I entered the world of school in search of the magic in the words. The sounds were no longer the soft sounds of Spanish which my grandfather spoke; the words were in English, and with each new awareness came my first steps toward a million volumes. I, who was used to reading my oraciones en español[3] while I sat in the kitchen and answered the litany to the slap of my mother's tortillas,[4] I now stumbled from sound to word to groups of words, head throbbing, painfully aware that each new sound took me deeper into the maze of the new language. Oh, how I clutched the hands of my new guides then!

Learn, my mother encouraged me, learn. Be as wise as your grandfather. He could speak many languages. He could speak to the birds and the animals of the field.

Yes, I remember the cuentos[5] of my grandfather, the stories of the people. Words are a way, he said, they hold joy, and they are a deadly power if misused. I clung to each syllable which lisped from his tobacco-stained lips. That was the winter the snow came, he would say, it piled high and we lost many sheep and cattle, and the trees groaned and broke with its weight. I looked across the llano[6] and saw the raging blizzard, the awful destruction of that winter which was imbedded in our people's mind.

And the following summer, he would say, the grass of the llano grew so high we couldn't see the top of the sheep. And I would look and see what was once clean and pure and green. I could see a million sheep and the pastores[7] caring for them, as I now care for the million words that pasture in my mind.

But a million books? How can we see a million books? I don't mean just the books lining the shelves here at the University of New Mexico Library, not just the fine worn covers, the intriguing titles; how can we see the worlds that lie waiting in each book? A million worlds. A million million worlds. And the beauty of it is that each world is related to the next, as was taught to us by the old ones. Perhaps it is easier for a child to see. Perhaps it is easier for a child to ask: How many stars are there in the sky? How many leaves in the trees of the river? How many blades of grass in the llano? How many dreams in a night of dreams? ●

---

3. **oraciones en español** (ô ra syôn´ ās en es pa nyōl´) prayers in Spanish.
4. **tortillas** (tôr tē´ yəs) *n.* thin, flat, round cakes of unleavened cornmeal.
5. **cuentos** (kwen´ tôs) *n.* Spanish for "stories."
6. **llano** (ya´ nō) *n.* Spanish for "plain."
7. **pastores** (pas tô´ rās) *n.* Spanish for "shepherds."

Cultural Connection

Mexican American Pride
Anaya's celebration of his grandfather's *cuentos* shares in the spirit of the Chicano movement of the 1960s.

- Participants in the movement cultivated pride in their Mexican American heritage.
- Leaders included Cesar Chavez (shown in the mural), who unionized grape pickers in California.
- Chicano artists use the symbol of the eagle and serpent to reflect their connection with the Aztecs, founders of a great civilization in Mexico.

Connect to the Literature

What is one way in which Anaya's essay celebrates his Mexican American heritage? Explain your answer.

Total U.S. Hispanic Population 2002: 37.4 million

Central and South American 14.3%

Puerto Rican 8.6%

Mexican 66.9%

Cuban 3.7%

Other Hispanic 6.5%

Source: U.S. Census Bureau, March 2002

So I worked my way into the world of books, but here is the **paradox**, a book at once quenches the thirst of the imagination and ignites new fires. I learned that as I visited the library of my childhood, the Santa Rosa Library. It was only a dusty room in those days, a room sitting atop the town's fire department, which was comprised of one **dilapidated** fire truck used by the town's volunteers only in the direst emergencies. But in that small room I found my shelter and retreat. If there were a hundred books there we were fortunate, but to me there were a million volumes. I trembled in awe when I first entered that library, because I realized that if the books held as much magic as the words of the old ones, then indeed this was a room full of power.

Miss Pansy, the librarian, became my new guide. She fed me books as any mother would nurture her child. She brought me book after book, and I consumed them all. Saturday afternoons disappeared as the time of day dissolved into the time of distant worlds. In a world that occupied most of my other schoolmates with games, I took the time to read. I was a librarian's dream. My tattered library card was my ticket into the same worlds my grandfather had known, worlds of magic that fed the imagination.

Late in the afternoon, when I was satiated with reading, when I could no longer hold in my soul the characters that crowded there,

Vocabulary

paradox (par´ ə däks´) *n.* a statement or situation that seems contradictory

dilapidated (də lap´ ə dāt´ id) *adj.* shabby; broken down

Literary Analysis
Reflective Essay What general idea connects this new experience to those Anaya has already narrated?

Reading Check

How does Anaya pursue his love of words?

I heard the call of the llano, the real world of my father's ranchito, the solid, warm world of my mother's kitchen. Then to the surprise and bewilderment of Miss Pansy, I would rush out and race down the streets of our town, books tucked under my shirt, in my pockets, clutched tightly to my breast. Mad with the insanity of books, I would cross the river to get home, shouting my crazy challenge even at la Llorona,[8] and that poor spirit of so many frightening cuentos would wither and withdraw. She was no match for me.

Those of you who have felt the same exhilaration from reading—or from love—will know about what I'm speaking. Alas, the people of the town could only shake their heads and pity my mother. At least one of her sons was a bit touched. Perhaps they were right, for few will trade a snug reality to float on words to other worlds.

And now there are a million volumes for us to read here at the University of New Mexico Library. Books on every imaginable subject, in every field, a history of the thought of the world which we must keep free of censorship, because we treasure our freedoms. It is the word *freedom* which eventually must reflect what this collection, or the collection of any library, is all about. We know that as we preserve and use the literature of all cultures, we preserve and regenerate our own. The old ones knew and taught me this. They eagerly read the few newspapers that were available. They kept their diaries, they wrote décimas[9] and cuentos, and they survived on their oral stories and traditions. ●

Another time, another library. I entered Albuquerque[10] High School Library prepared to study, because that's where we spent our study time. For better or for worse, I received my first contracts as a writer there. It was a place where budding lovers spent most of their time writing notes to each other, and when my friends who didn't have the gift of words found out I could turn a phrase I quickly had all the business I could do. I wrote poetic love notes for a dime apiece and thus worked my way through high school.

---

8. **la Llorona** (la yô rô′ na) *n.* spirit of many Spanish stories, famous for shouting and crying for her lost love.
9. **décimas** (dā′ sē mas) *n.* Spanish for "ten-line stanzas."
10. **Albuquerque** (al′ bə kʉr′ kē) *n.* city in central New Mexico.

And there were fringe benefits, because the young women knew very well who was writing the sweet words, and many a heart I was supposed to capture fell in love with me. And so, a library is also a place where love begins.

A library should be the heart of a city. With its storehouse of knowledge, it liberates, informs, teaches, and enthralls. A library indeed should be the cultural center of any city. Amidst the bustle of work and commerce, the great libraries of the world have provided a sanctuary where scholars and common man alike come to enlarge and clarify knowledge, to read and reflect in quiet solitude.

I knew a place like this. I spent many hours in the old library on Central Avenue and Edith Street. But my world was growing, and quite by accident I wandered up the hill to enroll in the University of New Mexico. And what a surprise lay in store for me. The libraries of my childhood paled in comparison to this new wealth of books housed in Zimmerman Library. Here there were stack after stack of books, and ample space and time to wander aimlessly in this labyrinth of new frontiers.

I had known the communal memory of my people through the newspapers and few books my grandfather read to me and through the rich oral tradition handed down by the old ones; now I discovered the collective memory of all mankind at my fingertips. I had only to reach for the books that laid all history bare. Here I could converse with the writers from every culture on earth, old and new, and at the same time I began my personal odyssey, which would add a few books to the collection which in 1981 would come to house a million volumes.

Those were exciting times. Around me swirled the busy world of the university, in many respects an alien world. Like many fellow undergraduates, I sought refuge in the library. My haven during those student university years was the reading room of the west wing of the old library. There I found peace. The carved vigas[11] decorating the ceiling, the solid wooden tables and chairs and the warm adobe color of the stucco were things with which I was familiar. There I felt comfortable. With books scattered around me, I could read and doze and dream. I took my breaks in the warm sun of the portal, where I ate my tortilla sandwiches, which I carried in my brown paper bag. There, with friends, I sipped coffee as we talked of changing the world and exchanged idealistic dreams.

Vocabulary
enthralls (en thrôlz´) *v.* captivates; fascinates

> A LIBRARY INDEED SHOULD BE THE CULTURAL CENTER OF ANY CITY.

Literary Analysis
Reflective Essay What general idea does Anaya use to relate this new period in his life to previous ones?

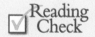
Reading Check
What vital services do libraries provide to cities?

---

11. vigas (bē´ gas) *n.* Spanish for "roof beams."

Vocabulary
poignant (poin´ yənt)
adj. emotionally mov-
ing; piercing

That is a rich and pleasant time in my memory. No matter how far across the world I find myself in the future, how deep in the creation of worlds with words, I shall keep the simple and poignant memories of those days. The sun set golden on the ocher walls, and the green pine trees and the blue spruce, sacred trees to our people, whispered in the breeze. I remembered my grandfather meeting with the old men of the village in the resolana[12] of one of the men's homes, or against the wall of the church on Sundays, and I remembered the things they said. Later, alone, dreaming against the sun-warmed wall of the library, I continued that discourse in my mind.

Yes, the library is a place where people should gather. It is a place for research, reading, and for the quiet fomentation of ideas, but because it houses the collective memory of our race, it should also be a place where present issues are discussed and debated and researched in order for us to gain the knowledge and insight to create a better future. The library should be a warm place that reflects the needs and aspirations of the people.

---

12. **resolana** (rā sô la´ na) *n.* Spanish for "place for enjoying the sun."

Critical Thinking

Cite textual evidence to support your responses.

1. **Key Ideas and Details (a)** According to Anaya, what did the stories of *los viejitos* teach him and other children? **(b) Compare and Contrast:** Identify a difference and a similarity between the riddles and *cuentos* Anaya learned in childhood and the books he later read.

2. **Craft and Structure (a)** At what point near the end of the essay does the author switch from the past to the present? **(b)** How does this order of ideas help him develop his main idea about libraries?

3. **Key Ideas and Details Interpret:** Why does Anaya associate libraries with freedom?

4. **Integration of Knowledge and Ideas (a)** In what ways do libraries make an impact on individuals? **(b)** In today's world, what do you think is the best way to awaken wonder and imagination in people and inspire them to learn? *[Connect to the Big Question: What kind of knowledge changes our lives?]*

Literary Analysis: Reflective Essay

1. Key Ideas and Details Using a chart like the one shown, analyze Anaya's use of libraries as a focus for his **reflective essay.** For each detail you list, explain its connection to libraries.

Feelings		Events or Facts
	Libraries	

from In Commemoration:
ONE MILLION VOLUMES
Rudolfo A. Anaya

2. Craft and Structure (a) Choose an item from your chart, and explain its association with something endless—an uncountable number, for example. What truth about imagination does the item illustrate? **(b)** Explain how Anaya organizes details to develop this idea.

Reading Skill: Main Idea

3. (a) Reread up to the paragraph on page 502 that begins, "But a million books?" What is the topic of this section? **(b)** What is the **main idea? (c)** What details support it?

4. (a) What is the next main idea you find in the essay? **(b)** Identify three **supporting details** for the idea.

5. (a) After reading the essay, identify one further question you have. **(b)** Where could you look to find the answer?

Vocabulary

Acquisition and Use For each sentence, write a new sentence with the same meaning using a word from the list on page 498.

1. Getting wet is a risk that is a built-in part of boating.

2. Their reunion was very emotional and touching.

3. My broken-down old bike is dangerous to ride.

4. That comic book is wildly interesting to him.

5. When she takes care of her little brother, her patience is endless.

6. It seemed like a contradiction that she loved to grow vegetables but did not like to eat them.

Word Study Use the context of the sentences and what you know about the **Greek prefix *para*-** to explain your answer to each question.

1. Would two *parallel* boards be crossing or touching each other?

2. Should you postpone a task of *paramount* importance?

Word Study

The **Greek prefix *para*-** means "beside" or "beyond."

Apply It Explain how the prefix *para*- contributes to the meanings of these words. Consult a dictionary if necessary.

paramedic
parameter
paraphrase

Integrated Language Skills

The Sun Parlor • *from* In Commemoration: One Million Volumes

Conventions: Subject Complements

Predicate nominatives and **predicate adjectives** are subject complements. They appear after a linking verb such as *be, is,* or *seem,* and they rename, identify, or describe the subject of the sentence.

A subject and a predicate nominative both name the same person, place, or thing. The linking verb joins them and makes them equal.

Examples: Their first <u>choice</u> was <u>you</u>.
Our vacation <u>destination</u> is the <u>beach</u>.

A predicate adjective appears with the linking verb and describes the subject of the sentence.

Examples: <u>Roses</u> are <u>red</u>.
Soccer <u>equipment</u> is <u>expensive</u>.

Practice A Identify the subject complement in each sentence and label it *predicate nominative* or *predicate adjective.*

1. The author is the narrator.
2. The sun parlor was beautiful.
3. West's aunt seemed healthy.
4. Children are our greatest treasures.
5. West felt remorseful.

Practice B Add a predicate nominative or predicate adjective, as indicated, to complete each sentence.

1. Anaya is (predicate nominative).
2. Anaya is (predicate adjective).
3. The stories of Anaya's youth seemed (predicate adjective).
4. One feature of libraries is (predicate nominative).
5. Books are (predicate adjective).

ⓔ **Reading Application** In "The Sun Parlor," find and copy one sentence that has a predicate nominative and one sentence that has a predicate adjective. For each sentence, label the complements, and underline the subject once and the linking verb twice.

ⓔ **Writing Application** Write a brief paragraph about a library. At least two sentences should have predicate adjectives, and at least two sentences should have predicate nominatives. After you draft, identify the subject complements you have included.

PH WRITING COACH Further instruction and practice are available in *Prentice Hall Writing Coach.*

Writing

Common Core State Standards

L.9-10.6; SL.9-10.4; W.9-10.3.d-e
[For the full wording of the standards, see page 486.]

Narrative Text Both authors reflect on an earlier time in their lives. Write a brief **memoir,** or recollection based on your personal experience, of a room or a building that holds meaning for you.

- Memoirs are autobiographical; write in the first person, using the pronoun *I* to refer to yourself.

- Develop your memoir with *precise words* to paint a vivid picture of the space or place you are recalling.

- Use concrete *sensory details* to describe the sights, sounds, and smells of the scene, and organize your ideas in a logical order.

- Conclude by sharing your insights with readers and revealing why the place has special meaning for you. Write in a style appropriate for your purpose and audience.

Grammar Application As you write your memoir, use at least one predicate nominative and one predicate adjective.

Writing Workshop: *Work in Progress*

Prewriting for a Letter to the Editor Using the Issues List in your writing portfolio, write an opening sentence for each item that identifies the main point of your letter. Save this Main Idea List in your writing portfolio.

Use this prewriting activity to prepare for the **Writing Workshop** on page 532.

Speaking and Listening

Comprehension and Collaboration Prepare an **oral recollection.** Focus on someone you know who is interesting and important to you or on a group you've been involved in, such as a sports team or a community organization.

- Provide key details to develop your subject. Organize them logically, and build toward a central insight.

- Make sure to clearly establish your point of view and relationship with the subject of your recollection.

- Include sensory details and concrete images.

- First, present your recollection to a classmate. Then, revise your draft based on feedback from your partner. Make sure the reasoning you use to connect details to your central insight is clear and that the style of your speech is appropriate for your audience and purpose.

- Present a revised version of your recollection to the class.

PHLit Online!
www.PHLitOnline.com
- Interactive graphic organizers
- Grammar tutorial
- Interactive journals

Test Practice: Reading

Main Idea

Fiction Selection

Directions: *Read the selection. Then, answer the questions.*

Nahuaca's family were cultivators of the *chinampas,* the raised lake gardens of the Aztecs. Nahuaca worked beside his father, placing rows of long poles to form the sides of the chinampas in the shallow lake surrounding the great city of Tenochtitlán. He paddled the canoe, scooping mud and plants from the lake bottom to build the chinampas several feet above the lake. He transplanted the tiny tomato plants in the garden. As he worked, he marveled at the garden's beauty.

One day his father spoke to him. "Nahuaca, someday you will choose your own path, but know that if you choose to farm with your family, you will be contributing to your people. Growing these tomatoes, maize, and chilies allows us all to thrive. Without us, the people in our city would have no food. Food is not all we get from the lake gardens, though; they are an important part of our culture as well."

1. Which of the following *best* states the main idea of this passage?

   A. Aztec people were great warriors.

   B. Aztec people grew a variety of food in lake gardens.

   C. Tenochtitlán was a beautiful city.

   D. Aztec people lived on gardens in lakes and worked very hard.

2. Which detail supports the idea that Nahuaca appreciated the gardens?

   A. His family were cultivators of the chinampas.

   B. He worked alongside his father.

   C. His father told Nahuaca he would choose his own path someday.

   D. He marveled at the gardens' beauty.

3. Which of the following details *does not* tell how the Aztec people lived?

   A. Chinampas were raised lake gardens.

   B. "We grow tomatoes, maize, beans, and chilies."

   C. Nahuaca paddled a flat-bottom canoe.

   D. One day his father spoke to him.

4. To understand the Aztec way of life better, what question might you ask?

   A. Did Nahuaca continue to grow food?

   B. Is it difficult to grow tomatoes?

   C. What did Aztecs do for recreation?

   D. Why should people build lake gardens?

Writing for Assessment

Consider the main idea and details in this passage. Then write an appropriate title for it. In a paragraph, explain why your title makes sense.

Nonfiction Selection

Directions: *Read the selection. Then, answer the questions.*

You may not be able to imagine pizza without tomato sauce, but tomatoes have not always been such a popular food. Tomatoes began as a wild species in what is now Peru and Ecuador. The plant was probably domesticated in Mexico centuries before Europeans arrived. Its name is from the Náhuatl (Aztec) word *tomati.* In the early 1500s, the Spanish brought the tomato to Europe, where it was used as food by the Spanish and Italians. In England, France, and Northern Europe, however, the tomato was believed to be poisonous. The English used the plant simply for its beauty.

From Europe, the tomato was introduced to North America, where it was used as food in the early 1800s. By the early twentieth century, the tomato was widely popular as food, and by the late twentieth century, the United States led the world in tomato production.

1. Which of the following *best* states the main idea of the passage?

    A. Tomatoes originated in South America, probably in Ecuador and Peru, and were probably domesticated in Mexico.
    B. At one time, tomatoes were considered poisonous and planted for their beauty.
    C. The tomato has a long history that spans the world, but it did not become widely popular as a food until the 1900s.
    D. The Aztecs were the first to cultivate tomatoes.

2. Which of the following details *does not* support the main idea of the passage?

    A. Some believed tomatoes were poisonous.
    B. *Tomato* originated from a Náhautl word.
    C. Tomatoes originated in Ecuador and Peru.
    D. The Spanish brought the tomato to Europe.

3. The author's purpose is most likely to—

    A. entertain readers with a humorous story about pizza.
    B. describe what it is like to eat a tomato.
    C. inform readers about how the tomato became a popular food.
    D. explain the process of growing tomatoes.

4. To learn more about the popularity of tomatoes in the United States today, what question might you research?

    A. What caused people to believe that tomatoes might be poisonous?
    B. How many tomatoes were sold in the United States last year?
    C. Do Europeans still plant tomatoes for their beauty?
    D. Do wild tomatoes grow in the U.S.?

Writing for Assessment

Connecting Across Texts

What details from the nonfiction passage might be used to support the fiction passage? In a paragraph, explain your answer.

www.PHLitOnline.com
- Online practice
- Instant feedback

Reading for Information

Analyzing Functional Texts

Technical Directions

User's Guide

Ⓒ Common Core
State Standards

Reading Informational Text
3. Analyze how the author
unfolds an analysis or series of
ideas or events, including the
order in which the points are
made, how they are introduced
and developed, and the
connections that are drawn
between them.

Writing
1. Write arguments to support
claims in an analysis of
substantive topics or texts, using
valid reasoning and relevant and
sufficient evidence. *(Timed Writing)*

Language
4.b. Identify and correctly use
patterns of word changes that
indicate different meanings or
parts of speech.

Reading Skill:
Follow and Critique Technical Directions

You can better understand technical directions if you first scan the text to get a sense of the information provided. Then, **critique the logic of the document by examining the sequence,** or structure, of information and directions. Analyze the order in which points are made, how they are introduced, and the connections that are drawn between them. Consider the clarity of the structure and determine whether any elements might cause confusion for the reader.

Once you have analyzed the text, be sure you can answer the following questions before **following the technical directions.**

Questions for Technical Directions

- What does the device do?
- What tools or materials are needed?
- What steps or directions are provided?
- What information is given in charts, diagrams, and illustrations?
- What are the safety warnings?
- What should the user do if something goes wrong?

Content-Area Vocabulary

These words appear in the selections that follow. You may also encounter them in other content-area texts.

- **degrees** (di grēz´) *n.* units of measurement for points on a circle

- **aligns** (ə līnz´) *v.* arranges in a straight line

- **defects** (dē´ fekts) *n.* faults or blemishes

How to Use a
Compass

Our compasses have been the accurate and easy-to-use choice of foresters, geologists, surveyors, scientific explorers, sports enthusiasts, military personnel, and many others for 50 years. Most of our compasses include these features:

- Magnetized tungsten steel needle
- Friction-free sapphire bearing
- Permanently clear, antistatic liquid
- Accurate from – 40° to +140°F

Inch Scale

Direction of Travel Arrow

Orienting Arrow

Base Lines

Magnetic Needle

Index Line

Mile Scale

Rotating Dial, 5°

Orienting Lines

Clear Base Plate

Features:

- step-by-step instructions for how to assemble, operate, or repair a product
- diagrams of the product with the parts listed and labeled
- text written for a specific audience

A diagram identifies the parts of the product with labels to help users follow the instructions.

Easy as 1-2-3

1

Point the Base Plate to Your Destination:
Place your compass on the map with the edge along the desired line of travel.

2

Set the Compass Heading:
Turn the compass Dial until "N" points to the north on your map. Your direction in degrees is read at the Index Line on the Dial.

NOTE: Align the Dial with magnetic north if it is marked on your map. If it is not marked on your map, align the Dial with true north and adjust for declination.

3

Follow Your Heading:
- Remove the compass from your map and hold it level, so the Magnetic Needle is free to turn.
- Turn your body until the red end of the Needle aligns with the Orienting Arrow and "N" on the Dial.

This section explains the easiest use of the compass. Other sections give instructions for other uses.

Find Your Way Without a Map:

Find a heading (field bearing):

1. Select a landmark along the route you want to travel. Hold the compass level and point the Direction of Travel Arrow at the landmark.
2. Find your heading to the landmark by turning the compass dial until the "N" aligns with the red end of the Needle. Read your heading in degrees to the Index Line.
3. Keep the Needle aligned with the "N"; look up; sight on your landmark and walk to it. Repeat this procedure until you reach your destination and walk to it.

When you know your heading:

1. If you've been given a heading in degrees to travel, turn the Dial so that the heading is set at the Index Line. Hold the compass level in front of you with the Direction of Travel Arrow pointing straight ahead.
2. Turn your body until the red end of the Needle is aligned with the "N" on the dial. You now face your direction of travel.
3. Pick out a landmark in line with your heading and move toward it. Repeat this procedure until you reach your destination.

NOTE: Be aware of nearby iron or steel objects. They may attract the Magnetic Needle if too close to the compass. Even a hidden nail can deflect the needle.

> Two ways of using the compass are explained, each in its own set of numbered steps.

Compass Warranty

What Is Covered?

We warrant your compass to be free from **defects** in materials or workmanship, and we guarantee its accuracy, for the life of the compass.

> Headings help users quickly locate answers to frequently asked warranty questions.

What Is Not Covered?

Normal wear, abrasion, melting, misuse, alteration, abuse, or taking apart the compass is not covered by this warranty.

How to Obtain Warranty Service or Repair of Your Compass

Should your compass become defective under the terms of this warranty, call the Customer Satisfaction Department toll free at 1 (800) 123-4567 for return authorization. If, after our inspection, we find that the product was defective in material or workmanship, we shall, at our option, either repair or replace it without charge. If repairs not covered under this warranty are required, we will contact you for approval to proceed. You will be charged for the components repaired or replaced, plus a nominal charge for labor.

There are no other express warranties beyond the terms of this limited warranty. In no event shall our company be liable for incidental or consequential damages arising from using our compasses.

GPS¹

Quick-Start Guide

Features:
- instructions for how to operate a device
- explanations of the different functions and features of the device and how to access them
- diagrams, illustrations, or photographs of the device
- text written for a specific audience

Using the Find Feature:

The features of the Map Page are defined and explained. Instructions are provided for how to utilize them.

1 Tap the **Find** icon on the Map Page tool bar to display the Find Menu.

2 Then select a category icon and tap it to open the search list. To narrow the list of items, tap the second field to display the list of search options. Choose "Near Current Location".

3 To shorten the list even more, tap the category field to display a list of sub-categories to refine the type of map item you are searching for.

4 Select the desired destination and tap to highlight it. Then tap the **Routes** icon at bottom of the page to begin route calculation. From the pop-up options window, select the calculation preference and then tap **OK** to complete route calculation.

5 When complete the route will be displayed on the Map Page along with navigation instructions and voice prompts.

Two sets of instructions are provided. The steps are numbered, and icons highlight key actions.

Managing a Route

Once you have selected a destination and calculated a route, you can modify the route, preview turns, and save it for later reuse.

1 Tap the **Routes** icon on the Map Page tool bar to display the Routes Page. Then tap the desired **Routes Options** icon.

2 Tap the **Turns Page** to view a list of turns for the route. Tap a turn entry to preview the turn on the map.

3 Tap **Recalculate** if you have left the route and want to calculate from your current location.

4 Tap the **Detour** icon if you want to detour the route around a traffic jam or road construction.

5 Tap the **Stop Navigation** icon if you want to quit the route.

6 Tap the **Route Preferences** icon if you want to change the way a route is managed in order to meet your personal requirements.

7 Tap **Edit Vias** if you want to add some new points to alter your route.

8 Tap **Saved Routes** if you want to save the current route or view a previously saved route.

9 Tap **Speak** if you want to listen to current route status voice prompts.

---

1. GPS An abbreviation that stands for Global Positioning System, a navigational system based on receiving signals from satellites orbiting earth.

Labeled graphics show what the user will see on the screen for key steps.

Routes

Navigation Using the Map Page

Navigation is the process of going from your current location to another, and the Map Page has features to help you do that.

Data Fields—Provide GPS Status when not moving, Direction of Travel or Next Street Ahead, Compass Direction, Speed and Current Location

Map Detail—With downloaded detailed maps: Residential Streets, Rivers, Lakes, Points of Interest and Individual Addresses. Oriented with North Up unless in Track Up mode.

The Position Arrow—Indicates your current location. Tap to center it on the map page. Points in the direction of travel.

The Map Pointer—Marks map locations using the stylus. Displays information for a location if available.

The Map Scale—Tapping the Map Scale Box in the lower left corner of the map displays the moving Map Scale. Tap the arrows to move up or down the scale. Tap the desired scale to close.

Navigating to a Destination

A destination can be determined in two ways: you use the Map Pointer to mark a point on the map and then tap the Routes icon . . . or use the Find Feature to search for a destination form the map database and then, when found and highlighted, choose the "Route To It" option from the Find Options Menu.

Using the Map Pointer:

1. Tap the point on the Map Page that you want to navigate to. If there is information about that point in the map database, it will display next to the point.

2. Then tap the Routes icon to display the Routes Page.

3. Tap the "Route To" field and the route will begin to calculate.

4. A pop-up window will offer three preferences for calculating the route. Select an option and tap OK to return to the Map Page to complete calculation.

5. When the calculation is complete, the route will display as a purple overlay on top of the map.

6. The first maneuver on your route is displayed at the top of the map page and is complemented by a voice prompt.

7. To view all of the turns on the route, open the Routes Page and tap the Turns Page icon. A list of turns will display and a preview page for each turn will display when the turn on the list is tapped.

Comparing Functional Texts

1. Key Ideas and Details (a) Critique the logic of the sequence of information in the technical directions. Explain which aspects of the structure help clarify information and which, if any, might cause readers to be confused. **(b)** Do the same for the user's guide. **(c)** Compare the structures of the two documents. Explain which is more logically structured and why.

Content-Area Vocabulary

2. (a) Using your knowledge of the word *aligns* and of word patterns, explain the meanings of these words: *aligned* and *alignment*. **(b)** Use each word in a sentence that reveals its meaning.

Timed Writing

Argumentative Text: Letter

Format and Audience
The prompt gives instructions to write a letter. Because the letter will be addressed to a business, the tone should be formal.

> Write a letter in which you request a repair under warranty for your compass. In your letter, describe a specific problem with the compass. Then, cite details from the warranty to explain the reasons you believe that the repair is covered. (20 minutes)

Academic Vocabulary
When you *describe* something, you use precise words to create a vivid picture in your reader's mind.

5-Minute Planner

Complete these steps before you begin to write:

1. Read the prompt carefully and completely.

2. Reread the technical directions to identify a problem that might occur with the compass. Then, decide on the repair that you will request and make notes about how you will describe the problem.

3. Reread the compass warranty to be sure that the repair you are requesting is covered. Then, note passages you will use as evidence to show why the company is obligated to make the repair.

4. Decide how to structure your letter. For example, you might include a brief introductory paragraph before presenting the reasons why the company should repair your compass. **TIP:** Your letter will be more convincing if you anticipate and answer your readers' objections.

5. Use your notes to prepare a quick outline. Refer to your outline as you draft.

Comparing Humorous Writing

In a **humorous essay** or **speech,** a writer presents a subject in an unexpected, amusing way. The writer may treat a serious situation lightly or a ridiculous situation seriously. Techniques for creating humor include the following.

- Using **hyperbole,** or exaggeration, a writer describes people, things, or events as if they were much more important than they are—for instance, calling the discovery of a missing sock a "joyous reunion."

- Using **understatement,** a writer speaks of people, things, or events as if they were less important than they are—for instance, saying that "the weather was not ideal" after a tornado carries off picnic tables.

When a writer uses humor to point out the foolishness of a particular type of human behavior or of a particular institution, the result is called **satire.**

Mark Twain's speech "A Toast to the Oldest Inhabitant . . ." and James Thurber's essay "The Dog That Bit People" use humor, but their comic techniques are different. Use a chart like the one shown to compare the elements that make these selections humorous.

Common Core State Standards

Reading Literature
7. Analyze the representation of a subject or a key scene in two different artistic mediums, including what is emphasized or absent in each treatment.

	Hyperbole	Understatement	Satire
Twain			
Thurber			

Diction, or word choice, is another literary element that contributes to humor. Authors try to select words that precisely convey the meaning they intend. To do so, they consider a word's **connotation**—the set of ideas associated with it—as well as the word's denotation, or definition. For example, the words *house* and *home* both mean "place to live," but the word *home* is associated with ideas like family and comfort. The word *house* does not have these connotations. As you read the selections, consider the connotations of the authors' diction and analyze how precise word choices contribute to both humorous meaning and **tone,** or the expression of the writer's attitude toward his or her subject and reader.

Reading Informational Text
4. Determine the meaning of words and phrases as they are used in a text, including figurative, connotative, and technical meanings; analyze the cumulative impact of specific word choices on meaning and tone.

Writing
2. Write informative/explanatory texts to examine and convey complex ideas, concepts, and information clearly and accurately through the effective selection, organization, and analysis of content.

2.a. Introduce a topic; organize complex ideas, concepts, and information to make important connections and distinctions. *(Timed Writing)*

www.PHLitOnline.com

- Vocabulary flashcards
- Interactive journals
- More about the authors
- Selection audio
- Interactive graphic organizers

What kind of *knowledge* changes our lives?

Writing About the Big Question

In each story, the narrator tolerates something that would otherwise be intolerable—terrible weather or an exceptionally bad dog—by treating it with good humor. Think about a bad situation that you or someone else might typically experience. What knowledge might change your attitude? Use this sentence starter to develop your ideas about the Big Question.

When I need to **adapt** to a bad situation, I try to remember _____.

Meet the Authors

Mark Twain (1835–1910)

Author of "A Toast to the Oldest Inhabitant"

Mark Twain is the pen name of Samuel Langhorne Clemens, one of America's greatest writers. He is most famous for two classic novels: *The Adventures of Tom Sawyer* (1876) and *The Adventures of Huckleberry Finn* (1884).

A Standup Comic Mark Twain became a sought-after, highly paid public speaker. He delivered "A Toast to the Oldest Inhabitant . . ." at the annual dinner of the New England Society on December 22, 1876.

James Thurber (1894–1961)

Author of "The Dog That Bit People"

A native of Columbus, Ohio, James Thurber went to work for the U.S. State Department after college. Soon afterward, however, he found his true calling—he became a humorist, writing essays and drawing cartoons for *The New Yorker*, a famous magazine.

Growing Fame, Failing Vision Thurber won fame for his whimsical depictions of human (and animal) silliness. By the 1940s, though, his failing eyesight forced him to reduce the number of cartoon drawings he created. By 1952, Thurber was almost totally blind, but he still wrote stories and articles for the magazine. His collections, including *The Thurber Carnival* (1945), are considered classics of humor writing.

A Toast to the Oldest Inhabitant:
The WEATHER
of New England
Mark Twain

▲ **Critical Viewing**
Based on this scene, what comments do you think Twain makes about New England weather?
[Preview]

Who can lose it and forget it?
Who can have it and regret it?
Be interposer 'twixt us Twain.[1]
—The Merchant of Venice, William Shakespeare

Gentlemen: I reverently believe that the Maker who made us all, makes everything in New England[2]—but the weather. I don't know who makes that, but I think it must be raw apprentices in the Weather Clerk's factory, who experiment and learn how in New England, for board and clothes, and then are promoted to make

---

1. **Twain** archaic word for "two" (and a pun on Twain's name).
2. **New England** the states of the northeastern United States: Maine, Vermont, New Hampshire, Massachusetts, Rhode Island, and Connecticut.

weather for countries that require a good article, and will take their custom elsewhere if they don't get it. There is a sumptuous variety about the New England weather that compels the stranger's admiration—and regret. The weather is always doing something there; always attending strictly to business; always getting up new designs and trying them on the people to see how they will go. But it gets through more business in spring than in any other season. In the spring I have counted one hundred and thirty-six different kinds of weather inside of four and twenty hours. It was I that made the fame and fortune of that man that had that marvelous collection of weather on exhibition at the Centennial[3] that so astounded the foreigners. He was going to travel all over the world and get specimens from all the climes. I said, "Don't you do it; you come to New England on a favorable spring day." I told him what we could do, in the way of style, variety, and quantity. Well, he came, and he made his collection in four days. As to variety—why, he confessed that he got hundreds of kinds of weather that he had never heard of before. And as to quantity—well, after he had picked out and discarded all that was blemished in any way, he not only had weather enough, but weather to spare; weather to hire out; weather to sell; to deposit; weather to invest; weather to give to the poor.

---

3. **Centennial** international trade fair held in 1876 in Philadelphia to mark the hundredth anniversary of the Declaration of Independence. The fair featured scientific and technological marvels of the day.

Vocabulary
sumptuous (sump´ cho͞o əs) *adj.* lavish

Literary Analysis
Humorous Writing
What hyperbole does Twain use here to make his point about New England weather?

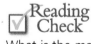
Reading Check
What is the main characteristic of New England weather according to Twain?

▼ **Critical Viewing**
Are you surprised there is such a wide variety of weather in such a small area of the United States? Why or why not? **[Make a Judgment]**

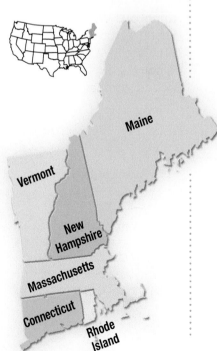

The people of New England are by nature patient and forbearing; but there are some things which they will not stand. Every year they kill a lot of poets for writing about "Beautiful Spring." These are generally casual visitors, who bring their notions of spring from somewhere else, and cannot, of course, know how the natives feel about spring. And so, the first thing they know, the opportunity to inquire how they feel has permanently gone by.

Old Probabilities has a mighty reputation for accurate prophecy, and thoroughly well deserves it. You take up the papers and observe how crisply and confidently he checks off what today's weather is going to be on the Pacific, down South, in the Middle States, in the Wisconsin region; see him sail along in the joy and pride of his power till he gets to New England, and then—see his tail drop. *He* doesn't know what the weather is going to be like in New England. He can't any more tell than he can tell how many Presidents of the United States there's going to be next year.[4] Well, he mulls over it, and by and by he gets out something about like this: Probable nor'-east to sou'-west winds, varying to the southard and westard and eastard and points between; high and low barometer, swapping around from place to place; probable

---

4. **how many Presidents of the United States there's going to be next year** The United States presidential election of 1876 was one of the most disputed, with two declared "winners" when Twain gave this speech. Rutherford B. Hayes was declared the final victor on March 2, 1877.

areas of rain, snow, hail, and drought, succeeded or preceded by earthquakes, with thunder and lightning. Then he jots down this postscript from his wandering mind, to cover accidents: "But it is possible that the program may be wholly changed in the meantime."

Yes, one of the brightest gems in the New England weather is the dazzling uncertainty of it. There is only one thing certain about it, you are certain there is going to be plenty of weather—a perfect grand review; but you never can tell which end of the procession is going to move first. You fix up for the drought; you leave your umbrella in the house and sally out with your sprinkling pot, and ten to one you get drowned. You make up your mind that the earthquake is due; you stand from under, and take hold of something to steady yourself, and the first thing you know, you get struck by lightning. These are great disappointments. But they can't be helped. The lightning there is peculiar; it is so convincing! When it strikes a thing, it doesn't leave enough of that thing behind for you to tell whether—well, you'd think it was something valuable, and a Congressman had been there.

And the thunder. When the thunder commences to merely tune up, and scrape, and saw, and key up the instruments for the performance, strangers say, "Why, what awful thunder you have here!" But when the baton is raised and the real concert begins, you'll find that stranger down in the cellar, with his head in the ash barrel.

Now, as to the size of the weather in New England—lengthways, I mean. It is utterly disproportioned to the size of that little country. Half the time, when it is packed as full as it can stick, you will see that New England weather sticking out beyond the edges and projecting around hundreds and hundreds of miles over the neighboring states. She can't hold a tenth part of her weather. You can see cracks all about, where she has strained herself trying to do it.

I could speak volumes about the inhuman perversity of the New England weather, but I will give but a single specimen. I like to hear rain on a tin roof, so I covered part of my roof with tin, with an eye to that luxury. Well, sir, do you think it ever rains on the tin? No, sir; skips it every time.

Mind, in this speech I have been trying merely to do honor to the New England weather—no language could do it justice. But, after all, there are at least one or two things about that weather (or, if you please, effects produced by it) which we residents would not like to part with. If we hadn't our bewitching autumn foliage, we should still have to credit the weather with one

Literary Analysis
Humorous Writing
How does Twain use understatement here to add humor?

Literary Analysis
Humorous Writing
What does Twain satirically imply about congressmen in this paragraph?

> Yes, one of the brightest gems in the New England weather is the dazzling uncertainty of it.

Reading Check
According to Twain, how easy is it to predict New England weather?

feature which compensates for all its bullying vagaries—the ice storm—when a leafless tree is clothed with ice from the bottom to the top—ice that is as bright and clear as crystal; when every bough and twig is strung with ice beads, frozen dewdrops, and the whole tree sparkles, cold and white, like the Shah[5] of Persia's diamond plume. Then the wind waves the branches, and the sun comes out and turns all those myriads of beads and drops to prisms, that glow and burn and flash with all manner of colored fires, which change and change again, with inconceivable rapidity, from blue to red, from red to green, and green to gold—the tree becomes a spraying fountain, a very explosion of dazzling jewels; and it stands there the acme, the climax, the supremest possibility in art or nature, of bewildering, intoxicating, intolerable magnificence! One cannot make the words too strong.

Month after month I lay up my hate and grudge against the New England weather; but when the ice storm comes at last, I say: "There—I forgive you, now—the books are square between us, you don't owe me a cent; go, and sin no more; your little faults and foibles count for nothing—you are the most enchanting weather in the world!"

---

5. Shah (shä) *n.* formerly, the title of the ruler of Persia (now Iran).

Critical Thinking

1. **Key Ideas and Details (a)** According to Twain, what quality or feature of New England weather "compels the stranger's admiration"? **(b) Connect:** What point does Twain support with the story of the man who collected and exhibited weather?

2. **Key Ideas and Details (a) Infer:** What is the profession of "Old Probabilities"? **(b) Interpret:** What point is Twain making in the anecdote about this character?

3. **Craft and Structure** Twain describes New England weather as having "inhuman perversity." **(a) Interpret:** Is the connotation of these words positive or negative? **(b) Analyze:** How does the connotation affect the tone of the writing?

4. **Integration of Knowledge and Ideas** What knowledge allows Twain to appreciate New England's tumultuous weather? *[Connect to the Big Question: What kind of knowledge changes our lives?]*

The Dog That Bit People

James Thurber

Nobody Knew Exactly What Was the Matter with Him, James Thurber

Probably no one man should have as many dogs in his life as I have had, but there was more pleasure than distress in them for me except in the case of an Airedale named Muggs. He gave me more trouble than all the other fifty-four or -five put together, although my moment of keenest embarrassment was the time a Scotch terrier named Jeannie, who had just had six puppies in the clothes closet of a fourth floor apartment in New York, had the unexpected seventh and last at the corner of Eleventh Street and Fifth Avenue during a walk she had insisted on taking. Then, too, there was the prize winning French poodle, a great big black poodle—none of your little, untroublesome white miniatures—who got sick riding in the rumble seat[1] of a car with me on her way to the Greenwich Dog Show. She had a red rubber bib tucked around her throat and, since a rain storm came up when we were halfway through the Bronx, I had to hold over her a small green umbrella, really more of a parasol. The rain beat down fearfully and suddenly the driver of the car drove into a big garage, filled with mechanics. It happened so quickly that I forgot to put the umbrella down and I will always remember, with sickening distress, the look of incredulity mixed with hatred that came over the face of the particular hardened garage man that came over to see what we

---

1. **rumble seat** *n.* in some early automobiles, an open seat in the rear, behind the roofed seat, which could be folded shut when not in use.

▲ **Analyze Representations**
Which elements of this drawing by Thurber suggest that Muggs has a difficult personality? **[Analyze]**

Vocabulary
incredulity
(in´ krə dōō´ lə tē) *n.* unwillingness to believe

Reading Check
What does Thurber say was his most embarrassing moment?

wanted, when he took a look at me and the poodle. All garage men, and people of that intolerant stripe, hate poodles with their curious hair cut, especially the pom-poms that you got to leave on their hips if you expect the dogs to win a prize.

But the Airedale, as I have said, was the worst of all my dogs. He really wasn't my dog, as a matter of fact: I came home from a vacation one summer to find that my brother Roy had bought him while I was away. A big, burly, choleric dog, he always acted as if he thought I wasn't one of the family. There was a slight advantage in being one of the family, for he didn't bite the family as often as he bit strangers. Still, in the years that we had him he bit everybody but mother, and he made a pass at her once but missed. That was during the month when we suddenly had mice, and Muggs refused to do anything about them. Nobody ever had mice exactly like the mice we had that month. They acted like pet mice, almost like mice somebody had trained. They were so friendly that one night when mother entertained at dinner the Friraliras, a club she and my father had belonged to for twenty years, she put down a lot of little dishes with food in them on the pantry floor so that the mice would be satisfied with that and wouldn't come into the dining room. Muggs stayed out in the pantry with the mice, lying on the floor, growling to himself—not at the mice, but about all the people in the next room that he would have liked to get at. Mother slipped out into the pantry once to see how everything was going. Everything was going fine. It made her so mad to see Muggs lying there, oblivious of the mice—they came running up to her—that she slapped him and he slashed at her, but didn't make it. He was sorry immediately, mother said. He was always sorry, she said, after he bit someone, but we could not understand how she figured this out. He didn't act sorry.

Mother used to send a box of candy every Christmas to the people the Airedale bit. The list finally contained forty or more names. Nobody could understand why we didn't get rid of the dog. I didn't understand it very well myself, but we didn't get rid of him. I think that one or two people tried to poison Muggs—he acted poisoned once in a while—and old Major Moberly fired at him once with his service revolver near the Seneca Hotel in East Broad Street—but Muggs lived to be almost eleven years old and even when he could hardly get around he bit a Congressman who had called to see my father on business. My mother had never liked the Congressman—she said the signs of his horoscope showed he couldn't be trusted (he was Saturn with the moon in Virgo)—but she sent him a box of candy that Christmas. He sent it right back, probably because he suspected it was trick candy. Mother persuaded herself it was all for the best that the dog had bitten him, even though father lost an important business association because of it. "I wouldn't be associated with such a man," mother said, "Muggs could read him like a book."

We used to take turns feeding Muggs to be on his good side, but that didn't always work. He was never in a very good humor, even after a meal. Nobody knew exactly what was the matter with him, but whatever it was it made him irascible, especially in the mornings. Roy never felt very well in the morning, either, especially before breakfast, and once when he came downstairs and found that Muggs had moodily chewed up the morning paper he hit him in the face with a grapefruit and then jumped up on the dining room table, scattering dishes and silverware and spilling the coffee. Muggs' first free leap carried him all the way across the table and into a brass fire screen in front of the gas grate but he was back on his feet in a moment and in the end he got Roy and gave him a pretty vicious bite in the leg. Then he was all over it; he never bit anyone more than once at a time. Mother always mentioned that as an argument in his favor; she said he had a quick temper but that he didn't hold a grudge. She was forever defending him. I think she liked him because he wasn't well. "He's not strong," she would say, pityingly, but that was inaccurate; he may not have been well but he was terribly strong.

One time my mother went to the Chittenden Hotel to call on a woman mental healer who was lecturing in Columbus on the subject of "Harmonious Vibrations." She wanted to find out if it was possible to get harmonious vibrations into a dog. "He's a large tan-colored Airedale," mother explained. The woman said that she had never treated a dog but she advised my mother to hold the thought that he did not bite and would not bite. Mother was holding the thought the very next morning when Muggs got the iceman but she blamed that slip-up on the iceman. "If you didn't think he would bite you, he wouldn't," mother told him. He stomped out of the house in a terrible jangle of vibrations.

One morning when Muggs bit me slightly, more or less in passing, I reached down and grabbed his short stumpy tail and hoisted him into the air. It was a foolhardy thing to do and the last time I saw my mother, about six months ago, she said she didn't know what possessed me. I don't either, except that I was pretty mad. As long as I held the dog off the floor by his tail he couldn't get at me, but he twisted and jerked so, snarling all the time, that I realized I couldn't hold him that way very long. I carried him to the kitchen and flung him onto the floor and shut the door on him just as he crashed against it. But I forgot about the backstairs.

Vocabulary
irascible (i ras´ ə bəl)
adj. quick tempered

Spiral Review
Series of Ideas
Explain what the story of "harmonious vibrations" adds to your understanding of the mother.

Reading Check
How does Muggs generally respond to people?

▲ **Analyze Representations**
How does this drawing of Muggs compare and contrast with the behavior described in the essay? **[Compare and Contrast]**

Muggs went up the backstairs and down the frontstairs and had me cornered in the living room. I managed to get up onto the mantelpiece above the fireplace, but it gave way and came down with a tremendous crash throwing a large marble clock, several vases, and myself heavily to the floor. Muggs was so alarmed by the racket that when I picked myself up he had disappeared. We couldn't find him anywhere, although we whistled and shouted, until old Mrs. Detweiler called after dinner that night. Muggs had bitten her once, in the leg, and she came into the living room only after we assured her that Muggs had run away. She had just seated herself when, with a great growling and scratching of claws, Muggs emerged from under a davenport where he had been quietly hiding all the time, and bit her again. Mother examined the bite and put arnica[2] on it and told Mrs. Detweiler that it was only a bruise. "He just bumped you," she said. But Mrs. Detweiler left the house in a nasty state of mind.

Lots of people reported our Airedale to the police but my father held a municipal office at the time and was on friendly terms with the police. Even so, the cops had been out a couple of times—once when Muggs bit Mrs. Rufus Sturtevant and again when he bit Lieutenant-Governor Malloy—but mother told them that it hadn't been Muggs' fault but the fault of the people who were bitten. "When he starts for them, they scream," she explained, "and that excites him." The cops suggested that it might be a good idea to tie the dog up, but mother said that it mortified him to be tied up and that he wouldn't eat when he was tied up.

Muggs at his meals was an unusual sight. Because of the fact that if you reached toward the floor he would bite you, we usually put his food plate on top of an old kitchen table with a bench alongside the table. Muggs would stand on the bench and eat. I remember that my mother's Uncle Horatio, who boasted that he was the third man up Missionary Ridge,[3] was splutteringly indignant when he found out that we fed the dog on a table because we were afraid to put his plate on the floor. He said he wasn't afraid of any dog that ever lived and that he would put the dog's plate on the floor if we would give it to him. Roy said that if Uncle Horatio had fed Muggs on the ground just before the battle he would have been the first man up Missionary Ridge. Uncle Horatio was furious. "Bring him in! Bring him in now!" he shouted. "I'll feed the — on the floor!" Roy was all for giving him a chance, but my father wouldn't hear of it. He said that Muggs had already been fed. "I'll feed him again!" bawled Uncle Horatio. We had quite a time quieting him.

In his last year Muggs used to spend practically all of his time outdoors. He didn't like to stay in the house for some reason or other—perhaps it held too many unpleasant memories for him. Anyway, it was hard to get him to come in and as a result the garbage man, the iceman, and the laundryman wouldn't come near the house. We had to haul the garbage down to the corner, take the laundry out and bring it back, and meet the iceman a block from home. After this had gone on for some time we hit on an ingenious arrangement for getting the dog in the house so that we could lock him up while the gas meter was read, and so on. Muggs was afraid of only one thing, an electrical storm. Thunder and lightning frightened him out of his senses (I think he thought a storm had broken the day the mantelpiece fell). He would rush into the house and hide under

Literary Analysis
Humorous Writing
Which details here suggest that Thurber is satirizing pet owners?

Reading Check
Why does Uncle Horatio get angry?

---

2. **arnica** (är′ ni kə) n. preparation once used for treating bruises.
3. **Missionary Ridge** hill near Chattanooga, Tennessee, that was the site of a Civil War battle.

Literary Analysis
Humorous Writing
Why is this anecdote about the thunder machine an example both of hyperbole and of understatement?

a bed or in a clothes closet. So we fixed up a thunder machine out of a long narrow piece of sheet iron with a wooden handle on one end. Mother would shake this vigorously when she wanted to get Muggs into the house. It made an excellent imitation of thunder, but I suppose it was the most roundabout system for running a household that was ever devised. It took a lot out of mother.

A few months before Muggs died, he got to "seeing things." He would rise slowly from the floor, growling low, and stalk stiff-legged and menacing toward nothing at all. Sometimes the Thing would be just a little to the right or left of a visitor. Once a Fuller Brush salesman[4] got hysterics. Muggs came wandering into the room like Hamlet[5] following his father's ghost. His eyes were fixed on a spot just to the left of the Fuller Brush man, who stood it until Muggs was about three slow, creeping paces from him. Then he shouted. Muggs wavered on past him into the hallway grumbling to himself but the Fuller man went on shouting. I think mother had to throw a pan of cold water on him before he stopped. That was the way she used to stop us boys when we got into fights.

Muggs died quite suddenly one night. Mother wanted to bury him in the family lot under a marble stone with some such inscription as "Flights of angels sing thee to thy rest" but we persuaded her it was against the law. In the end we just put up a smooth board above his grave along a lonely road. On the board I wrote with an indelible pencil "Cave Canem."[6] Mother was quite pleased with the simple classic dignity of the old Latin epitaph.

---

4. **Fuller Brush salesman** salesman for the Fuller Brush Company who went door-to-door demonstrating cleaning equipment; a figure celebrated in comic strips and movies of the 1920s through the 1940s.
5. **Hamlet** the main character of William Shakespeare's play *Hamlet*; in the play, he is visited by the ghost of his murdered father.
6 **"Cave Canem"** (kä´ vā kä´ nem´) Latin for "Beware of the dog."

Critical Thinking

Cite textual evidence to support your responses.

1. **Key Ideas and Details (a)** Which event was Thurber's "foolhardy" experience with Muggs? **(b) Analyze:** List reactions you expect the family to have to this experience, and explain which are missing in the essay.

2. **Key Ideas and Details Infer:** What do other people think of the family's tolerance for Muggs's behavior? Explain.

3. **Craft and Structure (a)** Is the connotation of Muggs's epitaph positive or negative? **(b)** Is the connotation appropriate? Explain.

4. **Integration of Knowledge and Ideas** Why did the family keep Muggs despite their knowledge of his bad nature? *[Connect to the Big Question: What kind of knowledge changes our lives?]*

Comparing Humorous Writing

1. Craft and Structure (a) Find an example of **hyperbole** in each work. **(b)** Find an example of **understatement** in each work. **(c)** Compare Twain's and Thurber's use of these devices, explaining which device each writer uses most.

2. Craft and Structure (a) Which author treats a potentially serious subject lightly? **(b)** Which treats an ordinary subject with exaggerated seriousness? **(c)** How do the forms—essay and speech—shape the way ideas are presented? Give examples.

3. Integration of Knowledge and Ideas (a) Find an example of **satire** in each essay. **(b)** Identify the type of person satirized in each. Do you think satirizing such people is fair or justified? Explain.

Timed Writing

Explanatory Text: Essay

In an essay, compare how Twain and Thurber use conflict to develop their humorous writing. Analyze how they use hyperbole, understatement, and precise diction to portray those conflicts and make them funny. **(30 minutes)**

5-Minute Planner

1. Read the prompt carefully and completely.

2. Before you write, complete a chart like the one shown to identify each conflict and the comic details that depict it.

3. Analyze the authors' diction, tone, and use of hyperbole and understatement. Take notes on specific details that support your analysis.

4. Develop an outline logically organizing your points.

5. Reread the prompt, and then draft your essay.

Writing Workshop

Write an Argument

Persuasion: Letter to the Editor

Defining the Form A **letter to the editor** is a formal business letter that presents the writer's viewpoints about important issues and is addressed to the opinion page of a newspaper or magazine. You might use elements of this form in position papers, speeches, and proposals.

Assignment Write a letter to the editor of a magazine, newspaper, or Web site. Give your opinion about a current event. Include these elements:

- ✔ *standard business letter format*, including a heading, an inside address, a greeting, a body, a closing, and a signature
- ✔ *formal, polite language* that creates an objective tone
- ✔ *a clear statement of opinion, or claim,* supported by sufficient evidence and by an argument refuting an opposing opinion
- ✔ *persuasive techniques* to convince readers to agree with you
- ✔ a conclusion that explains the importance of the claim
- ✔ error-free grammar, including *well-combined sentences*

To preview the criteria on which your letter to the editor may be judged, see the rubric on page 537.

 Writing Workshop: *Work in Progress*

Review the work you did on pages 485 and 509.

Prewriting/Planning Strategy

Find a hot topic. Watch television, scan newspapers, and listen to neighborhood discussions. List issues and note differing opinions about each one. Decide which prompt your strongest feelings.

Pro	Hot Topic	Con
Professional athletes have a responsibility to the public.	**Sports heroes as role models**	Excellent athletes are not models for behavior outside the court or off the field.
Restrictions can protect our youngest citizens.	**Laws restricting the Internet**	Freedom of speech is denied by restrictions.

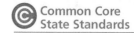 **Common Core State Standards**

Writing
1. Write arguments to support claims in an analysis of substantive topics or texts, using valid reasoning and relevant and sufficient evidence.
1.d. Establish and maintain a formal style and objective tone while attending to the norms and conventions of the discipline in which they are writing.

Finding Your Voice

Voice is the writer's distinctive "sound" or way of "speaking" on the page. It is created through elements such as word choice, sentence structure, and tone. Voice, in its written form, can be described in the same way the spoken word is described—fast, slow, blunt, and so on. Use the following tips to help you find the appropriate voice for your letter.

Choose effective words. Before you begin your letter, think about how you want to sound: for example, impassioned, concerned, reasoned, or detached. Your choice of words and the structure of your sentences communicate your voice. Try saying a few sentences aloud. You might tape-record your voice, or have a friend listen to you speak. Then, decide whether the sound of your voice is what you wish to convey on paper. Use a chart like the following to record words or phrases that reflect your voice.

> **PH WRITING COACH**
>
> Further instruction and practice are available in *Prentice Hall Writing Coach*.

Voice and/or Tone	Words and Phrases
impassioned	*We urgently need…; So much is at stake…*
concerned	*I am concerned…; The problem is serious…*
reasoned	*We all will benefit from…; We have the resources to…; Some people may disagree with me…*

Consider your audience and tone. Your voice in writing should reflect your audience. Your letter will address the general public, so include information that is essential to your case. Be respectful to your audience. Remember that the overall tone of a letter to the editor is usually objective. Even if you are voicing a complaint, maintain a calm and reasonable tone. Your goal is to persuade, not to insult.

Revise to create appropriate formality. Check that your tone is polite and your style is formal. Replace casual language with formal language.

Casual: The park's a big old mess.
Formal: The park is littered with trash.

Drafting Strategies

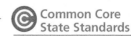

Common Core State Standards

Writing
1. Write arguments to support claims in an analysis of substantive topics or texts, using valid reasoning and relevant and sufficient evidence.
1.a. Introduce precise claim(s), distinguish the claim(s) from alternate or opposing claims, and create an organization that establishes clear relationships among claim(s), counterclaims, reasons, and evidence.
1.c. Use words, phrases, and clauses to link the major sections of the text, create cohesion, and clarify the relationships between claim(s) and reasons, between reasons and evidence, and between claim(s) and counterclaims.

Use the proper format. Your letter to the editor must follow a standard business letter format. Here are two commonly accepted conventions:

- **Block Format:** Each part of the letter begins at the left margin.

- **Modified Block Format:** The heading, closing, and signature align and are indented to the center of the page by using the tab function.

Ensure that you include all six elements of a formal business letter: heading, inside address, salutation, body, closing, and signature. (For more on business letters, see page R34.)

Organize ideas. Logically organize your ideas and use clear transitional words, phrases, and clauses so that your readers can follow your argument. Distinguish your opinions or ideas from those of others.

Use persuasive techniques. As you write, include persuasive techniques and rhetorical devices to convince your readers to adopt your opinion or take a course of action. The chart shown here provides some examples.

Persuasive Techniques	Rhetorical Devices
Appeal to Emotion Abandoned animals are suffering needlessly.	**Parallelism** Homeless animals deserve our compassion. Homeless animals deserve a home.
Appeal to Logic Taking care of these animals will help eliminate sources of diseases to our pets.	**Rhetorical Question** Can we allow this situation to continue?

Revising Strategy

Evaluate support. Review your draft, highlighting main ideas to ensure they are supported with sufficient evidence. Also ensure main ideas are valid and logical. If a point is not important or logical, omit it. If it is important, support it. Select different types of evidence to make your letter both convincing and interesting. Consider including evidence in these categories:

- facts and statistics
- real-life examples
- personal experiences
- expert opinions

Model: Highlighting to Add Supporting Details
Many pets in this city have been abandoned, left homeless by uncaring owners. These animals roam the city streets. Most are hungry, and many are sick and diseased. I personally rescued a puppy who was scavenging in our trash can for food. My vet said he had heartworms and fleas.

> The writer adds support in the form of personal experience.

Revising to Combine Short Sentences

If you use too many short sentences, your work can seem as if it was written for very young readers rather than a mature audience. To avoid this problem, combine short sentences that express related ideas.

Methods of Sentence Combining Use compound verbs to combine two short sentences:

Choppy: I *cancelled* my service. I *turned* my phone in for a refund.

Combined: I *cancelled* my service and *turned* my phone in for a refund.

You may use **compound objects:**

Choppy: I ate *a sandwich.* I ate *an ice cream cone.*

Combined: I ate *a sandwich* and *an ice cream cone.*

Use **compound predicate nominatives** or **predicate adjectives.**

predicate nominative	predicate adjective
a noun or pronoun that appears with a linking verb and identifies or explains the subject	an adjective that appears with a linking verb and describes the subject
Example: Parakeets are <u>birds.</u>	Example: Parakeets are <u>colorful.</u>

PH WRITING COACH

Further instruction and practice are available in *Prentice Hall Writing Coach*.

Choppy: My favorite celebrity *is a singer.* She is also *an actress.*

Combined: My favorite celebrity is *a singer and an actress.*

Choppy: The bicycle is *very lightweight.* It is *extremely fast.*

Combined: The bicycle is *very lightweight and extremely fast.*

Fixing Choppy Sentences Follow these steps to fix short sentences:

1. **Read your draft aloud,** listening for choppy sentences.

2. **Identify sentences to combine.** Determine which sentences share a common subject or a common predicate.

3. **Try a variety of sentence-combining techniques.** Use the methods above to create a variety of fluid sentences.

Grammar in Your Writing

Reread two paragraphs in your letter. Look for places where a single sentence would express related ideas better than a series of shorter sentences. Combine these sentences using one of the methods above.

Student Model: Clay Creamans, Independence, KY

Clay Creamans
2351 Any Drive
Independence, Kentucky 41051

September 25, 2005

Editor-in-Chief
The Daily Independent
552 Downtown Street
Ashland, Kentucky 41000

Clay uses a correct modified block format.

Dear Editor-in-Chief:

I am writing in response to the letter you published from Mr. Jones, who complained about our band's playing at the last football game.

Formal language shows that Clay takes both his opinion and his readers seriously.

The point of high school band programs is to train students to play together, to produce one stirring, harmonious sound. Because of a lack of instruction, education, and familiarity with music and instruments, this is difficult for some students. Band programs all over the country have inspired many students to go into the field of music, but many do not meet the requirements students need to compete after high school. I personally know students who have been denied scholarships and have had scholarships revoked because they have not been properly trained. The Kenton County School District needs to devise a class that will alleviate these problems.

Clay supports his argument with personal experiences.

This new music class should have a staff composed of teachers who can play and teach all of the band instruments. Students need one-on-one, as well as group, instruction. Of course, hiring a full staff of musicians for every school would cost a lot. Instead, full band directors could be hired for all the schools to share. This would allow students to gain a greater knowledge of music from a larger group of musicians. These teachers would offer more insight into the history and theory of music.

Clay points out an opposing argument and suggests an alternative plan.

With so many young people interested in fine arts, band directors cannot offer everyone the instruction that is needed. For the band to improve as a whole, everyone has to grow. Many of today's band directors try hard to develop better musicians, yet, because of a lack of time and staffing, they feel disappointed and discouraged.

With adequate time and staffing, students will be able to make music together and demonstrate their talents. With an experienced music staff and better classes, I believe that Mr. Jones will be happier with our band's performance.

The conclusion reinforces Clay's ideas.

Sincerely,

Clay Creamans

Clay Creamans

Editing and Proofreading

Check your draft for errors in format, grammar, and punctuation.

Focus on accuracy. Ensure that the names of people, periodicals, and quoted experts are spelled and capitalized correctly. Make sure that numerical data and street addresses are accurate.

Publishing and Presenting

Consider one of the following ways to share your writing:

Submit your letter. Send your letter to the editor of the media source you have addressed. When the letter is published, share the newspaper, periodical, or Web site with classmates.

Hold a speaker's corner. Organize a group of classmates in which you read your letters aloud and evaluate each speaker's point of view and reasoning. Point out any exaggerated claims or fallacious reasoning, such as overgeneralizations. As a group, set time limits for each speaker and negotiate rules, such as holding questions until a speaker is finished.

Reflecting on Your Writing

Writer's Journal Jot down your answers to this question:

How did writing about the issue you chose help you to understand it?

Rubric for Self-Assessment

Find evidence in your writing to address each category. Then, use the rating scale to grade your work.

Spiral Review

Earlier in the unit, you learned about **subject complements** (p. 508). In your essay, write at least one sentence that has a predicate nominative and one sentence that has a predicate adjective. To write effectively, choose sentences in which it is appropriate to use linking verbs rather than action verbs.

Criteria	Rating Scale not very very
Focus: How clearly do you state your opinion?	1 2 3 4 5
Organization: How accurately do you use standard business letter format?	1 2 3 4 5
Support/Elaboration: How relevant and logical are the facts, examples, or experiences you use to support your opinion?	1 2 3 4 5
Style: How formal and objective is your use of language?	1 2 3 4 5
Conventions: How correct is your grammar, especially your use of well-combined sentences?	1 2 3 4 5
Voice: How well do your word choice and sentence structure reflect your voice?	1 2 3 4 5

Leveled Texts

Build your skills and improve your comprehension of nonfiction with texts of increasing complexity.

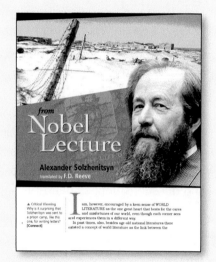

Read **"Keep Memory Alive"** to learn why a man has devoted his life to ensuring that the horrors of the Holocaust are not forgotten.

Read the excerpt from a writer's **Nobel Lecture** to find out how one author uses literature to fight against global forces of injustice.

Common Core State Standards

Meet these standards with either **"Keep Memory Alive"** (p. 542) or the excerpt from Alexander Solzhenitsyn's **Nobel Lecture** (p. 548).

Reading Informational Text
6. Determine an author's point of view or purpose in a text and analyze how an author uses rhetoric to advance that point of view or purpose. *(Literary Analysis: Persuasive Writing and Rhetorical Devices)*

8. Delineate and evaluate the argument and specific claims in a text, assessing whether the reasoning is valid and the evidence is relevant and sufficient; identify false statements and fallacious reasoning. *(Reading Skill: Evaluate Persuasion)*

Spiral Review: RI.9-10.5
Writing
1.d. Establish and maintain a formal style and objective tone while attending to the norms and conventions of the discipline in which they are writing. *(Writing: Letter)*

Speaking and Listening
3. Evaluate a speaker's point of view, reasoning, and use of evidence and rhetoric, identifying any fallacious reasoning or exaggerated or distorted evidence. *(Speaking and Listening: Debate)*

Language
5. Demonstrate understanding of figurative language, word relationships, and nuances in word meanings. *(Vocabulary: Synonyms and Antonyms)*

Literary Analysis: Persuasive Writing and Rhetorical Devices

Persuasive writing, including **speeches,** is intended to convince people to take a particular action or position. Persuasive writers present **arguments**, or series of logically linked ideas that support a conclusion, to defend their ideas. They also use **rhetorical devices,** or verbal techniques that create emphasis and appeal to emotions. Writers use both arguments and rhetorical devices to achieve a persuasive purpose. While rhetorical devices cannot replace arguments, they can move readers, helping them to understand, remember, and accept a writer's ideas. Here are some common rhetorical devices:

- **repetition:** the reuse of a key word or idea for emphasis
- **parallelism:** similar grammatical structures expressing related ideas
- **slogans and saws:** short, catchy phrases
- **rhetorical questions:** questions that are intended to have obvious answers; asked for effect

Reading Skill: Evaluate Persuasion

When reading persuasive writing, **evaluate the writer's argument.** Consider whether the writer supports claims with sound evidence and logical reasoning.

Determine when **persuasive techniques** are effectively used to enhance the impact of the supporting evidence and reasoning, and recognize when they are used to cover up a lack of logical support.

Using the Strategy: Argument Chart

Use an **argument chart** like the one shown to take notes as you read.

Position	Claim	Support	Persuasive Technique
People should oppose a new mall.	Local businesses will suffer.	Prices at malls are lower.	Rhetorical question: Do you want your neighbor to lose his business?

What kind of *knowledge* changes our lives?

Writing About the Big Question

In "Keep Memory Alive," Wiesel shows that testifying to the evils of the past can be a difficult but important duty. He argues that studying history is important not just for the facts and information it teaches us, but for the important lessons it reveals. Use these sentence starters to develop your ideas about the Big Question.

The kinds of facts we may learn through studying **history** include _____, and _____.

From these facts, we can learn important lessons such as _____.

Living in **ignorance** of problems of the past and present can be dangerous because _____.

While You Read Look for lessons the author learns in childhood that he carries with him as an adult.

Vocabulary

Read each word and its definition. Decide whether you know the word well, know it a little bit, or do not know it at all. After you read, see how your knowledge of each word has increased.

- **transcends** (tran sendz´) *v.* goes beyond the limits of; exceeds (p. 543) *The indescribable beauty of the Grand Canyon* <u>*transcends*</u> *the words used to describe it.* transcendent *adj.* transcendence *n.*

- **presumptuous** (prē zump´ choō əs) *adj.* overstepping appropriate bounds; too bold (p. 543) *It would be* <u>*presumptuous*</u> *of me to give medical advice, because I am not a doctor.* presume *v.* presumption *n.* presumptuously *adv.*

- **accomplices** (ə käm´ plis iz) *n.* people who help another person commit a crime (p. 544) *His* <u>*accomplices*</u> *kept a lookout while he robbed the bank.*

> ### Word Study
>
> The **Latin root -scend-** means "climb."
>
> In this speech, the author talks about receiving an honor that **transcends,** or climbs and goes beyond, him as just one person.

Author of
Keep Memory Alive

The Romanian-born teacher, philosopher, and writer Elie Wiesel was deported to the Nazi death camp at Auschwitz at age fifteen. His parents and sister all perished at the hands of the Nazis.

Survivor and Witness After surviving the war, Wiesel did not write a single word about his wartime experiences for ten years. Finally, in 1955, he wrote an account of his experiences, *And the World Kept Silent.* His English adaptation of the work, *Night,* was published in 1960. He says, "I wrote it for the other survivors who found it difficult to speak. And I wanted really to tell them, 'Look, you must speak . . . we must try.'"

BACKGROUND FOR THE SPEECH

The Holocaust

The Holocaust was the systematic persecution and murder of Jews and others deemed "unfit" by Germany's Nazi Party. The Nazis came to power in Germany in 1933. During World War II (1939–1945), Nazi forces killed Jews throughout German-occupied lands or sent them to concentration camps. There, prisoners like Elie Wiesel were worked to death, starved to death, or killed outright.

Did You Know?
Wiesel was perhaps the first to use the term *Holocaust* to describe the Nazis' brutal program of persecution.

Keep Memory Alive

Alive

Elie Wiesel

It is with a profound sense of humility that I accept the honor you have chosen to bestow upon me. I know: your choice transcends me. This both frightens and pleases me.

It frightens me because I wonder: do I have the right to represent the multitudes who have perished? Do I have the right to accept this great honor on their behalf? I do not. That would be presumptuous. No one may speak for the dead, no one may interpret their mutilated dreams and visions.

It pleases me because I may say that this honor belongs to all the survivors and their children, and through us, to the Jewish people with whose destiny I have always identified.

I remember: it happened yesterday or eternities ago. A young Jewish boy discovered the kingdom of night. I remember his bewilderment, I remember his anguish. It all happened so fast. The ghetto.[1] The deportation. The sealed cattle car. The fiery altar upon which the history of our people and the future of mankind were meant to be sacrificed.

---

1. The ghetto (get´ ō) During the Second World War, the Nazis forced Jews in European cities to live in crowded, restricted neighborhoods, or ghettos.

◄ **Critical Viewing** How does this image of children being sent to a Nazi concentration camp add force to Wiesel's point about the necessity of remembering? Explain. **[Support]**

Literary Analysis
Persuasive Writing
Identify two examples of parallelism in the second paragraph.

Vocabulary
transcends (tran sendz´) *v.* goes beyond the limits of; exceeds

presumptuous (prē zump´ chōō əs) *adj.* overstepping appropriate bounds; too bold

I remember: he asked his father: "Can this be true? This is the 20th century, not the Middle Ages. Who would allow such crimes to be committed? How could the world remain silent?"

And now the boy is turning to me: "Tell me," he asks. "What have you done with my future? What have you done with your life?"

And I tell him that I have tried. That I have tried to keep memory alive, that I have tried to fight those who would forget. Because if we forget, we are guilty, we are accomplices.

And then I explained to him how naive we were, that the world did know and remain silent. And that is why I swore never to be silent whenever and wherever human beings endure suffering and humiliation. We must always take sides. Neutrality[2] helps the oppressor, never the victim. Silence encourages the tormentor, never the tormented.

Vocabulary
accomplices (ə käm´ plis iz) *n.* people who help another person commit a crime

---

2. **Neutrality** (noo tral´ ə tē) *n.* state of not taking sides in a conflict; quality of being unbiased.

Critical Thinking

Cite textual evidence to support your responses.

1. **Key Ideas and Details** **(a)** On whose behalf does Wiesel accept the Nobel Prize? **(b) Draw Conclusions:** Why does he believe the award belongs to those people? **(c) Interpret:** Why does he say that receiving the award both "frightens and pleases" him?

2. **Key Ideas and Details** **(a)** What does the boy Wiesel ask the adult Wiesel? **(b) Interpret:** What do his questions imply about Wiesel's adult responsibilities? **(c) Draw Conclusions:** Why does Wiesel believe we have a moral duty to remember?

3. **Integration of Knowledge and Skills** Describe a situation in which silence might do harm.

4. **Integration of Knowledge and Skills** What lessons learned in a concentration camp have guided Weisel's actions as an adult? *[Connect to the Big Question: What kind of knowledge changes our lives?]*

Literary Analysis: Persuasive Writing and Rhetorical Devices

ⓒ **1. Key Ideas and Details** Identify the central **argument** in Wiesel's **persuasive speech**, and summarize his point of view.

ⓒ **2. Craft and Structure** What **rhetorical devices** does Wiesel use in his speech? Use a chart like the one shown to analyze examples.

	Repetition	Parallelism	Slogans or Saws	Rhetorical Questions
Example				
Effect				

ⓒ **3. Integration of Knowledge and Skills (a)** What assumptions does Wiesel make about a person's obligation to the community? **(b)** With a small group, discuss whether you agree with the assumptions.

Reading Skill: Evaluate Persuasion

4. (a) Wiesel says, "Because if we forget, we are guilty, we are accomplices." What are his reasons for making the claim? **(b)** Explain whether there are any important facts he has not taken into account. **(c)** Is the claim logical? Why or why not?

5. Use your answers to **evaluate** this claim. Consider the rhetorical power of Wiesel's statement as well as the support he gives.

Vocabulary

ⓒ **Acquisition and Use** Words that have similar meanings are called **synonyms**. Words that have opposite meanings are called **antonyms.** Explain whether each word pair contains synonyms or antonyms. Then, write a sentence using both words.

1. presumptuous, modest
2. transcends, exceeds
3. accomplices, collaborators

Word Study Use the context of the sentences and what you know about the **Latin root -scend-** to explain your answer to each question.

1. Are you going uphill or downhill as you *ascend* a mountain?
2. If a person is a *descendant* of a mayor, are the two related?

Word Study

The **Latin root -scend-** means "climb."

Apply It Explain how the root -scend- contributes to the meanings of these words. Consult a dictionary if necessary.

condescend
descend
ascend

What kind of *knowledge* changes our lives?

Writing About the Big Question

In the excerpt from Nobel Lecture, the author insists that writers should be the voices of truth against the lies and oppression of corrupt governments. Use this sentence starter to develop your ideas about the Big Question.

In order to develop a better **awareness** of and **insight** into issues such as free speech, one can _____.

While You Read Look for ways Solzhenitsyn suggests that writers can help one another to be the voice of truth.

Vocabulary

Read each word and its definition. Decide whether you know the word well, know it a little bit, or do not know it at all. After you read, see how your knowledge of each word has increased.

- **aggregate** (ag´ rə git) *n.* a group of distinct things gathered into a whole; a sum (p. 549) *The aggregate of ants worked together to rebuild their colony.* *aggregate adj. aggregate v. aggregation n.*

- **reciprocity** (res´ ə präs´ ə tē) *n.* relations of exchange; interdependence (p. 549) *Reciprocity between nations means helping each other out during difficult times.* *reciprocal adj. reciprocate v.*

- **jurisdiction** (joor´ is dik´ shən) *n.* sphere of authority or power (p. 549) *The mayor's jurisdiction does not extend beyond this town.* *jurisdictional adj. jury n.*

- **condemn** (kən dem´) *v.* disapprove of; pass unfavorable judgment on (p. 551) *The court is certain to condemn the traitor for his crimes.* *condemnable adj. condemnation n. condemned adj.*

- **inexorably** (in eks´ ə rə blē) *adv.* without the possibility of being delayed or stopped (p. 551) *The hurricane moved inexorably up the coast.* *inexorable adj. inexorability n.*

- **oratory** (ôr´ ə tôr´ ē) *n.* act of public speaking; strategies used in such speaking (p. 551) *The speaker's oratory fired up the crowd.* *orate v. orator n. oration n.*

Word Study

The **Latin root -jur-** means "law" or "right."

In this speech, the author asserts that a nation's government should not have **jurisdiction**, or the right to make laws, over the literature produced there.

Meet
Alexander Solzhenitsyn
(1918–2008)

Author of
Nobel Lecture

Russian writer Alexander Solzhenitsyn spent years in prison camps because of his political views. Yet he was never intimidated into silence. He experienced the hardship of being a dissident—someone who publicly disagrees with an established system.

A Powerful Voice During the Second World War, Solzhenitsyn was imprisoned for writing letters to a friend that were critical of the Soviet leader, Joseph Stalin. In his first novel, *A Day in the Life of Ivan Denisovich,* he described the harsh climate, backbreaking work, and poor diet at the camp in which he was imprisoned. In 1974, after the publication in Paris of parts of *The Gulag Archipelago,* Solzhenitsyn was tried for treason and exiled. In 1994, three years after the fall of the Soviet Union, he returned to his homeland.

BACKGROUND FOR THE SPEECH

A Writer in Exile

By writing critically about the U.S.S.R. (now Russia and other nations), Alexander Solzhenitsyn faced punishment and censorship. As he explains in his Nobel Lecture, writers and publishers around the world offered their support. When Solzhenitsyn was exiled in 1974, he was first welcomed by fellow author and Nobel Prize winner Heinrich Böll.

Did You Know?
Solzhenitsyn won the Nobel Prize in Literature in 1970.

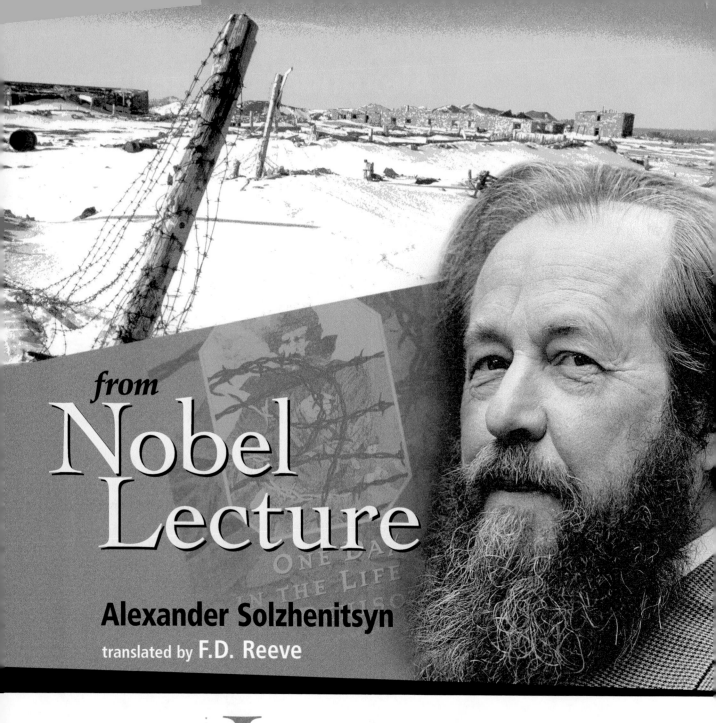

from
Nobel Lecture

Alexander Solzhenitsyn
translated by **F.D. Reeve**

▲ **Critical Viewing**
Why is it surprising that
Solzhenitsyn was sent to
a prison camp, like this
one, for writing letters?
[Connect]

I am, however, encouraged by a keen sense of WORLD
LITERATURE as the one great heart that beats for the cares
and misfortunes of our world, even though each corner sees
and experiences them in a different way.

In past times, also, besides age-old national literatures there
existed a concept of world literature as the link between the

summits of national literatures and as the aggregate of reciprocal literary influences. But there was a time lag: readers and writers came to know foreign writers only belatedly, sometimes centuries later, so that mutual influences were delayed and the network of national literary high points was visible not to contemporaries but to later generations.

Today, between writers of one country and the readers and writers of another, there is an almost instantaneous reciprocity, as I myself know. My books, unpublished, alas, in my own country, despite hasty and often bad translations have quickly found a responsive world readership. Critical analysis of them has been undertaken by such leading Western writers as Heinrich Böll.[1] During all these recent years, when both my work and my freedom did not collapse, when against the laws of gravity they held on seemingly in thin air, seemingly on nothing, on the invisible, mute surface tension of sympathetic people, with warm gratitude I learned, to my complete surprise, of the support of the world's writing fraternity. On my fiftieth birthday I was astounded to receive greetings from well-known European writers. No pressure put on me now passed unnoticed. During the dangerous weeks when I was being expelled from the Writers' Union,[2] THE PROTECTIVE WALL put forward by prominent writers of the world saved me from worse persecution, and Norwegian writers and artists hospitably prepared shelter for me in the event that I was exiled from my country. Finally, my being nominated for a Nobel Prize was originated not in the land where I live and write but by François Mauriac[3] and his colleagues. Afterward, national writers' organizations expressed unanimous support for me.

As I have understood it and experienced it myself, world literature is no longer an abstraction or a generalized concept invented by literary critics, but a common body and common spirit, a living, heartfelt unity reflecting the growing spiritual unity of mankind. State borders still turn crimson, heated red-hot by electric fences and machine-gun fire; some ministries of internal affairs still suppose that literature is "an internal affair" of the countries under their jurisdiction; and newspaper headlines still herald, "They have no right to interfere in our internal affairs!" Meanwhile, no such thing as INTERNAL AFFAIRS remains on our crowded Earth. Mankind's salvation lies exclusively in everyone's making everything his business, in the people of the East being anything but indifferent to what is thought in the West, and in the

---

1. **Heinrich** (hīn´ riH) **Böll** (böl) (1917–1985) German novelist and winner of the Nobel Prize in Literature.
2. **Writers' Union** official Soviet writers' organization, which enforced government policies on literature and gave privileges to writers. In addition to being expelled from this union, Solzhenitsyn was forbidden to live in Moscow.
3. **François** (frän swä´) **Mauriac** (mô´ rè ak´) (1885–1970) French novelist and essayist.

Vocabulary
aggregate (ag´ rə git) *n.* a group of distinct things gathered into a whole; a sum

reciprocity (res´ ə präs´ ə tē) *n.* relations of exchange; interdependence

jurisdiction (jo͝or´ is dik´ shən) *n.* sphere of authority or power

Spiral Review
Development of Ideas What do the details in this paragraph add to Solzhenitsyn's idea of "world literature"?

Literary Analysis
Persuasive Writing How does repetition of the words *common, unity, West,* and *East* add to the power of this paragraph?

Reading Check

Name one way in which writers in other countries helped Solzhenitsyn.

World Events Connection

Repression in the Soviet Union

◀ Many of Solzhenitsyn's difficulties with the Soviet authorities stemmed from his works exposing the evils of the Soviet Gulag.

The Gulag consisted of prison camps such as the one shown. Many were located in Siberia, where harsh weather, poor diet, and intensive labor led to much suffering among inmates. ▶

1929–1953 **Dictatorship of Josef Stalin** Millions are imprisoned for allegedly opposing the government.	**1956–1964** **The "Thaw"** New freedoms are permitted.	**mid-1960s–mid-1980s** Renewed Repression	**1985–1991** **Glasnost ("openness")** Mikhail Gorbachev introduces policies tolerating freedom of expression.

Connect to the Literature

Judging from Solzhenitsyn's Nobel Lecture, how might he have responded to news of Gorbachev's policies from 1985 to 1991?

people of the West being anything but indifferent to what happens in the East. Literature, one of the most sensitive and responsive tools of human existence, has been the first to pick up, adopt, and assimilate this sense of the growing unity of mankind. I therefore confidently turn to the world literature of the present, to hundreds of friends whom I have not met face to face and perhaps never will see.

My friends! Let us try to be helpful, if we are worth anything. In our own countries, torn by differences among parties, movements, castes, and groups, who for ages past has been not the dividing but the uniting force? This, essentially, is the position of writers, spokesmen of a national language, of the chief tie binding the nation, the very soil which the people inhabit, and, in fortunate circumstances, the nation's spirit too.

I think that world literature has the power in these frightening times to help mankind see itself accurately despite what is advocated by partisans and by parties. It has the power to transmit the condensed experience of one region to another, so that different scales of values are combined, and so that one people accurately and concisely knows the true history of another with a power of recognition and acute awareness as if it had lived through that history itself—and could thus be spared repeating old mistakes. At the same time, perhaps we ourselves may succeed in developing our own WORLDWIDE VIEW, like any man, with the center of the eye seeing what is nearby but the periphery of vision taking in what is happening in the rest of the world. We will make correlations and maintain worldwide standards.

Who, if not writers, are to condemn their own unsuccessful governments (in some states this is the easiest way to make a living; everyone who is not too lazy does it) as well as society itself, whether for its cowardly humiliation or for its self-satisfied weakness, or the lightheaded escapades of the young, or the youthful pirates brandishing knives?

We will be told: What can literature do against the pitiless onslaught of naked violence? Let us not forget that violence does not and cannot flourish by itself; it is inevitably intertwined with LYING. Between them there is the closest, the most profound and natural bond: nothing screens violence except lies, and the only way lies can hold out is by violence. Whoever has once announced violence as his METHOD must inexorably choose lying as his PRINCIPLE. At birth, violence behaves openly and even proudly. But as soon as it becomes stronger and firmly established, it senses the thinning of the air around it and cannot go on without befogging itself in lies, coating itself with lying's sugary oratory. It does not always or necessarily go straight for the gullet; usually it demands of its victims only allegiance to the lie, only complicity in the lie.

Vocabulary
condemn (kən dem´) *v.* disapprove of; pass unfavorable judgment on
inexorably (in eks´ ə rə blē) *adv.* without the possibility of being delayed or stopped
oratory (ôr´ ə tôr´ ē) *n.* act of public speaking; strategies used in such speaking

Reading Check

According to Solzhenitsyn, what does world literature have the power to do?

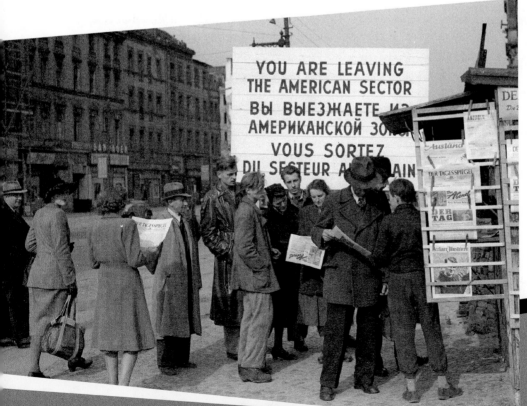

◄ **Critical Viewing** The Berlin Wall once separated East and West Berlin. How does this scene of newspaper readers by the wall support what the author says about truth? **[Connect]**

The simple act of an ordinary courageous man is not to take part, not to support lies! Let *that* come into the world and even reign over it, but not through me. Writers and artists can do more: they can VANQUISH LIES! In the struggle against lies, art has always won and always will. Conspicuously, incontestably for everyone. Lies can stand up against much in the world, but not against art.

Once lies have been dispelled, the repulsive nakedness of violence will be exposed—and hollow violence will collapse.

That, my friends, is why I think we can help the world in its red-hot hour: not by the nay-saying of having no armaments,[4] not by abandoning oneself to the carefree life, but by going into battle!

In Russian, proverbs about TRUTH are favorites. They persistently express the considerable, bitter, grim experience of the people, often astonishingly:

ONE WORD OF TRUTH OUTWEIGHS THE WORLD.

On such a seemingly fantastic violation of the law of the conservation of mass and energy are based both my own activities and my appeal to the writers of the whole world.

ONE WORD OF TRUTH OUTWEIGHS THE WORLD.

---

4. the nay-saying of having no armaments Solzhenitsyn is referring to the idea that nations should limit the number or kind of weapons that they hold ready for war.

Critical Thinking

1. Key Ideas and Details (a) According to Solzhenitsyn, what is a key difference between world literature today and in the past? **(b) Interpret:** Why does he call world literature "one great heart"?

2. Key Ideas and Details: (a) According to Solzhenitsyn, what were two ways in which European writers showed support for him? **(b) Connect:** How does this support confirm his view of world literature?

3. Key Ideas and Details Analyze: What role does Solzhenitsyn believe artists have in the struggle against injustice?

4. Integration of Knowledge and Ideas Solzhenitsyn wants writers to write about "the truth." **(a)** What issues would he think are most in need of this truthful examination? **(b)** Does he want the truth about these issues to change people? Explain. *[Connect to the Big Question: What kind of knowledge changes our lives?]*

Cite textual evidence to support your responses.

Literary Analysis: Persuasive Writing and Rhetorical Devices

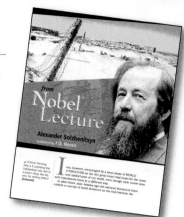

1. Key Ideas and Details Identify the central argument in and main purpose of Solzhenitsyn's **persuasive speech.**

2. Craft and Structure What **rhetorical devices** does Solzhenitsyn use to emphasize his message and achieve his purpose? Use a chart like the one shown to analyze examples.

	Repetition	Parallelism	Slogans or Saws	Rhetorical Questions
Example				
Effect				

3. Integration of Knowledge and Ideas (a) What assumptions does Solzhenitsyn make about the rights of individuals as opposed to the dictates of the state? **(b)** In a group, discuss whether you agree with his assumptions.

Reading Skill: Evaluate Persuasion

4. (a) Solzhenitsyn writes, "Once lies have been dispelled . . . hollow violence will collapse." Explain his reasons for making the claim. **(b)** Explain whether there are any important facts he has not taken into account. **(c)** Explain whether the claim is logical.

5. Evaluate Solzhenitsyn's claim. In your answer, consider the rhetorical power of the statement as well as the support he gives.

Vocabulary

Acquisition and Use Words with the same or similar meanings are **synonyms.** Words with opposite meanings are **antonyms.** Explain whether each item contains synonyms or antonyms. Then, write a sentence using both words.

1. reciprocity, independence

2. inexorably, avoidably

3. oratory, rhetoric

4. aggregate, total

5. jurisdiction, authority

6. condemn, approve

Word Study Use the context of the sentences and what you know about the **Latin root -*jur*-** to explain your answer to each question.

1. Would you expect to see a *jury* in a courtroom or in a gymnasium?

2. Why would it be a bad idea to commit *perjury* during a trial?

Word Study

The **Latin root -*jur*-** means "law" or "right."

Apply It Explain how the root -*jur*- contributes to the meanings of these words. Consult a dictionary if necessary.

abjure

injury

jurisprudence

Integrated Language Skills

Keep Memory Alive • *from* Nobel Lecture

Conventions: Degrees of Adverbs

An **adverb** is a word that modifies a verb, an adjective, or another adverb.

Most adverbs have three different forms, called degrees of comparison—the *positive,* the *comparative,* and the *superlative.* Use the positive form to describe a single action or quality. Use the comparative to compare two items. Use the superlative to compare more than two items.

There are several ways to indicate these degrees. For single-syllable words, add *-er* or *-est.* For longer words, use *more* or *most.* Some adverbs take on a completely different form. Look at these examples:

Positive	Comparative	Superlative
soon	sooner	soonest
impressively	more impressively	most impressively
well	better	best

Practice A Underline the adverb in each sentence. Tell whether its form is positive, comparative, or superlative.

1. Of all the writers, Wiesel spoke most convincingly.
2. He wrote powerfully about the concentration camps.
3. Wiesel painfully recalled his experiences during World War II.
4. We must be stronger than the person who wants to hurt us.

© **Reading Application** In "Keep Memory Alive," find at least one example of a positive and a superlative adverb.

Practice B Rewrite each sentence, replacing each positive adverb with either a comparative or a superlative adverb. You may need to add words to the sentences.

1. Solzhenitsyn wrote <u>passionately</u>.
2. The Russian government searched <u>often</u> for dissenting voices.
3. A courageous author writes <u>truthfully</u>.
4. Dedicated writers work <u>diligently</u> at uniting people.

© **Writing Application** Write a brief paragraph about the importance of free speech. Make sure to include at least one example of a positive, a comparative, and a superlative adverb in your writing.

PH WRITING COACH | Further instruction and practice are available in *Prentice Hall Writing Coach.*

Writing

Argumentative Text Write a **letter** taking a position on Weisel's claim that silence makes us accomplices *or* on Solzhenitsyn's claim that telling the truth can change the world.

If you are writing to Wiesel, follow these tips:

- Identify and state the general definition of "accomplice."
- Describe the specific results of silence that Wiesel points out.
- Use *rhetorical devices* to help reveal your point of view and purpose.

If you are writing to Solzhenitsyn, follow these tips:

- State a general definition of "changing the world."
- Describe the effects of truth that Solzhenitsyn identifies.
- Use *rhetorical devices* to help reveal your point of view and purpose.

In your letter, use evidence to support your reasoning. Also, be sure to use formal language and an objective tone. For example, use the objective word *illogical* instead of the emotional word *stupid*. Use the formal term *impressive* rather than the informal *awesome*.

Grammar Application Use the correct degree of adverbs in your letter.

Writing Workshop: *Work in Progress*

Prewriting for Persuasive Essay For a persuasive essay you may write, jot down five local or national practices that you would like to see changed or modified. Prioritize your list, numbering the items 1 through 5. Save this Topic List in your writing portfolio.

Speaking and Listening

Comprehension and Collaboration Hold a group **debate** about one of the following paraphrased claims.

Wiesel: *People who do not speak up against injustice are accomplices.*

Solzhenitsyn: *Telling the truth will bring down an unjust government.*

Choose a notetaker and moderator, and divide the group into teams to argue for and against the statement.

- Present your point of view, supporting it with evidence.
- During the debate, listen to the arguments presented and prepare to respond. Point out any instances of the opposing team's use of exaggerated evidence or fallacious reasoning.
- Conclude your argument by summarizing your position.

After the debate, review the notes to identify the best ideas.

Common Core State Standards

W.9-10.1.d; SL.9-10.3
[For the full wording of the standards, see page 538.]

Use this prewriting activity to prepare for the **Writing Workshop** on page 604.

www.PHLitOnline.com
- Interactive graphic organizers
- Grammar tutorial
- Interactive journals

Leveled Texts

Build your skills and improve your comprehension of nonfiction with texts of increasing complexity.

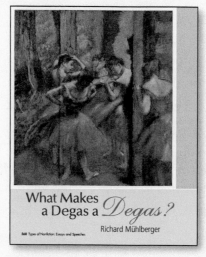

Read **"The American Idea"** to learn about the ideas that influenced the founding of the United States.

Read **"What Makes a Degas a Degas?"** to learn about a famous artist's life and work.

Common Core State Standards

Meet these standards with either **"The American Idea"** (p. 560) or **"What Makes a Degas a Degas?"** (p. 568).

Reading Informational Text
5. Analyze in detail how an author's ideas or claims are developed and refined by particular sentences, paragraphs, or larger portions of a text. (*Literary Analysis: Analytic and Interpretive Essays*)

Spiral Review: RI.9-10.3
Writing
7. Conduct short as well as more sustained research projects to answer a question or solve a problem; narrow or broaden the inquiry when appropriate; synthesize multiple sources on the subject, demonstrating understanding of the subject under investigation. (*Research and Technology: Cover Letter and Résumé*)

Language
1. Demonstrate command of the conventions of standard English grammar and usage when writing or speaking. (*Conventions: Degrees of Adjectives*)
5. Demonstrate understanding of figurative language, word relationships, and nuances in word meanings. (*Vocabulary: Analogies*)

Literary Analysis: Analytic and Interpretive Essays

An **analytic essay** is a brief work of nonfiction in which a writer explores an idea or claim by breaking it into parts. In an **interpretive essay,** a writer offers a view of the meaning or significance of an issue of general interest. A single essay may combine features of both types of essay.

To bring readers to accept an analysis or interpretation, a writer may develop it using **appeals** of the following types:

- *appeals to authority,* or calls upon the opinions of experts or other respected people

- *appeals to reason,* or calls upon logic

- *emotional appeals,* or calls upon feelings like fear, sympathy, or pride

- *appeals to shared values,* or calls upon beliefs shared by many about what is good, right, or fair

Reading Skill: Evaluate Persuasion

To **evaluate a writer's appeals,** decide whether the writer balances logic with emotional appeals. **Distinguish between fact and opinion.**

- A statement of **fact** can be proved true.

- A statement of **opinion** expresses a belief or a viewpoint and should be supported by facts or reason.

A weak essay may rely too much on persuasive appeal and not enough on fact. As you evaluate persuasive writing, look for ways in which the writer supports and develops his or her claims and ideas.

Using the Strategy: Fact and Opinion Chart

Record details on a **fact and opinion chart** like this one to help you decide if the writer has made a strong argument for a position.

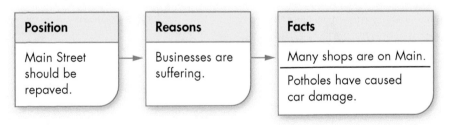

Position	Reasons	Facts
Main Street should be repaved.	Businesses are suffering.	Many shops are on Main.
		Potholes have caused car damage.

What kind of *knowledge* changes our lives?

Writing About the Big Question

In "The American Idea," the author explores the concept of America as a nation tied together by an idea of freedom. Use these sentence starters to develop your ideas about the Big Question.

The kind of knowledge that may **influence** a person's decision to move to another country is _____.

_____ can make it easier to **adapt** to life in a new land.

While You Read Look for the statement that White believes was most important to those who drafted the idea of American freedom. Then, consider White's proposal that this idea meant different things to different people.

Vocabulary

Read each word and its definition. Decide whether you know the word well, know it a little bit, or do not know it at all. After you read, see how your knowledge of each word has increased.

- **embodied** (em bäd´ ēd) *v.* gave form to; made concrete (p. 561) *The poem <u>embodied</u> her most hidden hopes and dreams.* *body n. embodiment n.*

- **emigrants** (em´ i grənts) *n.* people who leave their country or region to settle elsewhere (p. 561) *Many <u>emigrants</u> left Ireland in the 1840s and moved to other countries.* *emigrate v. emigration n. migrant adj.*

- **successive** (sək ses´ iv) *adj.* following one after another in sequence (p. 563) *Phil received an award after winning all five <u>successive</u> tennis matches.* *succeed v. succession n.*

- **subversion** (səb vur´ zhən) *n.* activity meant to overthrow something established (p. 564) *Disobedience is a <u>subversion</u> of authority.* *subversive adj. subversively adv. subvert v.*

Word Study

The **Greek prefix em-** means "in" or "into."

In this essay, the author explains that Jefferson's ideas about liberty are embodied, or put into concrete form, in the Statue of Liberty.

Meet
Theodore H. White
(1915–1986)

Author of
The American Idea

A Boston native, Theodore H. White worked as a newsboy for the *Boston Globe* to help pay for his education at Harvard University. At Harvard, he studied Chinese history and Asian languages. After he graduated, Henry Luce, founder of *Time* magazine, made him *Time*'s correspondent in eastern Asia.

The Making of a Reporter White earned fame writing about the election of John F. Kennedy in *The Making of the President, 1960*. "There is no excitement anywhere in the world, short of war, to match the excitement of the American presidential campaign," White observed. Today, he is viewed as one of the finest political reporters of the twentieth century.

Did You Know?
President Kennedy's widow, Jacqueline Kennedy, chose White to write a magazine essay honoring her husband.

BACKGROUND FOR THE ESSAY

Coming to America

In his essay, Theodore H. White asserts that immigration is key to the idea of America. Since its founding, the United States has welcomed more immigrants than any other nation. From 1820 to 1930, about 60 percent of all immigration worldwide was to the United States. From 1905 to 1914, more than a million people immigrated to the United States each year, seeking opportunity or fleeing oppression.

The
American
Idea

Theodore H. White

The idea was there at the very beginning, well before Thomas Jefferson put it into words—and the idea rang the call.

Jefferson himself could not have imagined the reach of his call across the world in time to come when he wrote:

"We hold these truths to be self-evident, that all men are created equal, that they are endowed by their Creator with certain unalienable rights, that among these are life, liberty, and the pursuit of happiness."

But over the next two centuries the call would reach the potato patches of Ireland, the ghettoes of Europe, the paddyfields of China, stirring farmers to leave their lands and townsmen their trades and thus unsettling all traditional civilizations.

It is the call from Thomas Jefferson, embodied in the great statue that looks down the Narrows of New York Harbor,[1] and in the immigrants who answered the call, that we now celebrate.

Some of the first European Americans had come to the new continent to worship God in their own way, others to seek their fortunes. But, over a century-and-a-half, the new world changed those Europeans, above all the Englishmen who had come to North America. Neither King nor Court nor Church could stretch over the ocean to the wild continent. To survive, the first emigrants had to learn to govern themselves.

---

1. **the great statue that looks down the Narrows of New York Harbor** Statue of Liberty.

Literary Analysis

Analytic and Interpretive Essays
What emotional appeals does White use in the opening paragraphs of this essay?

Vocabulary
embodied (em bäd´ ēd) *v.* gave form to; made concrete

emigrants (em´ i grənts) *n.* people who leave their country or region to settle elsewhere

Reading Check

According to Thomas Jefferson, what three rights do all men have?

But the freedom of the wilderness whetted their appetites for more freedoms. By the time Jefferson drafted his call, men were in the field fighting for those new-learned freedoms, killing and being killed by English soldiers, the best-trained troops in the world, supplied by the world's greatest navy. Only something worth dying for could unite American volunteers and keep them in the field—a stated cause, a flag, a nation they could call their own.

When, on the Fourth of July, 1776, the colonial leaders who had been meeting as a Continental Congress in Philadelphia voted to approve Jefferson's Declaration of Independence, it was not puffed-up rhetoric for them to pledge to each other "our lives, our fortunes and our sacred honor." Unless their new "United States of America" won the war, the Congressmen would be judged traitors as relentlessly as would the irregulars-under-arms in the field. . . .

The new Americans were tough men fighting for a very tough idea. How they won their battles is a story for the schoolbooks, studied by scholars, wrapped in myths by historians and poets. But what is most important is the story of the idea that made them into a nation, the idea that had an explosive power undreamed of in 1776.

All other nations had come into being among people whose families had lived for time out of mind on the same land where they were born. Englishmen are English, Frenchmen are French, Chinese are Chinese, while their governments come and go; their national states can be torn apart and remade without losing their nationhood. But Americans are a nation born of an idea; not the place, but the idea, created the United States Government.

The story we celebrate . . . is the story of how this idea worked itself out, how it stretched and changed and how the call for "life, liberty and the pursuit of happiness" does still, as it did in the beginning, mean different things to different people. ●

Reading Skill
Evaluate Persuasion
Identify one fact and one opinion expressed in the essay so far.

The new Americans were tough men fighting for a very tough idea.

▲ Thomas Jefferson

▲ John Adams

The debate began with the drafting of the Declaration of Independence. That task was left to Jefferson of Virginia, who spent two weeks in an upstairs room in a Philadelphia boarding house penning a draft, while John Adams and Benjamin Franklin questioned, edited, hardened his phrases. By the end of that hot and muggy June, the three had reached agreement: the Declaration contained the ringing universal theme Jefferson strove for and, at the same time, voiced American grievances toughly enough to please the feisty Adams and the pragmatic Franklin. After brief debate, Congress passed it.

As the years wore on, the great debate expanded between Jefferson and Adams. The young nation flourished and Jefferson chose to think of America's promise as a call to all the world, its promises universal. A few weeks before he died, he wrote, "May it be to the world, what I believe it will be (to some parts sooner, to others later, but finally to all), the signal of arousing men to burst their chains." To Adams, the call meant something else—it was the call for American independence, the cornerstone of an American state.

Their argument ran through their successive Administrations. Adams, the second President, suspected the French Revolutionaries; Alien and Sedition Acts[2] were passed during his term of office to protect the American state and its liberties

Vocabulary
successive (sək ses´ iv)
adj. following one after another in sequence

Reading Check

What document did the Founders draft to present their ideals?

---

2. **Alien and Sedition Acts** laws passed by Congress in 1798 restricting immigration and regulating the expression of criticism of the government.

Vocabulary
subversion (səb vʉr´ zhən) *n.* activity meant to overthrow something established

Spiral Review
Series of Ideas Why does White conclude with this story of Jefferson's and Adams's deaths?

against French subversion. But Jefferson, the third President, welcomed the French. The two men, once close friends, became archrivals. Still, as they grew old, their rivalry faded; there was glory enough to share in what they had made; in 1812, they began a correspondence that has since become classic, remembering and taking comfort in the triumphs of their youth.

Adams and Jefferson lived long lives and died on the same day— the Fourth of July, 1826, 50 years to the day from the Continental Congress's approval of the Declaration. Legend has it that Adams breathed on his death bed, "Thomas Jefferson still survives." As couriers set out from Braintree[3] carrying the news of Adams's death, couriers were riding north from Virginia with the news of Jefferson's death. The couriers met in Philadelphia. Horace Greeley,[4] then a youth in Vermont, later remembered: ". . . When we learned . . . that Thomas Jefferson and John Adams, the author and the great champion, respectively, of the Declaration, had both died on that day, and that the messengers bearing South and North, respectively, the tidings of their decease, had met in Philadelphia, under the shadow of that Hall in which our independence was declared, it seemed that a Divine attestation had solemnly hallowed and sanctified the great anniversary by the impressive ministration of Death."

---

3. Braintree town in Massachusetts (now called Quincy) where John Adams lived and died.
4. Horace Greeley famous American newspaper publisher.

Critical Thinking

Cite textual evidence to support your responses.

1. Key Ideas and Details (a) Identify three groups that White says heard the call of the American idea. **(b) Infer:** How did the call of the American idea affect each of them?

2. Key Ideas and Details Compare and Contrast: What differences does White see between early American settlers and people living elsewhere?

3. Key Ideas and Details Interpret: What does White mean when he writes, "Americans are a nation born of an idea"?

4. Integration of Knowledge and Ideas (a) Do you agree with White that "life, liberty, and the pursuit of happiness" means different things to different people? Why or why not? **(b)** How might these ideals shape a person's life? *[Connect to the Big Question: What kind of knowledge changes our lives?]*

The American Idea

Literary Analysis: Analytic and Interpretive Essays

1. Key Ideas and Details The author of this **interpretive essay** focuses on the "American idea." Briefly summarize White's view.

2. Craft and Structure (a) Use a chart like this one to summarize the development of ideas in the **analytic** sections of White's essay. **(b)** Explain how White uses the story about Adams and Jefferson along with other details and **persuasive appeals** to strengthen his presentation of an "American idea."

Reading Skill: Evaluate Persuasion

3. (a) List two **opinions** that White includes about people or events. **(b)** Which **facts** does he use to support each opinion?

4. Based on an analysis of his persuasive appeals and the facts and opinions presented, evaluate the validity of White's argument.

Vocabulary

Acquisition and Use Word **analogies** match the relationship in one pair of words with that in another. For each item, choose the word that will make the relationships in the first and second pair of words most similar.

1. immigrants : enter :: emigrants : **(a)** leave, **(b)** stay, **(c)** build
2. entertainment : comedian :: subversion : **(a)** film, **(b)** spy, **(c)** ship
3. build : construct :: embodied : **(a)** formed, **(b)** chosen, **(c)** broke
4. many : few :: successive : **(a)** logical, **(b)** interrupted, **(c)** finished

Word Study Use the context of the sentences and what you know about the **Greek prefix em-** to explain your answer to each question.

1. Would a person feel *embittered* after winning the lottery?
2. Is someone who is *emboldened* courageous or fearful?

Word Study

The **Greek prefix em-** means "in" or "into."

Apply It Explain how the prefix *em-* contributes to the meanings of these words. Consult a dictionary if necessary.

empathy
emphasize
empower

What kind of *knowledge* changes our lives?

What Makes a Degas a *Degas?*

Richard Mühlberger

Writing About the Big Question

In "What Makes a Degas a Degas?," the author "reads" two Degas paintings by combining his own knowledge of art with his knowledge about Degas's life. Use these sentence starters to develop your ideas about the Big Question.

Understanding how to interpret art is valuable because you gain **insight** into _____.

Artists can **influence** our understanding of the world by _____ and _____.

While You Read Consider the types of knowledge that interested Degas and influenced his work.

Vocabulary

Read each word and its definition. Decide whether you know the word well, know it a little bit, or do not know it at all. After you read, see how your knowledge of each word has increased.

- **immaterial** (im´ ə tir´ ē əl) *adj.* not consisting of matter (p. 569) *The baby does not understand that his shadow is <u>immaterial</u> and cannot be touched.* immaterialize *v.* immaterially *adv.* material *adj.*

- **silhouette** (sil´ ə wet´) *n.* an outline drawing filled in with a solid color (p. 569) *He drew a solid black <u>silhouette</u> of Emily's profile.* silhouette *v.*

- **simulating** (sim´ yoo lāt´ iŋ) *v.* giving the appearance of (p. 569) *The machine trained new pilots by <u>simulating</u> a realistic crash.* simulation *n.* simulator *n.*

- **lacquered** (lak´ ərd) *adj.* covered in tough, sticky varnish (p. 570) *The artist combined charcoal and sap to coat this <u>lacquered</u> music box.* lacquer *n.* lacquer *v.*

Word Study

The **Latin prefix** *im-* means "not" or "opposite of."

In this essay, the author explains that a painted landscape has an immaterial quality, which makes the picture seem as though it is not made of physical materials.

$\mathcal{T}$his was part of his lifelong quest:
to make viewers feel that they were
right there, beside him.

Ideas From the Exotic, Old, and New

Degas always enjoyed looking at art. One of the thrills of his school years was being allowed to inspect the great paintings in the collection of Paul Valpinçon's father. Throughout his life, the artist drew inspiration from the masterpieces in the Louvre in Paris, one of the greatest museums in the world. He also found ideas in Japanese prints. They were considered cheap, disposable souvenirs in Japan, but were treasured by artists and others in the West as highly original, fascinating works of art. Photographs, then newly invented, also suggested to Degas ways of varying his paintings. He eventually became an enthusiastic photographer himself.

In *Carriage at the Races*, the way in which the horses and carriage are cut off recalls figures in photographs and Japanese prints. For Degas, showing only part of a subject made his paintings more intimate, immediate, and realistic. He wanted viewers to see the scene as if they were actually there.

▲ **Degas self-portrait**

Critical Thinking

Cite textual evidence to support your responses.

1. **Key Ideas and Details** **(a)** Use details from the essay to describe the effect Degas seeks by outlining the dancers in black lines in *Dancers, Pink and Green.* **(b) Analyze:** What other elements contribute to this effect?

2. **Key Ideas and Details** **(a)** What is the dominant image in *Carriage at the Races*? **(b) Analyze:** How does Degas focus attention on this image?

3. **Integration of Knowledge and Ideas** What qualities in Degas's paintings suggest that he might have been a good photographer when he took up that hobby? Explain.

4. **Integration of Knowledge and Ideas** Degas and his art developed and changed based on knowledge he acquired throughout his life. Based on this essay, what subjects and areas of interest do you think influenced Degas and his painting? *[Connect to the Big Question: What kind of knowledge changes our lives?]*

Literary Analysis: Analytic and Interpretive Essays

© **1. Key Ideas and Details** Briefly summarize Mühlberger's view of Degas's "lifelong quest" in this **interpretive essay.**

© **2. Craft and Structure (a)** Use a chart like the one shown to analyze the development of ideas in the **analytic** sections of the essay. **(b)** Explain how **persuasive appeals** to reason strengthen Mühlberger's presentation of the idea that Degas intentionally incorporated qualities that might make his paintings seem incomplete.

Reading Skill: Evaluate Persuasion

3. (a) List two **opinions** that Mühlberger includes about Degas. **(b)** What **facts** does he use to support each opinion?

4. Based on an analysis of his persuasive appeals and the facts and opinions presented, evaluate the validity of Mühlberger's argument.

Vocabulary

© **Acquisition and Use** Word **analogies** match relationships between two pairs of words. For each item, choose the word that will make the relationships in the first and second pair of words most similar.

1. hatchback : car :: silhouette : **(a)** bracelet, **(b)** portrait, **(c)** carving
2. performing : do :: simulating : **(a)** pretend, **(b)** be, **(c)** own
3. chaotic : still :: immaterial : **(a)** dreamy, **(b)** personal, **(c)** solid
4. upholstered : chair :: lacquered : **(a)** table, **(b)** clean, **(c)** discolor

Word Study Use the context of the sentences and what you know about the **Latin prefix im-** to explain your answer to each question.

1. Would you be able to cross an *impassable* river?
2. Is it easy to solve a problem of *immeasurable* difficulty?

Word Study

The **Latin prefix im-** means "not" or "opposite of."

Apply It Explain how the prefix *im-* contributes to the meanings of these words. Consult a dictionary if necessary.

imbalance
immoderate
impudent

Integrated Language Skills

The American Idea •
What Makes a Degas a Degas?

Conventions: Degrees of Adjectives

An **adjective** is a word that describes a noun or a pronoun.

Most adjectives have three different forms, called degrees—the *positive degree*, the *comparative degree*, and the *superlative degree*. The positive is used to describe one item, group, or person. The comparative is used to compare two items, groups, or people. The superlative is used to compare three or more items, groups, or people.

For most two-syllable adjectives, add *–er* or use *more* or *less* to form the comparative, and add *–est* or use *most* or *least* to form the superlative. For adjectives of three or more syllables, use *more*, *most*, *less*, and *least*.

Positive	Comparative	Superlative
brave	braver	bravest
alert	more/less alert	most/least alert
good	better	best

Practice A Identify the degree of each italicized modifier.

1. Thomas Jefferson was a *brilliant* statesman.
2. Freedom is the *best* idea on which to build a nation.
3. The Declaration of Independence is an *important* document.
4. Some feel that Benjamin Franklin was *more pragmatic* than Thomas Jefferson.

 Reading Application In "The American Idea," find an example of a positive and a superlative adjective.

Practice B Determine if the italicized modifier is used correctly. Explain your answer.

1. Degas's ballerina painting is *prettier*.
2. Oil paints are *shiniest* than pastels.
3. In *Carriage at the Races*, the baby is *more important* than the carriage.
4. The center ballerina is the *taller* dancer in the entire group.

Writing Application Write about a style of art or music you enjoy. Use this sentence as a model to write a new sentence that incorporates the three degrees of adjectives. *Degas's oil paintings were quick, his pastels were quicker, and his drawings were quickest.*

PH WRITING COACH	Further instruction and practice are available in *Prentice Hall Writing Coach*.

Writing

 Argumentative Text Write a **critique,** or critical evaluation, of White's or Mühlberger's essay. Identify one of the central claims in the essay, and weigh the evidence the writer uses to support it.

- Before you draft, gather examples of the writer's *evidence.* For each piece of evidence, note whether it is effective.
- Consider discussing each piece of evidence in a separate paragraph.
- Identify ambiguities, nuances, and complexities within the text by looking for sections that confused you. Decide whether the writer clarified ideas for you. If not, determine the effect of the ambiguity.
- Conclude with a statement that evaluates the overall strength of White's or Mühlberger's evidence.
- Present your evaluation to the class. Ask whether listeners agree with your ideas. Summarize points of agreement and disagreement.

Grammar Application In your critique, use the correct degree of adjectives.

Writing Workshop: *Work in Progress*

Prewriting for Persuasive Essay Make a flowchart for the first choice on your Topic List. In each supporting box, write a detail that shows why the change is needed or what positive result it would have. Save this Topic Defense List in your writing portfolio.

Research and Technology

Use multiple reliable sources to research one of the people associated with the essay you read. For example, you might learn more about one of the nation's founders, such as Thomas Jefferson, or study an artist associated with French Impressionism, such as Mary Cassatt. Then, write a **cover letter** and **résumé** that he or she might have submitted for either the job of "Founder of the Republic" or "French Impressionist."

- Conduct research to identify the education and experience that make your subject suitable for the job.
- Consult reference works to find a suitable format for cover letters and résumés. Use action verbs and vivid descriptions to make your writing engaging.
- Use appropriate principles of design, such as correct margins, tabs, columns, and use of white space, to create a visually interesting document.
- Proofread carefully to ensure that you follow the format and use language accurately.

 Common Core State Standards

L.9-10.1; W.9-10.7
[For the full wording of the standards, see page 556.]

Use this prewriting activity to prepare for the **Writing Workshop** on page 604.

PHLit Online!
www.PHLitOnline.com
- Interactive graphic organizers
- Grammar tutorial
- Interactive journals

Test Practice: Reading

Evaluate Persuasion

Fiction Selection

Directions: *Read the selection. Then, answer the questions.*

Aaron called his best friend, Danny. "I just came from the city pound, looking for Jake. He got lost again," he told Danny. "You should see that place—crowded and smelly, no room for the dogs to run, not enough people to care for the animals. We need to do something."

"Like what?" asked Danny.

"We need to convince our city council to give more funds to the pound. We should treat animals humanely. These dogs are locked in small cages, with no place to exercise. Some of them look sick. They need better medical care. Also, if the pound were cleaner and the animals better cared for, more people would adopt pets from there. That would save the city money."

"Okay," said Danny. "Count me in. By the way, did you find Jake?"

"Yeah. He came home by himself!"

1. Which of the following *best* states the claim made by Aaron?
   A. There are too many stray dogs.
   B. The city pound is not a humane place for animals.
   C. The city pound is dirty.
   D. The city council is negligent.

2. What is Aaron's position?
   A. People should be convinced to adopt more animals from the pound.
   B. The city council should give the pound more money.
   C. Dogs should be taken for walks.
   D. People should be more humane.

3. The statement "We should treat animals humanely" appeals to—
   A. logic.
   B. economics.
   C. a sense of humor.
   D. a sense of ethics.

4. Which of the following persuasive techniques is *not* found in Aaron's appeal?
   A. logic
   B. emotion
   C. statistics
   D. a sense of ethics

Writing for Assessment

Which of Aaron's appeals do you find most persuasive? Explain your answer in three or four sentences, using details from the passage.

Nonfiction Selection

Directions: *Read the selection. Then, answer the questions.*

Adopting a family dog is a long-term commitment, so it is important to choose a dog wisely. The Labrador retriever is the most popular dog in the United States. More Labs are registered to owners than any other breed—for good reason.

Labs are affectionate and playful. They love the company of humans, and they always welcome attention. Labs also love any kind of active play. They love to play fetch, especially in the water. Toss a stick into the lake or pool, and you can be sure the Lab will never tire of retrieving it. Labs love to be part of a family, and they are patient and gentle with children. Labs are also easy to train, an important characteristic in a puppy. So when looking for a family pet, choose a Lab. You will not be sorry.

1. Which of the following is the *best* summary of the author's opinion?
   A. You should choose a pet carefully.
   B. Labrador retrievers are superior to other dogs.
   C. A dog's temperament is important.
   D. A Labrador retriever is the best family dog.

2. Repeated use of the word *love* serves to—
   A. help the reader identify with the writer's statements.
   B. emphasize the Lab's enthusiasm and good nature.
   C. show the writer's knowledge.
   D. show the superiority of Labs.

3. Which of the following persuasive techniques is found in the sentence *"More Labs are registered to owners than any other breed"*?
   A. fact
   B. repetition
   C. example
   D. humor

4. Which of the following statements can be verified?
   A. Labs love to be part of a family.
   B. More Labs are registered to owners than any other breed.
   C. You will not be sorry.
   D. Toss a stick in a pool, and you can be sure the Lab will never tire of retrieving it.

Writing for Assessment

Connecting Across Texts
What general attitude toward dogs is expressed in these two passages? In a well-developed paragraph, use details from the two passages to support your answer.

PHLit
Online!
www.PHLitOnline.com
• Online practice
• Instant feedback

Reading for Information

Analyzing Expository and Functional Texts

Research Source

Course Catalog

Common Core State Standards

Reading Informational Text
3. Analyze how the author unfolds an analysis or series of ideas or events, including the order in which the points are made, how they are introduced and developed, and the connections that are drawn between them.

Language
6. Acquire and use accurately general academic and domain-specific words and phrases, sufficient for reading, writing, speaking, and listening at the college and career readiness level; demonstrate independence in gathering vocabulary knowledge when considering a word or phrase important to comprehension or expression.

Reading Skill: Analyze Text Structures

Authors **structure and format** their texts in order to help achieve their purposes. **Scan,** or glance over, titles, headings, and subheadings to analyze how these features support the **author's purpose.** Also, **critique the document** by **skimming,** or quickly reading, key parts of the text to determine the **sequence,** or order, of information. Then, decide whether that sequence is logical. This chart lists some common text structures.

Common Text Structures	
Cause and Effect	action followed by consequences
Chronological Order	in order of occurrence
Comparison and Contrast	according to the similarities and differences
List	connected items stated consecutively or sorted into categories
Order of Importance	in a logical progression from most to least important or from least to most important
Spatial Order	according to location

Content-Area Vocabulary

These words appear in the selections that follow. You may also encounter them in other content-area texts.

- **linguistic** (liŋ gwis´ tik) *adj.* having to do with language
- **endeavors** (en dev´ ərz) *n.* earnest tries or attempts
- **spectrum** (spek´ trəm) *n.* range or scope

The History of the Guitar
Thomas A. Hill

When we attempt to pinpoint the origins of deliberately produced, carefully designed instruments, we run into problems, because the very first instrument makers were not very concerned with posterity. They did not leave written records. One approach we might try, in an effort to find out where the guitar came from, would be an examination of languages.

This paragraph is organized using a cause-and-effect structure.

Ancient Beginnings

The ancient Assyrians,[1] four thousand years ago, had an instrument that they called a *chetarah*. We know little more about it other than that it was a stringed instrument with a sound-box, but the name is intriguing. The ancient Hebrews had their *kinnura,* the Chaldeans[2] their *qitra,* and the Greeks their *cithara* and *citharis*—which Greek writers of the day were careful to emphasize were *not* the same instrument. It is with the Greeks, in fact, that the first clear history of the evolution of an instrument begins; some of this history can again be traced with purely **linguistic** devices. The cithara and citharis were members of a family of musical instruments called *fides*—a word that is ancient Greek for "strings." From the fides family it is easy to draw lines to the medieval French *vielle,* the German *fiedel,* the English *fithele* or *fiddle,* and the *vihuela,* national instrument of medieval Spain. Significantly, much of the music for the vihuela (of which a great deal survives to the present day) can easily be transcribed[3] for the guitar. In England, the influences of the cithara and citharis led to the evolution of such instruments as the *cither, zither, cittern,* and *gittern,* with which instrument the linguistic parallel we seek is fairly easy to draw. Gitterns dating back to 1330 can be seen in the British Museum. In Spain, there is music for the vihuela that dates back at least that far. What did these instruments look like? Superficially, they bore a substantial resemblance to the guitar as we know it today, although the sides seldom curved in as far as do the sides of the modern

The author gives information in spatial order, according to the regions in which the events took place.

---

1. Assyrians (ə sir´ ē ənz) founders of an ancient empire in the Middle East, flourishing in the seventh century B.C.

2. Chaldeans (kal dē´ ənz) a people that rose to power in Babylon, an ancient empire of the Middle East, during the sixth century B.C.

3. transcribed (tran skrībd´) *v.* adapted piece of music for an instrument other than the one for which it was originally written.

guitar. They were usually strung with *pairs* of strings, or *courses,* much like a modern twelve-string guitar. The two strings of each course were tuned either in unison or an octave[4] apart. For a while, there seemed to be no standard for the number of courses an instrument should have; there are both vihuelas and gitterns with as few as four courses and as many as seven. By the fifteenth century, the vihuela seems to have settled on six as the standard number of courses. . . In England, the gittern settled down to four courses. . . . Historians of this period do note the existence in Spain of an instrument called the *guitarra.* . . . But no music was being written for this instrument, and nobody seems to have been paying much attention to it.

The African Link

Meanwhile, in Africa, the Arabs had been playing an instrument that they called *al-ud,* or "the wood," for centuries. When the Moors crossed the Straits of Gibraltar[5] in the twelfth century to conquer Spain, they brought this instrument with them. It quickly became popular, and by the time anybody who spoke English was talking about it, al-ud had become *lute.* The lute's main contribution to the evolution of the guitar as we know it today seems to

have been the fret, a metal bar on the fingerboard. Until the arrival of the lute, the European forerunners of the guitar had no frets at all. Since the fret made it a little easier to play the same tune the same way more than once, and helped to standardize tunings, it was a resounding success. The first Arabic lutes in Europe had movable frets, tied to the neck, usually about eight in number. Consequently, the first vihuelas to which frets were added also had movable ones. The lute—or rather the people who brought it to Europe—made another important contribution. The Moorish artistic influence, blowing the cobwebs away from stodgy Spanish art and society, created an artistic climate that encouraged music to flourish. And so the instruments on which the music was played flourished as well, and continued to evolve and improve. This is a contribution that cannot be overestimated.

If any general lines can be drawn, perhaps it can be said that descendants of the original al-ud, crossing the Straits of Gibraltar, collided in Spain with the descendants of the Greek cithara and citharis. Sprinkled with a little bit of gittern influence from England, the result led ultimately to what we know today as the guitar.

---

4. **unison** (yōōn′ e sen) . . . **octave** (äk′ tiv) A unison consists of two tones of the same pitch. An octave consists of two tones that are eight notes apart in the scale. The pitches in an octave sound "the same" and are named by the same note.
5. **Moors** (mōōrz) . . . **Gibraltar** (ji brôl′ tər) Groups of Moors, an Arab people of North Africa, invaded Spain at various times, beginning in the eighth century A.D. The Straits of Gibraltar are waters dividing Spain from Africa.

CALIFORNIA STATE UNIVERSITY AT FULLERTON
Course Catalog

> Course Catalog
>
> **Features:**
> - descriptions of programs of study within each of the school's departments
> - explanations of the requirements for completing programs and attaining certificates or degrees
> - lists of the courses offered within each department and information about their value
> - text written for a specific audience

PROGRAMS OFFERED

> The text is organized by order of importance. The information becomes more specific through the document. This section lists all of the music programs offered.

Bachelor of Arts in Music
- Liberal Arts
- Music Education
- Music History and Theory

Bachelor of Music
- Composition
- Voice
- Instrumental
- Accompanying
- Keyboard
- Jazz and Commercial Music

Minor in Music

Master of Arts in Music
- Music History and Literature
- Music Education
- Piano Pedagogy

Master of Music
- Performance
- Theory-Composition

Single Subject (Secondary) Credential

INTRODUCTION

> An introduction provides an overview of the university's music program.

Music is one of the most rewarding of all human endeavors, and the faculty and students in the Department of Music share a deep love for their art and a common desire to achieve excellence in it. The department offers a wide spectrum of degree programs and options with an overall emphasis in the area of performance. The curriculum provides basic preparation for careers in music, music education, or further graduate study, and is designed to provide a balanced education in the many facets of musical experience. Artist-teachers offer instruction in all areas of performance; practicing composers and theorists teach courses in theory and composition; active musicologists provide instruction in history and literature; and specialists in music education teach the courses in that area. It is the goal of the department to develop each student's musical and intellectual potential to the highest level of individual capability. California State University at Fullerton is fully accredited by the National Association of Schools of Music and the Western Association of Schools and Colleges.

MUSIC DEGREE PROGRAMS

The Department of Music offers a variety of courses that lead to baccalaureate and graduate degrees. The baccalaureate degree may be earned in either of two degree programs (Bachelor of Arts or Bachelor of Music). Within these programs, a student will pursue a concentration in Liberal Arts, Music History and Theory, Music Education, Performance, Composition, Accompanying, or Jazz and Commercial Music.

> This section provides more specific information about one music degree program.

BACHELOR OF MUSIC

This degree program is designed to provide training for highly gifted students who show promise and capability of becoming professional performers and composers.

The degree consists of 132 semester units. A minimum of 70 semester units in music are required, at least 32 of which must be upper-division.

Core Requirements for the Bachelor of Music (38 units)

Music theory (*Music 109, 111, 112, 121, 122, 211, 221, 319, 320*) (16 units)

Music history and literature (*Music 151; 351A, B, C*) (11 units)

Principal performance area (*applied music*) (6 units)

Major performance ensemble (*Music 406*) (4 units)

Recital (*Music 498*) (1 unit)

> You can skim the information provided here to determine if it is logically presented.

KEYBOARD CONCENTRATION (70 units)

Second Language Graduation Requirement

Since the Keyboard Concentration within the Bachelor of Music is a high-unit program, majors in this concentration are exempt from the Second Language Graduation Requirement.

Core Requirements for the Bachelor of Music (38 units)

Music theory (*Music 109, 111, 112, 121, 122, 211, 221, 319, 320*) (16 units)

Music history and literature (*Music 151; 351A, B, C*) (11 units)

Principal performance area (*applied music*) (6 units)

Major performance ensemble (*Music 406*) (4 units)

Recital (*Music 498*) (1 unit)

Additional Requirements (32 units)

Music theory (*two courses from Music 418, 420, 422*) (4–5 units)

Music history and literature (*Music 454A, B*) (4 units)

Conducting (*Music 382A or 383A*) (2 units)

Recital (*Music 398*) (1 unit)

Principal performance area (*applied music*) (6 units)

Chamber music (*Music 407D, E, M, Y and/or 408B, G, K, S, W, X*) (3 units)

Piano-Vocal Collaboration (*Music 386*) (1 unit)

Pedagogy (*Music 467A, B, C*) (6 units)

Harpsichord or organ class (*Music 372 or 373*) (1 unit)

Electives in music (3–4 units)

Comparing Expository and Functional Texts

 1. Key Ideas and Details (a) Compare the **structures** and **formats** of each text. Make sure to explain the patterns of organization the writers use to order information, giving specific examples. **(b)** Explain ways in which structure and format affect how readers use each text.

Content-Area Vocabulary

2. The word *endeavor* can function as different parts of speech. Write one sentence using *endeavor* as a noun and another sentence using it as a verb. Use a dictionary if necessary.

 # Timed Writing

Explanatory Text: Letter

> **Format and Audience**
> The prompt directs you to write a letter to an author. Therefore, be sure you use letter formatting, formal language, and a respectful tone.

Write a letter to the author of the research source in which you comment on "The History of the Guitar" and the sequence of the information presented. Discuss whether the information was structured and developed effectively. Explain and support your comments with relevant details from the text. (25 minutes)

> **Academic Vocabulary**
> When you *explain* something, you describe it in terms that will help someone understand it more clearly.

5-Minute Planner

Complete these steps before you begin to write:

1. Read the prompt carefully. Look for key words, like those highlighted, to understand the assignment.

2. Scan the features and skim the text of the research source.

3. As you skim and scan, make notes about how the **sequence of information** helps you understand the text. Also note places where the sequence might confuse a reader.

4. Make a quick outline of your letter. Plan the order of the points you will make. Sequence your points in a way that will help the reader, the author, understand your ideas.

5. Use your outline and notes as you write to the author, Thomas A. Hill.

Comparing Literary Works

Comparing Authors' Purposes

An **author's purpose** is his or her main reason for writing. The following examples illustrate common purposes for nonfiction writers:

- A journalist might write to inform readers about a recent event.

- A humorist might write to entertain with a comical anecdote.

- An essayist might write to pay tribute to a person whom he or she thinks deserves honor.

A writer may have more than one purpose for writing. Generally, however, one purpose is the most important.

Both Yoshiko Uchida and N. Scott Momaday write about their personal connections to historic events. Both authors intend to inform readers about the past. However, writers who write about the past often have another, deeper purpose than informing: They may write to heal old wounds, to bear witness to past injustice, or to better understand themselves. As you read, use a chart like the one shown to compare Momaday's and Uchida's purposes and the details, or evidence, that they use for support.

	Uchida	Momaday
Details		
Purposes		

One important tool writers may use to accomplish a specific purpose in writing is **rhetoric,** or the use of language to persuade readers and shape their views of a subject. As you read, note the use of rhetorical strategies such as the following:

- Uchida's use of details appealing to readers' emotions, eliciting sympathy for her plight

- Momaday's blending of history with descriptions of landscapes and people to make vivid the Kiowa past and to help readers feel its loss

Common Core State Standards

Reading Informational Text
6. Determine an author's point of view or purpose in a text and analyze how an author uses rhetoric to advance that point of view or purpose.

Writing
2. Write informative/explanatory texts to examine and convey complex ideas, concepts, and information clearly and accurately through the effective selection, organization, and analysis of content.
2.a. Introduce a topic; organize complex ideas, concepts, and information to make important connections and distinctions. *(Timed Writing)*

PHLit Online!
www.PHLitOnline.com

- Vocabulary flashcards
- Interactive journals
- More about the authors
- Selection audio
- Interactive graphic organizers

Writing About the Big Question

Both Yoshiko Uchida and N. Scott Momaday write to record a vanishing past with a belief that passing down history is critical. Use this sentence starter to develop your ideas about the Big Question.

Reflecting on the past is important because _____.

Meet the Authors

Yoshiko Uchida (1921–1992)

Author of *Desert Exile*

Yoshiko Uchida's childhood was fairly uneventful—until history struck. In 1942, the United States and Japan went to war, and the United States government forced Japanese American families like Uchida's into relocation camps. Uchida and her family were sent to Tanforan Racetrack near San Francisco, where they lived in a stable. Later, they were relocated to a camp in Utah.

Supporting Awareness After the war, Uchida attended Smith College in Massachusetts. She became a teacher and an award-winning author who wrote more than thirty fiction and nonfiction books. Her ultimate goal, she said, was "to write of meaningful relationships between human beings, to celebrate our common humanity."

N. Scott Momaday (b. 1934)

©Thomas Victor

Author of *The Way to Rainy Mountain*

Growing up on the Native American reservations where his parents taught, N. Scott Momaday learned the traditions of his father's Kiowa culture, as well as those of the Navajo, Apache, and Pueblo Indians. At the same time, he received a modern education. "I grew up in two worlds and straddle both those worlds even now," he says. "It has made for confusion and a richness in my life."

A Creative Heritage Momaday has made much of this "richness," celebrating Native American traditions in novels, poetry, and essays. His first novel, *House Made of Dawn*, received a Pulitzer Prize.

from
Desert Exile:
The Uprooting
of a
Japanese-American Family

Yoshiko Uchida

Background On December 7, 1941, Japan attacked the American naval base at Pearl Harbor, Hawaii. Two months later, under strong political pressure, President Franklin D. Roosevelt ordered more than 100,000 Japanese Americans from their homes and into government-run relocation camps. More than thirty years after the war, President Gerald Ford officially apologized to Japanese Americans and signed a proclamation officially ending the old order.

Yoshiko Uchida tells of her own family's experience of wartime internment. In 1942, her father was arrested and taken to Montana by the Federal Bureau of Investigation. A few months later, the rest of the family was ordered to report to the assembly camp at Tanforan.

As the bus pulled up to the grandstand, I could see hundreds of Japanese Americans jammed along the fence that lined the track. These people had arrived a few days earlier and were now watching for the arrival of friends or had come to while away the empty hours that had suddenly been thrust upon them.

As soon as we got off the bus, we were directed to an area beneath the grandstand where we registered and filled out a series of forms. Our baggage was inspected for contraband,[1] a cursory medical check made, and our living quarters assigned. We were to be housed in Barrack 16, Apartment 40. Fortunately, some friends who had arrived earlier found us and offered to help us locate our quarters.

It had rained the day before and the hundreds of people who had trampled on the track had turned it into a miserable mass of slippery mud. We made our way on it carefully, helping my mother who was dressed just as she would have been to go to church. She wore a hat, gloves, her good coat, and her Sunday shoes, because she would not have thought of venturing outside our house dressed in any other way.

Everywhere there were black tar-papered barracks[2] that had been hastily erected to house the 8,000 Japanese Americans of the area who had been uprooted from their homes. Barrack 16, however, was not among them, and we couldn't find it until we had traveled half the length of the track and gone beyond it to the northern rim of the racetrack compound.

Finally one of our friends called out, "There it is, beyond that row of eucalyptus trees." Barrack 16 was not a barrack at all, but a long stable raised a few feet off the ground with a broad ramp the horses had used to reach their stalls. Each stall was now numbered, and ours was number 40. That the stalls should have been called "apartments" was a euphemism so ludicrous it was comical.

◀ **Critical Viewing**
Which details suggest that the family in this photograph is being forced to move to a relocation camp?

Literary Analysis
Author's Purpose
Which details here show that part of the author's purpose is to pay tribute, or honor the people she describes?

☑ **Reading Check**
What kind of building was Barrack 16 before it was turned into housing?

---

1. **contraband** (kän´ trə band´) *n.* prohibited goods.
2. **barracks** (bar´ əks) *n.* large, plain, often temporary housing.

The Uprooting of a Japanese-American Family *from* Desert Exile **587**

When we reached stall number 40, we pushed open the narrow door and looked uneasily into the vacant darkness. The stall was about ten by twenty feet and empty except for three folded Army cots lying on the floor. Dust, dirt, and wood shavings covered the linoleum that had been laid over manure-covered boards, the smell of horses hung in the air, and the whitened corpses of many insects still clung to the hastily white-washed walls.

High on either side of the entrance were two small windows which were our only source of daylight. The stall was divided into two sections by Dutch doors[3] worn down by teeth marks, and each stall in the stable was separated from the adjoining one only by rough partitions that stopped a foot short of the sloping roof. That space, while perhaps a good source of ventilation for the horses, deprived us of all but visual privacy, and we couldn't even be sure of that because of the crevices and knotholes in the dividing walls.

Because our friends had already spent a day as residents of Tanforan, they had become adept at scrounging for necessities. One found a broom and swept the floor for us. Two of the boys went to the barracks where mattresses were being issued, stuffed the ticking with straw themselves, and came back with three for our cots.

Nothing in the camp was ready. Everything was only half-finished. I wondered how much the nation's security would have been threatened had the Army permitted us to remain in our homes a few more days until the camps were adequately prepared for occupancy by families.

By the time we had cleaned out the stall and set up the cots, it was time for supper. Somehow, in all the confusion, we had not had lunch, so I was eager to get to the main mess hall, which was located beneath the grandstand.

The sun was going down as we started along the muddy track, and a cold, piercing wind swept in from the bay. When we arrived, there were six long weaving lines of people waiting to get into the mess hall. We took our place at the end of one of them, each of us clutching a plate and silverware borrowed from friends who had already received their baggage.

Shivering in the cold, we pressed close together trying to shield Mama from the wind. As we stood in what seemed a breadline for the destitute, I felt degraded, humiliated, and overwhelmed with a longing for home. And I saw the unutterable sadness on my mother's face.

This was only the first of many lines we were to endure, and we soon discovered that waiting in line was as inevitable a part of Tanforan as the north wind that swept in from the bay stirring up all the dust and litter of the camp.

---

3. **Dutch doors** two-part door in which the top half and the bottom half can be opened separately.

Once we got inside the gloomy cavernous mess hall, I saw hundreds of people eating at wooden picnic tables, while those who had already eaten were shuffling aimlessly over the wet cement floor. When I reached the serving table and held out my plate, a cook reached into a dishpan full of canned sausages and dropped two onto my plate with his fingers. Another man gave me a boiled potato and a piece of butterless bread.

With 5,000 people to be fed, there were few unoccupied tables, so we separated from our friends and shared a table with an elderly man and a young family with two crying babies. No one at the table spoke to us, and even Mama could seem to find no friendly word to offer as she normally would have done. We tried to eat, but the food wouldn't go down.

"Let's get out of here," my sister suggested.

We decided it would be better to go back to our barrack than to linger in the depressing confusion of the mess hall. It had grown dark by now and since Tanforan had no lights for nighttime occupancy, we had to pick our way carefully down the slippery track.

Once back in our stall, we found it no less depressing, for there was only a single electric light bulb dangling from the ceiling, and a one-inch crevice at the top of the north wall admitted a steady draft of the cold night air. We sat huddled on our cots, bundled in our coats, too cold and miserable even to talk. My sister and I worried about Mama, for she wasn't strong and had recently been troubled with neuralgia,[4] which could easily be aggravated by the cold. She in turn was worrying about us, and of course we all worried and wondered about Papa.

Suddenly we heard the sound of a truck stopping outside.

"Hey, Uchida! Apartment 40!" a boy shouted.

I rushed to the door and found the baggage boys trying to heave our enormous "camp bundle" over the railing that fronted our stall.

"What ya got in here anyway?" they shouted good-naturedly as they struggled with the unwieldy bundle. "It's the biggest thing we got on our truck!"

I grinned, embarrassed, but I could hardly wait to get out our belongings. My sister and I fumbled to undo all the

---

4. **neuralgia** (noo ral′ jə) *n.* severe pain along the path of a nerve.

Literary Analysis
Author's Purpose
How might these details affect the reader's opinion of the government relocation program?

Spiral Review
Development of Ideas How does Uchida develop the idea that the camp is an unpleasant place?

Vocabulary
unwieldy (un wēl′ dē) *adj.* hard to manage because of shape or weight

Reading Check
Identify three details showing that the family's first day in the camp is miserable.

The Uprooting of a Japanese-American Family *from* Desert Exile **589** knots we had tied into the rope around our bundle that morning and eagerly pulled out the familiar objects from home.

We unpacked our blankets, pillows, sheets, tea kettle, and, most welcome of all, our electric hot plate. I ran to the nearest washroom to fill the kettle with water, while Mama and Kay made up the Army cots with our bedding. Once we hooked up the hot plate and put the kettle on to boil, we felt better. We sat close to its warmth, holding our hands toward it as though it were our fireplace at home.

Before long some friends came by to see us, bringing with them the only gift they had—a box of dried prunes. Even the day before, we wouldn't have given the prunes a second glance, but now they were as welcome as the boxes of Maskey's chocolate my father used to bring home from San Francisco.

Mama managed to make some tea for our friends, and we sat around our steaming kettle, munching gratefully on our prunes. We spent much of the evening talking about food and the lack of it, a concern that grew obsessive over the next few weeks, when we were constantly hungry.

Our stable consisted of twenty-five stalls facing north which were back to back with an equal number facing south, so we were surrounded on three sides. Living in our stable were an assortment of people—mostly small family units—that included an artist, my father's barber and his wife, a dentist and his wife, an elderly retired couple, a group of Kibei[5] bachelors (Japanese born in the United States but educated in Japan), an insurance salesman and his wife, and a widow with two daughters. To say that we all became intimately acquainted would be an understatement. It was, in fact, communal living, with semi-private cubicles provided only for sleeping.

Our neighbors on one side spent much of their time playing cards, and at all hours of the day we could hear the sound of cards being shuffled and money changing hands. Our other neighbors had a teenage son who spent most of the day with his friends, coming home to his stall at night only after his parents were asleep. Family life began to show signs of strain almost immediately, not only in the next stall but throughout the entire camp.

One Sunday our neighbor's son fell asleep in the rear of his stall with the door bolted from inside. When his parents came home from church, no amount of shouting or banging on the door could awaken the boy.

"Our stupid son has locked us out," they explained, coming to us for help.

I climbed up on my cot and considered pouring water on him over the partition, for I knew he slept just on the other side of it. Instead

---

5. Kibei (kē′ bā′)

I dangled a broom over the partition and poked and prodded with it, shouting, "Wake up! Wake up!" until the boy finally bestirred himself and let his parents in. We became good friends with our neighbors after that.

About one hundred feet from our stable were two latrines and two washrooms for our section of camp, one each for men and women. The latrines were crude wooden structures containing eight toilets, separated by partitions, but having no doors. The washrooms were divided into two sections. In the front section was a long tin trough spaced with spigots of hot and cold water where we washed our faces and brushed our teeth. To the rear were eight showers, also separated by partitions but lacking doors or curtains. The showers were difficult to adjust and we either got scalded by torrents of hot water or shocked by an icy blast of cold. Most of the Issei[6] were unaccustomed to showers, having known the luxury of soaking in deep pine-scented tubs during their years in Japan, and found the showers virtually impossible to use.

Our card-playing neighbor scoured the camp for a container that might serve as a tub, and eventually found a large wooden barrel. She rolled it to the showers, filled it with warm water, and then climbed in for a pleasant and leisurely soak. The greatest compliment she could offer anyone was the use of her private tub.

The lack of privacy in the latrines and showers was an embarrassing hardship especially for the older women, and many would take newspapers to hold over their faces or squares of cloth to tack up for their own private curtain. The Army, obviously ill-equipped to build living quarters for women and children, had made no attempt to introduce even the most common of life's civilities into these camps for us.

During the first few weeks of camp life everything was erratic and in short supply. Hot water appeared only sporadically, and the minute it was available, everyone ran for the showers or the laundry. We had to be clever and quick just to keep clean, and my

Once we hooked up the hot plate and put the kettle on to boil, we felt better.

Reading Check
Name two major problems Uchida and other residents of the camp face.

---

6. Issei (ē′ sā′) *n.* Japanese immigrants to North America, especially those who came after 1907 and were ineligible until 1952 to become U.S. citizens.

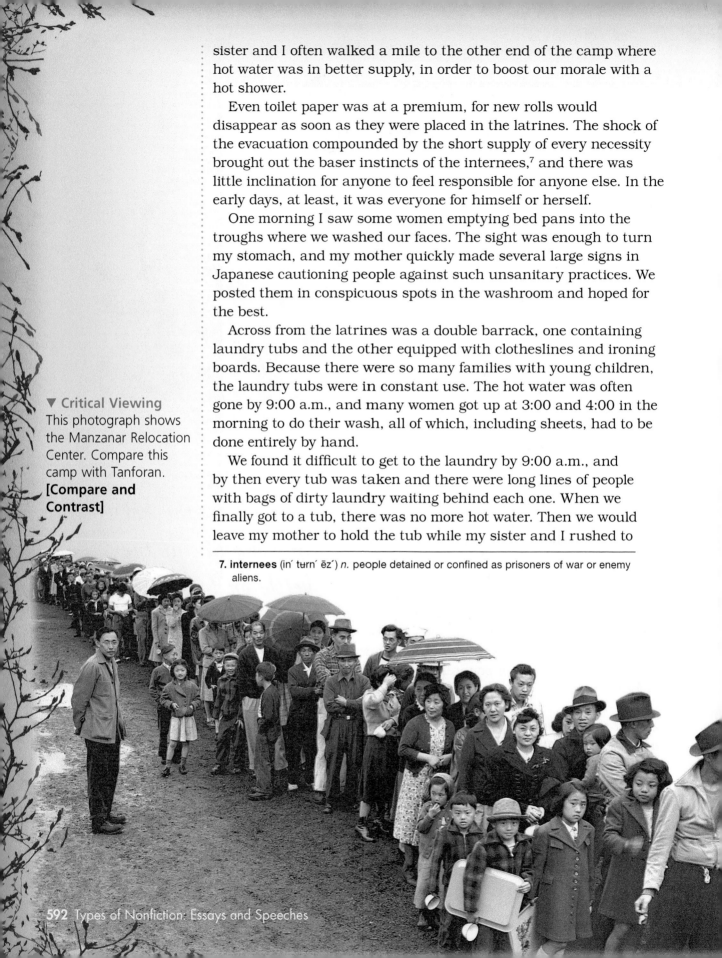

sister and I often walked a mile to the other end of the camp where hot water was in better supply, in order to boost our morale with a hot shower.

Even toilet paper was at a premium, for new rolls would disappear as soon as they were placed in the latrines. The shock of the evacuation compounded by the short supply of every necessity brought out the baser instincts of the internees,[7] and there was little inclination for anyone to feel responsible for anyone else. In the early days, at least, it was everyone for himself or herself.

One morning I saw some women emptying bed pans into the troughs where we washed our faces. The sight was enough to turn my stomach, and my mother quickly made several large signs in Japanese cautioning people against such unsanitary practices. We posted them in conspicuous spots in the washroom and hoped for the best.

Across from the latrines was a double barrack, one containing laundry tubs and the other equipped with clotheslines and ironing boards. Because there were so many families with young children, the laundry tubs were in constant use. The hot water was often gone by 9:00 a.m., and many women got up at 3:00 and 4:00 in the morning to do their wash, all of which, including sheets, had to be done entirely by hand.

We found it difficult to get to the laundry by 9:00 a.m., and by then every tub was taken and there were long lines of people with bags of dirty laundry waiting behind each one. When we finally got to a tub, there was no more hot water. Then we would leave my mother to hold the tub while my sister and I rushed to

---

7. internees (in′ tʉrn′ ēz′) *n.* people detained or confined as prisoners of war or enemy aliens.

▼ **Critical Viewing**
This photograph shows the Manzanar Relocation Center. Compare this camp with Tanforan.
[Compare and Contrast]

the washroom where there was a better supply and carried back bucketfuls of hot water as everyone else learned to do. By the time we had finally hung our laundry on lines outside our stall, we were too exhausted to do much else for the rest of the day.

For four days after our arrival we continued to go to the main mess hall for all our meals. My sister and I usually missed breakfast because we were assigned to the early shift and we simply couldn't get there by 7:00 a.m. Dinner was at 4:45 p.m., which was a terrible hour, but not a major problem, as we were always hungry. Meals were uniformly bad and skimpy, with an abundance of starches such as beans and bread. I wrote to my non-Japanese friends in Berkeley shamelessly asking them to send us food, and they obliged with large cartons of cookies, nuts, dried fruit, and jams.

We looked forward with much anticipation to the opening of a half dozen smaller mess halls located throughout the camp. But when ours finally opened, we discovered that the preparation of smaller quantities had absolutely no effect on the quality of the food. We went eagerly to our new mess hall only to be confronted at our first meal with chili con carne, corn, and butterless bread. To assuage our disappointment, a friend and I went to the main mess hall which was still in operation, to see if it had anything better. Much to our amazement and delight, we found small lettuce salads, the first fresh vegetables we had seen in many days. We ate ravenously and exercised enormous self-control not to go back for second and third helpings.

The food improved gradually, and by the time we left Tanforan five months later, we had fried chicken and ice cream for Sunday dinner. By July tubs of soapy water were installed at the mess hall exits so we could wash our plates and utensils on the way out. Being slow eaters, however, we usually found the dishwater tepid and dirty by the time we reached the tubs, and we often rewashed our dishes in the washroom.

Most internees got into the habit of rushing for everything. They ran to the mess halls to be first in line, they dashed inside for the best tables and then rushed through their meals to get to the washtubs before the suds ran out. The three of us, however, seemed to be at the end of every line that formed and somehow never managed to be first for anything.

Literary Analysis
Author's Purpose
Which details here reveal something about Uchida's personality?

Reading Check
Name two necessities that were in short supply at the camp.

One of the first things we all did at Tanforan was to make our living quarters as comfortable as possible. A pile of scrap lumber in one corner of camp melted away like snow on a hot day as residents salvaged whatever they could to make shelves and crude pieces of furniture to supplement the Army cots. They also made ingenious containers for carrying their dishes to the mess halls, with handles and lids that grew more and more elaborate in a sort of unspoken competition.

Because of my father's absence, our friends helped us in camp, just as they had in Berkeley, and we relied on them to put up shelves and build a crude table and two benches for us. We put our new camp furniture in the front half of our stall, which was our "living room," and put our three cots in the dark windowless rear section, which we promptly dubbed "the dungeon." We ordered some print fabric by mail and sewed curtains by hand to hang at our windows and to cover our shelves. Each new addition to our stall made it seem a little more like home.

One afternoon about a week after we had arrived at Tanforan, a messenger from the administration building appeared with a telegram for us. It was from my father, telling us he had been released on parole from Montana and would be able to join us soon in camp. Papa was coming home. The wonderful news had come like an unexpected gift, but even as we hugged each other in joy, we didn't quite dare believe it until we actually saw him. . . .

Critical Thinking

Cite textual evidence to support your responses.

1. **Key Ideas and Details** **(a)** Describe stall number 40. **(b) Analyze:** Why does Uchida feel that calling it an "apartment" was "ludicrous"?

2. **Key Ideas and Details** **Analyze Cause and Effect:** How do the shortages at the camp affect people's attitudes and behavior? Support your answer.

3. **Integration of Knowledge and Ideas** **Draw Conclusions:** What do the conditions at the camp suggest about the government's attitude toward Japanese Americans?

4. **Integration of Knowledge and Ideas** **(a)** In what ways did Uchida's experiences at the relocation camp change her? Support your answer with details from the selection. **(b)** What impact do you think Uchida hopes her narrative will have on readers? *[Connect to the Big Question: What kind of knowledge changes our lives?]*

from

The Way to Rainy Mountain

N. Scott Momaday

Background Like other Great Plains tribes, the Kiowa were buffalo hunters. When white settlers came to the Plains, the Kiowa fought them. By the late 1800s, however, United States troops had broken Kiowa resistance and white hunters had all but exterminated the buffalo. Traditional Kiowa life came to an end. In 1868, the Kiowas went to live on a reservation in southwestern Oklahoma.

A single knoll rises out of the plain in Oklahoma, north and west of the Wichita Range.[1] For my people, the Kiowas, it is an old landmark, and they gave it the name Rainy Mountain. The hardest weather in the world is there. Winter brings blizzards, hot tornadic winds arise in the spring, and in summer the prairie

---

1. Wichita (wich´ ə tô´) **Range** mountain range in southwestern Oklahoma.

▶ Chief Sa-tan-ta of the Kiowas

▲ Critical Viewing
Judging from Momaday's account, what hardships might this Kiowa person have experienced?
[Speculate]

Spiral Review
Development of Ideas How does Momaday develop the idea that the land was lonely and isolated?

is an anvil's edge. The grass turns brittle and brown, and it cracks beneath your feet. There are green belts along the rivers and creeks, linear groves of hickory and pecan, willow and witch hazel. At a distance in July or August the steaming foliage seems almost to writhe in fire. Great green and yellow grasshoppers are everywhere in the tall grass, popping up like corn to sting the flesh, and tortoises crawl about on the red earth, going nowhere in the plenty of time. Loneliness is an aspect of the land. All things in the plain are isolate; there is no confusion of objects in the eye, but one hill or one tree or one man. To look upon that landscape in the early morning, with the sun at your back, is to lose the sense of proportion. Your imagination comes to life, and this, you think, is where Creation was begun.

I returned to Rainy Mountain in July. My grandmother had died in the spring, and I wanted to be at her grave. She had lived to be very old and at last infirm. Her only living daughter was with her when she died, and I was told that in death her face was that of a child.

I like to think of her as a child. When she was born, the Kiowas were living the last great moment of their history. For more than a hundred years they had controlled the open range from the

Smoky Hill River to the Red, from the headwaters of the Canadian to the fork of the Arkansas and Cimarron.[2] In alliance with the Comanches,[3] they had ruled the whole of the southern Plains. War was their sacred business, and they were among the finest horsemen the world has ever known. But warfare for the Kiowas was preeminently a matter of disposition rather than of survival, and they never understood the grim, unrelenting advance of the U.S. Cavalry. When at last, divided and ill-provisioned, they were driven onto the Staked Plains in the cold rains of autumn, they fell into panic. In Palo Duro Canyon they abandoned their crucial stores to pillage and had nothing then but their lives. In order to save themselves, they surrendered to the soldiers at Fort Sill[4] and were imprisoned in the old stone corral that now stands as a military museum. My grandmother was spared the humiliation of those high gray walls by eight or ten years, but she must have known from birth the affliction of defeat, the dark brooding of old warriors.

Her name was Aho, and she belonged to the last culture to evolve in North America. Her forebears came down from the high country in western Montana nearly three centuries ago. They were a mountain people, a mysterious tribe of hunters whose language has never been positively classified in any major group. In the late seventeenth century they began a long migration to the south and east.

It was a journey toward the dawn, and it led to a golden age. Along the way the Kiowas were befriended by the Crows,[5] who gave them the culture and religion of the Plains. They acquired horses, and their ancient nomadic spirit was suddenly free of the ground. They acquired Tai-me, the sacred Sun Dance doll, from that moment the object and symbol of their worship, and so shared in the divinity of the sun. Not least, they acquired the sense of destiny, therefore courage and pride. When they entered upon the southern Plains they had been transformed. No longer were they slaves to the simple necessity of survival; they were a lordly and dangerous society of fighters and thieves, hunters and priests of the sun. According to their origin myth, they entered the world through a hollow log. From one point of view, their migration was the fruit of an old prophecy, for indeed they emerged from a sunless world.

---

2. **Smoky Hill River . . . Cimarron** (sim′ ə rän′) these rivers all run through or near Oklahoma. The area Momaday is defining stretches from central Kansas south through Oklahoma and from the Texas panhandle east to Tulsa, Oklahoma.
3. **Comanches** (kə man′ chēz) *n.* formerly warlike Native American people of the southern Great Plains, famed for their horsemanship.
4. **Fort Sill** fort established by the United States government in 1869 to guard against Kiowa and Comanche attacks.
5. **Crows** members of a Native American tribe of the northern Plains; like other Plains tribes, they hunted buffalo.

Literary Analysis
Author's Purpose
In this paragraph focusing on history, which details reveal something about Momaday?

Vocabulary
nomadic (nō mad′ ik) *adj.* moving from place to place; without a permanent home

Reading Check

Who gave the Kiowa the culture and religion of the Plains?

Literary Analysis
Author's Purpose
What does this
paragraph suggest about
Momaday's purpose in
writing about the Kiowa?

Although my grandmother lived out her long life in the shadow of Rainy Mountain, the immense landscape of the continental interior lay like memory in her blood. She could tell of the Crows, whom she had never seen, and of the Black Hills,[6] where she had never been. I wanted to see in reality what she had seen more perfectly in the mind's eye, and traveled fifteen hundred miles to begin my pilgrimage.

Yellowstone,[7] it seemed to me, was the top of the world, a region of deep lakes and dark timber, canyons and waterfalls. But, beautiful as it is, one might have the sense of confinement there. The skyline in all directions is close at hand, the high wall of the woods and deep cleavages of shade. There is a perfect freedom in the mountains, but it belongs to the eagle and the elk, the badger and the bear. The Kiowas reckoned their stature by the distance they could see, and they were bent and blind in the wilderness.

Descending eastward, the highland meadows are a stairway to the plain. In July the inland slope of the Rockies is luxuriant with flax and buckwheat, stonecrop and larkspur.[8] The earth unfolds and the limit of the land recedes. Clusters of trees, and animals grazing far in the distance, cause the vision to reach away and wonder to build upon the mind. The sun follows a longer course in the day, and the sky is immense beyond all comparison. The great billowing clouds that sail upon it are shadows that move upon the brain like water, dividing light. Farther down, in the land of the Crows and Blackfeet,[9] the plain is yellow. Sweet clover takes hold of the hills and bends upon itself to cover and seal the soil. There the Kiowas paused on their way; they had come to the place where they must change their lives. The sun is at home on the plains. Precisely there does it have the certain character of a god. When the Kiowas came to the land of the Crows, they could see the dark lees of the hills at dawn across the Bighorn River, the profusion of light on the grain shelves, the oldest deity ranging after the solstices. Not yet would they veer southward to the caldron[10] of the land that lay below; they must wean their blood from the northern winter and hold the mountains a while longer in their view. They bore Tai-me in procession to the east.

Devil's Tower

South Dakota

Wyoming

Nebraska

Colorado

Kansas

New Mexico

Texas

Oklahoma

Kiowa habitat

▲ Critical Viewing
Based on this map and
the details in the text,
why might the Kiowa
journey from Wyoming
to Oklahoma have
been challenging and
rewarding at the same
time? **[Connect]**

6. **Black Hills** mountain range running from southwestern South Dakota to northeastern Wyoming.
7. **Yellowstone** Yellowstone National Park, lying mostly in Wyoming but including strips in southern Montana and eastern Idaho.
8. **flax and buckwheat, stonecrop and larkspur** various types of plants.
9. **Blackfeet** tribe of the region that includes present-day Montana and parts of Canada.
10. **caldron** (kôl´ drən) *n.* pot for boiling liquids; large kettle.

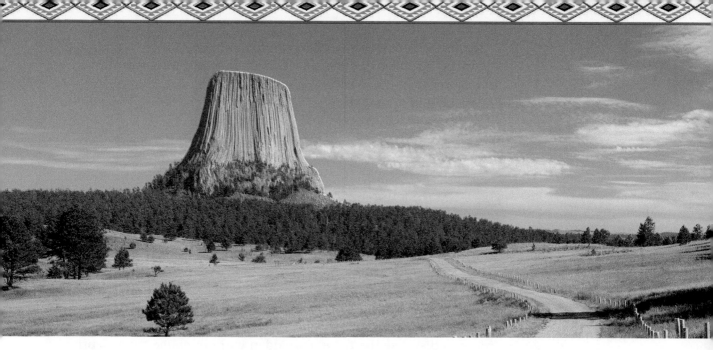

A dark mist lay over the Black Hills, and the land was like iron. At the top of a ridge I caught sight of Devil's Tower upthrust against the gray sky as if in the birth of time the core of the earth had broken through its crust and the motion of the world was begun. There are things in nature that engender an awful quiet in the heart of man; Devil's Tower is one of them. Two centuries ago, because they could not do otherwise, the Kiowas made a legend at the base of the rock. My grandmother said:

> *Eight children were there at play, seven sisters and their brother. Suddenly the boy was struck dumb; he trembled and began to run upon his hands and feet. His fi ngers became claws, and his body was covered with fur. Directly there was a bear where the boy had been. The sisters were terrified; they ran, and the bear after them. They came to the stump of a great tree, and the tree spoke to them. It bade them climb upon it, and as they did so it began to rise in the air. The bear came to kill them, but they were just beyond its reach. It reared against the tree and scored the bark all around with its claws. The seven sisters were borne into the sky, and they became the stars of the Big Dipper.*

From that moment, and so long as the legend lives, the Kiowas have kinsmen in the night sky. Whatever they were in the mountains, they could be no more. However tenuous their well-being, however much they had suffered and would suffer again, they had found a way out of the wilderness.

▲ **Critical Viewing**
Judging from this photograph of Devil's Tower, why might the landmark inspire Kiowa legends? **[Connect]**

Vocabulary
tenuous (ten´ yo͞o əs) *adj.* flimsy; not strong

Reading Check

What change did the Kiowa's beliefs undergo after they left the mountains?

My grandmother had a reverence for the sun, a holy regard that now is all but gone out of mankind. There was a wariness in her, and an ancient awe. She was a Christian in her later years, but she had come a long way about, and she never forgot her birthright. As a child she had been to the Sun Dances; she had taken part in those annual rites, and by them she had learned the restoration of her people in the presence of Tai-me. She was about seven when the last Kiowa Sun Dance was held in 1887 on the Washita River above Rainy Mountain Creek. The buffalo were gone. In order to consummate the ancient sacrifice—to impale the head of a buffalo bull upon the medicine tree—a delegation of old men journeyed into Texas, there to beg and barter for an animal from the Goodnight herd. She was ten when the Kiowas came together for the last time as a living Sun Dance culture. They could find no buffalo; they had to hang an old hide from the sacred tree. Before the dance could begin, a company of soldiers rode out from Fort Sill under orders to disperse the tribe. Forbidden without cause the essential act of their faith, having seen the wild herds slaughtered and left to rot upon the ground, the Kiowas backed away forever from the medicine tree. That was July 20, 1890, at the great bend of the Washita. My grandmother was there. Without bitterness, and for as long as she lived, she bore a vision of deicide.[11]

Now that I can have her only in memory, I see my grandmother in the several postures that were peculiar to her: standing at the wood stove on a winter morning and turning meat in a great iron skillet; sitting at the south window, bent above her beadwork, and afterwards, when her vision failed, looking down for a long time into the fold of her hands; going out upon a cane, very slowly as she did when the weight of age came upon her; praying. I remember her most often at prayer. She made long, rambling prayers out of suffering and hope, having seen many things. I was never sure that I had the right to hear, so exclusive were they of all mere custom and company. The last time I saw her she prayed standing by the side of her bed at night, naked to the waist, the light of a kerosene lamp moving upon her dark skin. Her long, black hair, always drawn and braided in the day, lay upon her shoulders and against her breasts like a shawl. I do not speak Kiowa, and I never understood her prayers, but there was something inherently sad in the sound, some merest hesitation upon the syllables of sorrow. She began in a high and

---

11. deicide (dē′ ə sīd′) *n.* killing of a god.

descending pitch, exhausting her breath to silence; then again and again—and always the same intensity of effort, of something that is, and is not, like urgency in the human voice. Transported so in the dancing light among the shadows of her room, she seemed beyond the reach of time. But that was illusion; I think I knew then that I should not see her again.

Houses are like sentinels in the plain, old keepers of the weather watch. There, in a very little while, wood takes on the appearance of great age. All colors wear soon away in the wind and rain, and then the wood is burned gray and the grain appears and the nails turn red with rust. The windowpanes are black and opaque; you imagine there is nothing within, and indeed there are many ghosts, bones given up to the land. They stand here and there against the sky, and you approach them for a longer time than you expect. They belong in the distance; it is their domain.

Once there was a lot of sound in my grandmother's house, a lot of coming and going, feasting and talk. The summers there were full of excitement and reunion. The Kiowas are a summer people; they abide the cold and keep to themselves, but when the season turns and the land becomes warm and vital they cannot hold still; an old love of going returns upon them. The aged visitors who came to my grandmother's house when I was a child were made of lean and leather, and they bore themselves upright. They wore great black hats and bright ample shirts that shook in the wind. They rubbed fat upon their hair and wound their braids with strips of colored cloth. Some of them painted their faces and carried the scars of old and cherished enmities. They were an old council of warlords, come to remind and be reminded of who they were. Their wives and daughters served them well. The women might indulge themselves; gossip was at once the mark and compensation of their servitude. They made loud and elaborate talk among themselves, full of jest and gesture, fright and false alarm. They went abroad in fringed and flowered shawls, bright beadwork and German silver. They were at home in the kitchen, and they prepared meals that were banquets.

There were frequent prayer meetings, and great nocturnal feasts. When I was a child I played with my cousins outside, where the lamplight fell upon the ground and the singing of the old people rose up around us and carried away into the darkness. There were a lot of good things to eat, a lot of laughter and surprise. And afterwards, when the quiet returned, I lay down with my grandmother and could hear the frogs away by the river and feel the motion of the air.

Now there is a funeral silence in the rooms, the endless wake of some final word. The walls have closed in upon my grandmother's

Literary Analysis
Author's Purpose
Which details here suggest Momaday writes to better understand his memories? Which details suggest he wants to pay tribute to his grandmother?

I do not speak Kiowa, and I never understood her prayers, but there was something inherently sad in the sound . . .

Reading Check

Who comes to visit Momaday's grandmother's house in the summer?

house. When I returned to it in mourning, I saw for the first time in my life how small it was. It was late at night, and there was a white moon, nearly full. I sat for a long time on the stone steps by the kitchen door. From there I could see out across the land; I could see the long row of trees by the creek, the low light upon the rolling plains, and the stars of the Big Dipper. Once I looked at the moon and caught sight of a strange thing. A cricket had perched upon the handrail, only a few inches away from me. My line of vision was such that the creature filled the moon like a fossil. It had gone there, I thought, to live and die, for there, of all places, was its small definition made whole and eternal. A warm wind rose up and purled like the longing within me.

The next morning I awoke at dawn and went out on the dirt road to Rainy Mountain. It was already hot, and the grasshoppers began to fill the air. Still, it was early in the morning, and the birds sang out of the shadows. The long yellow grass on the mountain shone in the bright light, and a scissortail hied above the land. There, where it ought to be, at the end of a long and legendary way, was my grandmother's grave. Here and there on the dark stones were ancestral names. Looking back once, I saw the mountain and came away.

Critical Thinking

Cite textual evidence to support your responses.

1. **Key Ideas and Details (a)** Describe two activities at Momaday's grandmother's house in summer. **(b) Connect:** In what ways are these activities connected to a vanishing way of life?

2. **Key Ideas and Details (a) Support:** In what sense is Momaday's grandmother one of the last representatives of traditional Kiowa culture? **(b) Draw Conclusions:** How does Momaday seem to feel about the disappearance of this way of life? Support your answer with details from the selection.

3. **Integration of Knowledge and Ideas (a) Interpret:** When Momaday imagines the cricket on the moon, why does he say, "there . . . was its small definition made whole and eternal"? **(b) Draw Conclusions:** In what sense is Momaday's memory of his grandmother similar to his vision of the cricket?

4. **Integration of Knowledge and Ideas (a)** In what ways did Momaday's relationship with his grandmother shape his appreciation of Kiowa culture? **(b)** How did his knowledge of Kiowa history impact his view of his grandmother? **(c)** How has the experience Momaday narrates changed his life? *[Connect to the Big Question: What kind of knowledge changes our lives?]*

After You Read

from **Desert Exile** •
from **The Way to Rainy Mountain**

Comparing Authors' Purposes

from *Desert Exile:*
The Uprooting
of a
Japanese-American Family

Yoshiko Uchida

© **1. Key Ideas and Details** **(a)** Choose two powerful details from each selection. Using a chart like the one shown, analyze the writer's use of these details. **(b)** In a statement, identify the writer's purpose in sharing the details you have chosen. Explain your reasoning.

	Detail	Writer's Response to Detail	What Detail Adds to Meaning
Uchida			
Momaday			

© **2. Key Ideas and Details** **(a)** What general purpose for writing do Momaday and Uchida share? **(b)** Identify one major difference in their views of the events and scenes they describe.

© **3. Craft and Structure** Give an example of each writer's use of **rhetoric,** or powerful language, and explain how it helps the writer achieve his or her purpose.

⏱ Timed Writing

Informative Text: Essay

Identify each author's purpose. Then, write a response to compare the effectiveness of the two selections. Address the success of both authors in meeting the purpose you have identified. Support your ideas with details from the selections. **(40 minutes)**

5-Minute Planner

1. Read the prompt carefully and completely.

2. Use these questions to get started:

   • Which passages best convey the author's purpose?

   • In these passages, are the details comprehensive enough to make the writing convincing or moving? Why or why not?

3. Plan your introduction to the topic. Make an outline in which you organize the ideas and concepts you plan to present. Think of ways to distinguish your ideas from alternative interpretations.

4. Reread the prompt, and then draft your essay.

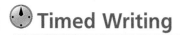

Writing Workshop

Write an Argument

Argument: Persuasive Essay

Defining the Form Persuasion is a part of daily life. Friends may use persuasion to convince you to try a new food or volunteer for a cause. A **persuasive essay** is a nonfiction literary work in which the writer tries to convince readers to accept a particular point of view or take a specific action. You might use elements of the persuasive essay in editorials, position papers, letters to the editor, and proposals.

Assignment Write a persuasive essay supporting your opinion about an issue that matters to you. Include these elements:

✓ a clear *description of the issue* and a clear, precise *statement of your opinion*—your position, or claim, about the issue

✓ reliable and varied *evidence* that supports your opinion, or claim

✓ *arguments* that acknowledge and refute opposing claims

✓ vivid, *persuasive language* that appeals to your audience

✓ a logical *organization* that shows the relationship among claims, counterclaims, and evidence

✓ error-free grammar, including *correct use of parallel structures*

To preview the criteria on which your persuasive essay may be judged, see the rubric on page 611.

 Writing Workshop: *Work in Progress*

Review the work you did on pages 555 and 575.

WRITE GUY
Jeff Anderson, M.Ed.

What Do You Notice?

Voice and Tone

Read the following sentences from Alexander Solzhenitsyn's *Nobel Lecture* several times.

The simple act of an ordinary courageous man is not to take part, not to support lies! Let that come into the world and even reign over it, but not through me. Writers and artists can do more: they can VANQUISH LIES!

Jot down the qualities that make the sentences interesting. Then, consider how to use voice and tone similarly in your essay.

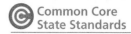 **Common Core State Standards**

Writing
1. Write arguments to support claims in an analysis of substantive topics or texts, using valid reasoning and relevant and sufficient evidence.

1.a. Introduce precise claim(s), distinguish the claim(s) from alternate or opposing claims, and create an organization that establishes clear relationships among claim(s), counterclaims, reasons, and evidence.

5. Develop and strengthen writing as needed by planning, focusing on addressing what is most significant for a specific purpose and audience.

7. Conduct short as well as more sustained research projects to answer a question or solve a problem; narrow or broaden the inquiry when appropriate; synthesize multiple sources on the subject.

Reading-Writing Connection

To get a feel for persuasive writing, read the excerpt from Alexander Solzhenitsyn's *Nobel Lecture* on page 548.

Prewriting/Planning Strategies

Brainstorm and freewrite. Think about topics that cause you and others to argue. Using a chart like the one shown, make a list of the subjects and issues that have prompted emotional reactions and circle the one that most intrigues you. Then, freewrite for three minutes about that topic. Review what you have written and circle any statements of opinion that have emerged. Select the subject with the clearest statement and use it as the starting point for your essay.

www.PHLitOnline.com
- Author video: Writing Process
- Author video: Rewards of Writing

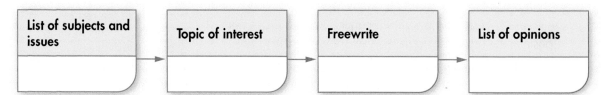

Conduct research. You may not have enough details about your topic to focus your ideas. More information can help you break the topic into meaningful parts. For example, freedom of speech is far too broad to discuss in a brief essay. However, after you learn more about it, you may choose to narrow your inquiry and research questions and write about balanced reporting in television news. Conduct research to identify an aspect of the topic that is manageable in the space of your essay.

Look at both sides of the issue. An effective persuasive essay anticipates and addresses differing opinions. It considers the knowledge level and concerns of readers and addresses their expectations. Use a pro-and-con chart like the one shown to identify counterarguments. In the left-hand column, list arguments that support your opinion, or claim. In the right-hand column, list opposing arguments. Use the chart to brainstorm for ideas, reasons, and evidence that counter the opposing claims.

Pro-and-Con Chart	
Topic: Honor Students Should Be Rewarded	
Supporting	**Opposing**
• Honor-roll students are responsible and dedicated. • They know the material.	• It is unfair to other students. • There would be inequality.

Drafting Strategies

Evaluate your arguments. Write each idea on a separate notecard. Then, consider whether your reasoning is valid and persuasive to your *intended audience*. Delete cards with faulty ideas that may not persuade readers. Then, organize the cards in order of persuasiveness.

Emphasize your strongest argument. Introduce your topic and state your claim in a precisely worded *thesis statement*. In the body of your essay, support your thesis with arguments and reasons. Use transitions to show the relationships between claims, reasons, and counterclaims and to create cohesion. Finish with a conclusion that urges readers to act. Consider the organization in the box shown at the right.

Offer evidence. Develop your claim and counterclaims fairly by providing evidence for each and by pointing out their strengths and limitations. For each point you make, provide convincing *support*, such as these types of evidence:

- **Facts:** information that can be proved true

- **Statistics:** numerical evidence

- **Expert opinion:** information or quotations from experts

- **Case studies:** analyses of examples that illustrate your opinions

- **Anecdotes:** relevant experiences, either your own or those of others

> **Model: Supporting Opinion With Evidence**
> Final exams are meant to test students' overall grasp of the course material. However, honor-roll students have already shown that they have mastered the course. School records show over 95% of honor-roll students have a straight "A" average.

Convincing statistical evidence supports the writer's opinion.

Identify your sources. The inclusion of *reliable sources* strengthens your arguments. When you present a fact or detail from your research, use a style guide to correctly provide the *source of the information*. If you quote someone, use quotation marks. When you use expert opinion, identify the expert and his or her qualifications. In addition, make sure to build a strong link between the quotation and your argument.

Organizing a Persuasive Essay

- Begin with a precise statement of your claim.
- Explain your second-best argument.
- Present and argue against a counterclaim.
- Organize the rest of your arguments in order of persuasiveness.
- End with your best argument.
- Wrap up with a concluding statement that follows from and supports the argument.

Common Core State Standards

Writing

1.a. Introduce precise claim(s), distinguish the claim(s) from alternate or opposing claims, and create an organization that establishes clear relationships among claim(s), counterclaims, reasons, and evidence.

1.b. Develop claim(s) and counterclaims fairly, supplying evidence for each while pointing out the strengths and limitations of both in a manner that anticipates the audience's knowledge level and concerns.

1.c. Use words, phrases, and clauses to link the major sections of the text, create cohesion, and clarify the relationships between claim(s) and reasons, between reasons and evidence, and between claim(s) and counterclaims.

1.e. Provide a concluding statement or section that follows from and supports the argument presented.

Writers on Writing

Erik Weihenmayer On Persuasive Techniques

> Erik Weihenmayer is the author of "Everest" from *Touch the Top of the World* (p. 452).

Atop Mt. Kilimanjaro, a sign reads, "You Are Now at the Uhuru Peak. . . ." Sitting on the summit, feeling exhausted, nauseated, and dizzy, I asked my guide, Baltazar, what "Uhuru" meant. He replied, "Freedom." In this passage, I try to persuade you to accept the conclusion about freedom I reached.

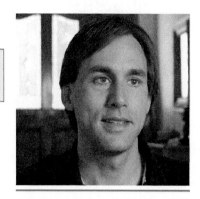

"Writing enables me to climb the mountain again."
—Erik Weihenmayer

Professional Model:

from *Touch the Top of the World*

Freedom. It was a word I didn't understand. Freedom from what? Freedom from the limits of my body? From pain? From disappointment? What did it mean? I wanted to believe that by standing atop mountains around the world, I was achieving this kind of freedom, . . . but when standing in these high places, the immense power of the mountains only served to magnify my own fragility, my human need for food, for oxygen, for the help that I received from my team. . . .

Then it came to me . . . Perhaps it was the freedom to make of my life what I wanted it to be, or at least the freedom to try, or to fail in the trying. Perhaps freedom itself was unobtainable and the goal was only to reach for it, strive for it, knowing all along that I would fall well short. Perhaps the importance was in the reaching out, and in the impossibility of it all, and in the reaching out through the impossibility, my body planted heavily on the earth but my spirit soaring up and coming impossibly close to its goal.

First, I ask you a series of difficult questions, which lead you to ponder whether freedom is obtainable.

Second, I try to shatter your traditional definition of freedom by emphasizing the obvious limits of our minds and bodies.

Lastly, I find the answer and suggest, without insisting on, a surprising new understanding of what freedom means.

Revising Strategies

Test your support. Every paragraph in your essay should play a clear role in *supporting your argument*. Use these steps to test each paragraph:

- Underline the sentence that states the main idea of the paragraph. If a topic sentence is missing, consider adding one.

- Put a star next to each sentence that supports the main idea. If a sentence is not starred, consider modifying or deleting it.

- If a topic sentence has fewer than two supporting details, add more evidence or reconsider whether the point is worth including.

Model: Revising to Strengthen a Paragraph

Even though honor-roll students have spent many hours studying for classes and completing assignments, they are forced to face even more stress in taking final exams. ★ Most honor-roll students are high performers who will spend extra time preparing for exams even though they do not need to.

★ A good friend of mine stayed up all night studying for his final chemistry exam, even though he already had an "A" in the class.

Additional anecdotal evidence helps to support the writer's claim.

Choose powerful words. Clear, strong language will help make your ideas memorable. Consider these options:

- **Comparatives and Superlatives** Comparative adjectives, such as *sharper* and *bolder,* clarify your ideas. Avoid overuse of predictable or subjective superlatives, such as *best, smartest, strongest,* or *bravest.*

- **Action Verbs** Strong verbs make your ideas more compelling.

  Linking verb: The policy *is* unfair. (weak)

  Action verb: The policy *cheats* us all. (strong)

- **Connotation** Be aware of **connotations,** the emotions a word sparks. Positive connotations can support ideas. Negative connotations can stress drawbacks of opposing arguments, but being overly negative can backfire. A neutral, objective tone shows fair-mindedness.

  Objective: We can look into this problem.

  Positive: We can rise to meet this challenge.

  Negative: We can attempt to approach this impossible task.

Peer Review

Review a classmate's work. Circle ten weak words in your partner's essay. In a peer conference, discuss possible replacements.

Common Core State Standards

Writing

1. Write arguments to support claims in an analysis of substantive topics or texts, using valid reasoning and relevant and sufficient evidence.

1.d. Establish and maintain a formal style and objective tone while attending to the norms and conventions of the discipline.

5. Develop and strengthen writing as needed by planning, revising, editing, rewriting, or trying a new approach, focusing on addressing what is most significant for a specific purpose and audience.

Language

1.a. Use parallel structure.

Revising to Create Parallelism

Parallelism is the use of similar grammatical forms or patterns to express similar ideas. Effective use of parallelism can connect your ideas and make them memorable.

Identifying Faulty Parallelism Parallel constructions place equal ideas in words, phrases, or clauses of similar types. Ideas are not parallel if the grammatical structure shifts.

	Nonparallel	Parallel
use of verbs	We want <u>to be learning, growing, and to succeed.</u>	We want <u>to learn, to grow, and to succeed.</u>
use of direct objects	Students benefit from <u>limits that are respectful, reasonable freedoms, and being inspired by classes.</u>	Students benefit from <u>respectful limits, reasonable freedoms, and inspiring classes.</u>

Fixing Errors Follow these steps to revise nonparallel constructions:

1. **Identify similar or equivalent ideas within a sentence.**

2. **Identify the form in which the ideas are expressed.** Then, read the sentence aloud to hear changes in rhythm or pattern.

3. **Rewrite the sentence so that all the elements match the stronger pattern.** Choose forms that produce the smoothest rhythm or require the fewest words. Look at these examples:

   Nouns: hand, heart, and mind

   Verbs: to seek, to question, and to learn

   Phrases: defining the borders, preserving our resources, securing the future

   Adverb clauses: wherever we go, whatever we do

   Adjective clauses: she who commits, who practices, who focuses

4. **Punctuate correctly.** Use commas to separate three or more words, phrases, or clauses in a parallel series.

PH WRITING COACH
Further instruction and practice are available in *Prentice Hall Writing Coach*.

Grammar in Your Writing
Review three paragraphs in your essay, circling sentences that present a series of equivalent ideas. If they have varying grammatical structures, revise them to build parallelism.

Student Model: Esther Herrera, Hialeah, FL

 Common Core
State Standards

Writing
6. Use technology, including the Internet, to produce, publish, and update individual or shared writing products, taking advantage of technology's capacity to link to other information and to display information flexibly and dynamically.

Language
2.c. Spell correctly.

True Reward for Our Achievements

Straight-A students have been rewarded in different ways for their hard work. They have been given the chance to eat breakfast with the principal, they have received gifts and certificates, and they have been publicly acknowledged. Schools hope that these policies will not only serve as a reward to students but also as an inspiration to others to do well in their classes. However, these honor-roll students show little interest in the awards; they want something else. These students should be exempt from taking the final exam because they have demonstrated responsibility and dedication, they know the material, and most importantly they feel that other students will likely be inspired to achieve the ultimate honor-roll goal.

> Esther clearly states her opinion on the issue.

Primarily, honor-roll students should be exempt from taking the final exam because they are responsible and dedicated. These students have stayed on task throughout the year, going out of their way to turn in a job well done. Sometimes, they sacrificed by staying up late to finish homework assignments. As one honor student recalled, "One time, I stayed up, literally, all night so that I could finish a project. The problem was not finishing it but making sure that it would come out perfect; it did."

> The writer states the argument and then supports it with valid evidence.

In addition, teachers should not have to give these students the final examination. Because they got A's in the first, second, third, and fourth quarters, it is clear that the students know the material very well. Furthermore, the final exam is added stress, because students worry and get nervous taking tests.

On the other hand, eleven out of twenty-five students whom I interviewed believe that such an exemption policy would not be fair to the other students. However, all students were given the same opportunity to get A's. The striking thing about this survey is that many students who were in favor of an exemption policy were not honor students. Instead, they were students who might work harder to earn the privilege of not taking the final exam. What I say to the first eleven students is: Accept the challenge.

> By referring to a survey she conducted, Esther shows her research and writes with authority.

> Here, the writer addresses those who oppose her ideas.

In conclusion, honor-roll students should be exempt from taking the final exam because they have already proved themselves. These students deserve a true reward: the knowledge that their efforts have been recognized.

> Esther restates her opinion in her conclusion.

Editing and Proofreading

Review your draft to correct errors in grammar, spelling, capitalization, and punctuation.

Focus on spelling. Some vowel sounds in words are silent, which can make correct spelling difficult. Generally, two vowels are used to spell a sound that usually takes only one vowel, as in the final syllable of *porcelain*. If a word gives you problems, create a memory aid to remember the spelling. For example, you may say, *"u hides in camouflage."*

Publishing and Presenting

Consider one of the following ways to share your writing:

Publish for an audience. If your topic relates to a school or community issue, submit your essay to a school or local newspaper, or post it on a class Web site. If you post on a Web site, create links to relevant information. Update the links when new information becomes available.

Deliver a speech. Use your persuasive essay as the basis for an in-class speech followed by a question-and-answer session. Survey your audience before and after your speech to see if you have changed their minds about your topic. Encourage the entire class to join in the question-and-answer period and clarify, verify, or challenge ideas.

Reflecting on Your Writing

Writer's Journal Jot down your answers to this question:
How did writing about an issue help you better understand it?

Rubric for Self-Assessment

Find evidence in your writing to address each category. Then, use the rating scale to grade your work.

Spiral Review
Earlier in the unit, you learned about **degrees of adjectives** (p. 574). Check your essay to be sure you have used the correct forms of adjectives.

Criteria	Rating Scale
	not very very
Focus: How clearly do you explain both the issue and your opinion?	1 2 3 4 5
Organization: How well do you organize the elements of your arguments?	1 2 3 4 5
Support/Elaboration: How reliable and varied is your evidence?	1 2 3 4 5
Style: How vivid and persuasive is your language?	1 2 3 4 5
Conventions: How correct is your grammar, especially your use of parallel structures?	1 2 3 4 5

Vocabulary Workshop

Words With Multiple Meanings

Common Core
State Standards

Language
4. Determine or clarify the meaning of unknown and multiple-meaning words and phrases based on grades 9–10 reading and content.
4.a. Use context as a clue to the meaning of a word or phrase.
4.c. Consult general and specialized reference materials, both print and digital, to find the pronunciation of a word or determine or clarify its precise meaning, its part of speech, or its etymology.
4.d. Verify the preliminary determination of the meaning of a word or phrase.

Many words in English have **multiple meanings.** Look at this dictionary entry for *coast*:

Dictionary

The first part of the entry gives meanings for the noun *coast.*

The second part of the entry gives meanings for the verb *coast.*

This means "obsolete," or no longer useful.

coast (kōst) *n.* [ME *coste,* coast < OFr, a rib, hill, shore, coast < L *costa,* a rib, side] **1.** land alongside the sea; seashore **2.** [Obs] frontier borderland **3.** a slide or ride, as on a sled going down an incline by the force of gravity— *vi.* **1.** to sail along or near a coast, esp. from port to port **2.** to go down an incline, as on a sled **3.** to continue in motion on momentum or by the force of gravity after propelling power has stopped **4.** to continue without serious effort, letting one's past efforts carry one along

To determine which meaning a writer is using in a sentence, look at the **context clues.** Context clues are in the information surrounding a word and can be used to determine the word's meaning. Look at the following sentence to identify context clues that help you determine the meaning used here:

My brother *coasted* through law school without opening a book.

One context clue is that *coast* is used as a verb. Another clue is *without opening a book,* which suggests "without much effort." Try each of the four definitions for verbs in the sentence. The definition that fits is 4— "to continue without serious effort, letting one's past efforts carry one along."

Practice A Read each sentence. Choose the multiple-meaning word that makes sense in each sentence pair: *vacuum, break, negative, police.*

1. (a) His _____ attitude kept him from succeeding in school.
(b) The _____ of a picture shows light and dark in reverse.

2. (a) I need to _____ the rug before company arrives.
(b) The absence of air creates a _____.

3. (a) We must _____ the campus for litter.
(b) My older sister went to the _____ academy when she was twenty.

4. (a) We definitely wanted to _____ free of our routine.
(b) The sun shone through a _____ in the clouds.

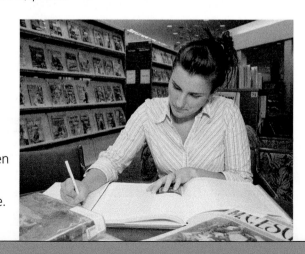

Practice B Using context clues, write your own definition for the under-lined word in each sentence. With a partner, discuss which context clues helped you to determine the meaning of the word. Then, look up the word in a dictionary to confirm or correct your definition.

1. The map didn't show the <u>cardinal</u> directions!

2. A cold <u>draft</u> came in under the door and through cracks around the window.

3. She didn't seem to <u>harbor</u> any hard feelings over what I'd said.

4. The <u>launch</u> sped across the choppy bay.

5. How can you <u>gauge</u> someone's interest in the drama?

6. To prepare for the long Alaskan winter, Andrew stocked his cabin with flour, cereal, potatoes, and other <u>staples</u>.

7. The truck bounced its way across the sandy <u>wash</u>.

8. Their <u>plot</u> to avoid the extra work failed completely.

9. Don't <u>force</u> the lock or you may break the key off.

10. The sailor could hardly stay on his feet as he walked across the heaving <u>deck</u> of the ship.

Activity Look in a dictionary to find the multiple definitions of these words: *litter, fan, coat, pump,* and *contract.* Write each word on a separate notecard like the one shown. Fill in the left column of the notecard according to one of the word's meanings. Fill in the right column according to another of the word's meanings. Then, trade notecards with a partner and discuss the different meanings and uses of the words that each of you found.

Word	First Meaning	Second Meaning

Comprehension and Collaboration

Find each of these words in a dictionary: *craft, switch, exhaust.* Select one of the mean-ings for each and write a sentence in which the context clearly illustrates the meaning. Trade sen-tences with a partner. Identify the definition of the word in each of your partner's sentences.

Communications Workshop

Delivering a Persuasive Speech

A convincing persuasive speech depends on two key elements: strong writing and a powerful delivery. Your words and presentation style must connect with your audience, so use standard grammar and language.

Learn the Skills

Use the strategies to complete the activity on page 615.

Support your opinion. Your persuasive speech will define and support a claim—your position, or point of view. Gather supporting evidence, such as facts, expert opinions, expressions of commonly accepted beliefs, and relevant anecdotes. Evaluate your evidence from your audience's point of view. Ensure that your line of reasoning is logical and free of fallacies, such as overgeneralizations and exaggerations.

Consider your purpose. Think about your purpose—to persuade—as well as your specific goals. For example, you might want to persuade your audience to take a particular action as well as to share your position. Organize your speech in a way that will make it easy for your audience to follow your reasoning.

Use rhetorical devices. Strengthen the argument by using rhetorical devices, such as repetition and parallel structure. Choose words carefully, paying attention to both their sounds and connotations. Work to appeal to your audience's emotions and beliefs while using formal English to maintain their respect.

Focus on your opening and closing. Grab your audience's attention in your introduction, and summarize your points in a memorable way in your conclusion.

Prepare a reader's script. Once you have written your speech, plan how you will present it. Mark a copy of your speech to show words you will emphasize and places you will pause, as modeled in the sample reader's script. Use effective pacing. Slow down to stress key statements; speed up to emphasize emotion. Use a casual tone when telling a personal anecdote. Use a serious tone when quoting an expert.

Establish eye contact. Keep your audience interested by making frequent eye contact. Practice your speech so that it is familiar to you.

Common Core State Standards

Writing

1. Write arguments to support claims in an analysis of substantive topics or texts, using valid reasoning and relevant and sufficient evidence.

Speaking and Listening

3. Evaluate a speaker's point of view, reasoning, and use of evidence and rhetoric, identifying any fallacious reasoning or exaggerated or distorted evidence.

4. Present information, findings, and supporting evidence clearly, concisely, and logically such that listeners can follow the line of reasoning and the organization, development, substance, and style are appropriate to purpose, audience, and task.

6. Adapt speech to a variety of contexts and tasks, demonstrating command of formal English when indicated or appropriate.

SAMPLE READER'S SCRIPT

start gradually

The plans for the new park at Elm Street call for a baseball field, ‖a

energetic

playground, ‖and a big lawn. It sounds <u>great</u>, but it could be <u>better</u>.

There is one thing missing: ‖dogs! ‖We need a dog run. We do not

slower

have a <u>single</u> public dog run in our city.   ‖ = pause

Practice the Skills

Presentation of Knowledge and Ideas Use what you have learned in this workshop to perform the following task.

ACTIVITY: Deliver a Persuasive Speech

Choose a topic that has two sides. Organize a presentation in which you take a stand. Practice in front of a classmate. Based on the feedback you receive, revise your presentation. Then, deliver the speech for the full class. Consider the following criteria as you develop your speech:

- How clear is the position, point of view, or claim?
- Is it supported by convincing evidence?
- Is the evidence logically organized?
- Is the line of reasoning easy for readers to follow?

As your classmates make their presentations, listen carefully. Use the Presentation Checklist to analyze and evaluate their presentations, and invite your classmates to use the checklist to analyze and evaluate your presentation.

Presentation Checklist

Presentation Content
Did the presentation meet all the requirements of the activity?
Check all that apply.
- ☐ Its organization and style supported the purpose and task.
- ☐ It did not contain fallacies; the reasoning was logical.
- ☐ It met all of the criteria listed in the activity assignment.

Presentation Delivery
Did the speaker effectively deliver the speech?
Check all that apply.
- ☐ The speaker used standard grammar and effective language.
- ☐ The speaker used effective pacing.
- ☐ The speaker made frequent eye contact with the audience.

Comprehension and Collaboration After all the class members have delivered their speeches, discuss which ones were the most effective and why. Offer positive suggestions for approaches or techniques that will help each student strengthen his or her presentation.

Cumulative Review

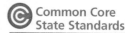
Common Core
State Standards

RI.9-10.1, RI.9-10.4, RI.9-10.6;
W.9-10.1
[For the full wording of the standards,
see the standards chart in the front of
your textbook.]

I. Reading Literary Nonfiction

Directions: *Read the passage. Then, answer each question that follows.*

Playing the Piano

You have heard it before: practice, practice, practice! Whether it is kicking a soccer ball, shooting hoops, or playing the piano, practice makes perfect. My parents sincerely believed that.

When I was nine years old, they bought a second-hand piano, hoping that my older sister would become the musical genius of our family. Unfortunately (or fortunately) she had about as much musical talent as I had athletic talent—in other words, zilch. On the other hand, I thought the piano wasn't the worst thing ever. I was <u>intrigued</u> that simply by pressing the right "buttons," you could make a song. I begged my parents for piano lessons. They agreed, on the condition that I vow to practice every day. I promised. I was excited. My music teacher told me I had "promise."

At first, I practiced every day. My parents marveled at my budding genius. My practice filled the house with heavenly music every day. Everyone but my sister thought I was wonderful. Gradually, the novelty of the piano and the praise grew stale. I still loved the piano, and I still loved to play—when I was in the mood. When spring came, I would rather be out riding my bike. When summer came, I would rather go to the beach. When fall came, I would rather be downloading music online.

So it went. Gradually, the praise stopped and the nagging started: "Have you practiced piano today?" Finally, the piano lessons were stopped. I didn't mind. I enjoyed the free time, and I still played the piano when I felt like it.

There is a moral to this story, of course: practice. Why? There are many reasons, but becoming a superstar is not necessarily one of them. With a physical skill, remember that muscles have "memories." Once you master a skill, such as biking, you never lose it. Even if the skill is more complex, such as playing a musical instrument, which requires both physical motor skills and mental skills, you never lose it. I have not played the piano for years, but I can still pick out a tune, and I can still read music. I still love the piano—and I love to bike-ride, too. So if there is something you enjoy doing, practice until you have mastered it. Then you will always have it. You may get rusty, but the skills will remain with you to enrich, expand, and enhance the rest of your life.

1. The second paragraph of this passage is an example of which type of **essay** writing?

   A. narrative
   B. argumentative
   C. humorous
   D. explanatory

2. The following passage is an example of which **persuasive** or **rhetorical device**?

   When spring came, I would rather be out riding my bike. When summer came, I would rather go to the beach. When fall came, I would rather be downloading music online.
   A. rhetorical question
   B. appeal to logic
   C. parallelism
   D. appeal to emotion

3. What best describes the **author's purpose**?

   A. to persuade readers to practice to become superstars
   B. to describe how it feels to practice
   C. to analyze the effect of practice
   D. to persuade readers to practice something they enjoy

4. Which sentence from the passage contains an example of **understatement**?

   A. My parents sincerely believed that.
   B. On the other hand, I thought the piano wasn't the worst thing ever.
   C. My parents marveled at my budding genius.
   D. There is a moral to this story of course: practice.

5. Which paragraph contains a **rhetorical question**?

   A. paragraph 2
   B. paragraph 3
   C. paragraph 4
   D. paragraph 5

6. Which of the following sentences from the passage contains **hyperbole**?

   A. I begged my parents for piano lessons.
   B. My practice filled the house with heavenly music every day.
   C. Gradually, the novelty of the piano and the praise grew stale.
   D. Finally, the piano lessons were stopped.

7. This passage reflects elements of which types of essays?

   A. analytic, argumentative
   B. reflective, humorous
   C. argumentative, humorous
   D. explanatory, reflective

8. **Vocabulary** Which is the closest definition of the underlined word *intrigued*?

   A. confused by   **C.** attracted by
   B. frightened by   **D.** angered by

9. With which of the following statements might the author agree?

   A. You should practice until you are perfect.
   B. An athlete should always strive to be the best in the world.
   C. Becoming skilled in a wide variety of activities is better than being perfect in one.
   D. Practicing daily makes you a better person.

 Timed Writing

10. Write a brief essay to **explain** whether you agree or disagree with the author's "moral." Cite evidence from the text to support your **argument.**

 GO ON

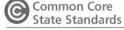

II. Reading Functional Texts

Directions: *Read the passage. Then, answer each question that follows.*

Common Core
State Standards
RI.9-10.3, RI.9-10.5; W.9-10.1, W.9-10.1.d, W.9-10.4; L.9-10.1
[For the full wording of the standards, see the standards chart in the front of your textbook.]

Using the Easy Smoothie Maker

Now create a nutritious, energy-packed smoothie in just a few seconds.

Read Safety Precautions Before Operation

- Do not immerse cord or base in water.
- Operate only on a clean, flat surface.
- Handle the cutting blade carefully to avoid injury.

Before beginning—

- Wash blade assembly and the cup in warm soapy water before using.
- Firmly place the four rubber suction cups on the feet of the base.

To create your own delicious smoothie—

1) Place the base on the counter, pressing firmly to secure the suction cups.

- Make sure the counter is free of water or grease.
- Do NOT plug in the Easy Smoothie until it is completely assembled.

2) Place ingredients in Smoothie Cup and screw on cutting blade.

- Place the solid ingredients in the cup, and then add milk or yogurt.
- Screw the cutting blade <u>assembly</u> on top of the filled Smoothie Cup.

3) Set the filled Smoothie Cup on base and engage the motor.

- Turn the cup over and place on the base, clicking it into place.
- Plug in the Smoothie base and press the "on" button for 10 seconds.
- Remove the cup from the base, unscrew the blade assembly, and enjoy!

---

1. Which of the following parts should you handle first when making a smoothie?

    A. the base assembly
    B. the suction cups
    C. milk or yogurt
    D. the plug

2. Why should you handle the blade carefully?

    A. It is worth a lot of money.
    B. It can be difficult to replace if you lose it.
    C. It is very sharp and can cause injuries.
    D. It can contaminate the cup's ingredients.

3. By **skimming** the article, one could learn—

    A. the dangers of improper appliance use.
    B. the steps for making a smoothie.
    C. how to care for the appliance.
    D. recipes for smoothies.

4. According to the directions, when should the Smoothie Maker be plugged in?

    A. before adding the ingredients
    B. after unscrewing the blade assembly
    C. before screwing on the cutting blade
    D. after placing the filled cup on the base

III. Writing and Language Conventions

Directions: *Read the passage. Then, answer each question that follows.*

(1) October 9, 2008

(2) Editor-in-Chief
The Sentinel Dispatch
700 Viewmont Street
Sentinel, South Dakota 96501

(3) Dear Editor-in-Chief:
(4) The school board of Sentinel High School has cut funds for after-school music programs. (5) I am writing to protest this action and to ask citizens of Sentinel to write to the school board to protest this as well.
(6) Students need options. (7) Music programs should receive as much funding as sports programs. (8) For students who are not athletic, music is an alternative to athletics. (9) All students should receive opportunities. (10) Please to the school board write. (11) Ask them not to cut funds.

(12) Sincerely,
Damon Fitzgerald

1. What section needs to be added to this letter?

- **A.** greeting
- **B.** closing
- **C.** return address
- **D.** date

2. The author's **tone** can best be described as—

- **A.** angry and disappointed.
- **B.** calm and reasonable.
- **C.** fearful and anxious.
- **D.** enraged and bitter.

3. Which sentences should be **combined?**

- **A.** sentences 4 and 5
- **B.** sentences 6 and 7
- **C.** sentences 8 and 9
- **D.** sentences 10 and 11

4. The author of this letter uses ____ language.

- **A.** formal
- **B.** informal
- **C.** sarcastic
- **D.** emotional

5. What is the correct way to revise sentence 10?

- **A.** To the school board write please.
- **B.** The school board please be written to.
- **C.** Writing to the school board please.
- **D.** Please write to the school board.

Performance Tasks

Directions: *Follow the instructions to complete the tasks below as required by your teacher.*

As you work on each task, incorporate both general academic vocabulary and literary terms you learned in this unit.

> © **Common Core State Standards**
>
> RI.9-10.2, RI.9-10.3, RI.9-10.4, RI.9-10.5, RI.9-10.6, RI.9-10.8; W.9-10.2.d., W.9-10.9.b.; SL.9-10.1, SL.9-10.1.a., SL.9-10.4; L.9-10.1.a., L.9-10.2.c
>
> [For the full wording of the standards, see the standards chart in the front of your textbook.]

Writing

© Task 1: Informational Text [RI.9-10.2; W.9-10.2.d.]

Analyze the Development of a Central Idea

Write an essay in which you analyze the development of the central idea in a nonfiction work from this unit.

- Provide a brief summary of the work in which you explain its most important points, especially the central idea.
- Explain how the author initially presents the central idea.
- Describe how the author shapes and refines the central idea throughout the work. Include specific details to support your analysis.
- Present your ideas concisely. Look for places where you can eliminate wordiness or choose more precise language.

© Task 2: Informational Text [RI.9-10.6; L.9-10.2.c.]

Determine an Author's Point of View and Analyze Use of Rhetoric

Write an essay in which you determine an author's point of view and analyze his or her use of rhetoric in a speech or an essay from this unit.

- Describe the author's point of view and explain how it affects his or her discussion of the topic.
- Discuss specific ways in which the author's rhetoric advances his or her point of view.
- Cite specific examples from the text to support your analysis.
- Edit your essay for correct capitalization and punctuation. Ensure that words are spelled correctly.

© Task 3: Informational Text [RI.9-10.8]

Evaluate an Argument

Write an essay in which you evaluate the argument in a persuasive work from this unit.

- Present the author's argument, delineating both the author's specific claims and his or her supporting evidence.
- Determine whether the author's argument is sound, the reasoning valid, and the evidence both relevant and sufficient. Explain your position.
- Identify any faulty reasoning or fallacious arguments in the work.
- Follow your class style guide when quoting sentences or short paragraphs from the argument.

© Task 4: Informational Text [RI.9-10.3, RI.9-10.5]

Analyze the Order and Development of Ideas

Write an essay in which you analyze the order and development of ideas in a nonfiction work from this unit.

- Identify the author's central idea.
- Describe the overall structure of the work, including the order in which supporting ideas are introduced.
- Discuss specific structural choices the writer makes, such as the ways in which he or she connects ideas. For example, explain how the writer uses transitional words and phrases, defines sections, or introduces contrasts and comparisons.
- Explain how the writer organizes sections, paragraphs, and individual sentences to develop key points and establish a logical flow of ideas.
- Maintain a consistent style and formal tone throughout your essay.

Speaking and Listening

Task 5: Informational Text [RI.9-10.6; SL.9-10.4]

Analyze an Author's Purpose

Deliver a speech in which you analyze an author's purpose in one work from this unit.

- Provide both a brief summary of the work and basic information about the author, including the era in which he or she wrote and his or her style and customary topics.

- Describe the author's purpose for writing this work. Explain specific concepts, attitudes, or feelings you think the author wanted to convey. Cite details from the work to support your thinking.

- Note specific ways in which the author uses rhetoric to support his or her purpose, and evaluate its effectiveness.

- Present your findings and supporting evidence clearly so that your audience can follow your reasoning.

Task 6: Informational Text [RI.9-10.4; SL.9-10.4; L.9-10.1.a.]

Analyze the Effect of Word Choice on Tone

Deliver an oral presentation in which you analyze the effect of word choice on tone in two works from this unit.

- Choose two works that offer clear and distinct tones. Explain your choices, describing how the tones of the two works differ.

- Identify specific word choices from each work and explain how these choices affect both meaning and tone.

- Use a graphic organizer to show how the tones of the two works differ.

- Present your ideas clearly and concisely so that your listeners can follow your reasoning.

- Use parallel structures to help engage your listeners.

Task 7: Informational Text [RI.9-10.5; SL.9-10.1, SL.9-10.1.a.]

Analyze an Author's Ideas

Lead a class discussion in which you analyze the ideas presented in a reflective essay from this unit.

- Prepare for the discussion by completing your own analysis of the work. Plan the key points you will address during the discussion.

- Introduce the discussion by offering a summary of the central ideas expressed in the work.

- Then, lead the class in a discussion of the work, including the significance of the title, as well as the development of ideas in specific paragraphs and sentences.

- Consider the author's uses of language, including rhetorical devices, word choices, and connotative meanings.

- As you lead the discussion, summarize points of agreement and disagreement and make connections among ideas.

THE BIG ? What kind of knowledge changes our lives?

At the beginning of Unit 3, you participated in a discussion of the Big Question. Now that you have completed the unit, write a response to the question. Discuss how your initial ideas have changed or been reinforced. Support your response with at least one example from literature and one example from an additional subject area or your own life. Use Big Question vocabulary words (see page 443) in your response.

Featured Titles

In this unit, you have read a variety of informational text, including literary nonfiction. Continue to read on your own. Select works that you enjoy, but challenge yourself to explore new topics, new authors, and works of increasing depth and complexity. The titles suggested below will help you get started.

Informational Text

Night
by Elie Wiesel

During World War II, approximately 6 million European Jews were killed in concentration camps set up by the Nazi regime. *Night* is a **memoir** that describes the author's experiences as a 15-year-old boy who survived the camps but was tormented by what he had seen and experienced.

Immigrant Voices: Twenty-Four Narratives on Becoming an American
Edited by Gordon Hutner
Signet, 1999

This collection of **autobiographical narratives** and **essays** explores the experience of becoming American from many different points of view, including those of a female doctor from Germany forbidden to practice and a man from India struggling to become a writer.

Today's Nonfiction

This collection of **autobiographical narratives** brings together different styles and cultures. From Ernesto Galarza's story of learning English in school to Joan Didion's description of her visit to Pearl Harbor, each real-life story in this collection vividly captures a moment as unique as it is universal.

Touch the Top of the World
by Erik Weihenmayer
Signet, 1999

Erik Weihenmayer had already climbed five of the world's highest peaks when he decided to climb Mount Everest—the "top of the world." Despite having lost his eyesight when he was a child, Weihenmayer achieved his goal. In this **memoir,** he recounts the challenges he faced and the fulfillment he experienced on his high-altitude adventure.

Bury My Heart at Wounded Knee
by Dee Brown
H. Holt, 1991   EXEMPLAR TEXT

In this work of **historical nonfiction,** Dee Brown explores the conflicts between nineteenth-century American settlers and native peoples. The author includes first-hand accounts by Native Americans, who reveal the hardships they faced in trying to maintain their culture and way of life.

The Longitude Prize
by Joan Dash
Farrar, Straus and Giroux, 2000   EXEMPLAR TEXT

During the eighteenth century, the British government offered a large monetary prize to the first person to develop a method for measuring longitude at sea. The government hoped to reduce the losses of both sailors and ships. This work of **historical nonfiction** tells the story of clockmaker John Harrison, who invented a creative answer to a national problem.

Literature

To Kill a Mockingbird
by Harper Lee
Warner Books, 1960   EXEMPLAR TEXT

In this classic **novel,** Harper Lee tells a story of racial prejudice in a fictional Alabama town during the Great Depression. The narrator is eight-year-old Scout Finch, a young girl whose father defends an innocent man in a trial that raises questions about race and justice in America.

In the Time of the Butterflies
by Julia Alvarez
Algonquin Books, 2010   EXEMPLAR TEXT

This **novel** is set in the Dominican Republic during the mid-twentieth century. It is based on the real-life stories of the Mirabal sisters, who took part in a plot to topple their oppressive government. Beginning with their childhoods, the author gives life to these courageous sisters and traces their development as political revolutionaries.

Preparing to Read Complex Texts

Attentive Reading As you read on your own, bring your imagination and questions to the text. The questions shown below and others that you ask as you read will help you learn and enjoy reading even more.

 Common Core State Standards

Reading Literature/Informational Text

10. By the end of grade 10, read and comprehend literature, including stories, dramas, and poems, and literary nonfiction at the high end of the grades 9–10 text complexity band independently and proficiently.

When reading literary nonfiction, ask yourself...

- Who is the author? Why did he or she write the work?
- Are the ideas the author conveys important? Do they merit my attention? If not, why?
- When did the author live and write? Do the attitudes of a particular time and place affect the ideas the author expresses? If so, how?
- Does any one idea strike me as being the most important? Why?
- How might the author's background and life experiences affect his or her views on the topic?
- How might the author's background and life experiences affect his or her use of language?
- How do my life experiences affect what I understand about the work? How do they affect what I feel about the work?
- What can I learn from this text?

Ⓒ Key Ideas and Details

- Does the author organize ideas so that I can follow them? If not, what is wrong with the way the text is ordered?
- Does the author capture my interest right from the beginning, or do I have to work to get into the text? Why do I think that is?
- Does the author give me a new way of looking at a topic? If so, how? If not, why?
- Is the author an expert on the topic? How do I know?
- Has the author made me care about the subject? If so, how? If not, why?
- Does the author use strong evidence? Do I find any of the evidence unconvincing? If so, why?

Ⓒ Craft and Structure

- Does the work seem authentic and true? Does any aspect of the work seem exaggerated, false, or unsupported?
- Do I agree or disagree with the author's basic premise? Why?
- Have I read other works about this or a related topic? What does this work add to my knowledge of the topic?
- How would I write about a similar topic? Would I follow an approach similar to the author's, or would I handle the topic differently?

Ⓒ Integration of Ideas

Resources

Glossary

Big Question vocabulary appears in **blue type**. High-utility Academic Vocabulary is <u>underlined.</u>

A

abruptly (uh BRUHPT lee) *adv.* happening suddenly; unexpectedly

abysmal (uh BIHZ muhl) *adj.* immeasurably deep; terrible

accomplices (uh KOM plihs uhz) *n.* people who help another person commit a crime

adamant (AD uh mant) *adj.* not giving in; unyielding; firm

<u>adapt</u> (uh DAPT) *v.* change or adjust

adept (uh DEHPT) *adj.* expert; highly skilled

adulation (aj uh LAY shuhn) *n.* high or excessive praise; intense admiration

adversaries (AD vuhr sehr eez) *n.* opponents

adversity (ad VUR suh tee) *n.* state of difficulty or misfortune

affable (AF uh buhl) *adj.* pleasant; friendly

affront (uh FRUHNT) *n.* open insult

aggregate (AG ruh giht) *n.* a group of distinct things gathered into a whole; a sum

aggrieved (uh GREEVD) *adj.* wronged; suffering grief or injury

allay (uh LAY) *v.* relieve; lessen; calm

alleviate (uh LEE vee ayt) *v.* to lighten; relieve

amenable (uh MEE nuh buhl) *adj.* responsive; open

amiably (AY mee uh blee) *adv.* in a cheerful, friendly way

anguish (ANG gwihsh) *n.* extreme suffering, as from grief or pain

<u>anticipate</u> (an TIHS uh payt) *v.* look forward to

apathy (AP uh thee) *n.* lack of interest or emotion

apprehension (ap rih HEHN shuhn) *n.* anxious feeling; fear

arable (AR uh buhl) *adj.* suitable for growing crops

ardent (AHR duhnt) *adj.* intensely enthusiastic; devoted

aspirations (as puh RAY shuhnz) *n.* strong ambitions

assuage (uh SWAYJ) *v.* lessen (pain or distress); satisfy (thirst or hunger)

attributes (AT rihb yoots) *n.* characteristics of a person or thing

audaciously (aw DAY shuhs lee) *adv.* in a bold manner

augmented (awg MEHNT ihd) *adj.* made greater; enhanced

august (aw GUHST) *adj.* impressive; majestic

<u>awareness</u> (uh WAIR nuhs) *n.* having knowledge

B

<u>background</u> (BAK grownd) *n.* conditions that surround or come before something

<u>bias</u> (BY uhs) *n.* point of view one has before the facts are known

blemished (BLEHM ihsht) *adj.* damaged; spoiled

bore (bohr) *v.* carried

brandished (BRAN dihsht) *v.* showed, waved, or shook in a threatening or triumphant manner

brazen (BRAY zuhn) *adj.* shameless; bold

buffer (BUHF uhr) *v.* lessen a shock; cushion

C

cajoling (kuh JOHL ihng) *n.* coaxing with flattery

calamity (kuh LAM uh tee) *n.* terrible misfortune; disaster

candid (KAN dihd) *adj.* honest; direct

canopied (KAN uh peed) *adj.* covered by a cloth suspended from poles or a framework

catalyst (KAT uh lihst) *n.* person or thing that triggers an event or action

cessation (seh SAY shuhn) *n.* halt; stopping

change (chaynj) *v.* become different; transform

<u>character</u> (KAR ihk tuhr) *n.* moral strength; self-discipline

chastisement (chas TYZ muhnt) *n.* severe criticism; punishment

choleric (KOL uhr ihk) *adj.* quick tempered; inclined to anger

circuit (SUR kiht) *n.* act of going around something; route

clenching (KLEHNCH ihng) *v.* closing; holding tightly

clustering (KLUHS tuhr ihng) *adj.* gathering; forming in a group

commemorates (kuh MEHM uh rayts) *v.* honors a memory

commences (kuh MEHNS ez) *v.* begins

commiserate (kuh MIHZ uh rayt) *v.* sympathize with; show sorrow for

<u>comprehend</u> (kom prih HEHND) *v.* grasp mentally; understand

compromise (KOM pruh myz) *n.* agreement where both sides give something up

compulsory (kuhm PUHL suhr ee) *adj.* required; mandatory

comrade (KOM rad) *n.* close companion; friend

concession (kuhn SEHSH uhn) *n.* act of granting or giving; allowance

concrete (KON kreet) *adj.* something specific or tangible

condemn (kuhn DEHM) *v.* disapprove of; pass unfavorable judgment on

condemned (kuhn DEHMD) *v.* declared to be guilty of wrongdoings; convicted

conduct (KON duhkt) *n.* the way a person acts; behavior

configuration (kuhn FIHG yuh RAY shuhn) *n.* arrangement of parts; pattern

confirm (kuhn FURM) *v.* establish the truth or correctness of something

confounded (kon FOWND ihd) *adj.* made to feel confused

confrontation (kon fruhn TAY shuhn) *n.* clashing of forces or ideas

confusion (kuhn FYOO zhuhn) *n.* state of disorder or distraction

conjured (KON juhrd) *v.* performed tricks in which things seem to appear, disappear, or change as if by magic

connection (kuh NEHK shuhn) *n.* relationship between things

consigned (kuhn SYND) *v.* handed over; gave up or delivered

conspicuous (kuhn SPIHK yu uhs) *adj.* easy to see

constricting (kuhn STRIHKT ihng) *adj.* preventing freedom of movement; limiting

contempt (kuhn TEHMPT) *n.* scorn; the attitude of someone who looks down on something or someone else

contested (KON tehst uhd) *v.* tried to disprove or invalidate something; disputed

context (KON tehkst) *n.* environment or situation in which something is found

context (KON tehkst) *n.* circumstances that form the setting of an event

contrive (kuhn TRYV) *v.* to bring about; manage

convalesce (kon vuh LEHS) *v.* to regain strength and health

converge (kuhn VURJ) *v.* to come together

convey (kuhn VAY) *v.* communicate or make known

convoluted (kon vuh LOOT uhd) *adj.* twisted in a complicated way

counsel (KOWN suhl) *n.* advice; discussion

countenance (KOWN tuh nuhns) *n.* face; the look of a face, showing a person's nature

courage (KUR ihj) *n.* willingness to deal with something dangerous

credulity (kruh DOO luh tee) *n.* tendency to believe too readily

customarily (kuhs tuh MEHR ih lee) *adv.* usually; by habit or tradition

D

debate (dih BAYT) *v.* argue or discuss

debut (day BYOO) *n.* first public appearance

decorum (dih KAWR uhm) *n.* behavior that is polite and is correct for an occasion

decrepitude (dih KREHP uh tood) *n.* feebleness; condition of being worn out by age or illness

deference (DEHF uhr uhns) *n.* a yielding to the ideas, wishes, and so on of another

deficiency (dih FIHSH uhn see) *n.* lack of something essential

deflects (dih FLEHKTS) *v.* wards off; turns aside

deftness (dehft nehs) *n.* skillfulness

defunct (dih FUHNGKT) *adj.* no longer in use or existence; dead

dejectedly (dih JEHK tihd lee) *adv.* in a depressed way

delusion (dih LOO zhuhn) *n.* an erroneous belief that is held despite evidence to the contrary

demeanor (dih MEE nuhr) *n.* way of conducting oneself; behavior

derisively (dih RY sihv lee) *adv.* in a mocking and ridiculing manner

derived (dih RYVD) *v.* reached by reasoning

desolate (DEHS uh liht) *adj.* empty; solitary

destitute (DEHS tuh toot) *adj.* lacking the basic necessities of life; poverty-stricken

determination (dih TUR muh NAY shuhn) *n.* firmness of purpose

detestable (dee TEHS tuh buhl) *adj.* deserving hate or scorn; offensive

dexterous (DEHKS tuhr uhs) *adj.* having or showing mental or physical skill

differentiate (dihf uh REHN shee ayt) *v.* distinguish between

dignity (DIHG nuh tee) *n.* quality of deserving respect and honor; self-respect

dilapidated (duh LAP uh dayt ihd) *adj.* shabby; broken down

diligence (DIHL uh juhns) *n.* constant, careful effort

dimpled (DIHM puhld) *adj.* marked with small hollows or indentations

dingy (DIHN jee) *adj.* dirty-looking; shabby

dire (dyr) *adj.* urgent; terrible; calling for quick action

discern (duh ZURN) *v.* tell the difference between two or more things; perceive

disconsolate (dihs KON suh liht) *adj.* so unhappy that nothing brings comfort; miserable

discord (DIHS kawrd) *n.* conflict; disagreement

discourse (DIHS kawrs) *v.* speak (on a topic) formally and at length

discourse (DIHS kawrs) *n.* ongoing communication of ideas and information

disdain (dihs DAYN) *n.* disgust for something or someone; scorn

disembarked (DIHS ehm BAHRKT) *v.* left a ship to go ashore

disparagement (dihs PAR ihj muhnt) *n.* comments expressing a low opinion of or lack of respect for

disreputable (dihs REHP yuh tuh buhl) *adj.* not respectable; having or deserving a bad reputation

dissent (dih SEHNT) *n.* refusal to accept a common belief or opinion; disagreement

distinct (dihs TIHNGKT) *adj.* clearly different; separate

distortion (dihs TAWR shuhn) *n.* anything that shows something in an untrue way

dogged (DAWG ihd) *adj.* stubborn

E

earnest (UR nihst) *adj.* serious and intense; not joking

eased (eezd) *v.* freed from pain or trouble; lessened

ebony (EHB uh nee) *adj.* black

edict (EE dihkt) *n.* public order; decree

edifying (EHD uh fy ihng) *adj.* instructive in such a way as to improve morally or intellectually

efface (uh FAYS) *v.* rub or blot out

elude (ih LOOD) *v.* avoid; escape by quickness or cleverness

elusive (ih LOO sihv) *adj.* hard to grasp mentally

emanating (EHM uh nayt ihng) *v.* coming forth, as from a source

embodied (ehm BOD eed) *v.* gave form to; made concrete

emigrants (EHM uh gruhnts) *n.* people who leave their country or region to settle elsewhere

emotion (ih MOH shuhn) *n.* strong feeling, such as love

empathy (EHM puh thee) *n.* sharing in another person's feelings

encroaching (ehn KROHCH ihng) *adj.* intruding on, especially in a gradual way

endeavored (ehn DEHV uhrd) *v.* tried to achieve a set goal

endure (ehn DUR) *v.* hold up under pain or hardship

engaging (ehn GAYJ ihng) *adj.* attractive; pleasant

enlighten (ehn LY tuhn) *v.* make clear through knowledge

enthralls (ehn THRAWLZ) *v.* captivates; fascinates

entreated (ehn TREET uhd) *v.* begged; pleaded with

ephemeral (ih FEHM uhr uhl) *adj.* short-lived

equilibrium (ee kwuh LIHB ree uhm) *n.* a state of balance

esoteric (ehs uh TEHR ihk) *adj.* beyond the understanding or knowledge of most people

estranged (ehs TRAYNJD) *adj.* kept apart; in the condition of having had affection turn into indifference or hostility

eternal (ih TUR nuhl) *adj.* without beginning or end; everlasting

evaluate (ih VAL yoo ayt) *v.* determine the worth of something

evidence (EHV uh duhns) *n.* information that indicates whether something is true or valid

evoking (ih VOHK ihng) *v.* to draw forth emotions or responses

evolve (ih VOLV) *v.* develop through gradual changes

exorbitant (ehg ZAWR buh tuhnt) *adj.* going beyond what is reasonable; excessive

expectations (ehks pehk TAY shuhnz) *n.* something looked forward to

explanation (ehks pluh NAY shuhn) *n.* clarifying statement

expound (ehk SPOWND) *v.* explain in detail

extolled (ehk STOHLD) *adj.* praised

extricating (EHKS truh kayt ihng) *n.* setting free; removing from a difficult situation

exuberance (ehg ZOO buhr uhns) *n.* good health and high spirits

F

falteringly (FAWL tuhr ihng lee) *adv.* spoken hesitatingly or with a wavering voice

fate (fayt) *n.* destiny; what happens to a person or thing; final outcome

fathom (FATH uhm) *v.* understand thoroughly

fawned (fawnd) *v.* flattered; act with excessive concern for the wishes and moods of another, as a servant might

flourishes (FLUR ihsh uhz) *v.* grows vigorously; thrives

fluttered (FLUHT uhrd) *v.* flapped or vibrated rapidly

foe (foh) *n.* enemy

forbore (fawr BAWR) *v.* prevented oneself from doing something; refrained from

foreboding (fawr BOHD ihng) *n.* a feeling that something bad will happen; premonition

formidable (FAWR muh duh buhl) *adj.* causing fear or dread

fraud (frawd) *n.* deceit; trickery

furtively (FUR tihv lee) *adj.* secretively; sneakily; stealthily

futile (FYOO tuhl) *adj.* not successful; useless

G

gauge (gayj) *v.* measure the size, amount, extent, or capacity of

grave (grayv) *adj.* very serious and worrying

grimacing (GRIHM ihs ihng) *v.* making a twisted face showing disgust or pain

growth (grohth) *n.* the process of developing

H

haphazardly (hap HAZ uhrd lee) *adv.* in an unplanned or a disorganized way

haste (hayst) *n.* quickness of motion; rapidity

heedless (HEED lihs) *adj.* careless; thoughtless

history (HIHS tuhr ee) *n.* account of what has happened

honor (ON uhr) *n.* strong sense of right and wrong

humble (HUHM buhl) *adj.* showing an awareness of one's shortcomings; modest

hypocrisy (hih POK ruh see) *n.* the act of saying one thing but doing another

I

idealistic (y dee uh LIHS tihk) *adj.* representing things as they should be rather than how they are

identity (y DEHN tuh tee) *n.* qualities of a person that make up who they are

idle (Y duhl) *adj.* useless; not busy

ignorance (IHG nuhr uhns) *n.* lack of knowledge or education

immaterial (ihm uh TIHR ee uhl) *adj.* not consisting of matter

imminent (IHM uh nuhnt) *adj.* about to happen

impeded (ihm PEED uhd) *v.* blocked; obstructed

impediments (ihm PEHD uh muhnts) *n.* things that slow something or someone down or that get in the way; barriers

impending (ihm PEHN dihng) *adj.* about to happen

imperceptibly (ihm puhr SEHP tuh blee) *adv.* so slowly or slightly as to be barely noticeable

imperiously (ihm PIHR ee uhs lee) *adv.* arrogantly

impervious (ihm PUR vee uhs) *adj.* not affected by (used with to)

impetuosity (ihm pehch oo OS uh tee) *n.* quality of acting suddenly, with great force and little thought; rashness

impression (ihm PREHSH uhn) *n.* an effect produced on the mind

improbable (ihm PROB uh buhl) *adj.* not likely to happen or be true

inaudibly (ihn AW duh blee) *adv.* in a way that cannot be heard

incessant (ihn SEHS uhnt) *adj.* not stopping; constant

incredulity (ihn kruh DOO luh tee) *n.* unwillingness to believe

indigence (IHN duh juhns) *n.* poverty

indignant (ihn DIHG nuhnt) *adj.* feeling anger, especially at injustice

indignation (IHN dihg NAY shuhn) *n.* anger that is a reaction to injustice or meanness

individual (ihn duh VIHJ oo uhl) *adj.* relating to a single person or thing

indulgence (ihn DUHL juhns) *n.* leniency; readiness to tolerate or forgive bad behavior

inexorably (ihn EHK suhr uh blee) *adv.* without the possibility of being delayed or stopped; unalterable

infinite (IHN fuh niht) *adj.* beyond measure or comprehension; endless

infirm (ihn FURM) *adj.* weak; feeble

infirmity (ihn FUR muh tee) *n.* weakness; physical defect

influence (IHN floo uhns) *n.* the power of people to change others

ingenuity (ihn juh NOO uh tee) *n.* cleverness

ingratiating (ihn GRAY shee ayt ihng) *adj.* acting in a way intended to win someone's favor

inhabit (ihn HAB iht) *v.* live in

inherent (ihn HIHR uhnt) *adj.* existing naturally in something

inheritance (ihn HEHR uh tuhns) *n.* gift handed down to a later generation in a family

innuendo (ihn yoo EHN doh) *n.* indirect insult or accusation; insinuation

insight (ihn syt) *n.* clear idea of the nature of things

instinct (IHN stihngkt) *n.* an inborn pattern of behavior, as opposed to a learned skill

insurrection (ihn suh REHK shuhn) *n.* rebellion

integrity (ihn TEHG ruh tee) *n.* willingness to stand by moral principles

interact (ihn tuhr AKT) *v.* relate to one another; affect another

interminable (ihn TUR muh nuh buhl) *adj.* seemingly endless

interpretation (ihn tur pruh TAY shuhn) *n.* explanation of the meaning of something

interred (ihn TURD) *v.* buried (said of a dead body)

intertidal (ihn tuhr TY duhl) *adj.* pertaining to a shore zone bounded by the levels of low and high tide

intervened (ihn tuhr VEEND) *v.* came between

intrigues (ihn TREEGZ) *n.* plots; schemes

irascible (ih RAS uh buhl) *adj.* irritable

irreproachable (ihr ih PROH chuh buhl) *adj.* above criticism

irretrievable (IHR ih TREE vuh buhl) *adj.* impossible to regain or recover

isolation (y suh LAY shuhn) *n.* being alone or set apart

itinerary (y TIHN uh rehr ee) *n.* route; travel plan

J

jauntiness (JAWN tee nuhs) *n.* carefree, easy attitude

jeered (jihrd) *v.* made fun of; mocked; taunted

jurisdiction (jur ihs DIHK shuhn) *n.* sphere of authority or power

K

keenest (KEEN uhst) *adj.* sharpest; most cutting

knowledge (NOL ihj) *n.* awareness and understanding of information

L

lacquered (LAK uhrd) *adj.* covered in tough, sticky varnish

lamentation (lam uhn TAY shuhn) *n.* act of crying out in grief; wailing; weeping

language (LANG gwihj) *n.* system used for expressing or communicating; word choice

languid (LANG gwihd) *adj.* without energy

lavished (LAV ihsht) *v.* gave with extreme generosity

lease (lees) *n.* contract by which something is rented for a specified period of time; rental

legacies (LEHG uh seez) *n.* money, property, or position left in a will to someone

legendary (LEHJ uhn DEHR ee) *adj.* extraordinary; memorable

livid (LIHV ihd) *adj.* discolored, as by a bruise; red with anger

lofty (LAWF tee) *adj.* elevated in rank or character; noble

looming (LOOM ihng) *adj.* appearing unclearly but in a threatening form; threatening to occur

lowly (LOH lee) *adj.* humble; of low rank

lucidity (loo SIHD uh tee) *n.* quality of being readily understood

lucrative (LOO kruh tihv) *adj.* producing wealth; profitable

lunar (LOO nuhr) *adj.* of the moon

M

maligned (muh LYND) *adj.* spoken ill of

manifestations (man uh fehs TAY shuhnz) *n.* appearances; forms

manipulate (muh NIHP yuh layt) *v.* control by use of influence, often in an unfair way

manipulated (muh NIHP yuh layt uhd) *v.* managed or controlled through clever moves

marginal (MAHR juh nuhl) *adj.* at, on, or near the edge

meager (MEE guhr) *adj.* of poor quality or small amount

meaning (MEE nihng) *n.* significance of something

meditates (MEHD uh tayts) *v.* thinks deeply

melancholy (MEHL uhn kol ee) *adj.* sad and depressed

millennial (muh LEHN ee uhl) *adj.* of 1,000 years

mirth (murth) *n.* joyfulness; merriment

misconstrued (mihs kuhn STROOD) *v.* misinterpreted

misinterpret (mihs ihn TUR priht) *v.* not understand correctly

modified (MOD uh fyd) *v.* changed; altered slightly

monotonously (muh NOT uh nuhs lee) *adv.* in a dull, unvarying way

motive (MOH tihv) *n.* something that causes a person to act in a certain way

multitudes (MUHL tuh toodz) *n.* large number of people or things

mutable (MYOO tuh buhl) *adj.* changeable

N

negotiate (nih GOH shee ayt) *v.* bargain with the hope of reaching an agreement

nevertheless (nehv uhr thuh LEHS) *adv.* in spite of that; however

nimbly (NIHM buh lee) *adv.* in a quick, easy, light way; with agility

nomadic (noh MAD ihk) *adj.* moving from place to place; without a permanent home

nonchalantly (NON shuh luhnt lee) *adv.* casually; indifferently

O

objective (uhb JEHK tihv) *adj.* not dependent on another's point of view

oblivious (uh BLIHV ee uhs) *adj.* unaware

obscured (uhb SKYURD) *v.* made dark; blocked from view; hid

oppose (uh POHZ) *v.* to set against; disagree with

oppressive (uh PREHS ihv) *adj.* causing great discomfort; distressing

oratory (AWR uh tawr ee) *n.* act of public speaking; strategies used in such speaking

overcome (oh vuhr KUHM) *v.* to master or prevail over

P

pallor (PAL uhr) *n.* lack of color; unnatural paleness

paradox (PAR uh doks) *n.* a statement or situation that seems contradictory

paranoia (par uh NOY uh) *n.* mental disorder characterized by delusions

perception (puhr SEHP shuhn) *n.* the way one understands the world through the senses

perpetually (puhr PEHCH oo uhl ee) *adv.* continuing forever; constantly

persevere (PUR suh VIHR) *v.* continue despite opposition; persist

perspective (puhr SPEHK tihv) *n.* the way one sees things; viewpoint

petulantly (PEHCH uh luhnt lee) *adv.* in a manner that expresses impatience or irritation

piety (PY uh tee) *n.* loyalty and devotion to family, the divine, or some other object of respect

piqued (peekt) *adj.* annoyed or upset

plague (playg) *v.* pester; harass; torment

plausibility (PLAW zuh BIHL uh tee) *n.* believability; seeming truth

plight (plyt) *n.* distressing situation

poignant (POY nuhnt) *adj.* emotionally moving; piercing

portentous (pawr TEHN tuhs) *adj.* ominous; giving signs of evil to come

presume (prih ZOOM) *v.* rely too much on; take advantage of

presumptuous (prih ZUHMP choo uhs) *adj.* overstepping appropriate bounds; too bold

pretense (prih TEHNS) *n.* a pretending; a false show of something

principles (PRIHN suh puhlz) *n.* rules for right conduct; basics

prodigious (pruh DIHJ uhs) *adj.* of great size or power

profuse (pruh FYOOS) *adj.* giving or pouring forth freely, often to excess; plentiful

progress (PROG rehs) *n.* development; improvement

prostrate (PROS trayt) *adj.* lying flat

prudent (PROO duhnt) *adj.* exercising sound judgment; cautious

purified (PYUR uh fyd) *v.* rid of impurities or pollution; made pure

Q

quench (kwehnch) *v.* satisfy; to fulfill the needs or desires of something

question (KWEHS chuhn) *v.* express uncertainty about; ask

R

radical (RAD uh kuhl) *adj.* extreme change

rash (rash) *adj.* too hasty in speech or action; reckless

rave (rayv) *v.* to talk incoherently or wildly

reality (ree AL uh tee) *n.* quality of being true to life

reapers (REE puhrz) *n.* people who gather or harvest grain

reciprocity (rehs uh PROS uh tee) *n.* relations of exchange; interdependence

reconciliation (rehk uhn sihl ee AY shuhn) *n.* restoring friendship and harmony

reflect (rih FLEHKT) *v.* think seriously about something

refuse (REHF yoos) *n.* waste; trash

rejoiced (rih JOYST) *v.* showed happiness

rejuvenation (rih joo vuh NAY shuhn) *n.* making new, youthful, or energetic again; revitalization

relent (rih LEHNT) *v.* become less strong, severe, or intense; ease up

relish (REHL ihsh) *n.* enjoyment

renounced (rih NOWNST) *v.* gave up formally

repertoire (REHP uhr twahr) *n.* stock of works, such as songs, that a performer is prepared to present

replenished (rih PLEHN ihsht) *v.* made complete or full again

replication (rehp luh KAY shuhn) *n.* duplicate; reproduction

resolute (REHZ uh loot) *adj.* showing a fixed purpose

resolution (rehz uh LOO shuhn) *n.* strong determination; a plan or decision

resolve (rih ZOLV) *v.* reach a conclusion or decision

respond (rih SPOND) *v.* answer

responsibility (rih spon suh BIHL uh tee) *n.* having to answer to someone or something else; being accountable for success or failure

reveling (REHV uhl ihng) *v.* taking great pleasure; celebrating

reverence (REHV uhr uhns) *n.* a feeling of deep respect, love, or awe

revise (rih VYZ) *v.* reconsider; modify

rudiments (ROO duh muhnts) *n.* basics; slight beginnings

S

sacrifice (SAK ruh fys) *v.* give up

sated (SAYT uhd) *adj.* satisfied; provided with more than enough

scrutinized (SKROO tuh nyzd) *v.* examined carefully

secular (SEHK yuh luhr) *adj.* of worldly, as opposed to religious, matters

self-expression (sehlf ehk SPREHSH uhn) *n.* sharing one's personality or emotions

selflessness (SEHLF lihs nuhs) *n.* being devoted to others' interests rather than one's own

self-sufficiency (sehlf suh FIHSH uhn see) *n.* independence

sententiously (sehn TEHN shuhs lee) *adv.* in a way that shows excessive fondness for wise sayings; in lecturing tones

serenity (suh REHN uh tee) *n.* state of calm or peace

servile (SUR vuhl) *adj.* slavelike; humbly submissive to authority

silhouette (sihl oo EHT) *n.* outline drawing filled in with a solid color

simulating (SIHM yuh layt ihng) *v.* giving the appearance of

skeptically (SKEHP tuh kuhl ee) *adv.* with doubt; questioningly

slumbering (SLUHM buhr ihng) *adj.* sleeping

sonorous (suh NAWR uhs) *adj.* having a rich or impressive sound

spare (spair) *adj.* lean; thin

spectacle (SPEHK tuh kuhl) *n.* strange or remarkable sight

squalid (SKWOL ihd) *adj.* foul; unclean

staidness (STAYD nuhs) *n.* state of being settled; calm

stance (stans) *n.* the way one stands, especially the placement of the feet

stark (stahrk) *adj.* bare; harsh

staunch (stawnch) *adj.* steadfast; loyal

steady (STEHD ee) *adj.* firm; sure in movement

stereotype (STEHR ee uh typ) *n.* overly broad and often incorrect notion of a group

stickler (STIHK luhr) *n.* person who insists on strict obedience to rules or standards

stifle (STY fuhl) *v.* smother; hold back

stipulates (STIHP yuh layts) *v.* includes specifically as part of an agreement

strife (stryf) *n.* struggle; conflict

struggle (STRUHG uhl) *v.* face difficulty

subdued (suhb DOOD) *adj.* quiet; lacking energy

subjective (suhb JEHK tihv) *adj.* based on or influenced by a person's feelings or point of view

subordinate (suh BAWR duh niht) *adj.* below another in importance or rank

subtle (SUH tuhl) *adj.* fine; delicate

subversion (suhb VUR zhuhn) *n.* activity meant to overthrow something established; rebellion

successive (suhk SEHS ihv) *adj.* following one after another in sequence

succinct (suhk SIHNGKT) *adj.* clearly and briefly stated

sullen (SUHL uhn) *adj.* gloomy and showing resentment

sumptuous (SUHMP choo uhs) *adj.* costly; lavish

supercilious (soo puhr SIHL ee uhs) *adj.* expressing an attitude of superiority; contemptuous

surmise (suhr MYZ) *n.* guess; idea based on evidence that is not conclusive

surpassed (suhr PAST) *v.* went beyond; excelled

T

tactile (TAK tuhl) *adj.* related to the sense of touch

tangible (TAN juh buhl) *adj.* able to be touched; actual

temperate (TEHM puhr iht) *adj.* mild; kept within limits

tempering (TEHM puhr ihng) *n.* changing to make more suitable, usually by mixing with something

tentative (TEHN tuh tihv) *adj.* hesitant; not confident

tenuous (TEHN yoo uhs) *adj.* not strong

threshold (THREHSH ohld) *n.* the bottom of a doorway; entrance or a point of beginning

titanic (ty TAN ihk) *adj.* powerful; of great size

toil (toyl) *n.* hard, tiring work

trace (trays) *n.* tiny amount; hint

transcends (tran SEHNDZ) *v.* goes beyond the limits of; exceeds

tremulous (TREHM yuh luhs) *adj.* trembling; quivering

tumult (TOO muhlt) *n.* noisy commotion

twinges (TWIHNJ uhz) *n.* sharp, sudden pains, either physical or mental

U

ulterior (uhl TIHR ee uhr) *adj.* further; beyond what is openly stated or implied

uncertainty (uhn SUR tuhn tee) *n.* inability to be sure

understanding (uhn duhr STAN dihng) *n.* power to comprehend and discern

unify (YOO nuh fy) *v.* combine into one

universal (yoo nuh VUR suhl) *adj.* existing in all things

unorthodox (uhn AWR thuh doks) *adj.* not typical; breaking with tradition

unwieldy (uhn WEEL dee) *adj.* hard to manage because of shape or weight; awkward

V

vagaries (vuh GAIR eez) *n.* erratic or unpredictable actions; whims

venerable (VEHN uhr uh buhl) *adj.* worthy of respect because of age or character

venturing (VEHN chuhr ihng) *v.* attempting to do something that involves taking risks

veracious (vuh RAY shuhs) *adj.* truthful; honest

verbal (VUR buhl) *adj.* relating to words

verified (VEHR uh fyd) *v.* proved to be true

verify (VEHR uh fy) *v.* prove that something is true

vile (vyl) *adj.* evil; low; extremely disgusting

W

waver (WAY vuhr) *v.* show indecision; fluctuate

wistfully (WIHST fuhl ee) *adv.* showing vague yearnings

wither (WIHTH uhr) *v.* dry up; shrivel from loss of moisture

wrathfully (RATH fuhl ee) *adv.* with intense anger

Spanish Glossary

El vocabulario de Gran Pregunta aparece en **azul**. El Vocabulario Academico de alta utilidad esta <u>subraydo</u>.

A

abruptly / abruptamente *adv.* que sucede de repente; inesperadamente

abysmal / abismal *adj.* inmensamente malo o extremo; terrible

accomplices / cómplices *s.* personas que ayudan a otros a cometer un crimen

adamant / obstinado *adj.* que no cede; inflexible; firme

<u>**adapt / adaptar**</u> *v.* cambiar o ajustar

adept / adepto *adj.* experto; altamente calificado

adulation / adulación *s.* grandes o excesivos elogios; intensa admiración

adversaries / adversarios *s.* opositores

adversity / adversidad *s.* estado de dificultad o infortunio

affable / afable *adj.* agradable; amistoso

affront / afrenta *s.* insulto abierto

aggregate / agregado *s.* grupo de cosas concretas que unidas forman un todo; una suma

aggrieved / agraviado *adj.* que sufre perjuicio; afligido o herido

allay / aliviar *v.* mitigar; reducir; calmar

alleviate / mitigar *v.* alivianar; aliviar

amenable / receptivo *adj.* sensible; abierto

amiably / amigablemente *adv.* de manera jovial y amistosa

anguish / angustia *s.* sufrimiento extremo, como de pena o dolor

<u>**anticipate / anticipar**</u> *v.* aguardar con interés

apathy / apatía *s.* falta de interés o sentimiento

apprehension / aprensión *s.* sentimiento ansioso; temor

arable / arable *adj.* apto para cultivar cosechas

ardent / ferviente *adj.* intensamente entusiasta; devoto

aspirations / aspiraciones *s.* ambiciones fuertes

assuage / aplacar *v.* aminorar (dolor o aflicción); satisfacer (sed o hambre)

attributes / atributos *s.* características de una persona o cosa

audaciously / audazmente *adv.* de manera intrépida

augmented / aumentado *adj.* hecho más grande; realzado

august / augusto *adj.* impresionante; majestuoso

<u>**awareness / conciencia**</u> *s.* tener conocimiento

B

<u>**background / antecedentes**</u> *s.* condiciones que rodean o preceden a algo

<u>**bias / prejuicio**</u> *s.* el punto de vista que uno tiene antes de conocer los hechos

blemished / manchado *adj.* dañado; estropeado

bore / portó *v.* cargó

brandished / blandió *v.* mostró, esgrimió o batió de manera amenazante o triunfante

brazen / descarado *adj.* sin vergüenza; audaz

buffer / amortiguar *v.* aminorar un golpe; suavizar

C

cajoling / lisonjeo *s.* persuasión de alguien con lisonjas

calamity / calamidad *s.* desgracia terrible; desastre

candid / candoroso *adj.* franco; directo

canopied / entoldado *adj.* cubierto por una tela suspendida de postes o una estructura

catalyst / catalizador *s.* persona o cosa que desata un evento o acción

cessation / cesación *s.* detención; alto

change / cambiar *v.* convertirse en algo distinto; transformar

<u>**character / temperamento**</u> *s.* fortaleza moral; autodisciplina

chastisement / castigo *s.* crítica severa; corrección

choleric / colérico *adj.* malgeniado; irascible

circuit / circuito *s.* acción de girar alrededor de algo; ruta

clenching / apretar *v.* cerrar; agarrar firmemente

clustering / amontonado *adj.* reunido; formado en un grupo

commemorates / conmemora *v.* honra la memoria de

commences / comienza *v.* inicia

commiserate / compadecer *v.* apiadarse de; tener lástima por

<u>**comprehend / comprender**</u> *v.* captar mentalmente; entender

compromise / acuerdo *s.* convenio donde ambas partes ceden algo

compulsory / obligatorio *adj.* requerido; exigido

comrade / camarada *s.* compañero cercano; amigo

concession / concesión *s.* acción de otorgar o dar; indulgencia

concrete / concreto *adj.* algo específico o tangible

condemn / condenar *v.* desaprobar de; emitir un juicio desfavorable sobre

condemned / condenado *v.* que ha sido declarado culpable de fechorías; sentenciado por un juez

conduct / conducta *s.* la forma de actuar de una persona; comportamiento

confirm / confirmar *v.* establecer la verdad o precisión de algo

confounded / aturdido *adj.* sentirse confundido

confrontation / confrontación *s.* choque de fuerzas o ideas

confusion / confusión *s.* estado de desorden o distracción

conjured / invocado *v.* llamado como por acto de magia

connection / conexión *s.* relación entre cosas

consigned / consignado *v.* entregado; cedido o entregado

conspicuous / conspicuo *adj.* fácil de ver

constricting / restrictivo *adj.* que evita la libertad de movimiento; limitante

contempt / desprecio *s.* desdén; la actitud de alguien que tiene a menos a algo o a alguien

contested / disputó *v.* que intentó refutar o invalidar algo; impugnó

context / contexto *s.* circunstancias que crean el entorno de un evento

context / contexto *s.* entorno o situación en la que algo se encuentra

contrive / ingeniar *v.* procurar hacer; lograr

convalesce / convalecer *v.* recuperar fuerza y salud

converge / converger *v.* unirse

convey / transmitir *v.* comunicar o dar a conocer

convoluted / intrincado *adj.* retorcido de manera complicada

counsel / consejo *s.* orientación; discusión

countenance / semblante *s.* rostro; la expresión de una cara que muestra la naturaleza de una persona

courage / valor *s.* la voluntad de lidiar con algo peligroso

credulity / credulidad *s.* tendencia a creer con demasiada facilidad

customarily / habitualmente *adv.* comúnmente; por hábito o tradición

D

debate / debatir *v.* argumentar o discutir

debut / debut *s.* primera aparición pública

decorum / decoro *s.* comportamiento cortés y apropiado para cierta ocasión

decrepitude / decrepitud *s.* debilidad; condición de estar desgastado por edad o enfermedad

deference / deferencia *s.* el ceder a las ideas, deseos, etc. de otra persona

deficiency / deficiencia *s.* falta de algo esencial

deflects / desvía *v.* que detiene algo; que rechaza algo

deftness / habilidad *s.* destreza

defunct / difunto *adj.* que ya no está en uso o existencia; muerto

dejectedly / abatidamente *adv.* estar desalentado; de forma deprimida

delusion / ilusión *s.* una creencia errónea que se mantiene a pesar de haber evidencia en contra

demeanor / comportamiento *s.* manera de comportarse; conducta

derisively / burlonamente *adv.* de manera irónica y ridiculizante

derived / derivado *v.* que se obtuvo mediante razonamiento

desolate / desolado *adj.* vacío; solitario

destitute / indigente *adj.* carente de las necesidades básicas de la vida; de gran pobreza

determination / determinación *s.* firmeza de propósito

dexterous / diestro *adj.* tener o mostrar destreza mental o física; experto

differentiate / diferenciar *v.* distinguir entre

dignity / dignidad *s.* cualidad de merecer respeto y honor; respeto de sí mismo

dilapidated / dilapidado *adj.* estado ruinoso; raído

diligence / diligencia *s.* esfuerzo constante y esmerado

dimpled / con hoyuelos *adj.* marcado con pequeños hoyos o hendiduras

dingy / manchado *adj.* de aspecto sucio; deslustrado

dire / abrumador *adj.* urgente; terrible; que exige una acción rápida

discern / discernir *v.* distinguir la diferencia entre dos o más cosas; percibir

disconsolate / desconsolado *adj.* tan infeliz que nada le reconforta; miserable

discord / discordia *s.* conflicto; desacuerdo

discourse / discurso *s.* comunicación continua de ideas e información

discourse / disertar *v.* hablar (sobre un tema) formal y detalladamente

disdain / desdeño *s.* disgusto por alguien o algo; desprecio

disembarked / desembarcó *v.* abandonó un buque para ir a tierra

disparagement / menosprecio *s.* comentarios que expresan una mala opinión o falta de respeto por alguien

disreputable / desacreditado *adj.* no respetable; que tiene o merece mala reputación

dissent / desacuerdo *s.* renuencia a aceptar una creencia u opinión común; desavenencia

distinct / distinto *adj.* claramente diferente; separado

distortion / distorsión *s.* cualquier cosa que muestra algo de manera engañosa

dogged / obstinado *adj.* terco

E

earnest / formal *adj.* serio e intenso; sin bromear

eased / alivió *v.* liberó de dolor o dificultad; alivianó

ebony / ébano *adj.* de color negro

edict / edicto *s.* mandato público; decreto

edifying / edificante *adj.* algo educativo que permite que la persona mejore moral o intelectualmente

efface / tachar *v.* borrar o suprimir

elude / eludir *v.* evitar; escapar con celeridad o astucia

elusive / elusivo *adj.* difícil de comprender

emanating / emanar *v.* brotar hacia afuera, como de una fuente

embodied / materializó *v.* dio forma a; concretó

emigrants / emigrantes *s.* personas que abandonan su país o región para establecerse en otro lugar

emotion / emoción *s.* sentimiento fuerte, como el amor

empathy / empatía *s.* compartir los sentimientos de otra persona

encroaching / invadir *adj.* cometer una intrusión, especialmente de manera gradual

endeavored / se esforzó por *v.* trató de alcanzar una meta fijada

endure / soportar *v.* aguantar con dolor o penuria

engaging / cautivador *adj.* atractivo; agradable

enlighten / ilustrar *v.* aclarar algo mediante el conocimiento

enthralls / encantar *v.* que cautiva; fascina

entreated / suplicó *v.* imploró; rogó

ephemeral / efímero *adj.* pasajero

equilibrium / equilibrio *s.* estado de balance

esoteric / esotérico *adj.* más allá de la comprensión o conocimiento de la mayoría de las personas

estranged / apartado *adj.* que se mantiene separado; condición en la que el afecto se torna en indiferencia u hostilidad

eternal / eterno *adj.* sin principio ni fin; sempiterno

evaluate / evaluar *v.* determinar el valor de algo

evidence / evidencia *s.* información que indica si algo es veraz o válido

evoking / evocar *v.* hacer salir las emociones o reacciones

evolve / evolucionar *v.* desarrollarse a través de cambios graduales

exorbitant / exorbitante *adj.* más allá de lo razonable; excesivo

expectations / expectativas *s.* algo que se aguarda con interés

explanation / explicación *s.* declaración aclaratoria

expound / enunciar *v.* explicar en detalle

extolled / elogiado *adj.* alabado

extricating / liberar *v.* dejar libre; sacar de una situación difícil

exuberance / exuberancia *s.* buena salud; vivacidad

F

falteringly / titubeante *adv.* dicho con titubeo o con voz trémula

fate / sino *s.* destino; lo que le sucede a una persona o cosa; resultado final

fathom / desentrañar *v.* comprender a fondo

fawned / aduló *v.* lisonjeó; actuó con preocupación excesiva por los deseos y antojos de otro, como lo haría un sirviente

flourishes / florece *v.* que crece vigorosamente; que prospera

fluttered / revoloteó *v.* agitó o vibró rápidamente

foe / adversario *s.* enemigo

forbore / abstuvo *v.* que desistió de realizar algo; que renunció a algo

foreboding / presentimiento *s.* una sensación de que algo malo ocurrirá; premonición

formidable / temible *adj.* que causa temor o pánico

fraud / fraude *s.* engaño; embuste

futile / fútil *adj.* ineficaz; inútil

G

gauge / aforar *v.* medir el tamaño, cantidad, alcance o capacidad de algo

grave / grave *adj.* que requiere de consideración seria; importante e inquietante

grimacing / haciendo muecas *v.* haciendo un gesto que muestre disgusto o dolor

growth / crecimiento *s.* el proceso del desarrollo

H

haphazardly / al azar *adv.* de manera no planeada o desorganizada

haste / apuro *s.* con rapidez de movimiento; prisa

heedless / desatento *adj.* descuidado; imprudente

history / historia *s.* relato de lo que ha pasado

honor / honor *s.* fuerte sentido del bien y del mal

humble / humilde *adj.* que muestra estar consciente de sus propios defectos; modesto

hypocrisy / hipocresía *s.* fingir ser o sentir lo que uno no es o siente

I

idealistic / idealista *adj.* que representa las cosas como deberían ser en lugar de como son en realidad

identity / identidad *s.* cualidades de una persona que representan lo que es

idle / ocioso *adj.* inútil; desocupado

ignorance / ignorancia *s.* falta de conocimiento o educación

immaterial / inmaterial *adj.* que no consiste de materia

imminent / inminente *adj.* a punto de suceder

impeded / impidió *v.* bloqueó; obstruyó

impediments / impedimentos *s.* cosas que retrasan a alguien o a algo, o que obstaculizan; barreras

impending / inminente *adj.* a punto de suceder

imperceptibly / imperceptiblemente *adv.* tan lento o leve que casi no se nota

imperiously / imperiosamente *adv.* arrogantemente

impervious / impenetrable *adj.* que no lo afecta algo

impetuosity / impetuosidad *s.* calidad de actuar repentinamente, con gran fuerza y poca consideración; temeridad

impression / impresión *s.* efecto que se produce sobre la mente

improbable / improbable *adj.* que no es factible que suceda o sea verdad

inaudibly / inaudiblemente *adv.* de forma que no se pueda oír

incessant / incesante *adj.* que no se detiene; constante

incredulity / incredulidad *s.* renuencia a creer

indigence / indigencia *s.* pobreza

indignant / indignado *adj.* que siente ira, especialmente por una injusticia

indignation / indignación *s.* ira en reacción a la injusticia o mezquindad

individual / individual *adj.* relativo a una sola persona o cosa

indulgence / indulgencia *s.* lenidad; estar dispuesto a tolerar o perdonar la mala conducta

inexorably / inexorablemente *adv.* sin la posibilidad de que lo atrasen o detengan; inalterable

infinite / infinito *adj.* más allá de medida o comprensión; interminable

infirm / enfermo *adj.* débil; endeble

infirmity / enfermedad *s.* debilidad; defecto físico

influence / influencia *s.* el poder de las personas para cambiar a otras

ingenuity / ingenio *s.* inventiva

ingratiating / congraciado *adj.* que actúa de cierta manera para ganarse el favor de alguien

inhabit / habitar *v.* residir en

inherent / inherente *adj.* que existe naturalmente en algo

inheritance / herencia *s.* dote que es pasada a la siguiente generación de una familia

innuendo / alusión *s.* insulto o acusación indirecta; insinuación

insight / discernimiento *s.* idea clara de la naturaleza de las cosas

instinct / instinto *s.* un patrón innato de comportamiento, en contraposición a una destreza aprendida

insurrection / insurrección *s.* rebelión

integrity / integridad *s.* voluntad para cumplir con los principios morales

interact / interactuar *v.* relacionarse entre sí, afectar a otro

interminable / interminable *adj.* que parece no tener fin

interpretation / interpretación *s.* explicación del significado de algo

interred / sepultó *v.* enterró (dícese de un cuerpo)

intertidal / entre marea alta y baja *adj.* característico de una zona litoral sujeta a los niveles de mareas alta y baja

intervened / intervino *v.* se interpuso entre

intrigues / intrigas *s.* tramas; maquinaciones

irascible / irascible *adj.* irritable

irreproachable / irreprochable *adj.* por encima de la crítica

irretrievable / irrecuperable *adj.* imposible de alcanzar de nuevo o recobrar

isolation / aislamiento *s.* estar solo o aislado

itinerary / itinerario *s.* ruta; plan de viaje

J

jauntiness / garbo *s.* actitud libre y desenvuelta

jeered / burló *v.* escarneció; mofó; ridiculizó

jurisdiction / jurisdicción *s.* esfera de autoridad o poder

K

keenest / más agudo *adj.* el más penetrante; cortante

knowledge / conocimiento *s.* conciencia y comprensión de información

L

lacquered / laqueado *adj.* cubierto con un barniz resistente y pegajoso

lamentation / lamento *s.* acto de vociferar con aflicción; gemido; llanto

language / lenguaje *s.* sistema usado para expresarse o comunicar; escogencia de palabras

languid / lánguido *adj.* falto de energía

lavished / derrochó *v.* dio con extrema generosidad

lease / arrendamiento *s.* contrato mediante el cual algo es alquilado por un plazo determinado de tiempo; alquiler

legacies / legados *s.* dinero, propiedades o posición que se deja a alguien en un testamento

legendary / legendario *adj.* extraordinario; memorable

livid / lívido *adj.* pálido, como por haber sufrido una herida; enrojecido por la ira

lofty / eminente *adj.* elevado en rango o temperamento; noble

looming / que aparece *adj.* que se asoma en forma vaga, indistinta, pero amenazante; que amenaza con ocurrir

lowly / inferior *adj.* humilde; de baja posición

lucidity / lucidez *s.* cualidad de ser fácilmente entendido

lucrative / lucrativo *adj.* que produce riqueza; rentable

lunar / lunar *adj.* de la luna

M

maligned / difamado *adj.* que se habló mal de

manifestations / manifestaciones *s.* apariciones; formas

manipulate / manipular *v.* controlar mediante el uso de influencia, a menudo de forma injusta

manipulated / manipuló *v.* que manejó o controló mediante jugadas astutas

marginal / marginal *adj.* en o cerca del borde

meager / escaso *adj.* de mala calidad o poca cantidad

meaning / significado *s.* el sentido de algo

meditates / medita *v.* que piensa profundamente

melancholy / melancólico *adj.* triste y deprimido

millennial / milenario *adj.* de 1.000 años

mirth / regocijo *s.* alegría; júbilo

misconstrued / malinterpretó *v.* entendió mal

misinterpret / malinterpretar *v.* no entender correctamente

modified / modificó *v.* cambió; alteró ligeramente

monotonously / monótonamente *adv.* de forma aburrida e invariable

motive / motivo *s.* lo que causa que una persona actúe de cierta manera

multitudes / multitudes *s.* gran cantidad de personas o cosas

mutable / mutable *adj.* cambiable

N

negotiate / negociar *v.* pactar con la esperanza de llegar a un acuerdo

nevertheless / sin embargo *adv.* a pesar de eso; no obstante

nimbly / ágilmente *adv.* de forma rápida, fácil y liviana; con agilidad

nomadic / nómada *adj.* que se traslada de un lugar a otro; sin hogar permanente

nonchalantly / indiferentemente *adv.* casualmente; imperturbablemente

O

objective / objetivo *adj.* que no está sujeto al punto de vista de otro

oblivious / olvidadizo *adj.* absorto

obscured / oscureció *v.* hizo oscuro; obstruyó la vista; escondió

oppose / oponer *v.* ponerse en contra; estar en desacuerdo con

oppressive / opresivo *adj.* que causa gran incomodidad; angustiante

oratory / oratoria *s.* acto de hablar en público; estrategias usadas en disertaciones

overcome / vencer *v.* conquistar o prevalecer sobre

P

pallor / palor *s.* carencia de color; palidez poco natural

paradox / paradoja *s.* declaración o situación que parece contradictoria

paranoia / paranoia *s.* trastorno mental que se caracteriza por delirios

perception / percepción *s.* la forma en que uno entiende el mundo a través de los sentidos

perpetually / perpetuamente *adv.* que continua para siempre; constantemente

persevere / perseverar *v.* continuar a pesar de la oposición; persistir

perspective / perspectiva *s.* la forma en que uno ve las cosas; punto de vista

petulantly / petulantemente *adv.* de forma que expresa impaciencia o irritación

piety / piedad *s.* lealtad y devoción hacia la familia, lo divino o algún otro objeto de respeto

piqued / molesto *adj.* enojado o irritado

plague / importunar *v.* molestar; fastidiar; atormentar

plausibility / admisibilidad *s.* credibilidad; verdad aparente

plight / aprieto *s.* situación difícil

poignant / conmovedor *adj.* que afecta emocionalmente; desgarrador

portentous / portentoso *adj.* ominoso; que da señales de cosas nefastas por venir

presume / presumir *v.* depender demasiado de; abusar de

presumptuous / descarado *adj.* que traspasa los límites de lo correcto; demasiado imprudente

pretense / pretensión *s.* jactancia; simulación fingida de algo

principles / principios *s.* reglas para una conducta correcta; normas

prodigious / prodigioso *adj.* de gran tamaño o poder

profuse / profuso *adj.* dar o vaciar libremente, a menudo en exceso; abundante

progress / progreso *s.* desarrollo; mejoras

prostrate / postrado *adj.* yacer tendido

prudent / prudente *adj.* practicar un razonamiento acertado; cauteloso

purified / purificó *v.* libró de impurezas o contaminación; hizo puro

Q

quench / aplacar *v.* satisfacer; llenar las necesidades o deseos de algo

question / preguntar *v.* expresar incertidumbre sobre algo; formular una pregunta

R

radical / radical *adj.* cambio extremo

rash / imprudente *adj.* demasiado apresurado en el dicho o en el hecho; precipitado

rave / desvariar *v.* hablar incoherentemente o decir disparates

reality / realidad *s.* calidad de ser conforme a la verdad

reapers / segadores *s.* personas que recogen o cosechan los granos

reciprocity / reciprocidad *s.* relaciones de intercambio; interdependencia

reconciliation / reconciliación *s.* reestablecer la amistad y la armonía

reflect / reflexionar *v.* pensar seriamente sobre algo

refuse / desechos *s.* desperdicios; basura

rejoiced / regocijó *v.* mostró alegría

rejuvenation / rejuvenecimiento *s.* hacer nuevo, más joven o energético una vez más; revitalización

relent / ceder *v.* volverse menos fuerte, severo o intenso; ablandarse

relish / deleite *s.* goce

renounced / renunció *v.* se rindió formalmente

repertoire / repertorio *s.* lista de obras, por ejemplo, canciones que un artista está preparado para presentar

replenished / reabasteció *v.* completó o llenó de nuevo

replication / réplica *s.* duplicado; reproducción

resolute / resuelto *adj.* que muestra un propósito fijo

resolution / resolución *s.* fuerte determinación; plan o decisión firme

resolve / resolver *v.* llegar a una conclusión o decisión

respond / responder *v.* contestar

responsibility / responsabilidad *s.* tener que responder ante alguien o algo; rendir cuentas por el éxito o el fracaso

reveling / deleitarse *v.* disfrutar; celebrar

reverence / reverencia *s.* un sentimiento de profundo respeto, amor o admiración

revise / revisar *v.* reconsiderar; modificar

rudiments / rudimentos *s.* fundamentos; inicios modestos

S

sacrifice / sacrificar *v.* ceder

sated / saciado *adj.* satisfecho; provisto con más que suficiente

scrutinized / escudriñó *v.* examinó detenidamente

secular / seglar *adj.* relativo a asuntos mundanos, en comparación con religiosos

self-expression / expresión del carácter propio *s.* compartir con otros la personalidad o las emociones

selflessness / desprendimiento *s.* tener devoción por los intereses de los demás por encima de los propios

self-sufficiency / autosuficiencia *s.* independencia

sententiously / sentenciosamente *adv.* que muestra un gusto excesivo por los proverbios; en tono de disertación

serenity / serenidad *s.* estado de calma o paz

servile / servil *adj.* semejante a un esclavo; humildemente sumiso a la autoridad

silhouette / silueta *s.* dibujo de un perfil relleno con un color sólido

simulating / simular *v.* dar la apariencia de

skeptically / escépticamente *adv.* con duda; interrogativamente

slumbering / soñoliento *adj.* adormecido

sonorous / sonoro *adj.* tener un sonido rico o impresionante

spare / frugal *adj.* enjuto; descarnado

spectacle / espectáculo *s.* presenciar algo extraño o extraordinario

squalid / escuálido *adj.* impuro; sucio

staidness / sobriedad *s.* estado de estar tranquilo; sosegado

stance / postura *s.* la forma en que uno se para, especialmente en cuanto a la colocación de los pies

stark / desolado *adj.* desierto; severo

staunch / firme *adj.* constante; leal

steady / estable *adj.* firme; de movimiento seguro

stereotype / estereotipo *s.* noción de un grupo que es demasiado amplia y a menudo incorrecta

stickler / rigorista *s.* persona que insiste en la obediencia estricta a las reglas o normas

stifle / sofocar *v.* asfixiar; reprimir

stipulates / estipula *v.* que incluye específicamente como parte de un acuerdo

strife / refriega *s.* lucha; conflicto

struggle / luchar *v.* enfrentar dificultades

subdued / alicaído *adj.* quieto; que le falta energía

subjective / subjetivo *adj.* basado en o influenciado por los sentimientos o punto de vista de una persona

subordinate / subordinado *adj.* inferior a otro en importancia o rango

subtile / sutil *adj.* fino; delicado

subversion / subversión *s.* actividad con intención de derrocar algo establecido; rebelión

successive / sucesivo *adj.* que uno le sigue al otro en secuencia

succinct / sucinto *adj.* expresado clara y brevemente

sullen / taciturno *adj.* adusto y que muestra resentimiento

sumptuous / suntuoso *adj.* costoso; espléndido

supercilious / altanero *adj.* que muestra una actitud de superioridad; desdeñoso

surmise / suposición *s.* conjetura; idea basada en evidencia que no es concluyente

surpassed / sobrepasó *v.* que fue más allá; superó

T

tactile / táctil *adj.* relativo al sentido del tacto

tangible / tangible *adj.* capaz de ser tocado; real

temperate / temperado *adj.* moderado; que se mantiene dentro de los límites

tempering / temperar *s.* cambiar para hacer más apto, generalmente al mezclarlo con otra cosa

tentative / tentativo *adj.* vacilante; incierto

tenuous / tenue *adj.* sin fuerza

threshold / umbral *s.* la parte inferior de un portal; entrada o punto de inicio

titanic / titánico *adj.* poderoso; de gran tamaño

toil / labor *s.* trabajo arduo y cansado

trace / trazo *s.* pequeña cantidad; pizca

transcends / trasciende *v.* que va más allá de los límites de; excede

tremulous / trémulo *adj.* tembloroso; que se estremece

tumult / tumulto *s.* conmoción ruidosa

twinges / punzadas *s.* dolores agudos y repentinos, ya sea físicos o mentales

U

ulterior / ulterior *adj.* subsecuente; más allá de lo que está abiertamente expresado o implícito

uncertainty / incertidumbre *s.* incapacidad de estar seguro

understanding / entendimiento *s.* poder de comprender y discernir

unify / unificar *v.* combinar en uno solo

universal / universal *adj.* que existe en todas las cosas

unorthodox / no ortodoxo *adj.* atípico; que rompe con la tradición

unwieldy / abultado *adj.* difícil de manejar debido a su forma o peso; incómodo

V

vagaries / caprichos *s.* acciones erráticas o impredecibles; antojos

venerable / venerable *adj.* digno de respeto debido a edad o posición

venturing / atreverse *v.* tomar el riesgo de

veracious / veraz *adj.* verdadero; honesto

verbal / verbal *adj.* relativo a las palabras

verified / verificó *v.* demostró que es cierto

verify / verificar *v.* probar que algo es cierto

vile / vil *adj.* malo; bajo; extremadamente detestable

W

waver / vacilar *v.* mostrar indecisión; titubear

wistfully / anhelantemente *adv.* mostrando vagos deseos

wither / marchitar *v.* secar; que se encoge por falta de humedad

wrathfully / coléricamente *adv.* con intenso enojo

Literary Terms

ACT See *Drama.*

ALLEGORY An *allegory* is a story or tale with two or more levels of meaning—a literal level and one or more symbolic levels. The events, setting, and characters in an allegory are symbols for ideas and qualities.

ALLITERATION *Alliteration* is the repetition of initial consonant sounds. Writers use alliteration to give emphasis to words, to imitate sounds, and to create musical effects. In the following line from Theodore Roethke's "The Waking" (p. 685), there is alliteration of the *f* sound:

I *f*eel my *f*ate in what I cannot *f*ear.

ALLUSION An *allusion* is a reference to a well-known person, place, event, literary work, or work of art. The title of the story "By the Waters of Babylon" (p. 314) is an allusion to the Bible's Psalm 137, in which the Hebrew people lament their exile in Babylon. It begins, "By the rivers of Babylon, there we sat down, yea, we wept. . . ."

ANALOGY An *analogy* makes a comparison between two or more things that are similar in some ways but otherwise unalike.

ANECDOTE An anecdote is a brief story told to entertain or to make a point. In the excerpt from "The Way to Rainy Mountain" (p. 595), N. Scott Momaday tells anecdotes about his grandmother to reveal her character and provide a glimpse into a vanishing way of life.

See also *Narrative.*

ANTAGONIST An *antagonist* is a character or force in conflict with a main character, or protagonist.

ANTICLIMAX Some stories end in an *anticlimax.* Like a climax, an *anticlimax* is the turning point in a story. However, an anticlimax is always a letdown. It is the point at which you learn that the story will not turn out in a way that truly resolves the problem or satisfies the reader.

ARCHETYPE An *archetype* is a type of character, detail, image, or situation that appears in literature throughout history. Some critics believe that archetypes reveal deep truths about human experience.

ARGUMENT See *Persuasion.*

ASIDE An *aside* is a short speech delivered by a character in a play in order to express his or her thoughts and feelings. Traditionally, the aside is directed to the audience and is presumed not to be heard by the other characters.

ASSONANCE *Assonance* is the repetition of vowel sounds followed by different consonants in two or more stressed syllables. Assonance is found in this phrase from Elizabeth Bishop's "The Fish" (p. 650): "frayed and wavering."

ATMOSPHERE See *Mood.*

AUTOBIOGRAPHICAL ESSAY See *Essay.*

AUTOBIOGRAPHY An *autobiography* is a form of nonfiction in which a writer tells his or her own life story. An autobiography may tell about the person's whole life or only a part of it. An example of an autobiography is Erik Weihenmayer's *Touch the Top of the World* (p. 449).

See also *Biography* and *Nonfiction.*

BALLAD A *ballad* is a songlike poem that tells a story, often one dealing with adventure and romance. Most ballads are written in four- to six-line stanzas and have regular rhythms and rhyme schemes. A ballad often features a *refrain*—a regularly repeated line or group of lines.

See also *Oral Tradition.*

BIOGRAPHY A *biography* is a form of nonfiction in which a writer tells the life story of another person. Biographies have been written about many famous people, historical and contemporary, but they can also be written about "ordinary" people.

See also *Autobiography* and *Nonfiction.*

BLANK VERSE *Blank verse* is poetry written in unrhymed iambic pentameter lines. This verse form was widely used by William Shakespeare.

CHARACTER A *character* is a person or an animal who takes part in the action of a literary work. The main character, or protagonist, is the most important character in a story. In Chinua Achebe's story "Civil Peace" (p. 358), Jonathan Iwegbu is the protagonist. This character often changes in some important way as a result of the story's events.

Characters are sometimes classified as round or flat, dynamic or static. A *round character* shows many different traits—faults as well as virtues. A *flat character* shows only one trait. A *dynamic character* develops and grows during the course of the story; a **static character** does not change.

See also **Characterization** and **Motivation**.

CHARACTERIZATION **Characterization** is the act of creating and developing a character. In direct characterization, the author directly states a character's traits. For example, in "The Masque of the Red Death" (p. 372), Poe directly characterizes Prince Prospero: "But the Prince Prospero was happy and dauntless and sagacious."

In indirect characterization, an author gives clues about a character by describing what a character looks like, does, and says, as well as how other characters react to him or her. It is up to the reader to draw conclusions about the character based on this indirect information.

The most effective indirect characterizations usually result from showing characters acting or speaking.

See also **Character.**

CLIMAX The **climax** of a story, novel, or play is the high point of interest or suspense. The events that make up the rising action lead up to the climax. The events that make up the falling action follow the climax.

See also **Conflict, Plot,** and **Anticlimax.**

COMEDY A **comedy** is a literary work, especially a play, that has a happy ending. Comedies often show ordinary characters in conflict with society. These conflicts are introduced through misunderstandings, deceptions, and concealed identities. When the conflict is resolved, the result is the correction of moral faults or social wrongs. Types of comedy include *romantic comedy,* which involves problems among lovers, and the *comedy of manners,* which satirically challenges the social customs of a sophisticated society. Comedy is often contrasted with tragedy, in which the protagonist meets an unfortunate end.

COMIC RELIEF **Comic relief** is a technique that is used to interrupt a serious part of a literary work by introducing a humorous character or situation.

CONFLICT A **conflict** is a struggle between opposing forces. Characters in conflict form the basis of stories, novels, and plays.

There are two kinds of conflict: external and internal. In an *external conflict,* the main character struggles against an outside force. This force may be another character, as in "Civil Peace" (p. 358), in which Jonathan Iwegbu struggles with the leader of the thieves. The outside force could also

be the standards or expectations of a group, such as the oppression and censorship that Juan struggles against in "The Censors" (p. 410). The outside force may be nature itself, as when Erik Weihenmayer struggles to climb Mt. Everest in *Touch the Top of the World* (p. 449).

An *internal conflict* involves a character in conflict with himself or herself. In *Julius Caesar* (p. 892), Brutus experiences an internal conflict when trying to decide whether to assassinate Caesar.

See also **Plot.**

CONNOTATION The **connotation** of a word is the set of ideas associated with it in addition to its explicit meaning.

See also **Denotation.**

CONSONANCE **Consonance** is the repetition of final consonant sounds in stressed syllables with different vowel sounds, as in *hat* and *sit.*

CONTEMPORARY INTERPRETATION A **contemporary interpretation** is a literary work of today that responds to and sheds new light on a well-known, earlier work of literature. Such an interpretation may refer to any aspect of the older work, including plot, characters, settings, imagery, language, and theme. T. H. White's *The Once and Future King* (p. 1156) provides a modern version of the legend of King Arthur.

COUPLET A **couplet** is a pair of rhyming lines, usually of the same length and meter. In the following couplet from Sonnet 29 by William Shakespeare, the speaker comforts himself with the thought of his love:

> For thy sweet love remember'd such wealth brings
> That then I scorn to change my state with kings.

See also **Stanza.**

DENOTATION The **denotation** of a word is its dictionary meaning, independent of other associations that the word may have. The denotation of the word *lake,* for example, is "an inland body of water." "Vacation spot" and "place where the fishing is good" are connotations of the word *lake.*

See also **Connotation.**

DESCRIPTION A **description** is a portrait in words of a person, place, or object. Descriptive writing uses sensory details, those that appeal to the senses: sight, hearing, taste, smell, and touch. Description can be found in all types of writing. Anita Desai's "Games at Twilight" (p. 138) has vivid descriptive passages.

DESCRIPTIVE ESSAY See *Essay.*

DIALECT *Dialect* is a special form of a language, spoken by people in a particular region or group. It may involve changes to the pronunciation, vocabulary, and sentence structure of the standard form of the language. Rudyard Kipling's "Danny Deever" (p. 652) is a poem written in the Cockney dialect of English, used by working-class Londoners.

DIALOGUE A *dialogue* is a conversation between characters that may reveal their traits and advance the action of a narrative. In fiction or nonfiction, quotation marks indicate a speaker's exact words, and a new paragraph usually indicates a change of speaker. Following is an exchange between two characters in "The Monkey's Paw" (p. 32):

> "*What's that?*" cried the old woman, starting up.
> "A rat," said the old man in shaking tones—"a rat. It passed me on the stairs."

Quotation marks are not used in *script,* the printed copy of a play. Instead, the dialogue follows the name of the speaker, as in this example from *Julius Caesar* (p. 892):

> **PORTIA.** Is Caesar yet gone to the Capitol?

DICTION *Diction* refers to an author's choice of words, especially with regard to range of vocabulary, use of slang and colloquial language, and level of formality. This sentence from "The Masque of the Red Death" (p. 372) is an example of formal diction containing many words derived from Latin: "This was an extensive and magnificent structure, the creation of the prince's own eccentric yet august taste."

See also **Connotation** and **Denotation.**

DIRECT CHARACTERIZATION
See **Characterization.**

DRAMA A *drama* is a story written to be performed by actors. The script of a drama is made up of *dialogue*—the words the actors say—and *stage directions,* which are descriptions of how and where action happens.

The drama's *setting* is the time and place in which the action occurs. It is indicated by one or more sets, including furniture and backdrops, that suggest interior or exterior scenes. *Props* are objects, such as a sword or a cup of tea, that are used onstage.

At the beginning of most plays, a brief *exposition* gives the audience some background information about the characters and the situation. Just as in a story or novel, the plot of a drama is built around characters in conflict.

Dramas are divided into large units called *acts,* which are divided into smaller units called *scenes.* A long play may include many sets that change with the scenes, or it may indicate a change of scene with lighting. *Julius Caesar* (p. 892) is a play in five acts.

See also **Dialogue, Genre, Stage Directions,** and **Tragedy.**

DRAMATIC IRONY See *Irony.*

DRAMATIC MONOLOGUE A *dramatic monologue* is a poem in which a character reveals himself or herself by speaking to a silent listener or thinking aloud.

DRAMATIC POETRY *Dramatic poetry* is poetry that utilizes the techniques of drama. The dialogue between the bride and the bridegroom at the end of "The Bridegroom" (p. 642) is an example.

END RHYME See *Rhyme.*

EPIC An *epic* is a long narrative poem about the deeds of gods or heroes. *Sundiata: An Epic of Old Mali* (p. 1094) and the *Ramayana* (p. 1108) are examples of the genre.

An epic is elevated in style and usually follows certain patterns. In Greek epics and in the epics modeled after them, the poet begins by announcing the subject and asking a Muse—one of the nine goddesses of the arts, literature, and sciences—to help.

An *epic hero* is the larger-than-life central character in an epic. Through behavior and deeds, the epic hero displays qualities that are valued by the society in which the epic originated.

See also **Epic Simile** and **Narrative Poem.**

EPIC SIMILE An *epic simile,* also called **Homeric simile,** is an elaborate comparison of unlike subjects. In this example from the *Odyssey,* Homer compares the bodies of men killed by Odysseus to a fisherman's catch heaped up on the shore:

> Think of a catch that fishermen haul in to a
> half-moon bay
> in a fine-meshed net from the whitecaps of the sea:
> how all are poured out on the sand, in throes
> for the salt sea,
> twitching their cold lives away in Helios' fiery air:
> so lay the suitors heaped on one another.

See also **Figurative Language** and **Simile.**

EPIPHANY An *epiphany* is a character's sudden flash of insight into a conflict or situation. At the end of the poem "The Fish" (p. 650), the speaker has an epiphany that causes her to release the fish.

ESSAY An *essay* is a short nonfiction work about a particular subject. While classification is difficult, five types of essays are sometimes identified.

A *descriptive essay* seeks to convey an impression about a person, place, or object.

An *expository essay* gives information, discusses ideas, or explains a process. In "The Spider and the Wasp"(p. 464), Alexander Petrunkevitch compares and contrasts the two creatures mentioned in the title.

A *narrative essay* tells a true story. In "The Dog That Bit People" (p. 525), James Thurber tells the story of a troublesome pet. An *autobiographical essay* is a narrative essay in which the writer tells a story from his or her own life.

A *persuasive essay* tries to convince readers to do something or to accept the writer's point of view. In "Keep Memory Alive" (p. 542), Elie Wiesel argues the importance of speaking out against evil.

See also ***Description, Exposition, Genre, Narration, Nonfiction,*** and ***Persuasion.***

EXPOSITION ***Exposition*** is writing or speech that explains a process or presents information. In the plot of a story or drama, the exposition is the part of the work that introduces the characters, the setting, and the basic situation.

See also ***Plot.***

EXPOSITORY ESSAY See ***Essay.***

EXTENDED METAPHOR In an ***extended metaphor,*** as in regular metaphor, a writer speaks or writes of a subject as though it were something else. An extended metaphor sustains the comparison for several lines or for an entire poem. In *Julius Caesar* (p. 892), Brutus uses an extended metaphor in Act II, Scene i, lines 21–27, when he speaks of "ambition's ladder."

See also ***Figurative Language*** and ***Metaphor.***

FALLING ACTION See ***Plot.***

FANTASY A ***fantasy*** is a work of highly imaginative writing that contains elements not found in real life. Examples of fantasy include stories that involve supernatural elements, such as fairy tales, and stories that deal with imaginary places and creatures.

See also ***Science Fiction.***

FICTION ***Fiction*** is prose writing that tells about imaginary characters and events. The term is usually used for

novels and short stories, but it also applies to dramas and narrative poetry. Some writers rely on their imaginations alone to create their works of fiction. Others base their fiction on actual events and people, to which they add invented characters, dialogue, and plot situations.

See also ***Genre, Narrative,*** and ***Nonfiction.***

FIGURATIVE LANGUAGE ***Figurative language*** is writing or speech not meant to be interpreted literally. It is often used to create vivid impressions by setting up comparisons between dissimilar things.

Some frequently used figures of speech are ***metaphors, similes,*** and ***personifications.***

See also ***Literal Language.***

FLASHBACK A ***flashback*** is a means by which authors present material that occurred earlier than the present time of the narrative. Authors may include this material in the form of a characters' memories, dreams, or accounts of past events, or they may simply shift their narrative back to the earlier time.

FOIL A ***foil*** is a character who provides a contrast to another character. In *Julius Caesar* (p. 892), the impetuous and resentful Cassius is a foil for the cooler and more rational Brutus.

FOOT See ***Meter.***

FORESHADOWING ***Foreshadowing*** is the use in a literary work of clues that suggest events that have yet to occur. This technique helps to create suspense, keeping readers wondering about what will happen next.

FREE VERSE ***Free verse*** is poetry not written in a regular pattern of meter or rhyme. Cornelius Eady's "The Poetic Interpretation of the Twist" (p. 633) is an example.

GENRE A ***genre*** is a category or form of literature. Literature is commonly divided into three major types of writing: poetry, prose, and drama. For each type, there are several distinct genres, as follows:

1. Poetry: Lyric Poetry, Concrete Poetry, Dramatic Poetry, Narrative Poetry, and Epic Poetry
2. Prose: Fiction (Novels and Short Stories) and Nonfiction (Biography, Autobiography, Letters, Essays, and Reports)
3. Drama: Serious Drama and Tragedy, Comic Drama, Melodrama, and Farce

See also ***Drama, Poetry,*** and ***Prose.***

HAIKU The ***haiku*** is a three-line verse form. The first and third lines of a haiku each have five syllables. The second line has seven syllables. A haiku seeks to convey a single vivid emotion by means of images from nature.

HOMERIC SIMILE See *Epic Simile.*

HYPERBOLE A *hyperbole* is a deliberate exaggeration or overstatement. In Mark Twain's "The Notorious Jumping Frog of Calaveras County," the claim that Jim Smiley would follow a bug as far as Mexico to win a bet is a hyperbole. As this example shows, hyperboles are often used for comic effect.

IAMB See *Meter.*

IDIOM An *idiom* or *idiomatic expression* is an expression that is characteristic of a language, region, community or class of people. Idiomatic expressions mean something more than or different from the meaning of the words making them up. Following is an example of an idiom from T. H. White's *The Once and Future King* (p. 1156): "Think what people will say about us, if we do not go and *have a shot* at that sword."

See also *Dialect.*

IMAGE An *image* is a word or phrase that appeals to one or more of the five senses—sight, hearing, touch, taste, or smell. Writers use images to re-create sensory experiences in words.

See also *Description.*

IMAGERY *Imagery* is the descriptive or figurative language used in literature to create word pictures for the reader. These pictures, or images, are created by details of sight, sound, taste, touch, smell, or movement.

INDIRECT CHARACTERIZATION
See *Characterization.*

INTERNAL RHYME See *Rhyme.*

IRONY *Irony* is the general term for literary techniques that portray differences between appearance and reality, or expectation and result. In *verbal irony,* words are used to suggest the opposite of what is meant. In *dramatic irony,* there is a contradiction between what a character thinks and what the reader or audience knows to be true. In *irony of situation,* an event occurs that directly contradicts the expectations of the characters, the reader, or the audience.

LITERAL LANGUAGE *Literal language* uses words in their ordinary senses. It is the opposite of *figurative language.* If you tell someone standing on a diving board to jump in, you speak literally. If you tell someone on the street to "go jump in a lake," you are speaking figuratively.

See also *Figurative Language.*

LYRIC POEM A *lyric poem* is a poem written in highly musical language that expresses the thoughts, observations, and feelings of a single speaker.

MAIN CHARACTER See *Character.*

METAPHOR A *metaphor* is a figure of speech in which one thing is spoken of as though it were something else. Unlike a simile, which compares two things using *like* or *as,* a metaphor implies a comparison between them. In "A Tree Telling of Orpheus" (p. 659), the speaker is a tree and describes music as if it were water: "my roots felt music moisten them."

See also *Extended Metaphor* and *Figurative Language.*

METER The *meter* of a poem is its rhythmical pattern. This pattern is determined by the number and arrangements of stressed syllables, or beats, in each line. To describe the meter of a poem, you must scan its lines. Scanning involves marking the stressed and unstressed syllables, as shown with the following two lines from *Julius Caesar* (p. 892):

> Wĕ bóth hăve féd ăs wéll, aňd wé căn bóth
>
> Eňdúre thĕ wíntĕr's cóld ăs wéll ăs hé . . .

As you can see, each stressed syllable is marked with a slanted line (´) and each unstressed syllable with a horseshoe symbol (˘). The stressed and unstressed syllables are then divided by vertical lines (|) into groups called *feet.* The following types of feet are common in English poetry:

1. *Iamb:* a foot with one unstressed syllable followed by a stressed syllable, as in the word "again"
2. *Trochee:* a foot with one stressed syllable followed by an unstressed syllable, as in the word "wonder"
3. *Anapest:* a foot with two unstressed syllables followed by one strong stress, as in the phrase "on the beach"
4. *Dactyl:* a foot with one strong stress followed by two unstressed syllables, as in the word "wonderful"
5. *Spondee:* a foot with two strong stresses, as in the word "spacewalk"

Depending on the type of foot that is most common in them, lines of poetry are described as *iambic, trochaic, anapestic,* and so forth.

Lines are also described in terms of the number of feet that occur in them, as follows:

1. *Monometer:* verse written in one-foot lines
   All things
   Must pass
   Away.

2. *Dimeter:* verse written in two-foot lines
   Thomas | Jefferson
   What do | you say
   Under the | gravestone
   Hidden | away?
   —Rosemary and Stephen Vincent Benét,
   "Thomas Jefferson, 1743–1826"

3. *Trimeter:* verse written in three-foot lines
   I know | not whom | I meet
   I know | not where | I go.

4. *Tetrameter:* verse written in four-foot lines

5. *Pentameter:* verse written in five-foot lines

6. *Hexameter:* verse written in six-foot lines

7. *Heptameter:* verse written in seven-foot lines

Blank verse, used by Shakespeare in *Julius Caesar* (p. 892), is poetry written in unrhymed iambic pentameter.

Free verse, used by Cornelius Eady in "The Poetic Interpretation of the Twist" (p. 633), is poetry that does not follow a regular pattern of meter and rhyme.

MONOLOGUE A *monologue* in a play is a long speech by one character that, unlike a *soliloquy*, is addressed to another character or characters. An example from Shakespeare's *Julius Caesar* (p. 892) is the famous speech by Antony to the Roman people in Act III, Scene ii. It begins, "Friends, Romans, countrymen, lend me your ears. . . ." (line 74).

See also **Soliloquy.**

MOOD *Mood,* or **atmosphere,** is the feeling created in the reader by a literary work or passage. The mood is often suggested by descriptive details. Often the mood can be described in a single word, such as lighthearted, frightening, or despairing. Notice how this passage from Edgar Allan Poe's "The Masque of the Red Death" (p. 372) contributes to an eerie, fearful mood:

> And now was acknowledged the presence of the Red Death. He had come like a thief in the night. And one by one dropped the revelers in the blood-bedewed halls

of their revel, and died each in the despairing posture of his fall.

See also **Tone.**

MORAL A *moral* is a lesson taught by a literary work, especially a fable—many fables, for example, have a stated moral at the end. It is customary, however, to discuss contemporary works in terms of the themes they explore, rather than a moral that they teach.

MOTIVATION *Motivation* is a reason that explains or partially explains why a character thinks, feels, acts, or behaves in a certain way. Motivation results from a combination of the character's personality and the situation he or she must deal with. In *Antigone* (p. 814), the protagonist is motivated by loyalty to her dead brother and reverence for the laws of the gods.

See also **Character** and **Characterization.**

MYTH A *myth* is a *fictional* tale that describes the actions of gods and heroes or explains the causes of natural phenomena. Unlike legends, myths emphasize supernatural rather than historical elements. Many cultures have collections of myths, and the most familiar in the Western world are those of the ancient Greeks and Romans. "Prometheus and the First People" (p. 1066) is a retelling of a famous ancient Greek myth.

See also **Oral Tradition.**

NARRATION *Narration* is writing that tells a story. The act of telling a story in speech is also called narration. Novels and short stories are fictional narratives. Nonfiction works—such as news stories, biographies, and autobiographies—are also narratives. A narrative poem tells a story in verse.

See also **Anecdote, Essay, Narrative Poem, Nonfiction, Novel,** and **Short Story.**

NARRATIVE A *narrative* is a story told in fiction, nonfiction, poetry, or drama.

See also **Narration.**

NARRATIVE ESSAY See **Essay.**

NARRATIVE POEM A *narrative poem* is one that tells a story. Alexander Pushkin's "The Bridegroom" (p. 642) is a narrative poem that tells how Natasha, a merchant's daughter, outwits a thief and murderer.

See also **Dramatic Poetry, Epic,** and **Narration.**

NARRATOR A *narrator* is a speaker or character who tells a story. The writer's choice of narrator determines the story's *point of view*, or the perspective from which the story is told. By using a consistent point of view, a writer controls the amount and type of information revealed to the reader.

When a character in the story tells the story, that character is a *first-person narrator*. This narrator may be a major character, a minor character, or just a witness. Readers see only what this character sees, hear only what he or she hears, and so on. Stephen Vincent Benét's "By the Waters of Babylon" (p. 314) is told by a first-person narrator. Viewing unfolding events from this character's perspective, the reader shares in his discoveries and feels more suspense than another point of view would provide.

When a voice outside the story narrates, the story has a *third-person narrator*. An *omniscient*, or all-knowing, third-person narrator can tell readers what any character thinks and feels. For example, in "The Monkey's Paw" (p. 32), we know the thoughts of the father, the wife, and the son. A *limited third-person narrator* sees the world through one character's eyes and reveals only that character's thoughts. In Jack Finney's "Contents of the Dead Man's Pocket" (p. 118), the narrator reveals only Tom's thoughts and feelings.

See also *Speaker.*

NONFICTION *Nonfiction* is prose writing that presents and explains ideas or that tells about real people, places, ideas, or events. To be classified as nonfiction, a work must be true. Dorothy West's "The Sun Parlor" (p. 490) is a true account of events related to a particular room in a house.

See also *Autobiography, Biography,* and *Essay.*

NOVEL A *novel* is a long work of fiction. It has a plot that explores characters in conflict. A novel may also have one or more subplots, or minor stories, and several themes.

OCTAVE See *Stanza.*

ONOMATOPOEIA *Onomatopoeia* is the use of words that imitate sounds. *Whirr, thud, sizzle,* and *hiss* are typical examples. Writers can deliberately choose words that contribute to a desired sound effect.

ORAL TRADITION The *oral tradition* is the retelling of songs, stories, and poems passed orally, or by spoken word, from generation to generation. Many folk songs, ballads, fairy tales, legends, and myths originated in the oral tradition.

See also *Myth.*

OXYMORON An *oxymoron* is a combination of words that contradict each other. Examples are "deafening silence," "honest thief," "wise fool," and "bittersweet." This device is effective when the apparent contradiction reveals a deeper truth.

PARADOX A *paradox* is a statement that seems contradictory but that actually may express a deeper truth. Because a paradox is surprising, it catches the reader's attention.

PARALLELISM See *Rhetorical Devices.*

PERSONIFICATION *Personification* is a type of figurative language in which a nonhuman subject is given human characteristics. Denise Levertov personifies a tree in her poem "A Tree Telling of Orpheus" (p. 659). In fact, the tree is the speaker in this poem: "I listened, and language came into my roots . . ."

See also *Figurative Language.*

PERSUASION *Persuasion* is writing or speech that attempts to convince the reader to adopt a particular opinion or course of action.

An *argument* is a logical way of presenting a belief, conclusion, or stance. A good argument is supported with reasoning and evidence.

PERSUASIVE ESSAY See *Essay.*

PLOT *Plot* is the sequence of events in a literary work. In most novels, dramas, short stories, and narrative poems, the plot involves both characters and a central conflict. The plot usually begins with an **exposition** that introduces the setting, the characters, and the basic situation. This is followed by the *inciting incident*, which introduces the central conflict. The conflict then increases during the *development* until it reaches a high point of interest or suspense, the **climax.** All the events leading up to the climax make up the *rising action*. The climax is followed by the *falling action*, which leads to the *denouement*, or *resolution*, in which the conflict is resolved and in which a general insight may be conveyed.

POETRY *Poetry* is one of the three major types of literature, the others being prose and drama. Most poems make use of highly concise, musical, and emotionally charged language. Many also make use of imagery, figurative language, and special devices of sound such as rhyme. Poems are often divided into lines and stanzas and often employ regular rhythmical patterns, or meters. Poetry that does not follow a regular metrical pattern is called **free verse.**

See also **Genre.**

POINT OF VIEW See **Narrator.**

PROSE **Prose** is the ordinary form of written language. Most writing that is not poetry, drama, or song is considered prose. Prose is one of the major categories of literature and occurs in two forms: fiction and nonfiction.

See also **Fiction, Genre,** and **Nonfiction.**

PROTAGONIST The **protagonist** is the main character in a literary work.

See also **Antagonist** and **Character.**

PUN A **pun** is a play on words involving a word with two or more different meanings or two words that sound alike but have different meanings. In *Julius Caesar* (p. 892), there is a pun on the phrase *mend you* (Act I, Scene i, lines 17–18): "yet if you be out [angry], sir, I can mend you." The speaker is a cobbler and by *mend you* he means both "mend your shoes" and "improve your disposition."

QUATRAIN A **quatrain** is a stanza, or section, of a poem made up of four lines, usually with a definite rhythm and rhyme scheme.

REPETITION **Repetition** is the use of any element of language—a sound, a word, a phrase, a clause, or a sentence—more than once.

Poets use many kinds of repetition. **Alliteration, assonance, consonance, rhyme,** and **rhythm** are repetitions of certain sounds and sound patterns. A *refrain* is a repeated line or group of lines. In both prose and poetry, repetition is used for musical effects and for emphasis.

See also **Alliteration, Assonance, Consonance, Rhyme,** and **Rhythm.**

RESOLUTION See **Plot.**

RHETORICAL DEVICES **Rhetorical devices** are special patterns of words and ideas that create emphasis and stir emotion, especially in speeches or other oral presentations. *Parallelism*, for example, is the repetition of a grammatical structure in order to create a rhythm and make words more memorable. In "Keep Memory Alive" (p. 548), Elie Wiesel uses parallelism: "Neutrality helps the oppressor, never the victim. Silence encourages the tormentor, never the tormented."

Other common rhetorical devices include *restatement*, expressing the same idea in different words, and *rhetorical questions*, questions with obvious answers.

RHYME **Rhyme** is the repetition of sounds at the ends of words. *End rhyme* occurs when the rhyming words come at the ends of lines, as in "The Desired Swan Song" by Samuel Taylor Coleridge:

> Swans sing before they die—'twere no bad thing
> Should certain persons die before they sing.

Internal rhyme occurs when one of the rhyming words appears within a line, as in these lines from "The Waking" (p. 685):

> God bless the Ground! I shall walk softly *there*,
> And learn by going *where* I have to go.

Exact rhyme involves the repetition of the same final vowel and consonant sounds in words like *ball* and *hall*. *Slant rhyme* involves the repetition of words that sound alike but do not rhyme exactly, like *grove* and *love*.

See also **Repetition** and **Rhyme Scheme.**

RHYME SCHEME A **rhyme scheme** is a regular pattern of rhyming words in a poem. The rhyme scheme of a poem is indicated by using different letters of the alphabet for each new rhyme. In an *aabb* stanza, for example, line 1 rhymes with line 2 and line 3 rhymes with line 4. "Meeting at Night" (p. 744) uses an *abccba* rhyme scheme in each of its two stanzas:

The gray sea and the long black land;	a
And the yellow half-moon large and low;	b
And the startled little waves that leap	c
In fiery ringlets from their sleep,	c
As I gain the cove with pushing prow,	b
And quench its speed i' the slushy sand.	a

Many poems use the same pattern of rhymes, though not the same rhymes, in each stanza.

See also **Rhyme.**

RHYTHM **Rhythm** is the pattern of *beats*, or *stresses*, in spoken or written language. Some poems follow a very specific pattern, or meter, whereas prose and free verse may use the natural rhythms of everyday speech.

See also **Meter.**

RISING ACTION See **Plot.**

ROUND CHARACTER See **Character.**

SATIRE A *satire* is a literary work that ridicules the foolishness and faults of individuals, an institution, society, or even humanity in general.

SCENE See *Drama.*

SCIENCE FICTION *Science fiction* is writing that tells about imaginary events involving science or technology. Many science-fiction stories are set in the future. C. J. Cherryh's science-fiction story "The Threads of Time" (p. 229) plays with the dimension of time.

See also *Fantasy.*

SENSORY LANGUAGE *Sensory language* is writing or speech that appeals to one or more of the senses.

See also *Image.*

SESTET See *Stanza.*

SET See *Drama.*

SETTING The *setting* of a literary work is the time and place of the action. Time can include not only the historical period—past, present, or future—but also a specific year, season, or time of day. Place may involve not only the geographical place—a region, country, state, or town—but also the social, economic, or cultural environment.

In some stories, setting serves merely as a backdrop for action, a context in which the characters move and speak. In others, however, setting is a crucial element.

See also *Mood.*

SHORT STORY A *short story* is a brief work of fiction. In most short stories, one main character faces a conflict that is resolved in the plot of the story. Great craftsmanship must go into the writing of a good story, for it has to accomplish its purpose in relatively few words.

See also *Fiction* and *Genre.*

SIMILE A *simile* is a figure of speech in which the words like or as are used to compare two apparently dissimilar items. The comparison, however, surprises the reader into a fresh perception by finding an unexpected likeness. In "The Guitar" (p. 648), for example, García Lorca says that the guitar "weeps monotonously / As weeps the water, / As weeps the wind / Over snow."

SOLILOQUY A *soliloquy* is a long speech expressing the thoughts of a character alone on stage. In William Shakespeare's *Julius Caesar* (p. 892), Brutus delivers a soliloquy in which he confirms and justifies his participation in the plot to assassinate Caesar (Act II, Scene i, lines 10–34): "It must be by his death . . ."

See also *Monologue.*

SONNET A *sonnet* is a fourteen-line lyric poem, usually written in rhymed iambic pentameter. The *English,* or *Shakespearean,* sonnet consists of three quatrains (four-line stanzas) and a couplet (two lines), usually rhyming *abab cdcd efef gg.* The couplet usually comments on the ideas contained in the preceding twelve lines. The sonnet is usually not printed with the stanzas divided, but a reader can see distinct ideas in each. (See Sonnet 18 by William Shakespeare on page 686.)

The *Italian,* or *Petrarchan,* sonnet consists of an octave (eight-line stanza) and a sestet (six-line stanza). Often, the octave rhymes *abbaabba* and the sestet rhymes *cdecde.* The octave states a theme or asks a question. The sestet comments on the theme or answers the question.

See also *Lyric Poem; Meter;* and *Stanza.*

SPEAKER The *speaker* is the imaginary voice assumed by the writer of a poem. In many poems, the speaker is not identified by name. When reading a poem, remember that the speaker within the poem may be a person, an animal, a thing, or an abstraction. The speaker in the following stanza by Emily Dickinson is a person who has died:

> Because I could not stop for Death—
> He kindly stopped for me—
> The Carriage held but just Ourselves—
> And Immortality.

STAGE DIRECTIONS *Stage directions* are notes included in a drama to describe how the work is to be performed or staged. These instructions are printed in italics and are not spoken aloud. They are used to describe sets, lighting, sound effects, and the appearance, personalities, and movements of characters.

See also *Drama.*

STANZA A *stanza* is a repeated grouping of two or more lines in a poem that often share a pattern of rhythm and rhyme. Stanzas are sometimes named according to the number of lines they have—for example, a *couplet,* two lines; a *quatrain,* four lines; a *sestet,* six lines; and an *octave,* eight lines.

See also *Sonnet.*

STATIC CHARACTER See *Character.*

STYLE *Style* refers to an author's unique way of writing. Elements determining style include diction; tone; characteristic use of figurative language, dialect, or rhythmic devices; and typical grammatical structures and patterns.

See also *Diction* and *Tone.*

SURPRISE ENDING A *surprise ending* is a conclusion that violates the expectations of the reader but in a way that is both logical and believable.

O. Henry's "One Thousand Dollars" (p. 308) and Saki's "The Open Window" (p. 195) have surprise endings. Both authors were masters of this form.

SYMBOL A *symbol* is a character, place, thing or event that stands for something else, often an abstract idea. For example, a flag is a piece of cloth, but it also represents the idea of a country. Writers sometimes use conventional symbols like flags. Frequently, however, they create symbols of their own through emphasis or repetition. In "The Garden of Stubborn Cats" (p. 384), for example, the cats come to symbolize nature's stubborn resistance to human development.

THEME A *theme* is a central message or insight into life revealed through a literary work.

The theme of a literary work may be stated directly or implied. When the theme of a work is implied, readers think about what the work suggests about people or life.

Archetypal themes are those that occur in folklore and literature across the world and throughout history. The hero who makes civilization possible, the theme of "Prometheus and the First People" (p. 1066), is an example of an archetypal theme.

TONE The *tone* of a literary work is the writer's attitude toward his or her audience and subject. The tone can often be described by a single adjective, such as *formal* or *informal, serious* or *playful, bitter* or *ironic.* When Valenzuela discusses the fate of Juan in "The Censors" (p. 410), she uses an ironic tone: ". . . another victim of his devotion to his work."

See also *Mood.*

TRAGEDY A *tragedy* is a work of literature, especially a play, that tells of a catastrophe, a disaster or great misfortune, for the main character. In ancient Greek drama, the main character was always a significant person—a king or a hero—and the cause of the tragedy was often a tragic flaw, or weakness, in his or her character. In modern drama, the main character can be an ordinary person, and the cause of the tragedy can be some evil in society itself. Tragedy not only arouses fear and pity in the audience, but also, in some cases, conveys a sense of the grandeur and nobility of the human spirit.

Shakespeare's *Julius Caesar* (p. 892) is a tragedy. Brutus suffers from the tragic flaw of blindness to reality and people's motives. His noble-mindedness is almost a form of arrogance. This flaw ultimately leads to his death.

See also *Drama.*

UNDERSTATEMENT An *understatement* is a figure of speech in which the stated meaning is purposely less than (or "under") what is really meant. It is the opposite of *hyperbole,* which is a deliberate exaggeration.

UNIVERSAL THEME A *universal theme* is a message about life that can be understood by most cultures. Many folk tales and examples of classic literature address universal themes such as the importance of courage, the effects of honesty, or the danger of greed.

VERBAL IRONY See *Irony.*

VILLANELLE A *villanelle* is a nineteen-line lyric poem written in five three-line stanzas and ending in a four-line stanza. It uses two rhymes and repeats two refrain lines that appear initially in the first and third lines of the first stanza. These lines then appear alternately as the third line of subsequent three-line stanzas and, finally, as the last two lines of the poem. Theodore Roethke's "The Waking" (p. 684) is a villanelle.

VOICE *Voice* is a writer's distinctive "sound" or way of "speaking" on the page. It is related to such elements as word choice, sentence structure, and tone. It is similar to an individual's speech style and can be described in the same way—fast, slow, blunt, meandering, breathless, and so on.

Voice resembles *style,* an author's typical way of writing, but style usually refers to a quality that can be found throughout an author's body of work, while an author's voice may sometimes vary from work to work.

See also *Style.*

Tips for Discussing Literature

As you read and study literature, discussion with other readers can help you understand, enjoy, and develop interpretations of what you read. Use the following tips to practice good speaking and listening skills while participating in group discussions of literature.

- ## Understand the purpose of your discussion

  When you discuss literature, your purpose is to broaden your understanding and appreciation of a work by testing your own ideas and hearing the ideas of others. Stay focused on the literature you are discussing and keep your comments relevant to that literature. Starting with one focus question will help to keep your discussion on track.

- ## Communicate effectively

  Effective communication requires thinking before speaking. Plan the points that you want to make and decide how you will express them. Organize these points in logical order and cite details from the work to support your ideas. Jot down informal notes to help keep your ideas focused.

  Remember to speak clearly, pronouncing words slowly and carefully so that others can understand your points. Also, keep in mind that some literature touches readers deeply—be aware of the possibility of counterproductive emotional responses and work to control them. Negative emotional responses can also be conveyed through body language, so work to demonstrate respect in your demeanor as well as in your words.

- ## Encourage everyone to participate

  While some people are comfortable participating in discussions, others are less eager to speak up in groups. However, everyone should work to contribute thoughts and ideas. To encourage the entire group's participation, try the following strategies:

  - If you enjoy speaking, avoid monopolizing the conversation. After sharing your ideas, encourage others to share theirs.
  - Try different roles. For example, have everyone take turns being the facilitator or host of the discussion.
  - Use a prop, such as a book or gavel. Pass the prop around the group, allowing whomever is holding the prop to have the floor.

- ## Make relevant contributions

  Especially when responding to a short story, a poem, or a novel, avoid simply summarizing the plot. Instead, consider *what* you think might happen next, *why* events take place as they do, or *how* a writer provokes a response in you. Let your ideas inspire deeper thought or discussion about the literature.

- ## Consider other ideas and interpretations

  A work of literature can generate a wide variety of responses in different readers—and that can make your discussions exciting. Be open to the idea that many interpretations can be valid. To support your own ideas, point to the events, descriptions, characters, or other literary elements in the work that produced your interpretation. To consider someone else's ideas, decide whether details in the work support the interpretation he or she presents. Be sure to convey your criticism of the ideas of others in a respectful and supportive manner.

- ## Ask questions and extend the contributions of others

  Get in the habit of asking questions to help you clarify your understanding of another reader's ideas. You can also use questions to call attention to possible areas of confusion, to points that are open to debate, or to errors.

  In addition, offer elaboration of the points that others make by providing examples and illustrations. To move a discussion forward, pause occasionally to summarize and evaluate tentative conclusions reached by the group members. Then, continue the discussion with a fresh understanding of the material and ideas you have already covered.

- ## Manage differing opinions and views

  Each participant brings his or her own personality, experiences, ideas, cultural background, likes and dislikes to the experience of reading, making disagreement almost inevitable. As differences arise, be sensitive to each individual's point of view. Do not personalize disagreements, but keep them focused on the literature or ideas under discussion.

  When you meet with a group to discuss literature, use a chart like the one shown to analyze the discussion.

Work Being Discussed:	
Focus Question:	
Your Response:	Another Student's Response:
Supporting Evidence:	Supporting Evidence:
One New Idea That You Considered About the Work During the Discussion:	

Literary Criticism

Criticism is writing that explores the meaning and techniques of literary works, usually in order to evaluate them. Writing criticism can help you think through your experience of a work of literature and can also help others deepen their own understanding. All literary criticism shares similar goals:

- **Making Connections** within or between works, or between a work of literature and its context
- **Making Distinctions** or showing differences between elements of a single work or aspects of two or more works
- **Achieving Insights** that were not apparent from a superficial reading
- **Making a Judgment** about the quality or value of a literary work

Critics use various **theories of literary criticism** to understand, appreciate, and evaluate literature. Some theories focus on the context of the work while others focus on the work itself. Sometimes critics combine one or more theories. These charts show a few examples of the many theories of criticism:

Focus on Contexts	
Human Experience	**Mythic Criticism** Explores universal situations, characters, and symbols called archetypes as they appear in a literary work
Culture and History	**Historical Criticism** Analyzes how circumstances or ideas of an era influence a work
Author's Life	**Biographical Criticism** Explains how the author's life sheds light on the work

Focus on the Work Itself
Formal Criticism Shows how the work reflects characteristics of the genre, or literary type, to which it belongs

Examples of Literary Theories in Action

- **Mythic Criticism:** discussing how the Greek myth "Prometheus and the First People," p. 1066, reveals Prometheus as an archetypal character
- **Historical Criticism:** showing how William Shakespeare was influenced by Elizabethan concepts of nature and politics in *Julius Caesar*, p. 892
- **Biographical Criticism:** showing how James Thurber's family relationships influenced the theme of "The Dog That Bit People," p. 525
- **Formal Criticism:** analyzing how "Contents of the Dead Man's Pocket," p. 118, combines short-story elements like plot, suspense, setting, character, and theme

Literary Movements

Our literary heritage has been shaped by a number of *literary movements,* directions in literature characterized by shared assumptions, beliefs, and practices. This chart shows, in chronological order, some important literary movements. While these movements developed at particular historical moments, all of them may still influence individual writers working today.

Movement	Beliefs and Practices	Examples
Classicism Europe during the Renaissance (c. 1300–1650)	• Looks to classical literature of ancient Greece and Rome as models • Values logic, clarity, balance, and restraint • Prefers "ordered" nature of parks and gardens	the clarity and restraint of Robert Frost's verse ("Mowing," p. 658)
Romanticism Europe during the late 1700s and the early 1800s	• Rebels against Classicism • Values imagination and emotion • Focuses on everyday life	the celebration of the natural world in Rachel Carson's writings ("The Marginal World," p. 156)
Realism Europe and America from the mid-1800s to the 1890s	• Rebels against Romanticism's search for the ideal • Focuses on everyday life	the faithful rendering of Russian life in Anton Chekhov's fiction ("A Problem," p. 256)
Naturalism Europe and America during the late 1800s and early 1900s	• Assumes people cannot choose their fate but are shaped by psychological and social forces • Views society as a competitive jungle	the indifference to human life that characters show in Guy de Maupassant's fiction ("Two Friends," p. 1233)
Modernism Worldwide between 1890 and 1945	• In response to WWI, questions human reason • Focuses on studies of the unconscious and the art of primitive peoples • Experiments with language and form	the experiments with free verse in Carl Sandburg's poetry ("Jazz Fantasia," p. 739)
Post-Modernism Worldwide after 1945; still prevalent today	• Believes works of art comment on themselves • Finds inspiration in information technology	the self-consciousness about tradition in John Phillip Santos's nonfiction (from *Places Left Unfinished at the Time of Creation,* p. 1053)

Tips for Improving Reading Fluency

When you were younger, you learned to read. Then, you read to expand your experiences or for pure enjoyment. Now, you are expected to read to learn. As you progress in school, you are given more and more material to read. The tips on these pages will help you improve your reading fluency, or your ability to read easily, smoothly, and expressively.

Keeping Your Concentration

One common problem that readers face is the loss of concentration. When you are reading an assignment, you might find yourself rereading the same sentence several times without really understanding it. The first step in changing this behavior is to notice that you do it. Becoming an active, aware reader will help you get the most from your assignments. Practice using these strategies:

- Cover what you have already read with a note card as you go along. Then, you will not be able to reread without noticing that you are doing it.

- Set a purpose for reading beyond just completing the assignment. Then, read actively by pausing to ask yourself questions about the material as you read.

- Use the Reading Strategy instruction and notes that appear with each selection in this textbook.

- Stop reading after a specified period of time (for example, 5 minutes) and summarize what you have read. To help you with this strategy, use the Reading Check questions that appear with each selection in this textbook. Reread to find any answers you do not know.

Reading Phrases

Fluent readers read phrases rather than individual words. Reading this way will speed up your reading and improve your comprehension. Here are some useful ideas:

- Experts recommend rereading as a strategy to increase fluency. Choose a passage of text that is neither too hard nor too easy. Read the same passage aloud several times until you can read it smoothly. When you can read the passage fluently, pick another passage and keep practicing.

- Read aloud into a tape recorder. Then, listen to the recording, noting your accuracy, pacing, and expression. You can also read aloud and share feedback with a partner.

- Use the *Prentice Hall Listening to Literature* audiotapes or CDs to hear the selections read aloud. Read along silently in your textbook, noticing how the reader uses his or her voice and emphasizes certain words and phrases.

Understanding Key Vocabulary

If you do not understand some of the words in an assignment, you may miss out on important concepts. Therefore, it is helpful to keep a dictionary nearby when you are reading. Follow these steps:

- Before you begin reading, scan the text for unfamiliar words or terms. Find out what those words mean before you begin reading.
- Use context—the surrounding words, phrases, and sentences—to help you determine the meanings of unfamiliar words.
- If you are unable to understand the meaning through context, refer to the dictionary.

Paying Attention to Punctuation

When you read, pay attention to punctuation. Commas, periods, exclamation points, semicolons, and colons tell you when to pause or stop. They also indicate relationships between groups of words. When you recognize these relationships, you will read with greater understanding and expression. Look at the chart below.

Punctuation Mark	Meaning
comma	brief pause
period	pause at the end of a thought
exclamation point	pause that indicates emphasis
semicolon	pause between related but distinct thoughts
colon	pause before giving explanation or examples

Using the Reading Fluency Checklist

Use the checklist below each time you read a selection in this textbook. In your Language Arts journal or notebook, note which skills you need to work on and chart your progress each week.

Reading Fluency Checklist

- ❑ Preview the text to check for difficult or unfamiliar words.
- ❑ Practice reading aloud.
- ❑ Read according to punctuation.
- ❑ Break down long sentences into the subject and its meaning.
- ❑ Read groups of words for meaning rather than reading single words.
- ❑ Read with expression (change your tone of voice to add meaning to the word).

Reading is a skill that can be improved with practice. The key to improving your fluency is to read. The more you read, the better your reading will become.

Types of Writing

Good writing can be a powerful tool used for many purposes. Writing can allow you to defend something you believe in or show how much you know about a subject. Writing can also help you share what you have experienced, imagined, thought, and felt. The three main types of writing are argument, informative/explanatory, and narrative.

Argument

When you think of the word *argument,* you might think of a disagreement between two people, but an argument is more than that. An argument is a logical way of presenting a belief, conclusion, or stance. A good argument is supported with reasoning and evidence.

Argument writing can be used for many purposes, such as to change a reader's point of view or opinion or to bring about an action or a response from a reader.

There are three main purposes for writing a formal argument:

- to change the reader's mind
- to convince the reader to accept what is written
- to motivate the reader to take action, based on what is written

The following are some types of argument writing:

Advertisements An advertisement is a planned communication meant to be seen, heard, or read. It attempts to persuade an audience to buy a product or service, accept an idea, or support a cause. Advertisements may appear in printed or broadcast form.

Several common types of advertisements are public-service announcements, billboards, merchandise ads, service ads, and political campaign literature.

Persuasive Essay A persuasive essay presents a position on an issue, urges readers to accept that position, and may encourage a specific action. An effective persuasive essay

- Explores an issue of importance to the writer
- Addresses an issue that is arguable
- Uses facts, examples, statistics, or personal experiences to support a position
- Tries to influence the audience through appeals to the readers' knowledge, experiences, or emotions
- Uses clear organization to present a logical argument

Forms of persuasion include editorials, position papers, persuasive speeches, grant proposals, advertisements, and debates.

Informative/Explanatory

Informative/explanatory writing should rely on facts to inform or explain. Informative/explanatory writing serves some closely related purposes: to increase readers' knowledge of a subject, to help readers better understand a procedure or process, or to provide readers with an enhanced comprehension of a concept. It should also feature a clear introduction, body, and conclusion. The following are some examples of informative/explanatory writing:

Cause-and-Effect Essay A cause-and-effect essay examines the relationship between events, explaining how one event or situation causes another. A successful cause-and-effect essay includes

- A discussion of a cause, event, or condition that produces a specific result
- An explanation of an effect, outcome, or result
- Evidence and examples to support the relationship between cause and effect
- A logical organization that makes the explanation clear

Comparison-and-Contrast Essay A comparison-and-contrast essay analyzes the similarities and differences between or among two or more things. An effective comparison-and-contrast essay

- Identifies a purpose for comparison and contrast
- Identifies similarities and differences between or among two or more things, people, places, or ideas
- Gives factual details about the subjects
- Uses an organizational plan suited to the topic and purpose

Descriptive Writing Descriptive writing creates a vivid picture of a person, place, thing, or event. Most descriptive writing includes

- Sensory details—sights, sounds, smells, tastes, and physical sensations
- Vivid, precise language
- Figurative language or comparisons
- Adjectives and adverbs that paint a word picture
- An organization suited to the subject

Types of descriptive writing include descriptions of ideas, observations, travel brochures, physical descriptions, functional descriptions, remembrances, and character sketches.

Problem-and-Solution Essay A problem-and-solution essay describes a problem and offers one or more solutions to it. It describes a clear set of steps to achieve a result. An effective problem-and-solution essay includes

- A clear statement of the problem, with its causes and effects summarized for the reader
- The most important aspects of the problem
- A proposal of at least one realistic solution
- Facts, statistics, data, or expert testimony to support the solution
- A clear organization that makes the relationship between problem and solution obvious

Research Writing Research writing is based on information gathered from outside sources. A research paper—a focused study of a topic—helps writers explore and connect ideas, make discoveries, and share their findings with an audience. An effective research paper

- Focuses on a specific, narrow topic, which is usually summarized in a thesis statement
- Presents relevant information from a wide variety of sources
- Uses a clear organization that includes an introduction, body, and conclusion
- Includes a bibliography or works-cited list that identifies the sources from which the information was drawn

Other types of writing that depend on accurate and insightful research include multimedia presentations, statistical reports, annotated bibliographies, and experiment journals.

Workplace Writing Workplace writing is probably the format you will use most after you finish school. In general, workplace writing is fact-based and meant to communicate specific information in a structured format. Effective workplace writing

- Communicates information concisely
- Includes details that provide necessary information and anticipate potential questions
- Is error-free and neatly presented

Common types of workplace writing include business letters, memorandums, résumés, forms, and applications.

Narrative

Narrative writing conveys experience, either real or imaginary, and uses time to provide structure. It can be used to inform, instruct, persuade, or entertain. Whenever writers tell a story, they are using narrative writing. Most types of narrative writing share certain elements, such as characters, a setting, a sequence of events, and, often, a theme. The following are some types of narration:

Autobiographical Writing Autobiographical writing tells a true story about an important period, experience, or relationship in the writer's life. Effective autobiographical writing includes

- A series of events that involve the writer as the main character
- Details, thoughts, feelings, and insights from the writer's perspective
- A conflict or an event that affects the writer
- A logical organization that tells the story clearly
- Insights that the writer gained from the experience

Types of autobiographical writing include autobiographical sketches, personal narratives, reflective essays, eyewitness accounts, and memoirs.

Short Story A short story is a brief, creative narrative. Most short stories include

- Details that establish the setting in time and place
- A main character who undergoes a change or learns something during the course of the story
- A conflict or a problem to be introduced, developed, and resolved
- A plot, the series of events that make up the action of the story
- A theme or message about life

Types of short stories include realistic stories, fantasies, historical narratives, mysteries, thrillers, science-fiction stories, and adventure stories.

Writing Friendly Letters

Writing Friendly Letters

A friendly letter is an informal letter to a friend, a family member, or anyone with whom the writer wants to communicate in a personal way. Most friendly letters are made up of five parts:

- ✔ the heading
- ✔ the salutation, or greeting
- ✔ the body
- ✔ the closing
- ✔ the signature

The purpose of a friendly letter is often one of the following:

- ✔ to share personal news and feelings
- ✔ to send or to answer an invitation
- ✔ to express thanks

Model Friendly Letter

In this friendly letter, Betsy thanks her grandparents for a birthday present and gives them some news about her life.

11 Old Farm Road
Topsham, Maine 04011

April 14, 20—

> The **heading** includes the writer's address and the date on which he or she wrote the letter.

Dear Grandma and Grandpa,

Thank you for the sweater you sent me for my birthday. It fits perfectly, and I love the color. I wore my new sweater to the carnival at school last weekend and got lots of compliments.

The weather here has been cool but sunny. Mom thinks that "real" spring will never come. I can't wait until it's warm enough to go swimming.

School is going fairly well. I really like my Social Studies class. We are learning about the U.S. Constitution, and I think it's very interesting. Maybe I will be a lawyer when I grow up.

When are you coming out to visit us? We haven't seen you since Thanksgiving. You can stay in my room when you come. I'll be happy to sleep on the couch. (The TV is in that room!!)

Well, thanks again and hope all is well with you.

Love,

Betsy

> The **body** is the main part of the letter and contains the basic message.

> Some common **closings** for personal letters include "Best wishes," "Love," "Sincerely," and "Yours truly."

Writing Business Letters

Formatting Business Letters

Business letters follow one of several acceptable formats. In **block format,** each part of the letter begins at the left margin. A double space is used between paragraphs. In **modified block format,** some parts of the letter are indented to the center of the page. No matter which format is used, all letters in business format have a heading, an inside address, a salutation, or greeting, a body, a closing, and a signature. These parts are shown and annotated on the model business letter below, formatted in modified block style.

Model Business Letter

In this letter, Yolanda Dodson uses modified block format to request information.

Students for a Cleaner Planet
c/o Memorial High School
333 Veteran's Drive
Denver, CO 80211

January 25, 20—

Steven Wilson, Director
Resource Recovery Really Works
300 Oak Street
Denver, CO 80216

Dear Mr. Wilson:

Memorial High School would like to start a branch of your successful recycling program. We share your commitment to reclaiming as much reusable material as we can. Because your program has been successful in other neighborhoods, we're sure that it can work in our community. Our school includes grades 9–12 and has about 800 students.

Would you send us some information about your community recycling program? For example, we need to know what materials can be recycled and how we can implement the program.

At least fifty students have already expressed an interest in getting involved, so I know we'll have the people power to make the program work. Please help us get started.

Thank you in advance for your time and consideration.

Sincerely,

Yolanda Dodson

Yolanda Dodson

The **heading** shows the writer's address and organization (if any), and the date.

The **inside address** indicates where the letter will be sent.

A **salutation** is punctuated by a colon. When the specific addressee is not known, use a general greeting such as "To whom it may concern:"

The **body** of the letter states the writer's purpose.

The **closing** "Sincerely" is common, but "Yours truly" or "Respectfully yours" are also acceptable. To end the letter, the writer types her name and provides a **signature.**

Writing a Résumé

Writing a Résumé

A résumé summarizes your educational background, work experiences, relevant skills, and other employment qualifications. It also tells potential employers how to contact you. An effective résumé presents the applicant's name, address, and phone number. It follows an accepted résumé organization, using labels and headings to guide readers.

A résumé should outline the applicant's educational background, life experiences, and related qualifications using precise and active language.

Model Résumé

With this résumé, James, a college student, hopes to find a full-time job.

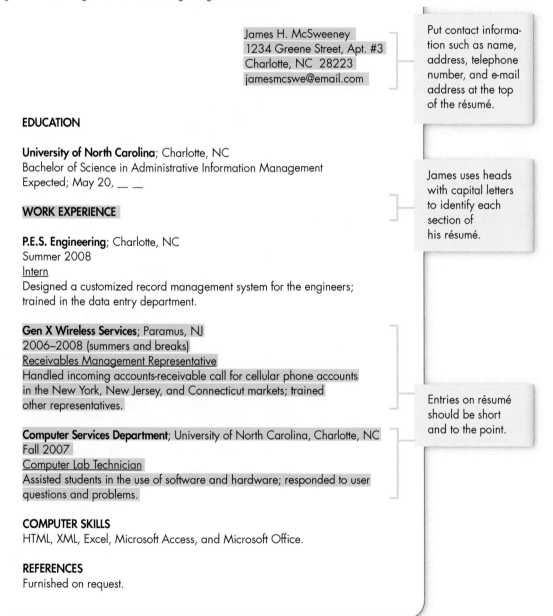

James H. McSweeney
1234 Greene Street, Apt. #3
Charlotte, NC 28223
jamesmcswe@email.com

> Put contact information such as name, address, telephone number, and e-mail address at the top of the résumé.

EDUCATION

University of North Carolina; Charlotte, NC
Bachelor of Science in Administrative Information Management
Expected; May 20, __ __

WORK EXPERIENCE

> James uses heads with capital letters to identify each section of his résumé.

P.E.S. Engineering; Charlotte, NC
Summer 2008
Intern
Designed a customized record management system for the engineers; trained in the data entry department.

Gen X Wireless Services; Paramus, NJ
2006–2008 (summers and breaks)
Receivables Management Representative
Handled incoming accounts-receivable call for cellular phone accounts in the New York, New Jersey, and Connecticut markets; trained other representatives.

> Entries on résumé should be short and to the point.

Computer Services Department; University of North Carolina, Charlotte, NC
Fall 2007
Computer Lab Technician
Assisted students in the use of software and hardware; responded to user questions and problems.

COMPUTER SKILLS
HTML, XML, Excel, Microsoft Access, and Microsoft Office.

REFERENCES
Furnished on request.

In research writing, cite your sources. In the body of your paper, provide a footnote, an endnote, or a parenthetical citation, identifying the sources of facts, opinions, or quotations. At the end of your paper, provide a bibliography or a works-cited list, a list of all the sources you cite. Follow an established format, such as Modern Language Association (MLA) Style.

Works-Cited List (MLA Style)

A works-cited list must contain accurate information sufficient to enable a reader to locate each source you cite. The basic components of an entry are as follows:

- Name of the author, editor, translator, or group responsible for the work
- Title of the work
- Place and date of publication
- Publisher

For print materials, the information required for a citation generally appears on the copyright and title pages of a work. For the format of works-cited list entries, consult the examples at right and in the chart on page R37.

Parenthetical Citations (MLA Style)

A parenthetical citation briefly identifies the source from which you have taken a specific quotation, factual claim, or opinion. It refers the reader to one of the entries on your works-cited list. A parenthetical citation has the following features:

- It appears in parentheses.
- It identifies the source by the last name of the author, editor, or translator.
- It gives a page reference, identifying the page of the source on which the information cited can be found.

Punctuation A parenthetical citation generally falls outside a closing quotation mark but within the final punctuation of a clause or sentence. For a long quotation set off from the rest of your text, place the citation at the end of the excerpt without any punctuation following.

Special Cases

- If the author is an organization, use the organization's name, in a shortened version if necessary.
- If you cite more than one work by the same author, add the title or a shortened version of the title.

Sample Works-Cited Lists (MLA 6th Edition)

Carwardine, Mark, Erich Hoyt, R. Ewan Fordyce, and Peter Gill. *The Nature Company Guides: Whales, Dolphins, and Porpoises.* New York: Time-Life. 1998.

"Discovering Whales." *Whales on the Net.* 1998. Whales in Danger Information Service. 18 Oct. 1999. <http://whales.magna.com.au/discover>.

Neruda, Pablo. "Ode to Spring." *Odes to Opposites.* Trans. Ken Krabbenhoft. Ed. and illus. Ferris Cook. Boston: Little, 1995.

The Saga of the Volsungs. Trans. Jesse L. Byock. London: Penguin, 1990.

List an anonymous work by title.

List both the title of the work and the collection in which it is found.

Sample Parenthetical Citations

It makes sense that baleen whales such as the blue whale, the bowhead whale, the humpback whale, and the sei whale (to name just a few) grow to immense sizes (Carwardine, Hoyt, and Fordyce 19–21). The blue whale has grooves running from under its chin to partway along the length of its underbelly. As in some other whales, these grooves expand and allow even more food and water to be taken in (Ellis 18–21).

Author's last name

Page numbers where information can be found

MLA Style for Listing Sources

Book with one author	Pyles, Thomas. *The Origins and Development of the English Language.* 2nd ed. New York: Harcourt, 1971.
Book with two or three authors	McCrum, Robert, William Cran, and Robert MacNeil. *The Story of English.* New York: Penguin, 1987.
Book with an editor	Truth, Sojourner. *Narrative of Sojourner Truth.* Ed. Margaret Washington. New York: Vintage, 1993.
Book with more than three authors or editors	Donald, Robert B., et al. *Writing Clear Essays.* Upper Saddle River: Prentice, 1996.
Single work in an anthology	Hawthorne, Nathaniel. "Young Goodman Brown." *Literature: An Introduction to Reading and Writing.* Ed. Edgar V. Roberts and Henry E. Jacobs. Upper Saddle River: Prentice, 1998. 376–385. [Indicate pages for the entire selection.]
Introduction to a work in a published edition	Washington, Margaret. Introduction. *Narrative of Sojourner Truth.* By Sojourner Truth. Ed. Washington. New York: Vintage, 1993. v–xi.
Signed article from an encyclopedia	Askeland, Donald R. "Welding." *World Book Encyclopedia.* 1991 ed.
Signed article in a weekly magazine	Wallace, Charles. "A Vodacious Deal." *Time* 14 Feb. 2000: 63.
Signed article in a monthly magazine	Gustaitis, Joseph. "The Sticky History of Chewing Gum." *American History* Oct. 1998: 30–38.
Newspaper	Thurow, Roger. "South Africans Who Fought for Sanctions Now Scrap for Investors." *Wall Street Journal* 11 Feb. 2000: A1+. [For a multipage article that does not appear on consecutive pages, write only the first page number on which it appears, followed by a plus sign.]
Unsigned editorial or story	"Selective Silence." Editorial. *Wall Street Journal* 11 Feb. 2000: A14. [If the editorial or story is signed, begin with the author's name.]
Signed pamphlet or brochure	[Treat the pamphlet as though it were a book.]
Work from a library subscription service	Ertman, Earl L. "Nefertiti's Eyes." *Archaeology* Mar.–Apr. 2008: 28–32. *Kids Search.* EBSCO. New York Public Library. 18 June 2008 <http://www.ebscohost.com>.
Filmstrips, slide programs, videocassettes, DVDs, and other audiovisual media	*The Diary of Anne Frank.* Dir. George Stevens. Perf. Millie Perkins, Shelley Winters, Joseph Schildkraut, Lou Jacobi, and Richard Beymer. 1959. DVD. Twentieth Century Fox, 2004.
CD-ROM (with multiple publishers)	Simms, James, ed. *Romeo and Juliet.* By William Shakespeare. CD-ROM. Oxford: Attica Cybernetics; London: BBC Education; London: Harper, 1995.
Radio or television program transcript	"Washington's Crossing of the Delaware." Host Liane Hansen. Guest David Hackett Fischer. *Weekend Edition Sunday.* Natl. Public Radio. WNYC, New York. 23 Dec. 2003. Transcript.
Internet Web page	"Fun Facts About Gum." NACGM site. 1999. National Association of Chewing Gum Manufacturers. 19 Dec. 1999 <http://www.nacgm.org/consumer/funfacts.html>. [Indicate the date you accessed the information. Content and addresses at Web sites change frequently.]
Personal interview	Smith, Jane. Personal interview. 10 Feb. 2000.

All examples follow the style given in the *MLA Handbook for Writers of Research Papers,* sixth edition, by Joseph Gibaldi.

Guide to Rubrics

What is a rubric?

A rubric is a tool, often in the form of a chart or a grid, that helps you assess your work. Rubrics are particularly helpful for writing and speaking assignments.

To help you or others assess, or evaluate, your work, a rubric offers several specific criteria to be applied to your work. Then, the rubric helps you or an evaluator indicate your range of success or failure according to those specific criteria. Rubrics are often used to evaluate writing for standardized tests.

Using a rubric will save you time, focus your learning, and improve the work you do. When you know what the rubric will be before you begin writing a persuasive essay, for example, you will be aware as you write of specific criteria that are important in that kind of an essay. As you evaluate the essay before giving it to your teacher, you will focus on the specific areas that your teacher wants you to master—or on areas that you know present challenges for you. Instead of searching through your work randomly for any way to improve it or correct its errors, you will have a clear and helpful focus on specific criteria.

How are rubrics constructed?

Rubrics can be constructed in several different ways.

- Your teacher may assign a rubric for a specific assignment.
- Your teacher may direct you to a rubric in your text-book.
- Your teacher and your class may construct a rubric for a particular assignment together.
- You and your classmates may construct a rubric together.
- You may create your own rubric with criteria you want to evaluate in your work.

How will a rubric help me?

A rubric will help you assess your work on a scale. Scales vary from rubric to rubric but usually range from 6 to 1, 5 to 1, or 4 to 1, with 6, 5, or 4 being the highest score and 1 being the lowest. If someone else is using the rubric to assess your work, the rubric will give your evaluator a clear range within which to place your work. If you are using the rubric yourself, it will help you make improvements to your work.

What are the types of rubrics?

- A holistic rubric has general criteria that can apply to a variety of assignments. See p. R-40 for an example of a holistic rubric.
- An analytic rubric is specific to a particular assignment. The criteria for evaluation address the specific issues important in that assignment. See p. R-39 for examples of analytic rubrics.

Sample Analytic Rubrics

Rubric With a 4-point Scale

The following analytic rubric is an example of a rubric to assess a persuasive essay.
It will help you evaluate focus, organization, support/elaboration, and style/convention.

	Focus	Organization	Support/Elaboration	Style/Convention
4	Demonstrates highly effective word choice; clearly focused on task.	Uses clear, consistent organizational strategy.	Provides convincing, well-elaborated reasons to support the position.	Incorporates transitions; includes very few mechanical errors.
3	Demonstrates good word choice; stays focused on persuasive task.	Uses clear organizational strategy with occasional inconsistencies.	Provides two or more moderately elaborated reasons to support the position.	Incorporates some transitions; includes few mechanical errors.
2	Shows some good word choices; minimally stays focused on persuasive task.	Uses inconsistent organizational strategy; presentation is not logical.	Provides several reasons, but few are elaborated; only one elaborated reason.	Incorporates few transitions; includes many mechanical errors.
1	Shows lack of attention to persuasive task.	Demonstrates lack of organizational strategy.	Provides no specific reasons or does not elaborate.	Does not connect ideas; includes many mechanical errors.

Rubric With a 6-point Scale

The following analytic rubric is an example of a rubric to assess a persuasive essay.
It will help you evaluate presentation, position, evidence, and arguments.

	Presentation	Position	Evidence	Arguments
6	Essay clearly and effectively addresses an issue with more than one side.	Essay clearly states a supportable position on the issue.	All evidence is logically organized, well presented, and supports the position.	All reader concerns and counterarguments are effectively addressed.
5	Most of essay addresses an issue that has more than one side.	Essay clearly states a position on the issue.	Most evidence is logically organized, well presented, and supports the position.	Most reader concerns and counterarguments are effectively addressed.
4	Essay adequately addresses issue that has more than one side.	Essay adequately states a position on the issue.	Many parts of evidence support the position; some evidence is out of order.	Many reader concerns and counterarguments are adequately addressed.
3	Essay addresses issue with two sides but does not present second side clearly.	Essay states a position on the issue, but the position is difficult to support.	Some evidence supports the position, but some evidence is out of order.	Some reader concerns and counterarguments are addressed.
2	Essay addresses issue with two sides but does not present second side.	Essay states a position on the issue, but the position is not supportable.	Not much evidence supports the position, and what is included is out of order.	A few reader concerns and counterarguments are addressed.
1	Essay does not address issue with more than one side.	Essay does not state a position on the issue.	No evidence supports the position.	No reader concerns or counterarguments are addressed.

Sample Holistic Rubric

Holistic rubrics such as this one are sometimes used to assess writing assignments on standardized tests. Notice that the criteria for evaluation are focus, organization, support, and use of conventions.

Points	Criteria
6 Points	• The writing is strongly focused and shows fresh insight into the writing task. • The writing is marked by a sense of completeness and coherence and is organized with a logical progression of ideas. • A main idea is fully developed, and support is specific and substantial. • A mature command of the language is evident, and the writing may employ characteristic creative writing strategies. • Sentence structure is varied, and writing is free of all but purposefully used fragments. • Virtually no errors in writing conventions appear.
5 Points	• The writing is clearly focused on the task. • The writing is well organized and has a logical progression of ideas, though there may be occasional lapses. • A main idea is well developed and supported with relevant detail. • Sentence structure is varied, and the writing is free of fragments, except when used purposefully. • Writing conventions are followed correctly.
4 Points	• The writing is clearly focused on the task, but extraneous material may intrude at times. • Clear organizational pattern is present, though lapses may occur. • A main idea is adequately supported, but development may be uneven. • Sentence structure is generally fragment free but shows little variation. • Writing conventions are generally followed correctly.
3 Points	• Writing is generally focused on the task, but extraneous material may intrude at times. • An organizational pattern is evident, but writing may lack a logical progression of ideas. • Support for the main idea is generally present but is sometimes illogical. • Sentence structure is generally free of fragments, but there is almost no variation. • The work generally demonstrates a knowledge of writing conventions, with occasional misspellings.
2 Points	• The writing is related to the task but generally lacks focus. • There is little evidence of organizational pattern, and there is little sense of cohesion. • Support for the main idea is generally inadequate, illogical, or absent. • Sentence structure is unvaried, and serious errors may occur. • Errors in writing conventions and spellings are frequent.
1 Point	• The writing may have little connection to the task and is generally unfocused. • There has been little attempt at organization or development. • The paper seems fragmented, with no clear main idea. • Sentence structure is unvaried, and serious errors appear. • Poor word choice and poor command of the language obscure meaning. • Errors in writing conventions and spelling are frequent.
Unscorable	The paper is considered unscorable if: • The response is unrelated to the task or is simply a rewording of the prompt. • The response has been copied from a published work. • The student did not write a response. • The response is illegible. • The words in the response are arranged with no meaning. • There is an insufficient amount of writing to score.

Student Model

Persuasive Writing

This persuasive letter, which would receive a top score according to a persuasive rubric, is a response to the following writing prompt, or assignment:

With the increased use of technology in the workplace, the skills that high-school graduates must possess have changed. Write a letter to your principal advocating new technology courses that could give high-school graduates a competitive edge.

Dear Principal:

I am writing to alert you to an urgent need in our school's curriculum. We need computer graphics courses!

> The letter begins with an engaging introduction that clearly states the persuasive focus.

Although you would have to find funds to buy the equipment, I've concluded that setting up this course would well be worth it. By adding this course, you would be adding many high paying career options for students. Computer graphics is a type of art, and businesses all around us involve art in some form. You see computer graphics in commercials, movies, news broadcasts, weather broadcasts, architectural design, and business presentations. Workers with computer graphics skills are well paid because they are in such high demand.

You may argue that the school already has computer science classes. Good point! I'm in a computer science class and it is mainly programming. Once we did have an assignment to design a graphic of a pumpkin. You wouldn't believe how much coding it takes to get a simple, animated drawing. In order to get a really creative image with definite lines, shading, lifelike colors, and texture, you need to use computer graphics software designed especially for that purpose. With software, you can make images that move and talk smoothly and environments with realistic colors and lighting. This is the same graphics software that businesses use for commercials, movies, and brochures. Students should be learning how to use this software.

> The author effectively counters an opposing argument to increase the persuasive power of her own argument.

Most important, computer graphics is a subject area that allows students to express their creativity. Adding a computer graphics course would have a positive effect on students. Course participants would enjoy doing their assignments, so they would earn good grades and turn in creative work. The energy and enthusiasm they would bring to their projects would catch the attention of the community at large. As a result, they would make the school and the principal look good.

> A positive argument that is well supported enhances the letter's persuasive appeal.

As you can see, adding a computer graphics course could be a very profitable idea for you, the students, and the community. You would be ensuring the success of the students who desire an art or computer career. You would be opening hundreds of different career pathways. Wouldn't it be great to know you were the reason for these students' success? Thanks for your time and consideration.

Sincerely,
Dawn Witherspoon

21st-Century Skills

New technology has created many new ways to communicate. Today, it is easy to contribute information to the Internet and send a variety of messages to friends far and near. You can also share your ideas through photos, illustrations, video, and sound recordings. *21st Century Skills* gives you an overview of some ways you can use today's technology to create, share, and find information. Here are the topics you will find in this section.

- ✔ Blogs
- ✔ Social Networking
- ✔ Widgets & Feeds
- ✔ Multimedia Elements
- ✔ Podcasts
- ✔ Wikis

BLOGS

A **blog** is a common form of online writing. The word *blog* is a contraction of *Web log*. Most blogs include a series of entries known as *posts*. The posts appear in a single column and are displayed in reverse chronological order. That means that the most recent post is at the top of the page. As you scroll down, you will find earlier posts.

Blogs have become increasingly popular. Researchers estimate that 75,000 new blogs are launched every day. Blog authors are often called *bloggers*. They can use their personal sites to share ideas, songs, videos, photos, and other media. People who read blogs can often post their responses with a comments feature found in each new post.

Because blogs are designed so that they are easy to update, bloggers can post new messages as often as they like, often daily. For some people blogs become a public journal or diary, in which they share their thoughts about daily events.

Types of Blogs

Not all blogs are the same. Many blogs have a single author, but others are group projects. These are some common types of blog:

- ✔ Personal blogs often have a general focus. Bloggers post their thoughts on any topic they find interesting in their daily lives.

- ✔ Topical blogs focus on a specific theme, such as movie reviews, political news, class assignments, or health-care opportunities.

Web Safety

Always be aware that information you post on the Internet can be read by everyone with access to that page. Once you post a picture or text, it can be saved on someone else's computer, even if you later remove it.

Using the Internet safely means keeping personal information personal. Never include your address (e-mail or real), last name, or telephone numbers. Avoid mentioning places you can be frequently found. Never give out passwords you use to access other Web sites and do not respond to e-mails from people you do not know.

Anatomy of a Blog

Here are some of the features you can include in a blog.

Posts Each post usually has a headline followed by the message.

THIS WEEK'S FOCUS

What are the manifestations of evil and good in the character Macbeth? Is he a man or a monster? Certainly he is traitor, killer, and tyrant, but is he a total monster? (See Mr. Y's in-blog post for more on this prompt.)

QUOTABLE

"[Macbeth] is forced to become a victim of his own horrified mind."
-- Jeff S.

" [S]ins have stayed the same, only the sinners have

ENGLISH 12 HONORS BLOG

☺ A Good Heart Gone Bad [private]

I firmly believe that Macbeth was simply a good man whose heart began to rot as he became more powerful. As Shakespeare began, Macbeth was a hero and a good man. He was a very courageous man who helped defeat Macdonald. Once he was named thane of Cawdor and learned of his prophecy, he had his first thoughts of evil. As Macbeth gained power, he became power hungry and kept wanting more and more power. This led to his murder of King Duncan. However, after the murder, Macbeth felt remorse and certainly not the happiness he expected. Macbeth told his Lady what he heard while committing the murder: "Listening their fear, I could not say 'Amen'/When they did say 'God bless us'"(II.i). This proves that Macbeth wanted to join in their prayers and be blessed, but the words "stuck in his throat". This is Macbeth showing that he is still a good man at heart; he just had evil actions.

Posted by **Briana K** on 1.8.08 4:29 PM | 6 comments
Labels: Shakespeare, Macbeth, tragedy

RECENT POSTS

A Good Heart Gone Bad
MACBETH: MAN OR MONSTER?
The Color Green
Shields and Armor
Honor in the Middle Ages
And the Band Plays On

LINKS

Write In Blog
Control Panel
Class Website
Macbeth E-text
RSC Macbeth Guide
Bard Net
Tips on Blog Comments

Blogroll Many blogs include a list of links to other blogs or sites.

Links Bloggers can add links to other Internet locations. Clicking a link sends readers to another place in the same blog, or to another site.

Labels Keywords are assigned by the blogger to categorize a post. Click a label to see other posts in this category.

Comments Clicking on this link allows visitors to read comments and add their own.

ID Entries include the name of the author and date the post was entered.

Creating a Blog

Keep these hints and strategies in mind to help you create an interesting and fair blog:

✔ Focus each blog entry on a single topic.

✔ Vary the length of your posts. Sometimes, all you need is a line or two to share a quick thought. Other posts will be much longer.

✔ Choose font colors and styles that can be read easily.

✔ Many people scan blogs rather than read them closely. You can make your main ideas pop out by using clear or clever headlines and boldfacing key terms.

✔ Give credit to other people's work and ideas. State the names of people whose ideas you are quoting or add a link to take readers to that person's blog or site.

✔ If you post comments, try to make them brief and polite.

SOCIAL NETWORKING

Social networking means any interaction between members of an online community. People can exchange many different kinds of information, from text and voice messages to video images.

Many social network communities allow users to create permanent pages that describe themselves. Users create home pages to express themselves, share ideas about their lives, and post messages to other members in the network. Each user is responsible for adding and updating the content on his or her profile page.

Here are some features you are likely to find on a social network profile:

Features of Profile Pages

- A biographical description, including photographs and artwork.

- Lists of favorite things, such as books, movies, music, and fashions.

- Playable media elements such as videos and sound recordings.

- Message boards, or "walls" in which members of the community can exchange messages.

You can create a social network page for an individual or a group, such as a school or special interest club. Many hosting sites do not charge to register, so you can also have fun by creating a page for a pet or a fictional character.

Privacy in Social Networks

Social networks allow users to decide how open their profiles will be. Be sure to read introductory information carefully before you register at a new site. Once you have a personal profile page, monitor your privacy settings regularly. Remember that any information you post will be available to anyone in your network.

Users often post messages anonymously or using false names, or *pseudonyms*. People can also post using someone else's name. Judge all information on the net critically. Do not assume that you know who posted some information simply because you recognize the name of the post author. The rapid speed of communication on the Internet can make it easy to jump to conclusions—be careful to avoid this trap.

Tips for Sending Effective Messages

Technology makes it easy to share ideas quickly, but writing for the Internet poses some special challenges, as well. The writing style for blogs and social networks is often very conversational. In blog posts and comments, instant messages, and e-mails, writers often express themselves very quickly, using relaxed language, short sentences, and abbreviations. However, in a conversation, we get a lot of information from a speaker's tone of voice and body language. On the Internet, those clues are missing. As a result, Internet writers often use italics or bracketed labels to indicate emotions. Another alternative is using emoticons—strings of characters that give visual clues to indicate emotion:

:-) smile (happy)	:-(frown (unhappy)	;-) wink (light sarcasm)

Use these strategies to communicate effectively when using technology:

✔ Reread your messages. Before you click *Send,* read your message through and make sure that your tone will be clear to the reader.

✔ Do not jump to conclusions—ask for clarification first. Make sure you really understand what someone is saying before you respond.

✔ Use abbreviations your reader will understand.

WIDGETS & FEEDS

A **widget** is a small application that performs a specific task. You might find widgets that give weather predictions, offer dictionary definitions or translations, provide entertainment such as games, or present a daily word, photograph, or quotation.

A **feed** is a special kind of widget. It displays headlines taken from the latest content on a specific media source. Clicking on the headline will take you to the full article.

Many social network communities and other Web sites allow you to personalize your home page by adding widgets and feeds.

MULTIMEDIA ELEMENTS

One of the great advantages of communicating on the Internet is that you are not limited to using text only. When you create a Web profile or blog, you can share your ideas using a wide variety of media. In addition to widgets and feeds (see page R45), these media elements can make your Internet communication more entertaining and useful.

Graphics	
Photographs	You can post photos taken by digital cameras.
Illustrations	Artwork can be created using computer software. You can also use a scanner to post a digital image of a drawing or sketch.
Charts, Graphs, and Maps	Charts and graphs can make statistical information clear. Use spreadsheet software to create these elements. Use Internet sites to find maps of specific places.

Video	
Live Action	Digital video can be recorded by a camera or recorded from another media source.
Animation	Animated videos can also be created using software.

Sound	
Music	Many social network communities make it easy to share your favorite music with people who visit your page.
Voice	Use a microphone to add your own voice to your Web page.

Editing Media Elements

You can use software to customize media elements. Open source software is free and available to anyone on the Internet. Here are some things you can do with software:

✔ Crop a photograph to focus on the subject or brighten an image that is too dark.

✔ Transform a drawing's appearance from flat to three-dimensional.

✔ Insert a "You Are Here" arrow on a map.

✔ Edit a video or sound file to shorten its running time.

✔ Add background music or sound effects to a video.

PODCASTS

A **podcast** is a digital audio or video recording of a program that is made available on the Internet. Users can replay the podcast on a computer, or download it and replay it on a personal audio player. You might think of podcasts as radio or television programs that you create yourself. They can be embedded on a Web site or fed to a Web page through a podcast widget.

Creating an Effective Podcast

To make a podcast, you will need a recording device, such as a microphone or digital video camera, as well as editing software. Open source editing software is widely available and free of charge. Most audio podcasts are converted into the MP3 format. Here are some tips for creating a podcast that is clear and entertaining:

✔ Listen to several podcasts by different authors to get a feeling for the medium. Make a list of features and styles you like and also those you want to avoid.

✔ Test your microphone to find the best recording distance. Stand close enough to the microphone so that your voice sounds full, but not so close that you create an echo.

✔ Create an outline that shows your estimated timing for each element.

✔ Be prepared before you record. Rehearse, but do not create a script. Podcasts are best when they have a natural, easy flow.

✔ Talk directly to your listeners. Slow down enough so they can understand you.

✔ Use software to edit your podcast before publishing it. You can edit out mistakes or add additional elements.

WIKIS

A **wiki** is a collaborative Web site that lets visitors create, add, remove, and edit content. The term comes from the Hawaiian phrase *wiki wiki,* which means "quick." Web users at a wiki are both the readers and the writers of the site. Some wikis are open to contributions from anyone. Others require visitors to register before they can edit the content.

All of the text in these collaborative Web sites was written by people who use the site. Articles are constantly changing, as visitors find and correct errors and improve texts.

Wikis have both advantages and disadvantages as sources of information. They are valuable open forums for the exchange of ideas. The unique collaborative writing process allows entries to change over time. However, entries can also be modified incorrectly. Careless or malicious users can delete good content and add inappropriate or inaccurate information.

You can change the information on a wiki, but be sure your information is correct and clear before you add it. Wikis keep track of all changes, so your work will be recorded and can be evaluated by other users.

Rules of Debate

A **debate** is a structured contest based on a formal discussion of opinion. In essence, it is a battle of intellect and verbal skill. The goal is mastering the art of persuasion. Who can best express, argue, and support opinions on a given topic? Who can best refute an argument, showing that the opponent's points are invalid? Which team, in the end, can convince the judges that their argument is the most sound?

Teams

A **formal debate** is conducted with two teams—an Affirmation team and a Negative team. As the names suggest, the Affirmation team is responsible for presenting the "pro" side of an issue, while the Negative team presents the "con" side of the issue. Each team has a main purpose and will offer both constructive and rebuttal speeches, practicing the art of persuasion and debate.

Affirmation team The Affirmation team as a whole carries the burden of proof for the debate. They must prove there is a problem. To do so, they need to cite credible sources, include relevant details, and present and support valid points. Each team member has a specific job. The first speaker has the most responsibility. He or she must

- define the issue or problem
- introduce the team line—a one-line summary of the team's position on the issue
- identify the point of the argument each speaker will discuss

The remaining team members have the job of presenting and supporting the main points of the argument.

Negative team Though the Negative team does not carry the burden of proof, the team must show that there is no problem or that the Affirmation team's solutions are invalid. Though their purpose is to rebut an argument, the rebuttal technique calls for a formation of their own argument. They must argue against the Affirmation team. To construct their argument, they must use—like the Affirmation team—credible sources, relevant details, and valid points. They should incorporate any available statistics, pertinent facts, or applicable testimonies to bolster their argument. Even though the first speaker of the Affirmation team lays out each point of the argument, the Negative team speakers cannot address points that have not been thoroughly discussed by an Affirmation team member.

Structure

Just like most other contests, debates have a set structure. Debates are divided into halves. The first half begins with the constructive speeches from both teams, which last ten minutes each.

After the first half, there is a short intermission. Then, the second half begins with the Negative team. This half is reserved for the rebuttal speeches, which last five minutes each and include rebuttals and refutations. This is each team's chance to rebuild their arguments that the other team broke down (rebuttal), and put forth evidence to show the other team is wrong (refutation). Although the Negative team begins the argument in the second half, every debate begins and ends with the Affirmation team.

Structure of Debate

1st Half: Constructive Speeches (10 minutes each)	2nd Half: Rebuttal Speeches (5 minutes each)
1st Affirmative Team Speaker	1st Negative Team Speaker
1st Negative Team Speaker	1st Affirmative Team Speaker
2nd Affirmative Team Speaker	2nd Negative Team Speaker
2nd Negative Team Speaker	2nd Affirmative Team Speaker
3rd Affirmative Team Speaker	3rd Negative Team Speaker
3rd Negative Team Speaker	3rd Affirmative Team Speaker

Speeches—Content, Organization, and Delivery

Debate speeches are the result of practicing the art of persuasion. To be effective, speakers must include pertinent content, use clear and logical organization, and have a powerful delivery. These combined elements make a strong speech.

Content Debates often focus on concrete issues that can be proved or disproved. The basis for a debate speech is its content. The Affirmation team should first determine their position. They should be sure to include any facts and/or statistics that concretely support the argument. Speech writers should cite specific instances and occurrences that solidify their position. Writers might also include testimonies or ideas from professionals. Finally, the Affirmation team needs to propose possible solutions to the problem or issue and examine the costs and effects of those solutions.

Though the Negative team does not have to state a position—their position is automatically the opposing position—they still need to include facts, statistics, testimony, and descriptions of specific instances or occurrences to make their counterpoints. They need to analyze the Affirmation team's proposed solutions and explain why they will not work. In essence, the Negative team must construct an argument around the Affirmation team's argument.

Organization Debate speeches are organized like other speeches and essays. They should have an introduction, transitions, body, and conclusion. The speeches should have clear main points and supporting details for those points. Because a debate is a structured discussion, there will be a specific order of points and the speakers who present them must be identified. Speakers can use note cards to help them stick to the planned organization, but they should only use brief notes, never reading directly from the cards.

Delivery The manner in which a speech is delivered can make or break the argument. The impression the speaker makes on the audience, including the judges, is key. To make a good impression, the speaker must present the material with confidence. He or she can portray confidence by forming a connection with the audience through eye contact, glancing away only briefly to consult notes. A speaker should focus on his or her voice, varying the tone, volume, and pace appropriately. Body movements should not include fidgeting or nervous movement. They should only be used if they are deliberate and help express or underscore a point. Finally, speakers should be concise, focusing on vivid and clear word choice and using words that emphasize the point.

Scoring

Debates are scored much like other contests. Each side is judged on the content and delivery of their speeches. Judges contemplate different elements of content and delivery in order to determine the number of points to give each team. They might ask themselves the questions in the chart below in order to determine the score.

Finally, judges look at the observation of debate etiquette. Speakers are expected to be mature and respectful of their opponents. Speakers should never attack an opponent, but instead should attack the argument. Judges will deduct points for personal attacks.

Scoring Criteria

Content	Delivery
Were arguments convincing?	Were speakers able to speak extemporaneously?
Were arguments supported with credible, valid and relevant reasons?	Were body movements deliberate and effective?
Were refutations and rebuttals effective?	Did speakers make a connection with the audience?
Were speakers confident and knowledgeable?	Did speakers stay within their time limits?

Grammar, Usage, and Mechanics Handbook

Parts of Speech

Nouns A **noun** is the name of a person, place, or thing. A **common noun** names any one of a class of people, places, or things. A **proper noun** names a specific person, place, or thing.

Common Noun	Proper Noun
city	Washington, D.C.

Pronouns A **pronoun** is a word that stands for a noun or for a word that takes the place of a noun.

A **personal pronoun** refers to (1) the person speaking, (2) the person spoken to, or (3) the person, place, or thing spoken about.

	Singular	Plural
First Person	I, me, my, mine	we, us, our, ours
Second Person	you, your, yours	you, your, yours
Third Person	he, him, his, she, her, hers, it, its	they, them, their, theirs

Antecedents are nouns (or words that take the place of nouns) for which pronouns stand. In the following sentence, the pronoun *it* stands for the noun *Florida.*

Florida is popular because it has a warm climate.

A **reflexive pronoun** ends in -*self* or -*selves* and adds information to a sentence by pointing back to a noun or a pronoun earlier in the sentence.

"If you were honest folk *yourselves* you wouldn't let a thief go free."

— Leo Tolstoy, p. 338

An **intensive pronoun** ends in -*self* or -*selves* and simply adds emphasis to a noun or a pronoun in the same sentence.

After a time, I *myself* was allowed to go into the dead houses and search for metal.

— Stephen Vincent Benét, p. 314

A **demonstrative pronoun** directs attention to a specific person, place, or thing.

this   these   that   those
These are the juiciest pears I have ever tasted.

A **relative pronoun** begins a subordinate clause and connects it to another idea in the sentence.

The poet *who* wrote "Fear" is Gabriela Mistral.

An **interrogative pronoun** is used to begin a question. The five interrogative pronouns are *what, which, who, whom,* and *whose.*

An **indefinite pronoun** refers to a person, place, or thing, often without specifying which one.

all   anyone   each   everyone   few   one   someone
And then, for a moment, *all* is still, . . .

— Edgar Allan Poe, p. 372

Verbs A **verb** is a word that expresses time while showing an action, a condition, or the fact that something exists.

An **action verb** indicates the action of someone or something.

An action verb is **transitive** if it directs action toward someone or something named in the same sentence.

He *dusted* his hands, muttering.

— Jack Finney, p. 118

An action verb is **intransitive** if it does not direct action toward something or someone named in the same sentence.

I *smiled* and looked up at the crew . . .

— Lynne Cox, p. 62

A **linking verb** is a verb that connects the subject of a sentence with a noun or a pronoun that renames or describes the subject. The noun, pronoun, or phrase acting as a noun that renames the subject is called a **predicate nominative.**

Romance at short notice was her specialty.

— Saki, p. 195

A **helping verb** is a verb that can be added to another verb to make a verb phrase.

Nor *did* I *suspect* that these experiences could be part of a novel's meaning.

Adjectives An **adjective** describes a noun or a pronoun or gives a noun or a pronoun a more specific meaning. Adjectives answer these questions:

What kind?	*blue* lamp, *large* tree
Which one?	*this* table, *those* books
How many?	*five* stars, *several* buses
How much?	*less* money, *enough* votes

The articles *the, a,* and *an* are adjectives. *An* is used before a word beginning with a vowel sound.

A noun may sometimes be used as an adjective.

diamond necklace   *summer* vacation

Adverbs An **adverb** modifies a verb, an adjective, or another adverb. Adverbs answer the questions *where, when, in what way,* or *to what extent.*

He could stand *there.* (modifies verb *stand*)
He was *blissfully* happy. (modifies adjective *happy*)
It ended *too* soon. (modifies adverb *soon*)

Prepositions A **preposition** relates a noun or a pronoun that appears with it to another word in the sentence.

before the end   *near* me   *inside* our fence

Conjunctions A **conjunction** connects words or groups of words.

A **coordinating conjunction** connects similar kinds or groups of words.

  mother *and* father   simple *yet* stylish

Correlative conjunctions are used in pairs to connect similar words or groups of words.

  both Sue *and* Meg   *neither* he *nor* I

A **subordinating conjunction** connects two complete ideas by placing one idea below the other in rank or importance.

  You would know him *if* you saw him.

Sentences, Phrases, and Clauses

Sentences A **sentence** is a group of words with a subject and a predicate. Together, these parts express a complete thought.

A **fragment** is a group of words that does not express a complete thought.

The Four Structures of Sentences There are two kinds of clauses: independent and subordinate. An independent clause can stand by itself as a sentence; a subordinate clause cannot. These can be used to form four basic sentence structures: *simple, compound, complex,* and *compound-complex.*

A **simple sentence** consists of a single independent clause.

A **compound sentence** consists of two or more independent clauses.

The clauses in a compound sentence can be joined by a comma and a coordinating conjunction *(and, but, for, nor, or, so, yet)* or by a semicolon (;).

A **complex sentence** consists of one independent clause and one or more subordinate clauses.

The independent clause in a complex sentence is often called the *main clause* to distinguish it from the subordinate clause or clauses.

A **compound-complex sentence** consists of two or more independent clauses and one or more subordinate clauses.

Phrases A **phrase** is a group of words, without a subject and a verb, that functions in a sentence as one part of speech.

A **prepositional phrase** is a group of words that includes a preposition and a noun or a pronoun that is the object of the preposition.

  outside my window   below the counter

An **adjective phrase** is a prepositional phrase that modifies a noun or a pronoun by telling *what kind* or *which one.*

  The wooden gates *of that lane* stood open.

An **adverb phrase** is a prepositional phrase that modifies a verb, an adjective, or an adverb by pointing out *where, when, in what way,* or *to what extent.*

  On a sudden impulse, he got to his feet. . . .

  — Jack Finney, p. 118

An **appositive phrase** is a noun or a pronoun with modifiers, placed next to a noun or a pronoun to identify it or add information and details.

  M. Morissot, watchmaker by trade but local militiaman for the time being, stopped short. . . .

  — Guy de Maupassant, p. 1233

A **participial phrase** is a participle with its modifiers or complements. The entire phrase acts as an adjective.

  Choosing such a tide, I hoped for a glimpse of the pool.

  — Rachel Carson, p. 156

A **gerund** is a form of a verb that is used as a noun. It ends in *-ing.* A **gerund phrase** is a gerund with modifiers or a complement, all acting together as a noun.

  . . . moving along the ledge was quite as easy as he had thought it would be.

  — Jack Finney, p. 118

An **infinitive** is the form of a verb using to. It acts as a noun, adjective, or adverb. An **infinitive phrase** is an infinitive with modifiers, complements, or a subject, all acting together as a single part of speech.

  To be dead, and never again behold my city!

  —Dreams, p. 676

Clauses A **clause** is a group of words with a subject and a verb.

An **independent clause** has a subject and a verb and can stand by itself as a complete sentence.

A **subordinate clause** has a subject and a verb but cannot stand by itself as a complete sentence; it can only be part of a sentence.

An **adjective clause** is a subordinate clause that modifies a noun or a pronoun by telling *what kind* or *which one.*

  The people *who read the book* loved it.

An **adverb clause** modifies a verb, an adjective, an adverb, or a verbal by telling *where, when, in what way, to what extent, under what condition,* or *why.*

  They read it as soon *as it was published.*

A **noun clause** is a subordinate clause that acts as a noun.

  Whoever reads it is overcome with joy.

Parallelism **Parallelism** is the placement of equal ideas in words, phrases, or clauses of similar type.

Parallel Words: The camp has excellent facilities for *riding, hiking,* and *swimming.*

Parallel Phrases: Jennings had gone to the country *to rest, to think,* and *to catch a few fish.*

Parallel Clauses: A news story should tell *what happened, when it happened,* and *who was involved.*

Verb Usage

The Four Principal Parts of Verbs A verb has four **principal parts:** the *present,* the *present participle,* the *past,* and the *past participle.*

Regular verbs form the past and past participle by adding *-ed* to the present form.

Present: walk
Present Participle: (am) walking
Past: walked
Past Participle: (have) walked

The past and past participle of an **irregular verb** are not formed by adding *-ed* or *-d* to the present form. Irregular verbs form the past and past participle by changing form. Whenever you are in doubt about the principal parts of an irregular verb, use a dictionary to check them.

Present: go
Present Participle: (am) going
Past: went
Past Participle: (have) gone

Pronoun Usage

Pronoun Case The **case** of a pronoun is the form it takes to show its use in a sentence. There are three pronoun cases: *nominative, objective,* and *possessive.*

The **nominative case** is used to rename the subject of the sentence. The nominative case pronouns are *I, you, he, she, it, we, you, they.*

As the subject: *She* is brave
Renaming the subject: The leader is *she.*

The **objective case** is used as the direct object, indirect object, or object of the preposition. The objective case pronouns are *me, you, him, her, it, us, you, them.*

As a direct object: Tom called *me.*
As an indirect object: My friend gave *me* advice.
As an object of preposition: The coach gave pointers to *me.*

The **possessive case** is used to show ownership. The possessive pronouns are *my, your, his, her, its, our, their, mine, yours, his, hers, its, ours, theirs.*

Agreement

Subject and Verb Agreement To make a subject and verb agree, make sure that both are singular or both are plural.

Many *storms are* the cause of beach erosion.

In the case of a plural and a singular subject joined by *or* or *nor,* choose the form of the verb that agrees with the closer of the two.

Either the *cats* or the *dog is* hungry.
Neither *Angie* nor *her sisters were* present.

Pronoun-Antecedent Agreement Pronouns must agree with their antecedents in number and gender. Use singular pronouns with singular antecedents and plural pronouns with plural antecedents. Many errors in pronoun-antecedent agreement occur when a plural pronoun is used to refer to a singular antecedent for which the gender is not specified.

Incorrect: Everyone did their best.
Correct: Everyone did his or her best.

The following indefinite pronouns are singular: *anybody, anyone, each, either, everybody, everyone, neither, nobody, no one, one, somebody, someone.*

The following indefinite pronouns are plural: *both, few, many, several.*

The following indefinite pronouns may be either singular or plural: *all, any, most, none, some.* Treat these pronouns as singular when the antecedent is singular.

All of the gold is gone, and we do not know who took *it.*

Treat these pronouns as plural when the antecedent is plural.

Most of my friends are going, and *they* will have a good time.

Using Modifiers

Degrees of Comparison Most adjectives and adverbs have three different forms to show degrees of comparison— the *positive,* the *comparative,* the *superlative.*

Use *-er* or *more* to form the comparative degree and *-est* or *most* to form the superlative degree of most one- and two-syllable modifiers.

Use *more* and *most* to form the comparative and superlative degrees of all modifiers with three or more syllables.

The irregular comparative and superlative forms of certain adjectives and adverbs must be memorized.

The form of some irregular modifiers differs only in the positive degree. The modifiers *bad, badly,* and *ill,* for example, all have the same basic form in the comparative and superlative degrees (*worse, worst*).

Capitalization and Punctuation

Capitalization Capitalize the first word of a sentence and also the first word in a quotation if the quotation is a complete sentence.

> "No matter," he concluded, "I'll go toward the
> rising sun."   — Leo Tolstoy, p. 338

Capitalize all proper nouns and adjectives.

> W. W. Jacobs   Flanders Fields   African writers

Capitalize a person's title when it is followed by the person's name or when it is used in direct address.

> Reverend Tallboys   Mrs. Prothero   "Hello, Major."

Capitalize titles showing family relationships when they refer to a specific person and are used with a name or as a name.

> Aunt Mae   Let's ask Grandmother.   *but*   his father

Capitalize the first word and all other key words in the titles of books, periodicals, poems, stories, plays, paintings, and other works of art.

> *Lord of the Flies*   "Spring and All"

End Marks Use a **period** to end a declarative sentence, an imperative sentence, an indirect question, and most abbreviations.

> The class will meet at noon.

Use a **question mark** to end a direct question, an incomplete question, or a statement that is intended as a question.

> Did you prepare your assignment?

Use an **exclamation mark** after a statement showing strong emotion, an urgent imperative sentence, or an interjection expressing strong emotion.

> Wait until you hear the news!

Commas Use a **comma** before the coordinating conjunction to separate two independent clauses in a compound sentence.

> His arms had begun to tremble from the steady strain
> of clinging to this narrow perch, and he did not know
> what to do now. . . .   — Jack Finney, p. 118

Use commas to separate three or more words, phrases, or clauses in a series.

> . . . he produced about fifteen hundred *drawings,*
> *prints, pastels,* and *oil paintings* with ballet themes.
>   — Richard Mühlberger, p. 568

Use commas to separate adjectives of equal rank. Do not use commas to separate adjectives that must stay in a specific order.

> With *pink, dimpled* knees, Henri, not yet a year old,
> sprawls on the lap of his nurse. . . .
> [In Degas's painting], the *creamy white* tones of the
> passengers stand out.
>   — Richard Mühlberger, p. 568

Use a comma after an introductory word, phrase, or clause.

> When Marian Anderson again returned to America,
> she was a seasoned artist.
>   — Langston Hughes, p. 98

Use commas to set off parenthetical and nonessential expressions.

> Now, *yes, now,* it was about to set!
>   — Leo Tolstoy, p. 338

Use commas with places, dates, and titles.

> Poe was raised in Richmond, Virginia.
> August 4, 2026
> Alfred, Lord Tennyson

Use a comma to indicate the words left out of an elliptical sentence, to set off a direct quotation, and to prevent a sentence from being misunderstood.

> Vincent Canby writes for *The New York Times*;
> Roger Ebert, for the *Chicago Sun Times*.

Semicolons Use a **semicolon** to join independent clauses that are not already joined by a conjunction.

> They could find no buffalo; they had to hang an old
> hide from the sacred tree.
>   — N. Scott Momaday, p. 595

Use a semicolon to join independent clauses separated by either a conjunctive adverb or a transitional expression.

> James Thurber wrote many books; moreover, he was
> a cartoonist and a journalist.

Use semicolons to avoid confusion when independent clauses or items in a series already contain commas.

> Thurber is remembered for his character Walter
> Mitty; for his cartoons, many of which illustrated his
> books; and for his terrifically funny essays.

Colons Use a **colon** in order to introduce a list of items following an independent clause.

> The authors we are reading include a number of
> poets: Robert Frost, Octavio Paz, and Emily Dickinson.

Use a colon to introduce a formal quotation.

> The next day Howard Taubman wrote enthusiastically
> in The New York Times: "Marian Anderson has
> returned to her native land one of the great singers
> of our time. . . ."
>   — Langston Hughes, p. 98

Quotation Marks A **direct quotation** represents a person's exact speech or thoughts and is enclosed in quotation marks.

> "Clara, my mind is made up."

An **indirect quotation** is a restatement or paraphrase of what a person said or thought and does not require quotation marks.

> The cops suggested that it might be a good idea to tie the dog up, but mother said that it mortified him to be tied up. . . .   — James Thurber, p. 525

Always place a comma or a period inside the final quotation mark.

> "Eh, you're a stranger," she said. "I thought so."
> — Josephina Niggli, p. 272

Place a question mark or an exclamation mark inside the final quotation mark if the end mark is part of the quotation; if it is not part of the quotation, place it outside the final quotation mark.

> He asked, "Which poetry do you like best?"
> Have you ever read the poem "Africa"?

Use single quotation marks for a quotation within a quotation.

Use quotation marks around the titles of short written works, episodes in a series, songs, and titles of works mentioned as parts of a collection.

> "Making a Fist"   "These Are Days"

Underline or italicize titles of longer works, such as plays, movies, or novels.

Dashes   Use **dashes** to indicate an abrupt change of thought, a dramatic interrupting idea, or a summary statement.

> It made her so mad to see Muggs lying there, oblivious of the mice—they came running up to her—that she slapped him and he slashed at her, but didn't make it.   — James Thurber, p. 525

Parentheses   Use **parentheses** to set off asides and explanations only when the material is not essential or when it consists of one or more sentences.

> When I finished (What a lot of facts I found out!), I turned in my report.

Hyphens   Use a **hyphen** with certain numbers, after certain prefixes, with two or more words used as one word, and with a compound modifier coming before a noun.

> fifty-two   greenish-blue water

Apostrophes   Add an **apostrophe** and s to show the possessive case of most singular nouns.

> Prospero's castle   the playwright's craft

Add an apostrophe to show the possessive case of plural nouns ending in -s and -es.

> the sailors' ships   the babies' mothers

Add an apostrophe and -s to show the possessive case of plural nouns that do not end in -s or -es.

> the children's games   the people's friend

Use an apostrophe in a contraction to indicate the position of the missing letter or letters.

> I *didn't* love any one of you more than any other.
> — William Melvin Kelley, p. 242

Glossary of Common Usage

among, between: *Among* is usually used with three or more items. *Between* is generally used with only two items.

> *Among* the poems we read this year, Eve Merriam's "Metaphor" was my favorite.
> "Like the Sun" tells of the conflict *between* telling the truth and telling white lies.

around: In formal writing, *around* should not be used to mean *approximately* or *about.* These usages are allowable, however, in informal writing or in colloquial dialogue.

> *Romeo and Juliet* had its first performance in *approximately* 1595.
> Shakespeare was *about* thirty when he wrote it.

as, because, like, as to: The word *as* has several meanings and can function as several parts of speech. To avoid confusion, use *because* rather than *as* when you want to indicate cause and effect.

> *Because* Cyril was interested in African American poetry, he wrote his report on Langston Hughes.

Do not use the preposition *like* to introduce a clause that requires the conjunction *as.*

> James Thurber conversed as he wrote—wittily.

The use of *as to* for *about* is awkward and should be avoided.

> Rosa has a theory *about* Edgar Allan Poe's style.

beside, besides: *Beside* is a preposition meaning "at the side of" or "close to." Do not confuse *beside* with *besides,* which means "in addition to." *Besides* can be a preposition or an adverb.

> As the men cross the lawn and approach the open window, a brown spaniel trots *beside* them.
> There are many other Indian oral epics *besides* the *Ramayana.*

can, may: The verb *can* generally refers to the ability to do something. The verb *may* generally refers to permission to do something.

> Dylan Thomas describes his childhood Christmases so vividly that most readers can visualize the scenes.
> Creon's edict states that no one may bury Polyneices.

different from, different than: The preferred usage is *different from.*

> The structure and rhyme scheme of a Shakespearean sonnet are *different from* the organization of a Petrarchan sonnet.

farther, further: Use *farther* when you refer to distance. Use *further* when you mean "to a greater degree" or "additional."

> The *farther* the ants travel, the more ominous and destructive they seem.

> The storm in Act I of *The Tragedy of Julius Caesar* *further* hints at the ominous deeds to come.

fewer, less: Use *fewer* for things that can be counted. Use *less* for amounts or quantities that cannot be counted.

> Poetry often uses *fewer* words than prose to convey ideas and images.

> It takes *less* time to perform a Greek tragedy than to perform a Shakespearean play.

good, well: Use the adjective *good* after linking verbs such as *feel, look, smell, taste*, and *seem*. Use *well* whenever you need an adverb or as an adjective describing health.

> Caesar remarks that Cassius does not look *good*; on the contrary, his appearance is "lean."

> Twain wrote especially *well* when he described eccentric characters.

hopefully: Do not attach this adverb to a sentence loosely, as in "*Hopefully*, the rain will stop by noon." Rewrite the sentence so that *hopefully* modifies a specific verb. Other possible ways of revising such sentences include using the adjective *hopeful* or a phrase such as *everyone hopes that*.

> Dr. Martin Luther King, Jr., wrote and spoke *hopefully* about his dream of racial harmony.

> Mr. White was *hopeful* that the monkey's paw would bring him good fortune.

> *Everyone hopes that* the class production of *Antigone* will be a big success.

its, it's: Do not confuse the possessive pronoun its with the contraction *it's*, used in place of "it is" or "it has."

> In *its* very first lines, "The Stolen Child" establishes an eerie mood.

> In "The Street of the Cañon," Pepe Gonzalez knows that *it's* dangerous to attend the party.

just, only: When you use *just* as an adverb meaning "no more than," be sure you place it directly before the word it logically modifies. Likewise, be sure you place *only* before the word it logically modifies.

> *Just* one wish changed the Whites' lives forever.

> A short story can usually develop *only* a few characters, whereas a novel can include many.

kind of, sort of: In formal writing, you should not use these colloquial expressions. Instead, use a word such as *rather* or *somewhat*.

> Poe portrays Prince Prospero as *rather* arrogant.

> The tone of the biography is *somewhat* harsh.

lay, lie: Do not confuse these verbs. *Lay* is a transitive verb meaning "to set or put something down." Its principal parts are *lay, laying, laid, laid. Lie* is an intransitive verb meaning "to recline." Its principal parts are *lie, lying, lay, lain*.

> They laid the monkey's paw on the table for a while before anyone dared to pick it up.

> La Belle Dame sans Merci enchants the knight as he *lies* in her "elfin grot."

leave, let: Be careful not to confuse these verbs. *Leave* means "to go away" or "to allow to remain." *Let* means "to permit."

> Threatening Antigone not to disobey his orders, Creon angrily *leaves* the stage.

> Creon did not want to *let* Antigone bury her brother.

raise, rise: *Raise* is a transitive verb that usually takes a direct object. *Rise* is an intransitive verb and never takes a direct object.

> In his speech, Antony unexpectedly *raises* the subject of Caesar's will.

> When the Cabuliwallah comes to call, Mini *rises* from her chair and runs to greet him.

set, sit: Do not confuse these verbs. *Set* is a transitive verb meaning "to put (something) in a certain place." Its principal parts are *set, setting, set, set. Sit* is an intransitive verb meaning "to be seated." Its principal parts are *sit, sitting, sat, sat*.

> Antigone's conduct *sets* a high standard for us.

> Jerry's mother *sits* in her beach chair while Jerry swims in the ocean.

so, so that: Be careful not to use the coordinating conjunction *so* when your context requires *so that*. *So* means "accordingly" or "with the result that" and expresses a cause-and-effect relationship. *So that* expresses purpose—what someone intends to achieve.

> He wanted to do well on the test, *so* he read *The Tragedy of Julius Caesar* again.

> Antony uses eloquent rhetoric to stir up the people *so that* they will rebel.

than, then: The conjunction *than* is used to connect the two parts of a comparison. Do not confuse *than* with the adverb *then*, which usually refers to time.

> I enjoyed "The Marginal World" more *than* "Flood."

Marian Anderson gave a triumphant singing recital in New York that evening, and she *then* embarked on a coast-to-coast American tour.

GRAMMAR, USAGE, AND MECHANICS HANDBOOK

that, which, who: Use the relative pronoun *that* to refer to things. Use *which* only for things and *who* only for people.

> The poem *that* Cheryl liked the most was "The street."
>
> Haiku, *which* consists of only seventeen syllables, is often built around one or two vivid images.
>
> The assassin *who* strikes Caesar first is Casca.

unique: Because *unique* means "one of a kind," you should not use it carelessly to mean "interesting" or "unusual." Avoid such illogical expressions as "most unique," "very unique," and "extremely unique."

> Emily Dickinson's bold experiments with form make her *unique* in the history of nineteenth-century American poetry.

when, where: Do not directly follow a linking verb with *when* or *where*. Be careful not to use *where* when your context requires *that*.

> **Faulty:** The exposition is *when* an author provides the reader with important background information.
>
> **Revised:** In the exposition, an author provides the reader with important background information.
>
> **Faulty:** Madras, India, is *where* R. K. Narayan was born.
>
> **Revised:** R. K. Narayan was born in Madras, India.
>
> **Faulty:** We read *where* the prizes were worth hundreds of dollars.
>
> **Revised:** We read *that* the prizes were worth hundreds of dollars.

Index of Skills

Boldface numbers indicate pages where terms are defined.

Writing

Writing Applications

Writing for Assessment.
See **TEST PRACTICE**

Writing Strategies

Prewriting:

Research and Technology

Activities:

Advertising poster, 1005
Biographical brochure, 1219
Bulletin board display on Vreeland, 27
Cover letter and résumé, 575
Daily observation journal, 87
Film "influences" chart, 1187
Literary history report, 731
Multimedia presentation, 1005
Report
   on sources, 267
Research summary, 399
Spreadsheet, 179
Visual arts presentation, 749
Women's history report, 1005

Steps/Tips:

Accuracy, evaluate, 267, 731
Action verbs, use, 575
Biographical dictionary, use, 1219
Chart, create, 87
Comments, ask for, 399
Complexities, identify, 267
Computer software, use, 87, 179, 1005, 1219
Data, review, 179
Design principles, use appropriate, 575, 1219
Details, include, 179, 1219
Director's influence, discuss/chart, 1187
Discrepancies, identify, 267
Expectations, anticipate/address, 399
Format, find/follow suitable, 575
Graph, create, 87
Ideas, jot down, 267
Information
   add interesting, 1005
   choose significant/integrate, 731
   order, 1005
Internet resources, use, 399, 731, 1005, 1219
Library resources, use, 399, 731, 1005, 1219
Misunderstandings, anticipate/address, 399
Opinions, jot down, 267
Paraphrase, 1005
Proofread carefully, 575
Props, use, 749
Questions, address, 267, 399
Quotations, add, 27
Reliability, evaluate, 267, 731
Sources
   document, 1005
   use variety/evaluate, 267, 731
Summary, write/share, 87
Technical terms, explain, 399
Text features, identify/evaluate, 267
Visual aids, use, 749, 1005

Test Practice

Reading for Information

Comparing, 95, 187, 305, 407, 517, 583, 699, 757, 867, 1013, 1127, 1227
Reading, 216, 436, 620, 784, 1040, 1258
Literary Skills, 214, 434, 618, 782, 1038, 1256
Reading Skills, 88, 180, 296, 400, 510, 576, 692, 750, 862, 1006, 1120, 1220
Vocabulary Skills, 217, 437, 621, 785, 1041, 1259
Writing and Language Conventions, 218, 438, 622, 786, 1042, 1260

Writing for Assessment:

Connecting Across Texts, 89, 181, 297, 401, 511, 577, 693, 751, 863, 1121, 1221
Drama, 862, 1007, 1039, 1043
Fiction/nonfiction, 88, 180, 215, 219
Nonfiction, 510, 576, 619, 623
Poetry, 692, 750, 783, 787
Short story, 296, 400, 435, 439
Themes in oral tradition, 1120, 1220, 1257, 1261
Timed, 95, 187, 305, 407, 517, 583, 699, 757, 867, 1013, 1127, 1227

Index of Features

Boldface numbers indicate pages where terms are defined.

Writing Workshop: Work in Progress

Index of Authors and Titles

Notes: Page numbers in *italics* refer to biographical information; Nonfiction and informational text appears in red.

Acknowledgments

Dr. Renee Friedman "Archaeology's Interactive Dig - Narmer's Temple: Week 1" by Renee Friedman from *http://www.archaeology.org* Copyright © 2003 Archaeological Institute of America. Used by permission.

Garmin International, Inc. "GPS Quick Start Guide" from *www.garmin.com.* Copyright © 2004 Garmin Ltd. or its subsidiaries. Used by permission.

Sanford J. Greenburger Associates "The Threads of Time" by C.J. Cherryh from *The Collected Short Fiction of C.J. Cherryh.* First Printing, February 2004. All rights reserved. Used by permission.

Grove/Atlantic, Inc. "Tanka: The Clustering Clouds" from *Anthology of Japanese Literature* by Minamoto no Toshiyori, translated by Donald Keene. Copyright © 1965 by Grove Atlantic, Inc. Used by permission.

Harcourt, Inc. "The Garden of Stubborn Cats" by Italo Calvino from *Marcovaldo of the Seasons in the City,* copyright © 1963 by Giulio Einaudi editore s.p.a., Torino. English translation by William Weaver copyright © 1983 by Harcourt, Inc. and Martin Secker & Warburg, Ltd. "How to React to Familiar Faces" from *How to Travel with a Salmon & Other Essays* by Umberto Eco, copyright © Gruppo Editoriale Fabbri, Bompiani, Sonzogno, Etas S.p.A., English translation by William Weaver copyright © 1994 by Harcourt, Inc. "Jazz Fantasia" by Carl Sandburg from *Smoke and Steel.* Copyright © 1920 by Harcourt, Inc. and renewed 1948 by Carl Sandburg. "Antigone" by Sophocles from *Sophocles: The Oedipus Cycle, An English Version.* The Oedipus Cycle: An English Version by Dudley Fitts and Robert Fitzgerald, copyright © 1939 by Harcourt Inc., and renewed 1967 by Dudley Fitts and Robert Fitzgerald. This material may not be reproduced in any form or by any means without the prior written permission of the publisher. **CAUTION:** All rights, including professional, amateur, motion picture, recitation, lecturing, performance, public reading, radio broadcasting, and television are strictly reserved. Inquiries of all rights should be addressed to Harcourt, Inc., Permissions Dept., Orlando, FL 32887. Used by permission of the publisher.

Harper's Magazine "The Leap" by Louise Erdrich from *Harper's Magazine.* Copyright © 1990 by Harper's Magazine Foundation. Used from the March issue by special permission.

Harvard Observatory "Classifying the Stars" by Annie J. Cannon from *The University of Stars.* Cambridge, Mass.: Harvard Observatory, 1926.

Harvard University Press "Tell all the Truth but tell it slant (#1129)", "The Wind-tapped like a tired man (#436)" by Emily Dickinson from *The Poems of Emily Dickinson,* Thomas H. Johnson, ed., Cambridge, Mass.: The Belknap Press of Harvard University Press, Copyright © 1951, 1955, 1979, 1983 by the President and Fellows of Harvard College. Used by permission of the publishers and the Trustees of Amherst College. Copyright © 1951, 1955, byt the President and Fellows of Harvard College. © Copyright 1914, 1914, 1918, 1919, 1924, 1929, 1930, 1932, 1935, 1937, 1942 by Martha Dickinson Bianchi.

Healdsburg Jazz Festival "Healdsburg Jazz Festival Winter 2007 Newsletter" from *www.healdsburgjazzfestival.org.* Used by permission.

Thomas A. Hill "The History of the Guitar" by Thomas A. Hill from *The Guitar: An Introduction of the Instrument.* Copyright © 1973 by Thomas A. Hill. All rights reserved. Used with permission of Thomas A. Hill.

Hispanic Society of America "The Guitar" by Federico García Lorca from *Translations From Hispanic Poets.* Copyright 1938 by The Hispanic Society of America. Used with permission of the Hispanic Society of America.

The Barbara Hogenson Agency, Inc. "The Dog That Bit People" by James Thurber from *My Life and Hard Times.* Copyright © 1933, 1961 by James Thurber. Used by arrangement with Rosemary Thurber and The Barbara Hogenson Agency. All rights reserved.

Houghton Mifflin Company, Inc. "The Marginal World" from *The Edge of the Sea* by Rachel Carson. Copyright © 1955 by Rachel L. Carson, renewed 1983 by Roger Christie. "Prometheus and the First People" (originally titled "The Creation of Man" and "The Coming of Evil") from *Greek Myths* by Olivia E. Coolidge. Copyright © 1949 by Olivia E. Coolidge; copyright renewed © 1977 by Olivia E. Coolidge. Adapted by permission of Houghton Mifflin Company. Text © 1949 by Olivia E. Coolidge. Used by permission of Houghton Mifflin Co. All rights reserved.

David Henry Hwang From "Tibet Through the Red Box" from Act II by David Henry Hwang. Used by permission.

The Jazz Society of Pensacola "The Jazz Society of Pensacola, March 2007 Newsletter" by Andrew R. Metzger from *http://www.jazzpensacola.com.* Copyright © 2001 Jazz Society of Pensacola. Used by permission.

Johnson & Alcock Ltd., London "The Bridegroom" by Alexander Pushkin from *The Bronze Horseman and Other Poems,* Secker & Warburg, 1982. Translation © D.M. Thomas. Used by permission of Johnson and Alcock Ltd., London.

Johnson Outdoors Inc. "Compass Directions and Warranty" by Staff from *www.silvacompass.com* Copyright 2002 Johnson Outdoors Inc. All rights reserved. Used by permission.

Alfred A. Knopf, Inc. From "Swimming to Antarctica: Tales of a Long-Distance Swimmer" by Lynne Cox. Copyright © 2004 by Lynne Cox. "The Weary Blues" by Langston Hughes from *Selected Poems of Langston Hughes,* copyright © 1994 by The Estate of Langston Hughes. Copyright © 1926 Alfred A. Knopf, Inc., Renewed 1954 Estate of Langston Hughes. Used by permission of Alfred A. Knopf, a division of Random House, Inc. All rights reserved.

Little, Brown & Company, Inc. "Theseus" from *Mythology* by Edith Hamilton. Copyright © 1942 by Edith Hamilton. Copyright © renewed 1969 by Dorian Fielding Reid and Doris Fielding Reid. By permission of Little, Brown, and Co., Inc.

Liveright Publishing Corporation "Reapers" by Jean Toomer from *Cane.* Copyright 1923 by Boni & Liveright, renewed 1951 by Jean Toomer. Used by permission of Liveright Publishing Corporation.

Los Angeles Public Library "Los Angeles Public Library: Borrower Services" from *http://www.lapl.org.* Used by permission of the City of Los Angeles.

The Jennifer Lyons Literary Agency, LLC "Fear" by Gabriela Mistral from *Selected Poems of Gabriela Mistral,* translated by Doris Dana. Copyright 1961, 1964, 1970, 1971 by Doris Dana. Used by permission.

Marco Mielcarek "Voices from the Wall: Ich bin ein Berliner" by Marco Mielcarek. Used by permission.

Edna St. Vincent Millay Society "Conscientious Objector" by Edna St. Vincent Millay from *Collected Poems*. Copyright © 1934, 1962 by Edna St. Vincent Millay and Norma Millay Ellis. All rights reserved. Copyright © 1917, 1921, 1923, 1928, 1931, 1933, 1934, 1936, 1937, 1938, 1939, 1940, 1941, 1950 by Edna St. Vincent Millay. Copyright © 1945, 1946, 1947, 1951, 1952, 1953, 1954, 1956 by Norma Millay Ellis. Used by permission of Elizabeth Barnett, literary executor.

Navarre Scott Momaday From "The Way to Rainy Mountain" by N. Scott Momaday. Copyright © 1969 by The University of New Mexico Press. Used by permission.

William Morris Agency "A Visit to Grandmother" by William Melvin Kelley from *Dances on the Shore*. Copyright © 1964, 1992 by William Melvin Kelley. Used by permission of William Morris Agency, LLC on behalf of the author.

National Aeronautics and Space Administration "Black Water Turns the Tide on Florida Coral" from *http://www.nasa.gov*

National Science Teachers Assocation Publications "An Interview with Firefighter Denise Dierich" by Megan Sullivan from *http://newsite.nsta.org* Copyright © 2003 NSTA. Used by permission.

Navajivan Trust From *Defending Nonviolent Resistance* by Mohandas K. Gandhi. Used by permission.

New American Library, a division of Penguin "An Enemy of the People" by Henrik Ibsen from *The Complete Major Prose Plays of Henrik Ibsen* translated by Rolf Fjelde, copyright © 1965, 1970, 1978 by Rolf Fjelde. Used by permission of Dutton Signet, a division of Penguin Group (USA) Inc.

New Directions Publishing Corporation "Do Not Go Gentle into That Good Night" by Dylan Thomas from *The Poems of Dylan Thomas*. Copyright © 1952 by Dylan Thomas. "Spring and All" by William Carlos Williams from *Collected Poems, 1909-1939, Volume I*. Copyright © 1938 by New Directions Publishing Corp. "A Tree Telling of Orpheus" by Denise Levertov from *Poems, 1968-1972*. Copyright © 1965, 1966, 1967, 1968, 1969, 1970, 1971 by Denise Levertov Goodman. Copyright © 1970, 1971, 1972, 1987 by Denise Levertov. Used by permission of New Directions Publishing Corp. "I Am Offering This Poem" by Jimmy Santiago Baca from *Immigrants in Our Own Land & Selected Early Poems*. Copyright © 1979 by Jimmy Santiago Baca. Reprinted by permission of New Directions Publishing Corporation.

The New York Times "Mr. Gorbachev's Role" by Staff from *The New York Times (Late Edition)* November 10, 1999. Copyright © 1999 by The New York Times Inc. All rights reserved. Used by permission and protected by the Copyright Laws of The United States. The printing, copying, redistribution, or retransmission of the Material without express written permission is prohibited.

The New York Times Agency "Feel the City's Pulse? It's Be-bop, Man!" by Ann Douglas from *The New York Times August 28, 1998*. Copyright © 1998 by the New York Times. All rights reserved. Used by permission and protected by the Copyright Laws of The United States. The printing, copying, or retransmission of the Material without express written permission is prohibited.

North Point Press, div of Farrar, Straus & Giroux "All" by Bei Dao translated by Donald Finkel and Xueliang Chen from *A Splintered Mirror: Chinese Poetry From the Democracy Movement*.

Translation copyright © 1991 by Donald Finkel. Used by permission of North Point Press, a division of Farrar, Straus and Giroux, LLC. "Also All" by Shu Ting, translated by Donald Finkel and Jinsheng Yi from *A Splintered Mirror: Chinese Poetry From the Democracy Movement*. Translation copyright © 1991 by Donald Finkel.

Norwegian Nobel Institute Keep Memory Alive" by Elie Wiesel from *Elie Wiesel's Nobel Prize Acceptance Speech*. Used with permission from the Norwegian Nobel Institute. Copyright © 1986 by the Nobel Foundation.

Naomi Shihab Nye "Making a Fist" by Naomi Shihab Nye from *Hugging the Jukebox*. Copyright © 1982 by Dutton: New York. Used by permission of the author, Naomi Shihab Nye.

Harold Ober Associates, Inc. From *Marian Anderson: Famous Concert Singer* by Langston Hughes. Copyright © 1954 by Langston Hughes. Renewed 1982 by George Houston Bass. Used by permission of Harold Ober Associates Incorporated.

Oxford University Press, UK "How Much Land Does a Man Need?" by Leo Tolstoy translated by Louise and Aylmer Maude from *The Raid and Other Stories*. Edited by Maude, Louise & Aylmer. Copyright © 1935 Oxford University Press. Used with permission of Oxford University Press.

Pantheon Books, a div of Random House Inc. "The Orphan Boy and the Elk Dog" by Blackfoot from *American Indian Myths and Legends* by Richard Erdoes and Alfonso Ortiz. Copyright © 1984 by Richard Erdoes and Alfonso Ortiz. Used by permission.

Pearson Education "Tides" by Staff from *Prentice Hall Science Explorer: Earth Science*. Copyright © 2001 by Pearson Education, Inc., publishing as Pearson Prentice Hall. All rights reserved. Used by permission.

Pearson Education Ltd. From "Sundiata: An Epic of Old Mali: Childhood, The Lion's Awakening" by D.T. Niane translated by G.D. Pickett from *Sundiata: An Epic of Old Mali*. Copyright © Longman Group Limited 1965, used by permission of Pearson Education Limited. Copyright © Presence Africaine 1960 (original French version: Soundjata, ou L'Epopee Mandingue) © Longman Group Ltd. (English Version) 1965.

Penguin Group (USA) Inc. "Everest" from *Touch the Top of the World: A Blind Man's Journey to Climb Farther than the Eye Can See* by Erik Weihenmayer. Copyright © 2002 by Erik Weihenmayer. All rights reserved.

Penguin Putnam, Inc From "Places Left Unfinished at the Time of Creation" by John Phillip Santos. Copyright © 1999 by John Philip Santos. All rights reserved. Used by permission.

G.P. Putnam's Sons, a division of Penguin "Arthur Becomes King" Part I, Chapter XXII from *The Once and Future King* by T.H. White. Copyright © 1938, 1939, 1940, © 1958 by T. H. White, renewed.

Random House, Inc. From "A Raisin in the Sun, Act I, Scene ii" by Lorraine Hansberry from *A Raisin in the Sun*. Copyright © 1984 by Robert Nemiroff, an an unpublished work. Copyright © 1959, 1966, 1984 by Robert Nemiroff. All rights reserved. "Occupation: Conductorette" from *I Know Why the Caged Bird Sings* by Maya Angelou. Copyright © 1969 by Maya Angelou. All rights reserved. Used by permission. "A Quilt of a Country" by Anna Quindlen from *Loud and Clear*. Copyright © 2004 by Anna Quindlen. All rights reserved.

Random House Children's Books "Ashputtle" by Jakob and Wilhelm Grimm translated by Ralph Manheim from *Grimm's Tales for Young and Old: The Complete Stories*, copyright © 1977 by Ralph Manheim. Translation copyright © 1977 by Ralph Manheim. All rights reserved. Used by permission of Random House Children's Books, a division of Random House, Inc.

Marian Reiner, Literary Agent "Metaphor" by Eve Merriam from *It Doesn't Always Have to Rhyme*. Copyright © 1964, 1970, 1973, 1986 by Eve Merriam. Used by permission of Marian Reiner.

Rogers, Coleridge and White, Ltd. "Games at Twilight" by Anita Desai from *Games at Twilight and Other Stories*. Copyright © 1978 by Anita Desai. Used by permission of the author c/o Rogers, Coleridge & White Ltd., 20 Powis Mews, London W11 1JN.

Heyden White Rostow "The American Idea" by Theodore H. White from *The New York Times Magazine, July 6, 1986*. Copyright © 1986 by Theodore H. White. Copyright © 1986 by The New York Times Company. All rights reserved. Used by permission.

St. Martin's Press "Circumference: Eratosthenos and the Ancient Quest to Measure the Globe" by Nicholas Nicastro from *The Astrolabe*. St. Martin's Press, 2008.

Scientific American "The Spider and the Wasp" by Alexander Petrunkevitch from *Scientific American, August, 1952*. Copyright © 1952 by Scientific American, Inc. Used by permission.

The Sheep Meadow Press "Pride" by Dahlia Ravikovitch translated by Chana Bloch and Ariel Bloch from *The Window*. Copyright © 1987 by Chana Bloch. All rights reserved. Used by permission.

Signet Classic *A Doll's House* by Henrik Ibsen from Act I. New York: Signet Classics, 2006. (1879)

Elyse Sommer "A Curtain Up Review: Antigone As Acted and Played by the Three Fates on the Way to Becoming the Three Graces". Review by Elyse Sommer in www.curtainup.com, the online theater magazine. Copyright 2004, Elyse Sommer. Used by permission.

Sonoma County "The County of Sonoma Volunteer Application" from *http://www.sonoma-county.org*. Used by permission.

Talkin' Broadway "Antigone (Theatre Review)" by Matthew Murray from www.talkinbroadway.com. Used by permission.

Jeremy P. Tarcher/Putnam "Making History with Vitamin C (originally titled: Ascorbic Acid)" by Penny Le Couteur and Jay Burreson from *Napoleon's Buttons: How 17 Molecules Changed History*. Copyright © 2003 by Micron Geological Ltd. and Jay Burreson. All rights reserved.

Anthony Thwaite "Tanka: "Was it that I went to sleep"" by Ono no Komachi translated and co-edited by Geoffrey Bownas and Anthony Thwaite from *The Penguin Book of Japanese Verse*. "When I went to visit" by Ki no Tsurayuki translated by Bownas & Thwaite from *The Penguin Book of Japanese Verse*. "One cannot ask loneliness" by Priest Jakuren translated by Bownas & Thwaite from *The Penguin Book of Japanese Verse*. Penguin Books copyright © 1964, revised edition 1998. Translation copyright © Geoffrey Bownas and Anthony Thwaite, 1964, 1998. Used by permission.

UCLA Office of Media Relations "Strong Earth Tides Can Trigger Earthquakes" from *http://www.newsroom.ucla.edu/*. Courtesy of UCLA. Used by permission.

David Unger "The Censors" by Luisa Valenzuela translated by Hortense Carpentier from *Open Door: Stories*. Copyright © translation by David Unger. Used by permission.

University of North Carolina Press The Street of the Canon" by Josefina Niggli from *Mexican Village*. Copyright © 1945 by the University of North Carolina Press, renewed 1972 by Josefina Niggli. Used by permission of the publisher.

U.S. News & World Report Will All the Blue Men End Up in Timbuktu?" by Stefan Lovgren from *US News and World Report, December 7, 1998*. Copyright © 1998 U.S. News & World Report, L.P. All rights reserved. Used by permission.

Viking Penguin, Inc. "Like the Sun" by R.K. Narayan, from *Under the Banyan Tree*. Copyright © 1985 by R. K. Narayan. "My City" by James Weldon Johnson from *Saint Peter Relates an Incident*. Copyright © 1935 by James Weldon John, © renewed 1963 by Grace Nail Johnson. All rights reserved. From "What Makes a Degas a Degas?" by Richard Muhlberger. Published by The Metropolitan Museum of Art, New York, and Viking, a Division of Penguin Putnam Books for Young Readers, copyright © 1993 by The Metropolitan Museum of Art. "What Makes a Degas a Degas?" is a registered trademark of The Metropolitan Museum of Art. All rights reserved.

Susan Vreeland "Artful Research" by Susan Vreeland from *The Writer, January 2002*. Copyright © 2001. "Magdalena Looking" by Susan Vreeland from *Girl in Hacinth Blue*. Copyright © 1999 by Susan Vreeland. Available in hardback: MacAdam-Cage; paperback: Penguin. Used with permission.

W. W. Norton & Company, Inc. "Don Quixote", excerpt from *Don Quixote: A Norton Critical Edition: The Ormbsby Translation, Revised*, by Miguel de Cervantes, edited by Joseph Jones and Kenneth Douglas. Copyright © 1981 by W.W. Norton & Company, Inc. Used by permission of W.W. Norton & Company, Inc.

Walker Publishing Company "Imaginary Lines" by Dava Sobel from *Longitude: The True Story of a Lone Genius Who Solved the Greatest Scientific Problem of His Time*. Copyright © Dava Sobel, 1995. All rights reserved. Used by permission.

Wallace Literary Agency, Inc. "Rama's Initiation" from *The Ramayana* by R.K. Narayan. Published by Penguin Books. Copyright © 1972 by R.K. Narayanan. Used by permission of the Wallace Literary Agency, Inc.

Wesleyan University Press "Glory" by Yusef Komunyakaa from *Magic City* (Wesleyan University Press, 1992) Copyright © 1992 by Yusef Komunyakaa and used by permission of Wesleyan University Press.

World Vision Magazine "Thank Heaven for Little Girls" by Rich Stearns from *World Vision Magazine*, Spring 2007. Used by permission.

The Wylie Agency, Inc. "The Garden of Stubborn Cats" by Italo Calvino from *Marcovaldo or the Seasons in the City*. Copyright © 1963 by Guilio Einaudi editore s.p.a., used with the permission of the Wylie Agency Inc. English translation copyright © 1983 by Harcourt Brace Jovanovich, Inc. and Martin Secker & Warburg Limited.

Note: Every effort has been made to locate the copyright owner of material reproduced on this component. Omissions brought to our attention will be corrected in subsequent editions.

Credits

Photo Credits

viii–ix: © James O'Mara/Taxi/Getty Images; x–xi: © James O'Mara/Taxi/Getty Images; xii–xiii: Flying Colours Ltd./Digital Vision/Getty Images, Inc.; xiv–xv: Flying Colours Ltd./Digital Vision/Getty Images, Inc.; xx–xxi: © Neil Brennan/Canopy Illustration/Veer; xxii–xxiii: © Neil Brennan/Canopy Illustration/Veer; xxiv–xxv: Ron Sanford/CORBIS; xxvi–xxvii: Ron Sanford/CORBIS; xxviii–xxix: Masterfile; xxx–xxxi: Masterfile; xlviii: Kompaniets Taras/Shutterstock; Gr10 U1 1: © James O'Mara/Taxi/Getty Images; 2: © Alexandra Day/CORBIS; 3: StockTrek/Getty Images; 5: Brand X Pictures/Getty Images; 6: *Speed Bump* © 2003 Dave Coverly. Reprinted with the permission of Dave Coverly and the Cartoonist Group. All rights reserved; 7: © Bob Krist/CORBIS; 9: *Detail of Head of a Young Woman,* Jan Vermeer, Francis G. Mayer/CORBIS; 10: Corel Professional Photos CD-ROM™; 12: *The Allegory of the Art of Painting,* c. 1670, Jan Vermeer, Kunsthistorisches Museum, Vienna/CORBIS; 15: Corel Professional Photos CD-ROM™; 16: Corel Professional Photos CD-ROM™; 21: t. Getty Images; 21: t. © Dorling Kindersley; 21: t. © Dorling Kindersley; 21: m. © Dorling Kindersley; 23: b. Courtesy of Susan Vreeland; 24: t. Images.com/CORBIS; 26: b. Hulton Archive/Getty Images Inc.; 26: bl. © Dorling Kindersley; 26: bm. Erich Lessing/Art Resource, NY; 26: br. Giraudon/The Bridgeman Art Library, London/New York; 26: br. Corel Professional Photos CD-ROM™; 26: b. © Dorling Kindersley; 31: b. © Alen MacWeeney/CORBIS; 31: tr. © Bettmann/CORBIS; 32: © Alen MacWeeney/CORBIS; 32: m. © Sebastian Derungs/Reuters/CORBIS; 33: istockphoto.com; 34: Frederick Ayer III / Photo Researchers, Inc.; 35: © Gregg Roth/Gregg Roth Studios/Sculpture by Andrew Leman; 36–37: border. © Alen MacWeeney/CORBIS; 37: Pamela Hodson/istockphoto.com; 38–39: border. © Alen MacWeeney/CORBIS; 40: istockphoto.com; 40–41: border. © Alen MacWeeney/CORBIS; 42: border. © Alen MacWeeney/CORBIS; 42: tl. istockphoto.com/Nathan Cox; 45: © Thomas Victor; 61: t. AP/Wide World Photos; 61: b. © Fergus Greer/Fergus Greer Studio; 62: © Patrik Giardino/CORBIS; 64: © bülent gültek/istockphoto.com; 66–67: © Patrik Giardino/CORBIS; 68: © Ty Milford/Aurora/Getty Images; 69: Galen Rowell/CORBIS; 70: Geoff Renner/Robert Harding World Imagery; 78–79: © Kit Kittle/CORBIS; 72: © bülent gültek/istockphoto.com; 73: © Keren Su/Digital Vision /Getty Images; 77: Mansell/Mansell/Time & Life Pictures/Getty Images; 77: tl. Getty Images; 80: Courtesy of the Market Street Railway, San Francisco; 80–81: © Bettmann/CORBIS; 82: Slim Aarons/Hulton Archive/Getty Images; 92: Maps.com; 97: mr. CORBIS; 97: bl. AP/Wide World Photos; 98: © Bettmann/CORBIS; 101: AP/Wide World Photos; 102: Department of the Interior; 104–105: Gina Martin/National Geographic/Getty Images; 105: br. Linda Whitwam/Dorling Kindersley/Getty Images; 106: © Macduff Everton/CORBIS; 137: t. Colin McPherson/CORBIS; 137: b. Nancy Sheehan/PhotoEdit; 138: bl. © Kamal Kishore/Reuters/CORBIS; 138–139: istockphoto.com; 141: © ADNAN ABIDI/Reuters/CORBIS; 142: © Photographer: Paul Butchard | Agency: Dreamstime.com; 143: Royalty-Free/CORBIS; 145: Chase Swift/CORBIS; 146–147: Nancy Sheehan/PhotoEdit; 155: Photofest; 155: b. © Peter Adams/JAI/CORBIS; 156–157: © Atlantide Phototravel/CORBIS; 158–159: © Brandon D. Cole/CORBIS; 161: © George D. Lepp/CORBIS; 162: © Riccardo Spila/Grand Tour/CORBIS; 163: © Arthur Morris/CORBIS; 167: ml. Courtesy of Jay Burreson; 167: tl. Courtesy Penny Le Couteur; 167: tl. RF © Slavoljub Pantelic/istockphoto.com; 168: tl. RF © Slavoljub Pantelic/istockphoto.com; 168: tl. istockphoto.com; 169: *As for Resolution* (oil on canvas), Brooks, Robin /Private Collection, /The Bridgeman Art Library International; 170: b. © Mike Kowalski/Illustration Works/CORBIS; 170: bl. © Stefano Bianchetti/CORBIS; 172: FoodCollection/Superstock; 174: t. James Cook (1728–79) from *Gallery of Portraits,* published 1833 (engraving) (later colouration), English School, (19th century) /Private Collection, Ken Welsh /The Bridgeman Art Library International; 176: Steve Gorton © Dorling Kindersley; 183: t. Barnabas Kindersley/© Dorling Kindersley; 183: b. Corel Professional Photos CD-ROM™; 184: Barnabas Kindersley/© Dorling Kindersley; 186: tl. © courtesy of the Hierakonpolis Expedition - Renee Friedman; 186: tr.

istockphoto.com; 186: m. Ivor Kerslake/The British Museum/© Dorling Kindersley; 186: b. © courtesy of the Hierakonpolis Expedition - Renee Friedman; 189: t. AP/Wide World Photos; 189: b. The Granger Collection, New York; 190: istockphoto.com; 191: istockphoto.com; 192: © John Foxx/Stockbyte/Getty Images; 193: © John Reader/Time Life Pictures/Getty Images; 194: © John Foxx /Stockbyte/Getty Images; 195: *Through a Window,* 1922, Farmer, Walter (1887–1947) /Private Collection /The Bridgeman Art Library International; 196: © Christie's Images; 198: THOMAS D. MCAVOY/Time & Life Pictures/Getty Images; 200: David Young-Wolff/PhotoEdit Inc.; 203: Prentice Hall; 208: © Alexandra Day/CORBIS; 210: © Bonnie Kamin/PhotoEdit Inc.; 218 (CL) © Associated Press, (BCR) © Classic Image/Alamy Images, (TR) Getty Images; Gr10 U2 220–221: Flying Colours Ltd./Digital Vision/Getty Images, Inc.; 222: © Stefano Bianchetti/CORBIS; 223: © Bettmann/CORBIS; 225: Mark Shaver/images.com; 226: © The New Yorker Collection 1999 David Sipress from cartoonbank.com. All Rights Reserved.; 227: © Jim West/Photo Edit; 241: t. Carl Van Vechten, photographer, Permission Van Vechten Trust; 241: b. *Young Man in Blue Suit,* Alice Kent Stoddard /SuperStock; 242: Smithsonian American Art Museum, Washington, D.C. /Art Resource, NY; 245: *Young Man in Blue Suit,* Alice Kent Stoddard /SuperStock; 246: *Haystack,* 1938 (tempera with oil glaze on linen on panel), Benton, Thomas Hart (1889–1975) /Museum of Fine Arts, Houston, Texas, USA, © DACS /Gift of Mr. Frank J. Hevrdejs /The Bridgeman Art Library International; 249: Stock Montage, Inc.; 255: t. © Bettmann/CORBIS; 255: b. © José Fuste Raga/Age Fotostock; 256: Private Collection, Roy Miles Fine Paintings /The Bridgeman Art Library; 258: Lebrecht Music & Arts; 261: *Candelabra,* 2003 (oil on canvas), Ireland, William (Contemporary Artist) /Private Collection, /The Bridgeman Art Library International; 263: © SuperStock, Inc. /SuperStock; 271: *Reina Xochtl* (gouache on newspaper) by Alfredo Ramos Martinez (1872–1946); 272: *Dance in Tehuantepec,* 1935, Diego Rivera, Los Angeles Museum of Art, Gift of Mr. and Mrs. Milton W. Lipper, from the Milton W. Lipper Estate. Photograph ©2003 Museum Associates/LACMA. ©Banco de Mexico Diego Rivera and Frida Kahlo Museums Trust Av. Cinco de Mayo No. 2, Col. Centro, Del. Cuauhtemoc 06059, Mexico, D.F. Reproduction authorized by the Instituto Nacional de Belles Artes y Literatura; 275: Images.com/CORBIS; 277: John Newcomb/SuperStock; 279: *Reina Xochtl* (gouache on newspaper) by Alfredo Ramos Martinez (1872–1946); 283: t. Thomas Victor; 283: b. *The Body of a House #5 of 8.* © Robert Beckmann 1993, oil on canvas, 69" x 96 1/2". Collection; Nevada Museum of Art, Reno. Photo by Tony Scodwell; 285: *The Body of a House #1 of 8.* © Robert Beckmann 1993, oil on canvas, 69" x 96 1/2". Collection; Nevada Museum of Art, Reno. Photo by Tony Scodwell; 286: *The Body of a House #2 of 8.* © Robert Beckmann 1993, oil on canvas, 69" x 96 1/2". Collection; Nevada Museum of Art, Reno. Photo by Tony Scodwell; 289: *The Body of a House #4 of 8.* © Robert Beckmann 1993, oil on canvas, 69" x 96 1/2". Collection; Nevada Museum of Art, Reno. Photo by Tony Scodwell; 291: *The Body of a House #5 of 8.* © Robert Beckmann 1993, oil on canvas, 69" x 96 1/2". Collection; Nevada Museum of Art, Reno. Photo by Tony Scodwell; 299: tl. W. Kenneth Hamblin; 299: tr. PhotoDisc, Inc./Getty Images; 299: b. W. Kenneth Hamblin; 299: bkgrnd. istockphoto.com; 300: istockphoto.com; 307: t. © Bettmann/CORBIS; 307: b. AP/Wide World Photos; 308: CORBIS; 312: Don Mason/CORBIS; 314–315: © David Tipling /Alamy; 317: *Sydney Harbour Bridge,* 1995 (oil on canvas), Blackall, Ted (Contemporary Artist) /Private Collection, /The Bridgeman Art Library International; 318: © Marshall Arisman; 320: © Marshall Arisman; 322: © Christel Tranberg/Getty Images; 324: *Tudor City at night, Overlooking East River,* 1998 (oil on canvas), Gibbs, Nicholas (Contemporary Artist) /Private Collection, /The Bridgeman Art Library International; 337: t. L. N. Tolstoi, I. E. Repin, Sovfoto/Eastfoto; 337: b. Scala /Art Resource, NY; 338: Corel Professional Photos CD-ROM™; 340: *The Toast,* G.K. Totybadse, Scala/Art Resource, NY; 342: Tate, London /Art Resource, NY; 345: Scala /Art Resource, NY; 346: Scala /Art Resource, NY; 350: © Bettmann/CORBIS; 353: © SuperStock, Inc. /SuperStock; 357: AP/Wide World Photos;

SuperStock; **703:** Scala /Art Resource, NY; **704:** *Marilyn Monroe,* Andy Warhol, ©Andy Warhol Foundation/CORBIS; **705:** *Marilyn Monroe,* Andy Warhol, ©Andy Warhol Foundation/CORBIS; **705:** *Marilyn Monroe,* Andy Warhol, ©Andy Warhol Foundation/CORBIS; **717:** t. Amherst College Archives and Special Collections, by permission of the Trustees of Amherst College; **717:** m. Time Life Pictures/Getty Images; **717:** b. Photo by Bachrach. Used by permission of Marian Reiner; **718:** istockphoto.com; **719:** © Howard J. Winter/zefa/CORBIS; **720:** © Michael A. Keller/CORBIS; **720:** inset © Lew Robertson/CORBIS; **721:** © Robert Michael/CORBIS; **722:** © Russell Tate/istockphoto.com; **725:** t. National Portrait Gallery, Smithsonian Institution /Art Resource, NY; **725:** m. Dina Gona; **725:** b. Amherst College Archives and Special Collections, by permission of the Trustees of Amherst College; **726:** © Regien Paassen; **727:** *The Cliffs of Moher,* 2003 (oil on board), Warmoth, Pip Todd (b. 1962) / Private Collection, Kings Road Galleries / The Bridgeman Art Library International; **728:** © Joel Barr /SuperStock; **735:** t. Photograph © The Estate of Carl Van Vechten Gravure and Compilation © Eakins Press Foundation; **735:** m. The Granger Collection, New York; **735:** b. The Granger Collection, New York; **736:** *Autumn Lamp* (*Guitar Player,* 1983), Romare Bearden, From the Mecklenburg Autumn Series, oil with collage, 40″ x 31″, Private collection, ©1997 Romare Bearden Foundation/Licensed by VAGA, New York, New York; **738:** © Oksana Struk/istockphoto.com; **739:** t. © istockphoto.com; **739:** b. © Aliaksandr Stsiazhyn /istockphoto.com; **743:** t. © Bettmann/CORBIS; **743:** m. Michael Nicholson/CORBIS; **743:** b. The Granger Collection, New York; **744:** Smithsonian American Art Museum, Washington, D.C. /Art Resource, NY; **745:** *Terror from the Deep* (gouache on paper), Frey, Oliver (b. 1948) /Private Collection, © Look and Learn / The Bridgeman Art Library International; **746:** © SuperStock, Inc. / SuperStock; **755:** t. Art Kowalsky/Alamy; **755:** b. Karsten Wrobel/Alamy; **755:** bkgrnd. Siephoto/Masterfile; **756:** Ariadne Van Zandbergen/Alamy; **756:** bkgrnd. Siephoto/Masterfile; **759:** t. © Kuntz Doug/CORBIS Sygma; **759:** m. Dorothy Alexander; **759:** b. Dorothy Alexander; **760:** Getty Images; **761:** l. Courtesy of Columbia Records; **761:** r. © Retna, LTD; **762–763:** istockphoto.com; **764:** AP/Wide World Photos; **765:** t. One of a series of paintings of birds and fruit, late 19th century (w/c on paper), Wang Guochen (19th century) /School of Oriental & African Studies Library, Univ. of London, / The Bridgeman Art Library International; **765:** b. AP/Wide World Photos; **766:** One of a series of paintings of birds and fruit, late 19th century (w/c on paper), Wang Guochen (19th century) /School of Oriental & African Studies Library, Univ. of London, /The Bridgeman Art Library International; **768:** Stewart Cohen/Photolibrary; **771:** Prentice Hall; **776:** © Spencer Grant /Photo Edit; **Gr10 U5** **778:** © Bettmann/CORBIS; **786** (TL, BR) © Associated Press; **788–789:** Ron Sanford/CORBIS; **790:** © Dave Reede/ Getty Images; **791:** © Elmar Krenkel/zefa/CORBIS; **794:** FOXTROT © 2003 Bill Amend. Reprinted with permission of UNIVERSAL PRESS SYNDICATE. All rights reserved.; **795:** © Bob Daemmrich /Photo Edit; **797:** © Chris Bennion/Seattle Children's Theater; **800:** © Chris Bennion/Seattle Children's Theater; **803:** © Peter Turnley/CORBIS; **804–805:** © Chris Bennion/ Seattle Children's Theater; **808** (T) © Per Andersen/Alamy Images, (B) Cardaf/Shutterstock; **809:** l. Robbie Jack/CORBIS; **809:** r. The Granger Collection, New York; **810A** Fedor Selivanov/Shutterstock; **810B** Khirman Vladimir/Shutterstock; **810C** Museo Nazionale Romano Rome/Collection Dagli Orti/The Art Archive; **810D** © The Art Gallery Collection/Alamy Images; **813** (B) © Ancient Art & Architecture Collection Ltd/Alamy Images, (T) akg-images/NewsCom; **814:** Images Courtesy of Old Dominion University Theatre Program. ANTIGONE, 2000. Directed by Dr. Erlene Hendrix. Designed & Photographed by Konrad Winters.; **817:** Images Courtesy of Old Dominion University Theatre Program. ANTIGONE, 2000. Directed by Dr. Erlene Hendrix. Designed & Photographed by Konrad Winters.; **819:** Images Courtesy of Old Dominion University Theatre Program. ANTIGONE, 2000. Directed by Dr. Erlene Hendrix. Designed & Photographed by Konrad Winters.; **821:** Images Courtesy of Old Dominion University Theatre Program. ANTIGONE, 2000. Directed by Dr. Erlene Hendrix. Designed & Photographed by Konrad Winters.; **823:** Liz McAulay/© Dorling Kindersley; **824:** ANTIGONE, 2000. Directed by Dr. Erlene Hendrix. Designed & Photographed by Konrad Winters.;

828: Images Courtesy of Old Dominion University Theatre Program. ANTIGONE, 2000. Directed by Dr. Erlene Hendrix. Designed & Photographed by Konrad Winters.; **830:** l. Robbie Jack/CORBIS; **830:** r. Bildarchiv Preussischer Kulturbesitz/Art Resource, NY; **839:** Images Courtesy of Old Dominion University Theatre Program. ANTIGONE, 2000. Directed by Dr. Erlene Hendrix. Designed & Photographed by Konrad Winters.; **842:** Images Courtesy of Old Dominion University Theatre Program. ANTIGONE, 2000. Directed by Dr. Erlene Hendrix. Designed & Photographed by Konrad Winters.; **846:** Images Courtesy of Old Dominion University Theatre Program. ANTIGONE, 2000. Directed by Dr. Erlene Hendrix. Designed & Photographed by Konrad Winters.; **849:** Images Courtesy of Old Dominion University Theatre Program. ANTIGONE, 2000. Directed by Dr. Erlene Hendrix. Designed & Photographed by Konrad Winters.; **852:** Etruscan Amphora, Black-figured, pontic Fighting soldiers, white dove on shield, National Museum, Warsaw, Poland, Erich Lessing/ Art Resource, NY; **854:** Images Courtesy of Old Dominion University Theatre Program. ANTIGONE, 2000. Directed by Dr. Erlene Hendrix. Designed & Photographed by Konrad Winters.; **857:** Images Courtesy of Old Dominion University Theatre Program. ANTIGONE, 2000. Directed by Dr. Erlene Hendrix. Designed & Photographed by Konrad Winters.; **869:** © Bettmann/CORBIS; **870:** AP/Wide World Photos; **874:** Robbie Jack/CORBIS; **884** (T) © Classic Image/Alamy Images, (BR) © V&A Images/Alamy Images, (BL) Scala/Ministero per i Beni e le Attività culturali/Art Resource, NY **885:** Adam Woolfitt/CORBIS; **886A** © Mary Evans Picture Library/The Image Works, Inc.; **886B** © Jeremy Hoare PCL/SuperStock; **886C** Superstock/ PhotoLibrary Group, Inc.; **889** © Robert Harding Picture Library / SuperStock; **890:** l. SuperStock; **890:** r. © Bettmann/CORBIS; **892:** bkgrnd. Roman/Bridgeman Art ARCHIVE/Getty Images; **892:** © Bettmann/CORBIS; **893:** istockphoto.com; **895:** Painting from the Villa Boscoreale (fresco), Roman, (1st century B.C.)/Museo Archeologico Nazionale, Naples, Italy, Giraudon/www.bridgeman.co.uk; **896:** Picture Post/Hulton Archive/Getty Images; **899:** Sunset Boulevard/CORBIS SYGMA; **900:** Scala /Art Resource, NY; **903:** The Art Archive/Jan Vinchon Numismatist Paris/Dagli Orti; **906:** Scala/Art Resource; **908:** The Art Archive/Provinciaal Museum G M Kam Nijmegen Netherlands/Dagli Orti; **911:** Nimatallah/Art Resource, NY; **916:** Reunion des Musees Nationaux/Art Resource; **916:** Roman/Bridgeman Art ARCHIVE/Getty Images; **917:** istockphoto.com; **922:** Culver Pictures, Inc.; **926:** Hulton Archive/Getty Images; **930:** Prisma/Ancient Art and Architecture Coll, Ltd; **931:** The Art Archive/Museo Nazionale Terme Rome/Dagli Orti; **933:** Reunion de Musees Nationaux/Art Resource, NY; **934:** Doug Pearson/CORBIS; **940:** *Death of Julius Caesar* (100–44 BC) (oil on canvas) by Vincenzo Camuccini (1773–1844). Museo e Gallerie Nazionali di Capodimonte, Naples, Italy/The Bridgeman Art Library; **940:** bkgrnd. Roman/Bridgeman Art ARCHIVE/Getty Images; **941:** istockphoto.com; **943:** Timothy McCarthy/Art Resource, NY; **944:** MGM /THE KOBAL COLLECTION; **951:** John Springer Collection/CORBIS; **954:** CORBIS; **958:** MGM/Photofest; **961:** Extispicium relief (inspection of entrails) from the Forum of Trajan, Rome. Early Hadrianic. Louvre, Paris, France, Alinari/Art Resource, NY; **966:** © Bettmann/CORBIS; **966:** bkgrnd. Roman/Bridgeman Art ARCHIVE/Getty Images; **967:** istockphoto.com; **969:** Hulton Archive/ Getty Images Inc.; **973:** The Art Archive/Rheinischeslandesmuseum Bonn/ Dagli Orti; **974:** Hulton Archive/Getty Images Inc.; **976:** Erich Lessing/Art Resource, NY; **982:** The Art Archive/Jan Vinchon Numismatist Paris/Dagli Orti; **986:** Bust of Brutus (85–42 B.C.) c. 1540 (marble) (see also 244606) by Michelangelo Buonarroti (1475–1564). Museo Nzaionale del Bargello, Florence, Italy/Alinari/The Bridgeman Art Library.; **986:** bkgrnd. Roman/ Bridgeman Art ARCHIVE/Getty Images; **987:** istockphoto.com; **991:** *A Roman Triumph,* 1838 (oil on canvas) by Frank Topham (1838–1924). New Walk Museum, Leicester City Museum Service. UK/The Bridgeman Art Library; **993:** Hulton Archive/Getty Images Inc.; **999:** Hulton Archive/Getty Images Inc.; **1009:** © Zacharias Dimitriadis/IML Image Group/drr.net; **1010:** © Zacharias Dimitriadis/IML Image Group/drr.net; **1011:** © Alan Schein Photography/CORBIS; **1012:** © David Frazier/CORBIS; **1015:** CORBIS; **1016:** Joan Marcus Photography; **1020:** Bluestone Productions/SuperStock; **1024:** Ted Thai/Time & Life Pictures/Getty Images; **1032:** © Dave Reede/ Getty Images; **1034:** istockphoto.com; **1042** (CL) © Bettmann/Corbis;